CLAN DONALD

KINGS AND LORDS OF THE ISLES

Origins of CLAN DONALD MAIN BRANCHES

Kings of Scots

Olaf. King of the Sudoreys and Man

1150 — Rex Insularum — SOMERLED Rex Insularum k.1164 — 1140 — Ragnhildi

David 1 d.1153

Malcolm IV "The Maiden" d.1165

1200 — Dugall — Ranald d.1207 — Bethag Prioress Iona — Angus k.1210

William the Lion d.1214

Clan Dugall of Lorne

Clan Donald — Donald d.1250 — Clan Ruairi — Ruairi d.1268 — James k.1210

1250

Angus Mòr d.c1292 — Alastair Mòr ante 1290 — Clan Alastair of Loup — Alan d.c1285 — Donald 6th Earl of Mar d.c1297 — Jane Heiress 1315 — Alexander eldest son of the Steward d.1291

Alexander II d.1249

Alexander III d.1286 William Wallace

Lords of the Isles — Ranald — Lachlan k.1318 — Ruairi d.c1325 — Christina MacRuairi — Duncan 2nd Son of Mar — Isabel of Mar 1295 — ROBERT BRUCE 1274-1329

1300

John Baliol 1292-1296

Robert 1 1306-1329 Edward Balliol 1332-1354

Alastair Og tapered 1308 — Agnes O'Cahan — Angus Og d.c1329 — Ranald k.ap1346 — Alan 5 p d.1310 — Marjory d.1316 1315 — Walter 6th High Steward

David II 1329-1371

to Ulster — John Sprangach 3rd son d.c1349 — MacIains of Ardnamurchan — Amie MacRuairi Heiress 1337 — JOHN Lord of the Isles d.1380 — 1350 — Margaret Stewart — RObert II 1316-1390

1350

Robert II 1st of Stewart Kings 1371-1390

Euphemia Countess of Ross — Antrim — Keppoch — Malcolm Earl of Lennox

1400 — Ranald d.1386 — Stewart Athol — Godfrey d.1401 — Ian Fraoch d.1358 — DONALD Lord of Isles claimant of Earl of Ross d.1423 — Lady Margaret Lesley — Ian Mòr k.1427 — Marion Bisset House of the Glens of Antrim — Alastair Carrach d.1440 — Mary of Lennox

Robert III d.1406 Regency of Albany 1406-1424

James 1 1424-1437

Clan Godfrey — Glencoe

Earls of Antrim

Alan d.c1430 — Stewart Appin — Donald d.1420 — Fraser Lovat — Elizabeth Seton — Alexander Lord of Isles Earl of Ross d.1449 — Lochalsh — Sleat

1450

James II 1437-1460

Clan Ranald — Glengarry — Earl of Argyll — John Lord of Isles Earl of Ross d.1503 — Elizabeth Livingston — Celestine of Lochalsh d.1476 — Finvola MacLean of Duart — Hugh of Sleat d.1498 — Elizabeth Gunn

James III 1460-1488

Sleat Chiefs & Lord Macdonald

Lady Margaret Campbell — Angus Og Master of the Isles k.1490 — Sir Alexander k.1495

1500

James IV 1488-1513

Donald Dubh dsp1545 — Sir Donald Gallda d.1519 — Margaret Heiress — Donald 6th Glengarry d.1560

James V 1513-1542

CLAN DONALD

BY

DONALD J. MACDONALD

OF CASTLETON

FOREWORD

by

The Rt. Hon. Godfrey James Macdonald of Macdonald

LORD MACDONALD

PELICAN PUBLISHING COMPANY

GRETNA 2008

First published by Macdonald Publishers
Published by Pelican Publishing Company, Inc., 2008

*The word "Pelican" and the depiction of a pelican
are trademarks of Pelican Publishing Company, Inc.,
and are registered in the U.S. Patent and Trademark Office.*

ISBN-13: 978-1-58980-390-9

Back-jacket photograph: Castle of Eilean Donan

Printed in Korea

Published by Pelican Publishing Company, Inc.
1000 Burmaster Street, Gretna, Louisiana 70053

Foreword

by

The Rt. Hon. Godfrey James Macdonald of Macdonald
LORD MACDONALD
Chief of the Name and Arms of Macdonald
High Chief of Clan Donald

Donald J. Macdonald of Castleton has spent many years of research in his endeavour to up-date the history of Clan Donald. The history of Clan Donald does not change, but over the years new facts inevitably come to light and it is in this respect that this volume is so valuable.

Our history is an exceedingly complex one, and certainly not a history to be absorbed readily at a first reading. It is only by constant reference, helped by the interesting style employed by Mr Macdonald, that the reader can understand the part played by Clan Donald throughout history.

Although this volume primarily deals with the Clan Donald history up to 1745, when the Clan System as it was ceased to exist, the history of Clan Donald is a continuing one, and more recently events have dictated the future rôle of Clan Donald in history with the formation of the Clan Donald Lands Trust.

This is a valuable work, and undoubtedly will become the reference book for all those many people interested in the history of our Clan, and indeed those interested in the history of the Kingdom of the Isles and of Scotland.

Ostaig House,
Isle of Skye

July 1978

Preface

IT HAS BEEN felt for a long time that a history of the Clan Donald was needed to meet the demands of the increasing number of Macdonalds world-wide who take an interest in the origins, background and history of their ancestors. Eighty years have elapsed since the three volumes of *Clan Donald* (1896-1904) were written by the Rev. Drs Archibald Macdonald of Kiltarlity and Angus Macdonald of Killearnan. It is with the greatest respect for their memory that I have used much of their work as a basis on which to build this history, which covers a period of 600 years, from the foundation of the Lordship of the Isles down to 1746 when the clans ceased to exist as separate organised entities. In order to satisfy this demand I was commissioned by Mr and Mrs Ellice McDonald, Jr., of Delaware to re-write the history of our Clan. I devoutly hope it will prove to be worthy of the confidence placed in me, and that it will be of real interest and use, not only to members of our Clan, but also to students of the Western Highlands and Isles generally.

The first 350 years of our history cover the long life of the Lordship of the Isles from its foundation by Somerled, *Rex Insularum,* and nine Lords who succeeded him, down to the last, John, who was forfeited of all his estates in 1493 by James IV. During that time ten important families with their clans branched off the main stem, but all continued to recognise MACDONALD as their high chief. Even after the death of the last Lord, John, in 1503, his grandson, Donald Dubh, twice headed rebellions in attempts to restore the Lordship to its former glory; but, when these failed, and he, the last scion of the House of Macdonald, died without issue in 1545, all was lost and the clans had to act independently in the pursuit and protection of their interests.

Thus, this book is not the history of a clan, but of several important clans, who descend from the old Kingdom of MACDONALD, and look back with pride to their origin and roots in the Lordship of the Isles. The history of each of these clans from 1500 to 1746 would warrant a book to itself. Each played its part in the history of Scotland until the final disaster of Culloden. What followed has been the subject of many books. The cruel fate of many of the clansmen, the wholesale emigration due to economic stress, and clearances by chiefs who had become feudal landlords, have been told over and over again, and are quite beyond the scope of this history.

Fortunately, following on that dark period, we are able in retrospect to admire the achievements of our clansmen and women in every field of human activity, who have pioneered the development of distant lands overseas and whose descendants return to seek their kinsfolk in the Highlands and visit the scenes about which they have read so much. It is to them we dedicate this work, hoping they will find it interesting, and in so doing will feel the urge to read and discover more about the old country that was the home of their ancestors.

DONALD J. MACDONALD

Acknowledgments

I should like to acknowledge with gratitude my indebtedness to all those who have helped me in producing this book, notably the following:

Mr and Mrs Ellice McDonald Jr. of Invergarry, Montchanin, Delaware, U.S.A., for their extreme generosity in covering all the heavy costs incurred in the publishing of this book. Without their help and encouragement it could never have been started;

Mr Malcolm Macdonald of Macdonald Publishers, who has gone to so much trouble in the editing and checking of my MS;

Mary Murray, D.A., and Beryl Pickering, A.T.D., F.S.D.-C., heraldic artists, for much of the art work involved in the coats of arms and seals which appear in these pages;

The staff of the Office of the Lord Lyon for their help in matters relating to heraldry and genealogies;

Sir Iain Moncreiffe of that Ilk, Albany Herald, for his help and advice, especially in the problems of succession in families of the Chiefs;

Rory MacDonald of Clachaig and Norman H. Macdonald (F.S.A. Scot.) for their help in respect of the Keppoch history;

The authors of the many books consulted in my study of the subject, which are listed in the Bibliography at the end of the volume;

The numerous clansmen and women world-wide for supplying information in response to my enquiries, and for their encouragement;

All those who kindly permitted the use of their illustrations;

All those, who have already subscribed, for waiting so patiently for the book to appear; and lastly,

My wife, whose patience and help have made it possible for me to live with this work for so long.

D. J. M.

Contents

Illustrations

GENEALOGICAL CHARTS

MAPS AND PLANS

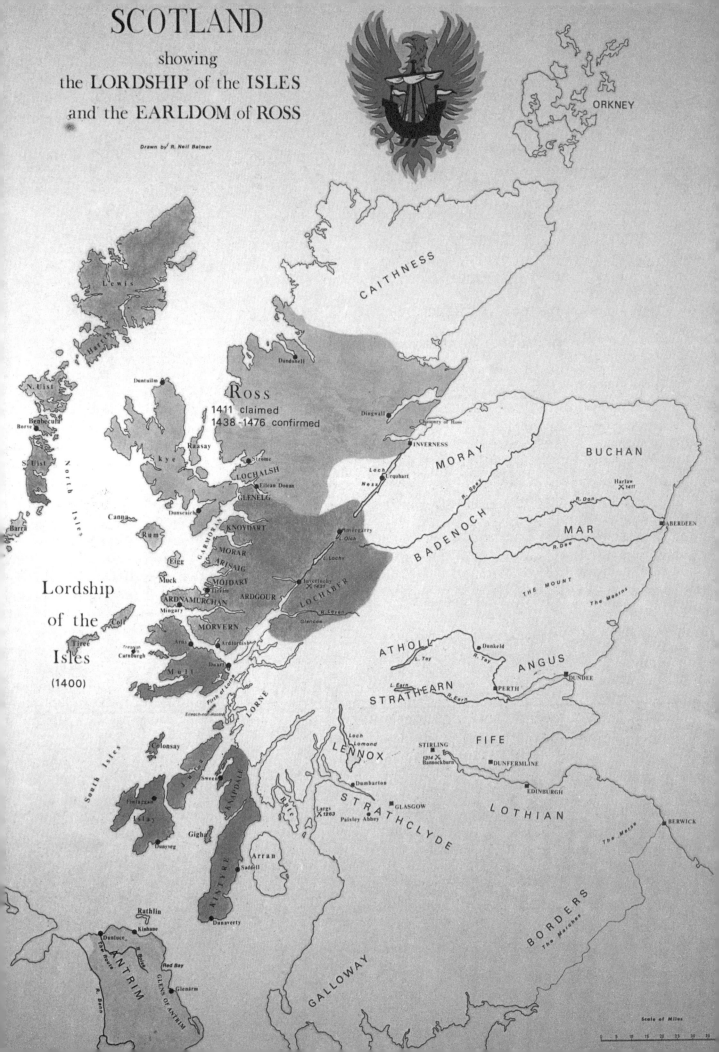

1

Introductory

"The descent and early history of the Clan Donald, like those of the other Highland clans, are involved in much obscurity. From the materials at the disposal of the historian it is difficult, if not impossible, to weave anything like a clear, reliable or consistent narrative. Fact and fiction are so often mixed up together, and tradition so frequently conflicts with what is regarded as authentic history, that the task of the historian sometimes assumes great, perhaps unmanageable, proportions. The Clan Donald, however, occupies so conspicuous and important a position in the annals of the country that any attempt to throw further light upon its rise and history may be regarded as worthy of commendation. . . ."

—from *Clan Donald*, by A. & A. Macdonald, 1896/1904, Volume I, Chapter 1, first paragraph.

WE HAVE CHOSEN this as a tribute to the two seanachies of the Clan who lived at the turn of the century and who did such a monumental task in writing the history of Clan Donald. Their work was spread over eight years and this is surely sufficient testimony to the time and trouble they took to produce what has been a standard work ever since. It is now out of print and almost unobtainable. Since their work was written, much has been done in the fields of history and archaeology to make us revise and in some instances correct their opening chapters on the early history of the Celts and our ancestors, the Gaels, as opposed to the Britons (Picts), and their arrival first in Ireland and thence in Scotland. This is very relevant to the history of our Clan; and it has been our endeavour to paint a picture of the nature of the Celts, their customs, culture and background generally, followed by their movements across Europe and their impact on other races, until they came to these shores and settled in Gaeldom—Ireland and Western Scotland.

We can only trace briefly within the scope of this book the movements of our Celtic ancestors from their country of origin until they arrived in Scotland. Some think they spread from as far East as Mesopotamia, the cradle of mankind, indeed one might say from the Garden of Eden itself. About 900 B.C. they were in and around the Danube valley, moving westwards all the time. In 800 B.C. we find some of their remains at Hallstatt, evidence of civilisation of a high order of the iron age. Moving still westwards, they invaded Italy and sacked Rome after the battle of the Allia in 390 B.C. So they were very powerful at that time; and, although they were defeated and repulsed, many of them remained in what the Romans called Cisalpine Gaul on the south side of the Alps. In fact there are many traces of them there still. In Northern Italy it is not uncommon to find completely blond people mixed with the darker inhabitants, and these blonds without doubt owe their colouring to the presence of Celtic blood.

Celts who remained on the Danube gave Greece a great deal of trouble in 290 B.C. They invaded Greece and conquered southwards right down as far as Delphi, but there they were halted and defeated. In 287 B.C. some of the survivors seem to have migrated eastwards again into Asia Minor where they lived and formed a province called Galatia, the inhabitants of which were the subject of one of Paul's Epistles. St Jerome records that a form of Celtic was still spoken in Galatia up to 400 A.D., although undoubtedly it would be much influenced by the Latin tongue. By 500 B.C. they had arrived in Spain. On their way they left traces in Galicia in Poland, and gave their name to another Galicia in Spain. There they mixed with the local inhabitants who were called Iberians, to form a tribe called the Celtiberi, to whom classical writers frequently refer.

On their way, the old Celtic language common to all Celts originally although now lost, split into two main branches. These are referred to by scholars as P-Celtic and Q-Celtic. Without going deeply into the subject, if we take two words, one in Welsh and one in Gaelic, we can see the meaning. In Welsh, the word for children is "plant," and the corresponding word in Gaelic is "clann." The P-Celts are represented today by the Welsh, the Cornish and the Bretons, and the Q-Celts by the Gaels of Scotland, Ireland and the Isle of Man. We shall call the P-Celts "Britons" and the Q-Celts "Gaels" in the rest of this work. These two branches of the original Celtic language are now well separated, although the time of their separation is very difficult to determine; but it must have taken place during their migration westwards across Europe.

The Celts have been described by many people over the years, classical writers and others. Professor Watson, in a talk on the Celts in Britain, said this: "The fair haired type has always been masterful and enterprising. The best representatives of the Teutonic people are now acknowledged to be Scandinavians. The Celts on the other hand have undergone racial mixture to a greater extent, the penalty of their wide diffusion over Europe and even beyond its bounds. Celtic culture on the other hand stands on a different footing. It has always possessed a wonderful attraction and was readily assimilated by subject races and sometimes even by others: as for instance those Normans who settled in Ireland and became more Irish than the Irish themselves." We all know the people of no Celtic blood whatsoever who come into contact with the Celtic race and become absorbed. Even those who have conquered and dominated the Celts for many years have frequently absorbed their culture and language and have become even more ardently Celtic than the Celts. The old saying *Hibernior Hibernis* applies equally to the Gaels of Scotland. Nowhere has this stubborn adherence of the Celt, in this case the Gael, to his traditions, lore, language and art (indeed to all things to do with the spirit), been more clearly demonstrated than in the persistence of the Gaelic language, art and culture during the 300 to 350 years of the Norse domination of the Western Isles. The children of Conn were able to sustain their traditions and language throughout all that period and even to impose on their conquerors some of their culture. This is proved by the way in which some of the Celtic art was taken back by the Norse invaders to their homeland. In a word, the Celt deals with the things of the spirit, and it is aptly put by St Paul in his epistle to the Celts of Galatia: ". . . things that are seen are temporal; things that are not seen are eternal." And so it has been with the Celt.

We shall have more to say about this in the course of the history of the Clan later on. The thorny question as to which branch of the Celtic peoples the early Britons in our country belonged has been argued for years. Who were the Picts? Who were the Britons that the Romans met on the shores of Kent and later throughout the country? When did the Gaels come to Britain and Ireland? A careful study of all the records would seem to point to the fact that the early Celtic inhabitants of Britain (England and Scotland), were Britons, and the Gaels came direct from the west of France and Spain into Ireland where they conquered and absorbed any Britons who may have been there at the time. They certainly absorbed the primeval inhabitants of that island, some of whom were Picts. Their own traditions point that way. We refer of course to the successive invasions of Ireland recorded in the works of the old Irish chroniclers. Their traditional origins go far back into pre-history, and some of them are mythical ones, but possibly with a foundation of some fact. Some of these traditions refer to the ancestors of the Gaels coming from the eastern end of the Mediterranean by sea to Spain and thence to Ireland. Accepting this, we must assume that there were no Scots in Scotland until they came over from Ireland. Historically and traditionally, it is certain that the Scots in Ireland carried out raids on the west coast of not only England and Wales, but of Scotland too, in early times. We know that Conn Ceud-Cathach in the second century A.D. did invade the West of Scotland for a time. Thus we have the Scots coming over in expeditions, but not for permanent settlement, from the second century during the Roman occupation of Britain. They came to help their friends and kinsmen, the Britons, against the Roman invaders.

Who were the people in these islands before the Celts came? Who were the people who built the stone circles, the wheel-houses, the vitrified forts—places like Dun Angus in the Aran Isles, and all the traces we find of long barrows and short barrows? The experts tell us about those; but in the course of this history, one type of people who lived here may interest us as Gaels more than any other, and these are the people who built and dwelt in wheel-houses. There are many of these to be found in the Highlands and in the Islands particularly. Wheel-houses were circular, of fairly large extent, divided radially into compartments for different families living on a communal basis, and earthed over the top—a form of dwelling that would be very useful in such windy and exposed areas as the outer isles of Scotland. These appear now in many cases in the form of grassy mounds, and are frequently referred to in place names as *sithean,* meaning in the Gaelic "the fairy mound." It may be that the stories of fairies and their doings have their origin in the inhabitants of these wheel-houses before the time came when they were completely absorbed by the incoming Gael.

In the folk tales of the Gael the fairies are portrayed as little people dwelling in "hollow hills" who came out mostly at night. They lived far from the Gaels' settlements, but visited them in secret, sometimes stealing an infant and substituting one of their own which was usually small, wizened and unattractive. At times they would perform menial tasks for reward such as bowls of milk or cakes. Late at night a man returning from a party (perhaps a rather convivial one) would be abducted by the "Little People" and kept prisoner for some time, but always in the most hospitable manner. One thing they dreaded most was cold iron. A dirk stuck in the doorpost was a sure way of keeping them out of a house, even if they were in a malevolent mood. Taking all these stories into account, it is surely plain that a small folk, driven into the forest fastnesses and distant glens by the incoming Gaels, arriving at first in small companies, could fit the description given of the fairies. They feared iron as all Neolithic and Bronze Age folk did when men of the Iron Age appeared. The hollow hills could be wheel houses or villages such as Skara Brae in Orkney whose passages, doorways, and beds could only have been used by people of short stature. Until completely destroyed they might well visit the incomers at night on friendly terms, working in return for reward on menial tasks. They seemed on the whole to be friendly, if the name given them by the Gaels is any indication. They were called *Daoine-Sithe* or Men of Peace, and their mounds *Sithean.* They were quite distinct from the other devilish sprites of malevolent intent who pervade some of the folk-tales, such as the *glaistig, uruisg, each-uisge,* and the like. Many of these are probably inherited from the aboriginal folk of our forefathers and incorporated in their tales.

Classical scholars, Greek and Roman, threw some light on the characteristics of the ancient Celts. For example, Philip of Macedon, father of Alexander the Great, in the 4th century B.C. concluded a treaty with the Celts who were then on his northern borders in Thrace and on the Danube, in order to set him free for his conquests southwards into Greece. They are described then as being tall, strong and fond of boastful words and high sounding speeches. They feared nobody, and they kept their bond when they took an oath. Another writer says that they trained themselves not to be stout, and that any of the younger men who exceeded the measure of his belt would be fined. Another states that they had handsome hounds for hunting, which they used against their enemies. We know that deer and wolf hounds were very popular in Ireland and the West of Scotland, and we know that St Patrick, after being enslaved in Ireland, escaped on a ship which was exporting deerhounds from Ireland to the Continent. They appear to have had quite a good export trade in that direction. The breeds of stag and wolf hounds were highly prized by the Gaels as is shown by place names in Argyll. Anchnacon in Glencoe and the same place-name in Appin show that rearing and training of hounds was a useful and probably lucrative occupation for the inhabitants. The hounds were exported, as we learn in the life of St Patrick, and are still to this day.

Their regard for horses was obviously great, as may be seen from some of the relics in museums, the bridles, saddles and head-pieces skilfully worked by the early Britons to adorn their steeds. The Gauls were great horse rearers and horse tamers, and they had used chariots up to the time of the Gallic war of Julius Caesar; but we know that the Britons in the South of England were using chariots in repelling the invasion of the Romans. It is interesting that in the old maps, the peninsula of Kintyre is shown to be inhabited by a people called the Epidii, who were named the Horse-Folk. They were horsemen and used horses freely. Right up to modern times, the name "MacEachran," which means "the son of the horse-man," is common in that area. The MacEachrans were Masters of the Horse to the Lords of the Isles at a later date.

As to their dress, we have a description by Virgil, who may himself have been of Celtic origin. He says, describing the Gauls who invaded Rome, "They had golden hair and vestures of gold, they gleamed bright in striped variegated cloaks [could these be tartans?]. Their milk-white necks are bound with gold, they brandish each of them two spears. Their bodies are protected by long shields." The two spears formed the regular armament of every ancient warrior —no doubt one for throwing and the other one for stabbing. Another classical writer describes the dress and armour at greater length. "The brightly dyed tunics with a diced or diamond pattern of many colours, the ornamental cloaks, light in summer and heavy in winter, the shields decorated according to taste, the helmets with horns. Some had breast-plates of iron links, others had none." The early Scottish or Irish warriors, or some of them, are described as wearing very complete body armour, and we know that this may have come later, but was not worn very much by our immediate ancestors. Another writer, describing the swords of the Gauls who defeated the Romans in 390 B.C., said that the iron of the Celts was soft and badly forged or tempered, and bent readily, so that they obviously had not acquired the art of making steel.

*   *   *

We have seen that what we now call England and Scotland was inhabited by the Britons, and the Gaels came to Ireland by sea from the west of France and Spain; and that the Gaels in Ireland, after absorbing the *Cruithne* (their name for the Picts) and the *Fir-bolg*, the original inhabitants, made frequent incursions into Britain. Coming down nearer to historical times, we find in Ireland the traditions and stories of what are called the Ultonian cycle of epic poems. These deal especially with a warrior called Cuchulain (the Hound of Ulster). He was contemporary with King Conchobar MacNessa, who flourished in the 1st century A.D. His first name was Setanta, but he was given the name by which he is best known because, when attacked by a fierce watch dog belonging to the chief blacksmith of the Ultonians, he killed it by seizing its hind-legs and dashing its brains out on a rock. The smith was furious at the loss and demanded how he was to guard his property without it. Setanta thereupon promised to train as good a hound for him; and until it was able to take up its duties, he himself would keep watch on his property.

Now Cuchulain is interesting to us for one simple reason. One of his adventures included a visit to the Isle of Skye, to the fortress of Dun Scaith, which in the matriculation of arms of the late Lord Macdonald as High Chief of the Clan Donald is called the "ancestral Seat" of Macdonald. It is one of the most interesting of all the castles within the Kingdom of the Isles. The derivation is Dun Sgàthaich, meaning the Castle of Sgàthach, a warrior queen who lived there. She was well versed in all the arts of war and the handling of all kinds of weapons. Warriors used to resort to her Dun to undergo a course of training in the use of weapons. Cuchulain is supposed to have gone there because somebody made a slighting remark about his ability and said that, if he would go and study under Sgàthach, he might in time become a good warrior. So he went to Scotland, went North to the Dun and stayed with Sgàthach in her fortress for a time. While there he aided this Amazon queen in a war against a neighbouring rival queen on the mainland whose name was Aoife. Cuchulain not only overcame Aoife in battle but also in love, and left her in a pregnant condition, telling her that, should the child be a son, he should be called Conlaoch. After a period of training with Sgàthach, Cuchulain went back to his former love, Emer, who had been waiting for him in Ulster. In due course Aoife's son was born, and was, in accord with Cuchulain's order, called Conlaoch. After a full course of training he was sent off to Ulster to meet Cuchulain. In parting, Aoife enjoined upon Conlaoch three promises, (1) to go to Ulster, (2) to refuse battle with none, and (3) not to divulge his name. Conlaoch duly went to Ulster, was challenged by his own father to a duel, and in a desperate battle, Conlaoch fell. In dying, he revealed his name. Aoife had her revenge. For a long time Cuchulain was out of action, stricken with grief, mourning his son.

Here it would be desirable to make a note of the Fianna (Fenians) who figure largely in many of these epics. They were a corps d'élite selected for the defence of the realm in the 1st and 2nd centuries A.D. They were led by Fionn (variously spelt Finn, or Fingal) who, although not the sturdiest of them in fight, was wise, generous, chivalrous, and trusted by all. They were picked warriors, who had to undergo severe tests of physical endurance and skill in arms, but also had to be men of education and culture. The Fianna were organised in battalions headed by leaders of renown—Diarmid, Raine, Goll, Caoilte, Oscar (Ossian's son), and others, whose banners were displayed heraldically to identify the bearers. Such a distinguished band of warriors proved in the end too powerful for the High King to countenance and were overcome at the Battle of Gabhra in 284 A.D. by King Cairbre Riata. In the battle the King was killed by Oscar, Ossian's son; but all the notable heroes of the Fianna were slain, only Ossian and Caoilte (who was noted for fleetness of foot) surviving.

To Ossian are attributed most of the epics recounting the feats of the Fianna. By some supernatural means he is supposed to have survived until the days of Patrick, and their conversation makes very amusing reading. Poor old Ossian cannot understand why Patrick tells him all the Fianna were very wicked and would undoubtedly end up in Hell, as in fact Ossian himself would unless he repented of his sins. Ossian put in a plea for his departed friends telling the saint that they were brave in battle, never did a mean thing, never refused help to the weak, were chivalrous to women, and hospitable to strangers. Even so, Patrick did not hold out much hope for the unfortunate Fianna: and Ossian saw no reason to repent. It is a good poem even if somewhat late in the catalogue of Gaelic poesy.

One of the earliest sources of the epics of our ancestors is the Book of the Dun Cow, which is still preserved in the Royal Irish Academy. It takes its name from the tradition that in its original form it was written on the skin of a favourite cow, the property of St Ciaran who was a contemporary of Columba. The book was copied in 1106 by the scribe, Maolmuridh. One of the most interesting poems in it is The Cattle Raid of Cooley (*Tàin Bò Chuailgne*) because of the light it throws on the customs and chivalry of the ancient Gaelic warriors. It tells of Maev of Connacht who was another Amazon queen like Sgàthach. She and her husband had large herds of fine cattle, and a rivalry existed between them as to who should have the finest. Now Maev owned a fine bull called "The White-Horned," and the only other able to match him was the Brown Bull of Cooley in Ulster. When the White-horned elected to desert Maev's herd and join her husband's she was furious and determined to get the better of him by acquiring the Bull of Cooley. Messages to the owner failed to produce results: in fact he was rather rude. Maev's anger knew no bounds and, gathering all her forces, she marched towards Ulster. Arriving at the ford over the river on the boundary she was confronted by one man alone. All the men of Ulster were afflicted with a crippling complaint and Cuchulain alone was fit to bear arms. Although Maev could easily have overrun the lone warrior, she generously met him and arranged that she should send one champion at a time to contest the ford. Day after day went by and warrior after warrior fell to the arms of Cuchulain. Many were the feats performed in that ford where the warriors met in their chariots. In the end a champion called Fergus, an old comrade of Cuchulain's, was prevailed upon by Maev to tackle him. Fergus left his famous sword behind and went to parley with his friend, who at last agreed to flee before Fergus, if he promised to flee from Cuchulain at some future date. Thus the Brown Bull went with Maev to Connacht. She did not profit by it because the Bull attacked the White-horned one, tore it limb from limb and then went mad and slew many of Maev's and her husband's finest cattle, at last expiring exhausted.

Many manuscripts exist recording deeds like these, the oldest and most notable being the Book of the Dun Cow, the Book of Leinster, the Yellow Book of Lecan and the Book of Ballymote of the 14th and 15th centuries, compiled from traditional sources handed down orally by the bards who were trained to commit to memory many hundreds of lines of poetry, and to hand them on to their successors, in many cases their sons who held the office of hereditary bard to some noble or royal family. The bardic profession was strictly maintained. They had to train in the use of many complicated rules of versification, metres, rhymes and alliteration. Their vocabulary was immense as is witnessed by the Incitement to Battle (*Brosnachadh Catha*) recited by the bard MacMhuirich before the Battle of Harlaw in 1411, in which some 350 adverbs were used, going through the alphabet from end to end, and all describing the one subject—the manner in which Donald's warriors were to acquit themselves in the forthcoming onset. To attain the rank of Ollamh (corresponding to a modern doctorate) the bard had to undergo some twelve years of training and have in his repertoire hundreds of epics, genealogies and stories.

The family of MacMhuirich (MacVurich) held office for 18 generations with the Lords of the Isles and later with the Clan Ranald down to the last of the family who lived in Staoiligary in Uist and in 1808 gave evidence before the Highland Society of London as to the authenticity of the works of Ossian. They descended from one Muireadach Albannach who in the 13th century fled from Ireland and took service with Macdonald in Islay. The Red and Black Books of Clanranald owe their origin to this famous family and are to be found in a translation in the two volumes of *Reliquiae Celticae* by Dr Cameron of Brodick in 1892. The MacMhuirichs recited their poems, composed more, related the history of the Clan, witnessed documents, and preserved the traditions of their patrons, who rewarded their services with grants of land and money.

There are many epics extant in various collections attributed to Ossian. Some were collected from the recitation of ordinary people, not in the least scholarly, who remembered hundreds of lines. A great many of Ossian's poems relate to the invasions of the Vikings—Danes and Norsemen. To defend Ireland from their incursions was the main task of the Fianna. One example will suffice to show the spirit of these warriors, and the code of behaviour to which they adhered. The *Brataichean nam Feinne* (Banners of the Fianna) tells how Magnus, King of Lochlann, lands on the shores of Erin and is confronted by the host of the Fianna. Both sides are drawn up in battle array on the beach. Magnus demands that all Ireland should be his, and he refuses to depart until the King cedes that realm. A parley is held; Ossian and Fergus, both bards, and vested with plenipotentiary powers and diplomatic immunity, talk with Magnus. Meantime the Fianna display their banners and in response to Magnus' enquiry about the regiments the bards tell the name of the leader of each and the name of his banner. These have high-sounding names: "The Black Venom," "The Grey Warlike One," and many others. Fionn's own is the "Deo-Greine," the Sun-ray. Ossian promises Magnus a desperate battle before any of them will yield. It proved to be a desperate battle indeed, fought from sun-rise to dark: the Norse are driven back to their ships with great loss. Magnus loses nine sons and escapes with a fraction of his host. The Fianna too lose heavily but their task is done, and Ireland saved.

Many of these epics deal with the invasions of the Norsemen. As Fionn and his Fianna are placed early in the Christian era, it is plain that the raids of the Danes and Norsemen began long before the wholesale invasions and subsequent occupation of the Isles and parts of Ireland in the 9th century.

* * *

We have recounted some of the traditions of the past to give a picture of the characteristics of our ancestors, many of which are reflected in the later generations of our people down to the present day. From the opening of the Christian era we are on firmer ground in the history of our Clan. Conn, from whom we derive the name Clann Chuinn, is an historical character who reigned from 123 A.D. to 173 A.D. and is supposed to have lived for 100 years although surrounded by some nebulous traditions. He had two sons by an early marriage, Connla and Art. By the time he wedded Becuma of the Fair Skin, who appears to have been a somewhat disreputable young woman, Connla had gone, and Art was alone (hence the name Art Aonarach). Becuma became jealous of him, presumably not having a son of her own. One of them had to go, so a chess game was arranged to decide (chess and backgammon were well known games in those days among our ancestors). Art won, and Becuma appears no more in our story. Art is famous only for the fact that he was father of Cormac.

Cormac Mac Art succeeded to the Kingship in 227 and reigned till 266 A.D. He was a wise king, a law-giver, and is said to have become a Christian in 254. During his reign the Fianna flourished with Fionn Mac Chumhail (Fingal) as their commander. Fionn was son-in-law of Cormac. Cormac was succeeded by his son Cairbre Riata, who was the first to found a settlement of any size in the West of Alba (Scotland). His marriage to Oileach, a lady of noble birth amongst the Picts of Alba, was important because when Cairbre's sons, the three Collas, migrated to Alba and expanded their father's settlements, their neighbours the Picts received them in a more friendly manner. The later Kingdom of Dalriada takes its name from Cairbre Riata.

Colla Uais, one of the three sons of Cairbre all named Colla, is the next in line that interests us. Clan Cholla is a name given to the Clan Donald by writers and bards for many years after. The three Collas had fallen out with the High King of Ireland and migrated to Alba. When recalled by the King two of them went back; but Colla Uais preferred to take his chance in Alba and continued to build up the power of Dalriada, which was still nominally subject to the Kings of Ireland. There he had four sons, the eldest of whom, Eochaidh, is claimed to be the direct ancestor of Somerled, founder of the Clan Donald. The generations between Colla and Somerled are somewhat obscure and vary from historian to historian; all, however, are agreed that Somerled was in the direct line of Conn and Colla. The "men of the Isles," whose opinions carried great weight in our early history, were satisfied of this fact when they invited Somerled to lead them in the 12th century rebellion by the Gaels against the Norse Kings of the Sudereys and Man.

*   *   *

During the latter years of the 4th century and whole of the 5th, much was happening in Britain and Alba.

1. The Romans were losing their hold on their Empire and had perforce to recall the legions to oppose the barbarians invasions. By 410 they had all gone leaving the Romanised Britons to their fate, defenceless, or nearly so, in the face of the increased pressure of the Anglo-Saxons on their eastern coasts. These pirates had been a menace during the Roman occupation; but now they were able to begin to occupy the country on a wide front from Kent to Forth.

2. The Scots of Dalriada were consolidating their hold on Argyll, Kintyre, and the isles south of Ardnamurchan. They had their set-backs and in 471 A.D. a strong king of the Picts, Angus, drove them back and occupied much of their territory. In the year 474, however, King Erc of Irish Dalriada died, leaving three sons: Fergus, Lorn and Angus. The succession was in dispute; and, when their uncle was made King in accordance with the Celtic Law of Tanistry, they left Ireland, migrated to Dalriada in Alba and divided the land between them. Lorn gave his name to the northern part: Fergus had Islay and Kintyre: and Angus ruled Arran and Cowal. Not long after, Fergus became King of Alban Dalriada, and is acclaimed as the first King of Scots in Scotland, although for another 60 years his realm was still part of the Irish Dalriada.

3. As we have seen, the Anglo-Saxon pirates turned colonists and conquerors. The Angle kingdom of Northumbria is the one that interests us most for two reasons: it occupied the south-east of Scotland for many years: and our Columban Church sent missionaries to convert the pagan Angles of Northumbria to Christianity.

4. The first organised Christian Church was founded at Whithorn in Galloway. Ninian was born in that area in 362 A.D. He was a Briton, son of a petty chief,

who was himself a Christian. His church, named *Candida Casa* (The White House), was built about the year 397 on the Isle of Whithorn where traces still exist. His cave with carvings on its wall is at some distance along the shore westwards. There he was wont to retire for meditation. From this centre missionaries went out all over Alba, especially to the Pictish regions of the north and east, although Dalriada was not neglected entirely. Ninian organised the Celtic Church in this island and died in 432, the same year as Patrick went to Ireland. Patrick's family may well have been converted by Ninian or one of his disciples, for they lived near to the Britons' fortress of Dumbarton on the Clyde whence Patrick was kidnapped by Irish pirates about the year 405. Ninian's disciples and followers left their names all over Alba. One of them, St Finnian the Great, had a great influence over Columba in his early training.

These four important developments in the period 397 to 500 mark one of the most important centuries in our history. The darkness and confusion of the following three centuries are relieved by few events, of which perhaps the most important was the coming of Columba.

This great man was born in Donegal in December 521 of the tribe of Conall Gulban. His father was a great-grandson of the famous King Niall of the Nine Hostages (397-405) and on his mother's side he was also of royal blood. He was of very strong character; and, while he is remembered mostly for his dedication to the Christian Church, he proved to be also very politically minded. He studied under St Finnian who was a disciple of Ninian's Candida Casa. He threw himself wholeheartedly into the cause of Christianity and was filled with the missionary spirit. The monasteries of Durrow and Kells were of his foundation between the years 546 and 563. In 561 there arose a quarrel about a manuscript he had copied while under the tutelage of Finnian. This was regarded as a serious offence at a time when manuscripts were so very valuable. The matter was even brought before the High King, Diarmait, who ruled that "To every cow belongs its calf," and Columba was ordered to hand his copy back. His anger was such that a civil war resulted between the King and his own Clan Niall in which the King was overcome. Columba was appalled at the bloodshed he had caused and to expiate his sins he vowed to leave Ireland never to return. He took twelve disciples and set sail for Dalriada in Argyll. It is said he kept going from isle to isle, at each looking back, and if Ireland was still in sight he continued northwards until in Iona he found his homeland had disappeared from view. The little hill he climbed to survey the scene is still called *Carn Cuil ri Eirinn* (Hillock of Back turned on Eire), and the cove in which he landed, *Port na Curaiche* (Haven of the Coracle).

His arrival amongst his kinsmen of Dalriada strengthened the Church in that realm, which had much need of revival. It had a "tincture of Christianity," but the flame was waxing faint. Columba threw himself into the task of reviving his kinsfolk not only in their religious faith, but politically too. In the year 560, before Columba's arrival, Brude, King of the Picts, had invaded Dalriada and reduced it to the status of a mere province of his kingdom. Gabhran Mac Domongart was slain and succeeded by Brude's nominee, Conall MacComgall, as Toiseach (Chief) of the province, and that is how Columba found matters when he landed. Once more the saint took a hand in politics and in 574 ordained Aidan MacGabhran King of Dalriada. This was probably the first coronation with Christian rites performed in Britain. The Clan Comgall revolted, but their leader, Duncan MacComgall, was killed and Aidan's kingship was assured. He proved to be a strong and wise king. With Columba's help and backing he consolidated his realm and successfully stemmed the Pictish tide. Aidan ruled from the year 574 to 606 A.D. and thereafter Dalriada may be regarded as a sovereign state no longer dependent on its parent kingdom of Irish Dalriada.

Columba's politics were as strong as his faith in his Master, and as successful as his efforts in the Christian mission field. The Columban Church thrived and sent missionaries far afield—many of them to the pagan kingdom of Northumbria where they converted the Angles and founded the famous church and monastery on Holy Island. No wonder he is remembered with affection as a faithful soldier of Christ and that many churches are dedicated to his name even in parts which he never visited in person.

The missionaries of the Celtic Church were active and numerous from the time of the foundation of their mother-church at Candida Casa in Galloway down to the time in the 11th century when it was overshadowed by the increasing power of the Roman Church ably assisted by Margaret, the Saxon princess who married Malcolm Canmore. Her influence on him and the kingdom by the introduction of Saxon ways and language, as well as the Roman priesthood, led in a comparatively short time to the extinction of the Celtic Church and the gradual supplanting of the Gaelic language at the Court by English. Later, in the time of her sons' reigns, Norman barons were invited to take up estates in Scotland to the exclusion of the native Gaelic chiefs. The feudal system followed close on their heels, and the government of Scotland completely changed its character. Gaelic culture, customs, language and even the Celtic Church, with its simple evangelistic form, were on the way out as far as the ruling class and central government of the realm were concerned.

During the centuries from 400 A.D. to the time of the serious incursions of the Vikings and the establishment of the Norse kingdoms of the Sudereys and Man, and Dublin, missionary zeal was at its height. Evangelists—Scots, Picts and Scoto-Picts—went out from end to end of the country. They left their names in numerous foundations and by these we can trace the enterprising nature of their movements amongst pagan and sometimes hostile tribes. Strangely enough not many of them suffered martyrdom at the hands of the native Gaels and Picts. Those who were murdered were mainly victims of the Norse invaders. St Donan and St Maelrubha were notable amongst these.

The rise and fall of the Celtic Church can for our purpose be told in few words; but these few cover a great many years of hard work, sweat and tears by many fine Christian saints. The Columban Church, begun in Iona and transferred to Dunkeld to escape the Viking atrocities, ended with the Culdees, scattered priests or monks who refused to join their other colleagues in conformity with the Roman Church. These last vestiges of the old Celtic Church (Gaelic and Pictish) disappeared with the arrival of Margaret, her marriage to Malcolm Canmore, and consequent influence over the Court. Gaelic ceased to be the language of the King and his Court, and the Roman Church took over. In Northumbria the Columban Church virtually died after the Synod of Whitby in 664.

The causes of the disappearance of the Celtic Church in Northumbria first and later in Scotland were the same. The old Celtic Church was a loosely organised edifice. It suited the tribal system of the pagans who accepted it. Each little area had its "bishop" who was virtually a parish priest on his own, distant from his neighbours, and owing allegiance to no central "High Church." There is a legend that one such "bishop" of the Celtic Church, when told he ought to render homage to and obey the Bishop of Rome, as head of Christ's Church world-wide, replied, "He may be bishop of Rome: I am bishop of this district: we both serve Christ, and I hope he is looking after Rome in the same way as I try to serve Christ here." Such a loosely-knit organisation confronted by the highly-organised Church of Rome, backed by a powerful Empire, and whose head claimed apostolic succession to St Peter, holding the keys of Heaven, was almost certain to be overshadowed and eventually absorbed. The differences between the two systems as cited by Wilfrid at Whitby, and later by Margaret, were after all very superficial; the tonsure, the date of Easter, the duration of Lent, and alleged immorality of the Celtic clergy in allowing a man to marry the widow of his deceased brother. The outcome for the Celtic Church was of course the result of political considerations which also determined its fate in Scotland some four centuries after the issue was raised.

It would take much time to record the expansion of Christianity during this period. One example must suffice.

St Comhgan was of noble birth, son of the King of Leinster born just before the year 700 A.D. He succeeded his father in 715, but had no heart in his kingship, preferring to give up all for Christ. He went to Candida Casa and trained there. His sister Kentigerna (*Ceann Tighearna,* Leader of the Lord), who was older and by this time a widow, went with him with one of her sons who also joined the Church. He was St Fillan, and he too left his name in places so well known in Scotland. Comhgan went through Dalriada leaving his name in various *teampuill* (oratories)—in Islay, on Loch Melfort-side, and Lochalsh—whence he went to Applecross where he met and worked with Maelrubha, a more famous saint and better known. Comhgan left his name in places as far apart as Ardnamurchan, North Uist, Knoydart and Skye. Kilchoan is a well-known name in these places; and there are two of his *teampuill* in Skye, both on the shores of Loch Eishort, one at Boreraig in the district of Strath, and the other at Ord on the west side of Sleat where traces are still to be seen on a knoll above Ord House looking out over the Coolins, Rum and Canna. It is a place of wonderful beauty, outlook and inspiration for any wishing to pass a moment in silent meditation. Comhgan went from the west over to Turriff in Buchan where his foundation lasted for many years after his death in or about 750 A.D.

* * *

We leave the obscurity of the seventh and eighth centuries during which Dalriada, Pictland, British Strathclyde, and the Angles in Lothians continued to be independent of each other, but not without strife and quarrels. The missionaries of the Celtic Church seemed to wander through these realms without hindrance. The ninth century brings developments of great importance.

Firstly, in 844 the kingdoms of Dalriada and the Picts were united in the person of Kenneth MacAlpin. This was achieved owing to the King's paternal grandmother being a Pict of royal blood. The Picts favoured descent through the female line, and it may be that males failed and they were content to accept a strong king and unite the two kingdoms rather than continue the strife with their neighbours, who were in any case Celtic. Both had in the past suffered attacks by their Anglo-Saxon neighbours in the South and increasing inroads by the Danes and the Norsemen all around their coasts. It is unlikely that the smaller Kingdom of Dalriada achieved unity with the Picts by conquest. Whatever the cause, Kenneth was accepted as King of the united peoples in 844 and reigned securely until his death in 860.

Secondly, the invasions of both Danes and Norsemen increased enormously from the year 880 and persisted for the next three hundred years. We have seen how, from the earliest recorded times, even in the myths, legends and books of the Celts and Ireland, the Kings of Lachlann (Norway) and their subjects were a menace all around the coasts of the West, the Isles and Ireland, leading to the formation of the warrior bands of the Fianna in the third century. In the ninth century, however, these incursions reached a sudden crescendo, for which there seems to have been two main causes.

In the case of the Danes, historians point to the savage attacks of the Emperor Charlemagne on the pagan inhabitants of Jutland and North Germany, which not only drove them to seek asylum elsewhere, but embittered them against the Christian religion. The Danes (known to the Gaels as *Dubhgall* — "Dark Strangers") were particularly brutal in their attacks on churches and monasteries. It was, however, the Norse (*Fionngall*—"Fair Strangers") who made the Northern Isles of Scotland (Orkney and Shetland) and the Southern Isles (from Lewis to Man) their especial target. The reason for this increase in raiding and settlement by the Norse is to be found in the fact that in the year 872 Harald Harfagr (Harold the Fair-haired) became the first king of Norway. He overcame many petty chiefs in the process, who, rather than submit, took to their ships to seek their fortune elsewhere. What more natural than to steer west to Orkney as their fore-fathers had done? This was soon occupied, and as they steered even further west to Cape Wrath (The Cape of Turning) and turned south, all the isles from there to Man were named by them the Sudereys (South Isles). All this in time became one Norse kingdom of the Sudereys and Man. In the Church of England there is to this day a Bishop of Sodor and Man. It is in this kingdom we of Clan Donald are specially interested, as it was here that our ancestors founded the fortunes of the Clan, and every Macdonald who traces his line back to Somerled has the blood of the Norse Kings of the Isles (*Rex Insularum*) in his veins. We shall see later how this was achieved.

In 888 Harald joined the Viking settlements in the Isles to the crown of Norway. The settlers at once revolted: after all they had come all that way to be independent of him. Harald contented himself by sending an emissary, "the happy possessor of the euphonious name," Ketil Flatneb, who quickly subdued them; but in a short time he himself threw off his subjection to Harald and was able to rule as sovereign in the Isles. His line died out in the year 900.

Kings of the Isles succeeded one another, sometimes by family inheritance, at times by intrigue and sheer force. In 938 we find Aulaf MacSitric, *Rex Insularum*, falling at the battle of Brunaburh against the Angles. He was followed by Godfra Mac Arailt (Godfrey Son of Harald) who died in 989. His son, Ragnal Mac Godfra, succeeded and reigned until 1004. Sigurd of Orkney followed. He led the Viking warriors to reinstate the Norse kingdom of Dublin and fell at the battle of Clontarf in 1014 at the hands of the Irish patriot, Brian Boroimhe. His son Thorfin the Mighty, Earl of Orkney, was the greatest leader of the Viking kingdoms for many years till he died in 1064. From the death of the great Thorfin to that of Somerled, founder of our Clan, was exactly one hundred years, a century packed with interest for us.

It is difficult to get anything like a true or faithful picture of the conditions in the Western Isles during the Norse occupation. It does not seem at all clear that the character of the Celtic population or its social institutions any more than its language underwent any material alteration. The native Gael largely pre-dominated all along. Considering that the Norsemen and the Gaels seem to have lived on terms of mutual friendship after the time of Harald Harfagr, it is singular that the former did not leave a deeper, more permanent impression. The explanation is to be found in the words of Gregory, when he states "that in all cases of conquest the changes in the population must have been most perceptible in the higher ranks, owing to the natural tendency of the invaders to secure their new positions where practicable by matrimonial alliance with the natives." While the Gaelic language was preserved unaffected by the invaders, place-names in the

Isles and West of Scotland bear extensive traces of Norse influence. Land tenure seems to have been modified and the system of rents (farthing land, penny land and merk land) is to be found in the ownership of landed property.

In addition to the Gaels and the Norse another folk appear in records and traditions called the *Gall-Gael* ("Stranger Gaels"). These appear to have been nothing more than Gaels, outlaws or characters who were not happy with their own people, who joined with Viking pirates to carry out depredations around the coasts to the annoyance of both the Gaels of the country and the Norse settlers. The name was applied by the Irish to the Picts of Galloway. Afterwards it came to be applied to the Western Gaels, or at least to those of them who had absorbed the customs and piratical habits of the Vikings. They were thus Gaels and at the same time by their behaviour, strangers, and as such were pirates after the fashion of the early Viking invaders ever since the days of the Fianna. Skene would have us believe that the Gall-Gael were a race of Celts with territorial dignities or positions; but we believe that they were nothing more than Gaelic pirates banded with Norsemen who followed the same mode of life.

Before describing the conquest of the Isles by Somerled, it would be fitting here to introduce an earlier ancestor whose family has a particular bearing on the fortunes of the Clan. This is Godred (Godfrey) Crovan whose father is recorded as Harald the Black De Yselandia (which may be taken to mean either Iceland, or Of the Isles, or as some prefer, Islay). Godred Crovan was also son-in-law of Harald Hardrada, King of Norway, who fell in the Battle of Stamford Bridge in 1066. Godred was present at the battle, but escaped to the west where he proceeded to improve his fortunes by the conquest of Man and the Isles. He seems to have been accepted by the men of the Isles. He was a great character, celebrated in song, and lived an eventful life, ending, it is believed, in battle in Islay where his grave is marked by the *Carraig Bhàn* on the road between Port Ellen and Kintraw. This stone is supposed to mark his grave, or perhaps the site of the battle, but it is quite probable that it is of much more ancient origin. Godred died in 1095 leaving three sons: Lagman succeeded him for a few years but deserted his kingdom for some reason unknown, unless his death in Jerusalem points to his having gone on Crusade. The second son was Haakon, of whom there is no certain knowledge. The third, Olaf the Red, succeeded Lagman in or about 1100, the year (as near as we can judge) of Somerled's birth.

Olaf the Red married twice. His first wife was Affreca, daughter of Fergus, Prince of Galloway, from whose line the famous Devorgilla sprang. She was mother of the puppet King of Scots, John Balliol, nominated by Edward the first of England in 1292. One of her sisters was the wife of John Comyn, Lord of Badenoch, enemy of Robert Bruce. Olaf the Red was thus connected in one way or another with some of the most powerful families in the kingdom during the turbulent years of the War of Independence. Unfortunately for the Gael, most of these were of Norman blood.

Olaf's second wife was Ingiborg, the Norse Princess in whose veins the blood of many Jarls of Orkney and Kings of the Isles ran. Her grandfather was Thorfin the Mighty, the celebrated Earl of Orkney who had divided northern Scotland with Macbeth, annexing Caithness and the old realm of the Northern Picts. It was the daughter of this second marriage, the Princess Ragnhilda, who married Somerled in 1140.

* * *

While the Kingdom of the Isles was being consolidated and achieving the position of strength it had reached on the eve of Somerled's birth, the neighbouring Kingdom of Scots had not remained free from turmoil within and attacks from without.

The raids of the Norse invaders on the West had intensified: Iona had been ravaged twice, with the martyrdom of many of the clerics of the Columban Church: even the headquarters of the new kingdom had been threatened in its old territory of Dalriada. In consequence the Mother Church had been moved to Dunkeld and the relics that remained taken to safety, some to Dunkeld and some of the most valuable to Ireland, to the Monastery of Kells which had been founded by Columba before he migrated to Iona. Fortunately for posterity, one of the most valuable of these was the famous Book of Kells, now preserved and on view in the library of Trinity College, Dublin. This beautifully illuminated book containing the four Gospels is one of the best examples of the intricate work done so lovingly by the monks of Iona. It is said that Columba himself began the work which must have been carried on by dedicated craftsmen for many years before its completion. The materials necessary to do such fine work must have been drawn from afar. The inks are of foreign origin, and other instruments used must have been imported. The work, however, is purely Celtic: the designs are distinctive in their intricate interlacing character with the addition of the zoomorphics so beloved by our ancestors. From the time of the first invasion Iona declined for a time. Later Somerled, his son and grandson, brought it back into its previous importance as the High Church of the Gaelic Principality of the Isles. Kings and Queens were buried there, some even from as far away as Norway and France.

The other consequence of the Norse raids and the eventual foundation of the Kingdom of the Isles was the removal of the capital of the new Kingdom of Scots to Scone where kings were crowned. Perth and Scone became the centre of government. It had been the chief seat of the kings of the Northern Picts before the union. The Scots kings brought the famous Stone of Destiny (Lia Fail) from Dunstaffnage Castle in Lorne to Scone and on it kings were crowned in accordance with the tradition that where it rested the Scots would reign. Edward I of England removed it to the Abbey of Westminster where it is kept in the coronation chair on which our kings and queens have been crowned ever since. Many Scots believe it is only a piece of local red sand-stone conveniently substituted by loyal Scots for Edward to steal, while the true Stone is still hidden in a place known only to a few.

Throughout the period the kingdom was beset by dangers from many quarters. The Norse in the Isles, the Danes in the East, the turbulent Earls of Orkney and the powerful Mormaers, Thanes or Earls in Ross and Moray, were a continual source of annoyance. South of the Tweed Saxon and Angle invaders were always ready to threaten the very existence of the kingdom. It nevertheless grew in strength and gradually expanded its borders. The Angles of Lothian were brought under its rule by Malcolm II's victory at Carham in 1018, to be followed 16 years later by the Britons of Strathclyde whose king was Duncan, Malcolm's grandson and heir. Duncan, in whose reign Scotland became united more or less in the form we know that country now, is best known as the innocent victim of the ambitious and unscrupulous Macbeth and his lady. It made a good tragic play, but it is bad history. Macbeth was Mormaer of Ross and Moray and a very powerful and ambitious potentate in the North. The fact that Duncan was killed on the borders of Macbeth's Earldom suggests that he was on a punitive expedition northwards to bring Macbeth to justice, but he fell in battle and Macbeth became king. He had a claim not only by killing Duncan, but through his wife Gruach, who was grand-daughter of an earlier king. Whatever his method of seizing power, Macbeth proved a strong king and for that reason a good one for Scotland. When Malcolm, the slain Duncan's son, avenged his father's death and became king, we entered upon a period which had a most drastic and important effect not only on Scotland, but on the history of the Western Clans in general and Clan Donald in particular.

Malcolm was crowned at Scone on the 25th April 1057, the first coronation with due ceremony and consecration we hear of since that of Aidan in 574. He was already imbued with Saxon ideas, absorbed while an exile at the English Court during Macbeth's reign, and English aid had assisted his return to his native land to wrest the kingdom from Macbeth. Nine years later, when disaster befell his English friends and the Conqueror with his Norman knights overran England, the relatives of the unlucky Harold had to flee. Amongst them Edgar Atheling and his sister Margaret fled to Scotland. Their landing on the shores of the Firth of Forth near to the Royal Burgh and Capital of Scotland, Dunfermline, is commemorated in the towns of North and South Queensferry and the bay called St Margaret's Hope. Malcolm welcomed the fugitives and made them at home in his Court, fell in love with the Princess Margaret and married her.

To the Scots the Norman Conquest must have seemed a very far off and unimportant event; but its sequel was soon felt. The Queen soon induced her infatuated husband to begin "reforms" in what she considered a backward and barbarous realm both in State and Church. Under her direction, and with the help of Malcolm, the Gaelic language was replaced by English in the Court and the Columban Church Romanised. Of the far-reaching significance of these reforms and the impact on the social and religious life of the country, a general appreciation may be gained from the following extract from A. & A. Macdonald's *Clan Donald*:

> No sooner, however, was the new kingdom established than English influence began to be felt, and the conquest, which force of arms could never effect, was not unlikely to be accomplished by more silent, imperceptible, yet no less powerful, influences. Malcolm Canmore had been early attracted by the English Court, where, during the misfortunes of his youth, he had found a friendly refuge. His admiration for England and its people was evinced when, from his warlike incursions to Durham and Northumberland, he carried back with him large numbers of young men and women, whom he settled in various parts of his kingdom. His marriage with the Saxon Princess Margaret was fraught with many consequences to the social and religious life of Scotland. The ancient language of the Court, with the manners and customs of his fathers, were changed by the unpatriotic King, and conformed to the English model. Still further to Anglicise his country, he offered an asylum to those Saxon refugees who were compelled to leave their native land during the reign of the persecuting Norman Conqueror. With the death of Malcolm the Saxon importation ceased for a time when Donald Bàn, his brother, who, according to Celtic law, succeeded him, issued a sentence of banishment against all foreigners, and an attempt was made to stem the tide of Southern influence, and place Celtic culture once more in the ascendant. This, however, was only temporarily successful. Donald Bàn was driven from the throne after a short and troubled reign, and the three sons of Malcolm Canmore, who followed him in succession, were steady supporters of the new order. It was in the reign of David I, who occupied the throne from 1124 to 1153, that the most momentous change took place in the civil policy and social life of Scotland. David, who had been educated

at the Court of Henry Beauclerc, became inspired by Norman ideas, and, before his accession to the throne, was advanced to the dignity of a Norman baron. In the feudal system which, for upwards of 100 years, had operated in England and transformed its institutions, he found an instrument ready to his hand for remodelling the customs of the Scottish people. He introduced a powerful Norman baronetage, by means of whom he planted, on an extended scale, the principles of feudal tenure, and a ruling idea of his reign was to suppress Celtic aspirations and institutions, as inconsistent with the new social system and with loyalty to the crown. Thus did the new feudal system take root in our Scottish soil, and under its shadow have flourished those Anglo-Norman institutions which have done so much to mould the national life.

We have dealt with this period at some length because the Anglicising and feudalising of the kingdom in the South and East left the Highlands and Isles to their ancient tribal patriarchal condition. Scotland was thus split into two very different parts. The difference between the Highlands and Lowlands has persisted down to the present day. Which of the two systems is the better is a matter of opinion. To Clan Donald and all the western clans, the imposition of feudal superiors was a disaster. Feudal barons with their vassals and serfs were foreign in every way to the Gaelic tribes. As time went on the clans had to conform. Clan Donald, with its traditions of leadership of the Gaels in its past, was the last to bow to the inevitable, and suffered in consequence. The clans were broken at Culloden, the chiefs became feudal land-lords, and the process was complete.

2

Somerled, *Rex Insularum*

(*c.* 1100-1164)

Reigning in Scotland
ALEXANDER I
1107-1124
DAVID I
1124-1153
MALCOLM IV
1153-1165

SOMERLED WAS BORN in the first decade of the 12th century. As we can now consult written histories, we are able to compile a fairly accurate account of this great warrior's career. The records which deal with him at greatest length are two, both by seanachies of the Clan Donald: the MacVurich histories contained in the *Red and Black Books of ClanRanald,* and the *History of the Macdonalds* written by the Sleat historian, Hugh Macdonald, in the reign of Charles II.

From the first we transcribe the following account:

Giolla Bride, son of GillAdamnan, son of Solamh, and from him, the Thanes of Argyle, having been among his kindred in Ireland, that is, from the Clann Colla, which are the Manchuidh and Mathdamnaidh, *viz.,* the tribes of Macguire and Macmahon, it happened that this tribe held a meeting and conference in Fermanagh, on the estate of Macguire, and among the matters to be transacted was that Giolla Bride should get some estate of his own country, since he had been in banishment from his inheritance, by the power of the Danes and Norwegians. When Giolla Bride saw a large host of robust young people in the assembly, and that they were favourable to himself, the favour he asked of his friends was that so many persons as the adjacent fort in the place could hold should be allowed to go to Scotland with him, in the hope that he might obtain possession of his own inheritance and portion of it.

Giolla Bride proceeded with that party to Scotland, where they landed. They made frequent onsets and attacks on their enemies during this time of trouble, for their enemies were powerful and numerous at that time. All the islands from Man to Orkneys, and all the border land from Dumbarton to Caithness, in the north, were in the possession of the Danes; and such of the Gael of those lands as remained were protecting themselves in the woods and mountains; and at the end of that time Giolla Bride had a good son, who had come to maturity and renown.

It happened that the small party who were followers of Giolla Bride and Somerled were in the mountains and woods of Ardgour and of Morven, and they were surprised there by a large force of Danes and Norwegians. All the soldiers and plundering parties which Somerled had gathered round him, and he arranged them front and rear. Somerled put them in battle order, and made a great display of them to his enemies. He marched them three times before them in one company, so that they supposed there were three companies there. After that he attacked them, and they were defeated by Somerled and his party, and he did not halt in the pursuit till he drove them

ORIGINS OF
SOMERLED AND RAGNHILDA

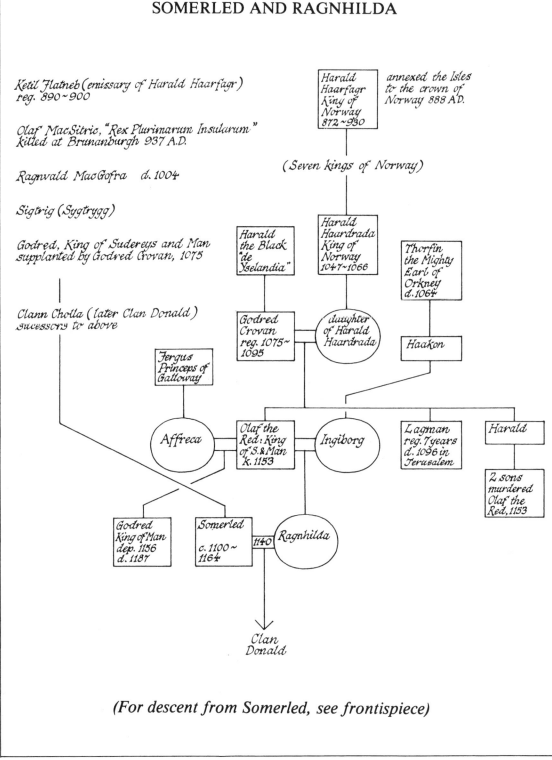

Ketil Flatneb (emissary of Harald Haarfagr)
reg. 890~900

Olaf MacSitric, "Rex Plurimarum Insularum"
killed at Brunanburgh 937 A.D.

Ragnvald MacGofra   d. 1004

Sigtrig (Sygtrygg)

Godred, King of Sudereys and Man
supplanted by Godred Crovan, 1075

Clann Cholla (later Clan Donald)
successors to above

Harald Haarfagr King of Norway 872~930 — annexed the Isles to the crown of Norway 888 A.D.

(Seven kings of Norway)

Harald the Black "de Yselandia"

Harald Haardrada King of Norway 1047-1066

Thorfin the Mighty Earl of Orkney d. 1064

Godred Crovan reg. 1075~1095

daughter of Harald Haardrada

Haakon

Fergus Princeps of Galloway

Affreca

Olaf the Red: King of S. & Man k. 1153

Ingiborg

Lagman reg. 7 years d. 1096 in Jerusalem

Harald

2 sons murdered Olaf the Red, 1153

Godred King of Man dep. 1156 d. 1187

Somerled c. 1100~1164

1140

Ragnhilda

Clan Donald

(For descent from Somerled, see frontispiece)

northward across the river Sheil, and a part escaped with their king to the Isles; and he did not cease from that work till he cleared the western side of Scotland of the Danes, except the islands of the Norwegians, called Innisgall; and he gained victory over his enemies in every field of battle. He spent part of his time in war and part in peace, until he marched with an army to the vicinity of Glasgow, when he was slain by his page, who took his head in the year of our Lord 1180 [1164]. His own people assert that it was not to make war against the king that he went on that expedition, but to obtain peace, for he did more in subduing the king's enemies than any war he waged against him.

From this brief account it appears that Gille Bride had made an abortive attempt to restore the fortunes of Clann Cholla in their ancient lands of Argyll. There, on the mainland, the Dalriadic Gaels were sustaining with difficulty their existence although continually raided by the Norse who dominated the adjacent Isles. Olaf the Red was in the process of carrying out one of these raids when we first meet Somerled in company with his father in the wilds of Morvern. They even had to shelter in a cave, the location of which is now unknown. *Gille Bride na h-Uaimh* (of the Cave), as he is known within the Clan, now disappears from our sight, and his great son emerges as the champion of the Gaels in the West. His first exploit was to repel an invasion in force by Olaf's Norsemen on the mainland of Morvern and Ardgour. Here the local tribes, notable amongst whom were the MacInnes clan and MacGillivrays who were kin to them, were anxious to oppose the invasion, but lacked a good leader. The MacInneses had lost their chief, a great and powerful warrior, in a previous encounter with the Norse while Somerled was still in hiding with his father. They now approached Somerled to be their chosen leader in the struggle.

How they came to see such promise in the young man we do not know; but they together with the other men of the Isles pointed out that he was in the direct line of the great Colla and Conn and it was his right and duty to take up the leadership and restore the fortunes of the Gael in those lands. This action of the "men of the Isles" is one instance of the power and initiative of the ordinary clansmen in choosing their chief. Chiefs did not always succeed to power by heredity or tanistry (the old Celtic law of succession whereby a chief was succeeded by his brother, especially if his son were a minor). The clan had to accept a chief before he could rule. This was most important in times of stress when the character of the chief had to be one of strength of purpose and skill in arms.

How Somerled came to accept the invitation to take the field against their enemies is the subject of a romantic story. The young man was more addicted to hunting and fishing than the serious problems of life. He had been fishing a pool in one of the rivers for days in an attempt to catch an especially fine salmon that lurked there. All his efforts had so far been unsuccessful, so he made a deal with the tribesmen, promising that, if he caught the salmon that day, he would take up the challenge and go to war with them. The salmon was caught, he kept his promise, and the salmon is to this day one of the quarterings on the arms of Clan Donald.

The first action undertaken by Somerled was a great victory. He saw that his forces were smaller than those of the invaders, and accordingly paraded his men several times within sight of the enemy, at times disappearing from sight, changing their attire in one way or another and emerging from behind a hill in different guise, until the Norsemen were quite deceived as to the strength of the force opposing them. A spirited charge with Somerled at its head spread confusion amongst the enemy, who expected the arrival of the considerable array they had seen. They were driven back to their ships with great loss, two of their chiefs being killed in the rout.

As Somerled's power and influence grew on the ancestral mainlands of the Dalriads, he began to turn his eyes to the Isles and his kinsfolk who lived under the domination of the Norse Kings. They had suffered long not only under the local kings, but even more from the punitive expeditions of the Kings of Norway. Some of these expeditions had been carried out with unbelievable ferocity. That of Magnus Barfod in 1102 was particularly vicious as contemporary accounts testify. The native Gaels must have suffered as much as their Norse overlords in these atacks. It was during this expedition which extended from Orkney to Man that Magnus came to an agreement with the King of Scots that all the Isles "between which and the mainland a helm-carrying ship should pass" should belong to the King of Norway. Magnus is said to have had his ship dragged across the isthmus between East and West Loch Tarbert with himself at the helm, thus claiming the whole peninsula of Kintyre, which ever after was deemed to be one of the Isles.

Olaf the Red must have recognised that the rise of the young Somerled was a force to be reckoned with. When the young Gaelic patriot sent messages to him desiring the hand of his daughter in marriage, the proud king at first refused disdainfully, telling him that the fair Ragnhilda's hand was to be bestowed upon someone much more important. Somerled bided his time—but not for long. It chanced that on an occasion when Olaf was on a voyage north with a few ships to administer justice in Skye, his galley was at anchor in the lee of the Point of Ardnamurchan. Somerled too was in his galley in the same bay, probably by design. The story goes that in Somerled's crew there was a skilful ship-wright, one Maurice MacNeil, who suggested a plan to make Olaf see reason in regard to the disposal of Ragnhilda's hand. The Gaelic chief agreed; and the *Saor Sleibhteach* (Sleat Carpenter) swam across under cover of darkness, bored several holes along the garboard strake of Olaf's galley, stuffed them with tallow and retreated. The two chiefs set sail for Skye next morning, the galleys rounded the headland and as they pitched and rolled in the Atlantic swell the tallow soon gave way and Olaf's galley began to sink. The haughty King hailed Somerled and requested help, but he refused any assistance until Olaf agreed to the marriage of Ragnhilda. Reluctantly the promise was given; and the carpenter of Sleat dived over the side and plugged the holes with wooden pins which he had thoughtfully provided. Thus were the fortunes of the MacIntyres assured, for Maurice was held high in the esteem of the ruling family from that time. As late as the 18th century, the famous bard, Duncan Ban Macintyre (*Mac an t-Saoir*), refers to the *Saor Sleibhteach* as his ancestor.

A romantic story, perhaps, but like some others there may be a grain of truth in it. In 1140 Somerled did marry his fair bride, and all Macdonalds who claim descent from that union, and there must be many thousands, may also claim to have the blood of this romantic princess in their veins.

During most of the period of Somerled's life the King of Scots was David I who reigned from 1124 to 1153. He was a strong king whose succession to his brother Alexander I, who died without issue, satisfied both the feudal law and that of the Celtic Law of Tanistry. He continued the policy of his predecessors in feudalising, Anglicising and Normanising his realm. During the reign of Donald Bàn there had been a reversal of these policies which succeeded for a short time only; but it showed that there were many in the Celtic parts of Scotland who disliked these processes, and none more so than the Gaels in the west and the Isles. David even descended to soliciting the aid of Norman knights from the North of England to suppress the rebellion of Angus, Celtic Mormaer (Earl) of Moray in 1130.

During his reign the insurrection of Malcolm MacHeth disturbed the kingdom. This Malcolm was said to have been an illegitimate son of the late Alexander I, King of Scots, but was at any rate accepted as the true representative of the Celtic Mormaers of Moray. The Mormaers had been rulers or viceroys, with the status of Earls, of the seven divisions of Celtic Alba. These divisions were Atholl, Angus, Caithness (with Sutherland), Fife, Mar and Buchan, Moray with Ross, and Stratherne—areas which bear the names to the present day, transcending modern county boundaries.

Malcolm gained strong support for his claims in all the Gaelic parts of Alba, and, as might have been expected, Somerled supported him, even giving him his sister in marriage to cement the alliance. At the time of Malcolm's rebellion we find an individual named Wymond, a monk, appearing in records as the rebel Earl. There is much uncertainty as to whether these were two persons or one and the same. Wymond was said to have been a son of Angus but had started life as a monk in the Cistercian Monastery of Furness. He gained influence in the priesthood and popularity with Olaf, King of Man, who put him in charge of a new monastery. Having gained power and popularity, he now proclaimed himself son of the late Angus, Mormaer of Moray. It is a strange story. Whatever the origin of the Mormaer who rebelled, he was known as Malcolm MacHeth and as such we refer to him. His rising, after a few years of strife and guerrilla warfare, ended in 1134 when he was caught crossing the River Cree in Galloway and imprisoned by David in Roxburgh Castle. Twenty years later the sons of Malcolm were again in rebellion with the support of their uncle Somerled, who gave his aid partly to strengthen his own position, partly in support of the Gaels of Alba, who disliked the way their age-old culture and customs had been suppressed by the unpatriotic monarchs, Malcolm Canmore and his successors.

About the same time events took a turn which greatly affected the policy of Somerled, working to his advantage because the Gaelic chief was able by energetic action to profit by it and consolidate his hold on the Isles. Olaf the Red died in 1153, murdered by two ambitious nephews, sons of his brother Harald. Godred, eldest son of Olaf by his first wife, Affreca of Galloway, was in Norway at the time. On hearing the news he returned to the Isles at once, executed the murderers, established his authority and almost at once embarked on a successful campaign in Ireland and in Man. He became overbearing and tyrannical, however, antagonising his nobles so much that one of their number, Thorfin son of Ottar, went to Somerled and asked him for his son, Dugall, in order to make him king over the Isles. This suited Somerled admirably and Thorfin took Dugall through all the Isles, proclaiming him king in defiance of Godred, who was "dismayed in mind" when the matter was reported to him.

Godred gathered his galleys and went north to assert his authority. Somerled was prepared and the two fleets met in early January 1156 off the north-west coast of Islay. A bloody battle was fought all night and when day dawned with both sides exhaused, an agreement was reached by which Somerled took all the Isles south of Ardnamurchan, including Kintyre, and Godred retained those north-wards of that peninsula. The latter part of this treaty did not last long, for two years later Somerled invaded Man with 53 ships and defeated Godred who fled to Norway. The behaviour of Somerled's followers during this campaign left much to be desired, and the memory of their brutalities to the people and violations of sacred property persisted in the island for centuries.

In the following year Somerled and the young King of Scots came to an understanding which restored peace between them for the next five years. By the same agreement a settlement was reached in the turbulent North by the release of Donald MacHeth, Malcolm's son, who had been imprisoned after the latest rising. This treaty was deemed of such importance that royal charters issued by Malcolm the Maiden in 1160 were dated *apud Pert natali domino proximo post concordium regis et Somerledi* (at Perth on the next Xmas Day after the Treaty between the King and Somerled).

Thus by 1158 in the space of some 40 years the great Somerled had restored the fortunes of Clan Cholla. From being a fugitive in the wilds of Morvern he had become *Rex Insularum* in succession to the Norse princes; still nominally under the Kings of Norway, while also nominally holding his mainland lands, part of old Dalriada, under the King of Scots. In actual fact he was an independent prince and acted as such, regarding the Norse and Scots kings as rather inconvenient sovereigns of distant realms, an attitude which prevailed in Clan Donald for many years to come. This is well reported by the Sleat historian (Hugh Macdonald), whom we quote from Dr I. F. Grant's *Lordship of the Isles*:

> What specially interested us at the moment was the speech that the seventeenth-century clan historian puts into Somerled's mouth in reply to an envoy sent from the king to order him to give up his mainland possessions. It is unlikely that anything more than the gist of what Somerled might have said should have survived for over five centuries; but what Macdonald makes him say embodies the claims to the status of more than that of a subject and feudal liegeman that were made over and over again by the Lord of the Isles, his heirs and descendants, and by the claimants to that shattered dignity in the years that followed the forfeiture. "Somerled replied, that he had as good a right to the lands upon the continent as he had to the Isles. As to the Isles, he had an undoubted right to them, his predecessors being possessed of them by the goodwill and consent of Eugenius the First, for obligations conferred upon him; That, when his forefathers were dispossessed of them by the invasion of the Danes, they had no assistance to defend or recover them from the Scottish king, and that he had his right of them from the Danes; but, however, he would be assisting to the king in any other affairs and would prove as loyal as any of his nearest friends, but, as long as he breathed, he would not condescend to resign any of his rights which he possessed to any; and that he was resolved to lose all or keep all, and that he thought himself as worthy of his own as any about the king's court."

In the years following his treaty with Somerled the King of Scots had been carrying out great changes in the Celtic districts of Moray and Galloway by the introduction of Saxon and Norman incomers who were displacing the native population. Somerled as a true leader of the Gael against all foreign usurpers reacted by threatening the King of Scots in his own realm. It is not likely that in mounting this final expedition he cherished any plan to conquer the whole of Scotland, but to relieve the pressure of the royal forces on his kinsmen in the North and South. However, having sailed up the Clyde with a large fleet of 160 galleys, the army camped near Renfrew. That night Somerled was murdered in his tent by one Maurice MacNeil (*not* the Sleat carpenter) whose presence there roused no suspicion as he is said to have been a near relative. If he was, some very strong reason must be found for such treachery. It has been assumed that Maurice was in the pay of Malcolm, which is a fair assumption. If there were a private vendetta leading to the murder, it does not appear on the surface, for in such a case secrecy would be essential. The first was the more likely. Perhaps the report, unconfirmed by any historian of the Clan, that King Malcolm sent Somerled's body at his own expense to be buried in Iona, might indicate some act of repentance to salve the King's conscience. The Clan, however, have always maintained that Somerled was buried in his newly endowed Abbey of Saddell in Kintyre, the foundation completed by his son Reginald.

Thus passed the great Celtic hero of the race of Colla and Conn, founder of a dynasty that lasted for 300 years. He had been a resourceful and brave warrior, as well as being a wise and prudent politician. In person he is described by the Sleat historian as "A well-tempered man, in body shapely, of a fair piercing eye, of middle stature and of quick discernment." In assessing the character and achievements of this great Chief we cannot do better than quote our seanachies from their *Clan Donald* (Vol. I, page 55):

Somerled was probably the greatest hero that his race has produced. It may seem strange that no Gaelic bard has sung of his exploits, but in his day and long afterwards, Gaelic singers were more taken up with the mythical heroes of the Feinn than with the genuine warriors of their native land. Others of his line may have equalled him in personal bravery and military prowess; but Somerled was more than a warrior. He possessed not only the courage and dash which are associated with the Celtic character; he had the organising brain, the fertile resource, the art not only of winning battles, but of turning them to account; that sovereign faculty of commanding the respect and allegiance of men which marks the true king, the able man of Thomas Carlyle's ideal. Without the possession of this imperial capacity he could never, in the face of such tremendous odds, have wrested the sovereignty

The Castle of Saddell in Kintyre, close to the Abbey founded by Somerled and in which he is said to be buried

of the Gael from his hereditary foes, and handed it to the Clan Cholla to be their heritage for hundreds of years. He was the instrument by which the position, the power, the language of the Gael were saved from being overwhelmed by Teutonic influence, and Celtic culture and tradition received a new lease of life. He founded a family which played no ignoble part in Scottish history. If our faith in the principle of heredity is sometimes shaken by degenerate sons of noble sires, when the last links of a line of long ago prove unworthy heirs of a great past, our faith is confirmed in it by the line of princes that sat upon the Island throne, and who as a race were stamped with the heroic qualities which characterised the son of Gillebride. Somerled's life struggle had been with the power of the Norseman, whose sun in the Isles he saw on the eve of setting. But he met his tragic fate in conflict with another and more formidable set of forces. This was the contest which Somerled bequeathed as a legacy to his successors. It was theirs to be the leading spirits in the resistance of the Gaelic race, language and social life to the new and advancing order which was already moulding into an organic unity the various nationalities of Scotland—the ever-increasing, ever-extending power of feudal institutions.

3

Reginald

(1164-1207)

Reigning in Scotland
WILLIAM THE LION
1165-1214

THE SONS OF Somerled by Ragnhilda, daughter of Olaf the Red, are taken by most authorities to be Dugall, Reginald (Raghnall, Ranald or Raonall to use the various spelling of that name) and Angus. That Dugall was the eldest seems to be accepted by all. One or two aspects of this problem make one wonder if Dugall was not perhaps a son by a marriage, "handfast" or other, previous to the official marriage in 1140. Dugall was old enough in 1153 to be installed by the rebellious Thorfin, son of Ottar, as King of the Isles over the head of Godred. If he was a son of Ragnhilda he could not have been more than twelve years old. That may be of little consequence, as at that time he was in any case only a pawn in the hands of the rebellious men of the Isles to oust the obnoxious Godred. Again, it would not be strange to assume that Ragnhilda would give her own name, or the equivalent, to her first-born son, for mothers sometimes do wish to perpetuate their own name after they have surrendered it to their husbands. In the event Reginald her son inherited the Isles of Islay and Kintyre, which were the centre of the Kingdom and remained as such during the whole history of the Kingdom and later Lordship of the Isles. From that nucleus the larger realm of Macdonald was built.

About the last year of Somerled's life the pressure on the Celtic Church to conform to the Roman rule was increased. In the later years of the 11th century Queen Margaret had restored the Abbey in Iona, but there is no evidence that she tried to insist on its Romanisation at that time. Iona had suffered five brutal violations of its monastery. Two have already been referred to (in 795 and 801). In 806, sixty-eight of the monks were martyred by Norse pirates and many valuable relics destroyed. Again in 825 in another raid the Abbot, Blathmac, prepared for it by ordering the remaining relics and books to be hidden without informing him of their hiding place, so that he would be unable, even under torture, to reveal them to the pirates. He was wise to do so for it happened just as he foresaw, and he and his monks were murdered; but the relics, which by this time could not have been very many, were saved. In 986 the last raid on the Isles took place. This time it was carried out by Danes from Dublin and the Abbot and fifteen monks were slain. Shortly after, the Kings of Norway and Dublin became Christians and tried to make some restitution for their predecessors' sins. The Church continued during Somerled's reign to be of the Celtic pattern as founded by Columba; but he saw that pressure would be brought to bear by the Kings of Scots who had suppressed the Culdees who followed the Columban tradition, and replaced them with the Roman Church.

The *Annals of Ulster* under date 1164 states that

> select members of the muinntir [community] of Iona: *viz.* the Arch-priest, Augustine, and the Lector, that is Dubsidhe, and the Disertach, that is

MacGilladuff, and the head of the Culdees, namely MacForcellaigh, and select members of the muinntir besides came to ask the Co-arb of Columkill, namely Flaherty O'Brolchan, to accept the Abbacy of Ia [Iona], by advice of Somerled and the men of Argyll and the Isles. But the Co-Arb of Patrick and the King of Erin, that is O'Lochlan, and the nobles of the family of Ewan prevented him.

Several interesting conclusions may be drawn. *First*, the "muinntir" of Iona seem to have been still of Gaelic origin as the names of these dignitaries are all Gaelic: *Second*, O'Brolchan must have been a very good and strong character to be so valued by the communities in both Ireland and Iona: *Third*, this would seem to have been an attempt on Somerled's part to retain the Celtic form in the Church of Iona and the rest of his realm: *Fourth*, in an important step such as this he sought and had the backing of the "men of Argyll and the Isles." The last is most important for here again we see that the men of the Isles take a large share in the policy of the kingdom, as they did at the very outset, and did later in the Council of the Isles which sat at Finlaggan in Islay. The new monarchy was very much a constitutional organisation which accounts for its long life with remarkably little internal strife. The Kings and the later Lords of the Isles ruled with wisdom and tolerance: the clans of which the realm was composed were consulted in matters of state, and for long periods dwelt in peace. As ever, until peace was disturbed, records are silent and one is safe in assuming that the intervening years were reasonably calm. The disturbance of the peace of the Isles came always from the adjacent Kingdom of Scotland, the sovereigns of which were continually seeking to impose their rule on the Islesmen, who knew very well that such an imposition meant feudalism with its concomitant serfdom of the ordinary folk and overlordship of superiors chosen by the King to regiment the chiefs. This did not recommend itself to the men of the Isles of whatever rank.

Besides the sons of Ragnhilda there were several other sons by unrecorded mothers. One, Gillecoluim, died with his father at Renfrew. Others were Gall MacSgillin by a Lowland woman (hence his name "Gall"), Gillies and Olave (Olaf). The Sleat historian, Hugh, states that Somerled's eldest son was also Somerled; but if this is correct he could not have survived very long. From other sources (Norse sagas) it seems likely that this Somerled was a grandson of the great founder; but even those sources agree he did not last long nor did he make much of an impression on the events of the period. We hear of only one daughter of Somerled and that was Beatrice (Beathag) whose brother Reginald installed her as the first Prioress of his newly founded priory of Benedictine nuns in Iona. Her grave-stone is on record as bearing the inscription *Behag Nyn Shorly Ilvrid Prioressa* (Beatrice, daughter of Somerled, Prioress).

We now return to the three sons of Somerled who left their mark on our clan history, the rest having faded into obscurity.

Dugall fell heir to Lorn, Mull and Jura: Reginald to Islay and Kintyre, the seat of power since the early days of Somerled's rise: and Bute with part of Arran and Garmoran, the territories from Ardnamurchan to Glenelg, went to Angus. The last named seems to have been a strange distribution of lands considering they were so widely separated, with Dugall's lands of Lorn and Mull intervening. In fact this division did not last long. We do not know if Somerled made these arrangements at all. His death was sudden and unexpected while he was at the height of his power and he may not have directed how his lands were to be apportioned. On the other hand it might be assumed that, inasmuch as Reginald entered into possession of the traditional centre of the realm, he was the prime heir of his father. In the end Reginald and his line did succeed to the leadership of Clan Cholla.

Before dealing with Dugall and Reginald, we should dispose of Angus and his line because it did not last long. We have seen he had Bute, part of Arran and Garmoran. This last part was known as The Rough Bounds (*Garbh Criochan*) and lay north of Ardnamurchan comprising Moidart, Morar and Knoydart. Meantime the North Isles—the Long Island (Lewis, Harris, the Uists and Barra)—had been taken over from Godred together with Man by one Reginald, a Norse King of Man. So at this time there were two kings named Reginald. It was not long before our Reginald fell out with his brother Angus. There was a battle in 1192 and Angus got the best of it; but later in 1210 Angus and his three sons were killed by "the men of Skye." This does not necessarily mean they were killed in Skye; and the men of Skye at that time must have been subjects of the Norse Reginald who probably resented Angus's occupation of Garmoran, which the former might well have regarded as his property. One account says the action took place in Moidart, which may bear out the theory that it was a Norse back-lash against the power of Somerled's family being extended into the realm left by Godred after his return from Norway. The male line of Angus being thus extinguished, there remained only Jane, an heiress, daughter of one of the sons of Angus. She married Alexander, son of Walter, the High Steward of Scotland, and the Stewarts thus came into possession of Bute and Arran after some resistance.

It falls now to examine the fortunes of the family of Dugall Mac Somerled. Seanachies and historians disagree as to whether this Dugall was the progenitor of the Clann Dugall who held lands in Lorn with their seat at Dunollie Castle at the mouth of Oban Bay. The family still lives there with a long history behind them.

The authors of *Clan Donald* (A. & A. Macdonald) deal with this knotty problem thus:

Angus' male line having thus become extinct, his possessions passed over to Reginald and his son Roderick. James the son of Angus, however, left a daughter Jane, who married Alexander, eldest son of Walter, the High Steward of Scotland. This led, in future years, to much trouble as regards the possession of the island of Bute. After the death of Angus and his sons in battle, the mainland and island possessions of the sons of Somerled were divided equally between the families of Reginald and Dugall. The relations between these two branches of the Clan Cholla were never of the most cordial description, and even at that early date a misunderstanding arose as to the ownership of Mull, which lasted over 100 years. The house of Somerled however, was all powerful in that region; the voice of the Campbell was not yet heard in the land, and the families of Argyll and the Isles were vassals of the Clan Cholla.

Reginald of Isla, according to the Irish historians, seems to have been popular both in Scotland and Ireland, feared in war but loved in peace. The exigencies of the time often led him to the field of battle, sometimes on the defensive sometimes as the aggressor; yet, as has often been true of the greatest heroes, he loved peace more than war, and we find him acting the part of peacemaker not only among his own people, but also on the other side of the Irish Channel.

It is probably at this stage that we can most conveniently discuss and, so far as possible, dispose of the question as to which of the sons of Somerled was the older, Reginald or Dugall. The seniority of Dugall would not, for reasons that will afterwards appear, constitute the Clan Dugall the senior branch of the house of Somerled, and therefore the question, though one of interest, is not of serious importance. In those days the feudal law of primogeniture, by which the oldest son succeeds to his father's lands, was not operative in the Isles; lands were gavelled equally among the male members of the family, and in more than one case it is difficult to arrive at definite conclusions when questions as to seniority arise. It is only inferentially that we can form an opinion as to the point at issue. The Seanachies give us no assistance. M'Vurich is silent on the subject, although, in mentioning the sons of Somerled, he names Dugall first. Hugh Macdonald, adopting what is with him a favourite rôle, bastardises Dugall, evidently with a view of placing beyond doubt or cavil the seniority of the house of Isla. Historians have followed one another slavishly in making Dugall the oldest of the sons of Somerled. One reason only can there be for the adoption of such a view. When the barons of Man and the Isles rose against Godred in 1153, it was Dugall who was carried through the Isles and proclaimed King. This has been taken as evidence of the contrary. Most probably it was because he was the younger son that he was put forward as his mother's heir for the possession of Man and the Isles, while Reginald, as the older son, was regarded as his father's successor in the hereditary domains of Oirthirghael. We have already stated that primogeniture did not rule in the Isles as regards the inheritance of lands. Yet the head of the race, whether brother or son to the last chief, enjoyed certain privileges. Preferably to others he possessed those lands which had always been connected with the residence of the head of the house. Hence, although the territories of Somerled were divided in somewhat equal portions, it is a significant fact that the occupancy of the lands of Kintyre and Isla remained with the descendants of Reginald. The modern Campbeltown became in after times the chief seat of the Lords of the Isles in the peninsula of Kintyre, and went under the name of Kinloch Kilkerran. It would thus appear that these lands, which were the seat of the Dalriadic power and the peculiar patrimony of the Clan Cholla, became after the days of Kenneth MacAlpin associated with that branch of the Scoto-Irish race which was represented by Somerled and his descendants. That Reginald and his posterity held this immemorial heritage of the Clan Cholla in preference to the line of Dugall seems to suggest the seniority of the house of Isla. Still further there is a prominence given in the records of the time to Reginald and his descendants, which clearly points to their being the chief inheritors of the name and honours of the house of Somerled.

Even if it were the case, which in our opinion it is not, that Dugall MacSomerled was the oldest of the three sons, that fact would not constitute the Clan Dugall, necessarily, the senior branch of the Clan Cholla. There are grave reasons for doubting whether the Clan Dugall, as represented by the head of that line for upwards of four hundred years, are at all descended from Dugall MacSomerled. A brief glance at the descendants of this Dugall may be helpful in the solution of the question. Dugall, son of Somerled, left three sons, Dugall Scrag, Duncan, and another son named Uspac Hakon, who appears in the Norwegian Sagas. Uspac stood high in the confidence of King Haco, who made him a King of the Sudereys. It is recorded by the same authority that in 1228-30, when the Norwegian forces came south to Isla Sound, the three brothers, Kings Uspac, Dugall and Duncan, were already there with a large armament, and it is interesting to find reference to the second Somerled as taking part in the expedition. The Sudereyan princes invited the Norwegians to a banquet, but the latter, having heard of the strong wine drunk at the Celtic symposia (does the potent national beverage possess this venerable antiquity?) and having their suspicions otherwise aroused, declined the proffered hospitality. A night attack was made on the Norsemen, when a considerable number of the Sudereyans, Somerled among the rest, were killed. Dugall Scrag was taken prisoner and protected by Uspac, who does not appear to have been implicated in the fray. With this incident Dugall Scrag passes out of history.

Shortly after this, Olave King of Man invaded Bute, then in the possession of the Scots, with a fleet of 80 ships, and besieged the Castle of Rothesay. The Norwegians were eventually successful with a loss of 390 men, and Uspac Hakon, who was among the assailants, was mortally wounded by a stone hurled from the battlements. He survived only till he reached Kintyre, whence his body was borne to Iona.

After this, Duncan the son of Dugall MacSomerled was the only member of the family who seems to have had any territorial position in the Isles; in fact, so far as history records, he was the sole representative of the line who left behind him a traceable posterity. As Duncan de Lorn he witnessed a charter to the Earl of Athole, and as Duncan de Ergalita he signs the letter and oath to the Pope of the nobles of Scotland, on the treaty of Ponteland in 1244. Duncan's son, King Ewin, or, as he is designated in the Sagas, King John, was the son of this Duncan, and the representative of the family in 1263. Historians have assumed that King John or Ewin was the father of Alexander de Ergadia, who with his son, John, was the determined enemy of Bruce in the war of Scottish independence. Now it is almost as certain as any historical fact connected with so remote a period can be, that Ewin of Lorn, the son of Duncan, left no male issue. It seems clear that his line terminated with two heiresses, one of whom married the King of Norway and the other Alexander of Isla, son of Angus Mor. It is on record that Alexander of Isla, through his wife Juliana, possessed lands in the island of Lismore, which was part of the lordship of Lorn, and Edward I summoned Edward Baliol before him for preventing them from enjoying possession of these lands. It is well established that, according to the feudal and Celtic laws of territorial possession, females could not inherit lands except on the failure of heirs male. Only because of such failure do we find, first Christina, and afterwards Amie MacRuairi, in the line of Roderick, the son of Reginald, inheriting the patrimony of the family. Hence the succession of Juliana of Lorn to a portion at least of her father's lands, forbids us to believe that he left any sons, and strongly suggests the conclusion that the male descendants of Dugall MacSomerled terminated with Ewin. Supposing, however, for the sake of argument, not only that Dugall MacSomerled was the oldest son, but that Alexander de Ergadia, who flourished in the time of Bruce, was his direct descendant, this is very far from proving that the Clan Dugall are the senior branch of the Clan Cholla. In truth, such a conclusion is impossible in view of the fact, that, in 1388 the line of Alexander de Ergadia terminated in an heiress, who brought over the lordship of Lorn to her husband, John Stewart. It is thus clear to a demonstration that the Clan Dugall, of whom the family of Dunolly is the leading branch, cannot, on any supposition, be traced back in the male line to Dugall, the son of Somerled. Although we are not writing a history of the Clan Dugall, it is desirable that their real origin should, if possible, be pointed out if for no other purpose than to give the Clan Donald their true position as the main branch of the Clan Cholla in the Western Highlands. An opportunity for looking at the question in its true bearings

THE MACDOUGALLS OF LORN
(from records of the family)

Dalriadic Kings

Gillebride

OLAVE II (Godredson)
King of Man and the Isles
1114-1154

SOMERLED   =   married (2) in 1140   =   RAGNHILDA

Rex Insularum
k. 1164 along with two
sons of his first marriage

DUGALL
Regulus of Lorn, Mull and Jura
Later King of the South Isles
1st of Dunollie

Reginald
King of the South Isles

Angus
Lord of Bute
and Arran
k. 1210

DUNCAN
2nd of Dunollie
d. 1248

Macdonald
Lords of the Isles

EWEN
"King John"
3rd of Dunollie

Sir ALEXANDER
4th of Dunollie

DUNCAN
6th of Dunollie

Juliana = Alexander
5th Lord of the Isles

Sir JOHN of Lorn
5th of Dunollie
d. 1317

ALAN
7th of Dunollie
from whom direct line to
present day in the person of
COLINE MACDOUGALL
30th of Dunollie

Ewen
5th of Lorn

Janet
m. Sir Robert Stewart
who took the Lordship of Lorn
which was transferred by charter
of 13 April 1388 to her sister

Isabella
m. Sir John Stewart
of Innermeath who took
the Lordship of Lorn
finally to Campbell of Argyll

will immediately occur. Meantime, our discussion of the question of seniority as between Reginald and Dugall, the sons of Somerled, has necessarily led us to anticipate, and we must now take up the thread of our history where we dropped it. Reginald, the son of Somerled, died in 1207. This is the date given by the Book of Clanranald, and is probably correct. The seal adhibited to his charter to Paisley Abbey is thus described: "In the middle of the seal on one side, a ship filled with men at arms; on the reverse side, the figure of an armed man on horseback with a sword drawn in his hand." By Fiona, daughter of the Earl of Moray, Reginald had three sons—Donald, Roderick and Dugall. Most authorities mention only two sons, excluding Dugall; nor do we find any record of him in the division of his father's lands. Yet the MS. of 1450, the most valuable genealogical authority we possess, includes Dugall among the sons of Reginald; and not only so, but traces the descent of the Clan Dugall to him instead of the son of Somerled.

As a matter of fact, and in view of all that has been said, this is the only theory of the descent of the Clan Dugall that appears on the evidence possible to adopt; and the value of the testimony of the 1450 MS on this question is immensely enhanced when we remember that it was in the years during which the writer of that MS flourished that the Dunolly family, the undoubted heads of their race, were invested by Stewart of Lorn in the posession of the lands from which they derive their designation and which they have held down to the present day.

On the other hand Gregory in his *History of the Western Highlands* states categorically that Dugall MacSomerled was the founder of the Clan Dugall "de Ergadia" (*i.e.* of Argyll) and Lorn. In the light of our own seanachies' treatment of the matter, this verdict of Gregory's seems too easy a way out of the dilemma. It is historical fact that the male line of Dugall MacSomerled died out in males in the person of the famous Ewan of Lorn (King John in some records) whose doings at the time of Haakon's expedition to Largs are interesting if a little complicated. We shall have to deal with this later. Ewan of Lorn left two daughters, one of whom, Julia, married Alasdair Og, brother of the famous Angus Og (*d.* 1329), friend of Robert Bruce.

We have seen that the Sleat historian gets out of the difficulty by stating that Dugall was illegitimate. This is too easy to say and too difficult to prove. Accepting that Dugall was the eldest son of Somerled, one asks who was his mother? If not the eldest by the marriage to the Princess Ragnhilda, could he have been the son of a "handfast" marriage of earlier date? Handfasting was like the old Scots custom of Marriage by Declaration by which a man and woman declared themselves man and wife in front of witnesses. This was deemed legal until 1939. The difference between this and handfasting was that the latter was taken to be valid for a year. Sometimes the "handfast" was performed by clasping hands through a hole in a monolith. Monoliths of this kind are common throughout the Isles. If the woman became pregnant during the year the union was usually confirmed by a proper marriage. In later years such marriages were very hard to confirm legally, and this led to many unfortunate individuals being regarded as illegitimate when they were nothing of the kind in Highland eyes. We do not therefore regard Hugh's verdict as final.

Whether we accept Gregory's ruling or that of our own seanachies matters little. Clan Dugall are undoubtedly of the line of Somerled.

Having thus dealt with the origins of Clan Dugall according to our own and other seanachies, it is only fair to record the views of that noble family itself. The accompanying chart has been supplied by the present Chief of the Clan

MacDougall, Mme. Coline MacDougall of MacDougall and Dunollie, 30th Chief. Their records state that two sons of Somerled by *his first marriage* fell with him at Renfrew in 1164. This is interesting as it would seem to bear out the theory already put forward. Might not Dugall MacSomerled, eldest son of Somerled, after all be one of the sons by this first marriage? We have seen that primogeniture did not necessarily hold under the Celtic Law of Tanistry.

Whether Dugall, founder of the family of the Lords of Lorn, was the eldest son of Ragnhilda, or of some other girl by the first marriage, matters little although it would be interesting to solve a problem which, at this distance of time, would seem to be insoluble.

* * *

Reginald, who carried on the main line of Somerled leading eventually to the Macdonald Kings and Lords of the Isles, was popular both in Scotland and Ireland if we believe the Irish historians. He was of peaceful disposition and showed it by his benefactions to the Church which by this time was of Roman form. Three monasteries were founded by him—a monastery of black monks in Iona in honour of God and Saint Columcille, a monastery of black nuns in the same place, and a monastery of grey friars at Saddell in Kintyre.

The latter foundation, which was begun by Somerled in his lifetime and received the body of the great man after his death, and also that of his son Reginald in 1207, is described thus by our seanachies (*Clan Donald*, Vol. I, p. 458):

> The oldest religious foundation connected with the Family of the Isles—at anyrate within the historical period—is the Abbey of Saddell, and a brief sketch of its origin and early history must be given before we pass on to the more widely known and still beautiful Church of St Mary's in Icolumkill. Tradition is not unanimous as to whether Saddell Monastery was founded by Somerled or his son Reginald, while Hugh Macdonald, the Seanachie of Sleat, ascribes its origin to Donald, the son of Reginald and the founder of the Clan. It is highly probable that so extensive a building would have been the work of several generations of the Lords of the Isles, and that while Somerled founded and endowed it and its erection was begun in his lifetime, his son and grandson enriched it with further gifts, and it was completed only in Donald's time. That it owes its original foundation to Somerled is confirmed by the almost universal tradition that his remains were interred within the Abbey, while one authority places the completion of the building as late as 1256— not long before the death of Donald de Ile and the succession of his son Angus Mor. The Church of Saddell was cruciform in structure, with the orientation and pointed arch characteristic of Gothic buildings; but, except in the windows, we miss the dressed sandstone which marked the full advance from the Celtic to the Gothic age. The Monastery lies in an exact position towards the four cardinal points. Its dimensions were at one time imposing, though little now survives beyond a mass of featureless confusion. Part of the gable of the transept and the aperture for a window alone survive; but vandalism here, as elsewhere, has done its unhallowed work, and the finished stonework of the window has almost all been removed. The cruciform minster was 136 feet long from east to west, by 24 feet broad, while the transepts from north to south measured 78 feet by 24. The conventual buildings were on the south; the dormitory was 58 feet long, and there are traces of the study room. The cloister girth was 58 feet square. Within the arched recess in the south wall of the choir, Somerled's tomb is pointed out. The sculpture

represents him as wearing a high pointed head-piece, a tippet of mail hanging over the neck and shoulders, and the body clad down to the knees with a skirt or "jupon" scored with lines to represent the folds. The right hand is raised up on to the shoulder, while the left clasps a two-handed sword. The inscription on the corner of the slab has been worn away by the elements, and has for ages been indecipherable.

The same historians describe Reginald's development of the Church in Iona thus:

The most important of the churches that owed either their origin or resuscitation to the Lords of the Isles was the Abbey Church of Iona. About 1072 Queen Margaret had restored the monastery and revived its establishment, but by the latter half of the twelfth century these had again fallen into ruin and decay. Reginald MacSomerled, whom M'Vurich describes as "the most distinguished of the Galls, that is, the Norwegians, and of the Gaels for prosperity, sway of generosity, and feats of arms," resolved to repair the waste places of the sacred island and restore its church and monastery to more than their pristine glory. According to the same authority, "three monasteries were formed by him—a monastery of black monks in I, or Iona, in honour of God and Saint Columchille; a monastery of black nuns in the same place; and a monastery of gray friars at Sagadule or Sadelle, in Kintyre," which latter we have already described. A column on the southeast, under the tower of St Mary's, bears the inscription—"*Donaldus O'Brolchan fecit hoc opus.*" This "Donaldus" was prior of Derry, and a relative of Flaherty O'Brolchan, bishop and Abbot of Derry, and although there is no distinct record on the subject, "Donaldus" must have been prior of Iona during the period these buildings were erected. As he died in 1203, the Church and Monastery of Iona must have been completed before that date, and this is further placed beyond doubt by the deed of confirmation of the Benedictine Monastery, which is still in the Vatican, and bears the date of 9th December 1203. The Tyronensis Order of Benedictine Monks, founded by Benedict, an Italian monk of the fifth and sixth centuries, and called black monks from the colour of their habits, was planted in the Monastery of Iona by Reginald of the Isles. He also established there, in connection with it, an order of Benedictine nuns, over whose convent his sister Beatrice was the first prioress; differing in this respect from the policy of the great Columkill himself, of whom tradition says that he would suffer none of the softer sex to set foot upon Iona, and to whom the somewhat acrid saying is ascribed.

> "Far am bi bo bi bean
> 'S far am bi bean bi mallachadh"

> (Where there is a cow there is a woman,
> And where there is a woman there is mischief)

Early this century the inscription on the monumental slab over the remains of the first Prioress was legible to this extent—"*Behag Nyn Shorle Ilvrid Priorissa.*" that is, "Beatrice daughter of Somerled Prioress." There is a tradition that the same pious lady built Trinity Temple, Carinish, the ruins of which are still standing in a state of comparative preservation. The historian of Sleat, on the other hand, ascribes its construction to another lady—also a descendant of Somerled—Amie Macruairi, famous in her day for works of piety and charity, and whose memory is still fragrant among the people of the North Isles. Trinity Temple is probably not the architectural product of any one age. There are traces of a foundation older than the days of Somerled, going back to the time of the Celtic Church, shown by indications of one at least of those bee-hive cells characteristic of that early phase of church architecture. It is also to be noted that Christina (daughter of Allan Macruari and aunt of Amie), who flourished about the end of the thirteenth and beginning of the fourteenth century, gave a grant of the chapel and lands of Carinish to the Monastery of Inchaffray, from which we infer that the Temple or Church in question is older than Amie, the wife of the "Good" John of Isla. Hence the probable correctness of the McVurich tradition that Trinity Church was built by the daughter of Somerled on a site formerly occupied by a Culdee establishment, though we may likewise adopt the tradition of Hugh Macdonald to the extent that, in later times, Amie Macruari did, as we shall see, repair and possibly enlarge the building. The Church of St Mary's, in Iona, measured 160 ft. × 24 ft., and 10 feet across the transepts, while its central tower, which still survives, is 70 feet in height. The high altar was of marble 6 ft. × 4 ft., but not a fragment now remains.

Another foundation that benefited from the generosity of Somerled and his successors was at Paisley. Why Paisley, which has never been within the territories of the Kingdom of the Isles? We can only assume that when Somerled fell at Renfrew the clerics who performed the last offices for the dead warrior came from that Abbey, the nearest to the scene of the tragedy. Some of them may have attended the funeral cortege when it set out for Saddell Abbey, founded by Somerled himself, where he was entombed. Reginald followed his father's example by making generous grants to the Abbey. So too did Donald, son of Reginald, and Angus Mor, his son and successor, as our seanachies relate:

Before 1200, Reginald became a monk of Paisley, and granted to the monastery eight cows and two pennies for one year, and one penny in perpetuity from every house on his territory from which smoke issued, and his peace and protection whithersoever the monks should go, enjoining his dependants and heirs in no way to injure them, and swearing by St Columb to inflict on the former the punishment of death, and that the latter should have his malediction if they disobeyed his injunction. His wife Fonia, who was a sister of the convent, granted to the monks the tithe of all her goods, whether in her own possession or sent for sale by land or sea. After the year 1210, Donald, the son of Reginald, who also had joined the brotherhood of Paisley, and whose wife became a sister of the convent, confirmed her father's grants both of the eight cows and of the smoke tax, for his salvation and that of his wife. Before 1295, Angus Mor, son of Donald, after the example of his father and grandfather, gave donations to the same institution as a friend and brother of the order. The annual smoke tax is continued in the same terms, while the eight cows are commuted for a half merk of silver for each of the houses whence smoke issues, and half a merk also from his own mansion, the donor giving also his peace and friendship. Also he grants them the right of fishing if they should desire it in any waters upon his territories. Still further, for the salvation of his Lord and King Alexander II and his son, Alexander III, also for his own and his heirs' he devoted to God and St James and Mirinus of the Monastery of Paisley and the monks there serving God and to serve God for ever, the Church of St Kiaran, in his lands of Kintyre, with all its pertinents. This was confirmed by his son, Alexander. We do not find any further grants or confirmations on the part of the Lords of the Isles until the time of the last Earl of Ross, whom we observe on the 21st May 1455, bestowing on the Abbey and Convent of Paisley, for the honour and glory of God, and of the Virgin Mary and Saint Mirinus, and of all the Saints, the Rectories of the Churches of St Kerran, Colmanell in Kintyre, and Knapdale, in the diocese of Argyle, given by his predecessors to them, for their and his salvation. We thus see that from the very beginning of the Island dynasty, reckoning from the time of Somerled, down to its direct close, this remarkable connection with Paisley Abbey is maintained, and what is still more strange, three in succession of these powerful and warlike Lords, Reginald, Donald and Angus Mor, and last of all the line, John, Earl of Ross, quitting the stormy scene of battle, and entering the quiet and peaceful haven of monastic life.

Reginald is described thus on his seal, *Reginaldus Rex Insularum Dominus de Argile*. The Galley of the Isles appears with sails furled and full of armed men. The Black Galley is of course the ancient Galley of the Kingdom of Man and the Isles, inherited from the Norse Kings of the Sudereys and Man. The heraldry of this seal is interesting and is dealt with by Sir Iain Moncrieffe of that Ilk, Albany Herald:

The Kingdom of the Isles was a mixed Scandinavian-Celtic realm. I think the Clan Donald probably descended in the male line from King Echmarcach of Dublin (who died on pilgrimage to Rome in 1065), that King Echmarcach descended in the male line from King Ranald "Higher than the Hills" (in whose honour Thiodolf wrote the Ynglingatal in the ninth century) and that they were all thus descended from the Frey-born pagan sacral Ynglingar "Peace Kings of Uppsala," who claimed descent from the male manifestation of the goddess Freya or Nerthus, whose emblem was the Galley—the Boat of Isis. Incidentally King Echmarcach's coins bore a Hand, the Gaelic symbol for the "true family" or *derbfine*.

Whether or not Somerled descended from King Echmarcach (Imergi or Ichmarc) he owed his kingship in the South Isles to his marriage with King Olaf Morsel's daughter.

All the families who had some inheritance in the Isles through descent (male or more often female) from King Olaf quarter, or quartered the Galley, but the only one that bears the Galley alone and unquartered is Lord Macdonald's House, the longest branch to reign in the Isles. I think that Olaf descended in the male line from King Harald of Limerick (killed 960), whose father was elder brother of the same King Echmarcach's ancestor and who was therefore also an Yngling of the line of the "Peace Kings of Uppsala," and whose ancestral emblem was thus also the Galley of Nerthus.

Families who quartered or quarter the Galley because of descent from the Norse Royal House of the Isles include the Macdonalds, the Macleods, the MacAlisters, the MacDougalls, the Stewarts of Appin, the Campbells of Argyll and Breadalbane, the Hamiltons of Arran, the Macleans of Duart (descended from a Macdonald girl), the MacNeils of Barra (which I suspect they got from a MacRuairi girl), and many other West Coast families. This Galley is always *black*.

Another group of Galley coats, but always a *golden* galley, is derived from the old Norse Jarls of Orkney, who were also Ynglings. To this group belong the Sinclairs.

The third group of galley coats, of many colours, but now settled by the Lord Lyon to be *blue* for the future, is derived from Clan Chattan descent.

The origin of this galley has not been established, although I suspect it comes off the black galley of the Isles; for Macdonald was for long the superior of the Chiefs of Clan Chattan, and there was doubtless much blood-relation between them.

The early use by the Macdonald Chiefs of the Galley is to be seen from their seals, on which it appears by the time of Angus of the Isles, who died *c.* 1292. Indeed they always used it. For Angus was the first *Macdonald*, son of that Donald from whom the family gets its name.

After they became Earls of Ross they added the Eagle which the Earls of Ross had long been using as a supporter behind the shield; but the Macdonalds instead hung the Eagle on the Galley's mast.

Clan Donald have borne arms ever since the days of Donald, the founder and eponymous of the Clan, and the Black Galley of the Isles is always displayed in some part of their arms.

Reginald married Fonia, daughter of the Earl of Moray, and had three sons: Donald, the eldest, who gave his name to the Clan; Ruairi, whose collateral line played a conspicuous part in the country's history until it merged in the main line with the marriage of its heiress, Amie MacRuairi, with John, Lord of the Isles in 1337; and Dugall, whom a MS of 1450 records as the progenitor of the great Clan Dugall.

4

Donald of Islay
(1207-1249)

Reigning in Scotland
ALEXANDER II
1214-1249

DONALD, WHO GAVE HIS NAME to our Clan, succeeded his father, Reginald, in 1207. Unlike his father, who had the reputation of being a man of peace and benefactor of the Church, and who was respected in both the Isles and Ireland, Donald seems to have been a man of blood and iron. That at least is the picture we gather from the only records available of his doings and character. There is no disguising the fact that he was a turbulent and forceful man as indeed he had to be at a time when the allegiance he owed to the King of Norway was being increasingly challenged by the King of Scots.

Donald fell heir to the lands of Islay, South Kintyre, and the other islands south of Ardnamurchan. Ruairi, his brother, received North Kintyre, Bute and Garmoran which extended from Ardnamurchan to Glenelg. The division, however, is not to be regarded as a permanent separation of the interests of the two brothers. Indeed they joined forces when it was to their mutual advantage to do so, for in 1211 we find them carrying out a concerted raid on the North of Ireland when, as noted in the *Annals of the Four Masters,* "Thomas Mac Uchtry, with the sons of Randal, the son of Somhairle, came to Derry Columkille, with a fleet of seventy-six ships: and, after plundering and destroying the town, they proceeded to Inishowen, and spoiled the whole peninsula." Nearer home they had to reconcile their differences in a common opposition to the Scottish king in his attempts to assert his authority in the West.

Alexander II had hardly ascended the throne before the descendants of the Mormaers of Moray, the MacHeths and their kindred, rebelled. It is extremely likely that Donald and Ruairi must have given the "rebels" some aid, a fact that did not endear them to Alexander, who reacted as soon as the MacHeth incident had been dealt with. In 1221 he descended upon Argyll and the Isles in an effort to settle once and for all the problems of Clan Cholla and its disturbing influence. This expedition does not seem to have been very successful. Next year he repeated the experiment with more success. Many of the island chiefs submitted at least temporarily, for it was their habit in cases of this sort all down through their history to pay lip-service while their pretended superior was present and revert to their former way of life once he had gone. In this case, although some seem to have submitted there is no certain record that Donald did so.

Once more, in 1249, Alexander made a last attempt to bring the Isles under control. He gathered a large force and declared "that he would not desist until he had set his standard on the cliffs of Thurso, and had reduced under himself all the provinces which the Norwegian monarch possessed to the westward of the German Ocean." He sailed to Kintyre, but Donald ignored his progress. He then made approaches to Ewan of Lorn, hoping to wean him from his allegiance to the Norse King. In this he failed as Ewan had been entrusted by Haakon with the management of his island estates. Moreover Ewan had aspirations to assuming the kingship of the Isles and Man, so that Alexander's presence was not welcome.

What happened in the island of Kerrera is not certain. Ewan may have plotted Alexander's death, as it would have been, and proved to be, of advantage to his plans. The King died there on Kerrera of some obscure illness: the army broke up and bore his body back to Scotland. A strange tale is told in a Norse saga (*Haakon Haakonson*). The King lay in his galley in the Sound of Kerrera opposite the Castle of Dunollie at the mouth of Oban Bay, the seat of Ewan, chief of the Clan Dugall. The King dreamed that three men came to him, a man of medium height, ruddy face and clad in royal robes: this one seemed friendly. The second was slim built and young: and the third very tall and of a menacing mien, bald in front. The last asked the King his intentions and on being informed that the subjection of the Sudereys was his object, he ordered him to turn back. On being told the dream in the morning his advisers begged the King to give up the enterprise, but he refused, and a little after took ill and died. The saga concludes that the men of the Sudereys believed that the three men were King Olaf, the saint: the saintly Earl Magnus of Orkney: and Saint Columba. The last named would seem to fit the description of the tonsure of the front half of the head used in the Celtic Church, and one of the usages of that ancient Church complained about by the Roman missionaries at Whitby in 664. That Alexander's body was taken so far back to Melrose for burial seems strange considering the sacred isle of Iona was not far away. Dr Grant concludes that this is an indication that the "orientation of the civilisation of Scotland had indeed been changed."

No sooner was Alexander dead than Ewan of Lorn embarked on his scheme of acquiring the realm of Man and the Isles. He was successful at first; but Haakon, hearing of it, asked for and obtained the aid of Donald and his brother Ruairi, who reacted promptly and effectively. Ewan, who was already unpopular with the Manxmen, had to flee north to his home in Lorn.

*   *   *

Hugh Macdonald of Sleat, writing in the seventeenth century, describes briefly and graphically the career of this warlike Chief thus:

Donald his son succeeded [Reginald] in the Lordship of the Isles and Thaneship of Argyll. He married the daughter of Gillies by whom he had Angus, Alexander and Somerled. He went to Denmark and brought with him many of the ancient Danes of the Isles namely, the MacDuffies and Macnagills: MacDougal his uncle went with him, whereby his own rights and the peculiar rights he had for the Isles by Olay the Red's daughter, were renewed by Magnus King of Denmark. For until that time the Danes on the north side of Ardnamurchan held off the King of Denmark. After this he and his uncle Dugall became enemies, so that at last he was forced to kill Dugall. After this, King Alexander sent Sir William Rollock as messenger to him to Kintyre, desiring him to hold the Isles of him which he had now of the King of Denmark. Donald replied that his predecessors had their rights of the Isles from the crown of Denmark, which was renewed by the present King thereof, and that he held the Isles of His Majesty of Denmark before he renounced his claim to his Majesty of Scotland. Sir William said that the King might grant superiority of the Isles to whom he pleased. Donald answered to this that Olay the Red, and Godfrey the Black's father, from whom he had the most of the Isles, had the Isles by their conquest and not from the King of

Denmark or Scotland. So that he and Sir William could not end their debate. In law or reasoning, Donald, being advised by wicked councillors in the dawning of the day surprised Sir William and his men. Sir William and some of his men were killed. He banished Gillies out of the Isles to the Glens in Ireland where some of his offspring remain to this day. He killed Gillies' young son called Callum Alin. He brought the MacNeills from Lennox to expel Gillies out of Kintyre.

After this he went to Rome bringing seven priests in his company to be reconciled to the Pope and Church. These priests declaring his remorse of conscience for the evil deeds of his former life, the Pope asked if he was willing to endure any torment that the Church was pleased to inflict upon him! Donald replied that he was willing should they please to burn him in a cauldron of lead. The Church seeing him penitent dispensed with him. Some writers affirm that he had his rights from the Pope of all the lands he possessed in Argyle, Kintyre, and the rest of the continent.

After his return home he built the Monastery of Saddell in Kintyre dedicated to the honour of the Virgin Mary. He mortified 48 merk lands to that monastery and the Isles of Heisker to the Nuns of Iona. He died in Shippinage [Skipness] in the year 1289 and was buried at Icolumkill [Iona].

This account is interesting even if not accepted as strictly accurate in one or two respects. For example Hugh calls the Norse King the "King of Denmark," although the distinction between Norse and Danes was explicit enough in the early accounts when they were known as "Fionngall" and "Dubhgall"—fair and dark strangers. Later writers like Hugh refer to them as "Danes." By the time Hugh was writing his history Denmark and Norway had become one kingdom, which may account for it. Then the date of Donald's death given as 1289 is obviously a slip. Donald succeeded his father, Reginald, in 1207. As he does not appear to have been a minor at this time, he could hardly have lived such an eventful life, eventful even for those days, to such a great age. Moreover, as we shall see later, he was not actively engaged in his affairs at the time of the invasion of Haakon in 1263. His son, Angus Mor, acted as regent then, while presumably Donald was leading a monastic life of spiritual repentance for his misdeeds. It is much more likely that Donald died in retirement about the year 1269 rather than 1289 as stated by Hugh.

The words put into Donald's mouth by Hugh in response to the King's presumptuous demands through his emissary, Sir William Rollock, are reminiscent of those used by Somerled when confronted with a similar demand by the King of Scots. Donald reacted even more strongly than his grandfather by killing the emissary.

The naive remark that Donald was "forced" to kill his uncle seems an over-simplification of such an impious deed. It certainly seems that Donald had much to do penance for and had many dark deeds on his conscience; so that it is not surprising that Hugh relates the pilgrimage of Donald to Rome to invoke the absolution of the Holy Father himself. It must have been a colourful party who approached the Pope on that occasion—the wild Chief from the outer limits of the known world accompanied by seven priests to interpret his confession. Whether in Rome or elsewhere, Donald received absolution and, as our seanachies so neatly put it, thereafter "brought forth fruits worthy of repentance." Like his father and grandfather he made generous gifts to the church. Saddell Abbey was particularly favoured, as was the Abbey of Paisley.

In sum, therefore, we may conclude that Donald of Islay, from whom the Clan takes its name, was a man of ruthless purpose, prepared to overcome any obstacle in pursuit of his ends. The times he lived in, surrounded as he was by jealous relatives and enemies eager to deprive him of his patrimony, may explain though not justify his actions. At least one cannot accuse him of mediocrity or vacillation, which were the most serious sins in any chief who wished to survive and protect his inheritance.

It was at this time that patronymics began to be used. Donald's brother was founding his own clan, the MacRuairis or Clan Ruairidh, and others followed. To differentiate the various lines stemming from Somerled it was necessary for clarity to give them separate names. Thus it is from this Donald that we take our name in Clan Donald. MacRuairi, MacDougall, MacAlister, Gorraidh and the others, in a variety of versions, followed soon after.

Donald had married a daughter of Walter, the High Steward of Scotland, by whom he had two sons: Angus Mor, who succeeded; and Alexander, progenitor of the Clan Alasdair of Loup, the oldest of the cadet families to leave the main stem. Thus early the Clan Donald became connected with the Stewart family which later became the Kings of Scots. Donald is said to have been buried in Iona, but his stone is lost.

5

The MacRuairis (Clann Ruairidh)
(1207-1346)

Reigning in Scotland
WILLIAM THE LION
1165-1214
ALEXANDER II
1214-1249
ALEXANDER III
1249-1286
MARGARET
1286-1290
Interregnum
1290-1292
JOHN BALLIOL
1292-1296
Interregnum
1296-1306
ROBERT I
1306-1329
DAVID II
1329-1371
ROBERT II
1371-1390

THE CLAN RUAIRI are not, strictly speaking, a cadet branch of the Clan Donald, seeing that Ruairi was a younger brother of Donald of Islay, from whom the Clan Donald takes its name. But the history and fortunes of the House of Garmoran are so closely connected with the House of Islay that a record of the one must be incomplete without some account being given of the other. Ruairi, the founder of the Family of Garmoran, who was the second son of Reginald of Islay, Lord of the Isles, was born sometime during the latter half of the twelfth century, and, on coming of age, his father bestowed upon him the Island of Bute, and other lands in Kintyre. The lands of Bute and Arran are said to have been bestowed by Malcolm II on Walter, the first Steward of Scotland. These lands afterwards changed hands several times, and became the subject of fierce contention, on the one hand between the Norwegians and the Scots, and, on the other hand, between the Scots and the descendants of Somerled. Towards the close of the eleventh century, both Bute and Arran were ceded to Magnus, King of Norway, by the Scots. On the marriage of the daughter of Magnus to Godred of Man, these lands were given to her as a portion of the marriage dowry. In the middle of the twelfth century they came by conquest into the possession of Somerled. When, on the death of Somerled, his extensive territories were divided amongst his sons, Bute and a part of Arran, with the Lordship of Garmoran, extending from Ardnamurchan to Glenelg, fell to the share of Angus. Reginald of Isla having driven Angus and his three sons out of Bute, they were in the year 1210 killed in a skirmish by "the men of Skye."

On the death of Angus MacSomerled and his sons, Reginald of Islay bestowed Bute and their other possessions on his son Ruairi. James, the son of Angus Mac Somerled, however, left a daughter, Jane, who married Alexander, eldest son of Walter, the High Steward of Scotland, and he claimed Bute in right of his wife. Ruairi, taking possession of the island, continued to resist this claim and, aided by the Lord of the Isles, was for a time successful in retaining his hold on it. Besides Bute, and the Lordship of Garmoran in the North, Ruairi also possessed lands in North Kintyre, as may be seen from the charter afterwards granted by him to the Abbey of Saddell. The position of Ruairi in Argyll and the Isles was now, in point of power and influence, second only to that of the Lord of the Isles himself. Together they formed a combination strong enough to repel the repeated attempts made by Alexander II and his Scots to conquer the territory of the Gael. The policy of Norway ever since the death of Somerled had been to conciliate the Clan Cholla, and, if possible, prevent any alliance between them and the Scots. Now that the foundations of the Norse

THE MACRUAIRIS (CLANN RUAIRIDH)

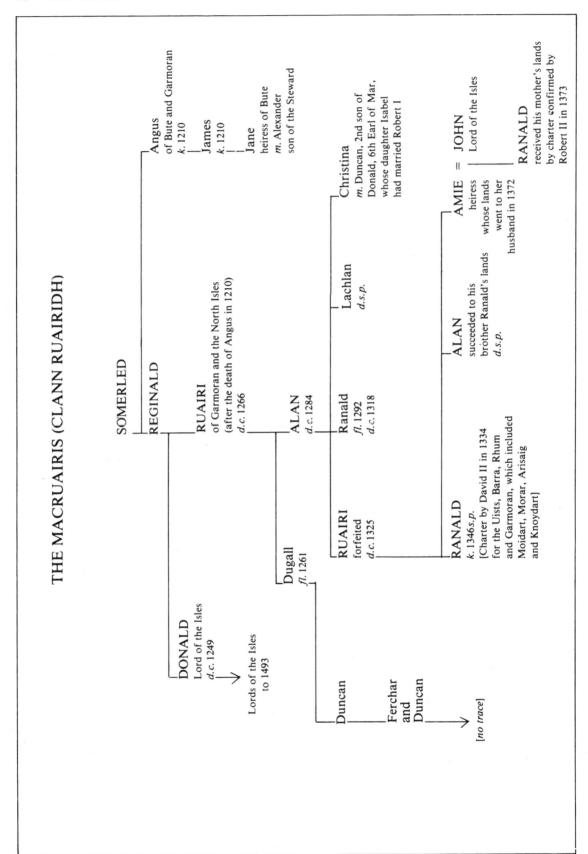

kingdom in the Isles were beginning to totter, it was necessary, if the aggressive Scot was to be kept at bay, that the leaders of the Clan Cholla should be drawn into yet closer friendship with their Scandinavian relatives.

During the final struggle between the two nations, of which the engagement at Largs was the crowning point, the conduct of the chiefs of the House of Somerled is ample evidence of the strong tie that bound them to their Norse ally. Ruairi of Bute had all along been a zealous partisan of the Norse interest in the Isles, and he, at an early stage in his stormy career, developed qualities which somewhat distinguished him from the other leaders of the Clan Cholla. He clearly inherited the wandering seafaring tendencies of his Scandinavian ancestors in a greater degree than any of his father's house, but, nevertheless, we should be slow to accept the character of sea robber ascribed to him by the Scottish historians. That he was a wild and restless man, even for the age in which he lived, appears to be sufficiently attested by the glimpses we get of him through the thick mist that envelops the history of that remote time. Not satisfied with the scope for his seafaring energies and wandering proclivities so temptingly offered by the Western seas, he went across the Irish Channel. In the year 1212, very early in his career, we find him on the Irish coast at the head of an armament of 76 galleys. Having landed in Ireland, he, his brother Donald, and Thomas of Galloway, at the head of their band, ravaged and plundered the town of Derry and the peninsula of Innisowen. In the following year, Ruairi, in company with Thomas of Galloway, again visited the North of Ireland, and sacrilegiously plundered the churches of that province.

We have no doubt Ruairi made ample penance for the atrocious conduct here laid to his charge by the Irish annalists. In any case, he atoned for his sin, probably after many qualms of conscience, by making grants of lands to the Church he had so grievously offended. To the Abbey of Saddell he granted the lands of Torrisdale and Ugadale, and in honour of St Mary and St John, for the service of the Church of St John in Kintyre, he gave five penny lands, three from the same Church of St John and two from the Church of St Mary.

In every attempt made by Alexander II to annex the Norwegian possessions in the Isles to his kingdom, he was strenuously opposed by Ruairi of Bute; and so effective was the opposition on the part of Ruairi and his brother, the Lord of the Isles, that the Scottish monarch utterly failed in the accomplishment of his object. During the long minority which followed the death of Alexander II, no effort was made to add the Isles to the possessions of the Scottish Crown. Ewan of Lorn had played a conspicuous part in the struggle with the Scottish monarch. To him had recently been committed the administration of Norwegian affairs in the Isles, and the present seemed a favourable opportunity for the accomplishment of the ambitious scheme which he had conceived, and which was neither less nor more than the conquest of the Norwegian Kingdom of Man. He accordingly invaded that island, and succeeded in getting himself proclaimed king in the face of much opposition on the part of the Manxmen. Haakon of Norway being informed of the conduct of his erstwhile lieutenant in the Isles, immediately took steps to deprive him of his newly acquired dignity. He appealed to Ruairi of Bute, amongst others, to help him to reduce that hero's relative to obedience. Ruairi, throwing all considerations of kinship aside, responded to Haakon's appeal and, with his brother Donald, invaded the Isle of Man at the head of considerable forces. They fell on the forces of Ewan of Lorn, and defeated them with great slaughter, the pseudo-king himself escaping with his life to the Highlands.

While Ruairi was thus engaged in the service of Haakon, advantage was taken of his absence by his Scottish neighbours who, invading Bute, took possession of it in the name of Jane, the heiress of James, the grandson of Somerled, and wife of Alexander, eldest son of the Steward of Scotland. Ruairi, on his return from the Manx expedition, finding that he had been forestalled, marshalled all his forces, and made a desperate effort to regain possession of his lost territory, but in this he utterly failed. Betaking himself to his Northern possessions he soon found scope for his energies in that region. In the North, Scottish interests were represented by Ferchar Macantagart, Earl of Ross. The possessions of the Earl lay along the western seaboard to Glenelg, while to the south lay the Lordship of Garmoran. To the west of the Earldom of Ross lay Skye and the Long Island, which formed part of the Norse possessions, with the Minch separating them from the territory over which Macantagart held sway. The family of Garmoran and the adherents of Norway in the North Isles were much molested and annoyed by the persistent and savage attacks made on them by the Earl of Ross and the Scottish party. The Norse sagas refer to the wanton cruelty and extreme barbarity which characterised the proceedings of Macantagart and his followers in the Isles. Their aggressiveness at length assumed such proportions that the chiefs, conspicuous among whom was Ruairi of Garmoran and his sons, Alan and Dugall, were forced to take counsel together with a view to taking united action in so critical an emergency. It was resolved to send a messenger to Norway to represent to Haakon the state of matters in the Isles, and the choice fell on the veteran Ruairi, who promptly took to his galley and sailed for Scandinavia.

The result of Ruairi's mission was the well-known expedition of Haakon to the Isles. From his knowledge of the western seas, it was thought desirable that Ruairi should remain at the Court of Haakon until such time as the Norse fleet got under way for the Western Isles. Early in the year 1263, Haakon sent messengers to Orkney to procure pilots for Shetland. Thence one of the messengers, John Langlifeson, proceeded to the Isles and informed Dugall MacRuairi of the elaborate preparations that were being made in Norway for Haakon's expedition. It had been rumoured that the Scots contemplated an invasion of the Isles that summer in quest of plunder. Dugall MacRuairi, styled in the Norse sagas "King Dougal," in order to ward off the intended Scottish descent, caused the report to be spread abroad that a fleet of forty sail was on its way from Norway to the Isles. At length the fleet appeared, and Dugall, with other Island chiefs, met Haakon at Kerrera. Both he and his brother Alan, with their father Ruairi, who had accompanied him from Norway, supported Haakon throughout his campaign in the Isles. The Norse King gave each of them an important command in his fleet, different divisions of which were sent hither and thither to devastate the country. He sent a squadron of fifty ships under the command of Dugall MacRuairi and Magnus of Man to plunder the lands of Ewan of Lorn. Another division of the fleet sailed up Loch Long. In this region Alan MacRuairi made himself conspicuous by acting as leader of a plundering party who penetrated into the country, doing havoc wherever they went, killing many of the inhabitants, and returning to their ships laden with much spoil.

The result of the Norwegian expedition so far had been the re-establishment of Haakon's authority in the Isles. The island of Bute was restored to Ruairi, and to Alan and Dugall Haakon gave the lands of Ewan of Lorn. He, besides, gave to Dugall "that Castle in Kintyre which Guthorme Bockakaly had besieged and taken."

Having now been reinstated in the possession of Bute, Ruairi was not slow in taking advantage of the opportunity with which fortune favoured him to punish the Stewarts and their Scottish followers. Not satisfied with the surrender of Rothesay Castle, he pursued the retreating garrison, and according to the Norse account, put nine of them to death. He followed up his pursuit by making a descent on the mainland, which he plundered and wasted with fire and sword for many miles into the heart of the country. The Castle of Rothesay, now represented by a magnificent ruin standing in the centre of the town of that name was for at least a hundred years identified with the history of one or other branch of the Clan Cholla. Ruairi made it his residence during his occupation of Bute.

Ruairi's triumph was of short duration, at least so far as Bute was concerned. On the annexation of the Norwegian possessions in the Isles of Scotland in 1266, both Bute and Arran were restored to the Stewart family; and Ruairi himself, now a very old man, probably died shortly after the Scoto-Norse Treaty of that year.

From the prominence given to Dugall in the Norse sagas, it is inferred that he was the eldest son of Ruairi. In 1261 he is mentioned as sole king in the Isles, and faithful to Haakon. Both Alan, his brother, and he are honoured with the title of king, but this distinction could only have meant that they were lords over wide territories, and exercised almost regal jurisdiction within these. Dugall, whether younger or older than Alan, drops out of view entirely after the annexation of the Isles to Scotland. The probability is that he refused to acknowledge the sovereignty of Alexander III. In any case, his family disappeared during the reign of that monarch from among the territorial families of Argyll and the Isles. Gregory asserts that Dugall died without leaving any issue, but in this he is contradicted by the MS of 1450 which, corroborated by other authorities, gives Ferchar and Duncan as two sons of Duncan, the son of Dugall, the son of Ruairi. The same MS gives the genealogy of the MacRuairi family back through Alan, from which it should not be inferred that Alan was the eldest son of Ruairi. What it proves beyond any doubt, however, is that the territorial line of the family was carried on by Alan and his successors, and not by Dugall and his successors.

Alan, therefore, succeeded his father in the lands of Garmoran, which included Knoydart, Moidart, Arisaig, and Morar, and also in his lands in North Kintyre. In all these Alexander III confirmed him, and added to the already extensive territory the lands of Barra, Uist and Harris, with the lesser islands of Eigg and Rum. The grant by Alexander III of lands in the Long Island, and elsewhere, is borne out by the terms of the charter granted afterwards by Robert Bruce to Ruairi, the son of Alan. Alan MacRuairi continued loyal to the Scottish throne during the remainder of his life. From his extensive territorial possessions he became one of the most powerful magnates in the Highlands. In the year 1284, when the Scottish Estates assembled at Scone, and declared Margaret, the Maid of Norway, heiress to the throne, the name of *Allangus filii Roderici* appears in the list of those present on that occasion. Alan MacRuairi, Angus of Islay, and Alexander of Lorn were the only Highland Chiefs who attended this Parliament, and all three were of the House of Somerled.

Alan MacRuairi, who appears to have died shortly after the meeting at Scone, was succeeded in his landed possessions by his daughter Christina. It may seem singular that Christina should have become her father's heiress, in view of the fact that Alan MacRuairi left at least three sons, Ruairi, Ranald and Lachlan. It is inferred from the circumstances that Ruairi, the eldest of the sons, was passed over in favour of Christina, that he was not a legitimate son of Alan MacRuairi. Whether Ruairi MacAlan was or was not feudally legitimate is a point which cannot now be definitely settled one way or the other, but that he was Celtically legitimate is conclusively proved by his succession in due time to the MacRuairi patrimony. In the charter granted to him by Bruce of the MacRuairi lands resigned in his favour by Christina, his sister, there is nothing indicative of a bar sinister, and in such an instrument, drawn out in feudal terms, reference, we think, would have been made to Ruairi's illegitimate descent if he had not been Alan MacRuairi's lawful son. The awkward fact, however, of Christina and not Ruairi inheriting the MacRuairi lands remains to be explained, and the only feasible explanation seems to be that Ruairi was the issue of a hand-fast marriage.

The MacRuairis made themselves conspicuous at a very early stage in the struggle for Scottish independence. In a letter of Alexander of Islay to Edward I, in the year 1292, that chief, who had the year before taken the oath of allegiance to the English King, accused Ranald, the son of Alan, and Duncan, the son of Dugall, of committing excesses in those regions subject to the authority of Edward. Again, in 1297, Alexander of Islay, who had now been appointed by Edward Admiral of the Western Isles, complains bitterly of the insubordination of the Island Chiefs, and invokes the aid of the English King in keeping them under subjection. Alexander of Lorn, who had not yet joined himself to the English interest, seems to have been the principal offender. Instigated by the Lord of Lorn, the MacRuairis invaded Skye and Lewis, the lands of the Earl of Ross, and some others of the Northern Isles, and after committing great ravages in these islands, they burnt all the ships engaged in the English service in the Western seas. The MacRuairi leaders engaged in this insurrection were Ruairi, Ranald and Lachlan, the sons of Alan, and grandsons of Ruairi of Bute, whose piratical tendencies they seem to have inherited. Ruairi, the Chief of the MacRuairis, though often warned of the serious consequences involved in his rebellious proceedings, continued obstinate. Alexander of Islay was at length obliged to adopt coercive measures against his kinsman. These resulted in the acknowledgment by Ruairi of the authority of the English King, whom he at the same time promised faithfully to serve.

Ruairi MacAlan kept his promise no longer than it was convenient to do so. The MacRuairis again broke out against English rule under his leadership, and perpetrated great atrocities in the islands under the sway of the House of Islay. The outraged islanders were obliged to send messengers to Alexander, complaining of the hardships to which they had been put by the tyrannical proceedings of the MacRuairis. Special mention is made of Lachlan MacRuairi as the prime mover and leader in the depredations committed by the plundering band who had invaded the Southern Isles. Lachlan, it appears, had previously offered homage to the English King, but his recent conduct roused the resentment of Edward's representative, the Lord of the Isles, and that chief soon succeeded in reducing the rebel to obedience. In pledge of his loyalty to the Island Lord, Lachlan MacRuairi offered his son as hostage, but no sooner had this been accomplished than his brother Ruairi, at the head of Lachlan's forces, and, it is said, at his instigation, raised the flag of revolt. The Lord of the Isles now determined to strike a final blow at the MacRuairis. Collecting his forces, and assisted by his brothers Angus Og and John Sprangach, he pursued Ruairi by sea and land, and at length seized and imprisoned him in one of his dungeons on the mainland.

How long Ruairi MacAlan remained in this situation we know not but in the year 1301, in a letter by Angus Og of Islay to Edward I, mention is made of Ruairi's sons, for whose loyalty Angus holds himself responsible. It appears that Ruairi himself still remained in custody, and that Angus Og acted as the guardian of his sons. The MacRuairis appear again on the scene in the year 1306. In that year Robert Bruce was crowned at Scone. After suffering defeat in two pitched battles, he found his way, a lonely fugitive, to Kintyre, where he was loyally received and hospitably entertained by Angus Og of Islay.

Here another of the family of Somerled played a prominent part in rendering aid to the King in his adversity. This was Christina MacRuairi, heiress of vast lands of her family—Knoydart, Moidart, Arisaig, Rum, Eigg, Uist, Barra and Gigha. In addition she had some lands in Kintyre so that her friendship, joined to that of Angus of Islay, made the King's sojourn in that region secure from attack. This lady, the only legitimate child of Alan MacRuairi, was related to the King by marriage though not by blood. This circumstance has led to some mistakes being made by our historians who link her name with Donald, Earl of Mar, by whom she is assumed to have had a daughter, Isabel, who married the King as his first wife. Donald, Earl of Mar (the 6th in most accounts), had died in or before 1297. By his wife, Helen, widow of Malcolm, Earl of Fife, he had five children: (1) Gartney (Gartnait) who succeeded as 7th Mar and married Christian Bruce, sister of the King; (2) Isabel, who married Robert Bruce, the King; (3) Duncan; (4) Alexander; (5) Mary who married the Earl of Atholl firstly and the Earl of Sutherland, secondly. Most sources agree that Christina MacRuairi married Duncan, the Earl's second son. She thus became a sister-in-law of the King's first wife and, in a distant way, sister-in-law of the King himself.

Christina seems to have met Bruce in or near his old lands of Carrick and brought some fifteen men to add to his slender force which was a welcome addition at the time. Fordun says that "the lady was a certain noblewoman, Christian of the Isles, and it was by her help and power and goodwill that Bruce was able to return to Carrack." Barbour in *The Bruce* states that "a lady of that country [Carrick], who was his near kinswoman, was wondrous glad at his arrival, and made haste to join him, bringing fifteen men, whom she gave to the King to help him in his warfare. He received them with much pleasure, and very greatly thanked her, and forthwith asked tidings of the queen and all his friends he had left in the country when he crossed the sea." After relating the sad news of his brother and the queen and how Sir Christopher Seton was slain, Barbour goes on with his story: "Thus the King sighed and mourned. And the lady took her leave and went home, and many a time she helped Bruce both with silver and with such food as she could get in the country."

Following on this timely assistance brought by Christina, it was resolved to find a safer place for the King to pass the winter. The Isle of Rathlin between Kintyre and Ireland was considered the safest refuge for him during the winter of 1306/07 and there he was supplied with all his needs by Christina and Angus Og. From this time onward Ruairi, Christina's half brother, followed the fortunes of Bruce. At Bannockburn he fought beside his kinsfolk, and it was the final onslaught of the Islesmen which set the seal on that decisive victory.

Ruairi was amply rewarded by Bruce for his loyalty and services. The King bestowed upon him the lands of Lorn, forfeited by Alexander MacDougall, and half the lands of Lochaber, forfeited by the Comyns. He also bestowed upon him a davoch and a half of Moidart, half a davoch of Arisaig, the six davoch lands of Eigg and Rum, with the patronage of the Church of Kildonan in Eigg, the six davochs and three-quarter of land in Kilpeter, in South Uist, the whole lands of Barra and Harris, all of which were resigned in his favour by Christina MacRuairi, his sister. The rest of the MacRuairi lands in Garmoran and the North Isles, including North Uist and a part of South Uist, appear to have been granted by Christina at this time, or shortly thereafter, to an Arthur Campbell, whose descendant put in a claim for them in the year 1427. There is no record, however, of a Campbell having ever obtained actual possession of these lands.

The lands resigned by Christina in favour of Ruairi were to be held by him for the service of a ship of 26 oars, with its complement of men and victuals, for the King's army, and on due warning; but if Ruairi, the son of Alan should have no male heir, then Ruairi, the son of Christina, should hold the lands in heritage, on condition that he should give in marriage the daughter or daughters of the said Ruairi, his uncle, if he should have any, with a portion of 400 merks sterling; and if, in the course of nature, it should happen that Ruairi, the son of Christina, could not succeed to the lands, then the daughter or daughters of Ruairi, the son of Alan, should succeed their father in the same, or if he had no surviving heirs, the lands should revert to Christina and her heirs.

Ruairi MacRuairi had now, by the acquisition of so large a territory, become a man of great power and influence in the Highlands, although a considerable share of the family inheritance still remained with his sister. Ruairi, as might have been expected, evinced his gratitude to his royal benefactor by loyally supporting the interests of the throne, at least for a time. One of his brothers, at the head of a number of Islesmen, joined Edward Bruce and fought under his banner in Ireland. When the brief but brilliant career of that restless prince came to an end by his death at Dundalk in 1318, MacRuairi fell fighting by his side. In the *Annals of Ulster,* under that year it is recorded that "Edward Bruce, the destroyer of Ireland in general, both foreign and Gaidheal, was killed by the foreigners of Ireland by dint of fighting at Dundelgain, and there was killed in his company MacRuadhri, King of Innis Gall." As Ruairi, the head of the MacRuairi family, lived for many years after this event, the "King of Innis Gall" referred to by the annalist must have been one or other of his brothers, Ranald or Lachlan.

The loyalty of the Chief of the MacRuairis was already on the wane. What the precise nature of his offence was is not recorded. It was no doubt some treasonable compact into which he had entered against the Crown, for his conduct was viewed in so serious a light that in a Parliament held at Scone, on the 28th March 1325, Ruairi was deprived of all his lands, both mainland and island. From the fact that there is no record of the old MacRuairi lands having been bestowed on another, we conclude that Ruairi continued to enjoy the undisturbed possession of these during the remainder of his life. The lands of Lorn and Lochaber, bestowed upon him by Bruce, were never restored to the family.

Ruairi MacRuairi must have died shortly after this forfeiture and was succeeded by his son Ranald. His other children, Alan and Amie, may have succeeded one after the other, to the family inheritance. Ranald still suffered under the forfeiture incurred by his father and was looking for an opportunity he would use to recover his territories. This was provided by the long minority following the king's death in 1329, when Ranald supported the cause of Edward of England and the Balliol faction. In 1341, however, the young King David returned from France and, anxious to strengthen his own position, adopted a policy of conciliation towards his rebellious subjects. In 1342, he confirmed Ranald in the ten davoch lands of Kintail, formerly granted to Ranald MacRuairi by William Earl of Ross. For these lands the King exacted a feu-duty of one penny sterling, to be paid annually at the Feast of Pentecost. In the following year, Ranald's loyalty having revived in the interval, the King granted him, for his services to his majesty, a charter of the whole lands of Uist, Barra, Rum, Moidart, Arisaig and Knoydart, with the patronage of the several churches within their bounds. Though Eigg and Harris are omitted from this charter, they continued in the possession of the MacRuairi family, as may be seen from the charter to John, Lord of the Isles, of the MacRuairi lands in 1372.

David II, taking advantage of the absence of Edward III in France, resolved to invade England in 1346. He accordingly issued a mandate summoning the Scottish barons to meet him at Perth with the purpose of submitting to them his plan of action. Ranald MacRuairi of Garmoran came to this meeting accompanied by a considerable train of followers, and took up his position in the Monastery of Elcho, in the immediate vicinity of the Scottish capital. William, Earl of Ross, was also among those who had answered the King's summons. That nobleman and Ranald MacRuairi had had a feud, the precise nature of which is not obvious, but very probably over the lands of Kintail, which the Earl had granted to the Lord of Garmoran, and which, as we have seen, the King had confirmed to that chieftain. Ranald, taking shelter under the royal confirmation, would likely enough have refused to render to the Earl the services due by the vassal to the superior. However this may be, the Earl, regardless of the sacredness of the building, broke into the monastery at the dead of night, and assassinated Ranald MacRuairi and several of his followers. On realising the heinousness of the double crime of sacrilege and murder which he had committed, and no doubt also fearing the consequences of his act, the conscience-stricken Earl hastened with all possible speed to his northern home. The MacRuairis, deprived of their leader, retired in confusion to the Isles.

Ranald MacRuairi, having left no issue, was succeeded by his brother Alan. References are made to Alan MacRuairi in several manuscript histories of the Clan, but there is nothing in these to indicate how long he survived the death of his brother Ranald. Were it not indeed for the charter conveying the MacRuairi lands to John, Lord of the Isles, in 1372, in which they are described as *terras tricentarum mercerum que fuerunt quondam Alani filii Roderici*, we should be

Castle Tirrim (*Tioram*), ancestral home of Clanranald, reputedly built by Amie MacRuairi

inclined to doubt that Alan MacRuairi ever existed. Alan MacRuairi having died without leaving issue, the male line of Ruairi of Bute became extinct, and the succession to the family inheritance is said to have devolved on Amie, the sister of Alan. There is no evidence, however, of Amie having ever been infefted in these lands, or indeed that she survived her brother Alan, if we except the testimony of the seanachies, who are unanimous in asserting that she carried the MacRuairi lands to her husband, John, Lord of the Isles. Before the year 1372, John granted a charter of these lands and others, to his eldest son, Reginald (Ranald), which was confirmed in that year by Robert II. Shortly after the latter charter of confirmation, the King granted a charter of the MacRuairi lands to John himself, and his heirs. In these charters there is no reference to Amie MacRuairi, or to the relationship between John and the MacRuairi family, and they are granted presumably for services rendered, and for the love and favour which the King bears to his son-in-law, the Lord of the Isles. The fact remains, however, that the MacRuairi lands were bestowed on Reginald (Ranald), the son and heir of Amie MacRuairi, who transmitted the inheritance to the great branch of the family of Macdonald which bears his name.

The position of importance occupied by the family of MacRuairi in the annals of the Clan Cholla is at once seen if we glance at the charters bestowed upon them by successive sovereigns. From the extensive possessions, therefore, over which they held sway, both on the mainland and in the islands, they stand in territorial significance second only to the family of the Isles itself. The residence of the family on the mainland seems to have been Castle Tirrim, and in Uist the Castle of Borve in Benbecula. Tradition points to Amie MacRuairi as having built both strongholds, but of this there is no historical confirmation. Though there is no reference to either in the charter granted by David II to Ranald MacRuairi, in 1344, yet as the MacRuairis must have had a residence on the mainland and in Uist, Castle Tirrim and Castle Borve, both of which are mentioned in Reginald's charter of 1372, are the only strongholds which, with any certainty, can be associated with the family. Possibly also Dunranald, in South Uist, as its name would seem to indicate, may have been a residence of the MacRuairis. This old stronghold which, if Uist tradition may be relied on, was occupied by the Macdonalds in the seventeenth century, was no doubt built by the Norsemen during their occupation of the Islands. Built without mortar, it is in its architectural style like many of the ruined forts to be met with elsewhere in the Outer Islands; and Ranald being a Norse name, Dunranald is as likely to have derived its name from a Scandinavian leader as from a chieftain of the MacRuairis.

It is worthy of notice that though the MacRuairi lands passed into the hands of another branch of the Clan Cholla, the MacRuairi name is still represented by a considerable number of clansmen in the land of their sires. The MacRurys, as they call themselves, a name which sounds perhaps more Irish than Highland, have been as a sept exclusively confined to the Island of Uist which, as we have seen, formed part of the MacRuairi territory from the year 1266 until all the MacRuairi lands came into the possession of Ranald, the son of Amie MacRuairi, prior to 1372. MacRury is, therefore, the oldest clan name in Uist. Though not many of them have risen to eminence either in Church or State, or as a sept have succeeded in retrieving the fallen fortunes of their house, they have at least succeeded in preserving the name from being lost, and they have done nothing to tarnish that name, or the fair fame of MacRuairi of Garmoran and the North Isles.

6

Angus Mor
(1249-1300)

Reigning in Scotland
ALEXANDER III
1249-1286
MARGARET
1286-1290
Interregnum
1290-1292
JOHN BALLIOL
1292-1296
Interregnum
1296-1306

WE HAVE SEEN in Chapter 4 that Donald, founder of the Clan, was in retirement when the invasion of Haakon of Norway took place in 1263 and Angus Mor, the first Macdonald, was ruling the realm of the Isles. The minority of Alexander III had left the Isles in freedom from aggression from the Scots Kingdom. The regents had quite enough to occupy them in keeping order amongst their turbulent barons. In 1262, however, just about the time Angus Mor had taken the reins, while his father was ending his days in pious exercises of repentance, the Scots King came of age, and began to rule his kingdom in earnest. One of his aims was to dominate and take control of the Isles, and by a mixture of diplomacy and aggression he tried to bring Angus Mor into the fold. His plans were initially frustrated by the arrival of Haakon with a large fleet, in which Clan Ruairi joined, as we have seen. Angus was not at first eager to support Haakon but was prevailed upon to lend his aid, albeit in a rather different manner to the enthusiastic participation of his uncle Ruairi. The final defeat of Haakon at Largs in 1263 placed the Clan Ruairi and Angus Mor in a very difficult position in regard to the victorious King of Scots. Nominal superiority over the Isles hitherto held by the Norwegian Crown passed to the King of Scots under the Treaty negotiated in 1266. Alexander at once demanded obedience from all the Gaelic chiefs of the Isles, and Angus Mor's young son was held hostage for his father's behaviour.

The terms of the Treaty of 1266 contained the "Annual of Norway" by which an annual payment of 4000 merks was to be made to the Norse Crown, payable at the Church of Magnus in Kirkwall. Permission was given to any Norse inhabitants in the Isles to go home, or to dwell under the new conditions prevailing in their isles. The terms offered by Alexander were not crippling, from which it would seem he was not yet too sure of his ground. He did not even execute some of the rebellious chiefs who had taken up arms against him. Perhaps he found it difficult to apprehend them, as later Kings discovered when the chiefs of Clan Donald got into trouble with the Crown. The Isles were still very far from the centre of the Scottish realm, and kings or royal emissaries found visits to these fastnesses perilous and even fatal. The mysterious sudden death of Alexander II in Kerrera, and the summary execution of Sir William Rollock already related, are good examples of the risks attending such excursions in those days.

From the point of view of the Scots King several of the island chiefs deserved the severest punishment for their part in the Largs campaign, and yet we find Angus Mor living in peace in his estates in Islay and Kintyre: Ewan of Lorn similarly in safe occupation of his lands: and Ruairi, who of them all had been the most active supporter of the invading King, holding his possessions in Garmoran and the North Isles with the title of "de Insulis." The reasons for such a state of affairs are perhaps explained by the peculiar position historically occupied by the Island principalities, the significance of which is clearly and concisely summed up in the following passage from *Clan Donald*:

It is not easy to define with clearness the exact relation of the House of Somerled to Norway and Scotland before and after the years 1263-66. The Southern Isles having been handed down by Somerled as an independent possession, were similarly held by his sons and grandsons. There are certain passages in the Saga on Haco's expedition, which convey the impression that these Southern Isles were re-conveyed to Norway. It is stated that Angus Mor was willing to surrender his lands to Haco, who afterwards, we are told, "bestowed Ila, taken by his troops, on the valiant Angus, the generous distributor of the beauteous ornaments of the hands." It cannot be true that the territories of Angus Mor were both willingly surrendered by him, and at the same time taken from him by force. The series of events leading to the battle of Largs; the mission of Roderick to Norway as ambassador of the Island chiefs; Haco's response to their representations in the equipment of his great armament, all this forbids the supposition of any hostile movement against the Island Lords. If Haco desired their loyal co-operation, it would have been bad policy to begin with a forcible annexation of their possessions. The association of Haco with the princes of the House of Somerled was neither more nor less than the formation of a league, offensive and defensive, to repel the aggressiveness of the Scottish realm. If Norway ceded the Southern Isles to Scotland in 1266, she gave over what she never possessed since these Isles were wrested from Godred of Man in 1156. There is not a scrap of evidence to show that from the days of Somerled down to Bruce's Charter to Angus Og, a period of 150 years, there was any effective acknowledgment of superiority by the princes of the Southern Isles either to Norway or Scotland, if we except Bute alone. It is now evident that a new chapter in the history of the Isles is opening. The feudal system has, theoretically at least, knit into a complete whole the social fabric of the Scottish nation. But, with the people of the Highlands, and particularly with the Lords of the Isles, the superiority of the Crown was but a name, and for hundreds of years there was witnessed a continual struggle on the part of the Celtic system to assert itself against the claims of feudal Scotland. In this struggle the Kings of Innse-Gall were the principal actors. Circumstances at times may have compelled them to accept of charters for their lands and render an insincere allegiance; but the traditions of independence long survived, and are largely accountable for the turbulence and disorder that mark the history of the Scottish Highlands.

The death of Alexander III in 1286 ended the reign of one of the wisest Kings the Scots ever had, and in its train brought thirty years of trouble such as Scotland has seldom seen. The Maid of Norway, grand-daughter of Alexander, who had in 1284 been acclaimed as the true heiress to the throne by a meeting of the Scots Estates at which three members of the Clan Cholla were present, amongst them Angus Mor of Islay, unfortunately died in Kirkwall on her way to her kingdom.

The circumstances surrounding the death of this unfortunate princess are clouded in mystery. Considering the importance of this girl, not only as a princess of the Royal House of Norway, but also as the obvious successor to the throne of Scotland, it is strange her death was not recorded with exactness at the time. Margaret, daughter of Alexander III, Queen of Norway, died in 1283 shortly after the birth of this sad little girl. Thus in 1286 when her grandfather died and the succession opened, she can have been only three years old. In 1290 when a brief announcement was made that she had died in Orkney on her way to her kingdom, she must have been about seven years old; but young as she was there had been much negotiation and plotting to affiance her to Edward of England's son. If she had lived and the union with the English prince been consummated, history would have been changed, and the aspirations of the numerous claimants to the throne rendered null and void.

Angus Mor's Seal
S. ANGUS DE YLE FILII DOANALDI

Although the descendants of Somerled had supported Haakon in his expedition to Largs, they continued as we have seen to enjoy their privileges unmolested by the Crown. Towards the end of Alexander's reign, however, Angus Mor seems to have been at variance to some extent with the King, who in 1282 called upon the other barons of Argyll to aid him in service against Angus *filius Dovenaldi* under pain of being disinherited. Later in 1282 Angus and the MacDougalls of Lorn with their friends were so seriously in rebellion that the Constable of Scotland, the Earl of Buchan, was called upon to take action against them. What happened does not appear in record. It was a time when nobles in Scotland were constantly involved in intrigues and sorely divided in their loyalties. The Islesmen were no exception. In 1284 Angus seems to have re-established friendly relations with the King as he was one of the three nobles of Argyll and the Isles who attended the Convention of Estates to settle the succession of the throne. The other two were Alexander of Lorn and Alan MacRuairi of Garmoran. These meetings seem to have been an earnest attempt on the King's part to secure the consent of all his nobles to the succession of the Maid of Norway to his throne.

The Parliament which met at Scone in 1286 appointed six guardians of the realm to govern in the name of the Maid of Norway. In 1288 the Regency became divided, and we find Angus with his son Alexander entering into a bond of association with James, High Steward of Scotland, and others who favoured the claims of Bruce. Angus was now well on in years, however, and therefore played no active part in the complicated negotiations that marked this period in Scots history. But it is clear he continued support of the elder Bruce, for in 1292 Balliol ordered Alexander of Argyll and his bailies of Lochow to summon "Sir Angus, son of Donald, and others, to do him homage within fifteen days after Easter wherever he might be at the time." This summons was repeated in 1293, but Angus of Islay paid no heed to either.

Angus died about the year 1300 at an advanced age, having been a great benefactor of the Abbey of Sagadull (Saddell) and granting to it lands by no fewer than four charters in the years 1253 and 1261.

*   *   *

Angus Mor married a daughter of Sir Colin Campbell of Lochow, by whom he had (1) Alexander, his heir; (2) Angus Og, who succeeded Alexander; (3) Iain Sprangach (Bold John), progenitor of the MacIains of Ardnamurchan; (4) Mora, who married Ferchard, 5th Chief of Mackintosh. The Clanranald seanachie of 1819 credits him with a fourth son, Duncan who, he states, was the progenitor of the Clann Donnachaidh, or Robertsons of Struan. This is confirmed by "Memoirs of a Memorial of The Antient Family of Robertson of Struan" (Macfarlane's *Genealogical Collections,* Vol. II, 1900, Scot. Hist. Socy., p. 301) but this authority says Duncan was a son of Angus Og.

7

Alexander (Alasdair Og) and Angus Og
(1300-1330)

Reigning in Scotland

Interregnum
1296-1306

ROBERT 1
1306-1329

DAVID II
1329-1371

THE EXTENSIVE TERRITORIES of Angus Mor were divided among his sons. Alexander succeeded him in Islay and other territories on the mainland of Argyll; Angus received the lordship of Kintyre; while the lands of Ardnamurchan were bestowed by King Balliol upon John Sprangach, the youngest of the sons.

Alexander's reign was not long, the shortest of all the Princes of the Isles. He lived in one of the most troubled periods in our history when recurring political changes rendered necessary the frequent readjustment of loyalties on the part of the whole Scottish hierarchy. It was Alexander's ill fortune that he gave his allegiance and continued his adherence to the wrong side in the struggle that followed. He appears for the first time on the historical stage with his father at the meeting in 1288 at which they engaged to further the Bruce interest. In 1291, the next time he comes before us, he is found acting an entirely different character, giving the oath of allegiance to the English King. He had become closely allied by marriage with the family of Lorn, and through them associated with the English interest, and although in his father's lifetime he does not appear to have taken a leading part on either side, now, as the struggle becomes keener, we find him throwing the whole weight of his power and influence into the scale of English aggression. There were, at an early stage in the conflict, many letters addressed to him from the English Court and in the interests of the English party, and from the rewards which afterwards followed, the services he rendered to that cause must have been very considerable.

Although the House of Islay has at this stage begun to take the part of England in the effort to accomplish the conquest of Scotland, it is only on an inadequate view of the situation that the historian can pronounce its representatives to be lacking in true patriotism. The Scottish claim to the Western Isles was of too recent date to admit of a strong feeling of loyalty to the Crown in that region; and to accuse the Island princes of that time of a lack of patriotism in the part they played is quite unfair, and ignores the political conditions of the time. Besides all this, it must not be forgotten that the sympathies of the Lords of the Isles must have been with the Old Celtic system, which was only gradually disappearing before the influence of Teutonic culture; that they regarded the Norman barons who had supplanted the old Mormaers not as the real children of the soil, but as strangers and interlopers in the land, and that the Crown itself, as the keystone in the arch of feudalism, must have appeared to them in the light of a comparatively modern institution. Hence there is nothing that need surprise us in the fact that, after the death of Angus Mor, his son and successor, Alexander of Islay, is found upon the side opposed to Scottish independence.

In the year 1295 we find the English King summoning King John Balliol before him to answer for withholding the lands of Lismore from *Alexandre de Insulis et Julianae uxore sua*. When Edward received the submission of the Scottish nobility in 1296, we are told that a grant of one hundred pounds worth of land was given to Alexander of Islay for services rendered to the English King. We find still further that Alexander held the office of Admiral of the Western Isles under the English Crown, after the ignominious termination of Balliol's reign, and it appears that the position was not by any means a sinecure. From letters addressed to the English King in 1297, it is evident that his lieutenant, however strenuously he exercised his commission, found it well nigh an impossible task to quell the insubordination and turbulence of the Western chiefs. Among the notables accused of lawless excesses in regions subject to the authority of Edward, there is reference to Ruairi, the son of Alan, grandson of Ruairi of Bute; also to Ranald, another son of Alan, as well as to Lachlan MacRuairi, probably a brother of the former two. The MacRuairi family seem to have inherited a large share of the piratical tendencies of the ancient Vikings, and we find these Highland rovers, in 1297, invading and carrying slaughter and depredations into the islands of Skye and Lewis, and burning the ships in the service of the King.

It is against Alexander of Lorn, however, also known as *de Ergadia,* as the arch offender, the leader and instigator in these irregularities, that the King's Admiral makes the chief complaint; and this is rather a singular fact, in view of the strong support which, very shortly thereafter, was given by Alexander and his son John to the English interest. In the previous year, 1296, Edward had received Alexander of Lorn's submission along with that of other Scottish noblemen, at Elgin, and he seems to have been subjected to a short term of imprisonment; but immediately after his liberation he, along with his accomplices, committed the crimes against the lieges to which the King's Admiral makes reference. One of his letters he winds up with a mild reminder of expenses incurred in the various expeditions conducted that year in the King's service, as well as of a sum of £500 promised him the previous year, but not yet paid. It is also interesting to note that, at the end of another letter, in which he invokes the royal aid in bringing the culprits to justice, he seeks to be excused for not having his own proper seal in his possession, and thus having to adhibit to "these presents" the seal of Juliana, his wife.

From these circumstances it appears that Alexander of Islay had received ample recognition of his services to the King of England, a recognition which stimulated him to still more zealous efforts in his patron's cause. From 1297 to 1308 we find no further mention of Alexander. In 1306 Robert Bruce was crowned at Scone, a King without a kingdom, and this was the beginning of a career as interesting as the most thrilling pages in the history of chivalry and romance. The enemies of his house now draw closer to one another, and a strong combination was formed against the heroic King. Alexander of Islay was a powerful and important factor in this combination. So in 1308 we find him fighting against Bruce in the district of Galloway, aided by MacDowall, lord of that region. This district continued obstinately to resist the King's authority and was at the time occupied by English troops. Bruce sent his brother Edward against them, and he prosecuted the campaign with such vigour and success that he soon reduced the country, defeated the combined forces of Sir Roland of Galloway and Alexander of Islay on the banks of the Dee, and compelled the inhabitants to swear allegiance to his brother the King.

In the pursuit that followed the dispersion of the Gallowegians and the Islesmen, Edward Bruce took prisoner "The Prince of the Isles." Alexander however, very soon escaped from Edward Bruce's custody, and betook himself to the stronghold of Castle Swein, in North Knapdale. This fortress commanded the entrance to Lochswein, and was regarded as the key to the districts of Knapdale and Glassary. As such, it was deemed a position of the greatest importance. In this Castle King Robert Bruce, fresh from his victory over Alexander of Lorn at the Pass of Ben Cruachan, besieged the Lord of the Isles, and Alexander, after defending himself for several days with the utmost determination and bravery, was obliged to surrender to the King. Bruce sent him forthwith a prisoner to Dundonald Castle in Ayrshire, where he is said to have died soon after. At all events we hear no more of Alexander of Islay in the struggle in which he had taken so prominent a part.

Alexander left four sons—Reginald, Black John, Angus and Charles. These and their progeny, victims of the fate which raised a younger brother to the dignity and honour of their father's house, lost the premier position in the Clan Cholla, though undoubtedly in the light of primogeniture they were the senior family of the line of Somerled. Their subsequent history must here be left to a later chapter.

* * *

Angus Og, second son of Angus Mor, succeeded his brother Alexander in 1308, both in his lands and in the chiefship of the Clan. In tracing his career, we must again traverse a portion of the ground of general Scottish history embraced in the period in which his predecessor flourished. In 1301 we find him equally zealous with his brother in his efforts to hold the Western Isles of Scotland in subjection to the English Crown, and along with Hugh Bisset he appears in a capacity similar to that which Alexander occupied four years previously. In a letter addressed to the English King, apparently written in October of that year, he reports that up to the Lord's day immediately preceding Michaelmas, he and the said Hugh Bisset had been with the English fleet in the island of Bute, and that, at the time he wrote, he was awaiting the royal commands. Apparently the loyalty of Alexander of Lorn to the English interest was still under suspicion. Angus Og, in his statement to the King, avoids committing himself to any opinion, either favourable or adverse, as to the fidelity of the Lord of Lorn. He humbly requests the King, if he believes in Lorn's loyalty, to order him to assist himself and Bisset in the reduction of the country, but, failing such belief, to forward written instructions that they may, with Divine help, be able to overcome Lorn and all other enemies of the King throughout the Western Isles. In the same letter the sons of Ruairi MacAlan, who seem to have been at the time in the custody of Angus Og, and whose loyalty is guaranteed, are recommended to the royal favour; and it is requested that they be allowed to enter into a pledge and compact of fidelity to King Edward as to their future subjection to his sway.

After this period, until the memorable events of 1306, history does not seem to record with any degree of definiteness the conduct of Angus towards either of the parties that strove for the mastery in Scotland. There is not much reason, however, to doubt that he continued consistently to support the authority of Edward I. But in 1306 there was a marked change. Bruce's coronation at Scone on 27th March of that year was soon followed by the disastrous defeat at Methven, and shortly thereafter by an unsuccessful encounter with John MacDougall of Lorn at Dalry, near the end of Strathfillan. Notwithstanding the magnificent prowess and courage of the King, his followers were obliged to retire in face of superior numbers. Under the guidance of the Earl of Lennox, whom Bruce, in the course of his subsequent wanderings, met on the shores of Loch Lomond, and assisted by Sir Neil Campbell, whom he had sent on in advance, the King reached the district of Kintyre, the country of Angus Og. And here we must pause for a moment to enquire as to the causes of this apparently sudden change of front on the part of the Lord of Kintyre, and his truly Highland and hospitable welcome to the royal fugitive. As to the warmth and friendliness of his reception, the poetic biographer does not leave us in doubt:

> And Angus of Ile that tyme was Syr
> And lord and ledar of Kintyr
> The King rycht weill resawyt he
> And undertook his man to be
> And he and his on mony wyes
> He abandowynt to his service
> And for mair sekyrness gaiff him syne
> His Castle of Donaverdyne.

In estimating the causes of this transference of allegiance from Edward I to Bruce, we may regard it as possible, though far from probable, that self interest may have had some weight. We know that the relations of Angus with the MacDougalls of Lorn were not of the friendliest, and that an old feud as to the possession of Mull had not yet been set at rest. Had Bruce's star been in the ascendant in 1306, we might understand that considerations of self interest might have weight in determining Angus' action. But his friendliness to Bruce was first shewn at a time when his fortunes were most depressed and his prospects of success least hopeful; and to all appearances there was nothing to gain, but everything to lose, by espousing the cause of the newly-crowned King of Scots. The motives by which Angus Og was actuated at this critical moment in the fortunes of Scotland are not such as have been suggested, but are to be found in less interested and more noble grounds. Angus Mor, as we have seen, was, in his latter years, a steady supporter of the claims of the elder Bruce, claims which appear to have been abandoned at the fall of Balliol in 1296, when Edward sought to reduce Scotland to the position of an English province. During the ten years that had elapsed since Balliol's deposition, the claims of the family of Bruce were in abeyance. But now, in 1306, these are once more advanced with most chivalrous daring by the young Earl of Carrick, and Angus Og, adopting the friendly attitude of his father, becomes associated with the stirring events of the war of Scottish independence.

Saddell, in whose castle Angus Og first received Bruce, had many associations with the family of the Isles, not the least of these being that the dust of the "mighty Somerled" reposed within the sacred precincts of its monastery. The Castle of Saddell, at the head of Saddell Bay, is a large, square battlemented tower still in a state of perfect preservation. It measures 17 yards by 10, and is about 50 feet in height. The walls are of great thickness, without buttresses, and a spiral stair-case leads through three sets of rooms up to the embattled parapet, whence a commanding view can be obtained of the wide Firth of Clyde as well as the shores of Kintyre and the picturesque isle of Arran. The inevitable dungeon in all its mediaeval gloom is still in evidence as a testimony to the power and sway of these Western Island Lords. As Barbour informs us, Angus Og took his royal guest for greater security to the Castle of Dunaverty, another Kintyre stronghold, and residence of the Lord of the Isles. Situated in the parish of Southend on Dunaverty Bay, five miles east by north of the Mull of Kintyre, it stood on the summit of a peninsula of pyramidal shape, 95 feet high, with a cliff descending perpendicular to the sea. Defended on the land side by a double rampart and ditch, it was, both as to site and construction, a fortress of remarkable strength, and commanded the approach to that part of Scotland where the sea between it and Ireland is narrowest. It was in after time the scene of some remarkable historical events. But there is now hardly a trace of the once almost impregnable walls. Even here Bruce did not tarry long. He knew that his asylum in Kintyre could not be concealed, and in the event of its becoming known prematurely, might expose his friendly host to the ireful vengeance of the English King. Angus now arranged to have Bruce quietly and secretly conveyed to Rathlin, a small island on the Irish coast inhabited and owned by members of the Clan Donald. Here the King, befriended by Angus Og, found a safe retreat during the following winter. This was the darkest time of Bruce's fortunes, and when the clouds rolled by and prosperity smiled upon the cause, Angus Og shared in the triumphs and rewards which accompanied the glorious day of revived Scottish freedom.

As the spring of 1307 drew nigh, the hopes of Bruce began to rise. The romantic interest that belonged to his career powerfully appealed to the female mind, and Christina of the Isles, the daughter and heiress of Alan MacRuairi of Garmoran and sister-in-law of Bruce, was among the first to render important aid. Receiving favourable news from the mainland, the King now began to meditate a descent upon Scotland, and having despatched messengers from his little garrison, he prepared to take his departure. In the beginning of 1307, Angus Og placed a chosen band of Highlanders under the command of Donald, son of Alasdair Mor, and these having crossed to Arran, were joined by the King, who meanwhile had taken the decisive step of quitting Rathlin Isle. From that day Angus Og of Islay, and with him the MacRuairis of Garmoran, were closely associated with Bruce in the task of vindicating the independence of Scotland. In his descent upon Carrick, where he regained his father's territory, the Islesmen bore an honourable part. The only cloud that darkened the political outlook in 1307 was the defeat and capture of the king's brothers, Thomas and Alexander, in Galloway by Roland MacDowall, lord of that region. It is recorded that Angus Og took part in that engagement, but escaped the disaster that overtook his friends. Next year, as has already been narrated, this reverse was amply avenged. Not only so, but in 1308 the King wreaked signal vengeance upon the MacDougalls of Lorn, the most implacable and determined of his foes. Marching towards Argyllshire, he totally defeated the Lords of Lorn, both father and son, took the Castle of Dunstaffnage, and laid the country waste. Alexander of Lorn was taken prisoner, but was permitted to depart with a safe conduct to England, where he is said to have died soon after in poverty.

On Angus Og becoming the head of the Clan Donald, after the defeat of his brother Alexander, already referred to, he was able to cast the whole influence of his Clan upon the patriotic side of the struggle. And so, when at last the King's toils and perils were crowned with victory on the field of Bannockburn, Angus Og and his Islesmen, estimated at about 5000 men, were an indispensable factor in determining the fortunes of the day. The incidents of that ever memorable field are well-known to readers of Scottish history, and need not here be detailed, save so far as they relate to Macdonald of the Isles and his followers. These formed a corps of the rear or reserve division, and were under the King's own immediate command. In Barbour's lines:

> Sir Angus of the Isles and Bute alswae
> And of the plain lands he had mae
> Or armed men, a noble rout,

In battle stalward was and stout.
He said the rear guard he wad maw
And even before him should gae
The vanguard, and on either hand
The other battle should be gaugand,
Behind ane side a litle space;
And the King that behind him was
Should see where there was maist maister
And there relieve them with his banner.

It was not until the critical moment arrived that the men of the Isles were summoned to the fray. Despite the enormous disparity of numbers, the chivalry of England was beginning to fall into confusion before Bruce's skilful dispositions and the stubborn courage of his army. It was then the King resolved to bring up his reserves. He directed Angus of Islay to march the Islesmen to the assistance of Edward Bruce, who was engaged with the enemy on the right, and addressed him in the memorable words which to this day illustrate the arms of the Clanranald Chiefs—"My hope is constant in thee." The stirring lines of Scott in "The Lord of the Isles" worthily interpret the spirit of that great and epoch-making scene:

"One effort more and Scotland's free!
Lord of the Isles, my trust in thee
    Is firm as Ailsa rock;
Rush on with Highland sword and targe,
I with my Carrick spearmen charge;
    Now forward to the shock!"

The attack of the Highlanders and the men of Carrick at that critical moment settled the fortunes of the day, and victory lay with the "fourth battle." Edward's great army fled before the prudent valour of the Bruce and the determined bravery of the Scots, and Bannockburn was won.

As a reward for the undoubted services rendered by Macdonald of the Isles and his Clan at Bannockburn, they always thereafter had allotted to them, at the express desire of the King, the honourable distinction of a place in the right wing of the royal army. Bruce, however, did not confine his patronage to sentimental favours of this kind. Out of gratitude for the yeoman service rendered by the Island chief in the momentous struggle, he bestowed upon Angus extensive possessions in addition to those which he already enjoyed. Besides Islay and Kintyre, the islands of Mull, Jura, Coll and Tiree, and the districts of Glencoe and Morvern fell to his lot. Lorn was bestowed upon Ruairi, son of Alan MacRuairi, who, not being considered feudally legitimate, received from his sister Christina, his father's legal heiress, a large share in her inheritance in Garmoran and the North Isles. Lochaber, which had for a long time been in the possession of the Comyns—the determined foes of Bruce—was forfeited, and divided between Angus of Islay and Ruairi of Garmoran; but the latter, having about 1325 entered into a treasonable league against the Crown, was afterwards deprived of that territory, and it was bestowed upon Angus Og. Bruce was no doubt well aware of the danger to the authority of the Crown involved in the bestowal of such possessions upon a subject, for although the loyalty of Angus Og himself was undoubted, his successors might not prove so friendly to the Scottish State. Indeed, one of the weighty counsels which King Robert left behind him for the guidance of the kingdom in future times, was not to let the lordship of the Hebridean Isles be in the hands of any one man. Still the services of the Lord of the Isles were too great to be overlooked, and the only precaution taken to neutralise the power which thus accrued to him was the erection of Tarbert Castle, in Kintyre, to be occupied as a royal stronghold.

Angus Og married a daughter of Guy or Conbuidh O'Cahan or O'Kane, one of the greatest barons of Ulster, Lord of Limvady, and Master of the whole County of Derry. The O'Cahans were originally a branch of the Cinel Eoghain,

Angus Og's tomb in Iona
HIC IACET CORPUS ANGUSII FILII DOMINI
ANGUSII MACDHOMHNILL DE ILA

descended from Neil of the nine hostages, King of Ireland. The Lord of the Isles obtained a unique dowry with his bride, whose name, according to the most generally accepted traditions, was Margaret, but according to another less known but more correct account, was said to be Ann, Aine or Agnes. The lady's portion took the form of 140 men out of every surname in O'Cahan's territory, and the descendants of those who left representatives are known to this day in the High-

lands as *tochradh nighean a' Chathanaich*—"the dowry of O'Cahan's daughter."
The importation of so many stalwart Irishmen shows that the Highlands were
somewhat sparsely peopled, and that there were no apprehensions of a congested
population in the days of Angus Og. It was still very much the time when might
was right and property could only be held by the strong hand of him who
could muster the biggest force of armed retainers. In these circumstances, the
arrival of this "tail" of youths from Antrim, to help the security of the lady's
new domains, was by no means an unwelcome occurrence. The names of some
of these immigrants have come down by tradition. Two families, the Munroes,
so called because they came from the innermost Roe water in the County of
Derry, their name being originally O'Millans, and the Roses of Kilravock, rose
to territorial distinction in the North Highlands. The other names preserved by
Hugh Macdonald are the Fearns, Dingwalls, Beatons, Macphersons, Bulikes of
Caithness, while the MS of 1700 mentions, in addition to these, Dunbar,
Maclinen, and the MacGilleglasses.

Angus Og's loyalty to Bruce never faltered. It stands in marked contrast to
the policy of the succeeding Lords of the Isles. Loyalty to Scottish nationality
was, however, a plant of slow growth, even among the great baronal families of
the South. These were, in blood and social ideas, as much Anglo-Norman as
Scottish, and swayed from one side to the other in the time of conflict just as
self-interest suggested. The case of the Lords of the Isles was similar, and, if
Angus Og was a notable exception to his line it was because in following the
impulses of friendship for the great deliverer of Scotland, he departed from what
was in reality the traditional policy of the Kings of Innse-Gall.

Angus Og died shortly after his illustrious patron (whose death occurred in
1329) in his residence at Finlaggan in Islay, and was buried in the tomb of his
ancestors in Iona. On his tombstone are his arms—a ship with sail furled, a
standard, four lions, and a tree—and the following inscription: *Hic jacet corpus
Angusii filii Domini Angusii MacDhomhnill de Ila.*

By his wife, Agnes O'Cahan, Angus Og had John, who succeeded, known as
"Good John" of Islay. He had also another son, known as Iain Fraoch, by a
daughter of Dugall MacEanruig, the "chief man of Glencoe," who is regarded as
illegitimate, but may have been by a handfast union, and thus legitimated by
Celtic usage. Iain Fraoch was the progenitor of the MacIains of Glencoe.

8

John of Islay
(1330-1386)

Reigning in Scotland
DAVID II
1329-1371
ROBERT II
1371-1390

JOHN OF ISLAY'S SUCCESSION to the extensive territories left by his father was almost contemporaneous with the accession of David II, then a mere child, to the Scottish throne. The problems that tend to accompany a long minority were for a few years mitigated by the firm and sagacious regency of Randolph, Earl of Moray; but when his strong hand was removed from the helm of State, Scotland was again plunged into anarchy and confusion. Disaster fell upon the Scottish arms at Dupplin; the power of the executive was shattered; English influence began to make itself felt once more, and Edward Balliol was crowned at Scone in 1332, and soon afterwards did homage as the vassal of Edward III. The cause of Scottish independence, though thus betrayed, was not by any means crushed; the spirits of Wallace and Bruce still ruled the people. For nine years the patriotic barons, backed by the national sentiment animating the great mass of the peasantry and middle class, were successful in maintaining the independence and integrity of the realm, in the face of domestic disloyalty fomented by the ambitious English monarch.

John of Islay's conduct throughout the stormy drama of Scottish politics during the fourteenth century is intelligible enough. Seeking to exercise independent sway within the Celtic sphere, he clearly saw that English influence in Scotland, with a weakened Scottish King, would serve his purpose best. This undoubtedly was his chief motive in espousing the cause of Balliol. But his attitude of hostility to the patriotic party was still further strengthened by a difference with the Regent regarding certain of the lands which he had inherited from his father. Randolph's successor refused to confirm him in these possessions, with the result that when Balliol assumed the crown the Lord of the Isles became associated with his party as that which was the more likely to establish him in his just and lawful rights. Hence it came to pass that on the 12th September 1335 John entered into a treaty of alliance with Edward Balliol in which he was put in possession of the lands inherited from his father and others. This treaty, which was concluded at Perth, was on the 6th October of the following year ratified by Edward III at Auckland, Balliol acknowledging the English King as his superior and Lord Paramount. Edward's confirmation of the treaty to which Balliol and John of Islay were parties throws an interesting light upon our subject. The substance of it is as follows:

> The King to whom, &c. We have examined certain letters of indenture drawn up between the magnificent prince Lord Edward King of Scotland, our illustrious and most dear cousin, and John of the Isles, in the following

terms: — In this indenture, made at the town of Perth on Tuesday, 12th December 1335, between the most excellent prince Lord Edward, by the grace of God the illustrious King of Scots, on the one part, and John of the Isles on the other part, it is certified that the said Lord the King has granted, in so far as in him lay, to the foresaid John for good and praiseworthy service rendered to himself, and in future to be rendered by him and his heirs,

>The Island of Ysle (Islay)
>The land of Kentyre (Kintyre)
>The land of Knappedoll (Knapdale)
>The Island of Githe (Gigha)
>Half the Island of Dure (Jura)
>The Island of Golwonche (Colonsay)
>The Island of Mulle
>The Island of Sky
>The Island of Lewethy (Lewis)
>The land of Kenalbadon and Ardinton (Morvern and Ardnamurchan)

to be held by the same John and his heirs and assignees. The same Lord the King has also granted to the same John the wardship of Lochaber until the attainment to man's estate of the son and heir of Lord David of Strathbolgy the last Earl of Athol. And for these foresaid concessions the foresaid John of the Isles binds himself and his heirs to be leal and faithful men to the said Lord the King and his heirs for ever, and he binds himself and his heirs to pursue all his foes and rebels whatsoever, on what days, in what places and ways he may be able to do so. And in security for the faithful performance of all these promises the oath shall be given by the said John on the holy eucharist, the cup of the altar, and the missal. Likewise the said John grants that if the foresaid King should desire to have from him a hostage or hostages for greater security, that a cousin or cousins of his own under age, very nearly related to him, may be delivered over to the said Lord the King when a suitable time has come, seeing that the said John has as yet neither son nor heir lawfully begotten of his own body. Besides, the foresaid Lord the King wishes and grants that at whatever time he may have an heir of his own body legitimately begotten the office of godfather to his heir may be granted to the foresaid John.

But we accept, ratify, approve, and confirm the whole and each of the contents of the foresaid letters for ourselves and our heirs so far as in us lies, as the foresaid letters more fully testify.

It is evident that John himself was present, and paid his respects to King Edward when these important negotiations were taking place. The Scottish records of the time indicate that on the very day on which John's league with Balliol was confirmed by the English monarch he received a safe conduct from that potentate. Intimation was made to all sheriffs, bailies and other faithful subjects that John and his retinue, servants and equipage, whether staying with the King, on their way to see him, or on their return home, were under his special protection and care. In all this we have evidence of the value placed by Balliol and his suzerain upon the power and resources of the Island Lord, and his adhesion to the anti-Scottish party.

This alliance with Edward III continued for several years, gathering rather than losing strength, and in the records of 1337 we find frequent traces of friendly intercourse between the English monarch and the Lord of the Isles. On 3rd December of that year John received a safe conduct couched in still more forcible language than that of 1335, and the most extreme pains and penalties are threatened against such as would cause injury or molestation to himself or his followers when coming, staying, or departing from the royal presence. This is followed on the day immediately succeeding by a commission to the Earl of Salisbury to enter into a league with the Lord of the Isles. On the same day a letter is sent by Edward to John by the hands of the same pleni-potentiary, abounding in the friendliest, most honeyed phrases—"*Epistola blandiloqua*" it is styled. He calls him his dearest friend, and offers him the best safeguards in his power, whether he comes with 60 or 80 or 100 attendants with the view of drawing closer the bonds of amity and concord between them. The relations between the English King and John, of which we have evidence in these transactions, seem to have lasted until a fresh crisis arose in the position of Scottish parties. Edward, recognising the power and capacity of the Island lord, seems to have done all he could to stimulate his discontent, secure his friendship, and establish his connection with the party of Balliol.

After a few years' struggle, the patriotic party was successful in vindicating the independence of Scotland, and the Steward, the nephew of David Bruce, having been appointed Regent, and finding his uncle's cause in the ascendant, arranged for his return from France to assume his father's sceptre in 1341. Owing to the attitude of John of Islay during the troublous times of David Bruce's minority, it might naturally be expected that the vengeance of the King would, on the overthrow of his enemies and his accession to the throne, be directed against him. As a matter of fact, in or about 1343, John was nominally forfeited in the lands of Gigha, Islay, Jura and Colonsay, all of which were granted by the King to Angus MacIain of Ardnamurchan, a kinsman of his own, and the head of a house that was yet to play a not unimportant part in the history of the High-lands. Ranald MacRuairi joined with John of Islay in offering a stout and effective resistance to the royal decree. His possessions seem also to have been involved in the confiscations of the time, although the MacRuairi tenure at that particular period is not altogether clear. The Island Chiefs were not, however, strong believers in the efficacy of parchments, and seem to have felt none the worse of their irregular relations to the crown.

It was not long before the exigencies of the Scottish State worked in favour of the Island interests. David Bruce, taking advantage of the absence of Edward III in France, resolved to invade England. Wishing to bring the whole military force of his kingdom into action, and with a view of conciliating all whose hostility might be feared, he pardoned both John of Islay and his kinsman, Ranald MacRuairi. The whirligig of time had brought about its revenges, and David Bruce repeated the work of Balliol. In 1343—before the invasion of England, and the very year of his forfeiture—he confirmed John in the lands of Duror, Glencoe, Morvern, Gigha, Ardnamurchan, Colonsay, Mull, Kerneburgh and Isleburgh Castles, with the lands pertaining to them; Tiree, Islay, Jura, Scarba, Lewis and Lochaber. It will be seen from this that Kintyre, Knapdale (South) and Skye, which formed part of Balliol's grant in 1335, are excepted, these lands having reverted to their former owners. To Ranald MacRuairi there were granted the Isles of Uist, Barra, Eigg and Rum, and the lordship of Garmoran, which included the districts of Moidart, Arisaig, Morar and Knoydart —all of which formed the ancient patrimony of the MacRuairi family.

On the eve of David Bruce's invasion of England, there occurred a tragedy which resulted in a considerable enlargement of the power and possessions of the House of Islay. Ranald MacRuairi met with a violent death. The Scottish barons having been convoked to meet at Perth, Ranald obeyed the summons and, accompanied by a considerable body of men, took up his quarters in the monastery of Elcho, a few miles from the ancient capital. Ranald held the lands of Kintail from the Earl of Ross, and as a bitter feud over the tenure of these lands had arisen between them, the opportunity of wreaking vengeance upon his foe seemed to the Earl too favourable to be lost. In the middle of the night he broke into the monastery, surprised the occupants, treacherously and sacrilegiously slew Ranald and seven of his men, and immediately thereafter betook himself to his northern fastnesses. It was considered a bad omen by many at the time that King David's campaign should have been immediately preceded by such a foul deed.

The incident materially affected the fortunes of John of Islay. In 1337, or shortly thereafter, he had married his third cousin, Euphemia (Amie) MacRuairi, sister of the slaughtered chief. In terms of the royal gift to her brother Ranald, she succeeded to the estates, and brought them over to her husband in 1346. Although John's right emerged through his marriage, he had also, as a male heir not remotely akin, a feasible right to the inheritance. In this way he had a double claim to Garmoran and the Northern Isles. The Scottish Government, however, did not regard the matter in this light. They considered John already too powerful a subject for the safety of the realm, and rightly feared that the vast territories to which he now laid claim threatened a revival of the ancient kingdom of the Isles. Consequently, they refused to acknowledge John as the rightful heir of the MacRuairis, or to give him legal investiture in their possessions.

It is therefore not surprising that the proud Chief of Clan Donald felt disposed again to espouse the fortunes of the Balliol party. In 1346, the year of Ranald MacRuairi's assassination, the fortunes of that faction seemed once more in the ascendant. King David Bruce's invasion of England opened with disaster. At the battle of Neville's Cross the Scottish army was defeated with great slaughter, and the King taken a prisoner to England. Yet although it might well seem that a fatal blow had been struck at Scotland's independence, and Balliol's position been re-established by England's success, neither of these results ensued. Balliol obtained not even the semblance of kingly authority; and the Scottish nobility were successful in placing the Steward, the next heir to the throne, in the regency of the kingdom. In 1351, Edward III, whose attention was largely taken up with his French wars, concluded a truce with Scotland, which he renewed from time to time, as he entertained prospects of replenishing his coffers by a large ransom for the royal captive.

Rather surprisingly in the circumstances, the friction caused between John of Islay and the Government in connection with the estates of Garmoran does not seem to have led the Island Chief into aggressive hostility. During the eleven years of David's captivity in England, John appears to have been left in undisturbed possession not only of the lands confirmed to him by the royal authority, but also of the MacRuairi territories, his right to which was still unacknowledged. Certain of the lands which were granted by David Bruce to John in 1343; namely the lands of Duror, Jura and Mull, and the fortresses of Kerneburgh and Isleburgh, of which John had received the custody, had been held by John of Lorn as the vassal of John of Islay. The privilege of holding these fortresses had been accompanied by certain conditions. One of these was that until John of Lorn delivered the Castle of Kerneburgh to John of Islay he should give him three hostages, and that John of Lorn should never give the keeping of the castle of Kerneburgh to any of the Clan Mackinnon, who at that time seemed to have had a settlement in Mull. These, with the exception of the three unciates of Tiree, next to Coll, were all resigned to John of Islay, it being stipulated that the Steward of the three unciates should not make a domestic establishment (*domesticatum*) or a dwelling (*habitaculum*) on those lands without leave obtained from the superior. The Island of Coll was retained by John of Lorn and, in the deed recording the transaction, was confirmed to himself and his heirs for ever. These negotiations took place in 1354, and in the record of the proceedings we find John of Islay described by the title "Lord of the Isles."

It may be true, as Gregory says, that there is no previous record of this particular chief of the Clan Cholla being called *Dominus Insularum* in the annals of that age. It is, however, a most unwarrantable inference to draw from that fact, as the same historian does, that the title "Lord of the Isles" was a new one in the history of the family. This particular question we propose to touch upon more fully in a subsequent chapter.

Shortly after this time an incident occurred in John's career which shows that English influence had lost its hold upon him, and that in his public conduct he had allowed himself to be drawn into the full tide of Scottish policy. In 1354-5, just as a treaty for the ransom of David Bruce was on the eve of being ratified, the Scots nobility were persuaded by a French offer of forty thousand moutons of gold to break the truce with England. This was followed by a series of hostilities both in Scotland and France, in both of which lands the able and ambitious Edward III still sought to obtain supreme dominion. In 1356, the Black Prince having penetrated far into the interior of France, the French King assembled an army vastly superior in numbers, and determined to cut off his retreat. A number of Scottish chiefs and nobles accompanied him to the field, and, among others, John of Islay, with a powerful body of Highlanders. With all his numerical advantages, the French King was unable to prevail against the valour of the English army. In the famous battle of Poitiers, fought on the 19th September 1356, the Scots contingent sustained great losses, and the Lord of the Isles was taken prisoner. From that date to 16th December of the following year he was in captivity, the greater part of the time in England. Once more John obtained from the English King a safe conduct for his return to his Island home, but it is notable that the terms of the document are less endearing than of old. Sheriffs and bailies and other lieges, however, are told that the Lord of the Isles, who was a prisoner of the Prince of Wales, his dear son, was in the King's safe conduct going to Scotland, accompanied by four knights, for the purpose of providing the means necessary for his ransom.

Two years after this we find John of Islay taking a prominent part in promoting the treaty for the liberation and ransom of David II, and thus still further indicating his abandonment of the English alliance and his assumption of a friendly attitude towards the Crown. It was stipulated in this treaty that, for the more sure payment of the ransom of 100,000 marks, twenty hostages were to be sent to England, amongst whom three of the following seven were always to be included, namely, the Steward of Scotland, the Earls of March, Marr, Ross and Sutherland, the Lord Douglas and Thomas de Moray; and that in the meantime, during the whole period of the ten years over which the payments were spread, an inviolable truce should subsist, in which truce were to be included "Monsieur Edward de Balliol and Johan des Isles."

Soon after the return of David Bruce to the Scottish throne, a complete revolution took place in the mutual relations of political parties. The party adhering to the King was regarded as patriotic and national, while that of Balliol as being favourable to English influence. But now David Bruce began to show symptoms that his long residence in England had cooled his patriotism. He expressed a willingness to admit English influence into the affairs of the realm, and even to promote the nomination of an English successor to the throne of

Scotland. The consequence was that the Balliol faction became the party of the court, while the national party, with the Steward at its head, ranged themselves in opposition. Yet although the Lord of the Isles found himself, for the first time, in a position in which antagonism to the Government was consistent with adherence to the party of Scottish independence; and although his connection with this party was further cemented by his marriage with Lady Margaret, daughter of the Steward, yet we do not find that he assumed a strenuous attitude in opposition to the policy of the King. The date of this marriage, in the absence of definite information, it is difficult to state with exactness, but it must have taken place about, and certainly not much later than, David Bruce's return from captivity.

We do not propose at this stage to discuss the merits of this union, the circumstances of which the history of the time has left, to a large extent, in obscurity. The voice of tradition is unanimous that, in order to carry out the marriage, the Lord of the Isles divorced or abandoned his first wife, Amie MacRuairi. In this he had the support and advice not only of the Steward, but—according to Hugh Macdonald, the Sleat historian—of his council, and, pre-eminently, MacInnes of Ardgour. The same authority—who, by the way, describes Amie as "a good and virtuous gentlewoman"—throws an interesting sidelight upon the pride of the great Highland Chief, who would not perform the unwonted act of obeisance— uncovering his head in the royal presence on the occasion of his marriage—but ingeniously evaded the courtesy by not wearing a head-dress at all. MacInnes's untoward intervention in the domestic affairs of the family of Islay was neither forgotten nor forgiven by Amie or her sons. It is alleged that a commission was given to Donald, son of Lachlan MacLean, to slay MacInnes with his five sons, and this having been done, he obtained possession of Ardgour, which his posterity still enjoy. Amie is said to have lived for a number of years after her separation from John of Islay, and to have built Castle Tirrim in Moidart, and Borve Castle in Benbecula, as well as places of worship which are described in a later chapter.

Although John's connection with the family of the Steward would naturally, as we have seen, lead him to espouse the policy of his party, yet his past conduct, both in war and diplomacy in recent years, continued to secure for him the favour of the Crown. He enjoyed certain high offices of State, his tenure of which does not seem to have hitherto attracted the attention of the historian. Such was the confidence that seems to have been reposed in him that, in or shortly before 1360, he was appointed Constable of Edinburgh Castle, a responsible and exalted military position, which reflected great credit upon the character and ability of the Chief of the Clan Donald. This, however, was not the only function which John, during these years of loyalty, discharged under the Scottish Crown. It is, indeed, a singular circumstance that, in 1364, we find him acting in the highest office which it was possible for a Scottish subject to occupy, that of Seneschal or High Steward of the King's Household, an office which had for generations come down by hereditary descent as the possession of a family nearly akin to the throne. The history of the time leaves little doubt as to the reasons for which, at the period under consideration, John of Islay, rather than the hereditary holder of the position, is found discharging the functions of High Steward of Scotland. Robert, the High Steward, had, by various Acts of Settlement passed by the Estates of Scotland, been designated as next heir to his uncle David Bruce, in default of the latter leaving heirs of his body. Queen Johanna died childless in 1363, and early in the following year the King, having contracted a violent fancy for a beautiful young woman named Margaret Logie— of comparatively humble origin—insisted, contrary to the advice of his Court, on bestowing his hand upon her in marriage. This unequal alliance caused an open rupture between David and his kinsman, the Steward, whose reversion of the Crown would certainly be nullified if the fair Margaret should bear a son. Such was the discord that arose out of this episode and the angry feelings to which it gave rise, that the Steward and his son, the Wolf of Badenoch, were thrown into prison, where they seem to have been detained for several years. The royal resentment does not seem, however, to have extended to the Steward's son-in-law, John of Islay, for undoubtedly he exercised the functions of Seneschal during a part, at least, of his father-in-law's imprisonment, a fact which seems to indicate that he must have been a special favourite with the King, and kept himself free from the contending factions of the time.

Two years after John of Islay first comes before us as Steward of Scotland, he appears as a royal envoy to Flanders to transact some business for the King. Again the records of the time help us to determine the nature of the negotiations in which the Lord of the Isles was engaged during his visit. The payment of the King's ransom was one of the chief obstacles in the way of a lasting peace between the two kingdoms, and to secure the regular payment of the first instalment the Scottish Parliament had made great sacrifices. It was ordained that the wool of the kingdom, apparently its most productive export at that time, should be sold to the King at a low rate, and it was afterwards disposed of under the King's instructions to merchants in Flanders, where textile industries seem at that early time to have flourished, and the profit from the transaction was applied in discharge of the royal ransom. John of Islay, in virtue of his office as Seneschal, had the management of the royal revenues, and his voyage to Flanders in 1366, accompanied by John Mercer, who was probably better versed than the Lord of the Isles in the price of wool, was no doubt undertaken for the purpose of negotiating with the Flanders merchants the value to be placed upon the precious commodity which was to yield a King's ransom.

The burdensome exactions which were thus necessary for completing the ransom of the King were felt to be a heavy impost by a country naturally poor and lately impoverished by a series of desolating wars. In the Highlands especially the taxation was found to be oppressive, and John of Islay, so recently a high official under the Scottish Crown, is found, along with other northern barons, refusing to pay the national taxation or attend a meeting of the Estates of the realm.

Some years before this outbreak of disaffection, as already stated, the King had thrown the Steward into prison for his opposition to the royal policy, but now finding himself unable to cope with the forces of disorder, he gave him his freedom, in the belief that he would lend his influence successfully to the vindication of the authority of the Crown. The Steward undertook a task dictated alike by policy and patriotism. His son-in-law, John of Islay, was the most difficult to reduce to subjection. There was peace, however, between Scotland and England; John of Islay had no foreign ally to whom to turn, and so David Bruce was able to bring all his resources to bear. At last, after years of open and successful defiance, the Steward prevailed upon John to meet the King at Inverness, when the following instrument of allegiance was finally drawn up in 1369:

To all who may see the present letters:—John de Yle, Lord of the Isles, wishes salvation in the Saviour of all. Since my most serene prince and master, the revered Lord David, by the Grace of God, illustrious King of Scots, has been stirred up against my person because of certain faults committed by me, for which reason, coming humbly to the presence of my said lord, at the Town of Inverness, on the 15th day of the month of November, in the year of grace 1369, in the presence of the prelates, and of very many of the nobles of his kingdom, I offered and submitted myself to the pleasure and favour of my said master, by suppliantly entreating for favour and for the remission of my late faults, and since my said lord, at the instance of his council, has graciously admitted me to his goodwill and favour, granting besides that I may remain in (all) my possessions whatsoever and not be removed, except according to the process and demand of law: Let it be clearly patent to you all by the tenor of these presents, that I, John de Yle, foresaid, promise and covenant, in good faith, that I shall give and make reparation to all good men of this kingdom whatsoever, for such injuries, losses, and troubles as have been wrought by me, my sons, or others whose names are more fully set forth in the royal letters of remission granted to me, and to whomsoever of the kingdom as are faithful I shall thus far make the satisfaction concluded for, I shall justly note purchased lands and superiorities, and I shall govern them according to my ability; I shall promptly cause my sons and my subjects, and others my adherents, to be in peaceable subjection, and that due justice shall be done to our lord the King, and to the laws and customs of his kingdom, and that they shall be obedient to, and shall appear before the justiciars, sheriffs, coroners, and other royal servants in each sheriffdom, even better and more obediently than in the time of Robert of good memory, the predecessor of my lord the King, and as the inhabitants of the said lands and superiorities have been accustomed to do. They shall answer, both promptly and dutifully, to the royal servants what is imposed regarding contributions and other burdens and services due, and also for the time past, and in the event that within the said lands or superiorities any person or persons shall offend against the King, or one or more of his faithful servants, and if he or they shall despise to obey the law, or if he or they shall be unwilling to obey in the premises, and in any one of the premises, I shall immediately, entirely laying aside stratagem and deceit, pursue that person or those persons as enemies, and as rebels of the King and kingdom, with all my ability, until he or they shall be expelled from the limits of the lands and superiorities, or I shall make him or them obey the common law: And for performing, implementing, and faithfully observing these things, all and each, I personally have taken the oath in the presence of the foresaid prelates and nobles, and besides I have given and surrendered the under-written hostages, *viz.* Donald, my son, begotten of the daughter of the Lord Seneschal of Scotland, Angus, son of my late son John, and one Donald, another and natural son of mine, whom, because at the time of the completion of this present deed I have not at present ready and prepared, I shall cause them to go into, or be given up at the Castle of Dumbarton, at the Feast of our Lord's birth now next to come, if I shall be able to otherwise on this side, or at the feast of the Purification of the Blessed Virgin (or Candlemas, 2nd February) next following thereafter, under pain of the breach of the oath given, and under pain of the loss of all things which, with regard to the lord our King, I shall be liable to lose, in whatever manner. And for securing the entrance of these hostages as promised, I have found my Lord Seneschal of Scotland, Earl of Strathern, security, whose seal for the purpose of the present security, and also for the greater evidence of the matter is appended, along with my own proper seal, to these presents in testimony of the premises. Acted and given, year, day and place foresaid.

Two years after the Treaty of Inverness was ratified, David II died and Robert II ascended the throne. Owing to his close connection by marriage with the reigning family, the subsequent relations of the Lord of the Isles with the

Court were of a friendly nature, and before his father-in-law was long upon the throne he was confirmed in possession of a domain which might well be called princely. It may be stated, generally, that the greater part of the territories that first belonged in their integrity to Somerled, but were afterwards divided among the houses of Islay, Bute and Lorn, were now consolidated under one powerful family. One of the first acts of King Robert II on his accession was to confirm his "beloved son, John of Isla," in the 300 merklands, once the property of Alan, the son of Ruairi, namely, the lands of Moidart, Arisaig, Morar, Knoydart, being in the lordship of Garmoran; also the Islands of Uist, Barra, Rum and Eigg, and Harris, being part of Lewis. This deed was executed at Scone, during the session of Parliament, on the 9th March 1371-2.

According to Skene this was the first time John of Islay had received feudal investiture of the patrimony of the MacRuairis. As a matter of fact, however, we find that on 4th July 1363—the time of John's enjoyment of high court favour and office—David II bestows upon him a Charter of Confirmation under the Great Seal for all lands possessed by him, by whomsoever these had been granted, a deed intended to make good all previous gifts granted by Balliol or by David or inherited through his first wife. In the same year there is a grant of these lands made by John to his son Ranald, born of the first marriage, with the addition that the castles of Benbecula and Island Tirrim, and also the lands of Sunart, Letterlochletter, Ardgour, Hawlaste, and sixty merklands in Lochaber, namely Kilmald and Locharkaig, are also included. This grant is accompanied by a royal confirmation. It is remarkable that neither John's first wife, through whom he received the lands, nor her brother Ranald, from whom she inherited them, receive any notice in the charter. This gift was further confirmed by Robert III in 1392.

One point only calls for remark in the disposition of lands provided for in this instrument; but it is of great importance, in view of future discussions, namely, that these lands of Garmoran and the North Isles and others were to be held by Ranald and his heirs from John and his heirs. Some years later, in 1376, the Lord of the Isles received three charters for the remainder of his lands, in which Colonsay, Lochaber, Kintyre and Knapdale, and other lands not previously disposed of, were granted by the King to himself, "John de Ile," and his heirs by his wife Margaret, the daughter of the King. The territories of John of Islay were, in this manner, divided into large divisions or lordships—the first, in the order of time, being the lordship of Garmoran and the Northern Isles, possessed by Ranald as the vassal of John and of John's feudal heirs—the other being the lordship of the Isles proper, with John himself as crown vassal, with a special destination of the lands in question in favour of the second family.

Some idea of the extent of this territory may be gained by enumerating the different districts in the following order:

Mainland Territories

The Lordship of Lochaber, including Kilmallie and Kilmonivaig.
The Lordship of Garmoran, including Moidart, Arisaig, Morar and Knoydart.
Also Morvern, Knapdale, Duror, Kintyre and Glencoe.

Island Territories

Islay, Gigha, Colonsay	Lewis, Harris
Jura and Scarba	N. Uist, Benbecula
Tiree, Eigg, Rum	S. Uist and Barra

After 1372 there is little left to record regarding John of Islay or his fortunes, until his death in 1386. Here, as elsewhere, the dulness of the annals would indicate a time of peace and prosperity. The Lord of the Isles breathed his last in the Castle of Ardtornish at an advanced age and his dust was laid in the Church of Oran, in Iona, where the ashes of his father, Angus Og, reposed. His obsequies were observed with great pomp and splendour by the Churchmen of the Isles, among whom he was known as the "Good John of Isla," on account of a munificence to their order in which he more than vied with the pious liberality of his fathers.

* * *

We have purposely refrained from disturbing the continuity of our narrative by dwelling upon certain controversial episodes in John's career which have an important bearing upon the future history of his family. These questions are in themselves so important that there is an obvious advantage in dealing with them in the closing part of the present chapter, where they can be treated with some measure of thoroughness rather than touched upon as mere passing details.

The two marriages of John of Islay open up far-reaching questions of genealogical interest. We cannot, however, avoid disposing of one question upon which future genealogical discussions must hinge, and that is the regularity, or the opposite, of John's union with Amie MacRuairi, the heiress of Garmoran.

Undoubtedly there has been a tradition which seems to have acquired a certain amount of weight, that this was one of those irregular unions known as handfasting which seem to have prevailed to some extent among the ancient Highlanders, and which, though recognised in the law of Celtic succession, were irregular in the eye of the feudal law. We are not, of course, surprised to find the historian of Sleat, Hugh Macdonald, stating, not that John was married, but that he lived for ten years with the mother of the first family, seeing that this seanachie is always ready to cast doubts upon the legitimacy of heads of branches of the clan whose claims to seniority might otherwise be preferred to those of the Chiefs of Sleat. We also place little reliance upon the conclusions of another document compiled in the same interest, in which—very unnecessarily for proof of the main contention—the legality of the marriage in question is scornfully put out of court. It is, however, somewhat surprising to find the Clanranald historian make an admission so damaging to the legitimacy of the line from which the Clanranald Chiefs were descended as that John of Islay "did not marry the mother of these men [his sons by Amie MacRuairi] from the altar."

How such a misconception of the true facts of the case should have arisen can only be accounted for in one way. The Scottish Government, when refusing to acknowledge John's right to the lands of Ranald MacRuairi, supported the refusal by the allegation that his marriage with Amie was irregular, and could not be reconciled with the principles of feudal tenure. This contention, however unfounded, and though a mere pretext for curbing a powerful subject, was quite sufficient, coming as it did from such high quarters, to impress the popular mind and create a tradition which appears to have received a considerable amount of credit.

That John's marriage with Amie was a perfectly legal and regular union is a fact simply attested. That a lady in Amie's position, belonging to a noble Highland family, should have contracted an irregular alliance of the nature suggested is in the highest degree improbable. But apart from this consideration, which is not without its own weight, two undoubted facts may be adduced in proof. First of all, there is a dispensation granted by Pope Benedict XII to John and Amie permitting them to enter the state of matrimony. According to the canon law of the Church of Rome, which was then very rigid, the parties, as third cousins, were within the forbidden degrees of consanguinity, and this barrier to their union could only be removed by the grace of the Church's earthly head. And it may be stated in passing that this very dispensation, implying as it did some sort of irregularity, may have been one ground upon which the Government based their refusal to confirm John in the MacRuairi lands.

But there is more than this. In the Treaty of Inverness the Lord of the Isles, in enumerating the hostages pledged for the performance of his sworn allegiance, draws a distinction between his "late son John and one Donald, another and natural son of mine." This John was the eldest son of Amie, and is spoken of in the same terms as Donald his son by the daughter of the Steward of Scotland. There seems, therefore, no ground for doubting—and in this the standard authorities are at one—that the first marriage of John of Islay was a perfectly valid and legal union. In point of fact, John's marriage with the daughter of the Steward is exposed to far more objections, both from a legal and moral point of view, than his first marriage. Assuming, as the evidence compels us to do, that the first marriage was regular, and there being nothing to show that Amie was guilty of any conduct unbecoming a true and faithful wife, the validity of the divorce and the power to contract a second marriage in her life-time is subject to very grave doubts.

By his first marriage with Amie MacRuairi, John of Islay had:

1. John, who predeceased his father, and whose son Angus appears to have left no issue;
2. Ranald, the ancestor of Clanranald and Glengarry;
3. Godfrey, from whom the Siol Ghorraidh (Clan Godfrey);
4. Mary, who married Lachlan Maclean of Duart (see *Highland Papers,* Vol. I, pp. 78/79, for reference to a Papal Dispensation absolving them from the excommunication incurred by marrying without banns).

By his second marriage with the Princess Margaret of Scotland, John had:

1. Donald, his successor;
2. John Mor Tanister, from whom the Clann Iain Mhoir Ile;
3. Angus, who left no issue;
4. Alexander, known as Alasdair Carrach, from whom the Keppoch chiefs of the Clanranald of Lochaber;
5. Hugh, who had a charter of the Thanage of Glentilt and whose descendants are said to have become a branch of the Mackintoshes;
6. Margaret, who married Angus Dubh Mackay of Strathnaver;
7. Agnes, who married Sir John Montgomery of Ardrossan, later of Eglinton.

DONALD OF HARLAW'S CHARTER OF 1408
The only surviving example in the Gaelic language, subscribed
with the Celtic or patriarchal title of the Lords of the Isles

9

Donald of Harlaw

(1386-1423)

Reigning in Scotland
ROBERT II
1371-1390
ROBERT III
1390-1406
JAMES I
1406-1437
Albany Regencies
1406-1424

JOHN OF ISLAY was succeeded by Donald, eldest son of his second marriage with Margaret, daughter of the Steward who was now the reigning King. We have seen in the previous chapter that there were two surviving sons of the first marriage, Ranald and Godfrey, of whom Ranald is regarded by most authorities as the elder. And since we cannot in the circumstances accept that the Celtic law of tanistry alone made Donald's accession possible, it is now necessary to examine the more powerful factors that helped to place Donald and not Ranald at the head of the Clan.

John, the eldest son of the first marriage, is referred to in the treaty of 1369 as then dead, while his son Angus, given as a hostage on that occasion for the future good behaviour of his grandfather, also did not survive, and left no issue. According to the MS of 1450, Ranald was the second son of the first marriage of John of Islay and, failing the issue of the first son, his father's feudal heir. This statement is supported by others, among whom MacVurich who, although he makes no mention of John, still places the name of Ranald before that of Godfrey. Ranald had already, in 1373, received a Crown Charter of the lands of Garmoran and the North Isles, all of which were included in the old MacRuairi lands; but the same Charter added also the lands of Sunart, Ardgour, and 60 merklands in Lochaber. In this Charter of 1373 Ranald is to hold his lands from John of Islay and his heirs. Who was John of Islay's heir? Not Angus, son of John, who had died without issue. It could not have been Ranald, now the eldest surviving son of John of Islay, for he could not be his own vassal. The next heir after Ranald is Godfrey, but he laid no claim to the Lordship of the Isles, and from what we know of his character, if he was his father's heir, he was not the man to stand tamely by while Donald took possession of the Lordship. The Charter of 1373 is itself the best evidence that Godfrey could not have been his father's heir. It seems amply clear that the policy of John of Islay in securing the Charter of 1373 for Ranald was to bribe him out of the succession. If Godfrey had been the eldest son, it is difficult to see how he could have been so utterly ignored by his father. Neither in the Charter of 1376, which conveys the lands of Colonsay and others to the sons of the second marriage, nor in Ranald's Charter of 1373 is there any mention made of Godfrey, or any disposition in his favour. The subsequent history of the Lordship shows very clearly who the heirs were referred to in the Charter of 1373. Ranald, although the eldest surviving son, came second to Donald, and the descendants of Ranald continued to be vassals of the future Lords of the Isles. Donald undoubtedly became, whether by feudal or Celtic law, superior to all his brothers, and his succession as "Donald de Ile" leaves no doubt as to the meaning of the Charter of 1373.

But Donald, besides being backed by the powerful influence of the King, his grandfather, and being in the advantageous position of eldest son of the family then in possession, appeared in every other way, as events afterwards proved, to have been fitter to rule over the vast territories of the family than Ranald. John of Islay himself took care to disarm opposition by making his heir in the Crown Charter of 1373 the feudal superior of Ranald. In all the circumstances, therefore, and in view of the unambitious character which we must ascribe to Ranald, the latter acted wisely in accepting the situation and offering no opposition to the succession of his brother. Accordingly, as we find from the *Book of Clanranald,* Ranald, as High Steward of the Isles, gave over all the rights and privileges of the Lordship of the Isles to Donald at Kildonan, in Eigg, and he was nominated Macdonald, and Donald of Islay, in presence of the principal men of the Isles.

Donald had now become not only the feudal superior of his brothers, but also, by the consent of the men of the Isles, the chief of the Clan Donald—another instance of the practical operation of the unwritten Celtic law which permitted the deposition of one chief, as well as the election of another who might not be the direct feudal heir.

Whatever opposition there may have been to Donald's succession, it appears, by his firm yet generous rule, to have gradually ceased; and the vassals of the Isles had never been so strongly cemented together, nor at any period in the history of the Lordship of the Isles do we find the followers of the Macdonald standard any stronger in their attachment to their chief than we now find them. This fact is sufficient proof of Donald's administrative powers, no less than of his wise and just rule in an age when the strongest often failed. He conciliated his brothers by the generous terms meted out to them in the division of the lands of Garmoran, the North Isles, and others, soon after his accession.

The position and attitude of Godfrey, the third son of Amie MacRuairi, does not, however, appear to be very clear, either at this juncture or during his subsequent history. We may infer from the Charter of 1373, by which Uist with the Castle of Benbecula and other lands are conferred on Ranald, that North Uist had been the portion allotted by John to his son Godfrey, and that he possessed it during the lifetime of his father. The same Insula de Wyst, mentioned in the Charter of 1373, is confirmed to Ranald MacAlan in the year 1498, and all the lands specified in that charter as being in Wyst are in South Uist. In a charter conveying the Trinity Church of Carinish, with the lands of Carinish and Illeray in North Uist to the Monastery and Convent of St John the Evangelist in Inchaffray, Godfrey styles himself *Godfridus de Insulis Dominus de Wyst.* But he dates his charter *apud castrum nostrum de Ellantyrum* (Castle Tirrim), the principal residence of the Clanranald. According to the *Book of Clanranald,* Ranald died in 1386, and Godfrey's Charter is dated 7th July 1389. It appears, therefore, that on the death of Ranald, Godfrey possessed himself of Garmoran and other lands granted to the former, and that he was allowed to keep possession, notwithstanding a confirmation in the year 1392 by Robert III of the Castle of Eilean Tirrim, the lands of Garmoran and others to Ranald's heirs. Whether Godfrey was encouraged or in any way assisted by Donald in this enterprise we have no means of knowing; but it is evident that he could not have kept possession long if Donald had chosen to oppose his pretensions, and in view of all the circumstances we are justified in concluding that Godfrey made out a plausible claim, as a descendant of the MacRuairis, to the lands of which he possessed himself. The sons of Ranald were likely enough to have assumed a defensive attitude, and resisted the aggressive pretensions of Godfrey to the utmost; but it is difficult to say, in the absence of any positive evidence, with what immediate result, even though supported as they were by the Crown Charter of

1373. It appears to be abundantly clear that, in the lifetime of Godfrey at least, the principal lands in the MacRuairi territory were not possessed by the sons of Ranald.

The sons of the second marriage of John of Islay were amply provided for out of the family inheritance. Donald himself, besides the superiority of the whole Macdonald territory included in the Lordship of the Isles, possessed directly the lands of Colonsay and others not included in the grants bestowed on the younger sons. John Mor Tanister, the second son, received a grant of 120 merklands in Kintyre and 60 merklands in Islay. He became the founder of the family styled of Dunnyveg and the Glens, the latter of which he acquired through his marriage with Margery Bisset, the daughter and heiress of MacEoin Bisset, Lord of the Antrim Glens. It will be observed that only certain lands in Islay were granted to John Mor, whose residence there was the Castle of Dun-Naomhaig (Dunny-veg), while Finlaggan in the same island was the residence of Donald, his brother, the Lord of the Isles. As a matter of fact, the family of John Mor never did possess the whole of the island of Islay, either before or after the forfeiture of the Lordship of the Isles, and they never arrogated to themselves the designation "de Ile," or "of Islay," which was the peculiar and exclusive designation of the head of the House of Macdonald, and ceased with John, the last Lord of the Isles, who died in 1503.

The next son of the second marriage of John of Islay was, according to the MS of 1450, Angus, who having died young without issue has nothing recorded of him but the bare name. The fourth son was Alasdair, afterwards known as Alasdair Carrach, progenitor of the Macdonalds of Keppoch. On him were bestowed lands in Mull, and also the lands of Lochaber, preferring these, according to the Sleat historian, to the lands of Trotternish in Skye, of which he had his choice.

Besides these, there appears also to have been another son of the second marriage of John of Islay, named Hugh, hitherto ignored by the historians of the family. Robert, the Steward of Scotland, before he succeeded to the throne, granted, as Lord of Atholl, a charter of the whole thanage of Glentilt to Eugenius (Hugh in Latinised form), Thane of Glentilt, and brother of Ranald of the Isles. From the fact that the lands were conferred by the Steward, we naturally conclude that Hugh was of the second family of the Lord of the Isles, and, therefore, the Steward's grandson. In 1382, a safe conduct, dated at Westminster on the 21st of October, is granted to Hugh of the Isles by Richard II, and an escort of six horsemen accompany him to the English borders. In the same year we find the following entry in the Scottish Exchequer Rolls: *Et Hugoni de Insulis, de dono regis, ut patet per literam suam de precepto sub secreto, ostensam super compotem sub periculo computantis iijli.* Again in the year 1403 we have: *Et domino quondam Hugoni de Insulis, de dono regis, prout pater per literas suas de recepto de anno hujus compoti ostensas super compotum vli.* Skene asserts that the family descended from Hugh became Mackintoshes from one of them whose name was Finlay Toiseach, Thane of Glentilt. This is highly probable, for we have never been able to identify any of the descendants of Hugh under the name of Macdonald, and from the fact that the heads of the family were styled Thanes or Toiseachs, there is every reason to suppose that in time they became Mackintoshes (Mac-an-Toisich).

Though the lands of the Lordship of the Isles were thus divided between the sons of the two marriages of John of Islay, the superiority of the whole still remained in Donald, now the acknowledged chief of the Clan Donald, and we are not by any means disposed to agree with Skene and others that this division of the lands of the Lordship weakened the power of the Clan Donald, and finally brought about the downfall of the Lordship itself. The real cause of the downfall of the Lordship of the Isles must be sought elsewhere, and may be summed up briefly in the struggle of Saxon against Celt, a struggle of unequal proportions, and therefore not surprisingly resulting in the triumph of the stronger over the weaker forces. Instead of weakening the power of the Lord of the Isles, the division of the heritage of the family seems very materially to have increased it. If the intention of the Charter of 1373 was partly to cripple the resources, influence and organic unity of the Island family, that policy certainly did not succeed, for the cadets of the family themselves, no less than the other vassals of the Lordship of the Isles, continued to adhere loyally to the Macdonald standard until the final attempt to set up the Celtic supremacy in the Isles failed in the rebellion of Donald Dubh.

The first mention we have of Donald, Lord of the Isles, in any record is in the year 1369 when, according to the treaty of Inverness, he was given as a hostage to the king for the future good behaviour of his father, John of Islay. Donald would then have been about ten years of age, if we are right in assuming that the second marriage of John of Islay took place in the year 1358. His compulsory residence in the Castle of Dumbarton could not in the nature of things have tended to make him loyal to the Scottish throne. The policy of the Scottish State in detaining Donald and the other sons of the Lord of the Isles, though the means of bringing about a temporary cessation of hostilities in the Isles, in the event proved unwise and short-sighted. Donald is no sooner set at liberty than he assumes a defensive attitude, biding his time for the opportunity to wreak vengeance on his former jailers. He felt he owed no loyalty to the Scottish State and, regarding its rulers from an early age as interlopers within the Island territory, began to prepare the groundwork of his policy to establish a Celtic supremacy in the West, secure from interference by his powerful neighbour.

The strained political relations between England and Scotland favoured negotiation with the former country, and accordingly Donald and his brothers are found visiting the English Court frequently during the years from 1378 to 1408. In the year 1378 a safe conduct is granted by Richard II to Donald, *filio Johannis de Insulis, clerico,* on his return from the University of Oxford, where he had been educated. In 1382, Hugh of the Isles, as we have seen, visits England, probably as ambassador from the Isles, and is honoured on his return with an escort of six horsemen. In 1388, the Lord of the Isles and his brothers, Godfrey and John Mor, visit the English Court and are received as independent Celtic princes, while at the same time they enter into a league with Richard II, to which John, Bishop of the Isles, is a party. In the year 1400, a safe conduct, dated at Westminster on 5th February, is granted to John of the Isles and Donald his brother with an escort of 80 horsemen. From the language of this document, it seems the brothers were received at the English Court with much distinction and ceremony. In July of the same year we find the two brothers again visiting England and entering into a defensive league with Henry IV. In the years 1405 and 1408, Donald and John repeat these visits, and renew their alliance with the English monarch.

Thus the exigencies of political warfare forced the Island family to seek the friendly alliance of England against an aggressive Scottish neighbour, and English statesmen were not slow to take advantage of so favourable an opportunity to advance the English policy towards Scotland. The conduct of the Island Lord may appear on the face of it unpatriotic, but in reality it was not so, though, as it ultimately proved, it was an unwise and short-sighted policy. It was a consistent and open declaration of the policy of his house, and an assertion of the ancient Celtic independence of his family. Meantime it served to disarm opposition on the part of the Scottish State, and secured his independence for a time, though ultimately it helped to bring about the downfall of his family.

Apart from political differences between Donald and his royal relatives, a purely domestic quarrel was provoked when he and his brothers, John Mor and Alasdair Carrach, were accused of want of filial affection towards their mother, the King's sister. Whatever the substance of the charge, of which there are no details on record, it so incensed the brothers that when in 1394 the Earl of Fife was enjoined by the King to protect his sister, Alasdair Carrach marched into the Earldom of Ross and took possession of the castle and lands of Urquhart. In this he was no doubt aided and abetted by Donald whose interest in the earldom, though not yet formally proclaimed, constrained him at least to keep a close watch on the course of events. Alasdair's tenure was short-lived, however, and he was taken and imprisoned, to be released a year later only after Donald had undertaken before Parliament to answer for his future conduct.

The next occasion on which we find Donald playing a significant rôle is in the drama of the year 1411. He does not appear to have taken any prominent part in the politics of the years immediately following the death of King Robert III, nor do we find him either opposing or acquiescing in the appointment of the Duke of Albany as Regent of the Kingdom, though we may conjecture from after events that he did not look upon it with favour. The remote situation of the Lordship, the assertion of independence on the part of Donald himself, together with an entire want of sympathy with southern aims, may explain the absence of a nobleman of his rank from the Scottish politics of this period. It is only when the interests of his own family and race are at stake that he chooses to play a prominent part. The rumoured resignation of her rights by Euphemia Leslie, the daughter and heiress of Alexander Leslie, Earl of Ross, is the cause that now draws him from his temporary retirement. The Earldom of Ross was too great a prize to be lightly neglected, and he eagerly watches his opportunity to possess it. In extent the earldom comprised the old district of Ross, Cromarty, and that portion of ancient Argyll extending westwards from Glenelg to Lochbroom, including the coast lands of Kintail, Lochalsh, Lochcarron, Applecross and Gairloch. It extended inland as far east as Urquhart, and included the parish of Kilmorack, now in the county of Inverness. In addition, the Earls of Ross were superiors of lands of which the following are the most important: in the County of Aberdeen, the lands of Auchterless and Kynedward; in the County of Inverness, the lands of Innermerky in the lordship of Badenoch; in the County of Nairn, the lands of Balmakayth, Both, Banchre, Rate, Kynowdie. Kinsteary, Kilravock, Easter Geddes, Dumnaglass and Cawdor.

This large territory, or at all events Ross proper, had formerly been under the sway of Celtic Mormaers, and for centuries had suffered from the incursions of both Norse and Dane. At this time the Scandinavian element largely preponderated over the original Pictish inhabitants, but the two had gradually become amalgamated into one people, and the Celtic spirit, which had survived the shock of centuries of Teutonic oppression, seems still to have pervaded the great body of the population. The introduction of feudal laws and institutions in the South affected almost simultaneously the old order of things in the North. The Celtic Mormaer gave place to the Norman baron. The last Mormaer of Ross of whom we have any record was Macbeth, who became King of Scotland in 1040, and was murdered in the year 1057. The first Earl of Ross of whom there is any notice was Gillanders, of the Celtic family of Obeolan, who were hereditary lay abbots of Applecross; but whether he assumed the dignity or had it conferred upon him, he is at all events referred to as Earl in the year 1160. The next Earl of Ross appears to have been Malcolm MacHeth, who held the earldom

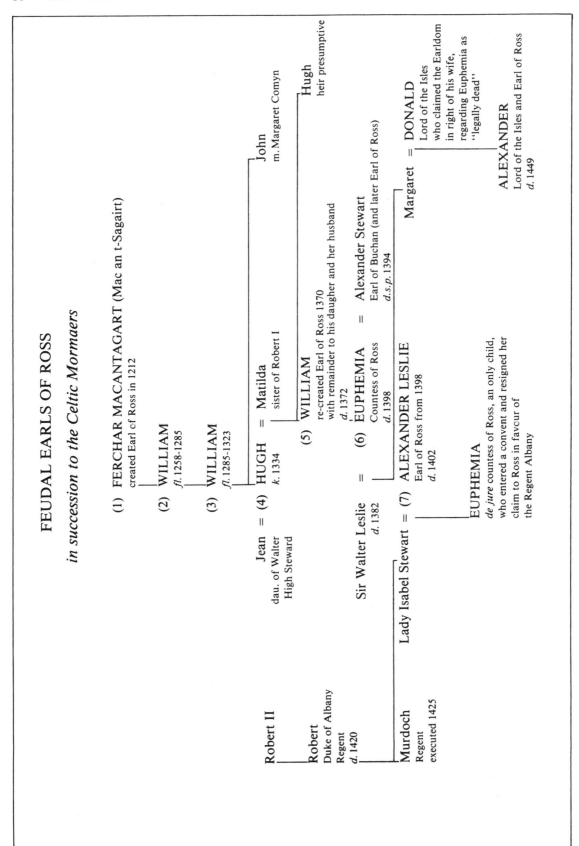

FEUDAL EARLS OF ROSS

in succession to the Celtic Mormaers

(1) FERCHAR MACANTAGART (Mac an t-Sagairt)
created Earl of Ross in 1212

(2) WILLIAM
fl. 1258-1285

(3) WILLIAM
fl. 1285-1323

Jean = (4) HUGH = Matilda
dau. of Walter   k. 1334   sister of Robert I
High Steward

John
m. Margaret Comyn

Hugh
heir presumptive

(5) WILLIAM
re-created Earl of Ross 1370
with remainder to his daughter and her husband
d. 1372

Sir Walter Leslie = (6) EUPHEMIA = Alexander Stewart
d. 1382   Countess of Ross   Earl of Buchan (and later Earl of Ross)
                          d. 1398   *d.s.p.* 1394

Robert II

Robert
Duke of Albany
Regent
d. 1420

Murdoch
Regent
executed 1425

Lady Isabel Stewart = (7) ALEXANDER LESLIE
                          Earl of Ross from 1398
                          d. 1402

EUPHEMIA
de jure countess of Ross, an only child,
who entered a convent and resigned her
claim to Ross in favour of
the Regent Albany

Margaret = DONALD
             Lord of the Isles
             who claimed the Earldom
             in right of his wife,
             regarding Euphemia as
             "legally dead"

ALEXANDER
Lord of the Isles and Earl of Ross
d. 1449

only for a very brief period. William the Lion then created Florence, Count of Holland, Earl of Ross, on his marriage with that King's sister. In or about the year 1212, the King created Ferchar Macantagart, of the Obeolan family of Applecross, Earl of Ross, for services rendered. He was succeeded by his son William as second Earl of the new creation. William was succeeded by his son William as third Earl. Earl Hugh, who was killed in the battle of Halidon Hill, was succeeded by his son William as fifth Earl. Earl William, on the death of his brother Hugh, his heir, resigned the earldom, but David II renewed a grant of it to him and his heirs male, with remainder to Sir Walter Leslie and his wife, the Earl's daughter. Thus the line of succession was diverted from heirs male exclusively to heirs general, and accordingly on the death of the fifth Earl in 1372, his daughter succeeded him as Countess of Ross. Sir Walter Leslie having died in 1382, his widow Euphemia, Countess of Ross, married Alexander Stewart, Earl of Buchan, to whom the King, at the desire of Euphemia, confirmed a grant of the earldom, and he afterwards appears in record as Earl of Ross, to the exclusion of Alexander Leslie, Euphemia's son. Alexander Leslie, however, ultimately succeeded to the earldom in the year 1398, and dying in 1402, his only daughter, who bore the family name of Euphemia, became Countess of Ross. The mother of the Countess of Ross was the Lady Isabella Stewart, daughter of Robert, Duke of Albany, the Regent of the kingdom, and her aunt was Margaret Leslie, daughter of Sir Walter Leslie and the Countess Euphemia of Ross. The Lady Margaret Leslie was the wife of Donald, Lord of the Isles, and therefore the nearest living relative in the line of succession to the Earldom of Ross after the Countess Euphemia.

In the event of Euphemia's death or resignation, it is obvious that we have abundant materials for a fierce domestic quarrel and, on account of the position of the parties, the elements of a stirring historical drama. The principal actors in the events that followed were all nearly related by blood to one another, as well as kindred to the Scottish throne. Chief in position was Albany, who for many years as Regent held the supreme power in the State. Devoid of the warlike qualities which his brothers possessed, in fact a man of suspected courage in the field, he was intellectually head and shoulders above all the other sons of Robert II. It is no unfounded suspicion that he condoned, if he did not actually arrange, the murder of the Duke of Rothesay, his nephew and heir apparent to the throne; and if he did not allow his other nephew James to be captured by the English, he offered no protest against his long imprisonment. Of determined resolution and unflinching purpose, he never amid the various and conflicting currents of State policy lost sight of his own ends, nor did he scruple to sweep out of his path whoever stood in the way of the execution of his designs. Had he been a single-hearted Scottish patriot, animated by zeal for the national welfare and the safety of the State, his policy in keeping the family of the Isles out of the succession to the Earldom of Ross would, from a national standpoint, have been worthy of all praise. If the addition of Garmoran and the North Isles to the House of Islay in the reign of David II constituted a source of danger to Scottish supremacy, the further addition of the Earldom of Ross to the already extensive Island domains would make the Island Lord a still more formidable antagonist.

Donald therefore had recourse to the argument which was best understood in the circumstances of the time. In addition to the conquest of Ross, he has been credited by some historians with designs extending far beyond the boundaries of the earldom, but no evidence exists to support the claim that he aspired to the mastery of the whole kingdom. The facts simply suggest the strength of Donald's resentment at the Regent's machinations and his determination not only to enforce his claim to the earldom but to secure his possession of it by a cautionary display of his military power.

According to the Sleat historian, Donald told the Regent that he would either lose all or gain the earldom to which he had such a good title. He maintained that Euphemia, the heiress to the earldom, having taken the veil and given up the world, might be regarded as legally dead, and Lady Margaret of the Isles had become *ipso facto* her successor. The contention seemed a sound enough one according to the canons of equity and our sympathies are naturally with Donald, who with chivalrous daring was prepared to fight for what he deemed to be rightfully his, rather than with the wily Regent, who pulled the wires of State and had the resources of a kingdom at his back.

Donald of Harlaw's Seal
(from the Inchaffray Charter of 1410)
SIGILLUM DONALDI DE YLE DOMINI INSULARUM

Donald chose Ardtornish in Morvern as the marshalling-point of his forces. Here in a commanding position stood a residence and stronghold of the Macdonalds, impregnable against attack by land or sea, and from here the fiery cross was sent blazing through the Isles and all the mainland territories of the Lordship and its vassals. Obeying the call to arms came the Macleans and MacKinnons, the hardy Clans of Mull, the Clan Chattan from Lochaber, the Macleods from Lewis and Harris, and many others who were eager to identify their interests with the cause. The best of these were selected and embarked in the fleet which now set sail for the west coast of Ross-shire.

It was a little after midsummer when the expedition disembarked at Strome. Marching through the great glens of Ross they soon reached the vicinity of Dingwall. But the conquest of Ross was not to be unopposed. The county of Caithness, as might be expected from its position, was from an early period subject to Norse influence, and in the course of time came to be occupied by a population largely Norse in composition. It formed part of the possessions of the great Norwegian Jarls of Orkney from the beginning of the 10th century down to the end of the 12th century. The district of Strathnaver, however, which formed the western portion of the ancient county of Caithness, differed from the rest of that region not only by reason of its wild and mountainous surface, but also in being the abode of a people who, amid the racial changes that took place in that time, retained their Celtic blood and speech largely unaffected by Norwegian admixture. The most powerful clan that occupied this portion of Caithness at the beginning of the 15th century was the Clan Mackay, and it is said that at that time Angus Dubh Mackay could bring into the field 4000 fighting men.

The news of Donald's march through Wester Ross having penetrated to far Strathnaver, Angus Dubh Mackay determined to oppose the progress and clip the wings of the Hebridean eagle. He hastily gathered his forces, said to have been 2500 strong, and marching to Dingwall, arrived just as the Islesmen were seen approaching. He immediately assumed the offensive, but failed to stem the tide of the advancing force. A fierce engagement took place, in which the men of Caithness, though they fought with the bravery and firmness characteristic of the Mackay clan, were routed. Rory Galld, brother of the chief, and many others were slain, whilst Angus Dubh himself was taken prisoner. Macdonald of the Isles, having taken possession of the Castle of Dingwall and garrisoned it, resumed his march and proceeded to Inverness by Beauly. At the latter place he halted, and diverting his line of march, proceeded to Castle Downie and administered a well-merited chastisement to the Laird of Lovat and his Frasers, who had the temerity to oppose the Island Lord's pretensions to the Earldom of Ross. Having at length arrived at Inverness, he planted his standard in the Highland Capital, and summoned all the fighting men of Ross and of the North to his banner. The summons met with a wide response from the purely Celtic regions of Scotland, and many, emboldened by the success that already attended Donald's efforts, took up arms to support his cause.

According to a MS history of the Mackenzies, quoted in the Macdonald Collections, "Murdoch Nichoil Mackenzie was the only chief in the North Highlands who refused assistance to Macdonald when he fought against the Governor's forces at Harlaw. He was taken prisoner by the Earl of Ross at Dingwall." The chief of the Mackenzies was at this time of so little consequence that it was hardly worth while keeping him in "durance vile" during the absence of the Island Chief at Harlaw. But he was not the only chief in the North who opposed Macdonald's invasion of Ross. A much more powerful individual, in the person of the Chief of the Frasers, had not only endeavoured to check Donald's progress through the earldom, but afterwards fought against him at Harlaw.

Instead of protecting his gains, Donald had no sooner mustered the full force of his followers than he launched what was apparently a fresh enterprise. It has by some been conjectured that, in addition to the invasion of Ross, there was another and more ambitious plan of campaign in which Donald expected to form a junction with his English allies. If this was so, and we can only speculate, England's difficulties in France proved to Scotland's advantage, and if Donald cherished any expectations of southern aid, he was doomed to disappointment. Though in possession of the Earldom of Ross, Donald well knew that he was not to be left long undisturbed in the enjoyment of his acquisition and, pressing his advantage, resolved to push his way eastwards in the expectation of swelling his ranks as he proceeded, and thus presenting such a formidable and imposing appearance as to strike terror into the heart of the opposing host. Besides, in the course of his quarrel with the Regent, Donald had threatened to burn the town of Aberdeen, and to put that threat into execution was at least one motive for his eastward march. The partial or total burning of the town of Inverness, in which the famous oak bridge over the Ness perished, though valiantly defended by a stalwart townsman of the name of Cumine, and the ravages committed by the Island host as they traversed the counties of Moray and Aberdeen must, however, be considered in the context of the time, when such conduct was accepted as the normal accompaniment of war; but the devastation left in the wake of the army on this occasion may have been unusually severe, especially in areas opposed or unsympathetic to its progress.

Three weeks of July of the year 1411 had elapsed when the Highland army, estimated at about 10,000 strong, set out from Inverness. Donald himself commanded the main body, which was composed of the Islesmen, including the Macleods of Lewis and Harris under their chiefs. The right wing was commanded by Hector Maclean of Duart, commonly known as *Eachunn Ruadh nan Cath,* while the left was under the command of Mackintosh. John Mor Tanister of Dunnyveg led the reserve. When the news arrived in Aberdeen that Donald and his host were on their way to consign the town to the flames, the panic may well be conceived. The terror which the approach of the High-landers struck into the popular mind has been reflected in the ballad poetry of the country.

An interesting side-light on the circumstances of this campaign is that the leaders of the opposing armies were first cousins. Donald, as we know already, was the son of the legitimate daughter of Robert II, while Mar was the illegitimate son of the infamous Wolf of Badenoch, who was himself an illegitimate son of the same King Robert.

Donald was not the illiterate chief of an uncivilised tribe as described by the Lowland chroniclers. He had had a University education in England and was accepted at the courts of England and France as a civilised prince in his own right. Mar, on the other hand, was heir to the Earldom of Buchan and displayed many of the unlovely propensities of his father, the Wolf. The followers of the Wolf and his son, Alexander, were sometimes described as "Wyld wykkyd Hielandmen" and no doubt the Wolf and his son, having feudal sway over the Eastern Highlands, employed some of the Gaelic tribes within their borders on their expeditions, as for example in the notorious sacking of Forres and Elgin with the destruction of the Cathedral in 1390. "Like father, like son" proved true in this case; for in 1392 Alexander, Earl of Buchan, carried out a raid on the braes of Angus and the Mearns and was met in Glen Isla at Gasklune by a force under Lord Lyndsay. It was a bloody fight and Buchan made off with the spoil, but twelve years later in 1404 he carried out a raid of a rather different sort.

The laconic account of the life of the warrior who met Donald at Harlaw, given in *Burke's Peerage,* tells only the bare facts about his acquisition of the Earldom of Mar.

> *Margaret, Countess of Mar,* died ante 1393 and was succeeded by her daughter Isabel, Countess of Mar, Lady of Garrioch, married firstly Sir Malcolm Drummond, and secondly, Alexander, natural son of Alexander, Earl of Buchan (the Wolf of Badenoch) who died 1435. The Countess made, 9th December 1404, a grant (confirmed by the King in 1405) of life rent in the Earldom to her second husband, thereafter 12th Earl of Mar, but reserved its heirship to her own lawful heirs.
>
> Alexander Stewart resigned the Earldom and got a re-grant to himself and his natural son, Thomas, who predeceased his father without issue. Thus the Earldom reverted to the kinsman and heir of his first wife, the Countess Isabel.

The underlying story is much more enlightening and even romantic. The widowed Margaret, Countess of Mar, after the death of her first husband, was living securely in her castle of Kildrummie on the Don, until in the year 1404 Alexander of Buchan arrived at the gates with a party of his banditti and demanded entrance. The Countess refused, but Alexander laid siege to the castle and eventually took it and forcibly married the widow who, after some pressure, reconciled herself to the marriage and indeed invested her new husband with the earldom which rightly belonged to her lawful heirs; so that Buchan now became the Earl of Mar, a great feudal lord with a high position in the State.

When the news of Macdonald's march through Moray went abroad, the gentlemen of Aberdeenshire, with their armed retainers, assembled under the leadership of the Earl of Mar. Mail-clad mounted knights, armed to the teeth after the manner of Norman chivalry, the number of which is not easily determined, but generally estimated at a little more than a thousand men, rode off to meet the foe. Inferior in numbers to the forces of the Isles, the disadvantage was heavily discounted by the completeness of their equipment and their strong defensive armour. Mar advanced by Inverury, and came in sight of the Highland army at the village of Harlaw, some ten miles from the county town of Aberdeen, whither had flocked to his standard the gentlemen of Aberdeen, Angus and the Mearns. The Ogilvies, the Lindsays, the Carnegies, the Leslies, the Lyons, the Irvings, the Gordons, the Abercrombies, the Arbuthnots, the Bannermans, the Leiths, the Douglases, the Barclays, the Mowats, the Duguids, the Fotheringhams, the Frasers and the Burnets—all were there in stern defence of hearth and home. Mar himself commanded the main body of his small force, while Sir Alexander Ogilvie, Sheriff of Angus, and Sir James Scrymgeour, constable of Dundee, led the vanguard.

Donald's army, consisting chiefly of the Macleans, the Mackintoshes, the Camerons, the Mackinnons, the Macleods, and all the vassals of the Lordship of the Isles, was drawn up in imitation of the old Pictish mode, in the cuneiform order of battle. Donald himself commanded the main body, with the Macleods of Lewis and Harris as his lieutenants while the right and left respectively were under the command of Hector Roy Maclean of Duart and Mackintosh. John Mor Tanister stood at the head of the reserve. The courage of the men of the Isles was roused to fervour by the stirring appeal of MacVurich to remember the ancient valour of the race of Conn:

> "A chlanna Chuinn, cuimhnichibh,
> Cruas an àm na h-iorghuill."

> "Sons of Conn remember
> Hardihood in time of strife."

The Highlanders, armed with broadswords, bows and axes, and bull-hide shields, rushing forward with furious onset and shouting the slogan of their clan, were received by the Lowlanders with steadiness and valour. Sir James Scrymgeour, Constable of Dundee, and Sir Alexander Ogilvie, Sheriff of Angus, who with a band of knights occupied the van of the Lowland army, endeavoured to cut their way through the Highland columns that were bearing down upon them like a flood, but they were soon overwhelmed and slain. In other parts of the field, the contest raged with fury. The brave Mar with his knights fought on with desperate courage till the Lowland army was reduced to a skeleton, but it was only after the long summer day had faded away at last that the exhausted combatants sheathed their blades. The Lowland army was annihilated, and the flower of the chivalry of Angus and the Mearns lay dead upon the field.

To the east of Scotland, Harlaw was a miniature Flodden, and the wail of a hundred years later over that bloody field "that the flowers of the forest were a' wede awa'," would not have been inappropriate here. On Mar's side, according to the Lowland chroniclers, 500 were killed and many wounded. Among the men of note who fell were Sir Alexander Ogilvie, Sheriff of Angus; Sir Thomas Murray, Sir James Scrymgeour, Sir Alexander Irvine of Drum, Sir Robert Maule of Panmure, Sir William Abernethy of Saltoun, Sir Alexander Straiton of Lauriston, Sir Robert Davidson, Provost of Aberdeen; James Lovel, Alexander Stirling and Leslie of Balquhain, with his six sons.

On Donald's side, 900 are said to have fallen, among whom were Gilpatrick MacRory of the Obeolan family and Lachlan Macmillan who, with Norman and Torquil Macleod, were the first at the head of their men to charge the Lowland host. Besides these, according to Hugh Macdonald, "two or three gentlemen of the name of Munro were slain, together with the son of MacQuarry of Ulva, and two gentlemen of the name of Cameron." The brave Hector Roy Maclean of Duart and Irvine of Drum fought hand to hand until they both fell together.

Trustworthy records of this famous fight there are none. Lowland historian and ballad composer, as well as Highland seanachie, described what they believed must and should have happened. Certain main facts, however, we are assured of. That both sides fought with valour and determination, and that Scotland alone was capable of being the nursing mother of such heroes, may well kindle the pride of Lowlander and Highlander alike. Yet the field of Harlaw, in proportion to the number engaged there, was one of the greatest reverses that ever befell the Scots. To say in the face of such a calamitious reverse that the Lowland army was victorious at Harlaw, as some historians have alleged, is to be blind to the most obvious facts. It is admitted on all hands that Macdonald's army could not have been under 10,000 strong. Of these, according to the Lowland estimate, 900 lay dead on the field, and granting that as many more lay wounded, Donald's force when the fight ceased numbered at least 8000 strong, ready to renew the contest with the returning day. The Earl of Mar himself lay covered in wounds on the field. Five hundred of his small force lay dead around him, while the remainder of his army lay mostly wounded, and unable to renew the fight. These are facts, if the Scottish historians are to be believed, but the conclusions they arrive at are not obvious, and cannot in reason be justified. That Macdonald of the Isles at the head of 8000 clansmen, or even half that number, retreated in dismay before a wounded leader lying prostrate on the field of battle surrounded by a mere handful of men, most of whom were crippled with wounds, cannot easily be believed by any unprejudiced person. If Donald ever expected English help, he now realised that he must do without it, and knowing well that all Lowland Scotland was arrayed against him, he judged it the wisest policy to betake himself to his Island fastnesses. There is every reason to believe that this was his main motive in not pursuing his campaign further against the Duke of Albany, while at the same time he must have experienced the same difficulty which confronted Montrose, Dundee and Prince Charles, in after times, of keeping a Highland army gathered from widely scattered districts for any length of time together in the field.

Ignoring all such considerations, some Scottish historians have chosen to interpret Donald's wise decision to withdraw from the field as an acceptance of defeat at Harlaw. Very different are the accounts of the famous engagement as given both by the Highland and Irish historians. Hugh Macdonald, MacVurich and many others refer in no vague terms to the complete overthrow of the Lowland army; while the Highland bards, who are never inspired by defeat, celebrate the victory of the men of the Isles in their loftiest strains. The Irish Annals are no less emphatic, as may be seen, among others, from the Annals of

Loch Cé: "A great victory by MacDomhaill of Alba over the foreigners of Alba; and MacGilla-Eoin of Macdonald's was slain in the counter wounding of that victory."

On the news of the crushing defeat at Harlaw reaching the ears of the Regent Albany, he made an unusual display of military spirit and activity. He resolved without delay on an invasion of the Earldom of Ross, and putting himself at the head of a sufficiently strong force, advanced on Dingwall, took possession of the castle, and established without any opposition his authority throughout Ross. Donald and his clansmen had retired to their Island strongholds. Within his own domains he was impregnable, for his naval force was superior to the whole Scottish fleet at that time. His mainland territories, however, were exposed and here the Regent, determined to crush his power, had his opportunity. In the following year, smarting from the humiliation of Harlaw, Albany resumed hostilities, proceeded at the head of an army to Argyll, and attacked Donald where alone he could do so with any chance of success. The records of the period are very obscure as to the fortunes and reverses alike of the Regent's campaign against the hero of Harlaw; but subsequent events indicate very clearly that Donald held his own, and that Albany was baffled in the effort to humble him.

The story of the treaty with the Regent at Polgilb, now Lochgilphead, where we find Donald coming forward humbly, laying down his assumed independence, consenting to become a vassal of the Scottish crown (which he was already—at least nominally), and delivering hostages for his future good behaviour, is given on the authority of that unreliable chronicler, John of Fordun; and as he is corroborated by no authority whatever, but, on the contrary, flatly contradicted by subsequent events, it must be regarded as nothing more than a story. Such a treaty would undoubtedly have been looked upon as an event of national importance, yet the national records are silent regarding it. No contemporary chronicler, Highland or Lowland—if we omit John himself—records this successful termination of a rebellion so formidable as to have shaken the Scottish State to its very centre. Both in the Chamberlain and Exchequer Rolls we find references made to the campaign of Albany against the Lord of the Isles in Argyll, but not the remotest reference is made to the alleged treaty of Polgilb. What we find is the complaint made that the Regent had not been recouped for conveying an army to Polgilb against the Lord of the Isles, and for his expedition to Ross against the Islesmen for the tranquillity of the realm. If the Lord of the Isles, as John of Fordun would have us believe, had surrendered at Polgilb and given hostages, the tone of the Scottish Chamberlain would have been more triumphant, and direct reference would have been made to such an important event. Donald well knew he could not take possession of the Earldom of Ross against all Scotland, and that he had resolved to make no further attempt in that direction his retreat from Harlaw clearly proves. His position in the Isles was too strong to be successfully attacked. Why, therefore, should he surrender at Polgilb? The fiction may be placed side by side with that other fable of the defeat, death and burial of Donald at Harlaw, where his tomb is pointed out to this day!

Ever since that July day in 1411 much has been written about the battle, its causes and results. Even allowing that, as some have put it, Donald had the victory and the Regent had the printer, the outcome from Donald's point of view was not satisfactory. He had all but annihilated the Royal army led by Mar, but saw fit to retire next day to his island realm and not long after to come to an accommodation with Albany whereby he retained his possessions. He had failed to win the earldom, however, and took no further steps to secure it although soon after his death it went to his son and successor, Alexander.

Albany undoubtedly took possession of the Earldom of Ross, and prevented the Lord of the Isles from pushing his claim to that important inheritance; but Donald held undisputed sway to the day of his death within his own Island principality. In no sense can Donald be said to have enjoyed the Earldom of Ross, save during those weeks when he invaded and occupied the district by force of arms. He never was, and never could have been *de jure* Earl of Ross. The Regent carried his point. In 1415, Euphemia resigned the earldom in favour of her grandfather, who thereafter conferred it on his son, John Stewart, Earl of Buchan.

Seal of Euphemia, Countess of Ross, 1394

The next time the Lord of the Isles emerges from his retirement is in a domestic quarrel with his brother, John Mor Tanister, a quarrel which seems to have assumed formidable proportions from the array of neighbouring clans that appear on either side. The cause of the quarrel arose from differences over some lands in Kintyre, claimed by John Mor as his share of his father's patrimony. The real instigator was the Abbot Mackinnon, who as a churchman was a man of considerable influence in Argyle, and with whose family John Mor's own relationship was none of the purest, if the historian of Sleat is to be believed. Maclean and Macleod of Harris espoused the cause of John Mor, while Donald was supported by Macleod of Lewis, the Mackintoshes, and other vassals of the Isles. The issue was not for a moment in doubt. John Mor was defeated and, passing into Galloway where Donald pursued him, found his way to Ireland and took refuge in the Antrim glens. The two brothers, however, were shortly thereafter reconciled.

The hero of Harlaw now passes finally from the public gaze and, joining one of the religious orders, he finds solace for his declining years in the exercise of quiet religious duties. The main features of his character have already passed under review. He stands before us, if not the greatest in a long line of distinguished chiefs of his family, yet a powerful and impressive personality, a leader who sustained the best traditions of the Clan Cholla, and who kept untarnished in peace and war the name and fame of Macdonald. By far the most powerful nobleman in the realm, both from the extent of his immense territories and the influence he exercised over his many vassals in the Isles and on the mainland, Donald also possessed the qualities of a statesman. He entered into repeated alliances with England. In the year 1389, among the allies of that country, consisting of several foreign princes and others, we find the name of Donald, Lord of the Isles, and commissions at different times are issued by the English Kings to treat with him on the footing of an independent prince. Some authorities affirm that the Lord of the Isles died in France in the year 1424, but these go on the assumption that Donald was Earl of Ross. The Earl of Ross who died in France that year, having been killed at the battle of Verneuil, was John Stewart, Earl of Buchan, on whom the Earldom of Ross was conferred on the resignation of Euphemia Leslie, in 1415. We have already assumed that the second marriage of John, Lord of the Isles, took place about the year 1358, and that he, the eldest son of that marriage, mentioned in the treaty of 1369, must have been ten years of age when in that year he was given as a hostage to David II. The year of Donald's death is somewhat uncertain, though 1423 seems approximately correct. If this is so, he must have attained the age of 64 when he died at his Castle of Ardtornish in Morvern and was buried with befitting pomp and solemnity in the tomb of his ancestors at Iona.

Donald married Lady Margaret Leslie, daughter of Sir Walter Leslie by Euphemia, Countess of Ross in her own right, with destiny to heirs general. By her, Donald had three sons:

1. Alexander, who succeeded to the Lordship and Earldom of Ross.
2. Angus, who became Bishop of the Isles.
3. Another whose name we do not know, who became a monk.

SEAL OF ALEXANDER
Lord of the Isles and Earl of Ross
of date 1440
S. ALEXANDRI DE YLE DOMINI INSULARUM ET ROSSIE

10

Alexander, Lord of the Isles and Earl of Ross
(1423-1449)

Reigning in Scotland
JAMES I
1406-1437
JAMES II
1437-1460

ALEXANDER, Donald's eldest son, succeeded on his father's death to the dignities and possessions of his house. Donald's heroic efforts to secure the Earldom of Ross as the lawful inheritance of his wife, had not met with complete success. After Euphemia's resignation, the earldom was given by the Regent to his son, the Earl of Buchan, but it again fell vacant in 1424 when the Earl fell in the battle of Verneuil at the head of the army he had taken to the aid of France.

When Robert, Duke of Albany, died in 1420 the Regency of the kingdom came to his son Murdoch, who was a man of inferior capacity to his father and proved unable to govern strongly in a country which was gradually falling into anarchy. At last Murdoch negotiated with England for the ransom of the young King James I, who had spent many years in captivity in that country, and James accordingly returned to his kingdom and took up the reins of government.

Some historians allege that one of the earliest acts of James after his restoration was to restore the Earldom of Ross to the heiress of the line, the mother of Alexander, Lord of the Isles. Reference is made in record that in 1426 Alexander, Lord of the Isles and Master of Ross, was one of the "assiers" condemning the Regent, his two sons, and the Earl of Lennox to death. It is also on record that in 1427 Alexander in a charter dated at the Island of Finlaggan in Islay and also in another charter bestowed a grant of the lands of Barra and Boisdale in South Uist on one Gilleownan, one of the family of Macneill, and called himself Master of Ross. From this reference it has not unnaturally been inferred that the mother of Alexander, "Lady Mary of the Yles and of Rosse," had been invested by the Crown with her hereditary rights and that the Lord of the Isles had thus been acknowledged as heir apparent to the earldom. But nothing could be clearer than the tenure by the Crown of the powers and privileges of the earldom at a much later date than 1426. However, "Lady Mary of the Yles" had every right in law and equity to the earldom so long as she lived, with reversion to her heir, and the continued assumption of its rights by the Crown was rightly considered an illegal act.

Alexander appears on the jury before which many nobles were summoned for treason in 1426, which seems to show that he had gained some measure of royal favour. It was not long, however, before his relations with the Crown changed completely. James I devoted the first two years of his reign to the reduction of the lawlessness which had so long prevailed in the southern parts of his Kingdom. Now, in 1427, he turned his attention to the Highlands. James was undoubtedly one of the ablest statesmen that ever occupied the throne of Scotland. It was essential for his policy to curb the power of the nobility, as a powerful sovereign was the only guarantee for the maintenance of law and order and liberty among all classes of the people. The struggle of the Crown with these great nobles who exercised so much power in their own areas, explained much of the civil strife that prevailed in Scotland during the 15th century. The policy of the King, while succeeding in its main design very well, was prosecuted in many cases with much harshness, which eventually led to his tragic fate.

After the battle of Harlaw, the Castle of Inverness had been fortified and reconstructed on a large scale by the Earl of Mar. In 1427 it played an important part in the royal policy of reformation. In this, the third year of his reign, James marched to Inverness at the head of a large army and accompanied by the leading Lowland barons. There he convened a parliament and summoned the vassals of the Crown and others to attend. There was a large response. From the far North came Angus Dubh Mackay who in 1411 unsuccessfully opposed Donald of the Isles at Dingwall, but who was a powerful chief in the Celtic regions of Caithness and Sutherland, and a leader of some four thousand men. Kenneth Mor Mackenzie with two thousand men, and his son-in-law, John Ross, and others responded to the call. John MacArthur of the family of Campbell, leader of a thousand men, and James Campbell came to the meeting. The principal leaders of Clan Donald, Alexander, Lord of the Isles and Alexander MacGorrie of Garmoran, also obeyed the summons and came. This was to prove an important meeting, especially from the point of view of the family of the Isles.

One incident of significance in the relations between the King of Scots and the Lordship of the Isles had taken place before this meeting at Inverness. This was the murder of John Mor Tanister, founder of the family of Dunnyveg and the Glens, who was described even by George Buchanan as a man illustrious among his own countrymen. John Mor's death was the culmination of a series of intrigues promoted by the courtiers of King James, and was apparently connived at by the King himself. Many of the Scottish Barons who were powerful at Court were jealous of the Lords of the Isles and King James resolved to break the power of Alexander who by this time was becoming impatient at the continued neglect of his mother's claims to the Earldom of Ross. The King therefore tried to take John Mor into his confidence with a view to investing him with the territories of the Isles in preference to Alexander. It may be that the King thought that John Mor, being Alexander's uncle, was nearer by blood to the Crown. John did not agree with this proposal and an individual by the name of James Campbell is said to have received a commission from the King to arrest him under cover of a friendly interview. Whatever powers were granted him under this commission, it is certain that John Mor was a victim of the most detestable treachery. He received a message from the King's delegate to meet him at Ard Dubh in Islay to receive a communication from the King. John Mor came, attended by only a few of his guard, and in the course of the interview was attacked and murdered. The King cannot be absolved completely from the planning of this treachery. There is strong reason to believe that the King's orders were very vague, and his commissioner well understood the spirit and purpose of his instructions. In Campbell he found a willing instrument, and it has to be noted that now, for the first time, the shadow of the ill-omened house of Campbell fell across the path of the family of the Isles.

The murder of John Mor caused deep resentment among many powerful and noble families who saw in it just another instance of the King's overbearing and treacherous behaviour. This was especially true throughout the Highlands. The King protested he had not planned the murder, and had the assassin tried for his life, while Campbell continued to state that although he did not have it in writing he did have royal authority for the murder. These were only some of the circumstances which, on account of the turmoil they created in the Highlands, led James to march on Inverness, summoning a Convention of the Highland chiefs.

To make matters worse, John MacArthur, a member of the house of Campbell, advanced a claim to a portion of the land of Garmoran in the North Isles. His claim was based upon a charter by Christina, daughter of Alan MacRuairi to Arthur, son of Sir Arthur Campbell, Knight, early in the 14th century. Christina, being her father's heir, was acting within her legal rights in this disposition, but her reasons for overlooking her brother Roderick in this matter, while making him heir to the rest of her property, is a question which it is impossible to answer now. Whatever validity this document may have possessed, any claim founded upon her charter must have been of a very nebulous kind. In 1427 Garmoran was occupied by Alexander MacGorrie, the son (or perhaps grandson) of Godfrey, son of Good John of Islay, Lord of the Isles, by his wife, Amie MacRuairi.

The Clan Gorrie had apparently the ascendancy over the family of Ranald and were in possession of Garmoran and the Castle of Eilean Tirrim which had been seized by Godfrey in 1389. Alexander, the representative of that family in the year of the Inverness Convention, was the leader of some two thousand men and would be very unlikely to submit to the MacArthur claim. All this was aggravated by the feud that undoubtedly existed between the Clan Ranald and the Clan Godfrey about the possession of the vast regions conferred upon Ranald and his descendants in 1373.

The events which took place in connection with the King's visit to Inverness can only be estimated by the known outcome of that meeting, which revealed the ruthlessness and measure of treachery the King was prepared to employ in the assertion of his authority. The chiefs came from all over to attend the Convention with the nobles of the North, trusting to the faith and honour of the King, and yet on their arrival at Inverness they were all immediately apprehended. Some were led to prison, each being in solitary confinement, while others became victims of judicial murder, more unjustified than almost any others in our country's history. The King is said to have been much amused at the success of his plot. James Campbell justly expiated his crime, which after all was one in which the King himself was implicated. The slaughter of Alexander MacGorrie along with others without any sort of trial was less easy to explain or forgive, and seemed a flagrant exercise of arbitrary power.

These events considerably damaged the already unfriendly relations of the Lord of the Isles with the King. The murder of his uncle, John Mor, and his cousin, Alexander MacGorrie, must have greatly increased Alexander's discontent and displeasure. Little is definitely known beyond the fact that Alexander and his mother, the rightful Countess of Ross, were among those whom the King imprisoned at Inverness.

The Lord of the Isles was detained in custody on this occasion for only a brief period. He had to accompany the King to Perth where in the presence of the Estates of the realm he is said to have received a royal admonition for his past actions, and on promise of amendment was restored to favour and set at liberty. His mother, meantime, was kept prisoner as a hostage for his loyalty on the island of Inchcolm in the Firth of Forth. It was unlikely in the light of these extraordinary events and the dark and treacherous conduct of the King, that the Highlands and Islands would settle down peacefully. Alexander had been taken prisoner and humiliated, his mother imprisoned, and his countrymen and followers in the West were not unnaturally filled with hatred of the King. No sooner had Alexander returned to the Isles than rebellion broke out. With a force of 10,000 men from the Isles and the Earldom of Ross, he invaded the mainland in 1429, making his headquarters in Lochaber. Thence he marched to Inverness, a town which on all such occasions was unfortunately the target of the Islesmen. Alexander burnt Inverness and laid waste the lands in its neighbourhood to avenge to some extent the indignities he had suffered. He found. however, that the King, however unscrupulous and treacherous in his nature, was prompt and vigorous in action when aroused. Thus Alexander was soon forced to retire before the royal army whose rapid approach was followed by the defection from his cause of the Camerons and the Mackintoshes. These two large clans were the most easterly of the mainland possessions of the Lord of the Isles and consequently probably more susceptible to threats from the King than those living in the happier regions further west and in the Isles. Alexander's situation became desperate when these two large clans joined the royal standard and the Lord of the Isles was forced to sue for peace. The King insisted on unconditional surrender, but Alexander was not at first inclined to obey on such terms.

According to Buchanan in his history, Alexander returned to the Isles and planned to retire to the North of Ireland where Donald Balloch, son of the murdered John Mor, was now head of the family of Dunnyveg and possessed great influence in that region. If Alexander had retired as so many of the Clan Donald were forced to do in the troublous times that followed right down to the end of the 17th century, the unfortunate surrender of Alexander and his humiliation need never have occurred. Time and again the leaders of the Clan Donald, in their opposition to the King, retreated for safety to Ireland and in time, although declared rebel, their sins were conveniently forgotten, owing to the difficulty of running them to ground. In the end Alexander had to surrender.

On Easter Sunday the King and his court were assembled in the church of Holyrood, and it is said that Alexander appeared in attire so scanty that the congregation was deeply impressed. The authorities are so conflicting as to be untrustworthy. The description of the attire in which Alexander appeared is exaggerated, especially by Lowland historians who would seem to go to any lengths to dishonour their Highland neighbours. It is said that he appeared in his shirt. If one examines the attire of the Celtic warrior in Ireland and the west, they are clad in long shirt-like garments, many of them quilted, over which they wore shirts of mail, which by their very nature demand some fairly substantial form of padding between the chain mail and their skin. The saffron shirt was no doubt of this nature, and naturally, all form of armour having been discarded, the chain mail would be removed, leaving only the "shirt" worn underneath it. We are inclined to think that Alexander would still have worn the garb of his country, which we have just described, and which was unfamiliar to the Court, and hence the tradition may have obtained currency that he appeared before the King in his shirt. On bended knee, holding his bonnet in one hand and the point of his sword in the other, he made submission. His life was spared, but he was committed prisoner to Tantallon Castle in the custody of William Douglas, Earl of Angus.

The fortunes of the Lord of the Isles had now fallen very low, with Macdonald himself for the second time imprisoned, and his mother still a prisoner on Inchcolm. It might well be thought that the Clan Donald and their associate clans in the Isles might think that the end was very near. However, this proved not to be the case, for the Clan was rallied under the leadership of the young Donald Balloch, Lord of Dunnyveg, who was a redoubtable champion and a distinguished warrior.

He was only about eighteen years of age at this time, but had already shown great promise and his clansmen accepted him at once as natural regent for the unfortunate prisoner in Tantallon. Donald was the senior cousin-german of Alexander, as his father, the recently murdered John Mor of Dunnyveg, was the second son of John of Islay by the Princess of Scotland. The leadership of the Lordship therefore fell to his lot for two reasons; by right of blood and by his reputation in the field of battle. He took up his duties with zest, and not long after the imprisonment of Macdonald, he raised the clansmen and friends of the Lordship. The imprisoned Lord contrived by some means to send a message to him and the Island chiefs encouraging them to continue the struggle regardless of what might happen to himself in the process. Donald Balloch accordingly summoned his clansmen and friends to a meeting on the Island of Carna in Loch Sunart, where he met with MacIain of Ardnamurchan, Alan MacAlan of Moidart, and his own brother, Ranald Ban of Largie, as these were the principal men of the name, who picked out the best of their warriors to the number of 6000, mostly gentlemen and free-holders, and came in their galleys to Inverskipnish, two miles south of Inverlochy; and here Alasdair Carrach, Macdonald's younger uncle, who held the lands of Lochaber from the time of Good John of Islay, joined the party with some two hundred and twenty men, all of them skilled archers.

The Royal army lay encamped in Lochaber, which had always been a natural strategic centre in the mainland possessions of the Lordship. They were led by the Earls of Mar and Caithness, charged with the function of extinguishing any sparks of disaffection with the Crown that might still exist in that area. Thus by a strange fate it was destined that Mar should again meet Clan Donald in combat, and another Donald, nephew of him who fought at Harlaw, was to prove

quhart Castle, on the shore
of Loch Ness, frequently
seized and occupied during
insurrections under the
Lordship

himself a worthy opponent. Strangely enough, Mar seems to have underestimated the quality of his opponent, although it is possible that the recent "daunting" of the men of the Isles in Lochaber which led to the imprisonment of their Chief may have caused him to scorn their fighting abilities. He relied on his superior armour and discipline, and sat calmly in his tent playing cards with Mackintosh, who was still a disloyal vassal of the Isles. Mar and his friends continued to play their cards although news came that Donald Balloch was approaching, having left his galleys along the lochside. Mar's lieutenants became exasperated with his carelessness, for he appeared to think that he would be able to finish the game and then defeat the enemy. When the battle was joined Donald led the main battle in front of his men. The front was commanded by MacIain of Ardnamurchan, and John Maclean of Coll. The main force was commanded by Ranald Ban, Alan MacAlan of Moidart, MacDuffy of Colonsay, MacQuarrie of Ulva, and MacGee of the Rhinns of Islay. Alasdair Carrach and his archers took up a position on a hill on the flank, and shot their arrows into the Royal army so as to compel them to give way. Alan, Lord of Caithness, and the son of Lovat were killed with 990 men. Hugh Mackay of Strathnaver was taken prisoner, and strange to say, later married the daughter of Alasdair Carrach, from whom are descended the race of Mackays called Sliochd Iain Abraich. On Donald's side only 27 men were lost.

The gathering of the forces of Donald Balloch has been commemorated in a famous pibroch known as the Pibroch of Donald Dubh. Sir Walter Scott made a well-known ballad on the subject of the gathering of the clansmen in Inverlochy, and the tune has always been associated with this battle and later the second battle of Inverlochy in 1645. The metre adapted by Scott in his ballad copies very well the tempo of the urlar (theme) of the pibroch. The tune is claimed by the Camerons on the ground that MacDhomhnail Dhuibh is a patronymic of the chiefs of the Clan Cameron. Considering that the Clan Cameron, as we have seen, had defected with Mackintosh from Macdonald's side during the troubles with the Crown, and that this pibroch has always been associated with the battle of Inverlochy, it seems strange that it should be linked with the Clan Cameron. The pibroch has been adapted as a Regimental March used to this day by the Cameron Highlanders, and makes a very fine marching martial tune.

The defeat of the Royal forces was so complete that Mar, who had been wounded in the thigh by an arrow, took to the hills accompanied only by his servants, and was soon in a starving condition. At last he fell in with some women who were tending cattle and who had a little barley meal with them which they gave to the Earl, and his servants mixed it with a little water in the heel of the Earl's shoe. Mar composed a very interesting couplet extolling the virtues of barley meal mixed in the heel of a shoe when one is in a really starving condition. Thus he went on eastwards, and fell in with a poor man who gave him liberal hospitality, washed the Earl's feet with warm water and cleaned and washed the wound. The story is told very fully by Hugh Macdonald, the Sleat historian. Mar is said to have been so impressed with the hospitality thus extended to him that he told the man that if he was ever in trouble he should remember to go to Kildrummie Castle, the Seat of the Earl of Mar, and ask for Alexander Stewart, who would cause the Earl to reward him suitably. In the process of time the man was reduced to a very low condition and made his way to Kildrummie, knocked on the gate and said that he wanted to speak to Alexander Stewart. The porter said that there was no such man there, but the applicant would not take no for an answer, until the Earl of Mar himself heard about him, and called to the porter asking who was at the gate. The porter replied that he was some fool enquiring for Alexander Stewart, and the Earl immediately started up, opened the gate, and embraced him. The good man was well cared for, and after entertaining him for some time, the Earl sent him home with 60 cows, telling him to send his son, who came some time afterwards and was made laird of a small estate—from which one learns that a good turn done to a generous or noble person is not always lost.

The reason for the arrival of Mar at the head of the Royal forces is said to have been that the King proposed to deprive the Macdonalds of their rights in Lochaber and bestow these on Mar himself, but there seems to be no evidence to prove this point. It would, however, have made Alasdair Carrach even more eager to oppose Mar and his army than he was already as a loyal relative of Macdonald.

After the battle of Inverlochy, the first but not the last fought by Clan Donald there, Donald Balloch ravaged the country of the Camerons and Mackintoshes in revenge for their desertion of the Lord of the Isles during his misfortunes. Donald returned with much booty to the Isles. As Lord of Dunnyveg he held extensive lands in Islay and Kintyre, but in the right of his mother, the heiress of the Bisset fortunes, he owned also large estates in Antrim. To these he now retired to escape the vengeance the King was preparing to exact.

The news of the revolt and the result of the battle enraged the King, believing as he did that the chiefs had been effectively quelled at Inverness and Lochaber during the period before the imprisonment of Macdonald in Tantallon. He immediately took steps to put down disturbers of the peace. A land tax was raised to defray the expenses of a new campaign. He soon made his appearance at Dunstaffnage Castle with a view to proceeding to the Isles and capturing Donald Balloch with his associates. The results of this expedition are very hard to assess. Some say that Donald Balloch came with his accompanying chiefs and made submission, that 300 of them were hanged or beheaded, and that as a conclusion to the matter Donald's head was sent from Ireland to the King. The truth of this version may be decided by the inaccuracy of including Donald in the number taken by the King. Moreover it is extremely unlikely, as most of our historians agree, that as many as 300 were hanged or beheaded. Some may have suffered, but there is no doubt that Donald himself was by then dwelling in safety on his Irish estates. James must have known that Macdonald had gone to Ireland, because in time word was sent to O'Neill, the important Irish chief of Ulster, that as a friend he should return Donald Balloch alive or dead, if he still desired to keep the friendship of King James. James knew that he could not attack O'Neill, Lord of Antrim, or Donald on his estates in that country, with any chance of success. However, a human head was somehow got hold of and sent to James with the statement that this was indeed the head of Donald Balloch. As we are well aware that Donald lived for many years after this period, the head must have belonged to some other unfortunate person, but it was enough to satisfy James that he had at last run his enemy to earth, and the Scottish King flattered himself that the most formidable warrior of Clan Donald would now cease from troubling him. Meantime, Donald was living happily on his estates and had married O'Neill's daughter, through which alliance a bond was soon afterwards made between the two families. The Lowland historians, amongst them Buchanan, were taken in by this subterfuge, but many years after the first two Jameses were dead, Donald Balloch was still very much alive, as we shall see later.

The battle of Inverlochy was fought in the early weeks of 1431, by which time the Lord of the Isles had been pining a prisoner in Tantallon Castle for a space of well-nigh three years. But now the time was rapidly approaching when he was to be set at liberty. At first sight it seems somewhat remarkable that a King who had proved himself so inexorable to offenders against his authority should have displayed such leniency to the Lord of the Isles, when others had been executed. His conduct in this particular instance towards a subject who had been more than once guilty of rebellion, was not characteristic of his policy or methods. It is hardly to be accounted for by Alexander's kinship to the throne, as the blood of many of the King's relatives had already flowed upon the scaffold. The reasons, however, may not be far to seek. It is probable that by this time the King had discovered the impolicy of harsh measures, and that at a time when murmurs of discontent were beginning to be heard in other quarters, the more prudent course was to put an end, if possible, to the quarrel with the Lord of the Isles. The supposed death of Donald Balloch had also removed the most formidable disturber of the peace, and a favourable opportunity alone was lacking to open the gates of Tantallon Castle and set the prisoner free. Such an opportunity soon arose. In October 1431 the heir to the Scottish Crown— afterwards James II—was born, and it is said that during the public rejoicing connected with this auspicious event, an amnesty was granted to a number of political delinquents, among them Alexander, Lord of the Isles, who was restored to his freedom, dignities and possessions.

If the early years of Alexander's public life were crowded with troublous events, after 1431 his career was peaceful and prosperous, his life being spent in the enjoyment of the honours and the discharge of the duties of his high position. It has been the prevailing belief among historians that at the date of Alexander's liberation from Tantallon he not only received restitution of his ancestral rights as Lord of the Isles, but likewise full investiture of the Earl of Ross. Of this latter, however, there does not seem to be anything like adequate or satisfactory proof. The evidence seems to point the other way. It is unquestionable that the functions of the Earldom of Ross lay in the Crown as late as 1430 when Alexander, Lord of the Isles, was still a prisoner at Tantallon, which might be adduced as a reason for the Crown possessing the earldom, since the possessions and dignities of the family had been forfeited. The contrary will appear from consideration of the following facts:

On the 11th April 1430 there was an enquiry made at Nairn, in presence of Donald, Thane of Cawdor, regarding the tenure of the lands of Kilravock and Easter Geddes, an enquiry rendered necessary by the destruction of the ancient writs in the burning of Elgin Cathedral in 1390. In the record of that inquisition, it is stated with the utmost clearness, that the lands in question were held from the Crown in ward for the Earl of Ross, who had not received the Crown confirmation as such since the death of the last Earl of Ross in France some years previously. Still stronger testimony to the same effect is borne by a Crown Charter of James I to Donald, Thane of Cawdor, on 4th September 1430 which opens with the words, "James, by the Grace of God King of Scots and Earl of Ross." Nor is this all. It appears from the evidence of contemporary records from 1431 down to 1435 that payments of £10, £24 and £34 were made out of the Royal Treasury to the Countess of Ross as "Dowager Lady of the Isles." Two inferences may be drawn from these references without straining the probabilities of the case. In the first place, it may reasonably be supposed that the King, who drew the revenues of the earldom, acknowledged by these payments a certain moral right to them on the part of the Lady of the Isles, and, in the second place, her designation in these accounts, not as Countess of Ross, but as Dowager Lady of the Isles, seems an undoubted proof that, as late as 1435, James continued to withhold his formal recognition of her title to the earldom.

There is, in fact, the best reason to believe that the Lord of the Isles did not enter into possession of the Earldom of Ross during the life-time of James I; and, however good and equitable his claim was, no effective right could come to him without the acknowledgment of the royal source of property, as well as honour, in the realm. James I was assassinated on the 21st February 1437, and the first charter proceeding from Alexander, in his capacity as Earl of Ross, is dated September of the same year. This seems to suggest that in the interval the Regents acting for the young King had given the Lord of the Isles investiture of the earldom, which the late King so long continued to withhold. During the half dozen years that intervened between Alexander's restoration and the death of James, the chronicles of the age have little to say about the Lord of the Isles, and although we may naturally suppose that he would have occupied an attitude of opposition to the Court, it is evident that he stood apart from the conspiracy by which the murder was plotted and carried out.

Following the tragic death of the King and the minority of the young prince, now only six years old, Alexander and the Island clans enjoyed a period of peace with the central government. Internally, within the Lordship, some old scores had to be settled. Alexander had not forgotten that the defection of the Clan Cameron and Clan Chattan had led to his sorry humiliation under James I. Inverlochy still rankled.

Two Regents were appointed to rule during the minority: Sir William Crichton and Sir Alexander Livingstone, who appointed Archibald, Earl of Douglas, Lieutenant-General of the realm. The latter had always been friendly towards Alexander and a year after James's death he appointed him Warden or High Sheriff of Scotland north of the Forth. He was answerable to the central authority of the Regents through the agency of John Bullock, Bishop of Ross, in matters pertaining to peaceful rule in the North. Records of events during this period show that Alexander discharged his duties ably, his name appearing frequently in the transactions of the time as touching the rule of his district. The town of Inverness was within that region and its burgesses must have viewed the arrival of Alexander in his new office as somewhat strange after his previous visits to their town, which could by no means have been forgotten. They seem to have been treated very fairly, however, as no serious complaints are recorded.

Naturally Alexander had not forgotten Inverlochy and the disloyal clans Cameron and Chattan. Now that he had the power to punish the defectors he was able to rectify that wrong, but his manner of accomplishing this appears in the circumstances most capricious. The chief of Clan Cameron was dispossessed of his lands in favour of Maclean of Coll who, however, had but a brief enjoyment of them because the Cameron chief was soon back and able to regain his patrimony. But the Mackintoshes, who had been equally guilty of disloyalty at Lochaber, now received generous grants of lands from Alexander, some of them at the expense of his own close relatives. Any matrimonial connections that may have existed could scarcely account for these transactions since marriage ties at no time invariably led to peaceful relations between the parties concerned: an outstanding example of this being the case of Donald Dubh, last scion of the main family of Macdonald of the Isles, who from childhood was kept prisoner at Inchconnel by his grandfather, the Earl of Argyll. Whatever the motives, the treatment of the Clan Chattan to the detriment of Alexander's own blood relations of Keppoch is very hard to understand. In 1443 Mackintosh was given a grant of Keppoch's lands in Brae Lochaber, not that Mackintosh had much joy from his "vassals." The chiefs of Keppoch continued to occupy their lands and hold them by the sword, scorning "sheep-skins." Not content with this unfair action the fickle Alexander also bestowed upon Mackintosh the bailiary of all Lochaber, a valuable and prestigious office.

There is reason to believe too that Alexander flirted with the Douglas family in plans which later bore so much bitter fruit. He met and conferred with

Douglas in Bute in 1438, but what passed we do not know. In view of the later history of John, last Lord, it does seem very suspicious. In Alexander's lifetime, however, matters went no further than a league, defensive and offensive, between the Earls of Crawford, Douglas and Ross, signed and sealed on the 7th March 1445.

Little remains to be told about Alexander except that he died in his Castle of Dingwall and was buried in the Chanonry of Ross on the 8th May 1449. No stone marks his resting place today. Oliver Cromwell utterly destroyed the Cathedral of Fortrose, turning it into a quarry for building stone. Why Alexander's body was not conveyed to Iona for burial, as his forebears had been, is a mystery. Perhaps the family hoped that by burying him within his Earldom of Ross a seal would be placed upon the occupation of those valuable estates by his posterity. It was a vain hope, as we shall see in the next chapter.

If Alexander had a somewhat chequered career, and seemed to be vacillating at times, he did at least manage to convey the Lordship of the Isles and the Earldom of Ross intact to his son. He was three times married:

First. Elizabeth, daughter of Alexander Seton, Lord of Gordon and Huntly, by whom he had John, his successor.

Second. A daughter of MacPhee of Lochaber, by whom he had Celestine, who was given the lands of Lochalsh.

Third. A daughter of Gilpatrick Roy, son of Ruairi, son of the Green Abbot of Applecross, by whom he had Hugh, founder of the family of Sleat.

Although the two later marriages are in dispute by some historians, their offspring have been accepted as legitimate, with no bar to succession to their names, titles and estates.

11

John, Lord of the Isles and Earl of Ross
(1449-1493)

Reigning in Scotland
JAMES II
1437-1460
JAMES III
1460-1488
JAMES IV
1488-1513

ON THE DEATH of Alexander of Islay, Earl of Ross, in 1449, his son John succeeded him both in his island and mainland territories. The period was a comparatively quiet and prosperous one in the history of the family of Macdonald. Alexander, after many struggles and vicissitudes, had succeeded at length in uniting to the Lordship of the Isles the mainland inheritance of his mother, and thus both in extent of territory and influence he had elevated himself to a position of power unequalled even by the Lord of Douglas in the South. The policy of Alexander seems to have been dictated by the wise and firm resolution not to involve himself again in an open quarrel with the Scottish State. Though his sympathies lay entirely with Crawford and Douglas, having, as stated in the last chapter, entered into a league with them, he played no active part in the civil commotions in which these noblemen were such able actors. Far removed from the base of operations, he remained an interested spectator of a kingdom torn asunder by factions and transformed into a stage on which the actors played each for his own hand.

This wise and prudent policy evidently did not commend itself to Alexander's son and successor, John. The state of matters in the Highlands at the death of Alexander favoured the continuation of a defensive rather than an aggressive policy. Conditions in the South were very different. The kingdom was still in the throes of a long minority. The assassination in 1437 of James I, whose wise, if sometimes harsh, rule had done so much to restore order and tranquillity throughout his kingdom, was contemplated with secret satisfaction by those turbulent noblemen whose excessive power the King had so successfully curbed. Now that his powerful personality was removed and the reins of State placed in other hands, we can readily conceive how those ambitious and powerful barons, on whose feudal privileges the King had encroached, would seize the opportunity and devote their energy towards the restoration of lost power and prestige. The moving spirits in the struggle of place and power were the Douglases, the Livingstones and the Crichtons, the great object governing the policy of each being the destruction of the other, while the majority of the people groaned under the cruellest oppression.

While Lowland Scotland was thus distracted by petty feuds and tumults, the Highland portion of the kingdom seems to have enjoyed comparative peace and prosperity. This is true in an especial manner of the extensive domain over which John, Lord of the Isles, held sway, due mainly to the wise policy of his father, Alexander. There was no call for an aggressive policy on the part of John in the circumstances in which he found himself on his accession to the honours and dignities of his house. By taking part in the quarrels of his southern neighbours, he had everything to lose and it is difficult to see what, under the most favourable circumstances, he could have ultimately gained by pursuing a course so unwise and unpatriotic. He was already in possession of a vast territory, and surrounded by loyal vassals and cadets of his house. But John was a minor at the time of his father's death, and this, no doubt, largely accounts for the rash policy which he pursued on the very threshold of his career. From an entry in the Chamberlain Rolls, it would appear that this official charges himself with the rents of the lands of the barony of Kynedward for two years, that barony being in ward through the death of Alexander, Earl of Ross. This means that John was either a minor or had not at this time received confirmation of the lands of the barony of Kynedward. But an entry in the Exchequer Rolls of the year 1456 leaves no doubt as to the age of the Earl of Ross when he succeeded to that dignity. In this entry reference is made to the barony of Kynedward as having been in ward for three years, during which the Earl of Ross was a minor. John was, therefore, eighteen years of age when he succeeded his father in 1449. But though thus still of tender years, he would not have lacked for counsel at so critical a moment in his career as head of the House of Macdonald. The veteran Donald Balloch, Lord of Dunnyveg and the Antrim Glens, was the principal councillor of the Island Lord, as well as Captain of the Clan Donald, and there were other cadets of the family who attained to considerable power and influence in the Highlands and Islands. These were the Clanranald branch, the MacIains of Ardnamurchan, the MacIains of Glencoe, and the Macdonalds of Keppoch. Surrounded by these, as well as by the other vassals of the family, whether at Dingwall or at Ardtornish, John had little to fear from his foes inside or outside the Highland boundary.

Both at Dingwall and at Ardtornish, the Earl of Ross held court on a scale approaching that of a sovereign prince. From several charters granted by him, we find the names of his councillors and the offices held by them in the government of the Isles. Donald Balloch comes before us as President of the Council, while Maclean of Ardgour and Munro of Foulis were Treasurer of the Household and Chamberlain respectively: other offices were held by Maclean of Duart, Macneill of Barra, Macdonald of Largie and others of the vassals of the Isles. One of the first charters granted by John on his becoming Earl of Ross was that to the Master of Sutherland of the lands of Easter Kindeace for his homage and faithful service, and among the witnesses are the names of several members of the Island Council.

The Earl of Ross, however, did not confine himself to the affairs of his own principality. It would have been well if he had. He had barely succeeded to his patrimony when (in 1451) we find him in league with the Earls of Douglas and Crawford. These noblemen had raised the standard of revolt in the Lowlands, and had set all law and order at defiance. Both were selfish, cruel and ambitious, and being possessed of great power and influence, their rebellious attitude was a constant menace, and a source of danger, to the Scottish State. Their extensive estates gave them the command of a powerful army of military vassals, but this only stimulated their ambition to grasp at still greater power, and they seem to have set themselves no less a task than the dismemberment of the kingdom. A mutual oath was entered into between them "that each of them should be aiding and assisting against all the world, to the friends and confederates of one another." Into this dangerous league the young Earl of Ross threw himself, prompted, no doubt, by the vain ambition of acquiring yet greater power and adding to his already far too extensive domains. It was not in the north alone that the standard of revolt was raised; the whole kingdom was thrown into a turmoil of rebellion. The Earl of Ross, who had married the daughter of Sir James Livingstone, the King acting in the interesting capacity of matchmaker, was no doubt somewhat disappointed at not receiving the dowry, with the promise of which His Majesty had clinched the matrimonial bargain. But the disgrace and attainder of Livingstone intervening was the cause, no doubt, why the royal promise was not implemented. Neither the non-payment of the dowry, however, nor the disgrace of Sir James, was the prime motive for the conduct of the Earl of Ross in the present revolt against the King's authority. It was, as we have seen, part of a great scheme, into which John had entered with the insurgent Lords of Douglas and Crawford, and from which he hoped to gain a much greater prize than Elizabeth Livingstone's dowry.

The details of this formidable rebellion have not been recorded, but the great outlines of the transaction remain. John, at the head of a large body of his vassals, marched to Inverness, and without much opposition took the Castle, garrisoned it and proceeded to Urquhart. He claimed the lands of Urquhart as part of the Earldom of Ross, which lands, with the Castle, had formerly been in the possession of his family. The stronghold of Urquhart, which was almost impregnable in its great size and strength, was held for the King. John at once attacked it and, after a short but stout resistance on the part of the garrison, became master of the situation. His father-in-law, Livingstone, who on hearing of the commotion in the North had escaped from the King's custody, was made governor of Urquhart Castle. Intoxicated with the success which attended him at Urquhart and Inverness, he marched southwards through Moray and, taking the Castle of Ruthven, another royal stronghold, he committed it to the flames. The King, who had evidently not yet discovered the treasonable league between Douglas, Crawford and Macdonald, devoted all his energy and resources to the southern portion of his kingdom. At all events, no immediate step was taken to punish the Island rebel, who remained defiantly in possession of his recent conquests.

James II, who had just come of age, was not by any means wanting in administrative capacity or military ardour. Both were very soon put to the test. The Southern portion of his kingdom, torn and distracted by the feuds of the Lowland barons, had become a fertile region for all confusion and rapine. It required the possession of a steady judgment and a firm hand to restore order and good government, and the energy of the young monarch was taxed to the utmost. The King's whole attention, therefore, being meanwhile devoted to his unruly subjects in the South, the Earl of Ross and his clansmen enjoyed the benefit of complete immunity from the royal vengeance. But the tide of affairs, after a brief interval, took a sudden turn, and John of the Isles appears in a new light. The treasonable league between Macdonald, Douglas and Crawford, very probably recently renewed, was at length discovered by the King, and he at once realised the powerful combination arrayed against him.

Meanwhile an event happened which changed the King's plans, and helped to break up the league between the confederate lords in an unexpected manner. The Earl of Douglas, on his return to Scotland, and at the instigation of the English Court, put himself without delay in communication with Macdonald and Crawford, and in order to carry out the elaborate scheme against the Scottish State, Douglas opened the campaign by summoning his vassals and retainers to his standard. One only, it would appear, disobeyed the call, and, asserting his independence, refused to join in the insurrection. This bold vassal, whose name was Maclellan, was closely allied by blood to Sir Patrick Gray, a courtier of high standing in the King's household. Douglas, highly incensed at the conduct of his retainer, ordered his arrest and imprisonment at Douglas Castle. On the news of Maclellan reaching the court, the King at once despatched a messenger demanding the release of the prisoner. Divining the purport of the royal messenger's visit, and knowing well that his presence betokened no good omen, Douglas gave orders privately to have Maclellan beheaded. This defiant conduct on the part of Douglas, so utterly regardless of the King's authority, roused the indignation of James, who would have taken immediate steps to bring him to justice if he had not dreaded his power. Instead the King, suppressing his indignation, prudently determined to have a secret conference with Douglas in the Castle of Stirling, ostensibly with the purpose of making a better citizen of the haughty baron. James gave his assurance under the Great Seal for the personal safety of the Earl. Relying on the Royal assurance, Douglas sped to Stirling, where the King and Court then resided, and presented himself before His Majesty. The King remonstrated with him for his treasonable proceedings, and especially for the league he had entered into with Macdonald and Crawford. The proud Lord of Douglas listened with impatience to the reproaches of his Sovereign, and at length defied James, whereupon the King, losing all control of his temper, drew his dagger and stabbed the rebel lord. It is impossible to justify the conduct of the King. Whether premeditated or in a fit of temper, no justification can be pleaded for an act committed in direct violation of his solemn promise to protect the person of his victim. There can be little sympathy, on the other hand, for the murdered nobleman, whose own hands were not free from blood, and whose career throughout was marked by the most cruel and tyrannical actions.

Thus the first blow was aimed at the Macdonald, Crawford and Douglas league, but it did not prove effective. The leading spirit was removed only to make room for another Douglas, whose chief aim was to perpetuate the policy of his house towards the Scottish State.

The temporary discomfiture of the Douglas party, and the strong measures taken by the King and his advisers to put down the rebellion of Crawford, were not without their effect on the Earl of Ross. The Earl of Huntly, at the head of the royal forces, devoted his attention in the first place to Crawford, whom he defeated in a pitched battle near the town of Brechin. Though not personally present in this engagement, the Earl of Ross sent a contingent of clansmen to the assistance of the Earl of Crawford. Huntly's plan of campaign was to attack the rebel lords one after the other, and defeat them in turn. Macdonald, who still held his own in the North, realising his danger, began to make elaborate preparations to resist the threatened invasion of the King's lieutenant. The formidable defence made by the Earl of Ross discouraged the invading host, and Huntly, who had penetrated as far as Moray, retired in dismay. No further attempt was made for a time. The Earl of Huntly's services were required elsewhere, and the Douglases seem to have taken up the whole attention of the King. In any case, the Earl of Ross still continued to hold the castles of Inverness and Urquhart, and suffered no diminution of his power in the North. Though in league with Crawford and Douglas, he cannot be said to have taken an active part with them in the recent revolt against the Scottish Government. He prudently remained at home, and allowed his confederates to fight for their own hand. The King was too busy elsewhere to attack him in the North.

Though free from Southern interference, the Earl of Ross was not without his troubles at home. Ever since the Macdonald family settled in Ross-shire, the neighbouring clans, and even some of the vassals of the earldom, looked with a jealous eye on their growing power and influence. Chief among these were the Mackenzies, at this time of no great account as a clan, the Mackays and the Sutherlands. It was seldom the House of Islay was free from those domestic feuds which bulk so largely in the traditions of the country. The seanachies, embodying these traditions in their manuscripts, give us vivid, if sometimes exaggerated pictures of the marauding and piratical expeditions engaged in by the restless spirits of those times. The stories told by some, when brought under the light of authentic history, are found in many instances to be wonderfully reliable. Both MacVurich and Hugh Macdonald refer to a raid on the Orkney Islands by the young men of the Isles, led by Hugh Macdonald of Sleat, brother of John, Earl of Ross. Authentic records of the time not only confirm this raid but refer to a series of other raids on Orkney, and other Norse possessions, by the men of the Isles. In a manifesto by the bailies of Kirkwall and community of Orkney the complaint is made that the Orkneys were habitually overrun by bands of Islesmen sent thither by the Earl of Ross, designated as *ab antiquo inimicus capitalis.* These invasions were of yearly occurrence during the reign of James II. The Islanders, according to the manifesto, plundered, burned and ravaged the country, and carried off cattle and whatever else they could lay their hands on. In a letter by William Tulloch, Bishop of Orkney, dated 28th June 1461, the same complaint is made against the men of the Isles, and the Bishop alludes to the efforts which he was then making to come to an arrangement with the Earl of Ross to put a stop to these marauding expeditions. What success attended these laudable efforts on the part of the good Bishop history does not record. The Earl of Ross and his Islesmen were soon required elsewhere, and little time was left for raids, naval or other, in the North.

The Earl of Douglas, who had long kept the Lowlands in a perfect turmoil of civil war, was finally defeated by the King's forces at Arkinholme, in Annandale. Disappointed of expected English aid, and having been declared traitor to the Scottish State, Douglas as a last resort fled to Argyllshire where, in the Castle of Dunstaffnage, he was received by Donald Balloch, who may not inappropriately be called the Lieutenant-General of the Isles. Here the Earl of Ross, who had come from the North, and Douglas met in solemn conference to decide which steps should be taken in the present emergency. The result of their deliberations was soon apparent. Douglas, having persuaded the Island Lord, apparently without much difficulty, to support him in his cause, hastened across the border into England, where he was cordially received by the Duke of York. Macdonald immediately prepared for an invasion of the King's lands and summoning his clansmen and vassals, he soon gathered to his standard a force 5000 strong. The command of this force he bestowed on the veteran Donald Balloch, whose prowess in many a field has been the admiration alike of friend and foe. A fleet of 100 galleys was equipped for the expedition, and Donald, directing his course towards the mainland, proceeded to Inverkip, where he landed his force. There appears to have been no opposition offered to this formidable armament, and Donald was allowed, not only to land unmolested, but on penetrating into the country he carried fire and sword everywhere he went with impunity. From Inverkip he directed his course towards the island of Arran, which with the Cumbraes and Bute he invaded in turn, burning and plundering wherever he went.

Donald's primary object, however, was not plunder but revenge, and this he was now able to gratify to the full. After besieging the Castle of Brodick and burning it to the ground, he next attacked the Castle of Rothesay, took it and made himself master of Bute. According to the *Auchinleck Chronicle,* he carried away immense spoil from this and the adjacent islands and mainland including a hundred bolls of meal, a hundred bolls of malt, a hundred marts and a hundred marks of silver, five hundred horses, ten thousand oxen and kine, and more than a thousand sheep and goats. The loss in lives and property does not appear to have been very great in proportion to the strength of the invading forces. If we are to believe the chronicler, there was slain only "of good men fifteen, of women two or three, and of children three or four." It would appear from this that Donald's object was not so much to punish the natives as the superiors of the lands which he had invaded.

In the episode which followed, however, Donald's conduct is deserving of the severest condemnation. Lauder, the Bishop of Lismore, a Lowlander, had evidently through over-zeal in the exercise of his sacred calling made himself obnoxious to the men of Argyll. Instead of going cautiously to work, and making himself acquainted with the mode of living of the people, with the oversight of whom he had been entrusted, he exercised discipline with a strong hand, and sought to bring the inhabitants into conformity with the ways and manners of the South. This he found by no means an easy task. The people, of whose language and manners the bishop was utterly ignorant, stubbornly resisted his reforms, and were driven by his high-handed policy to commit outrages on his person and ravage and plunder the sacred edifices of his diocese. The bishop had besides, as one of the King's Privy Council, affixed his seal to the instrument of forfeiture against the Earl of Douglas, and this only added another to his already many offences against the Lord of Dunnyveg. Donald now had his opportunity of punishing the obnoxious prelate, and without delay he proceeded to Lismore, where the bishop resided, and besieged him in his sanctuary. After ravaging the island with fire and sword, he put to death the principal adherents of the bishop, in all likelihood natives of the Lowlands, while the prelate himself escaped with his life by taking refuge in the Cathedral Church of his diocese. Without wishing to condone the conduct of Donald Balloch in any way, it may be permissible to say that this prelate, by his short-sighted and unwise policy, had himself done much to provoke this and other outrages on his sacred calling and jurisdiction. That, however, does not warrant the outrages committed on this or on former occasions on the Bishop of Argyll, and Donald Balloch nowhere comes before us in a worse light than in his expedition to Lismore.

No immediate action seems to have been taken by the King to punish the rebel Lord of Dunnyveg, or his chief, the Earl of Ross, in the recent treasonable proceedings. In Argyll and the Isles it would have been vain to attack them. The Scottish navy at this time was not fit to cope with the strong maritime power of the Isles, and this probably was the principal reason why the King thought it prudent not to hazard an expedition to Argyll. In any case there is no record of the pains and penalties which should have fallen on the head of the sacrilegious spoiler of Lismore. One incident may be recorded which throws light on the turmoil into which the Douglas-Macdonald league had thrown the Highlands and Islands. Feeling no longer safe in these regions, John of Islay's consort, the Lady Elizabeth Livingstone, escaped with all haste from the country, and, finding her way to Court, threw herself on the protection of the King. According to one of the Scottish historians, this lady married the Island Lord with the laudable view of toning down his rugged disposition and making him a loyal Scottish subject. In this, it would appear, the Lady Elizabeth utterly failed, and her return to Court at the present juncture is a clear indication of the policy of the Earl of Ross towards the executive government, as it also makes only too apparent the wide gulf that separated racially the North from the South. The King received the Countess of Ross with much cordiality, and a suitable maintenance having been assigned her, she appears to have remained at Court during the remainder of her life.

The Earl of Ross, weakened by the defeat of the Douglas party, finally sent messengers to the King offering to repair the wrongs he had committed on his lieges, and promised in anticipation of the royal clemency to atone with good deeds in the future for his rebellious conduct in the past. The Earl well knew that his wisest policy in the present state of affairs was to make his peace with the King. He could not very long stand out in his present attitude and expect much success to attend his efforts in opposition to the Scottish Government. He appears to have been perfectly sincere in his desire to be reconciled to the King. The King at first was not disposed to treat with John on any terms, but finally granted John a period of probation during which he was to show the sincerity of his penitence. Meanwhile the King summoned a meeting of Parliament to consider the affairs of his realm. Whether the Earl of Ross was present at this meeting, or was represented, does not appear very clear, but it seems that much attention was devoted to the Highlands and Islands, and that many good laws were passed for the welfare and peace of the realm generally. The Earl of Ross, it would appear, was now on his good behaviour, for, according to the good Bishop Lesley, the King in this Parliament "maid sic moyennis with the principallis capitanis of the Ilis and hielands that the same wes als peacable as ony parte of the Lawlandis, and obedient as weill in paying of all dewties of thair landis to the King, als redy to sarve in wearis with greit cumpanyis." "The principallis capitanis of the Ilis," including no doubt the hero of the recent naval raid, had from all appearances been suddenly converted, but like most sudden conversions, there do not appear to have followed any results of a permanent kind.

Notwithstanding the friendly relationship in which the Earl now stood to the Crown, the King, in a Parliament held at Edinburgh in 1455, deprived him of both the castles of Inverness and Urquhart. Next year, however, the Castle of Urquhart, together with the lands of Urquhart and Glenmoriston, were granted to John at an annual rent of £100. To these were added at the same time the lands of Abertaff and Stratherrick, and to still further confirm his loyalty, the King conferred upon him the lands of Grennane in Ayrshire.

What conspicuous services were rendered to the State by the Earl of Ross after his sudden conversion history does not record, but the King must have received some proof of his loyalty, for in the year 1457 he appointed John one of the Wardens of the Marches, an office of great importance and responsibility. No doubt the King's policy was to attach John to his person and Government. In bestowing upon him this office of trust under his Government, the King evinced his desire to cure the northern potentate of his rebellious tendencies, and wean him from the influence of those factions which had been so baneful in the past. As a further proof of his confidence, the King appointed John with other noblemen to conclude a truce with England.

The history of the Highlands during the next few years, so far as the Earl of Ross is concerned, is almost a blank. The only reference to him in his official capacity which we have been able to find is a document preserved in the Kilravock Charter Chest, which tells us that in 1460 at Inverness the Earl granted Rose of Kilravock permission to "big ande upmak a toure of fens" (build and erect a tower of defence).

The time soon arrived when the Earl of Ross acted a part very different from that which he was accustomed to play. In the year 1460, James II entered on his campaign against England. The truce between the two countries to which, as we have seen, John, Earl of Ross, was a party had not lasted long. The King opened his campaign by attacking the Castle of Roxburgh, an important frontier stronghold, then and for long prior to this time in the possession of the English. Here he was joined by the Earl of Ross at the head of 300 clansmen, "all armed in the Highland fashion, with habergeons, bows and axes, and promised to the

King, if he pleased to pass any further in the bounds of England, that he and his company should pass a large mile afore the rest of the host, and take upon them the first press and dint of the battle." John was received with great cordiality by the King, who commanded him, as a mark of distinction, to remain near his person, while his clansmen meanwhile set themselves to the congenial task of harrying the English borders. The unfortunate and melancholy death of the King from the bursting of a cannon at the very commencement of the siege of Roxburgh virtually brought the campaign against England to an end, and the Earl of Ross had no opportunity of proving his own fidelity, or the courage and bravery of his clansmen.

Seal of John, Lord of the Isles and Earl of Ross
(from the Cawdor Charter of 1449)
S. JOHIS DE YLLE COMIS ROSSIE DNI INSULARUM

The untimely death of the King in the flower of his youth and at the very beginning of his vigorous manhood exposed the country once more to the dangers attendant on a long minority. James, during his comparatively short reign, had proved himself a wise and judicious ruler. Of this we have ample evidence in the success which attended his efforts in destroying the overgrown power of the house of Douglas, and attaching to his interests such men as the Earl of Ross.

The Earl of Ross, whose loyalty, as we have seen, was so conspicuous during the latter portion of the reign of the late King, now allowed himself once more to become the victim of the Douglas faction. By a judicious combination of firmness and moderation, the King had disarmed the enmity of John, and had James not been cut off so prematurely, there is every reason to believe that John would have continued loyal to the Scottish throne. The death of the King, however, soon plunged the Scottish State into the difficulties that always attend a minority. It will be remembered that the last Earl of Douglas had been forfeited in all his estates, and was now undergoing his sentence of banishment at the Court of Edward IV. Douglas had, in the days of his prosperity, maintained friendly intercourse with the family of York, and now that Edward IV seemed in a fair way to crush the House of Lancaster, Douglas hoped that the power and influence of England might be directed towards the restoration of his lost territories and position in Scotland. Meantime the banished Earl watched with deepest interest the passing phases of political feeling between the English and Scottish crowns, and he made every effort to win his old ally, the Earl of Ross, from his friendly relations with the Government of Scotland.

As had often happened in the past, the difficulties which England had to deal with at home and in France had hitherto proved a barrier against active interposition in the affairs of Scotland, and the Wars of the Roses had particularly absorbed all the energies of the House of York. In the year 1461, however, the two events already referred to, the accession of Edward IV to the English throne and the death of James II of Scotland, seemed to shed a gleam of hope on the broken fortunes of the exiled Douglas. Edward lent his countenance to the Douglas scheme all the more readily because the Scottish Court had afforded an asylum to his opponent, Henry of Lancaster, whose defeat at Taunton had driven him to Scotland, while it placed Edward on the English throne. Various schemes were devised in Scotland for the restoration of the English monarch, all of which proved futile. To counteract these and divert the Scottish rulers from their object and neutralise their efforts, Edward lent a willing hand to Douglas in his desperate scheme. The King of Scotland was a child, and past experience had taught that a Scottish regency, accompanied as it often was by faction and conspiracy, would afford ample scope for the execution of such a scheme as Douglas might devise for his restoration to the honours he had forfeited.

The time had evidently come when the old league with the Macdonald Family might be revived. In these circumstances we are not surprised to find that a few weeks after the King's death the first overtures were made to the Earl of Ross for the formation of an offensive and defensive league with England. That the English Government was the first to move in the matter is evidenced by the fact that the writ empowering the Commissioners from England to treat with the Lord of the Isles was issued on the 22nd of June 1461, while the ambassadors from the Isles were not formally commissioned until the 19th October following. The English Commissioners to the Isles were the banished Earl of Douglas, his brother, John Douglas of Balveny, Sir William Wells, Dr John Kingscote and John Stanley. The following is the text of the writ appointing the English Commissioners:

AMBASSADORS ARE APPOINTED TO TREAT WITH THE EARL OF ROSS

The King to all of whom, &c., salvation. Know ye that we, trusting very fully in the faithfulness and prudence of our dearest cousin James Earl of Douglas and of our dear and faithful William Welles, Knight, and John Kyngescote, Doctor of Laws, also of our dear John Douglas and John Stanley, have nominated and appointed these same, the Earl, William, John, John and John our special ambassadors, commissioners or messengers, for meeting with our dearest cousin John Earl of Ross and our dear and faithful Donald Balloch or their ambassadors, commissioners, or messengers having sufficient power from our same cousins the Earl of Ross and Donald Balloch —on that part. Also for treating and communicating with these same concerning and with regard to all matters and affairs touching and concerning ourselves and our cousin Earl of Ross and with regard to what is contained in the matters and affairs aforesaid that have to be proceeded with, determined, agreed upon and concluded. And other matters all and each which ought to and must needs be granted carried out and arranged as in the premisses and their conclusions. Promising in good faith and by our royal word in these documents that all and each of the items in or bearing upon the premisses that shall have been appointed agreed upon and concluded by the foresaid ambassadors, commissioners or messengers we shall hold settled agreeable to us and fixed for ever. In testimony of which, &c.

T.,R. At Westminster 22nd day of June 1461. By The King Himself.

For consideration of the proposals about to be submitted to the English envoys, the Lord of the Isles with his Council, a body that had existed in connection with the family from the earliest times, met and deliberated in the Castle of Ardtornish, which, in the time of John, Earl of Ross, was the meeting place on important and State occasions. The Douglases and the other Commissioners of Edward seem to have come all the way to Ardtornish to lay their proposals before John and his privy council. Of the conclusion arrived at, after mature and solemn deliberation, we are not informed. In any case it was necessary that the tentative compact must be considered and ratified in the great English capital itself. To represent the interests of the Macdonald Family at Westminster, two commissioners were appointed. Ranald Ban of the Isles, son of John Mor Tanister, and founder of the family of Largie, and Duncan, Archdean of the Isles, were appointed to meet the English Commissioners; and it was no ordinary sign of confidence that they were entrusted with such important and delicate negotiations. The English Commissioners appointed to meet the Commissioners of the Isles at Westminster were Lawrence, Bishop of Durham, the Earl of Worcester, the Prior of St John's, Lord Wenlock, and Robert Stillington, Keeper of the King's Seal.

The treaty that was concluded in the name of the English King and the Earl of Ross, with the Earl of Douglas as the moving spirit of the plot, was bold and sweeping in its provisions. It was undoubtedly treasonable to the Scottish State, but the whole history of the family of the Isles, and in a measure, of that of Douglas, was a continued protest against the supremacy of the Crown. From the terms of the treaty, it would appear that the object in view was nothing less than the complete conquest of Scotland by the Earls of Ross and Douglas, assisted by the English King. The Earl of Ross, Donald Balloch and John, his son and heir, agreed to become vassals of England, and with their followers to assist Edward IV in his wars in Ireland and elsewhere. For these services, and as the reward of their vassalage, the Earl of Ross was to be paid a salary of £200 sterling annually in time of war, and in time of peace, 100 merks; Donald Balloch and his son John were to be paid salaries respectively of £40 and £20 in time of war, and in time of peace half these sums. In the event of the conquest of Scotland by the Earls of Ross and Douglas, the portion of the kingdom north of the Forth was to be divided equally between the Earls and Donald Balloch. Douglas was to be restored to his estates in the south. On the division of the north being completed the salaries payable to the Macdonalds were to cease. In the case of a truce with the Scottish monarch, the Earl of Ross, Donald Balloch, and John, his son, were to be included in it.

Such was the Treaty of Ardtornish, 1462, a diplomatic instrument daring in its conception and fraught with great risk to the Lordship of the Isles. Considering the commanding position John already occupied, it is strange he should have allowed himself to be entangled in a scheme so wild and perilous. He was already by far the most powerful noble in Scotland, with a vast territory and almost regal sway. But he seems to have been ambitious of acquiring still greater power and prestige. The bribe held out to him proved a strong temptation, and undoubtedly influenced his conduct in the step he took; yet the scheme was so wild that we are amazed at the eagerness with which he entered into it, and at his simplicity in allowing himself to be blindly led into so hollow an alliance. It is plain that the scheme did not emanate from the brain of the Earl of Ross. On this, as on critical occasions before, John was under the controlling influence of wills stronger and more persistent than his own. It was the scheme of a bold and desperate man who was playing a hazardous game for tremendous odds. For the provisions of the Treaty of Ardtornish we are indebted mainly to the banished and forfeited Earl of Douglas. But there was another party to the contract who must not be overlooked. Donald Balloch was thoroughly imbued with the Celtic spirit, keen, restless and eager, the determined foe from his early years of the Scottish State, and still in his declining years burning for dangerous and exciting adventures. From these and other circumstances we may well believe that he strongly supported the league embodied in the Treaty of Ardtornish.

This remarkable compact between the Lord of the Isles and the English King, with the Earl of Douglas as the moving spirit of the plot, implied the adoption of military measures to carry its provisions into effect. The events that followed almost immediately after the ratification of the Treaty seem to suggest an understanding between the parties that no time was to be lost in taking the contemplated action. On the side of the Earl of Ross proceedings were taken with almost precipitate haste. The two foremost Clan Donald warriors of the day were placed at the head of the vassals of Ross and the Isles. First in command was Angus Og, son of the Lord of the Isles, who now for the first time makes his appearance upon the arena of war, but who had already, though scarcely more than a boy, begun to show indications of the dauntless courage, the

e Castle of Ardtornish in
rvern, an ancient strong-
hold of the Lords of the
and scene of the negotia-
s leading to the notorious
Treaty

unconquerable spirit which he showed in the future. Second in command was Donald Balloch, the hero of Inverlochy, a fight the memory of which was beginning to grow dim in the minds of the generation that witnessed it.

The Lord of Dunnyveg and the Glens of Antrim had only once unsheathed his sword since he overthrew the Earl of Mar in Lochaber, but he was still, though past his prime, well nigh as formidable an antagonist as of old, always to be found where the hurricane of battle was brewing, now, as of yore, the stormy petrel of Clan Donald warfare. Angus Og, destined to play the leading part in the decline and fall of the Lordship of the Isles, was a natural son of the Earl of Ross. The historian of Sleat, whether inadvertently or of set purpose, would make it appear otherwise, and says that Angus Og was the issue of a marriage with a daughter of the Earl of Angus. There is no evidence that such a marriage ever took place, and John had no male issue by his wife, Elizabeth Livingstone. The question is placed beyond dispute by a charter which was afterwards given to John in confirmation of his possessions, and in which it was provided that failing legitimate heirs male, the title and estates were to descend to his natural son Angus. The mother of Angus is said to have been a daughter of Macphee of Colonsay, so that the heir of the Lordship of the Isles was of gentle if not legal origin.

The army of the Isles, under the leadership of Angus Og and Donald Balloch, marched to Inverness, once more the theatre of warlike operations. Taking possession of the town and castle, the latter one of the royal strongholds in the north, they at once, in the name of the Earl of Ross, assumed royal powers over the northern counties, commanded the inhabitants and all the Government officers to obey Angus Og under pain of death, and to pay to him, as his father's lieutenant, the taxes that were levied by the Crown. In this way did the Earl of Ross attempt to carry into immediate and forcible execution the provisions of the Treaty of Ardtornish. It is hardly credible that John would have taken a step so daring and extreme had he not expected that the English portion of the Treaty would have been carried out at the same time by the dispatch of a strong body of auxiliaries to form a junction with the Highland army. There is evidence that an English invasion of Scotland was contemplated at the time, and that apprehensions of its imminence prevailed in the Eastern Counties. Especially in the town of Aberdeen the Provost and inhabitants were warned to keep their town, sure intelligence having been received that an English fleet was on the way to destroy not only Aberdeen but other towns upon the coast. Had Edward iv been able to support the action of the Earl of Ross in the North by throwing an army across the border in aid of the Earl of Douglas, it is quite possible that the State might have fallen, and Scotland have lost the independence for which she had made such heroic struggles. Fortunately for the Kingdom of Scotland, this was not to be. The Wars of the Roses were still raging in the sister country, and the resistance of the heroic Margaret of Anjou to the pretensions of the House of York absorbed the energies of the reigning power. Edward iv was unable to dispatch the expeditionary force to the assistance of the Highland insurgents, the scheme for the division of Scotland, after the manner prescribed in the Treaty of Ardtornish, came to naught and the rebellion finally collapsed.

What actually followed the campaign of Angus Og and Donald Balloch, whether they were called to account and subdued by force of arms, or whether matters were allowed to adjust themselves without any active measures being undertaken by the State, are questions upon which the annals of the age do not throw much light. It seems clear, however, that, whether through want of will or power, no decisive steps were taken against the Earl of Ross. It must be remembered, however, that the full measure of the treason was very far from being known. The invasion of the northern counties, with the seizure of Inverness, and whatever hostilities accompanied the proclamation of sovereignty, must have come to the knowledge of the Government; but the serious aspect of the whole affair, the negotiations embodied in the Treaty of Ardtornish, still remained a secret buried out of sight in the archives of the English Crown at Westminster. It needed but a favourable opportunity for that explosive document to bring dismay and consternation to the minds of those involved.

The Earl of Ross does not appear to have suffered either in dignity or estate after the rebellion of 1463. For at least twelve years after that maddest of engagements, the Treaty of Ardtornish, he pursued the even tenor of his way with little or no molestation from the Scottish State. That John maintained his position intact is evidenced by Crown confirmations of grants of land bestowed upon his brothers, Celestine and Hugh. These twelve years, from 1463 to 1475, are years of well-nigh unbroken darkness so far as the Lordship of the Isles and the Earldom of Ross are concerned. The rebellion of 1463, short-lived though it was, and comparatively little as we know of its details, left abundant seeds of future trouble. There is undoubted reason to believe that John was summoned to appear before the Parliament of 1463 to answer for his conduct under pain of forfeiture, but despite the threatened penalties, the Earl of Ross, whose love for these conventions seems never to have been strong, did not put in an appearance. Whether it was that his command of the Scots tongue was limited, and he did not care to mix with the Southern nobles for that reason, or whether he ignored the jurisdiction of that august body, we know not, but certain it is that on almost all occasions he was represented at the Scottish Parliament by procurators. Owing to John's non-compearance at the Parliament of 1463, his case was postponed, and the Parliament adjourned to meet in the city of Aberdeen on the Feast of St John the Baptist the same year. Of neither of these Parliaments have any records survived, but subsequent proceedings clearly show that John still elected to remain in his Castle of Dingwall rather than respond to the summons of the High Court of the realm.

That same year there is evidence that efforts were not lacking to bring the rebel to task, though these do not appear to have been conducted with much resolution. Several Royal Commissioners, including the Earl of Argyll and Lords Montgomery and Kennedy, and Treasurer Guthrie, came North to lay the Royal commands before the Earl of Ross, for it is on record that expenses amounting to £12 10s 4d were allowed them for two days' sojourn at Perth on their way to Dingwall Castle. There is no definite knowledge of the result of this mission. The probability is that John was neither punished nor forgiven, but was left in a condition of suspense as to his standing with the Crown, and this leaving of the matter undecided explains why, in after years, the Government was enabled to go back upon the delinquencies of 1463. Although the Treaty of Ardtornish was still a secret, the government seems to have had sufficient evidence that John had been guilty of treason against the Crown by the assumption of royal prerogatives in the North, and the appropriation of taxes and revenues pertaining to the Crown alone. He and his brother Celestine, were justly accused of having retained the Crown lands in 1462-3, as well as £542 5s 7d of the Rents of Petty, Leffare, Bonach, Ardmannoch, the vacant See of Moray and others, wrongfully and without the King's warrant. It was probably no easy task for the Earl of Ross to prevent disturbances breaking out between the restless Islesmen by whom he was surrounded and the occupants of the lands adjacent to his territories. We find, in 1465, reckoning made of the wasting and burning of the lands of Kingeleye, Bordeland, Drumelcho, Buchrubyn, Drumboye, Turdarroch, and Monachty, to the extent of £31, for all of which the Earl of Ross and his followers were held responsible. Quarrels were likewise breaking out occasionally between the Earl of Ross and his neighbours in the East of Scotland. Thus, in 1473, and in the month of August there is strife between himself and Alexander of Setoun regarding the lands of Kinmundy, in Aberdeenshire, so much so that the matter evokes the royal displeasure, and an Act of Parliament is procured to provide for the punishment of the culprits, though we are not enlightened as to the nature of the penalty administered. A feud also arose with the Earl of Huntly in 1474, and this also was the theme of remonstrance by the King, who, in the month of March, sent letters to both Earls "for stanching of the slachteris and herschippes committit betwixt theer folkis."

Whatever may have been John's relations with the Scottish Crown on the one hand, or his neighbours in the North and West on the other, his intercourse with his own dependants seems to have been of the friendliest and most peaceful character. So true is this that beyond the granting of charters to some, and the confirmation of grants to others, the records of the period have almost nothing to say as to the relations between the superior and his vassals of the Earldom of Ross, while in the Lordship of the Isles, since the last outbreak of Donald Balloch, a wonderful and unwonted calm seems to have reigned from 1462 to 1475. All this is an indication that whatever may have been the foreign relations —if we may use the term—of the Earl of Ross and Lord of the Isles, there seems to have been harmony and concord between his subjects and himself.

At last the ominous quiet is broken, and all at once there is a great convulsion and upheaval. The Treaty of Ardtornish is exhumed, dug out of the oblivion to which for twelve years it had been consigned, and in which, no doubt, its perpetrators prayed that it might for ever rest, and the rash and daring instrument, which aimed at the destruction of a great State, is thrust upon the notice of an astounded and indignant nation. The Scottish Government felt that the ship of State had been sailing among hidden yet dangerous rocks, and that serious disaster had by no means been a remote contingency. It was determined to take resolute and immediate action against the only party to the compact on whom the hands of the Executive could be laid. The Earl of Douglas was an outlaw beyond Scottish jurisdiction; Donald Balloch was secure from danger amid the Antrim glens; and so the Earl of Ross, perhaps the least culpable of the contracting parties, became the victim and scapegoat of the conspiracy.

Highland historians do not afford us much assistance in tracing the causes which led to the disclosure of this treaty, a disclosure which was, to all appearance, a gross breach of faith on the part of England in whose archives the document must have been preserved. Yet the causes that led to the revelation of the secret may be estimated with tolerable accuracy, if not with absolute certainty. In 1474 Edward IV was contemplating the invasion of France, and, in the circumstances, he deemed it his wisest policy to secure his frontiers at home by a treaty of friendship with the Northern Kingdom. A treaty was consequently drawn up, the main provision of which appears to have been, that a contract of marriage should be entered into between the Prince of Scotland, son of James III, and Cecilia, daughter of the English King, the subjects of this interesting arrangement having attained respectively to the mature ages of two and four years. We refer to it because it indicates new and friendly relations between the two countries, and because it would be impossible for Edward IV, under the conditions that had arisen, to continue promises of support to the Earl of Douglas, or abide by a treaty which was a standing menace to the quiet and integrity of the sister land. There was nothing therefore more natural than that in the course of friendly negotiations between the two kingdoms, in 1474, the Treaty of Ardtornish should have emerged and become the signal for hostile proceedings against the Earl.

After the discovery of the Treaty, the Government seems to have lost little time in calling John of Islay to account for his twelve-year-old treason, and an elaborate process was instituted against him in the latter months of 1475. On the 20th November of that year, Parliament met, and an indictment containing a formidable record of his political offences was drawn up. In the forefront of the crimes of which he was accused stands the treaty of Ardtornish, but other charges of treasonable conduct were likewise included in the document. The various letters of safe conduct to English subjects passing to and fro between the two countries, the rebellion of 1463 and the imperative commands issued then to the King's lieges to obey his bastard son Angus on pain of death; the campaign of Donald Balloch, his siege of Rothesay Castle, and his depredations in Bute and Arran, with the slaughter of many of the King's subjects, events of a much earlier date than the Treaty of Ardtornish; in fact the whole sum of John's offences from the beginning are all narrated in full. John himself, hereditary Sheriff of Inverness, being under the ban of the law, Alexander Dunbar of West-field, Knight, Arthur Forbes, and the King's herald, were conjointly and severally appointed Sheriffs of Inverness, by special royal warrant for the legal execution of the summons. These emissaries of the law were commanded to present the summons personally to John, Earl of Ross, in presence of witnesses, and it was enjoined that this be done at his Castle at Dingwall, but the prudent proviso was inserted, *if access thereto should with safety be obtained.* Failing this safe delivery of the citation at the Castle, it was provided that it should be made public proclamation at the cross and market place of Inverness, while it bore that the Earl of Ross must appear in presence of the King at Edinburgh, at the next Parliament to be held there on the 1st December following. It is noticeable that, while the Parliament which authorised the summons met on the 20th November 1475, the document was issued under the great seal at Edinburgh on the last day of the previous September. It is evident that Parliament was simply called together to endorse what the royal prerogative had already enacted.

The next step in the process was the execution of the royal summons, and this also took place before the meeting of Parliament on 20th November.

Two other similar instruments containing wearisome repetitions of the summons follow after the foregoing, the sum and substance of the enormous mass of verbiage being that John is cited to appear at Edinburgh before a Parliament to be held on the 1st December 1475. In due course the Convention of the Estates of Scotland met, and evidence was given that the Earl of Ross had been lawfully cited at the cross and market place both of Dingwall and Inverness. John not compearing, Andrew, Lord of Avondale, Chancellor of Scotland, by command of the King charged him in presence of the assembled nobles with the high crimes and misdemeanours already fully detailed; upon which it became the unanimous finding of Parliament that his guilt was established. Finally, judgement was given by the mouth of John Dempster, Judge for the time being of the Court of Parliament, that for the treason proven against him, John, Earl of Ross and Lord of the Isles, had forfeited his life as well as his dignities, offices and possessions, which latter were thereby alienated not only from himself, but also from his heirs forever, and attached to and appropriated by the Crown.

These drastic proceedings of the Scottish Parliament were immediately followed by formidable preparations to wring from the attainted noble by force what he would not voluntarily concede. Colin, Earl of Argyll, willingly adopted the rôle of public policeman, and accepted a commission to execute the decree of forfeiture which had recently been pronounced. It does not appear, however, that Argyll was entrusted with the reduction of the Earl of Ross to submission, for in the following May a strong expeditionary force was raised and divided into land and naval sections, under the command of the Earls of Atholl and Crawford respectively, for the invasion of John's extensive territories. As it turned out, forcible measures ceased to be necessary when, on the advice of Atholl, the King's uncle, John at last agreed to make a voluntary submission and throw himself upon the royal mercy. Once more Parliament met, and on 1st July 1476 John appeared before it with all the semblance of humility and contrition. On the intercession of the Queen and the express consent of the nobles, John was there and then pardoned and restored to all the honours and possessions he had forfeited. Apparently this investiture was only a form for enabling him to denude himself of a large portion of his inherited estate. The same day on which he was reinstated he made a voluntary resignation of the Earldom of Ross and Sheriffdom of Inverness and Nairn, with all their pertinents, castles, and fortalices to the king. He did so, the record says, of his own pure and free accord, but we may well believe that this renunciation was the condition of his being restored to favour. On the same day the King confirmed to Elizabeth, Countess of Ross, all the grants of lands within the Earldom formerly made to her by the Crown, as not being included in the foregoing renunciation. John, having made these concessions, received in recognition of his obedience a new distinction. He still remained John de Ile, and retained the ancient heritage of his house with the old historic dignity, the Lordship of the Isles, which no Scottish monarch had bestowed and, from the Celtic standpoint, none could take away; but the ancient honour, with all the proud memories it enshrined, was now combined with a brand new title of Baron Banrent and Peer of Parliament.

It soon appeared that the King and Parliament were not completely satisfied with the reduction which had thus been made in the power and possessions of the Chief of Clan Donald. On the 26th July, the same month that witnessed his surrender, resignation and partial re-investiture, he received a formal charter for all the territories which it was resolved by the Government he should be permitted to retain. This charter contains evidence that John was deprived of territories other than those he gave up in his resignation of 1st July, namely, the lands of Kintyre and Knapdale, with which exception all the other estates which belonged to him in the Lordship of the Isles were allowed to remain in his possession. The historian of Sleat connects the loss of these lands with certain dealings which John had with Colin, Earl of Argyll, and while the details of his story do not seem very probable, there is every likelihood that that wily and unscrupulous nobleman and courtier may have had something to do with that unfortunate occurrence. This charter of 1476 contained other important provisions connected with the transmission of the still important possessions and honours of the House of Islay. John had no legitimate male issue, but the family succession was secured to his natural son Angus, and failing him, to his natural son John and their heirs after them, failing legitimate issue of their father's body.

It is thus plain that the situation, however disastrous, was not without its compensations, and that John issued out of the terrible ordeal in which the Treaty of Ardtornish placed him, with as little loss of outward estate as could possibly have been expected in the circumstances. Others not more guilty had lost life and property. The comparative fortunate result may be attributed, less to his own sagacity and force of character, than to the leniency of the Crown, and contemporary records are pretty clear in showing that, in the eyes of the King, blood was thicker than water, and that John's kinship to the royal line of Scotland had much to do with the large measure of clemency that was displayed.

Had John been a stronger man than he was, with the political calibre of his namesake "the Good," or had he possessed the qualities of his father and grandfather, he might either have avoided the pitfalls that lay in his path, or made a better fight for the interests at stake when the hour of trial came. But John, even discounting the forces he had to contend with, was the weakest potentate of his line, and there must be something after all in the verdict of Hugh Macdonald, that he was a "meek, modest man . . . more fit to be a churchman than to rule irregular tribes of people."

Taking all these things into consideration, the position in which John found himself after the convulsion of 1475-6 was still not unworthy of the traditions of his house; and the family of Islay, though the glory of their territorial position was much bedimmed, still occupied one of the highest places among the nobles of the land. It also appeared as if an era of peace and friendship with the Crown was beginning to dawn upon the House of Macdonald when, not long after the reconstruction of John's estate, his son Angus married a daughter of that eminent Scottish courtier, Colin, Earl of Argyll. That instead of a time of peace, a period of almost unprecedented turmoil and conflict was at hand, events were soon to show.

The scant records of the time distinctly prove that the large sacrifice of his status and possessions, which the head of the Clan Donald had been compelled to make, were exceedingly unpopular among those chieftains and vassals who were directly descended from the family of the Isles. The exalted station of the head of the House of Somerled shed a reflected lustre, not only on the chiefs of the various branches, such as the Clanranalds, the Sleats, the Keppochs, and others, but upon every individual who bore the name of Macdonald, and they bitterly resented John of Islay's undignified surrender of their birthright without affording them the chance of striking a blow in its defence. And none was more upset by these circumstances than Angus Og, the son and heir whose proud and resolute spirit was henceforth dedicated to the restoration of the Clan's prestige and recovery of its heritage.

It is equally intelligible that the other vassals should have regarded the crisis from a somewhat different point of view. The clans other than Clan Donald, who held their lands from John, had greatly increased in power and dignity under the kindly rule of the Lord of the Isles. The loss of power by their superior did not, however, imply their decadence. On the contrary, the greatness of the Family of the Isles overshadowed their attempts at self-assertion, and the signs of a new order of things, in which they might rival the historic house in property and influence, were naturally not unwelcome. Thus there came to be a parting of the ways between those clans that held their territories, less on account of ties of kinship, and more by the bonds of feudal tenure, and those other tribes who regarded the Lord of the Isles, not merely as the superior of their lands, but as the acknowledged head of their race. No doubt these other clans, forming as they did a component part of the Island lordship, were still deeply interested in the preservation of the Celtic system which that lordship represented, and, as a matter of fact, we find them in after years fighting strenuously for its restoration. Yet at this particular crisis these clans were undoubtedly less zealous for the maintenance of the honour and glory of the House of Islay than the Clan Donald itself probably for the reasons that have been assigned. Hence we find them adhering to the Lord of the Isles in his attitude of concession and submission, while the Clan Donald, eager for the maintenance of the ancient power of the Family, sympathised with a policy of greater boldness and less compromise, and looked to Angus Og, the son and heir of John, as the hero and exponent of their aspirations.

Whatever estimate may have been formed of Angus Og by the outside world —and, no doubt, he proved himself a terror to his foes—he was certainly a great favourite with those of his name and lineage. Not only did they esteem his heroism and regard him as the restorer of their pristine greatness, but they loved him for his own sake. He possessed the popular manners and generous impulses of his race. He was open-handed and liberal with his means, and while he was brave as a lion on the field of battle, he followed with zest those sports and recreations with which even the most warlike beguiled the tedium of peace. He was a keen lover of the chase, and his unbounded hospitality in the banquetting hall was affectionately remembered in after times. Such was unquestionably the verdict of his contemporary clansmen, and their devotion was evinced by the unanimous support accorded him in all his undertakings. Such could hardly have been the case had Angus Og been the deep-dyed villain whom certain historians have portrayed.

There is very great uncertainty as to the sequence of events during the years that followed the forfeiture and partial restoration of John, Lord of the Isles. Down to the fall of the Lordship of the Isles, chronological difficulties abound. There is evidence, however, that from 1476 onward, Angus Og, supported by the general sentiment of the Clan, resisted what with some reason was considered his father's pusillanimous surrender. Undoubtedly the beginning of the long series of troubles, which filled the remaining years of the history of the Lordship of the Isles, was associated with John's deprivation of the lands of Knapdale and Kintyre. Castle Swein, in North Knapdale, long ago the scene of Alexander of Islay's discomfiture by Bruce, and destined in a future century to play a part in the annals of the Clan, was from 1476 to 1478 the scene of operations evidently carried on for the restoration of the surrounding territory to the family from which, in the opinion of its vassals, it had been unrighteously diverted. Whether the Lord of the Isles had been art and part in the rebellious proceedings or not, he was held responsible for what was done, although he appears to have satisfied the Government that the irregularities complained of had been perpetrated if not without his knowledge, at any rate contrary to his wishes, and was successful in procuring pardon for his son, Angus Og, who was now beginning to display decided symptoms of unwillingness to accept the situation created by the misfortunes of his father.

From 1478 to 1481 a fair condition of tranquillity seems to have prevailed in the Highlands and Islands generally. The Government seem to have been so convinced of the loyalty of John of Islay that in the latter year large tracts of land in Kintyre, formerly in his possession, were now re-conveyed by royal charter for his life-time, as an acknowledgment of faithful service. In 1481, however, Angus Og took the initiative and mounted a formidable expedition with the object of curbing the rising power of the Mackenzies and re-establishing the influence of his Clan in the Earldom of Ross. He collected a large force in the Isles, as well as in those regions of the mainland where the Macdonald influence was still predominant. The Keppochs, Glengarrys and many other clansmen from the Isles rallied to his standard and with a formidable force he set out for Ross. The government, by this time realising that they were face to face with a rebellion of some magnitude, commissioned the Earl of Atholl to march against and subdue the Islesmen. That nobleman, putting himself at the head of the Northern clans, including the Mackenzies, Mackays, Brodies, Frasers and Rosses, took the field against the Western host. The two armies met at a place called Lagabraad, and a sanguinary battle was fought, which resulted in the triumph of Angus Og and the utter rout of his opponents. There were slain of Atholl's army 517 men, the chief of the Mackays was taken prisoner, while Atholl and Mackenzie narrowly escaped with their lives. The outcome proved that Angus Og, as a brave and accomplished warrior, was second to none of his race, and that if he had received the possessions of his house intact he would have died sooner than surrender them.

Soon after Lagabraad, the Government gave instructions to the Earls of Huntly and Crawford to lead a new expedition against this formidable and enterprising rebel; but it is not clear whether they took hostile action or did so with complete success. We are equally in the dark as to the result of Angus's victory in Ross, or whether he was able to maintain his hold upon any part of that extensive region. The next time light falls upon this obscure period we find Angus in the Isles when the Earls of Argyll and Atholl have brought about an interview between himself and his father for the purpose, it is said, of effecting a reconciliation. Well might father and son, like the Trojans of old, fear the Greeks when they came with gifts, and it is not strange that under such auspices peace would not descend. The old Lord was dominated by the party of the Court, Angus commanded the steadfast devotion of the Clan, and with a record of triumphant success behind him he was not likely to yield to the representations of the Government without the restoration of some of the rights that had been surrendered.

The Earls of Argyll and Atholl undertook to subdue the undaunted rebel, and prepared an expedition for the purpose. The lords and chief men of the Isles, those favouring a policy of concession and those that supported the attitude of Angus, sailed in their galleys up to the Sound of Mull, and ranged along the opposite side of the beauteous waterway and prepared for the conflict. The combination against Angus Og had been organised by the Earls of Argyll and Atholl, but when the day of battle came they seem to have kept at a safe distance. Thus it came to pass that in this fight of saddest omen, the most noted naval battle in the Isles since the days of Somerled, in which the ancient Lordship of the Isles was being rent in twain, the Lord of the Isles was left in command of the force which was to engage the warriors of his race and name under the leadership of his own son. The battle fought in the neighbourhood of Tobermory was fiercely contested and sanguinary. Little is known of the details of this memorable engagement beyond what has been preserved by the historian of Sleat. Angus Og's galleys were drawn up on the north side of Ardnamurchan, and detained by stress of weather for a space of five weeks. At the end of that time the Laird of Ardgour was observed sailing up the Sound, and he, on observing Angus Og and his fleet, at once displayed his colours. Donald Gallach, son of Hugh of Sleat, and Ranald Ban, son of Alan MacRuairi, chief of Moidart, were in the company of Angus Og, and they steered towards Maclean's galley. This was the signal for the opposing force coming to the assistance of Ardgour, conspicuous among the rest being William Macleod of Harris. Ranald Ban grappled Macleod's galley, while one of Ranald's company, Edwin Mor O'Brian by name, put an oar in the stern-post between the helm and the ship, which immediately became unmanageable, and was captured with all on board. Macleod was mortally wounded and died shortly afterwards at Dunvegan. Maclean of Ardgour, who was taken prisoner, had a narrow escape for his life. Angus Og is said to have suggested hanging, and this would probably have been his end were it not that the Laird of Moidart, with a touch of humour, interceded for him on the ground that, if Maclean's life was taken, he himself would have no one to bicker with. This view seems to have commended itself to the leader and on Ardgour taking the oath of fealty he was spared, presumably to save Clanranald from too monotonous a life. Here we are afforded but a glimpse of an incident in this famous sea fight, the result of which was the discomfiture of Angus Og's opponents and his own secure establishment as the Captain of the Clan Donald.

So far as we can calculate without accurate data, the Battle of Bloody Bay was fought in 1484.

Fateful events followed each other in rapid succession during these later years of the Lordship of the Isles, and very shortly after this victory of Angus Og, an incident occurred which aggravated the enmity between the opposing parties, and became a fruitful cause of trouble for many years to come. It is not to be forgotten that the agents in provoking this outburst of renewed bitterness were the two noblemen who, a few short months before, are alleged to have done their utmost to bury the hatchet of strife. Angus Og, as has already been stated, was married to a daughter of Colin, Earl of Argyll, probably about 1480, and at the time of the battle of Bloody Bay this lady, and an infant son Donald, were living in the family residence at Finlaggan. The Earl of Atholl, with the connivance and assistance of Argyll, who furnished him with boats, crossed secretly to Islay, stole the infant son of Angus, and delivered him to Argyll, who immediately sent him under careful guardianship to the Castle of Inchconnel in Lochawe. The reasons for this shameful abduction do not appear to us very far to seek. We do not wish to censure unfairly the inveterate enemy of the House of Islay, but facts, however repulsive, must be stated unreservedly. Even the most strenuous apologists of the House of Argyll can hardly get the facts of history to prove that they were unselfish or unrewarded in their vaunted support of Scottish nationality, or that their conduct amid the turmoil of Highland politics was disinterested. The abduction of the infant Donald Dubh was an act of unspeakable meanness, and was instigated by the basest motives. So long as there was an heir to the Lordship of the Isles, there was a likelihood of the Macdonalds retaining the family inheritance; and this must lead to a postponement of the family of Argyll usurping the Macdonald estates. To prevent, if possible, the Macdonald succession, Argyll seized the heir presumptive, with the view of retaining him a perpetual prisoner. Still further to prevent the succession of his grandson, he concocted and got the Government to believe the story of Donald's illegitimacy—a pure fabrication to promote his sinister ends. If Donald Dubh were really illegitimate, that fact would of itself suffice to prevent his succession to the honours and possessions of the Clan Donald; and, in the circumstances, the Government would be most unlikely to grant a charter of legitimation in his favour. Hence, if the story had been true, the measure of consigning Donald to perpetual captivity would have been altogether unnecessary. It was because of Donald's legal birth, and his undoubted right to succeed his father, that the dastardly device was adopted of stealing the unoffending child, and making him virtually a prisoner for life. Our criticism of the conduct of Argyll in connection with this particular event is supported by the testimony of history. How, indeed, can we contemplate without indignation the character of a man who, to further his own schemes of policy, not only consigned an innocent grandchild to a living death, but cast an unfounded suspicion on the fair name of his own daughter?

It is not by any means surprising that this abduction, in which Atholl was the catspaw of the crafty Argyll, caused the deepest resentment in the breast of Angus Og, and no sooner did it come to his knowledge than he took immediate steps to execute vengeance on the actual perpetrator of the deed. Collecting a band of warriors in the Isles, Angus sailed with a fleet of galleys up to Inverlochy, a landing-place which, from its position in the far interior, was well adapted for a descent upon any part of the North of Scotland. The Highland host, disembarking in this historic scene, marched through the great mountain passes of Lochaber and Badenoch until at last, swooping down upon the lowlands of Perthshire, they passed into the region of Atholl. Tidings having reached Blair of the rapid approach of the Islesmen, and time not availing for the organisation of defence, the Earl and Countess of Atholl, with a number of dependants and retainers, and a large quantity of valuable effects, took refuge in the sanctuary of the Church of St Bridget's.

There is great uncertainty as to the events that followed. The facts of history have in this connection been so twisted and misplaced, and the religious preconceptions of the narrators have so obscured the issue, that it is well nigh impossible to extricate the real occurrences from the mythological haze in which they are enveloped. The consequence is that modern Scottish historians have presented us with a blend of legend and fact which does great credit to their imagination. The historian of Sleat, who at no time is the apologist of Angus, flatly denies the story of the burning of St Bridget's, and it is, no doubt, to be placed in the same category of fabulous traditions as other conflagrations with which the family historians of the North of Scotland have credited the Clan Donald. The same authority remarks with truth that the Lords of the Isles were generous benefactors, and not the destroyers of churches, and this is more than can be said of some of the historical houses that rose upon the ruins of their fallen state. Certain facts connected with the raid of Atholl seem beyond dispute. That Angus and his followers invaded the sanctity of St Bridget's; that they took captive within that shrine the Earl and Countess of Atholl, in revenge for the abduction of Donald, Angus' infant son, and that probably a quantity of valuable booty at the same time was seized; that Angus took the high-born captives with him, by way of Inverlochy, to Islay, as hostages for the restoration of his son; that the hurricanes of the wild western sea may have engulfed some of the treasure-laden galleys on their homeward voyage; that the leader and his captains in after times went back on a pilgrimage, probably directed by Mother Church, to seek the divine mercy at the shrine which, in their wrath, they had desecrated but not destroyed, doing so with all the outward symbols of contrition which the piety of the age prescribed; and that the Earl and Countess of Atholl were unconditionally set free from their captivity in Islay after the expiry of a year—all this appears to be fairly well authenticated. But the exaggerations and improbabilities that have gathered round the facts in the pages of the credulous chronicler belong to the large mass of fable with which the history of the period so much abounds.

Little is known of the subsequent career of Angus Og, until the tragic close which seems to have taken place some five years later. So far as the government of the Isles was concerned, his position was unquestioned, and had his life been prolonged, the vigour and determination of his character would not improbably have done much to restore the ancient power of his family. A pleasing feature in these latter years lay in his reconciliation with his father. Angus Og seems never to have abandoned his scheme for the conquest of Ross, and it is probably with the view of reducing to subjection the old vassals of the Earldom, and particularly of chastising the Mackenzies, that he took his last fatal journey to the North. Angus halted at Inverness, where, as was his wont, he gave hospitable entertainment to his friends and allies in that region. The story is told by the historian of Sleat and bears upon the face of it the mark of truth.

The heir of the Macleod of Lewis had been recently a minor under the tutelage of Ruairi Dubh Macleod, whose daughter was married to the Laird of Moidart. Ruairi Dubh coveted the succession, and refusing to acknowledge the true heir, assumed the lordship himself. His schemes, however, were thwarted by Angus Og, who displaced Ruairi from the position he usurped, and put the rightful heir in possession, acting in the matter as the representative of his father, of whom the Macleods were vassals. The Lady of Moidart, Ruairi Dubh's daughter, moved by hatred of Angus for thus vindicating a righteous cause, compassed his death. There was a harper of County Monaghan, named Art O'Carby, who was either in Macdonald's retinue or a frequenter of his establishment. This minstrel conceived a violent passion for the daughter of Mackenzie of Kintail, who was at feud with Angus Og, and it would appear that the Lady of Moidart put Mackenzie up to the scheme of promising his daughter in marriage to O'Carby if he did away with the heir to the Isles. He made the harper swear never to disclose the secret of who instigated the deed. The Irishman undertook to carry out the dark conspiracy, and in token of his villainous intention was wont, when in convivial mood, to repeat doggerel verses of his own composition, of which the following is a couplet:

> T'anam do Dhia a mharcaich an eich bhall-bhric,
> Gu bheil t' anam an cunnart ma tha puinnsean an Gallfit.

> Rider of the dappled steed, thy soul to God commend,
> If there is poison in my blade, thy life right soon shall end.

One night after Angus had retired to rest, the harper entered his apartment, and perceiving he was asleep, killed him by cutting his throat. O'Carby was apprehended, but never confessed who his tempter was, or what inducement was held out as a reward for the murderous act. Jewels found upon him which formerly belonged to Mackenzie and the lady of Moidart proclaimed their complicity in the crime. The harper, according to the cruel fashion of the time, was torn asunder, limb from limb, by wild horses.

Thus fell Angus Og, and although the Sleat historian tells us that his father's curse visited him, his theory of retribution hardly fits in to the facts of his own narrative. Angus fell a victim, as better men have done before him, to the malignant spite of an unscrupulous and designing woman, and that not for any deed of cruelty or oppression, but for upholding the cause of justice in the succession to the lordship of Lewis. With Angus vanished the best hopes of the Clan Donald for the restoration of their proud pre-eminence, and there is surely pathos in the thought that, as the Founder of the Family in historic times had his warlike career cut short by treachery, so now three hundred years later the last direct representative of the line save one, also died by the assassin's knife. Our estimate of his character, and the date at which we have placed his death, are both confirmed by the Irish Annals of Loch Ce, in which under the year 1490 the tragedy is thus referred to: "MacDhomnaill of Alba, *i.e.* the best man in Erin or in Alba of his time, was unfortunately slain by an Irish harper, *i.e.* Diarmaid Cairbrech, in his own chamber."

At the period to which we have now come, it may well be said that, although many bright pages of the story of the House of Somerled still remain to be written, yet its heroic age as the dominant power in the Western Isles of Scotland is beginning to pass away. After the death of Angus, the Clan Donald were never afterwards united under a leader so able, or in whom they reposed such confidence. From 1476 down to his death his father's headship of the house was nominal, and it was round Angus that the kindred clans rallied at every juncture that arose. On his death, John again became the effective ruler in the Isles, and there was still a possibility, had he possessed the necessary spirit, of the Lordship of the Isles being maintained. Not long after Angus's death, John, though still far short of extreme age, ceased to take an active part in the government of his territories, which he seems to have surrendered to his nephew, Alexander, son of Celestine of Lochalsh. Alexander acted ostensibly in the interests of Donald Dubh who, though still in prison, was undoubtedly heir apparent to John; but as there was little hope of his ever being released, Lochalsh doubtless contemplated, with few misgivings, his own succession to the Lordship of the Isles. At the same time it is clear from subsequent events that, notwithstanding Donald's continued captivity, the Islesmen were unanimous in regarding him as his grandfather's rightful heir.

It had often been the fate of the last Earl of Ross to be under the influence of wills more imperious and resolute than his own, though strangely enough he had offered a stubborn resistance to the aim and policy of his son. It was so now in his declining years. He who had so strenuously resisted the resolute stand made by Angus against the encroachments upon the family estates, now abandoned every attempt to curb the turbulence of his nephew, Alexander of Lochalsh. Whether he approved of the rising of 1491, or whether he made unavailing protestations against it, we are unable to say. All we know is that Alexander seems, without any delay, to have taken up the scheme for the invasion of Ross, which was interrupted by the death of Angus Og. Owing to his territorial position in Wester Ross. Alexander naturally possessed great influence in that region. The extensive lands of Lochbroom, Lochcarron and Lochalsh were his, and he doubtless expected that the other vassals of the earldom, always of course excepting the Mackenzies, would attend the summons to his banner. In this he was to a large extent disappointed, but his following was nevertheless a formidable one. The whole power of the island and mainland Macdonalds, along with the other vassals of the Lordship, and the Clan Cameron, who were vassals of Alexander for the lands of Lochiel, formed no inconsiderable array, and with all these resources at his back he might hope to win back the inheritance which his uncle had lost. Indeed, he possessed far greater resources than Angus Og was ever able to command in the divided state of the Lordship in his time.

We have no reason to doubt the personal bravery and prowess of Alexander, but he seems to have lacked that inexplicable power of organising forces and leading them to victory which is born with a man, and constitutes the true commander. Alexander and his army, taking the time-honoured highway, marched through Lochaber into Badenoch where they were joined by the Clan Chattan, under the command of Farquhar Mackintosh, Captain of the Clan. Arriving at Inverness, which he stormed and garrisoned, and where he was joined by Hugh Rose, younger of Kilravock, the only vassal of the earldom that seconded his undertaking, Alexander next directed his march towards Ross. Invading the Black Isle, he and his host penetrated to its uttermost limits, plundering the lands of Sir Alexander Urquhart, Sheriff of Cromarty. Authorities are agreed that at this stage Lochalsh divided his forces into two sections, one detachment having been sent home with the spoils, while the other marched to Strathconan to ravage and lay waste the Mackenzie lands. Like almost all the chronicles of the age bearing upon the history of the Highlands, the annals of this campaign abound in absurd inaccuracies and exaggerations. When we find a mythical Celestine performing deeds of valour, and meeting a hero's death; Angus Og or his father taken prisoner, but soon thereafter magnanimously released by *Coinneach a' Bhlàir*; *Alasdair Ionraic*, who had died in 1488, giving his benediction to his son before going to battle; a supernatural being of diminutive stature appearing and vanishing mysteriously, and in the interval doing great havoc among the invaders—when we find all this described as having taken place at the Battle of Park in 1491, it is well to remember that the stories of the Northern chronicles of the time must be accepted with great reserve. In these circumstances, we do not attach the slightest credence to the legend of Contin Parish Church being set on fire by Alexander of Lochalsh and his men on their march from Strathconan. Nor do we believe that Alasdair Ionraic, having departed this life three years previously, could have congratulated his people—as he is said to have done—that now this sacrilegious act had enlisted the Almighty on the side of the Mackenzies. The whole bombastic and inflated Mackenzie history of the battle of Park is correct only in the one essential—namely that the Macdonalds were worsted, and had to retire from Ross.

So far as we can gather, the sober facts of history in this connection are clear enough. Alexander and his men arrived at Park late in the evening after harrying and laying waste the lands of Strathconan. Wearied with the day's labours, they slumbered on the field, and apparently committed the fatal oversight of keeping neither watch nor ward. Meanwhile Kenneth of Kintail, who was by all accounts a brave warrior, had assembled his available strength, and in the silence of night bore down upon the sleeping encampment. The Macdonalds were taken completely by surprise, and there followed a panic-stricken confusion which spread throughout the whole force and was intensified by the boggy nature of the ground between them and the river Conon. Taking full advantage of their familiarity with the ground, the Mackenzies were able to put many to the sword, and many more met their death in the river, towards which they were driven by their triumphant foes.

Such was the Battle of Park, which illustrates the advantage possessed by an enemy, resolute and wary, who takes an encampment by surprise. The result was the retirement of Alexander of Lochalsh from Ross, and his abandonment for the time being of all attempts to accomplish its conquest. It has been held by some that Park was fought in 1488, but the evidence is all in favour of the later date. Angus Og was alive in 1488, and it is not likely that he would have played a subordinate part in such a campaign, or that Alexander would have borne the prominent part he did had Park been fought in the lifetime of John of Islay's son. We find also that in 1492 Sir Alexander Urquhart obtained restitution on behalf of himself and others for the spoil carried away by the Islanders, and it is very unlikely that a claim of such magnitude would have lain dormant from 1488. Hence there seems little doubt that the Battle of Park was fought in 1491.

The invasion of Ross, undertaken undoubtedly with the view of gaining forcible possession of the earldom, which had since 1476 been vested in the Crown, could not fail to be regarded as an insurrection against the State and, as such, calling for the severest measures. Whether John of the Isles approved of his nephew's rebellion or not, it appeared to the authorities that the time had come for depriving him finally of every vestige of power. If he aided and abetted the proceedings of 1491, he must appear to the Government as an incorrigible rebel, incapable of absorbing the lessons in loyalty administered to him throughout his long years of rule. If, on the other hand, he had disapproved but failed to prevent the disorders of that year, his deprivation would also seem justified on the ground of his utter inability to exercise authority in the regions subject to his sway. It was on one or other of these grounds that in May 1493 John was forfeited in all his estates and titles, and this measure was formally implemented by himself in 1494, when he made a voluntary surrender of all the lands of the Lordship.

Thus fell the Lordship of the Isles, and with it the dynasty which for hundreds of years had continued to represent, in a position of virtual independence, the ancient Celtic system of Scotland. The natural result of such a catastrophe was that for a long term of years the region that had been ruled by these Celtic princes was subject to prolonged outbursts of anarchy and disorder. There arose a vacuum in the social system which the authority of the Scottish

State, anti-Celtic as it had increasingly become, failed adequately to replace. Social order depends as much upon sympathy with the governing power as upon force, and the amalgamation of the Celtic and Saxon elements of Scottish society must inevitably prove a long process. Further, while the feudal status of the Lordship of the Isles was one that Parliament could abolish, the Highlands regarded it not as a feudal, but as a Celtic dignity, older than the Scottish State and independent of it—a dignity which no individual could surrender and no King or State could destroy. Thus it was that for two generations after John's forfeiture Highland politics swayed between efforts on the part of the Crown, on the one hand, to reduce the clans to subjection, and spasmodic movements by the clans, on the other, to restore the Celtic order which they loved, by rallying to the banner of one scion of the Family of the Isles after another, each of whom laid claim, with some appearance of justice, to the ancient honours of his house.

The events of consequence that took place between John's political demise in 1494 and his death in 1503 will more appropriately be dealt with in a succeeding chapter. The details of his personal life during these years present a sad picture of departed greatness. The descendant of a long and princely line, who for almost half a century in his own person had wielded immense power and authority, was now reduced to the level of a humble pensioner living on the King's bounty, his clothes, shoes and other simple necessities doled out to him like a pauper. It has been generally accepted that after his forfeiture John lived and died an inmate of the Monastery of Paisley, an institution that had in former years enjoyed the munificent patronage of the House of Islay. The records of the period, however, tell a somewhat different tale. The monastery doubtless was his home, but he sometimes left it, paying visits, among other places, to his old dominions in Lochaber and the Isles. At last we find him falling sick at Dundee, where he dies in an obscure lodging-house, and the sum due to his landlady and the expenses of his "furthbringing" are charged to the Scottish Treasury. All this is quite consistent with the tradition that his remains were buried at his own request in the tomb of his ancestor, Robert ii, in the ancient Abbey of Paisley, whither they must have been conveyed all the way from Dundee.

By his wife Elizabeth Livingstone, daughter of the Chamberlain of Scotland, John had no issue. He had, however, two natural sons: (1) Angus Og, Master of the Isles, who predeceased his father in 1490, as we have seen; and (2) John, who also predeceased his father. Both sons were expressly legitimised feudally in the charter granted to their father in 1476. Angus Og, Master of the Isles, was accordingly the feudal and Celtic heir of John, the last Lord, and acted as heir presumptive during his lifetime, leaving Donald Dubh, his only son, as the last represener of the noble House of the Isles, recognised and accepted as such until his death in 1545.

SEAL OF ALEXANDER OF LOCHALSH
(from the Mackintosh Charter of February 1492/3)
S. ALEXANDRI DE LOCHALSH

12

After the Lordship

Reigning in Scotland
JAMES IV
1488-1513
JAMES V
1513-1542
MARY
1542-1567

THE FALL OF THE House of the Isles in the person of John, the last Lord, did not, as the King no doubt devoutly hoped, lead to peace in the West and the Isles. We have seen, towards the end of John's reign, the vigorous action taken by leading members of his family in resisting the constant encroachments of the royal power. Alexander of Lochalsh, heir presumptive after Angus Og and Donald Dubh, had made his attempt to prop up the weakened realm and failed. Angus Og before him had made determined efforts to stem the tide, and had he lived might have postponed the evil day; but the writing was on the wall. The efforts of succeeding aspirants to the Lordship during the next fifty years were the cause of much disorder and bloodshed, and in the end came to naught.

James IV was a strong king who saw the wisdom and necessity of reaching a peaceful settlement in the Isles. On 18th August 1493 he held court at Dunstaffnage Castle where he met some of the chiefs and received their homage. Amongst these were John of Dunnyveg, chief of the Islay Macdonalds, his son John Cathanach, John MacIain of Ardnamurchan, and Alexander of Lochalsh, who had led the recent rebellion. The royal progress was marked by a policy of conciliation, culminating in the knighting of John of Dunnyveg and Alexander of Lochalsh. That the latter was so honoured is remarkable not only on account of his recent rebellion but also because, with Donald Dubh still languishing in his prison of Inchconnel, Lochalsh was the one claimant most likely to take active steps for the restoration of the Lordship. It was no doubt the King's hope in conferring the knighthood that Lochalsh would become attached to the royal interest and cause no further trouble by prosecuting his claim to the forfeited Island honours.

Of the other Clan Donald chiefs, MacIain of Ardnamurchan alone responded to the King's pacific overtures. The rest were still doubtful of his motives, finding it difficult to believe that he was serious in his efforts to inspire their loyalty and establish peaceful conditions in the West. To hasten their submission, the King mounted another expedition the following year, this time to Kintyre where he restored the Castle of Tarbert, making it a royal fortress as Robert Bruce had done before him. Leaving a garrison there, he continued his march to the extreme south of the peninsula, where he seized Dunaverty Castle without opposition, and installed a governor and a garrison before setting sail for home. If he thought he had overawed the Clann Iain Mhoir by leaving these two heavily fortified castles in their borders, he soon discovered his mistake. He had hardly set sail before Sir John and his son, John Cathanach, laid siege to Dunaverty and took it in time to hang the King's governor from the battlements in full view of the departing monarch. Who instigated this bold deed is not known, but Sir John was now getting on in years and it is probable that the younger John Cathanach was the prime mover. He had never been reconciled to the King and deeply resented the presence of a military force in the midst of his territories.

From the King's standpoint, such a flagrant act of defiance must be punished at all costs. The tool James found ready to his hand was John MacIain of Ardnamurchan, the only chief of Clan Donald who had responded favourably to James's attempt at conciliation in 1493. MacIain had married a daughter of the Earl of Argyll, and this may have been one of the factors which led him to betray his own kith and kin. The story is told in another chapter of the base action whereby Sir John of Dunnyveg, his son John Cathanach "and their accomplices" were arrested by MacIain and taken to Edinburgh to be summarily hanged on the Boroughmuir outside the city. It seems incredible that MacIain could have accomplished this act of baseness without resort to the most treacherous conduct, when we consider that the unfortunate Sir John and his party are said to have been arrested within their own residence of Finlaggan.

James made several more visits to the West and the Isles in pursuance of his policy of pacification. He garrisoned the castles of Mingary in MacIain's country and Cairnburgh in the Treshnish Isles west of Mull as a preparation for a more formidable expedition. In the summer of 1495 he led a strong force from Glasgow to Dumbarton, took ship and sailed round Kintyre north to Mingary again. Here he set up his court. The chiefs were suitably overawed and arrived in some numbers to make their peace with the sovereign, amongst them Alan of Clanranald, Donald of Keppoch, and John of Sleat, the ineffective successor to the founder, Hugh, who had laid the fortunes of his House. MacIain was also there, now in proud possession of sundry lands in Islay as reward for his base betrayal of his kinsmen of Clann Iain Mhoir. Glencoe and Dunnyveg alone were absent from this gathering where so many of the Chiefs of Clan Donald had to make their peace with James.

Encouraged by the improvement in his relations with the Western chiefs, the King on his return secured an Act requiring them to keep their people in order, and making them responsible to King and Council for misdemeanours committed in their domains. As a result of these proceedings, some of the chiefs duly appeared before the Council and bound themselves in the sum of £500 each to observe the provisions of the Act. Whether these measures were effective or not is a matter for conjecture but James seemed to have been satisfied with his arrangements, for he was able to embark on a Northern progress and enjoy the hospitality of his subjects in Dingwall.. The northern clans had never been wholeheartedly attached to the Macdonald Earldom of Ross, having suffered too much at the hands of successive Island chiefs who had invaded the territory in their attempts to acquire and maintain their hold over Ross. Their lives had been more peaceful after the forfeiture of that earldom and its attachment to the Crown in 1476. It is true that when James visited Mingary, two northern chiefs had been thrown into prison by the King. These were Mackenzie of Kintail and Farquhar Mackintosh, Captain of Clan Chattan. It is hard to see why Kenneth of Kintail should have been thus treated unless it was because of his unruly behaviour after the rebellion of Lochalsh in 1491; but it was unusual in these times of frequently changing loyalties for such a long period to elapse before retribution was exacted. The case of Mackintosh was different. He was nearly related to the blood of the Isles and his fortune had been greatly enhanced by gifts from the Lord of the Isles, including grants of lands in Lochaber which at a later date were a continual source of friction between him and the Keppoch Macdonalds.

Not long afterwards, Sir Alexander of Lochalsh once more essayed to restore the Lordship on his own behalf, although claiming to act as representative of the captive Donald Dubh. He did not get far on his raid on Ross and was defeated at Drumchatt by the Munros and Mackenzies who had combined to oppose him. He now retired to Colonsay hoping to raise more men to recover his lands in Ross, and thereafter to revive the Lordship. But the King's recent policy of conciliation was beginning to bear fruit, and few of the men of the Isles rallied to Sir Alexander's call. Many of those who had received grants of land after the fall of the Lordship were no longer interested in its restoration, and chief amongst them was MacIain of Ardnamurchan who continued steadfast in his aim of currying favour with the King. Failing the expected support, Sir Alexander became an easy prey to the treachery of MacIain who surprised and killed him at Oronsay.

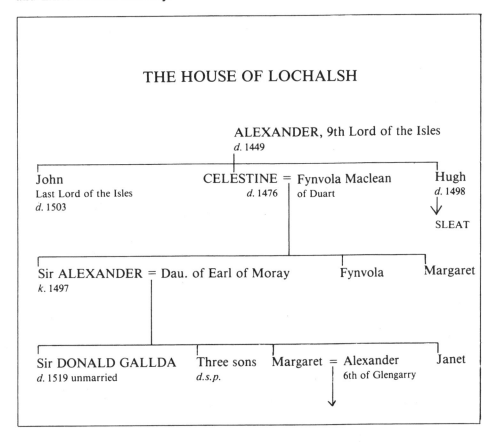

THE HOUSE OF LOCHALSH

ALEXANDER, 9th Lord of the Isles
d. 1449

John
Last Lord of the Isles
d. 1503

CELESTINE = Fynvola Maclean
d. 1476   of Duart

Hugh
d. 1498
SLEAT

Sir ALEXANDER = Dau. of Earl of Moray
k. 1497

Fynvola   Margaret

Sir DONALD GALLDA
d. 1519 unmarried

Three sons
d.s.p.

Margaret = Alexander
             6th of Glengarry

Janet

In 1498 the King paid another visit to the Isles and held court in his recently built Castle of Kilkerran (on the Loch now called Campbeltown Loch), where some of the chiefs renewed their allegiance. He seems to have spent at least a month there, during which he issued several charters. On the 3rd of August a charter was given to Ranald MacAlan, Chief of Clanranald, for lands in Uist "for services rendered," and again on the 5th of the same month more lands in Uist, Eigg and Arisaig. This last confirmed the action of John, son of Hugh of Sleat, when he had resigned these lands in favour of Clanranald. On the same day more lands in Uist, Benbecula, Morar and Arisaig were given to Angus Riabhach, a younger son of Ranald, the founder of the lines of Clanranald and Glengarry. Trotternish in Skye was given to Torquil Macleod of Lewis and his heirs by his wife, Katherine, daughter of Archibald, Earl of

Argyll. Most of these dispositions held seeds of future dissension amongst the Islesmen, which may have been the object of the King's policy; for the more the western chiefs quarrelled amongst themselves, the easier it would be for the King to intervene and assert the royal authority.

The King had hardly returned home, however, before he revoked all the charters thus granted during his visit. The reason became clear in the following year when he again visited Kilkerran to inaugurate his new plan for "daunting the Isles." The Earl of Argyll was given a commission as royal lieutenant over the whole of the Lordship, with Tarbert Castle as his headquarters. In addition Argyll received a lease of the whole Lordship except for Islay and Kintyre. The influence behind the King's change of mind thus becomes apparent. It was the beginning of the policy to expel as many Macdonalds as possible from the South Isles, a process which was almost complete by 1615 when the last Macdonalds of Islay were driven out and Campbell of Cawdor took over the cradle of Macdonald power. All who could claim to be of the main line of the House of Somerled were to be hounded out and destroyed. Such a policy held little hope of the Isles settling down to peaceful co-existence with their Lowland neighbours under the rule of the Royal House, and its conception and prosecution must be taken as sufficient evidence of the sinister influence now being exerted by Argyll and other chiefs who were eager to profit from the ruins of the Lordship. Thus was established the pattern on which successive governments based the conduct of their policy for the next two hundred and fifty years.

The lands of the forfeited Lordship were now relentlessly parcelled out and and granted to those friendly to the Crown. John MacIain of Ardnamurchan received lands in Islay and Jura; Stewart of Appin, Glencoe and Duror; and Lord Gordon, the Earl of Huntly's son, vast lands in Lochaber. The displaced chiefs of Clan Donald were summoned to appear and prove their charters to their lands. None were able to do so, and were accordingly deemed to have no right to the lands, which were thereupon apportioned to the King's friends. The result was inevitable, and the disinherited Islemen rose up once again in rebellion.

The young Donald Dubh had been named the heir to his father, Angus Og, who was deemed legitimate heir to John, the last Lord. Angus Og had been named and accepted as legitimate in the Act of Parliament of 1476, and Donald was now accepted by the Islesmen as the true heir to the Lordship and their natural leader. He was however still in prison on the Isle of Inchconnel in Loch Awe under the not too friendly eye of Argyll. The men of Glencoe rectified this by invading the heart of the Campbell country in what was noted at the time as a feat worthy of the Fianna of old. Donald Dubh was freed and at once raised the standard of revolt. He was accepted as the *de jure* Lord of the Isles by Torquil Macleod of Lewis, the Macleans, Camerons, Mackinnons, MacQuarries, MacNeils and others. According to the records of the Parliament of 1503, Donald also looked for aid to England and Ireland. But no help reached him from these quarters, and little is known about the revolt except that Donald got as far as Badenoch, which was laid waste with fire and sword.

The King realised the magnitude of the revolt against his authority and without delay took the strongest measures to quell the rebellion. A Parliament was convened at which Torquil MacLeod was declared rebel and all his estates forfeited to the Crown. Efforts were made to win over the other chiefs, but few paid heed to the King's advances. Accordingly Huntly, Lovat and Munro of Foulis were commissioned to bring the rebels to heel. They had no success, so a concerted effort by sea and land was planned. Letters were first sent to MacIain of Ardnamurchan, Maclean of Lochbuy, Macleod of Dunvegan, Ranald of Clanranald, MacNeil of Barra, Mackinnon, Macquarrie, and even Torquil of Lewis, informing them of the forfeiture of Maclean of Duart and Cameron of Lochiel for their alleged treason in supporting the rebellion. These chiefs were now offered a grant of half of their forfeited lands in return for their aid in apprehending the rebellious Donald Dubh and his associates. Delivery of the letters was entrusted to Argyll, Huntly and the Bishop of Ross. It is surprising to find Torquil Macleod, so recently declared traitor, amongst those to whom these overtures were being made, and it is likely that his name was included at the instigation of Argyll who hoped, even at this late hour, to win his son-in-law over to the side of law and order. There is no record of the fate of these letters, but the one clear thing that emerges is that no heed was paid to them by the rebel chiefs. In these circumstances there remained only one course open for the Government, and preparations were made to mount a massive expedition to the West and the Isles.

The Earl Marshal with Argyll was to invade from the south by way of Dumbarton, while Huntly with Crawford and Lovat undertook the northern part of the operation. Huntly asked for ships and artillery to reduce the strong fortresses of Strome and Eilean Donan. This aid does not seem to have been forthcoming. In the South, as the castles of Kintyre, Tarbert and Dunaverty had been in the King's hands ever since 1493, there was not much to do except to try to bring an elusive foe to a decisive battle. The terrain favoured the insurgents as they could move from isle to isle without their enemies being able easily to catch up with them. Not much is recorded about this expedition, but one can assume that no solid gains were made by the royal forces. If there had been any real success, it would surely have been recorded in the annals of the time.

In 1505 the King once more mounted another expedition which he himself

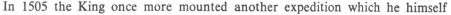

The Castle of Mingary in Ardnamurchan, frequently ~~ted~~ by James IV after the fall of the Lordship

intended to lead. Trouble in the South demanded his attention, however, and he had to leave the enterprise in other hands. This time he saw that an attack by sea was the best way to make progress against the Islesmen, and a naval force was despatched under Sir Andrew Wood of Largo and Robert Barton, able men who had distinguished themselves in repelling the incursions of the English fleets on the East coast. On land they were supported by forces under the Earl of Arran. The success of these operations disheartened the chiefs, and most of them were now inclined to make their peace with the King. Torquil Macleod alone stood out, probably knowing that he could expect little mercy from the outraged sovereign. Few details of this campaign exist, but it was obviously a success, as the arch-rebel, Donald Dubh, was made prisoner and lodged in Edinburgh Castle. Torquil had been obliged to hand Donald over to Maclean of Duart, who surrendered the fugitive when that chief himself gave in his submission. Torquil continued to hold out. He was again declared traitor and his extensive lands on the mainland in Coigeach and Assynt were given in life-rent to Mackay of Strathnaver in return for his services in the recent rebellion. Huntly pursued Torquil to his island fastness of Lewis, and took his castle of Stornoway. Torquil made good his escape and he does not appear ever to have been caught. If he had been, there is little doubt that records would have told us with some satisfaction that such a notable rebel and stout warrior had been dealt with. By the time the lands were restored to Torquil's family, he himself was no doubt dead, for it is extremely unlikely the King would ever have forgiven him. Nor would he, if alive, have stood by and allowed his estates to be given to his brother Malcolm, as indeed they were in 1511.

With the end of the rebellion, a period of comparative peace and order prevailed in the Highlands and Isles. The wise provisions enacted by the Parliament of 1503, which radically transformed the administration of justice in these regions, were in time productive of good results. The appointment of Argyll to the Sheriffship of Kintyre and the Southern Isles, and of the Earl of Huntly to that of Inverness and Dingwall, did much to extend the Royal authority in the North and West. Moreover, the King's expressed concern for the impartial dispensation of his justice was successful in attaching the Islesmen to his interest for the remainder of his reign, and it speaks much for his sagacity as a ruler that he was able to produce such a remarkable change in face of such adverse circumstances.

The chiefs of Clan Donald who had remained firm in their adherence to the Royal cause reaped the reward of their loyalty. We have already noted the grants made in 1498 to Ranald of Clanranald and MacIain of Ardnamurchan. During the remainder of his reign, although the Macdonald chieftains were allowed to retain possession of their lands without, however, any formal title, no further grants were made except to MacIain of Ardnamurchan whose obedience and good services to the King were now amply rewarded. After the revocation of the charters in 1498, MacIain had been granted extensive lands in Jura and Islay. In 1505 and again in 1506 these lands were confirmed to him together with lands in Ardnamurchan and Sunart, with the castles of Mingary and Dunnyveg. At the same time he was confirmed in the office of Bailie of the lands of Islay which he had formerly held under the Lord of the Isles. With these acquisitions MacIain had now become the most powerful chieftain of all Clan Donald.

The chief who came off worst of all was Alexander of Dunnyveg who, from the time of his father's death till the end of the reign, had to content himself with living on the lands in Antrim which his family had inherited from the Bisset heiress. Hugh, the Sleat historian, relates that MacIain of Ardnamurchan sent his two sons with a body of men to the Glens of Antrim to take him prisoner.

Alexander, son of the murdered John Cathanach, at once attacked and defeated the invaders, killing most of them including MacIain's two sons. During the fight the blacksmith of Islay deserted to the side of his rightful chief. Alexander promptly seized the enemy's boats and crossed to Islay, received the surrender of Dunnyveg from the Constable, and then besieged MacIain who had taken refuge on the island fort of Lochgorm. MacIain submitted on terms, one of which strangely enough was that Alexander undertook to marry his daughter, and he also agreed to surrender his lands in Islay. It is to the credit of Alexander that he did not immediately execute this inveterate enemy of his family.

The part played by the separate branches of Clan Donald during this eventful period may be noted more fully when we deal with each of them in subsequent chapters. Hugh of Sleat and his son John took no part in Donald Dubh's efforts to restore the Lordship, but Donald Gallach, third Chief of Sleat, played a prominent part in the insurrection. He was murdered by his bastard half-brother, Gilleasbuig Dubh, at Kishorn in 1506. Gilleasbuig was *de facto* head of the Sleat family until 1517 when he in turn was murdered by Donald Gruamach, son of Donald Gallach, assisted by Ranald, son of Donald Hearach, another of Gilleasbuig's victims.

The Clanranald seemed generally to be in favour with the King and continued thus at least until Donald Dubh escaped from his prison in Edinburgh Castle, when there is little doubt that they rallied round his standard.

The men of Glencoe, after their spectacular expedition to release their Lord from his prison on Inchconnel, would no doubt have rendered assistance in the revolt which followed, although they do not appear in the record of these events.

The brave Keppoch men continued their support of Donald Dubh unswervingly. Royal charters and King's favours did not interest them much, as we shall see from their history in a later chapter.

The Chief of Lochalsh was a minor at the time of the insurrection. After Sir Alexander's death at the hands of MacIain of Ardnamurchan, his three sons were taken to Edinburgh where they were brought up and educated under the supervision of the Royal household, no doubt in order to ensure their future attachment to the interests of their sovereign. The eldest, Donald Gallda—so called from his Lowland upbringing—was in high favour with the King, who gave him possession of his father's lands and is said to have knighted him on the field of Flodden.

Glengarry is not mentioned in the records of the period, but we may confidently assume that they allied themselves with their kinsfolk in support of Donald Dubh.

From this brief outline it is clear that all the branches of the Clan, with one exception, had joined in the attempt to restore the old order in the West. James IV's energetic administration of affairs, combined with the patience and moderation that characterised most of his efforts to restore order and good government, was successful in winning the loyalty and co-operation of the chiefs and produced a lull which lasted for the rest of his reign. The underlying discontent was contained by the power of the King's personality and, had he lived, it is possible that harmonious relations between the Crown and the clans might have been established at an early stage. Such a prospect was rendered remote by the character of the men to whom successive rulers entrusted the government of the Highlands and Isles. With Huntly in the North and Argyll in the South, two grasping and rapacious men whose excess of authority provided them with the means of satisfying their cupidity at the expense of the old Island vassals, peace could not be expected to continue for long in these regions.

Scarcely had the Highland chiefs returned from Flodden when Sir Donald Gallda raised his standard and was proclaimed Lord of the Isles, although he affirmed that he was claiming the Lordship on behalf of the unfortunate Donald Dubh. Donald Gruamach of Sleat, whose claim may have been at least as good, was also proposed, but the Islesmen were not so much concerned with strength of claims as with the leader most likely to accomplish the change in government they desired, and they accordingly rallied to Sir Donald of Lochalsh. Sir Donald's following included the Macleods of Lewis and Harris, Maclean of Duart, Alexander of Dunnyveg and Alexander of Glengarry who by his marriage to Sir Donald's sister was in due course to inherit the Lochalsh estates. With a large force Donald invaded Glen Urquhart and took the Castle, laying waste the land and carrying off a vast spoil. Maclean seized the royal castle of Cairnburgh in Mull, and Macleod of Harris took the Castle of Dunscaith in Skye, both of which were held for the new Lord. The Regent Albany with his Council at once ordered Argyll to attack Maclean and the other rebels in the South Isles. Mackenzie of Kintail and Munro of Foulis were asked to harass Sir Donald in the North, while the Chiefs of Lochiel and Mackintosh were appointed royal lieutenants in Lochaber. MacIain of Ardnamurchan was sent to treat with the less violent insurgents, offering bribes and remission for their crimes to those who were willing to submit. These measures proved successful in many cases, and the powerful influence of Argyll secured remission for Maclean of Duart and Macleod of Harris for their part in the seizure of Cairnburgh and Dunscaith. His support having thus been effectively undermined, Sir Donald had perforce to come to terms. It was agreed that outstanding disputes with MacIain of Ardnamurchan should be submitted to the decision of an impartial tribunal, and in August 1515 Sir Donald and the Regent were reconciled.

In the light of the government's lenient treatment of Sir Donald, it is difficult to account for the course of conduct on which he now embarked. Apparently not satisfied with the outcome of his dispute with MacIain of Ardnamurchan, he saw in the rebellion of Lord Home a favourable opportunity for again raising his standard and prosecuting designs which soon became suspect even to his foremost supporters. Having raised a considerable body of men, he invaded Ardnamurchan and seized the Castle of Mingary, which he then burned to the ground. Not content with the expulsion of MacIain from his domain, he proceeded to lay waste the whole district with fire and sword. Lachlan Maclean of Duart and Alexander Macleod of Dunvegan, suspecting that Donald's excesses were inspired by motives of personal vengeance against the inhabitants no less than against MacIain himself, and moreover that his aim was now directed to the restoration of the Lordship in his own person, at length resolved to put an end to his reckless actions and hand him over to the government. Warned of their design, however, Sir Donald made his escape, but his two brothers were seized by Maclean and taken to Edinburgh where they were placed on trial and executed.

This act by an erstwhile member of the Lordship is severely criticised by the Maclean seanachie in the history of his own Clan. Lachlan Cattanach, who succeeded to the chiefship in 1513, was a very despicable character, as the seanachie's account shows:

> The death of the brave Hector Odhar introduces us to the name of one, in writing of whom I could wish the pen were in other hands than those of a Maclean; but as I have set out avowedly with the purpose of giving a faithful record of our race, I shall certainly "nothing extenuate." Lachlan Cattanach

succeeded his father in the year 1513: this chief, whose natural violence of temper and neglected education led to acts of the most savage cruelty, was altogether such a character as to make one regret that the noble line of Duart's lords had ever been tarnished by his being of their number.

Lachlan Maclean of Duart and Alexander Macleod of Dunvegan now offered their services to the Regent in the campaign against Donald Gallda. They sent in petitions asking pardon for their offences in aiding the rebels, and further asked for grants of lands in Mull, Tiree and Skye in consideration of their future services, adding a demand that Sir Donald be forfeited of all his lands to ensure the peace of the Isles. At the same time Argyll asked for and received a commission to act as the deputy of the Regent and Council in the West and the Isles with powers to grant remissions and find security for the payment of Crown dues in those regions. But "Sir Donald of the Ilis his brethir and Clan and Clan-donale" were expressly excluded from any such remission. This three year commission granted to Argyll ordered him to "persew Donald of the Ilis and expell him" from the Isles, and to secure hostages from those who continued to support him. There is no record of any success attending Argyll's efforts. Indeed, Sir Donald once more resumed his claim, and with the aid of Alexander of Dunnyveg and the Macleods of Lewis and Raasay he again attacked his arch-enemy MacIain. In the bloody battle of Creag-an-Airgid, near Kilchoan, he utterly defeated MacIain, killing him and his two sons, Angus and Iain Sunartach. This success brought more support to his standard, and Donald was again proclaimed Lord of the Isles.

The Regent and Council were dismayed and instituted measures to have the rebel forfeited in Parliament for treason. While these preparations were going on, however, the restless Chief died, according to MacVurich in the Castle of Cairnburgh on the west of Mull, but according to the Sleat historian at Teinlipeil in Tiree. A stone on the Isle of Finlaggan in Islay is thought by some to mark his grave, although the inscription is not quite accurate. It reads *Donaldus Filius Patrici Celestini*. As we know of no son of Celestine of Lochalsh named Patrick, one interpretation is given as "Donald son of the noble Celestine," but then Donald was the grandson, and not the son, of Celestine. The inscription is now nearly destroyed by vandals but Graham in his *Carved Stones of Islay* has preserved it on record.

Sir Donald's career, extraordinary even in the annals of Clan Donald, was both short and spectacular. Brought up at Court, knighted by the King he followed to Flodden, resolute in his efforts to restore the fallen Lordship, he stands out as a remarkable man, single-minded in his ambition to uphold the honour of his race and family. With his death in 1519 the House of Lochalsh ended. He never married. His brothers also died without issue, and his sister Margaret carried what remained of the estates to the Glengarry family by her marriage with Alexander, 6th of that line.

Sir Donald Gallda's death, and the continued imprisonment of Donald Dubh, left the Islanders for the time being without a natural leader and for some years a state of comparative peace and order continued in the West. The most striking feature in the history of this period is the rapid advance of the power and influence of the House of Argyll. The fall of the Lordship furnished this family with the opportunity to use their position as heads of a powerful clan and highly favoured courtiers to promote their political and territorial interests at the expense particularly of the vassals of the Isles. We have seen that in 1517 Argyll was given a royal commission as Lieutenant of the Isles, an office possessing almost regal authority in a sphere in which the King's writ seldom ran. With his brother Sir John Campbell of Cawdor and Archibald Campbell of Skipness, Argyll began to extend his power in the first instance by the acquisition of dormant claims and Bonds of Manrent followed by other devious measures in the ruthless pursuit of his family's aggrandisement.

Bonds of Manrent engaged the vassal to provide certain services to the superior in exchange for protection, and were intended to attach isolated clans to a House loyal to the Crown. In the Western Highlands by far the greatest number of these Bonds were entered into with Argyll or members of his family as superiors. The Chief of Glengarry gave a bond of manrent to Argyll, Donald Gruamach, 4th Chief of Sleat, gave a similar bond to Sir John Campbell of Cawdor. In 1520 Dugall, Chief of the Clanranald, gave a bond to Cawdor, confirmed later by his successor, Alexander. In the same year Alexander of Dunnyveg gave a similar bond to Cawdor. By entering into these engagements, the chiefs became virtual vassals, in the feudal sense, of a Campbell superior. It is not to be thought that they were contented and loyal vassals. They simply found themselves compelled by their circumstances to cultivate the goodwill of powerful men who were eager to assume the functions and exploit the position left vacant by the forfeiture of the Lordship.

During the young King's minority numerous grants of land were made to powerful individuals whose interest the Regent wished to attach to his party. The resulting loss of revenue led to the impoverishment of the Royal estate, the undermining of the machinery of justice and consequent widespread disorder in the land. In 1528, at the age of sixteen, James succeeded in escaping from the domination of the Regent Angus and assumed control of the government. Resolved to restore some of the revenues and to strengthen the authority of the Crown in the most effective manner, the young King and his Council as a first step revoked all the grants of land which had been made during his minority, and further provided that no future grants should be bestowed in the West Highlands and Isles without the sanction of the Council and the Earl of Argyll, the King's Lieutenant in the Isles.

This revocation, equitable as it may appear from a national standpoint, was followed by considerable discontent amongst the Western clans whose confidence in the government it did nothing to restore. A more or less direct consequence of the reversal of the government's policy is to be found in the disturbances which broke out in the Isle of Skye.

Hugh of Sleat had held his lands of Trotternish, Sleat and North Uist under charter from his brother John, Earl of Ross, in 1469. At that time Skye lay within the Earldom of Ross. This charter was confirmed by the Crown in 1495. Hugh's ineffectual son John, on the death of his father in 1498, resigned all these lands in favour of Alan, 4th of Clanranald. Donald Gruamach of Sleat, a strong chief, paid no attention to this claim, and Clanranald were unable to take possession. Later when the Regent conveyed the lands to Macleod, Donald Gruamach with the help of his brother-in-law, Torquil of Lewis, expelled Macleod from Trotternish and held Sleat and North Uist by force of arms. Although the grant of the lands to Macleod had been made during the King's minority, and was later revoked with so many others when the King came of age, nothing positive was done to restore them to their rightful owner. Macleod naturally continued to maintain that he had a legal right to Trotternish, and this quarrel was a festering sore between these two clans for many years to come. It would seem that the Crown regarded the Sleat family as strong potential claimants to the defunct Lordship, and wished to limit their territorial expansion in order the more effectively to frustrate a future attempt on their part to revive the Island principality. Their situation is representative of the general conditions of this period when the powerful influence of the Crown is employed to withhold from them their patrimonial rights and, like their kinsmen of Keppoch, they are compelled to hold their lands by the most ancient of all instruments of tenure, the power of their strong right arms.

These troubles in the North were matched by similar disquiet in the South. Alexander of Dunnyveg, Chief of Clann Iain Mhoir, son of the murdered John Cathanach, was a worthy successor to his warlike father and grandfather. He was driven to rebellion against the Crown in 1528 when the King revoked the grants given during his minority. Alexander had been granted Crown lands in Islay and elsewhere in addition to the 60 merklands already owned by his family. As noted earlier, the Argyll family gained some hold on many lands during the Regency by bonds of manrent. One such bond between Sir John Campbell of Cawdor and Alexander of Dunnyveg concerned some lands in Islay, Jura and Colonsay, and was to run for five years. Before the expiry of this period Cawdor appears to have made an unprovoked assault on Colonsay, and although a remission was granted by the Crown for having laid waste the lands, relations between Cawdor and Dunnyveg naturally remained very strained. It is probable that in 1528 Cawdor seized the opportunity provided by the revocation of the grants to enforce his claims on the lands of Colonsay and thus drove Alexander and his followers into open insurrection.

In this rebellion Alexander was joined by the Macleans of Duart whose long-standing friendship with the Macdonalds of Islay was re-inforced on this occasion by the prospect of avenging the insult offered to their clan by the murder of their late though unlamented chief at the hands of the Campbells. In 1529, aided by the Macdonalds of Largie, the two clans fell upon the Campbell lands of Roseneath, Lennox and Craignish which they ravaged with fire and sword. The Campbells retaliated and, selecting the Macleans as their target, attacked and harried their possessions in Coll, Tiree and Morvern. This was a patent act of private vengeance by the Campbells and not the disciplinary or punitive legal action that might be officially countenanced by the holder of the office of the King's Lieutenant in the Isles.

In the light of these proceedings it is somewhat surprising to find Campbell of Cawdor, on behalf of his brother the Earl of Argyll, self-righteously coming forward and presenting proposals to the Government for the restoration and maintenance of order in the West. These proposals suggested the assembly at Lochranza in Arran of an expeditionary force composed of levies from Dumbarton, Renfrew, Carrick, Kyle and Cunningham—all districts, be it noted, whose inhabitants might be most favourably disposed to the objects of such an expedition. The whole force was to be at the service of Argyll and employed by him for the reduction of the King's rebellious subjects in the Isles.

The proposals were considered, but not endorsed by the Council, some of whose members were beginning to question the Argyll family's professions of zeal for the service of the Crown. Many perceived the danger that the office of Lieutenant of the Isles might well be used by unscrupulous hands to extend the power and influence of a single ambitious family which thus would pose as great a problem to the central government as the ancient Lordship had presented in the past.

Instead of acting on the Campbell proposals, the Council decided on the wiser and more pacific course of sending the herald Robert Hart to treat with Dunnyveg and the Western chiefs. His mission was to order Alexander of Dunnyveg "and his complices" to disband their forces under pain of treason. Upon their compliance Alexander was to be offered safe conduct to come before the King and state his grievances in person, provide pledges for his future conduct and for the payment of rents and dues of such lands as the King might be pleased to grant to him.

Whether because of the obduracy of the chiefs or duplicity on the part of Argyll, the result of the negotiations failed to satisfy the Council and directions were thereupon given to Argyll to proceed to the Isles and "persew the said Alester and all utheris inobedient liegis" until they were reduced to obedience to the laws of the realm. Argyll was furnished with a roll of all the tenants of the Isles who were to be summoned to the King's presence "to commune with His Majesty upon good rule in the Isles," and under pain of treason were prohibited from rendering aid to the rebels or engaging with them in any offensive action. The Islesmen who obeyed the King's summons were offered a safe conduct for a period before and after their visit to the King, and as an additional assurance of protection and good faith hostages were to be taken from the Earl of Argyll. From a list which included the names of the Campbell Chiefs of Glenorchy, Auchinbreck, and Skipnish, two were to be selected for confinement in Edinburgh Castle until the Islanders had returned safely home.

By the same decree most of the fighting men of the Lowlands were summoned to meet the King at Ayr, with provisions for forty days to accompany him to the Isles. The calling out of these levies was, however, delayed as the King and his Council continued to entertain hopes of a peaceful solution, and a further postponement was caused by the illness and death of the Earl of Argyll. The new Earl inherited all the honours and offices held by his father, including the Lieutenancy of the Isles, and forthwith undertook to discharge the duties of his commission faithfully, promising to exact from the Islanders the punctual payment of all lawful dues and to destroy all those who opposed his measures to restore peace and order. It was not till some months later, in the early spring of 1531, that it was decided to move against the Islanders. In addition to the forces assembling at Ayr under Argyll, the men of the northern regions were mustered under the Earl of Moray, the King's Lieutenant in the North, who was to proceed to Kintail and there await the King's orders. Here we may detect a significant departure from the methods hitherto adopted by the government in its policy towards the Isles. Both these operations, the one under Argyll in the South and the other under Moray in the North, were to be conducted under the personal supervision of the King. It marked the beginning of that royal policy, pursued by James for the rest of his reign, by which he was determined to make the personal acquaintance of the warlike chiefs who had so long troubled the state and thus inspire them with that sense of loyalty to his House which they were to express in such full measure to the last of his line.

In the meantime, and in furtherance of the King's new line of policy, the rebel chiefs continued to be cited to the Royal presence. The Clan Donald chiefs listed in the summons of 28th April included Alexander of Dunnyveg, Donald Gruamach of Sleat, John "Moidartach" of Clanranald, Alexander MacIain of Ardnamurchan, Alasdair of Glengarry and Donald of Largie. Impressed no less by the King's sincere desire to treat directly with him on a personal basis than by the extent of the military operation being prepared, and having received assurances of safe conduct for himself and his retinue, the Chief of Dunnyveg came to the King at Stirling and on 7th June received the royal pardon. The conditions on which he was restored to royal favour recognised his influence amongst the Islesmen and bound him to assist the government in the maintenance of law and order in Kintyre and the South Isles. Many other Island vassals gave in their submission at the same time and under conditions which reflected the King's genuine desire to establish an orderly relationship with them.

The Royal intervention had thus secured the voluntary submission of the principal chiefs without resorting to extreme and costly military action. Such a successful vindication of his policy served to add to the growing suspicion, long held by some members of his Council and now harboured by the King himself, that Argyll's commission as Lieutenant of the Isles was being used as an instrument for his personal aggrandisement, and that much of the trouble in the Isles was being fomented to secure forfeitures of lands from which his family would be most likely to benefit. This suspicion tended to be strongly confirmed when Argyll, frustrated by the submission of Alexander of Dunnyveg and Maclean of Duart, cast around for some pretext which would cause them to break the peace. Failing to provoke these two chieftains, Argyll had recourse to the incident of the combined raid of 1529 which he used to present a complaint to the Council accusing them of various violent crimes against him and his followers.

Alexander of Dunnyveg promptly appeared to answer these charges. After fruitlessly waiting for his accuser to present himself, Alexander submitted to the Council a written statement remarkable for its honesty and candour, and for its indictment of Argyll and the barrier his power had erected between the King and his Island subjects. The document is quoted here in full because of the light it casts on the history of the period, and in particular for the significance it bears in the history of the Clan Donald:

STATEMENT BY ALEXANDER OF DUNNYVEG ANENT CERTAIN COMPLAINTS PREFERRED AGAINST HIM BY THE EARL OF ARGYLE

In presence of the Lords of Council compeared Alexander John Cathanachson, and gave in the articles underwritten, and desired the same to be put in the books of Council; of the which the tenor follows: — My Lords of Council, unto your Lordships huimlie menis and schawis I, your servitor Alexander John Cathanachson, that quhar lately Archd. Earl of Argyle of verray proven malice and envy gave in ane bill of complaint of me to your Lordships, alleging that I had done divers and sundry great faults to him and his friends, which is not of verities; for the which your Lordships commanded me by ane maiser to remain in this town to answer to his complaints. And I have remained here continually these 13 days last by past daily to answer to his said bill; and because he perfectly knows that his narration is not nor may not be proved of verities, he absents himself and bydis away and will not come to follow the same. And since so is that that his narration is all wrong and feynyeit made upon me without any fault of very malice as said is as manifestly appears, because he will not come to pursue and verify the same, I answer to the points of his bill in this wise—In the first, I understand that no person has jurisdiction of the Lordship of the Isles but my master the King's grace alanerly. And insafer as his highness gave command and power to my sympilnes at my first incoming to his grace at Stirling, I have obeyed and done his highness's commands in all points and fulfilled the tenor of all his acts made in Stirling in every point as I was commanded. And gif it please his grace to command me to give his malis and duties of his lands and Lordship of the Isles to any person, the same shall be done thankfully after my power. And in sa fer as the said Earl alleged that I did wrong in intromitting and uptaking of the malis and dewities of the Isles, he failyeit thairin, because I did nothing in that behalf but as I was commanded by the King's grace, my master.

Further, my Lords, I at your Lordships' command has remained in this town thir days last by past ready to answer to the said Earl in anything he had to lay to my charge to my great cost and expense. He as I am informed is past in the Isles with all the folks that he may get and with all the men that the Earl of Murray may cause pass with him for heirschip and destruction of the King's lands of the Isles and for slaughter of his poor lieges dwelling therein; which as I trust is done without his grace's advice, license, authority or consent. And if so be the whole fault is made to his highness considering both the land and the men and the inhabitants thereof are his own; and well it is to be presumed that his grace would give no command to destroy his own men and lands. And if the King's grace my sovereign Lord and Master will give power or command to me or any other gentleman of the Isles to come to his highness to pass in England in oisting or any other part in the mainland within this realm, I shall make good we shall bring more good fighting men to do his grace honour, pleasure, and service than the said Earl shall do.

And, if the said Earl will contempne the King's grace's authority his highness giving command to me and his poor lieges of the Isles, we shall cause compel the said Earl to dwell in any other part of Scotland nor Argyle, where the King's grace may get resoun of him.

And further, there is no person in the Isles that has offended to the said Earl or any others in the Lowlands but I shall cause him to come to the King's grace to underly his laws and to please his highness and the party be ressoun, suchlike as other Lowland men does, the brokynes and heirschip of the Isles being considered made by the said Earls father, the Knight of Calder, and Gillespy Bane his brother.

And mairattour, what the King's grace and your Lordship will command to me to do for his highness honour and weal of his realm the same shall be done with all diligence of my power without my dissimulation.

And further, my Lords, I have fulfilled your lordships' command and bidden aye in this town and kept the day that your Lordships assigned to me to answer to the said Earl's complaint and that he came not to follow the same, that ye will advertise the King's grace thereof, and of my answer to his complaint, and give command to the Clerk of Council to subscribe the copy of my answer here present to be sent to the King's grace for information to his highness of the veritie. And your answer humbly I beseech.

The King seems to have been deeply struck by Alexander's indictment, and with characteristic sense of justice caused a minute enquiry to be made into its leading allegations, as well as into the whole question of the Argyll policy in the Isles. The result was a complete vindication of Alexander of Dunnyveg. It was clearly brought out that the policy of the Argyll family in the Isles had been animated by motives of private interest rather than by zeal for the peace and welfare of His Majesty's lieges in that part of his dominions, and that they were largely to blame for fomenting much of the turbulence and disaffection which had arisen within recent years. Still further it was brought out that Argyll's handling of the Crown rentals was not so advantageous to the royal revenues as with strictly honest accounting it should have been. The Earl was thrown into prison, and although his liberation soon followed, he was discredited and disgraced, while the public offices he filled were all taken from him, and some of them bestowed upon Alexander of Dunnyveg, who continued for the rest of his life to receive numerous marks of royal favour. From the Clan Donald point of view, the pleasing but unwonted spectacle is now witnessed of the head of a great branch of the Family of the Isles raised high in the confidence of the Crown, while the Chief of the Clan Campbell has to retire into obscurity and disrepute.

From 1532 down to 1538 the history of the Isles appears to have been quiet and uneventful; at anyrate the surviving records of the age have little to say regarding the history of the Macdonald Family, a clear vindication of the methods of governing the Highlands adopted by James v and his advisers. The problem of the Hebridean clans, especially, proved not hopelessly insoluble when approached in a spirit of generosity and firmness; while, looked at through Argyle spectacles, and treated in the tortuous methods of Argyle policy, it was a standing menace to the peace of Scotland.

In 1539, however, the Isle of Skye and the western border of Ross-shire became the scene of a fresh attempt to restore the Lordship of the Isles. One of the most remarkable features of the history of this period is the almost unanimous support that the various claimants to the Lordship received from the Western clans. Although Donald Dubh was still regarded as the rightful heir he was, and was likely to continue, a closely guarded prisoner in Edinburgh, and failing him the one family that could justly claim the heritage was now represented by Donald Gorm, the Chief of Sleat and son of Donald Gruamach, an earlier aspirant who had striven valiantly to protect and extend the patrimony of Clan Uisdein.

Donald Gorm was supported by most of the chiefs, and especially by the Macleods of Lewis with whom his family had long been united in bonds of friendship and marriage. He opened his campaign by regaining the district of Trotternish in Skye from Macleod of Dunvegan who had succeeded in seizing it on a previous occasion. He thereupon turned his attention to the mainland of Ross and laid siege to the Castle of Eilean Donan, at that time in the

The Castle of Eilean Donan, at the siege of which Donald Gorm met his death in 1539

possession of the Mackenzies who not only had assisted Macleod of Dunvegan in past attempts to occupy Trotternish, but were now well known to be actively opposed to the restitution of the Lordship. In the course of the siege, however, Donald Gorm was killed by an arrow, and the rebellion collapsed. The incident has been embellished by the Mackenzie seanachies in much the same way as their account of the Battle of Park. Their story is that there were only three men in the Castle during the siege—the Governor, the Watchman and one Duncan Macrae—and they are supposed to have successfully withstood the onslaught of fifty boat-loads of warriors until Donald Gorm approached too near the battlements and received the wound from which he later bled to death on the spot ever since known as *Larach Tighe MhicDhomhnaill* (the site of Macdonald's house). That Donald Gorm's followers did not retire, as alleged by the seanachies, is amply attested by authentic documents of the time which record the capture and burning of the Castle, the destruction of Mackenzie's fleet of galleys, and the ravaging of the surrounding countryside.

Donald Gorm's insurrection, which but for his death might have reached serious proportions, provided ample proof of the continuing depth of feeling amongst the clans for the revival of the Lordship. In the following year, therefore, the King made preparations on a formidable scale for an expedition to the Isles that he hoped would effectively put an end to similar attempts in the future. An armada of twelve ships was fitted out with all the necessary weapons of war and set sail from Leith in the early summer. Six of the ships were occupied by the King and the troops under his special command, three were assigned to Cardinal Beaton and the Earls of Huntly and Arran, each of them accompanied by a strong body of men, and the remaining three carried supplies for the whole force. Touching at several places on its way round the north of Scotland, the expedition eventually reached Trotternish and dropped anchor at Portree, so called after this royal visit. Here a number of the Western chiefs had assembled to meet their sovereign, amongst them John of Moidart, the proudly independent Captain of Clanranald, Archibald the Clerk, acting as Captain of Sleat on behalf of his young nephew Donald Gormson, Alexander of Glengarry and Macleod of Dunvegan. John of Moidart and Macleod of Dunvegan were obliged to accompany the King on his southward voyage, but it is interesting to note that the head of the family responsible for the recent insurrection was left in peace and in the following year was granted the royal pardon for the excesses committed in the course of that campaign.

Proceeding south the King called at Kintail, where he met the Chief of the Mackenzies, and in his further progress through the Isles took on board Hector Maclean of Duart and James Macdonald of Dunnyveg. Landing at Dumbarton he sent the fleet, with the captive chiefs still on board, back to Leith. Those chiefs who were considered the most dangerous were lodged in Edinburgh Castle as hostages for the good behaviour of their clansmen. Several of them were released after a short period after having provided sureties for their future conduct, but the most turbulent of them remained in confinement until some time after the King's tragic death. As a further assertion and confirmation of the royal authority the whole of the Isles were formally re-annexed to the Crown and future grants of lands were henceforth to be made as rewards for public service or as inducements to keep the peace. Garrisons commanded by men of proved loyalty were placed in the most important Island fortresses, including those of Dunnyveg in Islay and Dunaverty in Kintyre. The effect of these measures to all appearances was to give the finishing blow to future attempts to restore the Lordship, and to introduce a period of unaccustomed peace which, had the King lived, held the promise of lasting stability in the Isles and the West.

This prospect was destroyed as a result of the King's death and the confusion into which the country was plunged by the conflicting interests of powerful personalities intent on pursuing their selfish and unpatriotic aims without regard for the security of the State. There was an English party and a French party, the former led by the Regent Arran, a man of weak and vacillating character, the latter by Cardinal Beaton, able and ruthless in his opposition to the progress of the Reformation and hostility to Henry of England's designs upon the young Queen and the independence of the country. The influence of the Earl of Angus and the Douglases, returned by Henry with the more important prisoners captured at Solway Moss, was used to secure the Regent's attachment to the English King's policy of the eventual absorption of the Scottish State by a marriage between his son and the infant Queen. Beaton retaliated by recalling the Earl of Lennox, a man of royal Stewart blood, and with the object of undermining Arran's position proposed him for the Regency in his place. The alarm occasioned by this action, and the simultaneous disclosure of Henry's real designs, led to Arran's coalition with the Cardinal and to the abandonment of the marriage treaty. Now that the Cardinal had achieved his purpose, he had no further use for Lennox who thereupon switched his allegiance from the French to the English party and with the Earl of Glencairn intercepted and seized a French shipment of stores and money intended for employment in the French interest. From then on Lennox was to play a prominent rôle in the troubles that afflicted the Western Highlands.

In 1543, and in the midst of these intrigues in the Scottish State, Donald Dubh succeeded in making his escape from Edinburgh Castle where he had been incarcerated since the time of his first rebellion forty years before. At that time he had been proclaimed Lord of the Isles with all the traditional rites and ceremonies. Now as then he was accepted with enthusiasm by his own clan and by many other vassals of the old Lordship. He also revived his claim to the Earldom of Ross, and immediately began his preparations to expel both Argyll and Huntly from the possessions they had acquired in his patrimony. Both these noblemen had largely kept aside from the intrigue and political corruption that marked the centre of government only because their interests were bound up with the maintenance of the established order, but the extent of these interests and the envy and jealousy they aroused now became factors which seemed likely to lend powerful assistance to the prospects of Donald Dubh.

The most powerful of the Highland chiefs, whose presence was essential to the success of the rebellion, were still prisoners in Edinburgh Castle. Foremost among them was John of Moidart who, at the instigation of the Earl of Glencairn, was released with the others by the Regent for no apparent reason other than to embarrass Argyll and Huntly by strengthening the forces arrayed against them under the new Lord of the Isles. The liberation of the chiefs was immediately followed by the invasion and ravaging of the territories of Argyll, in which Donald Dubh had the unanimous support of the Island chiefs with the sole exception of James of Dunnyveg, whose attitude no doubt was influenced not only by his matrimonial connection with Argyll, but also by his family's long and friendly relationship with the late King's Government. In the North also Huntly suffered constant harassment at the hands of John of Moidart whose victory at the noted battle of Blar-na-leine not only marked the successful outcome of his feud with Lovat but was also an important factor in a sustained diversion in support of Donald Dubh.

On his conversion from the English interest, the Regent Arran realised the magnitude of his error in releasing the Island chiefs and made overtures to Donald Dubh with the object of securing his submission on the most favourable terms. In this he was unsuccessful, however, and he was prevented from taking active measures against Donald because of the rapidly deteriorating relations between the English and Scottish governments. In August 1544 an English expedition under the command of the Earl of Lennox attacked and ravaged the islands of Bute and Arran, but was thwarted in his attempt to capture Dumbarton by the patriotic action of the Governor. After further ineffectual attacks on Argyll and the districts of Kintyre, Kyle and Carrick, Lennox retired to England to prepare for an invasion in force which the traitorous Scottish Lords now invited Henry to mount against their country. Negotiations were opened with Donald Dubh to secure his support, and when news of these reached the ears of the government a proclamation was issued against "Donald, alleging himself of the Isles," condemning his "invasions" carried out with English assistance, calling upon him and his followers to desist from their treasonable conduct, and threatening him with utter ruin and destruction if he continued obdurate. No attention was paid to this proclamation, and the processes for treason which immediately followed served only to expedite the negotiations which were to cement the alliance between the Lord of the Isles and the English King.

On 23rd July 1545 a commission was granted by Donald "Lord of ye Ilis and Erll of Roiss," with the consent of his "barronis and counsaill of ye Ilis," to two plenipotentiaries for assisting the Earl of Lennox to complete negotiations with the English King. This document, drawn up on the Island of Eigg, has an additional interest in the full list it contains of the Island vassals, all of whom signed with their hands "at ye pen" (as was not unusual at the time, none of the seventeen chiefs could write his name). The Council of the Lord of the Isles, here constituted in the traditional manner, was composed of the following members: Hector Maclean of Duart, John of Moidart, Ruairi Macleod of Lewis, Alexander Macleod of Dunvegan, Maclaine of Lochbuie, Maclean of Torloisk, Archibald of Sleat (representing the young chief), MacIain of Ardnamurchan, Maclean of Coll, MacNeil of Barra, Mackinnon of Strath, MacQuarrie of Ulva, Maclean of Ardgour, Alexander of Glengarry, Angus of Knoydart, Maclean of Kingairloch, and Angus, brother of James of Dunnyveg. The solidarity presented by such an imposing array of chiefs is sufficient evidence of the strong attachment borne by the Islesmen to the ideals of the old Lordship and of their determination to restore it to its former position of political and territorial power. The total unity of the Island chiefs is confirmed by the presence of Angus of Dunnyveg who, although his brother still stands aside, was undoubtedly accompanied by his complement of fighting clansmen. Even the inveterate hatred of the chief of Ardnamurchan seems to have dissolved in a new-found loyalty and devotion to the aspirations of his fellow-chiefs.

The Commissioners appointed to treat with the English King were John of Moidart's brother Roderick, Dean of Morvern and Bishop-designate of the Isles, and Patrick Maclean, brother of Maclean of Duart, described as Bailie of Iona and Justice Clerk of the Isles. The clerical work of the Council in all its proceedings bears the stamp of these two skilled and highly competent men. A week after their appointment, Donald and his Island Council had moved to Knockfergus in Ireland with a fleet of 180 galleys and 4000 men, the composition of which is described in despatches to Henry as being "three thousand of them very tall men, clothed for the most part in habergeons of mail, armed with long swords and long bows, but with few guns: the other thousand, tall mariners, that rowed in the galleys." The meeting of the Council was held in the Monastery of Greyfriars at Knockfergus and was attended by Patrick Colquhoun and

Walter Macfarlane, Commissioners of the Earl of Lennox, and also, it is interesting to note, by John Carswell, later to be the first Protestant Bishop of the Isles and author of the Gaelic prayer-book. It is clear from Donald's correspondence with the English King that he had already received from that monarch a sum of 1000 crowns with the promise of an annual pension of 2000 crowns for his continued allegiance. Articles were now drawn up defining the conditions of the alliance and these, with some modifications introduced by Lennox, were approved by the Council and despatched by the hands of the Commissioners to the English Court. The gist of the proposals was as follows:

1. Lennox was to be sent to Scotland with an army "for settin fast of the Kingis enemys."

2. The Lord of the Isles and Earl of Ross undertook to destroy "the tane half" of Scotland and compel its submission to Henry and his "subject" Lennox.

3. Henry was to make no "aggreance" with Scotland, and especially with the Earls of Argyll and Huntly, without the consent of Donald and his "barronis" of the Isles.

4. Donald was to have an annual pension of 2000 crowns for past and future services, and security in the enjoyment of his possessions.

5. Donald undertook to serve Lennox with 8000 men, of whom 4000 were already in Ireland and the other 4000 in Scotland facing Argyll and Huntly. Henry was to pay the wages of 3000 men, and 5000 were to serve under Lennox without wages, for which presumably Donald himself was to be responsible.

There follows a catalogue of offences committed in the past by Argyll and Huntly against the men of the Isles, the hanging, beheading, imprisonment and destruction of many of their kin, and the long confinement of the Lord of the Isles himself "from his mother's womb, and not released by their will but now lately by the grace of God." Considerable astuteness is shown not only in emphasising the advantages to Henry of keeping Argyll and Huntly's forces engaged and thus preventing them from taking part in the defence of the kingdom, but also in the appeal to the King's vanity suggesting that any delay might be interpreted by the French as an indication of weakness caused by his war against their country.

On 4th September 1545 agreement was reached with Henry on the basis of these proposals, and the Commissioners returned to Knockfergus bearing with them a personal letter from Henry to Donald expressing his satisfaction with the outcome of the negotiations and adjuring him now "to proceed like a noble man" to revenge the dishonours committed by their common enemies. Another letter in similar terms was addressed to Hector Maclean of Duart whose leading part in all the proceedings would seem to suggest that he had resumed his hereditary rôle of Steward of the Isles, a position for which his outstanding ability in war and council well qualified him.

In accordance with the agreement, the Earl of Lennox was to lead the expedition against the West of Scotland with Donald's 8000 men and a force of 2000 Irish levies under the Earl of Ormond. Before preparations were completed, however, he was ordered to England to concert plans with the Earl of Hertford who was to lead the invasion from that country. Lennox's prolonged absence proved fatal. The Island forces became disheartened as a result of the continued inaction, and Donald's impatience with Lennox together with his increasing concern for his interests in Scotland, eventually prompted him to withdraw his army to the Isles. The arrival of Henry's gold shortly thereafter, and its reputedly unfair distribution by Maclean of Duart, added to the discontent and caused serious dissension which led to the break-up of the army. This was the situation which confronted Lennox when at length he returned to Ireland. He nevertheless decided to make a descent upon Scotland as soon as the Irish levies were ready, and therefore despatched Patrick Colquhoun to secure the Lord of the Isles' support with whatever force he was still able to muster. Records are silent concerning the result of Colquhoun's mission, and it is uncertain if Island forces accompanied Lennox when he set out from Dublin on 17th November with the capture of Dumbarton as his main objective. The expedition appears to have been abandoned when news came that the Castle had fallen into the hands of the Regent, and the records of the period cast no light on Lennox's subsequent activities. It seems certain, however, that Donald Dubh returned to Ireland in the hope of raising fresh forces to pursue his original design, and that on the way to Dublin he died of a fever in Drogheda.

Thus ended the direct line of the Lords of the Isles in the person of one who had spent a lifetime in confinement and yet in two brief periods of freedom proved himself possessed of the courage and intrepidity of his forefathers, capable of surmounting misfortune and preserving his spirit unbroken in face of prolonged injustice and adversity. With him ended all serious attempts to restore the Lordship. It has been said that Donald Dubh, whose only son was illegitimate, named James Macdonald of Dunnyveg as his successor since the natural heir, the young Chief of Sleat, was a minor and therefore considered incapable of providing the mature and able leadership essential to the success of any future attempt to recover the ancient heritage. Dunnyveg was elected in due course, but mainly by the voice of the cadet branches of the Clan, and his position was rendered untenable by the opposition of the older vassals of the Lordship, including such powerful families as the Macleans and the Macleods of Lewis and of Harris, many of whom wished to disown the English alliance and make their peace with the Regent. Nevertheless in February 1546 James of Dunnyveg attempted to revive the English alliance by despatching an envoy to Henry with proposals for joining Lennox with his forces on the same terms and conditions as Henry had offered to Donald Dubh. To this Henry appears to have made no reply, no doubt because he had lost confidence in the Islanders' ability to provide the sustained action he needed for the success of his policies. James of Dunnyveg decided to abandon his claim and, fortunate to escape the punishment he had earned, once again became a loyal and obedient subject.

There is no record of further attempts to restore the Lordship. A common devotion to the ideals it represented in the past had served more than any other circumstance to unite the clans in a single purpose, and Donald Dubh's rebellion is the last occasion on which we find the vassals of the Lordship almost totally combined to achieve a common objective. Once this bond of unity was broken, the peace of the Highlands became even more disturbed when clan after clan directed its energies towards the protection of its own interests and the extension of its power at the expense of its neighbours, thus creating the conditions which Argyll and Huntly as royal lieutenants adroitly and ruthlessly used to expand the influence and territorial possessions of their families.

13

The Nature of the Lordship

AT THIS POINT in our history, when we have seen the end of the Lordship and the efforts made to revive it, it may be appropriate to consider the nature of that institution, and the social and economic conditions which governed its survival and provided its strength. In earlier chapters we have noted the continuing conflict of Gael against Saxon and Norman, with the patriarchal and tribal system of the Gael constantly resisting the inroads of feudalism. The latter, coupled with a process of Saxonising and Normanising, had been growing in strength ever since Queen Margaret used her influence over her husband to replace the Gaelic tongue with English as the language of the Court, and to promote the suppression of the old Celtic Church in favour of the more highly organised Roman Catholic establishment. Her sons accelerated the process and by the time Somerled took power in the Isles the Kingdom of Scots was quite alien to the Kingdom of the Isles. The result was inevitable—a clash between the feudal and the tribal regimes. In the end the highly organised feudal system overcame the tribal. The chiefs became feudal superiors, and Culloden, followed by the Clearances, completed the destruction of all that was best in the old Gaelic way of life. Material and financial forces went hand in hand to make the old way of life under a tribal system impossible.

At the top of the social structure of the Lordship, the descendants of Somerled were paramount in the leadership, and accepted as such by all ranks. Their inauguration as Lords of the Isles was conducted according to the ancient Gaelic ritual, and we are indebted to the Sleat historian, Hugh Macdonald, for the following description of the ceremonial with which it was attended:

At this the Bishop of Argyle, the Bishop of the Isles, and seven priests were present; but a bishop was always present with the chieftains of all the principal families and a Ruler of the Isles. There was a square stone, seven or eight feet long and the tract of a man's foot cut thereon, upon which he stood, denoting that he should walk in the footsteps and uprightness of his predecessors, and that he was installed by right in his possessions. He was clothed in a white habit to show his innocence and integrity of heart, that he would be a light to his people and maintain the true religion. The white apparel did afterwards belong to the bard by right. Then he was to receive a white rod in his hand, intimating that he had the power to rule, not with tyranny and partiality, but with discretion and sincerity. Then he received his father's sword, or some other sword, signifying that his duty was to protect and defend them from the incursions of their enemies in peace as in war, as the obligations and customs of his predecessors were. The ceremony being over, mass was said after the blessings of the bishop and seven priests,

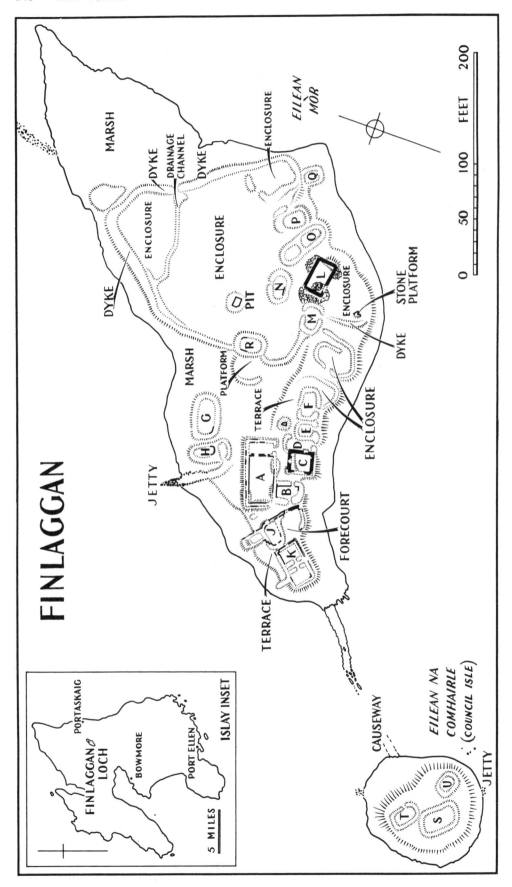

FINLAGGAN

MARSH

DYKE

ENCLOSURE

DYKE

DRAINAGE
CHANNEL

DYKE

ENCLOSURE

*EILEAN
MÒR*

DYKE

MARSH

ENCLOSURE

PIT

N

P

O

L

M

ENCLOSURE

STONE
PLATFORM

DYKE

PLATFORM

R

G

H

TERRACE

D

E

F

ENCLOSURE

JETTY

A

B

C

J

K

FORECOURT

TERRACE

0   50   100   FEET   200

PORTASKAIG

FINLAGGAN
LOCH

BOWMORE

PORT ELLEN

ISLAY INSET

5 MILES

CAUSEWAY

*EILEAN NA
COMHAIRLE*
(COUNCIL ISLE)

JETTY

T

U

S

the people pouring out their prayer for the success and prosperity of their newly created Lord. When they were dismissed, the Lord of the Isles feasted them for a week thereafter; gave liberally to the monks, poets, bards and musicians. You may judge that they spent liberally without any exception of persons.

This description is interesting as it shows conformity with the ancient practices of the Gaels in Ireland, where there is evidence of the survival of similar customs to a late period. The commemoration of important events by monuments of stone was a common custom among ancient peoples, and the Stone of Destiny, although it bears no footprint, may be regarded as another feature of these Celtic ceremonials. One footprint stone was found a few years ago in Loch Finlaggan near the larger of the two isles on which the manor house of Macdonald stood. Smaller than that described by Hugh, it may have been one used by the Chiefs of Islay after the fall of the Lordship, but experts disagree about it.

In the 18th century Martin describes a somewhat similar ceremony at the installation of the Chiefs of Sleat. In this case a pyramid of stones was used for the new Chief to stand upon, indicating the superiority of his station; and after the proclamation, the family bard recited the merits of his ancestors as an incentive to follow in their steps in equity and justice. In Scotland, even after the introduction of feudalism, the crowning of the King was followed by a bard reciting the genealogy of the Kings of Scots back to the old Gaelic days. It is interesting to note that Edmund Spenser, the English poet, who went to Ireland as secretary to Lord Grey of Wilton, describes the installation of an Irish chief thus:

They used to place him that shall be their Captain upon a stone always reserved to that purpose, and placed commonly upon a hill. In some of which I have seen formed and engraven a foot; whereon he, standing, receives an oath to preserve all their ancient customs inviolate; and to deliver up the succession peacably to his Tanist: and then hath a wand delivered to him by some whose proper office that is, after which, descending from the stone, he turneth himself round thrice forwards and thrice backwards.

KEY TO PLAN

Eilean Mor: (A) The Great Hall (61′ × 29′); (B) Stores and service building (25′ × 18′); (C) The servants' quarters; (D), (E), (F) Outbuildings; (G), (H) Guard-houses; (J) The personal apartment of the Lord of the Isles (19′ × 12′), which adjoins the family dwelling (K). There is also a forecourt (61′ × 26′) facing south, which was possibly roofed in to form a verandah. (L) is the Chapel with its burial ground, and the nearby stone platform no doubt served as the plinth of a carved cross similar to others found in Islay.

The enclosures were probably used as gardens and to accommodate a small number of domestic animals for the household's immediate needs.

Eilean a' Chomhairle (Council Isle) contains three buildings, the largest of which is the Council Chamber (36′ × 22′). The two islands were connected by a timber bridge.

The suggested purpose of the various buildings is subject to confirmation by the results of further excavation and study.

Loch Finlaggan, showing th
main island (*Eilean Mor*)
and the smaller Council Isle

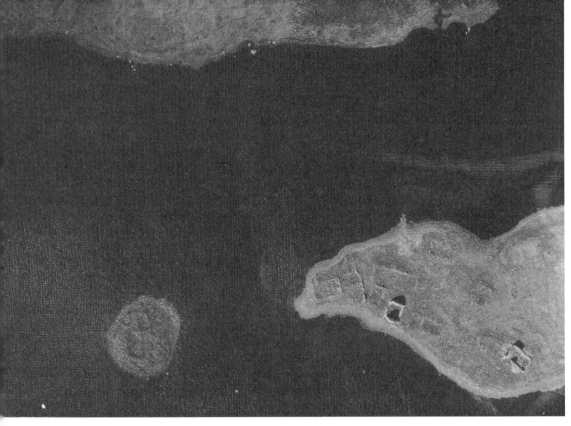

An aerial view of the two
islands, revealing the outli
of the ancient structures

It is certain that most of the installations of the Lords thus so fully described by Hugh of Sleat took place at Finlaggan on the Eilean Mor, probably in and around the Chapel, the remains of which can still be seen. This place was not essential to the ceremony, any more than it was necessary for Macdonald to issue and ratify charters at his residence at Finlaggan. The notable occasion on which a new Lord was installed elsewhere was when Donald of Harlaw was proclaimed at Kildonan in the Island of Eigg. The reason why this site was chosen for that particular function was doubtless that the island was part of the patrimony of the MacRuairi family, whose heiress Amie brought it to Good John of Islay by her marriage in 1337. Her son Ranald showed his acquiescence in the choice of Donald, eldest son by John's second marriage, by attending the ceremony and publicly handing over his rights to Donald. It may therefore have been politic for Donald to be "crowned" in Eigg. Eigg was also a place of meeting for special purposes, such as the gathering of an expeditionary force. It was more central in the extent of the Lordship than Islay.

With Macdonald as the head or apex of the pyramid of power, the next layer in that edifice was the Council of the Isles. This was the Privy Council of the Lord which met on the little *Eilean a Chomhairle* or Council Isle, on Loch Finlaggan. The island is not a large one but has the foundations of three fairly large halls, enough to seat the members of Council during their deliberations, after which they would be entertained at the Lord's manorial residence on the adjacent Eilean Mor. Once more Hugh of Sleat comes to our aid by describing the constitution of the Council, from which it will be seen that it was truly representative of the "men of the Isles," that potent body of opinion which controlled their mode of government, and influenced the conduct of Macdonald himself. The phrase "by the will of the men of the Isles" has appeared several times in our history. Hugh says:

Macdonald had his Council at Island Finlaggan in Isla to the number of sixteen, namely, four thanes, four armins, that is to say four lords or sub-thanes, four bastards, *i.e.* squires or men of competent estates, who could not come up with Armins or Thanes, that is freeholders or men that had the land in factory as Magee of the Rinds of Isla, MacNicoll in Portree in Skye, and Maceachren, Mackay, and MacGillivray in Mull. There was a table of stone where this Council sat in the Isle of Finlaggan: the whole table with the stone on which Macdonald sat were carried away by Argyle with the bells that were in Iona. Moreover, there was a judge in every isle for the discussion of all controversies, who had lands from Macdonald for their trouble and likewise the 11th part of every action decided. But there might still be an appeal to the Council of the Isles. MacFinnon was obliged to see weights and measures adjusted, and MacDuffie or MacPhee of Colonsay kept the Records of the Isles.

In these two excerpts we have a picture of a self-contained autonomous principality, well-organised on liberal lines, where justice was done, and in which a fully representative body ruled under one benign head. The position of the kingdom of Somerled and his successors was rather different to that of other sub-divisions of Scotland which existed up to the time of Kenneth MacAlpin, who had united the Scots with the Picts in the ninth century. In these days there were seven "Mortuaths" or provinces each under the rule of a Mormaer, the High Steward who in his district was answerable only to the King or "Ardrigh," on the lines of the old five provinces of Ireland. The provinces ruled by the Mormaers were Moray, Fife, Monteith, Strathearn, Buchan, Mar, and Caithness. The latter was at times under the Norse Earldom of Orkney. None of them contained the districts of Argyle and the Isles, for since the ninth century these had been in the kingdom of the Sudereys and Man taken over by Somerled in the twelfth century. The Kingdom of the Isles, therefore, was quite separate from the later earldoms which followed the "Mortuaths" within the kingdom of the Scots. And so it remained during the 300 years of the Lordship, and Macdonald owned no allegiance to any Celtic or Saxon king, except when forced to do so, a condition which lasted only as long as the king, whether Norwegian or Scottish, was present in person.

Much can be written about the history of the Isles and the West in the years following the foundation of the Kingdom of Dalriada, which in territorial extent was not much greater than one of the provinces ruled by the Mormaers. When Kenneth MacAlpin united that kingdom with the Pictish Kingdom in 843, it became the Kingdom of Alba or Scotland, as it was termed later. Not long after, towards the end of the ninth century, the Norse kings of the Sudereys and Man dominated the Isles and the western seaboard of Argyll from Kintyre to Loch Broom. This forced the kings of the race of Kenneth to move the capital of their realm to Scone, and the High Church of Iona to Dunkeld. Iona had been ravaged and many of the relics and books found asylum back in Ireland, fortunately for posterity.

For three hundred years the Norse kings and nobles ruled in the Isles but the indigenous population of Gaels held strongly to their traditions and customs. The long period of subjection had not blurred their memories of the family whose right it was to rule over them, and when Somerled came on the scene the "men of the Isles" were quick to acclaim him head of the family and to incite him to action against their oppressors. Their tribal organisation rested on the recognition and acceptance of a family head whose right to that position was based on descent from the founder, and his tenure of it conditioned by the benevolence and justice of his patriarchal rule. As distinct from feudalism with its well-nigh absolute property in land, and its absolute claim upon the service of the vassals, such a patriarchal system was largely limited by the will and interests of the tribe. The chief was the father of his people, but that power must be exercised for the good of the entire family. That was the fundamental law of the duties of the patriarch. He was the superior of the land for and on behalf of the people, and was supposed to rule in a manner productive of the greatest happiness of the greatest number. It was a conception that worked out reasonably well in practice. The chief who abused his power and became oppressive was apt to find himself in trouble with his clan, as happened more than once in the history of the clans, as we shall see. It is significant that the notable instances of a chief being thus dealt with by his clan occur in the Clan Ranald, who of all the branches of our Clan were the most devoted custodians of the ancient customs of the Gael. Perhaps it was because their origins, going back through Ranald, son of Amie MacRuairi and John of Islay, were much more Gaelic than the other rulers of the Isles who descended from John's second marriage. The admixture of "foreign" blood may be regarded with some misgiving by any who love and respect the old Gaelic traditions.

Because the duties of the chief as father of his family entailed his duty to defend their lands and property, it became necessary to have a strong head of the family, able to rule fairly within his tribe, and lead the fighting men into battle when occasion demanded. The age-old law of Tanistry thus came into being and was observed throughout Gaeldom for many generations. While a chief ruled, his brother or nearest relative of full age was nominated Tanister, or heir apparent. The heir himself might be a minor at the time of the chief's death, and minorities are always times of stress when rival factions or hostile neighbours become a threat to peace and internal order. The law of Tanistry was useful in circumventing these dangers, whilst not precluding the heir's succession to his rightful position in due course.

The chief in his rôle of military commander was also called the Toiseach, and when it was necessary for the chief to remain at home for any reason, the office of Toiseach was delegated usually to the oldest cadet most·fitted to lead in the field of battle. Thus the duties of the chief were divided. He was the father of the clan or family and ruled their lands: the Toiseach, or senior cadet, led the men to battle, and also had the responsibility of dealing with the fiscal administration of Crown lands within the chief's domain. The latter function became important only later and was not so much in evidence before the advent of feudalism. Another function of the chief was that of judge. We have seen that Macdonald delegated his authority as judge to a "judge in every isle," but in the smaller clan units the chief continued personally to act as judge of differences and quarrels within his family.

In relation to material possessions, it can be said that in early Celtic times private property in land did not exist. The land belonged to the community and the chief had a superiority of it not as a private individual but as head of, and in the name of, the tribe. Personal property was confined to what we may call "moveable assets," which in the main were livestock and household chattels. Private property in land was an innovation accelerated by the inroads of feudalism, and was foreign to the Gael. The land was held by the Chief and his kindred in common, and all within the limits of three generations from the head of the race had a claim on the family inheritance in accordance with the law of Gavel (*Gabhail,* taking, seizing). The consequent division of the land among the nearest of kin to the Chief tended to modify the principle of common property in land and promoted the growth of a privileged class of landowners, those who inherited the Orba, as it was called. There was in addition the tribe's land proper occupied by the *Ind-fine,* the ordinary clansmen who were not so close to the main stem, but still of the blood. This land was called the *duchas* and was the right of the clan free of taxation, later to be attached to the Crown. In course of time, however, the increase in numbers of those who still claimed justly to be of the blood of the founder of the tribe, however distant the connection, made the operation of the old laws more difficult to implement.

We have thus dealt with the true clansmen, related however distantly to the Chief and founder of their tribe. There were others, however, who dwelt on the tribal lands side by side with the true clansmen or *Saor-chlann,* the free-holders. These were the *Daor-chlann,* or bondmen, who were the original occupiers of the lands conquered by the incomers, or outsiders who came in either as fugitives from neighbouring tribes or for some personal reasons. In Ireland they provided the main recruiting material for the "galloglasses" (*galloglaich,* foreign servants, armed retainers), notorious in the history of that country in the wars with the English and Norman invaders. They were in some sense mercenary troops, paid in cash or kind, well trained and armed, and prepared to lay down their lives in the service of their employers, as so frequently happened in those wars. The *Daor-chlann* were obliged to render military service and pay taxes in the form of *calpe,* that is a horse or cow instead of cash. This was a tax the *Saor-chlann* did not pay. The status of these stranger septs or broken men who sought refuge in a Clan's lands led later to the engagements known as "Bonds of Manrent" by which, in return for services rendered, the superior undertook to protect them so long as they dwelt in his bounds. All or most of the clans have acquired these "septs" in the course of their history, though none perhaps as many as the Clan Donald.

The word "sept" is given in dictionaries as "a branch of a clan in Ireland." This definition is rather inadequate since it implies that a sept must be connected to the main stem by blood. The evidence in fact points to a two-fold origin, especially in the case of the larger and more powerful clans. Of the septs of Clan Donald, one category comprised those definitely connected by blood to our eponymous, Donald of Islay, grandson of Somerled. A second developed from those best described as "adherents," who lived within the Clan Donald lands, pursuing their specialist vocations and owing allegiance to the chiefs of Clan Donald in their separate regions.

The first class of septs, however far removed from the main stem, still regarded themselves as *fior-Dhomhnallaich* (true Macdonalds) and of the blood of the Lords of the Isles. Travellers in the Highlands even down to modern times state that those bearing the name "Macdonald," however humble or impoverished their circumstances, bore themselves nobly and displayed no hesitation in claiming descent from princes.

In the second category of "adherents" were to be found most importantly those who held appointments in the Council of the Isles or were employed in the more distant parts, as, for example, the judges who ruled in "every isle." The MacVurichs are a notable example of these. They were for eighteen generations bards to the Lords and later the Chiefs of Clanranald, and had lands allotted to them for their services. As late as the year 1800 the last official bard of Clanranald had the lands of Staoiligary in Uist. The Beatons were the physicians to the Lords and other clans too. The MacEachrans were the Masters of Horse, and the name was common in Kintyre, which in Roman times was known as the country of the horse-folk. The MacLaverties were the spokesmen or speech-makers to the Lords, and we have seen that MacFinnon (Mackinnon) adjusted the weights, while MacDuffie of Colonsay kept the records. The holder of the latter office was not necessarily the actual scribe as the gentry, even in Scotland, were seldom able to write and preferred to wield the sword rather than the pen. The task was usually assigned to the clergy, the monks and parish priests, who carried out their work under the direction and supervision of the office-holder. The services of the clergy were invariably employed in the administration of any office requiring some measure of education and learning. For example, Thomas Dingwall, sub-deacon of the Diocese of Ross, acted as Chamberlain for the earldom during the reign of John, the last Lord. Such an office demanded a knowledge of accounting, revenue and estate management, and this knowledge was almost entirely a prerogative of the clergy. It was such a rare accomplishment that if a member of the ruling family were capable of reading and writing in an expert manner, he was sometimes given the second name of *Cleireach* (the Clerk). An instance of this we find occurring on two occasions in the chiefly line of Sleat.

The Beatons (variously spelt Bethune, Beton, Beath) were the hereditary physicians of the Lordship, and members of the family also served other clans down through history. They were taken to be one of the "seven score" names of those sent by O'Cahan of Ulster as the dowry of his daughter Agnes, when she married Angus Og of Islay, fifth in line from Somerled. Their knowledge of medicine was much needed in Angus's realm and contributed much to the welfare of the clan throughout their long and active history.

The records of the Isles have suffered sadly as a result of wars and raids ever since the ravages of the Vikings in the ninth century on Iona, where so many valuable documents reposed. The later forfeiture of the Lordship added to the destruction, and the virtual obliteration of all traces of the Macdonalds in Islay was effectively accomplished by the incoming Campbells in the early seventeenth century. It is not surprising that little remains of the records kept by the MacDuffies and others of our Clan, and that so much has been lost which could have provided a clearer picture of our ancestors and their way of life during the long period of their sway in the West and the Isles.

Apart from the scant records that survive, it is mainly in the sphere of unwritten law and custom that evidence is found of the social, economic and political factors which governed the life of the Clan. One peculiarly Celtic law was the ancient law of tanistry which operated during the Lordship and later amongst the clans who succeeded that realm after its break-up. A notable instance where it worked very well, and for the benefit of the Clan Donald, was in 1308 when Alexander was deposed in favour of his younger brother, Angus Og. Angus was Tanister of Alexander, and his natural successor. In describing this event our seanachies concisely present the principle and practical operation of the law as follows:

> Succession to the chiefship of a clan was quite a different matter from lord-ship over the lands, and was governed by totally different principles. If succession to lands was now affected by feudalism, succession to the chiefship was still, and long after, a question upon which the voice of the Clan, which was a potent element in the law of tanistry, made itself effectually heard. The succession of Angus Og to the exclusion of the son of Alexander could hardly have been accomplished so quietly, and without any apparent dissent, were it not that the succession of one brother to another appealed to the traditional sentiments of the race. We may be sure that the question was well weighed by the Council of Finlaggan, and that the assumption of the sceptre of Clann Cholla by Angus Og, only took place after due and earnest consideration on the part of the officials of the Clan.

The operation of the same law is to be seen in the succession of Donald of Harlaw in preference to his brother Ranald, the son of John of Islay by his first marriage, although here there were other circumstances affecting the issue. The whole train of events was set in motion by the influence exerted by Robert II to divert the honours of the House of Islay to the family of his own daughter. It is clear that Ranald, the eldest surviving son of Amie MacRuairi, was the lawful son, and by the law of primogeniture the heir of John of Islay. It is equally clear that he abandoned his position as heir of his father, both to the chiefship and to the estates, by two acts which are undoubtedly vouched for. First, he resigned his rights as the heir of his father's lordship by accepting in return a charter for the lands brought to the Lordship by his mother. However princely in extent the domain he thus received, the charter in question reduced him from the position of prospective Lord of the Isles to that of a vassal of the Lordship. In the second place, he deprived himself of the Chiefship of the Clan, and made himself a vassal Celtically as well as feudally by handing over the sceptre of Innse-Gall to Donald at Kildonan. The ceremony took place as a purely Celtic function, and not in any sense as a feudal investiture; and it seems that in accordance with the law of tanistry, by which Celtic succession was hereditary in the family but elective in the individual, Donald, on the surrender by Ranald of his reversion to the Chiefship, became *with the approval of the Clan* Donald of Islay, Lord of the Isles and Head of the Family of Macdonald.

Another example of the application of the law was in the case of John Mor, second son of John of Islay by his second marriage, who was known as Iain Mor Tanister (*i.e.* Tanist of Macdonald). There is no record of a formal installa-tion of John Mor in this office, but his brother Donald's son and heir Alexander, who succeeded eventually to the Headship, was still young enough to justify such an appointment as a provision against Donald's early death. John Mor was thus accepted as the probable successor for a time on Donald's death, and his designation must be regarded as a wise precaution not only because of Alexander's youth but also because his only brother had renounced his claim by entering the Church. Other instances of the operation of this law occur later in our history; but these examples suffice to show that the old Celtic laws persisted in what was in essence a Celtic principality.

The office of Toiseach, or military leader, of the clan, was at times separate from that of the Chief. Often it devolved upon the senior cadet, the representative of the family which first branched off from the main stem. The Toiseach could aptly be described as the Lieutenant-General of the Clan. A good instance of this is that of Donald Balloch who, although not called Toiseach, wielded that power very effectually for many years, as leader of the Clan in the field, during the reigns of Alexander and John, the last Lords of the Isles. From 1431 to 1463 Donald Balloch, son of John Mor Tanister, and 2nd Chief of the large Clann Iain Mhoir Ile, led the forces of the Lordship in every enterprise during those turbulent years. He was also the head of the leading cadet family of the Isles, and thus fulfilled in two capacities the rôle of Toiseach of Clan Donald.

In more recent times the office of Toiseach, although not given that name, was filled by the "Captain" of a Clan. John of Moidart and his father were each termed the Captain of Clanranald, at a time when their opponents were not disposed to recognise them as patriarchal heads; and in 1545 Gilleasbuig Cleireach (Archibald the Clerk) was termed the Captain of Clann Uisdein during the minority of his nephew, Donald Gormson, 6th Chief of Sleat.

As the Celtic law of tanistry and not the feudal law of primogeniture originally governed succession to the chiefship, so the Celtic law of *gavel* operated in the transmission of lands. The father's lands were divided in approximately equal portions amongst his sons. In those days younger sons could not usually leave home and seek their fortunes in distant parts of an Empire, or in industrial employment nearer home. The land was their living and their world. Moreover manpower at home was essential to the well-being of the tribe, and to its very existence in times of strife. The operation of the law is clearly seen in the history of our Clan from the time of Somerled, who divided his vast domains among his three sons, Ranald, Dugall and Angus. Donald left his patrimony to his two sons, Angus Mor and Alasdair; and Angus Mor provided in a similar manner for his three sons, Alexander, Angus Og and Iain Sprangach. It would be a reasonable assumption that such fragmentation inevitably undermined the power and authority of the Lordship, but in effect the younger brothers held their lands from the head of the family, usually the eldest, whose name "de Ile" indicated his position as Macdonald, Lord of the Isles. When John of Islay, son of Angus Og, succeeded, the law worked in reverse, because he inherited the the lands of the deposed Alexander, and those also of the forfeited MacDougalls and Comyns; and still further to increase his estates his marriage with Amie MacRuairi brought him the extensive holdings of the Clan Ruairi in Garmoran and the North Isles. The law of gavel operated once again on the death of John of Islay, when he divided his estates amongst seven sons. Of these, Godfrey, Ranald, Donald, John Mor Tanister, and Alasdair Carrach founded notable clans within the Lordship and owned allegiance to the head, Donald of Harlaw, whom we saw installed with his brothers' consent at Kildonan in 1386. Although the Lord's personal estate might be comparatively small, the lands over which he was superior were vast, held under his rule by near relatives as heads of septs or separate clans, as well as by other clans who were within the Lordship

The exterior and interior of a weaver's cottage in Islay as seen by Pennant on his 18th-century tour

although not of Macdonald blood. These were not vassals in the feudal sense, rather partners in the Gaelic realm with Macdonald as *primus inter pares*. The lands were bestowed by verbal gift or by written charter. From the time of Somerled to the reign of Angus Og, verbal charters were common, and one example which has survived is of a grant of the lands of Kilmahumaig in Knapdale to one, Mackay, for ever:

Mise Domhnull Mac Dhomhnuill	I, Donald Mac Donald
Am shuidh air Dun Domhnuill	sitting on the Seat of Donald
Toirt coir do Mhac Aigh air Kilmahumaig	give the right to MacAigh
'S gu la brath'ch mar sin.	over Kilmahumaig for ever.

It is assumed that, as Macdonald calls the place where he sat **Dun Domhnuill**, any place where such a transaction was done was for the time being his "seat." Grants of land, when written, were almost always in Latin, drawn up by the Lord's scribes, clerics or others who could write.

The Lord of the Isles was maintained in his dignity by lands set aside for his own use, and by tribute paid to him by his vassals, but there were also other Celtic forms of taxation which he enjoyed. The charter given by Alexander, Earl of Ross, to Mackintosh of the Lordship of Lochaber in 1443, mentions the "service of wardship and relief." The right of wardship usually belonged to the King. It consisted of the guardianship of an estate during the minority of the heir, and the guardian or tutor, as he was sometimes called, held actual possession of the estate as if it were his own. On the heir resuming possession "relief" was exacted from him as compensation to the guardian.

The same charter throws some light too on the old tax or levy called *eirig* which by derivation may be called "the price of a man." The effect of the tax was that, when a man's life was taken either by culpable homicide or murder, his kinsmen were compensated in cash or kind. The deceased's kin were not obliged to be satisfied with anything short of the blood of the murderer, but when a fine was agreed to, the amount was determined by the rank and status of the deceased, and by the heinousness of the crime in relation to the community.

Another tax mentioned in the same charter is the *herezeldis* which was similar to the *calpe* paid by "native men" living under the protection of a conquering chief. It consisted of the best horse in the deceased's estate being taken by the landlord or chief. This practice lingered on in North Uist for nearly a hundred years after Government had abolished it.

A third tax referred to in the Mackintosh charter is the *Mulierum Mercheta*, which was a payment made by a vassal to his superior upon the marriage of his daughter. It was in effect a form of compensation exacted by the lord for the loss of the bride's services, especially when the marriage involved the transfer of her allegiance to another superior. Although there is considerable difference of opinion concerning the origin of this tax, most authorities are agreed that it was a feudal imposition which found its way at an early period into Celtic social culture.

Of all the laws and customs relating to marriage among Celts, the curious practice of "handfasting" should perhaps here be singled out because of the genealogical problems it has generated in the history of the clans. Handfasting was a temporary marriage for a year and a day arranged by the fathers of the bride and groom. The important factor was of course the matter of any issue consequent on the union. If the lady became pregnant during this period the marriage became legal and binding even if not solemnised by the Church. The survival of this practice, so contrary to the laws of the Church, can only be accounted for by the fact that it was traditionally allowed amongst the Celts because the welfare of the clan or family depended upon the birth of heirs to carry on the line. Instances of this occur in many families in the Highlands and Isles. One such was in the family of Maclean of Ardgour, the 4th laird, when he hand-fasted his daughter with MacIain of Ardnamurchan, who took the lady "upon the prospect of marriage if she pleased him." After two years he sent her back to her father, but his offspring by her were reputed lawful children because their mother was taken "upon a prospect of marriage." The outstanding case in Clan Donald where a handfast marriage is alleged to have taken place is that of John of Islay, whose first marriage with Amie MacRuairi appears to have presented some historians with problems which have already been discussed elsewhere in these pages, and especially in the chapter devoted to John, seventh Lord.

* * *

In concluding our examination of the nature of the Lordship, it may well be appropriate here to present a brief survey of the dignity, sway, and wealth of the family whose story we have tried to tell. As we have seen, the chiefs of Clan Cholla became independent rulers within Dalriada after Kenneth MacAlpin had moved eastward to become King of the new realm of Alba. Somerled, after he had vindicated his rights, assumed like his forebears the title King of the Isles, and was to all intents and purposes an independent prince. This sense of independence he transmitted to a long line of successors and, although at times compelled by the force of circumstances to profess allegiance to the Scottish Kings, no amount either of force or conciliation could make them long adhere to a submissive attitude. Reginald, son of Somerled, styled himself Lord of Argyll and King of the Isles, a two-fold designation which seemed to indicate that the relation of his dynasty to the Isles was of an older and more independent character than their relation to Argyll. Reginald was also the first of the family known as *de Ile*, though the Isles must have been the home of the race several centuries before his day. This title of *de Ile* was the oldest territorial designation of his family, and always stood first and foremost in the order of their honours and dignities. It was confined to the heads of the race, and while cadets of Macdonald might designate themselves *de Insulis* or assume any other title they chose, they never presumed to adopt that of *de Ile*. It is from this fact, mainly, that we conclude the seniority of the Clan Donald line over all other branches descended from Reginald, son of Somerled. Reginald was himself *de Ile,* as were his ancestors probably for many generations, and while other junior families branched off, that of *de Ile,* from Donald down to the last John, were undoubtedly the heads of the Clan Cholla. While they had this territorial title, they were also known by others. Both in Ireland and Scotland, they were frequently designated *Righ Innsegall* (Kings of the Isles) and in the beginning of the fifteenth century we find MacVurich the Bard addressing his *Brosnacha Catha* to Donald of Islay, *King of Innse-gall.*

On the other hand it is undoubtedly the case that the Celtic or patriarchal title of the heads of the family, down from the time of the first Donald de Ile, was *MacDhomhnuill.* There is only one signed charter from any of the heads of the House of Islay, namely, the Gaelic Charter by Donald of Harlaw in 1408, and in this deed he styles himself without any territorial addition, simply as Macdonald. The Chiefs of Islay were all Macdonald, from the time of Angus Mor down to Donald Gallda and Donald Dubh, who were both proclaimed "Macdonald" in their unsuccessful efforts to revive the fallen principality of the Isles. In the arming of the last Lord of the Isles, MacVurich speaks of

John as "Macdonald," the noble son of Alexander, the heroic King of Fingall, and a poem by a contemporary bard, quoted by the same seanachie, begins with the words "True is my praise of Macdonald." In Ireland, also, from very early times, the heads of the race were known by the same Celtic title. In the *Annals of Loch Ce*, 1411, we read of a "great victory of the Macdonalds of Alba," and in the *Annals of Ulster* we find that "in the year of Christ 1490, Angus, son of Macdonald of Scotland, who was called the young lord, was murdered by his Irish harper Dermod O'Cairbre, and at Inverness he was slain." It seems necessary to dwell with some emphasis on this fact, inasmuch as Gregory, and others who have followed him, have persisted in maintaining that Macdonald is a comparatively modern surname adopted by the Barons of Sleat and the Lords of Dunnyveg, from one or more noted chiefs who bore the name of Donald.

We find in those heraldic emblems, which can with certainty be regarded as belonging to the Lords of the Isles, evidence of their premier position among the western clans of Scotland. Amid all the variations which the taste and fancy of later ages have introduced into the Macdonald arms, there are two features that stand out prominently as belonging unquestionably to the Family of Islay, and these are the galley and the eagle. We find the galley as far back as the time of Reginald, and the galley with an eagle against the mast we find in the seal of John, last Lord of the Isles, after he was forfeited in the Earldom of Ross in 1476. The galley is intended to convey the idea of the sovereignty of these Celtic Lords over the western seas, and the eagle symbolises, under another form, the royal superiority of the Macdonald Chiefs. No doubt other western clans have the galley in their armorial bearings, but these in every case have borrowed the emblem from the arms of the house of which in previous ages they had been feudatories and vassals.

All the information we can obtain suggests the possession of great power and wealth by these Island Lords. Somerled seems to have had the command of immense maritime resources, for from the time that he conquered Godred down to his last struggle with the Scottish Crown the number of galleys that accompanied him to sea varied from 60 to 160. Angus Og led 10,000 Highlanders to the field of Bannockburn, and Donald commanded no less a force at the battle of Harlaw. From the large numbers which at various times these Lords of the Isles were able to assemble on the day of battle, we conclude that the population of the Western Highlands must have been larger than is usually supposed. Nothing of the nature of a standing army seems to have existed beyond the *luchd tighe* (bodyguard, or garrison) who kept ward on Isle Finlaggan, where the Macdonald Lords held court, and where the remains of their dwellings are still to be seen. Martin tells us that "the *luchd tighe* attended the chief at home and abroad. They were well trained in managing the sword and target, in wrestling, swimming, jumping, dancing, shooting with bows and arrows, and were stout seamen." They were composed of the strongest and most active young men in the best families in the Isles and were called *Ceatharnaich* (warriors), from their great strength and feats of daring. They were known in the Lowlands, where their forays were rich and frequent, as "Kerns" or "Caterans." The military strength of the Lordship was not, however, to be measured by the *luchd tighe*. The vassals of the Isles, not only those of the same blood and lineage, but others who held lands of the House of Islay by feudal tenure, were bound to provide a certain number of men when the fiery cross went round. While the Stewart kings, with all the encouragement they gave to the cultivation of archery, were never able to bring a band of efficient bowmen to the field, the Islesmen were expert archers, and when fighting in the royal army were always placed in a position in which their superiority in this respect would have the best effect.

Remains of the butts of Imiriconart, in Islay, where the archers of Macdonald practised their art, survived long after they had outlived their use.

While the Lords of the Isles thus encouraged the cultivation of warlike courage and skill, we are not to suppose that the arts of peace were neglected according to the standards of their day. The numbers, extent, and solidity of the castles, fortifications and religious houses, whose ruins are scattered over the Western Highlands and Islands, show that encouragement of a distinct kind must have been given to the crafts of masonry, carpentry and others, while they at the same time suggest the expenditure of great wealth. No doubt some of this wealth would have been derived from the tribute paid by the vassals, which must have amounted to a considerable sum, measured by the conditions of the time. There are also other ways of accounting for the well-filled coffers of the Macdonald Chiefs. They were acquainted, through their seafaring habits, with the navigation of foreign seas, and made many descents upon the maritime countries of Western Europe, carrying with them to the Islands golden vases, silks, armour, money and other spoils. An art which the seafaring habits of the Kings of Innse-Gall must have greatly promoted was that of shipbuilding. In this particular craft, doubtless, the Norwegians would have promoted their instruction, but the Western Gaels must very early have become skilled in an art so necessary in an insular region like the Lordship of the Isles. It is also extremely probable that timber grew more plentifully in the Hebrides then than in modern times, a supposition which is supported by the numerous roots of trees which now and then are exposed to view in the extensive bog-lands of Lewis and Uist. In 1249, Hugh de Chatillon, one of the richest and most powerful of French barons, consented to accompany Louis ix of France to the crusades, and the ship that was to carry him was built in the Highlands, a fact to be seriously considered by those who would fasten the stigma of barbarity upon the Scottish Gael of a bygone age.

Various other proofs of the wealth of these Island Lords might be adduced, but one significant proof will suffice. Reginald, son of Somerled, in 1196 purchased the whole of Caithness from William the Lion, an exception being made of the yearly revenue due to the Sovereign, which the Lord of the Isles did not acquire. That the chronicler does not, in recording this transaction, confuse Reginald of the Isles with the potentate of the same name who became King of Man, is clear from the fact that the Lords of the Isles for many ages thereafter continued to possess lands in Caithness, for we find both Donald of Harlaw and John, last Earl of Ross, giving charters of land in that county during the fifteenth century.

A certain amount of trade must have been encouraged by the Lords of the Isles, and frequent intercourse with Ireland on the one hand, and Norway on the other, led to the exchange of commodities which were useful to both. An official mentioned by Hugh Macdonald as exercising an important function under the Lords of the Isles was the Chief of Macfinnon, who looked after the adjustment of weights and measures, a fact which shows that encouragement was given to trading. The stately and even royal Court kept by these potentates involved the distribution of wealth around them whether they held their court in Islay, Ardtornish, or Dingwall, and it is on record that after the Earldom of Ross was forfeited and Dingwall Castle had to be abandoned, that burgh for a long time languished and decayed through the withdrawal of the business which the presence of the Island Chiefs and their numerous retainers created. The trade of the Islands would probably consist of the staple commodities produced in those regions, and by means of which the rents and tiends would to some extent have been paid, such as wool, cloth, flax, linen, fish, butter, eggs, and corn.

It is interesting to note that, when the Earl of Douglas visited the Earl of Ross at Knapdale in 1453, the former brought presents of wine, silken cloths, and silver, while the Highland Chief in return gave mantles and Highland plaids. We find in some of the older accounts that the spinning of wool and flax and the manufacture of cloth were industries practised in the Hebrides from a very remote period. The cultivation of the arts and sciences has with every appearance of probability been ascribed to the influence of the Gaelic clergy who were established over the Western Isles prior to the arrival of the Norwegians, as well as to numbers of Britons flying thither from the ravages of the Saxons, who bore with them the remains of Roman culture and of the arts of life. At any rate, it is a fact that an Icelandic Skald, describing an elegant dress for a hero of the seventh century, says *"Enn Sudreyskar spunnu,"* which is, being interpreted, "Sudereyans spun the web." This manufacture of cloth from home-grown wool and flax was an art universally cultivated and always preserved under the sway of the Lords of the Isles. It is evident that whatever trade existed in the Isles and with foreign countries must have been conducted by the medium of barter or exchange. Money as an instrument of commerce must have been scarce in these ages, down from the time of Angus Mor, "the generous dispenser of rings," to his latest successor in the sovereignty of the Isles.

Considering the character of the times in which they flourished, it is not difficult to see that the influence of the Lords of the Isles was exercised for the good of the lands which owned their sway, and the terrible state of anarchy and darkness which for generations followed the fall of their Lordship is alone sufficient to prove the fact. To the Kings and State of Scotland they were turbulent and dangerous, because they never forgot their ancient traditions of independence, but to their own vassals and subjects they were kindly, generous, and just, abounding in hospitality, and profuse in charitable deeds. Had this not been the case, it is hardly possible to conceive that the Highlanders should have rallied to so many forlorn hopes aimed at re-establishing the fallen dynasty. In their proud independence, they were to the Highland people the representatives of what was best in Gaelic history, who never owned a superior, either Celt or Saxon. Only the king of terrors himself could lay Macdonald low: such must have been the feeling of the devoted subject who engraved the brief but expressive legend on his tomb, *Macdonald fata hic.*

14

Clann Alasdair
MacAlisters of Loup and Alexanders of Menstrie

I

THE MACALISTERS

THIS IMPORTANT FAMILY is the first to branch off the main stem of Clan Donald. Its origin has been the subject of considerable speculation, chiefly because of the existence of two Alexanders, uncle and nephew, to whom its posterity has variously been ascribed. The confusion caused by the conflicting accounts of the chroniclers is discussed at length by our own seanachies in their *Clan Donald,* and their examination of all the available evidence would appear to lead to the conclusion that, in their own words, "there is no reason to doubt that the Clan Allister are the descendants of 'Alastair Mor,' son of Donald de Ile, the younger brother of Angus Mor." The other Alasdair or Alexander was the eldest son of Angus Mor, whom he succeeded as Lord of the Isles until his deposition by Robert Bruce in favour of his younger brother Angus Og. The sons of Alexander, the deposed Lord of the Isles, fled for refuge to Ireland where they became noted captains of galloglasses, and there is no record of a family of importance being founded by them in Scotland.

We may therefore accept Alasdair Mor, younger brother of Angus Mor, as progenitor of the MacAlister branch of the Clan, the oldest of all the families that sprang from the main stem. Alasdair Mor first appears on record as witness to a charter granted by his brother Angus Mor to the Monastery of Paisley in 1253. As only brother to the Lord of Isles he would have received his *gavel* in the division of the family inheritance in accordance with established custom, but the absence of charters or other documentary evidence connecting himself and his descendants with the main family patrimony has left their early history somewhat obscure. The only other mention of Alasdair Mor is to be found in the *Annals of the Four Masters,* where it is related that in 1299 "Alexander MacDonnell (of Antrim), the most distinguished of his name either in Ireland or in Scotland for hospitality and feats of arms, was slain by Alexander MacDugall, together with many of his people." From this it would appear that he fell victim to the feud then raging between the MacDougalls of Lorn and the family of the Isles in the conflict of interests and loyalties aroused by the contenders for the Scottish throne. The designation "of Antrim" suggests that Alasdair Mor

THE ARMS OF THE MACALISTERS OF LOUP

Lyon Register, Vol. 4, Folio 105 (1847)

had a territorial interest in that region a full century before John Mor Tanister, progenitor of the great House of Dunnyveg, laid the foundation of his family influence in the Glens by his marriage with the Bisset heiress.

Alasdair Mor is said to have had five sons, Donald, Godfrey, Duncan, John and Hector. Donald and his son Alexander appear on record in 1291, when they swore fealty to Edward I of England. Again in 1314 "Donald of the Isles" and his brother Godfrey are both named as such and in that order as being received into the peace of the English King—from which it has been inferred that Donald, contrary to the opinions of some chroniclers, was the oldest of his brothers and the undoubted head of his house. Another and unfortunate inference that may be gathered from the same source is that the family were on the losing side in the struggle that led to Bannockburn and suffered the consequences of their hostility to Bruce by the forfeiture of their possessions and banishment from the country.

Probably as a result, from this time there is a complete blank in the history of the family until 1366 when, as the Irish annalist tells us:

Donal O'Neill and the Clan Donnell, namely Torlough Mac Donnell and Alexander his son, collected their forces to attack Niall O'Neill: they expelled Mac Cathmail from the country, who went and joined O'Neill. . . . Randal, son of Alexander, heir of the clan of Alexander, arrived at the same time from the Hebrides to join O'Neill. The kerns from either side of the Clan Donnells having approached each other Randal sent messages to Torlough and his son, Alexander, entreating them to let him pass in respect of his seniority and of their friendship with each other; but they however treated that application with indifference, for they advanced to the ford over which they saw him preparing to pass, and a determined and fierce engagement ensued in which many were slain and wounded on both sides: a son of Randal was slain by Torlough in the thick of the fight, and Alexander, a son of Torlough, was taken prisoner by Randal's party, whom they resolved instantly to put to death; Randal would not consent to the proposal, for he said that he should not be deprived both of his son and of his kinsman on the same day.

Apart from the evidence it affords of close involvement in Irish disturbances at an early stage, the passage confirms the line of succession through Alexander, Donald's son. Ranald appears to have had other sons besides the one who was killed in Ireland, but after 1366 he and his descendants as a Highland family disappear from history for several generations. If Kintyre was the home and nursery of the race, and it seems impossible to associate Clan Alasdair as a Highland family with any other region, their history is buried in obscurity for upwards of one hundred years, and no records whatsoever exist which might relieve the darkness of the period.

Many of the members of this House migrated to the lowland regions where they entered peaceful walks of life, and where the surname of MacAlister was changed to the simpler form of Alexander. Their history is treated at length in a later part of this Chapter.

The lands of "Lowb" (best known to us in connection with the Clan Alasdair as "Loup"), appear first in a charter for certain lands in Kintyre bestowed by King James III upon John, Lord of the Isles. In 1481, Charles MacAlister was appointed by the King to the Stewardry of the lands of Kintyre and at the same time received a charter for a considerable grant of lands in that district. Loup is situated to the south of West Loch Tarbert, and the name is derived from the Gaelic word *lub*, equivalent to the English "loop," and signifying a curve or bend, this being the shape of the shore which bounded the ancient lands of the Clan Alasdair. Charles MacAlister was succeeded in the leadership of the family by his son John, who is styled Angus John of the Lowb. He was succeeded by Alexander MacAlister whom we find on 23rd July 1529 coming under the displeasure of the Government. He had been involved with the Macleans and Macdonalds in the invasion of the Campbell territories of Roseneath, Lennox and Craignish in that year, and was put to the horn for his inability to find security for his future behaviour. Men of rank in the Lowlands were often prepared to provide these friendly securities, but on this occasion none seemed willing to take the risk either in the case of the Chief of Loup or his companions. Upon this, the King called upon the Justice Clerk to receive James Macdonald, the son of Alexander, Lord of Dunnyveg, "to relax them from our horne."

For about a generation, nothing of importance is on record regarding Clan Alasdair. During the remainder of the 16th century they seem to have sheltered themselves under the protection of the Macdonalds of Dunnyveg and the Houses of Argyll and Hamilton. They were not Crown vassals, but held their possessions from Dunnyveg and Argyll, especially Dunnyveg. During the period 1540-72 they appear to have been very active in the North of Ireland which was in a state of constant warfare. The Western Isles-men often fought in Ulster on the side of the famous Sorley Buy, whose story is told elsewhere in this volume. The Clan Alasdair gave Sorley their most strenuous support. In 1568 Sorley was successful over the English government on all fronts, and succeeded in occupying almost all the garrisons on the coasts of Antrim. On 19th February 1569 a bloody battle was fought between Owen MacGilleasbuig, who seems to have commanded a detachment of Sorley's Scottish troops, and the English forces. We are unable to give the battle a name or location, or to determine exactly the result, but the State Papers of the time leave no doubt as to its having been fought, and that a number of the Clan Alasdair (Randal, Donough, Gilleasbuig and others, described as Scottish Captains of the Clan Alasdair) were slain. A few years after this, in the winter of 1571-72, another engagement took place at Knockfergus in which, according to the only available authority, a body of Scottish Highlanders were defeated by Cheston, Captain of the English forces. This fight was still more disastrous to the Clan Alasdair for "Owen McOwen Duffe McAlasterain, called the Lord of Loup" was slain. He was probably the son of the last named Alexander, and the record which chronicles the event gives him the high praise that he was "one amongst them more esteemed than Sorley Buy." This John (Owen, Eoin, Iain, are all other forms of the name) was succeeded by his son Alexander who in 1573 obtained a charter from the Earl of Argyll, and about the same time his name appears on the roll of those who, by Act of Parliament, were called upon to deliver hostages for their behaviour. In 1580 a bond was entered into between Angus Macdonald of Dunnyveg and the MacAlisters, which illustrates the dependence of the family on that powerful branch of the Clan Donald.

In the latter half of the 16th century a new branch of the Clan Alasdair of Kintyre appears. The lands owned by this family lie by the shores of East Loch Tarbert, adjoining the estates of the main branch, while the Heads of the House became Hereditary Constables of Tarbert Castle, which had been fortified by Robert the Bruce many years before to assert his sovereignty over the power of the Lords of the Isles. In 1580, Charles MacAlister appears as Constable of Tarbert, for on 8th May of that year Alexander MacAlister, perpetual Vicar of the Parish Church of Kilcalmonell in Knapdale, granted in fee-farm as well as life-rent to this same Charles, his cousin, and to his heirs and assignees, the two merklands of old extent called Balleneile in the lordship of Knapdale and the sheriffdom of Tarbert. In the instrument of gift Charles is described as Constable of Tarbert, thus holding an official position under the Scottish Crown. The charter given at Tarbert was confirmed at Holyrood on the 5th September following. Another family of some consequence, connected with the House of Loup, had some kind of holding at Barr towards the close of the sixteenth century, for on 27th March 1588 "Johannes alias Ewyn Bane M'Ane M'Alexander in Bar" is among those to whom James VI gave a Commission of Justiciary against the chief of the Clan Cameron and others who had incurred the displeasure of the Government.

As already observed, the Clan Alasdair were vassals of Argyll for, at any rate, a portion of their lands; but this did not prevent the occurrence of feuds and the outbreak of hostilities between themselves and the Clan Campbell. Donald Campbell of Kilmore and Dougal, his son, were particularly aggressive and unruly, and gave much trouble to the family of Tarbert, whose estates lay in their immediate neighbourhood. Matters came to such a height that on 9th February 1589, Sir James Campbell of Ardkinglas had to sign a bond of caution for his lawless kinsmen, for Donald £1000, and for Dougal 100 merks, to secure freedom from hurt to Archibald MacAlister, apparent of Tarbert, his tenants and servants.

We have seen that the Clan Alasdair sought the friendship and protection of the great territorial houses in their vicinity, and in further evidence of this we find in 1590 that professions of fealty, dependence, and services were rendered by the Clan Alasdair to Lord John Hamilton, while shortly thereafter a similar bond was given by the Tutor of Loup and others of his clan to the same superior. The Clan Alasdair in Kintyre were in no way dependent upon the Hamiltons, but those of them who had settled in Arran and Bute occupied the position of a stranger sept, and such a bond was expedient in a region where the heads of the House of Hamilton were lords of the soil. In 1591 Godfrey MacAlister of Loup received a charter from the Earl of Argyll. On 1st October 1596, "Gorrie M'Aichan Vc Allaster of the Lowpe," along with others, attests a letter of renunciation by Angus Macdonald of Dunnyveg in favour of Sir James, his son, by which he proposed to surrender to him all his lands, possessions, and rights.

In 1598 a serious quarrel arose between Godfrey MacAlister and his kinsman Charles MacAlister, who had been his tutor and guardian during his minority. Of the causes that led to this difference, we are left in ignorance, but the consequence was a domestic tragedy. The Tutor of Loup fell beneath the sword of Godfrey, and his sons, apprehensive of a similar fate, fled to Askomull House, The laird of Loup, who received the aid of Sir James, younger of Dunnyveg, surrounded the house at Askomull with several hundred armed men, but the family refused to surrender. The incidents that followed opened an important chapter in the story of the House of Dunnyveg, but records are silent concerning the fate of the Tutor's sons or their subsequent relations with their wrathful kinsman.

During the next few years the annals of the Clan Alasdair of Kintyre are enlivened by outbreaks of lawlessness. In 1600, Hector MacAlister, probably the heir of Tarbert, was in ward in Edinburgh, no doubt in consequence of crimes that were committed by the Clan during that year. The authorities, doubtful of the sufficiency of the King's prison to hold Hector with absolute security, accepted a bond of caution from Aulay MacAulay of Ardincaple for 1000 merks that the prisoner would keep ward until it was his Majesty's pleasure to relieve him. It was this year also that, while John Montgomery of Skelmorlie was in the Lowlands, his house and lands of Knockransay in Arran were invaded and captured by the Clan Alasdair, his wife and children taken prisoners, and his furniture and other possessions, amounting in value to £12,000 Scots, seized by the marauders. On seeking redress from the Clan Alasdair, Montgomery caused Alexander, the son of the late Tutor of Loup, and leader of the raid, to be given up to him in security for reparation of his loss and for the good order of the Clan pending his obtaining satisfaction. This measure for the vindication of Montgomery's rights was, however, so fenced round with restrictions and precautions that the advantage he derived from it was more apparent than real. Montgomery was compelled to give a bond for £40,000 in security for the delivery of Alexander MacAlister to Angus of Dunnyveg and Archibald, his natural son, and this security not being regarded as sufficient, he also had to pledge his lands in Arran for the payment of this large sum. Some time having elapsed without Alexander's surrender to the authorities, John, Marquis of Hamilton, feudal superior of Arran, procured letters of horning against Montgomery of Skelmorlie, and was on the eve of denouncing him for his apparent disobedience in failing to bring the wrongdoer to justice, and charged him under the pain of rebellion to do so without delay.

Montgomery now occupies the anomalous position of being the aggrieved party in the case, and at the same time the object of a formidable legal prosecution by this potentate of the West. He excused himself on the ground that the time allowed for letters of horning was too brief, in respect that the distance of the complainer's house from the seat of justice was twenty miles of sea, and from the mainland to the coast sixty or eighty miles, the King being at the time resident in the town of Perth. It was therefore impossible for the complainer, being in the Lowlands at the time, either to deliver up Alexander MacAlister or to seek remedy at Court within so short a time, the charge having been made at his house at Knockransay. If he delivered Alexander to the Marquis he would be in danger not only of forfeiting the penalty of £40,000, but also the lands in security, and thus losing all chance of remedy. The Clan Alasdair, he went on to say, were "sic unhappie peple and of sic force as the complainer is unable to resist," and he feared that they would, under pretence of the bond, put themselves into possession of his lands to the utter "wrak" of his tenants and servants. He, however, concluded his complaint by saying he had found caution to surrender Alexander, if it should be found that he ought to do so. The cautioner was Hugh Montgomery, bailie of the regality of Kilwinning, who pledged himself for £1000 that Montgomery of Skelmorlie would enter Alexander MacAlister before either of the Justices of the Privy Council, on the 10th November following, if ordered to do so, and also to pay, within forty days, to the Treasurer, £100 for his escheat, or else obtain nullity of the horning used against him for not having delivered Alexander to John, Marquis of Hamilton. This bond was subscribed on 21st September 1601. We have no information as to the punishment inflicted upon Alexander for his violence in the isle of Arran. Whether moderate or severe, it did not prove remedial, for in the course of a few years the same chieftain became involved in a broil fraught with results of a far more serious nature than the invasion of Bute seems to have entailed.

Alexander MacAlister was not the only scion of the Clan who cast covetous glances upon the fertile fields and well-stocked homesteads of Bute. In 1603 Archibald MacAlister, heir-apparent of Tarbert, took part in another invasion of that long-suffering island. This time, however, the MacAlisters were not alone concerned. Chieftains from North Kintyre, including Campbell of Auchinbreck, were parties to the attack, with the hereditary champion of law and order, the Earl of Argyll covertly aiding and abetting a common "herschipp." A force of 1200 men, all supplied with arms, "hagbutts and pistolettes," set sail for Bute.

On their arrival they proceeded first to damage the property of Marion Stewart, and to harry her lands of Wester Kames. Thence they passed on to the lands of Ninian Stewart, Sheriff of the County, where all sorts of atrocities were committed. The raiders being vassals of Argyll, that nobleman was accountable to the Council for their behaviour, and when he and they were summoned to appear and failed to do so, all of them—the Earl, Archibald MacAlister, and the the other delinquents—were ordered to be denounced as rebels. With this denunciation, which was apparently inoperative so far as punishing the guilty was concerned, the episode appears to have closed.

Two years later, on 13th June 1605, an order was issued by the Privy Council to Archibald MacAlister of Loup, and John MacAlister, Tutor of Loup, to exhibit their infeftments and rentals, as well as to find sureties for the payment of Crown rents, on pain of having the titles declared null and void, and being denounced as rebels. Loup appears to have been one of the few who attended, and we find that he received titles from Argyll for his lands of Loup and others during that year.

So far as the public records of the age can indicate, the history of the Clan Alasdair of Kintyre is a blank for the next nine years. In 1614, however, Alexander MacAlister, the hero of the Knockransay raid, appears as an actor in a much more portentous drama, the events that consummated the final downfall of the House of Dunnyveg. Alexander left Kintyre ostensibly to help in carrying out the policy of his feudal superior, Argyll, and take part in the capture of the castle of Dunnyveg, in the King's name; but no sooner did he arrive at the seat of war in Islay than he quickly threw in his lot with Angus Og, the leader of the Macdonalds of Islay. Donald MacAlister, the Tutor of Loup, appears among the friends who, with Angus Og, drew up terms of settlement with the Bishop of Argyll, the King's representative in the island. Although Alexander does not appear as a party to the bond, yet his share in the rebellion is shewn in the evidence he gave before the Council in 1615, for the vindication of Angus Og, and he shared in the punishments inflicted on the rebels. While awaiting his trial in the Tolbooth prison in Edinburgh, the Lords of Council made provision for his "interteynment and charges," to the amount of ten shillings per day, while a kinsman of his, Angus MacEachan MacAlister, apparently his social inferior, received five shillings daily. Other members of the Clan Alasdair—"Ronald Oig MacAllister, Soirlle MacAllister, Angus MacAchane MacAllister, and Donald MacAllister Wrik"—were charged with complicity in the taking of Dunnyveg. Alexander MacAlister, the principal member of the Clan involved in these unfortunate proceedings, became the victim of the same tragic fate which overtook Angus Og. Both were found guilty of treason, and hanged for having resisted the Royal forces by the defence of that historic fortress.

In 1617, Donald MacAlister, a cadet of Loup, from Barr, appeared among those to whom, with the Earl of Argyll, a commission was given for the pursuit and apprehension of Alan Cameron of Lochiel and a number of clansmen and associates, who were at the horn for armed convention and slaughter, and various acts of lawlessness. In 1618, we find the Laird of Loup among those who appeared before the Council with proposals for keeping the peace within Argyll, while, in 1623, MacAlister of Loup is on the Commission of Justices of the Peace in Argyllshire.

The tranquillity of these years was eventually broken in 1623 when Godfrey MacAlister, who was at this date the active head of the house of Tarbert and apparently a man of position, energy, and enterprise, is found to be at feud with a number of the landowners of Renfrew and Ayr, against whom forays were conducted on quite an extensive scale. Among the victims of his attacks were

Sir Archibald Stewart of Castlemilk, John Shaw of Greenock, Ferlie of that Ilk, John Crawford of Kilbirnie, John Brenshaw of Bishoptown, and James Crawford of Flatterton. Godfrey was evidently able to hold his own against these Lowland barons to such effect that they had to seek the intervention of the Government. On 7th September 1623, a bond of caution had to be signed on Godfrey's behalf by John Lamont of Auchnagaill in £1000, pledging that Godfrey was not to molest these Lowland lieges or their families. It appears, however, that the chief of Tarbert was not always the aggressor, for on the very day on which this bond of caution was registered, Joseph Millar, advocate, registered two bonds of caution for his protection, one by Archibald MacVicar of Blairrowne in £1000 for Malcolm MacNaughtan of Stronseir, and another by John Dunlop in Kirk-michael, Stirling, for £500 on behalf of Dougall Campbell in Knockdarrow, securing that both would abstain from molesting Godfrey MacAlister, fiar of Tarbert, and his servants. Both bonds were dated at Inveraray on 24th September 1623. On 5th November, however, Godfrey has to find caution for both himself and Ronald Roy MacAlister for 3000 and 500 merks respectively not to molest Walter MacAulay of Ardincaple, Malcolm MacNaughtan of Stronseir, Robert Colhoun, fiar of Cumstrodone, and Dougal Campbell in Mamoir, nor their families, and that Godfrey would pay 40 merks and Ronald £10 for their escheat to the Treasurer. The bond of caution granted by Andrew MacEachan of Kil-blane contained a clause of relief by Godfrey in favour of the granter.

Before we part with this turbulent chief there remains to be recounted the story of a serious quarrel that broke out between himself and Walter MacAulay of Ardincaple. The Government, having adopted a policy of reform for the Western Highlands, sought to make the herring of Lochfyne an instrument of that "civilising" policy. The Admiral of the Western Seas, with his deputies, protected the fishermen of those waters. Macaulay of Ardincaple had apparently been ousted from the deputy admiralship in favour of Godfrey MacAlister of Tarbert. In the record of the dispute Godfrey is called "Admiral Depute," while Ardin-caple receives the title of "pretended Admiral." This disagreement was injurious to the industry which the Government sought to protect. The "slayers of herrings" were, as might be expected, greatly embarrassed by this dual control. Sometimes they were summoned to the courts of the real, sometimes to those of the pretended Admiral, while fines for absence were imposed sometimes by the one, sometimes by the other. The real and pretended Admiral were, in the usual form, bound to keep the peace, and on 1st October 1623, Mr Matthew Forsyth, advocate, as procurator for the cautioners, registers a bond of caution by Hector MacNeill of Kilmichell and John Lamont of Achnagaill in 3000 merks for Godfrey MacAlister, fiar of Tarbert, Admiral Depute of the West Seas; and in 1000 merks each for Hector MacAlister of Glenranloch, Godfrey's brother; Ewen MacGilleasbuig Vc Kenneth, one of his officers; John Stewart, his bailie substitute; and James Bruce, notary, his clerk of court, not to molest Walter Macaulay of Ardincaple, pretended Admiral Depute of the said West Seas, and his family. As often happens regarding Highland quarrels and delinquencies, the records do not state how this matter was settled, if it was settled at all.

After 1624 the annals of the Clan Alasdair of Kintyre are few and meagre. On 5th December 1627, Godfrey MacAlister, heir apparent of Tarbert, granted a bond in favour of Archibald, his father, whereby he disponed to him certain lands in the parish of Glassary. This was done for the security of Archibald, as cautioner for the granter in a contract with Hector MacAlister and Margaret Campbell, his wife. In 1631 the same Archibald MacAlister of Tarbert visited his distinguished clansman, William Alexander, Earl of Stirling, at Menstrie, and was with him elected a burgess of Stirling on 10th August of that year. It is said that during this visit MacAlister acknowledged the Earl as his chief; but, though there seems to be some ground for the statement in the records of the Lyon Court, we should suppose that the Laird of Loup, the real head of the clan, would have something to say to such a proceeding.

Meantime the records have been very silent as to the history of the main family and, even when the head of the house is referred to, identification is rendered doubly difficult by the fact that the Christian name is often omitted. For a long period up to 1661 little can be gathered regarding the family of Loup. In that year Godfrey MacAlister of Loup is apparently no more, for Hector MacAlister of Loup is a commissioner in the shire of Argyll for regulating, ordering, and lifting the annuity of £40,000 granted to Charles II by the estates of the realm. Two years later the heads both of Loup and Tarbert were Justices of Peace in their districts, appointed under an Act of Parliament. In 1667, when an Act of the Convention of the Estates was passed voting a sum of money to the King, Ranald MacAlister, Captain of Tarbert, was commissioner for Argyll.

We find no further notice of the Clan Alasdair until 1689. By that time the great bloodless Revolution was an accomplished fact, and the son of the late Earl of Argyll, whose titles and possessions, as well as his life, had been forfeited, returned home from William's Court at the Hague. The presence of Argyll in Scotland is witnessed in a display of loyalty shown by the chief of Loup. A French vessel which had sailed from Ireland touched at some port in Kintyre, and was taken possession of by MacAlister and Angus Campbell of Kilberry. The two local chiefs put her under a guard of thirty men, and wrote Argyll, who was attending the Convention of Estates, asking for instructions as to how to dispose of the ship. The Convention issued orders that a sufficient crew should be placed on board to take the ship to Glasgow, and, if necessity should arise, to press seamen into the service, and that as much of the loading should be disposed of as would defray the expense of taking her from Kintyre to her destination. It would appear, however, that the Laird of Loup's loyalty was short-lived, for there is evidence that the Clan Alasdair, probably under the leadership of their chief, shared with their kinsmen of Clan Donald in the brilliant victory of Killiecrankie.

From 1689 to 1704 we lose sight of the Clan Alasdair, and the fact that heads of the family do not appear as acting in any public capacity in their district, either as Justices or Commissioners of Supply, is an indication that the shadow of the Revolution rested on them, along with all loyal adherents of the House of Stewart. In 1704, however, during the first Parliament of Queen Anne we find Alexander MacAlister of Loup and Archibald MacAlister of Tarbert, both acting as Commissioners of Supply for Argyll, which suggests that under the reign of a member of the historic House suspicions of disloyalty were removed. In 1705 we find Archibald MacAlister of Tarbert promoting the commercial interests of his property by an Act which passed the Scottish Parliament, ordaining quarterly fairs and a weekly market to be held at the town of East Tarbert. Each of the quarterly fairs was to last for two days, and the weekly market was to be held every Tuesday. By 1706 Tarbert had ceased to belong to the Clan Alasdair, having passed into the possession of a Maclean.

Alexander MacAlister of Loup, who flourished at and after the Revolution, was succeeded by his son, Godfrey. He had another son, Duncan, who went to Holland and settled there in 1717, and *his* son Robert rose to the rank of a general in the Dutch service, commanding the Scots brigade. His descendants are still in that country, and continue to cherish their connections with the MacAlisters of Loup. Since the time of the Revolution, son has succeeded father

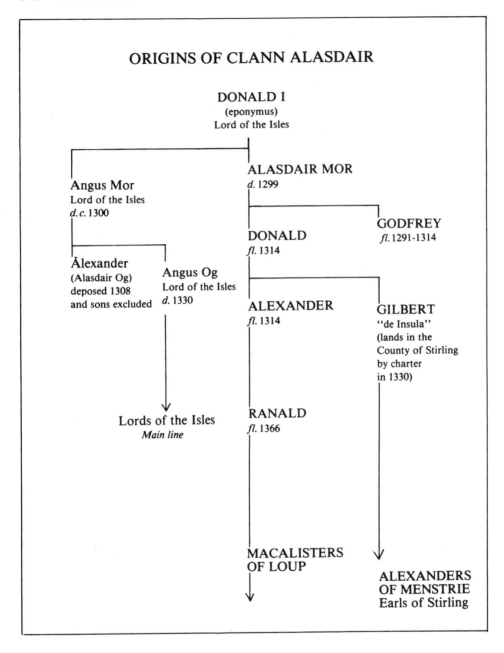

ORIGINS OF CLANN ALASDAIR

DONALD I
(eponymus)
Lord of the Isles

Angus Mor
Lord of the Isles
d.c. 1300

ALASDAIR MOR
d. 1299

GODFREY
fl. 1291-1314

DONALD
fl. 1314

Alexander
(Alasdair Og)
deposed 1308
and sons excluded

Angus Og
Lord of the Isles
d. 1330

ALEXANDER
fl. 1314

GILBERT
"de Insula"
(lands in the
County of Stirling
by charter
in 1330)

Lords of the Isles
Main line

RANALD
fl. 1366

MACALISTERS
OF LOUP

ALEXANDERS
OF MENSTRIE
Earls of Stirling

in unbroken and uneventful succession. Many years ago this family severed its immemorial connection with the peninsula of Kintyre, when Colonel Charles Somerville MacAlister, great-grandfather of the present head of Loup, sold his Highland estates.

II

THE ALEXANDERS OF MENSTRIE

It is accepted that this family derive their descent from Alasdair Mor, younger son of Donald (eponymous), in the 13th Century. Our seanachies link them with Gilbert, a son of Donald, eldest son of the founder of the MacAlisters of Loup.

This Gilbert is found early in the 14th century receiving a charter for lands in Stirlingshire, identified as Glorat in the Parish of Campsie. By the 16th century the descendants of this Gilbert (called *de Insula*) were settled on the estates of Menstrie in the County of Clackmannan, at the base of the Ochil Hills and some five miles north-east of Stirling.

During the generations which followed Gilbert, the "Mac" was dropped and the family adopted the more Lowland name of "Alexander," by which they have been known ever since. They first come to our notice in 1505 when Thomas Alexander is named as arbiter in a dispute between the Abbot of Cambuskenneth Abbey, which is near the lands of Menstrie, and Sir David Bruce of Clackmannan. Again in 1518 William Alexander is found in possession of the estate of Tullibody and Menstrie, with which the family were connected right down to 1739 when the last Earl of Stirling died without issue. They were in the position of lesser barons holding their lands of a feudal superior, in this case the Earl of Argyll. Andrew Alexander, son of the arbiter Thomas, had a charter from Argyll of the lands of Menstrie, dated 8th April 1526, granted to himself and his wife Catherine Graham in life-rent, and in fee to his son Alexander, who succeeded him in 1527.

In the following years the terms of tenure were frequently changed by Argyll but, apart from a confusing detail of charter and sasine, testament and succession, which nevertheless left the Alexanders firmly established in their estates, the history of the family continued its uneventful course until the end of the century and the advent on the public stage of its most distinguished member. William Alexander was born about 1567 and on his father's death in 1580 was entrusted to the care of his grand-uncle James, whom his father in his will had designated guardian of his children and thereafter was known as the Tutor of Menstrie. Since James lived in Stirling it is likely that William received his early education in the Grammar School of that town. He later attended the University of Leyden where he completed his studies before returning to assume his position as head of his house.

Beyond these meagre facts, nothing is known of his early manhood, and the first incident connected with his life that remains on public record is his infeftment in the five pound land of the Mains of Menstrie, in 1597, by Archibald, Earl of Argyll. The precept of sasine is dated 18th March, 1597-8. From Archibald, Earl of Argyll, he subsequently received the lands and barony of Menstrie for the yearly payment of 24 bolls of wheat, 6 score bolls malt, 52 bolls oatmeal, and 23 bolls oats, together with 4 dozen "sufficient capons, and 2 dozen hens, and 30 unclipped lambs, with 100 merks of money, and 40 merks at the entry of an heir in place of the duplicand of the feu duty." On 24th September 1607, a charter was granted to him, under the Great Seal, of the minerals and metals of every kind with the lands and barony of Menstrie, one-tenth of the proceeds being payable to the sovereign.

William Alexander's entrance into public life dates from his introduction to the Scottish Court by the Earl of Argyll, the hereditary patron of his house, upon which he was appointed tutor to Prince Henry, the heir apparent to the throne. On the union of the Crowns in 1603, Alexander followed James to England, and was enrolled as one of the thirty-two gentlemen extraordinary of Prince Henry's private chamber. His gifts as a poet, his culture as a scholar, and his high intellectual endowments, strongly commended him to King James, and the influence he brought to bear on that monarch's susceptibilities soon began to bear fruit. In 1607, Sir William Erskine of Balgonie, commonly called Parson of Campsie, received a Royal warrant for an Exchequer pension of £200 a year to be shared with his son-in-law, William Alexander, and it was stipulated that after Erskine's death half the amount should continue to be payable to his son-in-law. In 1608, William Alexander and his relative, Walter Alexander, a member of the Prince's household, received authority to uplift all arrears of taxes due to the Crown from the first year of the reign of Edward VI up to the thirtieth year of Elizabeth, amounting to £12,000, a sum on which they were to receive a commission of one half; but what benefits, if any, they derived from this concession history does not record. About 1609 William Alexander received the honour of knighthood from the King. The death of Prince Henry, the heir to the throne, on 6th November 1612, at the early age of eighteen, plunged the nation into mourning, and Sir William Alexander's elegaic poem on the life cut short in its early prime worthily commemorates the sad event. In token of appreciation James appointed the poet to the same position in Prince Charles' household as he occupied in that of the late Prince.

The project with which Sir William Alexander's name is chiefly connected is his scheme for the establishment of an American colony under the name of "New Scotland." The foundations of the great Republic of the West were laid in the famous patent of 1620, by which forty English subjects, incorporated as a Council "for planting, ruling, ordering and governing New England," acquired lands extending from the 40th to the 48th degree of latitude, and from the Atlantic to the Pacific Ocean. Sir William believed he saw in these settlements an opportunity for relieving the poverty of his needy fellow-countrymen and at the same time advancing his own private interests. He therefore secured the Royal consent for his establishment of a new Scottish Colony in Canadian territory and he was given a grant of the vast district known since then as Nova Scotia, consisting of the lands lying east of the St Croix, and south of the St Lawrence. The patent for acquiring this large territory was enacted on 10th September 1621, and on the 29th of the same month a charter passed under the Great Seal appointing Sir William Alexander hereditary Lieutenant of the new Colony.

When loss and disaster attended the initial stages of his colonial enterprise, Sir William had recourse to an expedient already successfully employed by James for the replenishment of a depleted treasury. To encourage the settlement of Ulster a new order of baronets had been devised, and the sale of these titles had proved a valuable source of much-needed revenue. Now Sir William Alexander, adopting the same methods, obtained the Royal consent, with that of the Lords of Council, to the establishment of a baronetcy of Nova Scotia among Scottish landowners, the fees of enrolment and the purchase money to go towards the expenses of the colony. The death of James I, in 1625, somewhat retarded the progress of events; but Charles I continued to show Sir William the same royal favour by confirming him in the office of Lieutenant of Nova Scotia, and the charter of 12th July 1625 contained additional clauses regarding the new order of baronets, restricting the number to one hundred and fifty, and promising that the former grant would be confirmed by Parliament. All who paid £150 for six thousand acres were to receive the honour of a knight baronetcy, while the King, by letter to the Scottish Privy Council dated 19th July 1625, fixed the amount of land that was granted to the new baronets at "thrie myles in breadth, and six in lenth, of landis within New Scotland, for their several proportions." When a technical difficulty arose as to the infeftment of the newly made baronets in their freshly acquired territories without their own presence on the spot, recourse was had to a curious legal fiction. The soil of the Castle Hill of Edinburgh was, by a Royal mandate, converted into that of Nova Scotia, and there they were invested with their dignities, and took sasine of their lands.

Meantime, Sir William Alexander continued to advance in royal favour. The Earl of Melrose having been removed from the office of Chief Secretary for Scotland, Sir William was promoted to the vacant post. The difficulties encountered by the settlers in the young colony were causing grave concern, and early in 1627 preparations were made for a new expedition. On the eve of its departure alarming rumours were brought to Britain as to claims actively pressed by French Canadian settlers to a territory which embraced the whole of the region in which Nova Scotia was situated. This was not be wondered at, since the region in question belonged to the French, if only by right of prior discovery and occupation. The English Government, however, acted with energy. In an engagement which ensued the French suffered a serious defeat, and the Scottish settlers were meanwhile left masters of the situation. The news of the victory gave a new impetus to the colonial enterprise; fourteen new patents of baronetcy were recorded, new vessels were chartered, and Sir William Alexander's eldest son was appointed to accompany the fleet as his father's deputy-lieutenant. It was found on their arrival at Port Royal, the headquarters and stronghold of the colony, that a number of English adventurers were seeking to gain a footing there, and the difficulties arising from their pretensions necessitated the return of young Sir William to Britain in the following year. The result was the frustration of the Englishmen's design, the confirmation of the original grant, and an increase of the powers of the promoters to settle colonies in those regions of the new world.

While Sir William Alexander's colonial ambition now seemed likely to be satisfied, his private fortunes bade fair to be prosperous. In 1627 he was appointed Keeper of the Signet, while his office of Scottish Secretary was enhanced by an addition of £500 by the commutation of certain perquisites which belonged to his predecessors. About this time he resolved to establish a shipping port upon the West of Scotland, and for this purpose obtained a royal charter of the lands of Largs, with permission to erect them into a barony and to construct a free port for the advancement of trade and commerce. On 14th January 1627, he received Irish citizenship, and following the example of several Ayrshire land-owners who had sought to improve their shattered fortunes by acquiring lands in the province of Ulster, he obtained a grant of 1000 acres in the County of Armagh. The Scottish Secretary also enlarged his family estate at home. In 1628 he obtained from Archibald, Lord Lorne, a new charter for Menstrie by which the lands and barony were granted him and his wife on an annual payment of £80 Scots. By another charter under the Great Seal he received the lands and barony of Tullibody, bounding the lands of Menstrie on the south east.

In 1629-30, a crisis arose in the history of the colony with which Sir William's fortunes were so closely identified. Great Britain had been at war with France, but when peace was concluded Port Royal was ceded to France, and with it the extensive district upon which Sir William had staked his fortune. He was promised £6000, and £10,000 was actually voted in recompense for his losses in connection with what was really a national enterprise, but neither he nor his successors ever actually received payment. In view of the vast expenses he incurred on behalf of a colony, first promoted but afterwards abandoned by the Crown, the increasing embarrassments of his private affairs may not perhaps be surprising. The King, however, amid all changes of fortune, continued to favour him with the highest honours. On 4th September 1630 Sir William Alexander was elevated to the state and dignity of Viscount of Stirling and Lord Alexander of Tullibody. The same year Lord Stirling visited Scotland, and sold for £12,000 Scots the lands and port of Largs.

Charles I cannot be absolved from gross inconsistency in his relations with Lord Stirling and the Colony of Nova Scotia; but probably his increasing domestic difficulties prevented him from taking a firm stand at the risk of a rupture with France. Down to the very last he declared his purpose to maintain the Colony, while almost in the same breath with this declaration, Lord Stirling was charged in a Royal missive to abandon it.

In 1631, Viscount Stirling was visited at Menstrie by Archibald MacAlister of Tarbert, who on that occasion acknowledged his Chiefship over the Clan Alasdair. Whatever other significance such a proceeding possessed it seems to confirm the view that the Alexanders of Menstrie were, like the Clan Alasdair of Kintyre, descended from Alasdair Mor's eldest son. Lord Stirling and MacAlister of Tarbert were both elected burgesses of Stirling on the 10th of August of that year. It was about this time also that Lord Stirling matriculated arms. The Royal letter instructing the Lyon King-at-Arms ordered him "to marshall his Coate Armour, allowing it to him, quartered with the armes of Clan Allaster, who hath acknowledged him for chief of the familie." The coat of arms granted to Lord Stirling, combined with the motto, is a clear acknowledgment by him of his Clan Donald descent, and confirms the statements of the genealogists. It is thus described in the MS in the Lyon Office:

Alexander Erle off Stirline, Lord Alexander of Canada, etc., Bairyeth quarterlie—First parted per pale arg. and sable a chiveron with a croisant in bass counterchanged for his paternall coat. Secondlie, or, a lumfad raes in croce sable betwixt thrie croce croslet gules by the name of Mc----; the thrid as the second; the fourt as the first. Over all ane Inscutcheon with the armes of Nova Scotia, viz. arg. a crose azur with the armes of Scotland; abune the schield his comitall crounet; upon the same, his helme and mantle guls doubled ermine. For his creist, on a wreath arg. sable, a bever proper. For supporters a Sacaidge and a Marmaid, combe in hand. His Motto, *Per Mare per terras.*

Lord Stirling had already rebuilt or enlarged the old house of Menstrie; but now, in the town of Stirling, whence he derived his new title, his son Anthony, who had studied architecture, designed a handsome residence. In 1634 the family possessions were further extended when he received under the Great Seal a charter of the lands and town of Tillicoultry. These were erected into a burgh of barony, to be held of the King on the annual payment of £55 Scots.

The latter years of the Earl's life were clouded by domestic sorrow, his oldest son, Lord Alexander, and his second son, Sir Anthony, dying in 1637-38. On 12th February 1640, the Earl of Stirling himself died, and his remains were buried in the family vault of his own town. His character as a public man was in his own day severely criticised by opponents of some of his projects. Yet there is no incident in his life that might be deemed unworthy of an honourable man. His errors were those of a lofty ambition and if he displayed imprudence in his financial transactions, it was not in the pursuit of sordid gain, but of extending to a new continent the power and prestige of his native land. As a poet and as a private gentleman he was esteemed beyond most: Drummond of Hawthornden remained his devoted friend to the last, and Sir Thomas Urquhart, on occasions one of his bitterest critics, addressed to him lines extolling his virtues as poet and as statesman.

The Earl of Stirling seems to have been haunted by the apprehension that the honours he had acquired might pass out of the line of his direct descendants to some collateral branch. With the object of preventing such a contingency, he surrendered his titles of Baronet of Nova Scotia, Lord Alexander of Tullibody, Viscount of Canada, and Earl of Stirling into the King's hands shortly before he died. Thereupon the King, by a charter under the Great Seal dated 7th December 1639, granted these titles *de novo* to the heirs male, and failing them to the eldest heirs female. Yet although several sons had been born to him, and numerous descendants of later generations were present in the male line, by a singular fatality his titles became extinct in less than a century after his death.

William Alexander, the Earl's eldest son, did not succeed his father, having pre-deceased him by about a year, yet some reference to his short but promising career must be made. He received his higher education in the University of Glasgow, which he entered in 1618, his name appearing in the Register as *Gulielmus Alexander haeres Dom. de Menstrie.* In 1628 he received the honour of knighthood, and was appointed by his father governor of Nova Scotia. On 28th March of that year he was granted authority to proceed with four ships to Newfoundland, the river of Canada, and Nova Scotia, for settling colonists in these parts. He returned from Canada in the autumn, and on Christmas day, "after his return from the sea voyage, gave to the puir of Stirling fiftie aucht pundis money." On 11th May 1630, Sir William Alexander received a Royal patent for thirty-one years "for the sole trade in all and singular the regions, countries, dominions and all places adjoining, for beaver skins and wool and all other skins of wild beasts." When his father was created Earl of Stirling, he assumed the courtesy title of Lord Alexander. He was sworn a member of the Privy Council of Scotland in November 1634, and on 20th December Royal letters were issued at Hampstead appointing him an extraordinary Lord of Session in succession to his father. On 22nd April 1635 he received a grant from the Council of New England "of all that part of the mainland in New England from St Croix adjoining New Scotland along the sea coast to Pemo quid and so up the river to the Kuibequi to be henceforth called the County of Canada, also Long Island called the Isle of Stirling." It is said that the hardships which he endured from the rigours of an American winter as his father's deputy in Nova Scotia injured his constitution and led to his premature death, which took place at London on 18th May 1638.

Anthony, the second son of the Earl of Stirling, was, like his brother, a young man of talent and culture. He also received his education at the College of St Mungo, having been registered as a student in March 1623. By letter addressed to the Privy Council in July 1626, Charles I gave him leave to "proceed for three years on foreign travel, the better to qualify him for the gaining of languages and for otherwise doing his Majestie and his countrie service." It appears that while on the Continent, Anthony devoted himself to the study of architecture, and on his return in 1628 he was, on the King's advice, appointed Master of Works conjointly with James Murray of Kilbaberton. In October 1630 he was admitted an honorary burgess of Stirling, and five years later he was knighted at Whitehall.

During these years he had held the office of Joint Master of the King's Works and Buildings in Scotland; but the Scottish Lodge of Free Masons had opposed his nomination, on the ground that the office rightly belonged to their hereditary Grand Master, Sir William St Clair of Roslin, and acting on this objection, the Commissioners of Exchequer delayed giving effect to the Royal warrant for his appointment, as well as the payment of his salary. Before these objections could be disposed of, Sir Anthony died on 17th September 1637, and his remains were laid to rest in the family vault in Stirling.

Henry Alexander, third son of the Earl of Stirling, was educated, like his two elder brothers, in the University of Glasgow. Henry followed mercantile pursuits, and on 13th October 1634 received letters patent under the Great Seal, along with Patrick Maule of Panmure, James Maxwell of Inverwick, and Sir Thomas Thomson of Duddingston, Kt., granting them a monopoly for thirty years of exporting goods from Scotland to America. On 21st April 1636, the same privilege was extended so as to include Africa. Like his brothers, he also received the honour of being made a burgess of Stirling on 9th November 1636, and about the same time was appointed Agent of the Convention of Royal Burghs.

Lord Alexander, the Earl of Stirling's heir, who died in 1638, left an infant son, William, who succeeded his grandfather as second Earl of Stirling. He seems to have survived only a few months, and was succeeded by his uncle, Henry Alexander, as third Earl of Stirling in May 1640. This position he held for ten uneventful years, when he died in 1650, leaving an only son Henry, who succeeded him as fourth Earl of Stirling. The fourth Earl of Stirling was a child at his father's death, and was still a minor in 1661. In that year his guardians submitted to the Privy Council a memorandum bearing upon the youthful Earl's hereditary claim to Nova Scotia and, as the sum of £10,000 voted to the first Earl had never been paid, praying the King to continue to the present Earl the grant of the Colony for which his grandfather had sacrificed his fortune. It does not appear that the petition was granted. Henry, fourth Earl of Stirling, died in February 1690, and his remains were on the 11th of that month interred in the family burial place at Binfield. In his will, dated 13th June 1683, he named as his executors Robert Lee, Esquire, and his "dear sister Dame Jane Alexander," to whom he bequeathed "goods, plate, jewells, and personall estate wheresoever and whatsoever, in trust, that they shall sell and dispose of the same to pay debts and divide surplusage amongst all my children except the eldest, Lord Alexander." He left a large family of sons and daughters, the eldest son, Henry, succeeding him as fifth Earl. He was born on 7th November 1664 and led a life of privacy and retirement, taking no part in public affairs. In the autumn of 1733 he waited on the King and Queen at Court in his 69th year, not having previously paid his respects to royalty since 1691. He was introduced by Sir Robert Walpole, and was graciously received. He died, without issue, on 4th December 1739, and with him the Earls of Stirling, though their patent of nobility could be transmitted through all legal heirs, became extinct. Since his time more than one claimant to the dormant honour has appeared, but none has been able to satisfy the House of Lords as to the unimpeachable validity of his claim, nor is it likely that any of the old line, though morally sure of his descent, will be successful in placing his right of succession genealogically beyond dispute.

The various estates of the first Earl of Stirling were disposed of after his death for the satisfaction of his creditors, while the Stirling mansion, which was never occupied by any of his successors, passed into possession of Archibald, ninth Earl of Argyll, in 1666. In 1764 it was sold on behalf of John, fourth Duke of Argyll, and about the beginning of the present century it was transferred to the War Department, being used as a military hospital.

The name of the first Earl of Stirling will always be remembered in connection with the colony of Nova Scotia. Though ceded to the French in the reign of Charles II, in 1763 it finally came into the undisputed possession of Great Britain, and since that time has been a favourite field of emigration for the many members of Clan Donald who have been forced, by adverse fortune, to leave the country of their birth.

*   *   *

As a foot-note to this history it is interesting to note that in our own time, the "legal fiction" of the Royal Mandate was removed by the action of a Premier of Nova Scotia. The purpose of the Mandate was to enable the barons and baronets of Nova Scotia to take sasine (*i.e.* seizing) of their newly acquired lands without having to cross the Atlantic. In taking sasine the aspirant to the lands was required to take in his hands some of the actual soil of his estates in token of his occupation thereof.

In October 1953, the Rt. Hon. Angus L. MacDonald, Premier of Nova Scotia for twenty-five years, and Minister of Marine for Canada in World War II, visited Edinburgh. At a ceremony on the Castle Esplanade attended by many barons and baronets of Nova Scotia, the Premier scattered a bag of Nova Scotian soil into the moat of the Castle. A plaque commemorating this occasion is on the wall of the moat today at the north-west end of the parade ground.

THE ARMS OF MACIAIN OF ARDNAMURCHAN

Lyon Register, Vol. 18, Folio 20 (1905)

15

The MacIains of Ardnamurchan

ARDNAMURCHAN FORMED PART of the original mainland patrimony of Clann Cholla, and the Castle of Mingary, the stronghold of the MacIain chiefs, is in all probability on the site of an earlier fort of the Norse chief who ruled the district under the Kings of the Sudereys and Man. The long peninsula of Ardnamurchan was traversed in the 6th century by St Columba whose historian, Adamnan, comments on its rough and rocky character when he describes the saint's journey *"per asperam et saxosam regionem quae dicitur Ardamuirchol."*

It was here that Somerled is said to have fought and won his first victory over the Norsemen. The lands first appear in public records in 1292, when they were included by John Balliol in the newly created Sheriffdom of Lorn. There is little doubt that at an earlier period they formed part of the vast lands of Garmoran (the Rough Bounds) given to Angus of Bute, son of Somerled, and which passed from his line, on its extinction, to Ruairi, founder of the Clan Ruairi. About the middle of the 13th century Ardnamurchan appears to have formed part of the Lordship of Lorn and was thus in the possession of the MacDougalls, whose opposition to Bruce led to their forfeiture and in 1309 both Ardnamurchan and Sunart, with other lands, were transferred by charter to Angus Og, Lord of the Isles. It is believed that Ardnamurchan and Sunart, comprising a large estate of some 85,000 acres, were later granted by the Lord of the Isles to his younger brother John, otherwise known as *Iain Sprangach,* whom most authorities accept as the progenitor of the MacIains of Ardnamurchan.

John Sprangach (the Bold or Imperious), like his brother Alexander before and during his tenure of the Lordship, played an active part in the political struggle surrounding the Scottish throne, supporting the cause of Balliol and taking a leading rôle in negotiations with the English King. In the Ragman Rolls we find his name as "Johan de Ile" amongst the two thousand Scottish nobles, clergy and landholders who signed away their freedom and allegiance to Edward I in 1296. John's constant devotion to the interests of the English King brought him many marks of royal favour, not the least of which included his preferment to the high dignity of Baron of the Exchequer in England. In 1305 he was appointed Justice of the Lothians with a salary of 60 merks, and in Edward's subsequent campaign his services were employed to an extent which leaves no doubt of the value placed upon the contribution he was considered capable of making to the cause he served.

There is nothing in the records to indicate whether John Sprangach, after the accession of Bruce, continued to subscribe to the English interest or if he followed his brother Angus Og in his stalwart support of the Scottish King and the cause of Scottish independence. There is no further mention of the family until 1341, the year in which David II returned to his kingdom and set about restoring the authority of the Crown. John, Lord of the Isles, who had given his support to Edward Balliol during the King's absence, was in that year forfeited in all his lands, and many of them were now granted to Angus, the son of John Sprangach. The lands thus conveyed were extensive: the charter mentions "the whole island called Yla, the whole land of Kintyre, the island of Gychay, 24 unciates of Colonsay and two unciates of Morvern."

It may be noted that no reference is made in this charter to Ardnamurchan, which had been granted by Bruce to Angus Og in 1309 and was subsequently confirmed to his son John, Lord of the Isles, by Edward Balliol in 1335. If Angus had possessed Ardnamurchan he must have held it from the Lord of the Isles, and it is therefore not apparent why it was not included in his charter of 1341, unless the grounds of his existing tenure were regarded as of sufficient validity.

Down to the fall of the Lordship, the history of the MacIains of Ardnamurchan is merged in that of the main family of the Isles, whose cause they loyally supported in its frequent confrontations with the power of the State. We hear no more of Angus after the charter of 1341. His son and successor Alexander must have been a man of advanced age in the year 1411, but he loyally responded to his Chief's call to arms and supported him throughout the campaign which culminated in the bloody field of Harlaw. Alexander is thought to have met his death in that battle, or at any rate very shortly thereafter, because in 1420 his son John is found witnessing the resignation by William de Grahame of the Barony of Kerndale in Ross.

John of Ardnamurchan next comes before us in the events following James I's notorious visit to Inverness in 1427, when many of the Highland chiefs were treacherously seized by the King. The story is told in Chapter 10 of the manner in which the royal justice was administered on that occasion, some of the leading disturbers of the peace being summarily tried and executed, while many more, including Alexander, Lord of the Isles, were committed to various prisons. No sooner was Alexander released than he launched his punitive expedition against the crown lands near Inverness, and John of Ardnamurchan played a prominent part in the extensive ravaging that took place over a wide area. His activities attracted the particular attention of the Frasers of Lovat who, on the defeat of Alexander by the royal forces, proceeded to lay waste the Clan Donald lands as far as Ardnamurchan. There they were met by the MacIains who had marshalled the support of their kinsmen, and the Frasers were thrown back with great slaughter.

When **Donald Balloch** raised the standard of revolt on behalf of his imprisoned Chief in 1431, John of Ardnamurchan and his men contributed their full share to the overwhelming victory that followed at Inverlochy. On regaining his freedom Alexander rewarded John MacIain with certain lands in Islay, together with the bailiary of that island. His services were at the same time recognised by Donald Balloch who bestowed upon him the gift of lands in Jura.

On the accession of John, last Lord of the Isles, in 1449, John MacIain became a member of his Island Council. The last time he appears on record is as witness to a charter in 1463. His death must have taken place before 1467, for in that year his son Alexander is named as one of the Island Council and witnesses a charter granted by the Lord of the Isles to his brother, Celestine of Lochalsh. Two years later he again appears as a member of the Council and as signatory to the charter granted by the Island Lord to his brother, Hugh of Sleat. The last mention we have of Alexander is in connection with another charter in 1478. There is no record of the part, if any, he played in Angus Og's gallant struggle to restore the fortunes of the Lordship, and he died some years before the final forfeiture.

Alexander was succeeded by his nephew John, whose legitimacy has been questioned by the Sleat historian. Hugh Macdonald asserts that John was a natural son of Alexander and that he usurped the estates, thus dispossessing the sons of his uncle, Donald Ruadh, for whom he acted as Tutor. John's legitimacy, however, and his right to the succession appear to be confirmed by the charter granted by James IV in 1506, in which he is referred to as "grandson and heir of John, the son of Alexander, the son of John of Ardnamurchan." The position to which John succeeded was already one of considerable influence and power in the Highlands. Besides Ardnamurchan and Sunart, he had lands in parts of Kintyre, in Islay and in Jura; and his extraordinary abilities, adjudged and condemned by his contemporaries as symptoms of mental instability, were to be skilfully employed throughout his career in adding to his possessions at the expense of clansmen left defenceless in the void of the fallen Lordship.

When James IV came to Dunstaffnage in 1493 to receive the submission of the Island vassals, John MacIain was one of the first to make a show of loyalty to the monarch, and from that time he consistently supported the royal policy in opposition to the aspirations of other vassals of the fallen Lordship. He received his first reward in June 1494, when the King granted him a charter of lands in Islay formerly held by him under the Lord of the Isles. Such a charter was not likely to relieve the enmity already existing between MacIain and the powerful Chief of Dunnyveg over the latter's claims to the lands of Sunart, and especially MacIain's possessions in Islay. The opportunity for putting an end to the dispute once and for all was soon provided by events which, precipitated by the rashness of the Dunnyveg Chief, played into the hands of the designing MacIain and, while confirming him in his attachment to the service of the Crown, condemned him for ever in the eyes of Clan Donald for an act of perfidy outstanding in its annals.

John of Dunnyveg was one of the Chiefs who made his submission with MacIain at Dunstaffnage and on that occasion received from the King the honour of knighthood. In the following year the King, impatient to establish his authority throughout the whole peninsula of Kintyre, proceeded to fortify the stronghold of Tarbert in the north and occupied and garrisoned the Castle of Dunaverty in the south. The whole district of Kintyre was regarded by the Islay family as an inviolable part of their possessions, and the royal action in placing garrisons in their territory provoked their strong and active resentment. The King had scarcely embarked before Sir John of Dunnyveg and his son John Cathanach laid siege to Dunaverty, took the castle by storm, and hanged the Governor from the battlements in full sight of the departing King.

The King responded to this affront by issuing a summons for treason against the Dunnyveg Chief. Sir John ignored the summons, and the King cast about for other means of executing his vengeance. He found it in MacIain of Ardnamurchan, already high in the royal favour, and ready to seize any opportunity for finally resolving his private feud with the Islay family. He was no doubt also prompted by his father-in-law, the Earl of Argyll, whose predatory gaze was fixed upon the territorial advantages to be gained from internecine divisions in the defunct Lordship. Towards the end of 1494 MacIain and his men proceeded to Finlaggan in Islay and, by employing what must in the circumstances have been a subtle and devious stratagem, succeeded in apprehending the Chief of Dunnyveg, his son John Cathanach, "and their accomplices," all of whom were later tried and executed in Edinburgh. For this dark deed MacIain was expressly rewarded in 1499 when he received a royal charter of 20 merklands in Sunart, 10

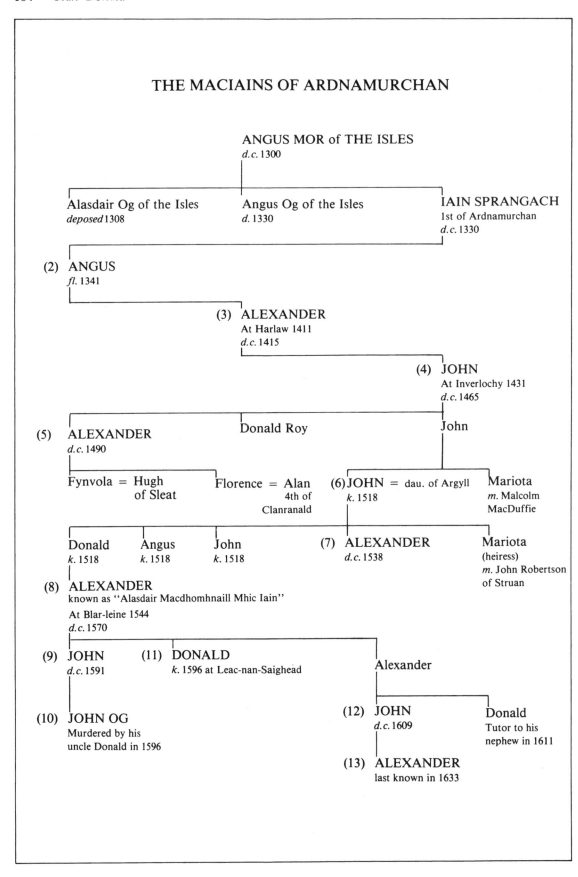

THE MACIAINS OF ARDNAMURCHAN

ANGUS MOR of THE ISLES
*d.c.*1300

Alasdair Og of the Isles
*deposed*1308

Angus Og of the Isles
*d.*1330

IAIN SPRANGACH
1st of Ardnamurchan
*d.c.*1330

(2) ANGUS
*fl.*1341

(3) ALEXANDER
At Harlaw 1411
*d.c.*1415

(4) JOHN
At Inverlochy 1431
*d.c.*1465

(5) ALEXANDER
*d.c.*1490

Donald Roy

John

Fynvola = Hugh
of Sleat

Florence = Alan
4th of
Clanranald

(6)JOHN = dau. of Argyll
*k.*1518

Mariota
m. Malcolm
MacDuffie

Donald
*k.*1518

Angus
*k.*1518

John
*k.*1518

(7) ALEXANDER
*d.c.*1538

Mariota
(heiress)
m. John Robertson
of Struan

(8) ALEXANDER
known as "Alasdair Macdhomhnaill Mhic Iain"
At Blar-leine 1544
*d.c.*1570

(9) JOHN
*d.c.*1591

(11) DONALD
*k.*1596 at Leac-nan-Saighead

Alexander

(10) JOHN OG
Murdered by his
uncle Donald in 1596

(12) JOHN
*d.c.*1609

Donald
Tutor to his
nephew in 1611

(13) ALEXANDER
last known in 1633

merklands in Jura, and more lands in Islay. Although at the same time he had to surrender his lands in Kintyre, he was amply recompensed by another royal charter of the lands of Ardnamurchan and the Castle of Mingary, the scene of many a royal visit in years to come.

In the meantime MacIain continued unflagging in his zeal for the royal service. When Sir Alexander of Lochalsh was defeated by the Mackenzies at Drumchatt in 1497, he was forced to retire to Colonsay where he sought the aid of the Island chiefs in his attempt to restore the Lordship. The firm measures taken by the King, however, were still fresh in the minds of the Islesmen, and they were not yet ready to join in an insurrection against the government. The isolation in which Sir Alexander was thus placed exposed him to the machinations of his enemies, and MacIain of Ardnamurchan became their willing instrument. Sir Alexander's subsequent death at MacIain's hands provoked a reaction which forced the government to take steps to protect MacIain from reprisals by his infuriated kinsmen and neighbours. The Chiefs of Clanranald and Keppoch, Maclean of Duart and Cameron of Lochiel were all bound in the sum of £500 each as surety for the safety of MacIain from molestation or injury by them or their followers.

In spite of these pledges, we find the Chief of Clanranald soon afterwards involved in a serious quarrel with MacIain over the lands of Sunart, of which the former claimed possession by virtue of a lease alleged to have been granted by Sir John of Dunnyveg. The dispute was resolved only by the intervention of the King, and the right of possession of these lands was finally decided in favour of MacIain and was confirmed in one of the royal charters granted to him in 1499.

All these marks of royal favour had helped to raise John of Ardnamurchan to a position of power and pre-eminence in Clan Donald, and his loyalty to the King remained constant throughout his reign. In the rebellion of Donald Dubh, he ranged himself against his kinsmen and rendered conspicuous service in the suppression of that forlorn attempt to restore the Lordship. For this he was rewarded in 1505 when, "for the good, faithful and willing service done to him by his dear John Makkane of Ardnamurchan," the King confirmed him in all the lands formerly granted to him in Ardnamurchan and Sunart, with the Castle of Mingary and Dunnyveg, and the bailiary of Islay. His exercise of the latter office was a cause of considerable friction in Islay and resulted in a serious dispute between MacIain and Maclean of Duart, who also possessed lands in the island. Here again the King intervened, settling the dispute in MacIain's favour, and binding Maclean and his kinsman of Lochbuie to abstain from molesting MacIain and his followers. In 1506 a final charter confirmed MacIain in all his possessions, with the addition of certain other lands in Islay and Jura which were claimed as crown property by virtue of the forfeiture of 1493.

The death of the King at Flodden left MacIain exposed to the vengeance of the many enemies created by his activities in the service of the monarch. Foremost among them was Alexander of Dunnyveg, whose father and grandfather had been treacherously seized by MacIain and were later executed at Edinburgh. The story has been told in another Chapter of MacIain's relentless pursuit of Alexander and his brother into the Glens of Antrim, and his usurpation of the family's estates in Islay. With the death of James IV Alexander saw the way clear for his return to Scotland and the recovery of his lands. Although MacIain's subsequent expulsion from Islay is said to have been accomplished on terms which included Alexander's promise to marry his daughter, there is no evidence to suggest that such a matrimonial alliance influenced his resolve to exact the fullest retribution for the injuries inflicted on his House.

Alexander's opportunity, like that of MacIain's other enemies, arose with the enterprise launched by Sir Donald of Lochalsh for the restoration of the Lordship. Apart from the over-riding aim, the two Chiefs were united in the common purpose of avenging the death of their parents at the treacherous hands of MacIain. They were supported by the Macleods of Lewis and Raasay, and together they formed a powerful combination which MacIain, deserted even by many members of his own clan, had no hope of resisting. Ardnamurchan was invaded, the Castle of Mingary taken, and the whole district wasted with fire and sword. In a second incursion in 1518, the lands were again ravaged and MacIain was eventually forced to make his last stand at Creag-an-Airgid. Here, after a bloody and stoutly-fought engagement, MacIain and many of his followers were killed, including his sons Iain Sunartach and Angus. MacIain was taken for burial to Iona, where a stone placed on his grave by his sister Mariota's husband, Malcolm Macduffie of Colonsay, bears the inscription: *Hic jacet Johannes Macceain dominus de Ardnamurchan et Mariota Macceain soror eius sponsa Malcolmi Macduffie de Deneuin in Colonse hanc lapidem emit sua fratri.*

John MacIain had achieved for himself a position of great power and influence in the Isles and in his relations with the central Government, but the methods he employed in advancing the interests of his family bore the seeds of its eventual destruction. His death marked the beginning of a decline in the fortunes of his House, which was accelerated by the long minority of his successor. Alexander, his surviving son and heir, was a mere child on his accession and appears to have died before reaching his majority. The wardship was granted by the Crown to the Earl of Argyll, who thus received into his hands the control of vast estates. These included, at least nominally, the lands in Islay granted by charter to young MacIain's father but in the actual possession of Alexander of Dunnyveg. It would appear that Argyll delegated some of his duties as guardian of the young MacIain to his brother, Sir John Campbell of Cawdor, and in pursuance of his policy of family aggrandisement, determined to make the most of the opportunities presented by the situation. Thus in 1520 we find Alexander of Dunnyveg entering into a bond of service with Sir John Campbell of Cawdor in return for which he received a five-year lease of 45 merklands in Islay. Alexander's concern was at any cost to recover possession of lands which were deemed to belong to him as of right, and he had no intention of implementing his engagement to Cawdor. Nor had Cawdor's assumption of superiority any legal basis except in so far as it derived from Argyll as guardian of the young MacIain. The whole transaction marks a stage in the insidious process by which Argyll and Cawdor were in course of time to divide between them the greater part of the patrimony of Clan Donald.

Young MacIain died some time before 1538, for in that year his sister Mariota, who was married to Robert Robertson of Struan, was named heiress to all the lands possessed by her father at his death. Two years later Mariota resigned these lands in favour of the Earl of Argyll, but in the following year the Earl surrendered them to the Crown in return for a payment of £5000. In 1543 the same lands were leased by the Crown to Argyll for a period of 12 years, but in 1550, on account of some alleged irregularity in the transaction, and by virtue of the original resignation by Mariota in his favour, the 80 merklands of Ardnamurchan were granted to the Earl by Crown charter. Although these lands were almost immediately bestowed by Argyll on James Macdonald of Dunnyveg, whose matrimonial alliance with his influential neighbour was thus redounding to his advantage, the superiority of the lands remained with Argyll and his family. The MacIains, however, remained in actual possession for many years to come, and this situation appears to have been tacitly accepted by their superiors, either of whom at any time had the power if not the will to expel them from their ancestral lands.

It is difficult to understand the motives which led the Government to deprive the MacIains of the legal titles they had acquired by their long and dedicated service to the Crown. The explanation is probably to be found in the view taken by the Government of the activities of young MacIain's successor. This was his cousin, another Alexander, who played a prominent part in the rebellious proceedings that marked the decade following his accession. He gave his loyal support to the newly liberated John of Moidart, the avenging chief of Clanranald, and joined that doughty warrior in his ravaging expeditions to Urquhart and Glenmorison. He was also by his side at the battle of Blar-na-leine where the Frasers were virtually annihilated. Four years later his name appeared with that of other chiefs in a remission granted for the slaughter of the Frasers in that battle, and for his failure in 1547 to attend the hosting at Fala Muir to repel the English invader.

Alexander was also closely involved in Donald Dubh's second attempt to restore the Lordship, and was among the first to join his standard. He rendered loyal service as a member of the Island Council, and was furthermore selected as one of the commissioners appointed by Donald Dubh to conduct negotiations with the English king. After these events we lose sight of Alexander except for one appearance on record in 1561, when he is mentioned as holding lands in Ardnamurchan as tenant of the Abbot of Iona, and the Isle of Muck as tenant of the Bishop of the Isles.

Alexander died about the year 1570 and was succeeded by his son John, whose claim to fame centres around the bitter feud between Lachlan Mor Maclean of Duart and the Macdonalds of Dunnyveg. John MacIain followed the rest of Clan Donald in supporting their kinsmen in Islay. The immediate cause

ngary, the stronghold of the
Maclains of Ardnamurchan
from about 1300

of the revival of the feud, which is described in detail in a subsequent Chapter, was Maclean's treacherous seizure of hostages from Angus Macdonald of Dunnyveg when the latter paid him an innocent visit at Duart. Angus in turn seized Lachlan Mor himself and his uncle, John Dubh Maclean of Morvern, when they later came to Islay to enforce the terms of the agreement exacted from Angus. According to the Maclean historians, Lachlan Mor was shortly afterwards conditionally released and returned to Duart, whereupon John MacIain sped to Islay and falsely reported to the Dunnyveg Chief that Lachlan had executed two of his Macdonald hostages. The Islay Chief retaliated by ordering the instant execution of John Dubh Maclean. The immediate outcome was the invasion of MacIain's lands of Ardnamurchan by Alan Maclean of Ardtornish, John Dubh's son. After several bloody encounters, a settlement was eventually achieved by the marriage of Alan Maclean with MacIain's daughter Una, and certain lands that were surrendered with her as her dowry.

No such settlement, however, was possible with Lachlan Mor Maclean who was not disposed to forget MacIain's part in the death of John Dubh and the vigorous support he continued to give to the Macdonalds of Dunnyveg. Maclean soon found an opportunity for exacting a barbarous revenge. MacIain had for some time sought the hand of Lachlan's mother in marriage, and Lachlan, realising how well this might serve his purpose, now gave his consent to the alliance. When everything was prepared, MacIain and his retinue proceeded to the Maclean residence at Torloisk in Mull, where the ceremony was performed without delay. Accounts of what afterwards transpired tend to differ in certain details, but MacIain's own version of the affair has the ring of truth and is likely to be accurate since it is recorded in the complaint he afterwards made to the Privy Council. In that complaint MacIain states that, after mutual expressions of friendship and goodwill, the marriage was solemnised by the "accustomed forme and ordour of the countrey, the banquet made, good countenance and entertainment shewn by all parties, and at nycht the said John MacIain was conveyed by the said Lachlan by the hand to his mother's own chamber and bed purposely to cover his mischief, and that the said John MacIain and his friends might be careless of their own saftey as indeed they departed immediately to take their night's rest in any other house or barn nearest to the place where John MacIain himself was looking for no harm or injury from anyone and least of all from the said Lachlan MacLean or any of his people in respect of his former behaviour, nevertheless immediately after they had fallen asleep said Lachlan and his complices armed with haberschois swerdis and durkis entered per force within the said house or barne and in most cruel and barbarous manner without pity or compassion unmercifully slew the said John MacIain's friends being therein to the number of 18 persons, gentlemen besides others: and not satisfied therewith immediately thereafter repaired to the chamber where the said John MacIain was lying and with equal cruelty pursued him and would have bereft him of his life were it not his own better defence and the lamentable crying out and suit of the said Lachlan's mother for whose sake at last they spared the said John's life, detaining his mother notwithstanding ever since with Alester MacIain and Angus MacIain his page in close captivity; putting his person to daily torture and pains and will in no ways put their prisoners until they be compelled."

MacIain's complaint produced immediate results. Lachlan was summoned to appear personally before the Council to answer for his barbarous conduct, and to produce the persons of his prisoners. On his failure to appear, Lachlan was denounced rebel, but his only response was the tardy release of MacIain. Whatever measures the government chose to take, he obviously regarded them with less apprehension than the more imminent danger presented by the attitude of his powerful neighbours of Clanranald, whose anger and sympathy had been provoked by the treatment meted out to their kinsman of MacIain. Lachlan was aware of the weakness of his position in face of a combination of the MacIains and Clanranald and, in ·the best military tradition, took immediate steps to forestall their attack by striking before the junction of their forces. It so happened that the *Florida*, one of the ships of the dispersed Armada, had sought shelter in Tobermory Bay, and Maclean had supplied the provisions she needed for her homeward voyage. Lachlan now asked for the service of a hundred marines in return for these provisions and, using them as a spearhead, launched an attack on the islands of Rum, Canna, Eigg and Muck, killing many of the inhabitants and carrying off much plunder. He then proceeded to invade Ardnamurchan, laying siege· to the Castle of Mingary. By this time, however, the MacIans and Clanranald had marshalled their forces, and the invaders were defeated with great slaughter, Maclean himself with difficulty escaping. with the remnants of his forces to the safety of his Castle of Duart. The only notice we find the Government taking of these violent proceedings is in the record of a remission granted soon afterwards to both MacIain and Maclean for all the crimes they had recently committed against each other.

John MacIain died not long after these events, and was succeeded by his son John Og, who seems to have inherited in large measure the spirit of his father. In 1592 King James, anxious to replenish his treasury, issued a decree requiring the Western Chiefs to find surety for the payment of their dues to the Crown. Many of the chiefs failed to obey, among them John Og MacIain, and they were duly put to the horn. This had the desired result in the case of MacIain, who appears to have found the required sureties, for he was later released from the consequences of his disobedience by a special decree of the Council.

The feud with Maclean of Duart was not forgotten, and John Og lost no opportunity of thwarting that Chief in his designs. Elizabeth of England had purchased the support of the Duart Chief in her struggle against the Irish rebel Tyrone, and John Og at once joined the Island host that was speeding to answer Tyrone's call for aid. But as the southward-bound fleet sheltered for the night in the Sound of Mull it was surprised by the watchful Chief of Duart, whose "bauld stratagem and prettie feit of weir" secured for him many prisoners. Among them was MacIain, and both he and Clanranald were thrown into a dungeon where they remained until Lachlan's proceedings came to the notice of the Government and he was forced to release them.

In the following year (1596) a renewal of the feud with Maclean was brought about by an unfortunate incident which resulted in the death of John Og. MacIain, it appears, had been betrothed to Lochiel's daughter. His uncle Donald and he had not been on amicable terms for some time past owing to differences which had arisen between them regarding the possession of Sunart, to which Donald laid claim. Donald was, besides, presumptive heir to his nephew, and would, therefore, in the event of the latter dying without issue, succeed him as head of the family of Ardnamurchan. While preparations were being made for the celebration of the marriage of the young chieftain, and as he was returning from a visit to Lochiel, accompanied by a small retinue, he was attacked and slain by his uncle, who was lying in wait for him at a place in Ardnamurchan called ever since *Faoghail Dhomnuill Chonulluich* (Donald Macdonald's Ford). On hearing of MacIain's death, Alan Cameron of Lochiel vowed vengeance on the murderer, who immediately after committing the crime took refuge in Mull, and put himself under the protection of Lachlan Mor of Duart. Donald MacIain had no difficulty in persuading Lachlan Mor to help him against the Camerons and the adherents of the late chieftain. Lochiel had already pursued him to the

Sound of Mull. Lachlan Mor accordingly collected a force of 220 men, and sent his eldest son, Hector, and Donald MacIain, at their head to the mainland. The Camerons and the MacIains met them in Morvern at a place in Black Glen ever since called *Leac-nan-Saighead* (Rock of the Arrows), where a sanguinary conflict resulted in the total defeat of the Macleans, and the death of Donald MacIain. The local traditionary account of the death of Donald MacIain is to the effect that one of the Clan Cameron, observing him "uplifting his helmet, instantly bent his bow, took aim, and drove his arrow into MacIain's head, pinioning his hand, which at that time was passing over his forehead, to his skull. He fell, but for a moment regaining his strength he arose and expressed a desire, it is feared a treacherous one, to deliver his sword to Lochiel. But the last spark of life was fast expiring. He clenched the huge weapon, and, in the ire of death, transfixed it to the hilt in the opposite bank, and fell on it to rise no more."

On the death of Donald MacIain, his brother Alexander's son John succeeded as head of the family, but his succession to the lands of Ardnamurchan was disputed by the Earl of Argyll. The Clan Iain being weakened by internal strife, Argyll seized his opportunity to enforce the deed of conveyance granted in favour of the fourth Earl by the heiress, Mariota MacIain. Argyll accordingly forced MacIain into a contract whereby he became bound to exhibit to the Earl his writs of the 80 merklands of Ardnamurchan. He also bound himself to resign the same lands to the Earl, who agreed to feu them out again to MacIain, and certain heirs mentioned in the contract, to be held of the Earl for the payment of 13s 4d of feu-duty. The Earl further promised faithfully to protect MacIain in the possession of these lands. It is not apparent if this contract was ever fulfilled by either party, but the tradition of the country suggests that MacIain delivered up his old title-deeds without, however, receiving the promised charter in return. There is also a tradition that the title-deeds came into the possession of Argyll by his having found them with a burgess of Edinburgh, with whom MacIain left them as a pledge for a debt incurred in educating his son. Be this as it may, the old charter of 1499 granted to John MacIain for apprehending the Macdonalds of Dunnyveg was from now on in the hands of the family of Argyll.

The departure of King James from his native Scotland to take possession of the English Crown, and the turmoil which followed and continued for some time, no doubt prevented Argyll, who was busy elsewhere extending his influence and possessions in the name of law and order, from taking actual possession of Ardnamurchan. The history of the Ardnamurchan family from this juncture is one long and desperate struggle, in which they succeeded for a time in holding their own against several branches of the Clan Campbell. In 1605 MacIain, with many other Island Chiefs, was summoned to exhibit his title deeds to Lord Scone, Comptroller of Scotland, at Kilkerran in Kintyre, and at the same time to find surety for the regular payment of Crown rents and duties for the lands possessed by him, under penalty of having his title deeds declared null and of being prosecuted with fire and sword. From all this it would appear that the authority of the Argyll family had not been established in Ardnamurchan, and that the MacIains still possessed that territory, though illegally, upon the old charters. Though elaborate preparations were made to compel the Island Chiefs to wait on Lord Scone, none put in an appearance at Kilkerran. MacIain had probably no title deeds to exhibit, but he at all events ignored the summons, and he seems to have incurred no penalty for his disobedience.

When Lord Ochiltree was appointed Lieutenant in 1608, and held court at Aros in Mull in that year, MacIain of Ardnamurchan wisely avoided falling into the trap which was so skilfully and successfully laid for the other Chiefs. Lord

Ochiltree, however, on his return from his expedition, reported to the Privy Council "anent the House of Ardnamurchan that he held the bond of James Campbell of Lawers that it should be delivered whenever required under a penalty of £10,000." Whether James Campbell was acting for Argyll, or what his connection with Ardnamurchan at this time was, does not appear. Shortly thereafter, on 14th November 1609, the Lords of the Privy Council ordered MacIain to be summoned before them, for a certain day, to "underly such order as shall be taken with him touching his obedience to his Majesty, under the pain of rebellion." There is no evidence that MacIain ever answered the summons, and the probability is that he was dead before the day appointed for his personal appearance before the Council.

John MacIain left a son, Alexander, who was a minor at the time of his father's death. In the year 1611 we find, from the Register of the Privy Seal, that the Clan Iain of Ardnamurchan were led by Donald MacIain, uncle of the minor, who is referred to as Tutor of Ardnamurchan. The year 1612 was one of unaccustomed peace in the region of Argyll. Taking advantage of this lull, and no doubt also of the minority of the young chieftain of the MacIains, the Earl of Argyll made one more effort to establish his authority in the district of Ardnamurchan. Early in that year he granted a commission to Donald Campbell of Barbreck "to take and receive the Castle and place of Meigarie and upon our expences to put keepers thereinto," with power to summon before him all the tenants and indwellers in Ardnamurchan, and generally to manage that territory, both in fixing the rents to be paid, in collecting them with regularity, and in punishing by expulsion the refractory tenants. From the tenor of this commission, it is clear that Ardnamurchan was then in a very disturbed state, arising doubtless from the hostility of the old family to Argyll. Donald Campbell, originally a churchman, and afterwards, by the force of his talents both in civil and military affairs, the person most trusted by Argyll and the Campbells against the refractory Islanders, was a natural son of John Campbell of Cawdor, and first distinguished himself by the zeal with which he pursued those who had any share in his father's murder. He was a man of uncommon ability, a brave and skilful soldier, but reputed to be of a stern and even cruel disposition, and little disposed to conciliate those he was appointed to govern by the mildness of his measures.

In return for his services as Commissioner, Donald Campbell now received from Argyll a lease of the lands of Ardnamurchan. The MacIains, who had not yet been expelled from the district, complained bitterly of the severity of the churchman's rule which, though kept within legal bounds, so exasperated them by his harsh dealings that they broke out into open rebellion against his authority. Campbell was obliged to appeal to the Privy Council, who compelled Donald MacIain, Tutor of Ardnamurchan, to give a bond for himself and on behalf of his nephew, and all persons for whom his nephew was by law obliged to answer, that they should keep good order in the country and obey the laws. Donald MacIain further gave a pledge that he would make his appearance before the Council on the 10th July annually to render his obedience, and oftener if so directed, upon 60 days' warning. The penalty for non-fulfilment of every point of this bond was fixed at 2000 merks.

Donald MacIain's bond, as far as he was concerned, was a mere matter of convenience. Between the Privy Council on the one hand, and the Campbells on the other, the Tutor of Ardnamurchan found himself in a situation that whether he pleased either or both the results would be much the same. If he was to be extricated from the difficulties of his position, he had to look for help to a third party; and now there appeared for him a gleam of hope. Sir James Macdonald of Dunnyveg had just escaped from his long confinement in Edinburgh Castle, and betaken himself to the Highlands to marshal support for his cause. On his way to Islay he was joined by the MacIains of Ardnamurchan. Sir James was received with great enthusiasm by the Clan Donald, both North and South; but his efforts to restore the fallen fortunes of his family proved futile, and he was compelled to take refuge in exile. During his short and ill-planned campaign, the MacIains rendered conspicuous service, and thus only succeeded in making themselves still more obnoxious to the Government and the Clan Campbell. Donald MacIain, as might have been expected, failed to make his appearance in terms of his pledge to the Privy Council, and therefore incurred the penalty of 2000 merks stipulated in his bond. The Council accordingly gave a decree against him, and Donald Campbell, now that fortune had put the MacIains in his power, hastened to put into force the sentence against Donald MacIain.

So cruelly treated were the unfortunate MacIains that the Tutor was obliged to appeal even to his enemy Argyll himself. He sent his son John to Edinburgh for the purpose of representing to the Earl and his brother, Campbell of Lundy, the straitened circumstances in which he found himself owing to the tyrannical proceedings of Donald Campbell. In the absence from town of the Earl and his brother, William Stirling of Auchyle, the principal manager of all the Argyll estates, undertook to write a letter to Donald Campbell, the delivery of which he entrusted to John MacIain. In this letter he urged Campbell to be more lenient to the MacIains. "It is not," he wrote, "without reason and some foir-knowledge in preventing further inconvenience I have written to you which I am assured ye will consider out of your own wisdom. I hope ye will press to win the people with kindness rather nor with extremitie specially at the first." Stirling's letter evidently had the desired effect, for peace seems to have prevailed in the region of Ardnamurchan during the two following years. In midsummer 1618, however, John Macdonald, younger of Clanranald, appeared suddenly on the scene, and the result was a renewal of hostilities between the opposing parties. Argyll played the double part of granting a lease of Ardnamurchan to Sir Donald Macdonald of Clanranald several years before the expiry of the lease to Donald Campbell, in consideration of a certain sum of money in name of *grassum*. This transaction is explained partly, at least, by the financial straits in which the Earl of Argyll undoubtedly found himself at that time. Young Clanranald, with the assistance of the MacIains, invaded Ardnamurchan and put Donald Campbell and his garrison to flight. It was thereupon arranged that Argyll should pay back the money advanced by Sir Donald of Clanranald, the dispute being submitted to arbitration. The arbiters were Sir George Erskine of Innerteill and Sir George Hay of Kinnoull who, finding that Campbell's lease was the best in law, ordered him to be repossessed in the lands of Ardnamurchan.

Thus the MacIains were now again at the mercy of the Campbells, and they had to find sureties for their dutiful obedience to the House of Argyll. They pledged themselves to Donald Campbell that they would remain peaceable tenants under him, and pay all rents or other damages that might be due to him. Campbell accepted the Chiefs of Clanranald and Macleod, and Maclean of Coll, as sureties for the good behaviour of the MacIains. In this submissive attitude, however, they did not remain long. Within a year Donald McEan in Ormisage, John, Angus, and Donald, his sons, Alaster McAngus VcEan in Ardsliginish, Alaster McConeill VcEan in Camisingle, and a number of others of the Clan Iain, were put to the horn and denounced rebels. Campbell himself, two years later, complained to the Privy Council that Alexander MacIain, at a meeting of his followers, had bound them to support him in recovering his possessions, either by law or by force. Though Alexander MacIain afterwards swore before the Privy Council that there was no truth in the charge preferred against him by Campbell, it is pretty certain that the latter had some cause of complaint, as in less than two years thereafter MacIain is found at the head of his men in open rebellion, bidding defiance to the whole Campbell Clan. On the 22nd September 1624, Sir Ruairi Mor Macleod, John of Clanranald and Maclean of Coll were summoned before the Privy Council for not exhibiting certain rebels of the Clan Iain, for whose good behaviour, as we have seen, they had pledged themselves. From the charge it appears that the Clan Iain "pretend to be a branch of the Captain of Clanranald's House, quhilk he lykwayes acknowledgeit and takis the patrocine and defence of thame in all their adois." Having failed to obey the summons, Macleod, Clanranald, and Coll were all declared rebels.

The MacIains now seem to have broken loose from all ordinary modes of warfare, and taking to a piratical life, they became the terror of the Western seas. It must be allowed that, judged by the standard of their time, and their peculiar circumstances, there was much to justify their conduct. They had been hard pressed for years by their enemies, the Campbells, who had by unfair means dispossessed them of their lawful inheritance. For the repressive measures of the Government itself, it is difficult to find excuse, for the MacIains of Ardnamurchan were not sinners above all the other Islesmen. In this fresh direction of their efforts at survival, a piratical band of clansmen seized an English ship, which they manned and armed, and the Government at once took steps to destroy such a powerful threat to coastal shipping. Warrant was given to James, Archbishop of Glasgow, and Sir William Livingston of Kilsyth, to go to the Burgh of Ayr and "provide a ship and a pinnace well armed and provided for the pursuit of the Clan Ean." For the same purpose a commission of fire and sword was also given to Lord Lorne, the lairds of Lochnell, Auchinbreck, Cawdor, and Ardkinglas, or any three of them, Lord Lorne always being one.

The MacIains, notwithstanding the formidable armament arrayed against them, continued to plunder all ships, home and foreign, that came their way. The extent of their piratical operations may be gathered from a letter dated 29th July 1625, from the Council to the King, in which they are referred to as "rebellis of the Clan Eane be whom not only your maiesties awne subjects, bot the subjectis of otheris princes yor maiesties friends and confederates were havelie distrest and robbed of thair shippis and goodis and some of them cruellie and barbarouslie slain." The rebels, being now hotly pursued by Lord Lorne, were driven by him from the Southern to the Northern Isles. Finding themselves on the coast of Skye, they were pursued by Sir Ruairi Mor Macleod of Dunvegan, and driven across the Minch to the mainland. They landed in Clanranald's country, and hid themselves in the woods and caves of Arisaig and Moidart. From the list of the names of the ringleaders, it appears that not a few of the followers of the Chief of Clanranald had joined the MacIains, and this no doubt accounts for the latter seeking and finding refuge amongst their kindred. The MacIain rebellion being at length suppressed, Lord Lorne landed at Ardnamurchan and made a pretence of driving away the few followers of the Clan Iain that still remained there. Lorne was thanked by the Privy Council for his services, and Donald Campbell became proprietor of Ardnamurchan for an annual feu duty of 2000 merks, payable to Argyll as superior.

The Clan Iain now ceased to exist as a territorial family. It appears, however, that Alexander MacIain, the head of the family, received a considerable sum of money in name of compensation for his claims on the lands of Ardnamurchan. At Edinburgh, on 22nd April 1629, he gave his bond for £40,000 Scots to Robert Innes, burgess of Fortrose, a sum which represented at that time a very large fortune. It would appear from this transaction that however much the family of Ardnamurchan may have suffered otherwise, they were now, financially at least, in a very flourishing condition.

Very little is known of the history of the MacIains as a family from the time of their landing in the Moidart district in 1625. There is some evidence, however, that they continued for a time to annoy the new possessor of their old inheritance. In the year 1633, Sir Donald Campbell "dischargis and exoners" the leader of the Clan Iain for committing "sundrie wrangis" within his bounds of Ardnamurchan. According to the Morar MS, John Macdonald of Clanranald became answerable to the King for the future good behaviour of the Clan Iain. As we have seen, they had already acknowledged Clanranald as their Chief, and the small remnant now left of them identified themselves with his branch of the Clan Donald. Many years ago, when the old churchyard of St Columba in Kingussie was being improved, a tombstone was brought to light bearing the following inscription: HEIR LYES ALX MCDON SON TO IO MCDON IN RVTHEN WHO DIED 13 AP. 1719 ALSO ALX & ALX MCDONALDS HIS FATHER & UNCLES SOMETIME REPRESENTING THE ANCIENT FAMILY OF ARDNAMOURACH. The unearthing of the tombstone in Badenoch shows at least that some members of the MacIain family lived for some time in that district, but there is no evidence besides that of the inscription itself that the Macdonalds in Ruthven represented directly or at all the ancient family of Ardnamurchan. It is very probable that those whose names are inscribed on the tombstone found their way to Badenoch at the time of the general dispersion of the Clan Iain, and that Alexander Macdonald, whose father lived in Ruthven, represented for a time, in that district at least, the MacIains of Ardnamurchan.

16

The Macdonalds (MacIains) of Glencoe

THE MACDONALDS OF GLENCOE (known as MacIains after their founder) originated in the 14th century from Iain Fraoch, a natural son of Angus Og of the Isles by the daughter of Dugall MacEanruig (MacHenry), "the chief man in Glencoe" at the time. Tradition has it that Dugall MacEanruig was the son of Henry MacNaughtan who migrated to Callart on Loch Leven, opposite Glencoe, in the late 13th century and settled finally in Glencoe.

To trace the history of this Clan, we have to depend upon tradition and meagre references in the annals of Scotland. These references deal mainly with their misdeeds, and in consequence they are always regarded as outlaws and disturbers of the peace. In the 16th century, when the other branches of Clan Donald emerge as separate entities, the history of the Clann Iain is almost a total blank. Even the Chiefs, whose names were always John for about eight generations, leave no definite trace of their births and deaths.

Glencoe is so well known now that it seems almost unnecessary to describe it; but the fact that it is a narrow trough between some of the highest mountains in Argyllshire, having little arable land and poor hill pastures, greatly influenced the way of life of its inhabitants. The Glen runs down from the wild tract of the Moor of Rannoch through a steep defile broken only by the little Loch Triochtan until it turns north. Here the River Coe runs through the main stretch of arable land to flow into Loch Leven. The Glen is not wide and parts are subject to flooding. On the south side it has two passes leading over to Dalness in Glen Etive where one branch of the Clan lived. Three passes only break through the rocky wall of the massif of mountains topped by the highest two, Bidein nam Bian and Stob Coire an Lochain. These are the Lairig Gartain, Lairig Eilde and Lairig Fhionnghail. The sheer wall of Aonach Eagach to the north shuts off any access to that side from end to end of the valley. Where the Glen turns north at the Signal Rock near Achnacon another glen opens up to the north west. This is Gleann Leac nam Muidhe and from it a fairly practicable pass leads over into Appin at the head-waters of Glen Ure and Glen Duror. This proved to be the only safe escape route for the fugitives who fled after the Massacre in 1692. In a glen so narrow and with so little land for the plough, and yet supporting at times as many as some five hundred souls, the way of life must have been grim indeed. The enterprising warriors of the Clan had to find sustenance for their families by other means than peaceful pursuits. To the east and south lay the fat lands of Moray and the Lennox, both of which were the traditional hunting grounds of the men of Glencoe.

The Arms of
Lieutenant-General **SIR JOHN MACDONALD**
(Glencoe)

Quarterly; 1st, Argent, a lion rampant Gules and in a canton of the last a mural crown Or; 2nd, Or, a dexter arm in armour couped in fess proper, the hand also proper, holding a cross-crosslet fitched Sable; 3rd, Or, a lymphad with her oars and sails Sable, flags flying Gules; 4th, Vert, a salmon naiant proper.   ❖
Crest, out of an Eastern Crown Or a cubit arm erect proper encircled by a laurel wreath Vert, in the hand a dagger erect also proper, pomel and hilt Or.   ❖
Motto over the Crest NEC·TEMPORE·NEC·FATO.   ❖   ❖   ❖   ❖

Lyon Register (Volume 2, Folio 173).

The earliest accounts of the Glen begin in the 6th century when an early saint or missionary of the Celtic Church passed that way. This was Kenneth, a Pict born in 516 A.D. in Ireland. After being educated and ordained in that country he crossed over to Dalriada (Argyll) in 562, just one year before Columba came to Iona. He left his name in many places as he travelled through the country from west to east: a small flat island in Loch Leven near Ballachulish bears his name (Eilean Choinnich). He passed through Glencoe on his way eastwards. He did not stay there long, but a strange story is told about him. While he tarried in the narrowest part of the Glen for a few days, an angel came to him and offered to remove the mountain on the south side, which made the place so dark. Kenneth prevailed upon the angel to desist, as he did not propose to dwell there indefinitely. The initial efforts of the angel are pointed out on the face of Aonach Dubh; but the fissure which marks his labours is now called Ossian's Cave. At last Kenneth died in his own country of Ireland, but in A.D. 600, as he prepared for death, he declared that a holy man not of his own community would come to perform the last offices for him. He was right: one did arrive and that was Fintan-Mundus whose name is preserved in the little isle on which the Macdonalds of Glencoe and the Camerons of Callart are buried. This is Eilean Munde. Fintan came to Iona not long after Columba died and began his travels from there, returning eventually to Ireland.

The founder of the Clan Iain of Glencoe was Iain Fraoch, natural son of Angus Og, as we have said. He must have been born about the beginning of the 14th century, but dates of his birth and death are unrecorded. He was given the lands of Glencoe by his father. No charter or deed of transfer exists. Perhaps the agreement was only verbal. But from then down to the middle of the 19th century, the Macdonalds held those lands without charters. They made no attempt to regularise their tenure even after the fall of the Lordship, when other chiefs were trying to obtain charters to their lands from the Crown. We have seen in other chapters how charters were given, taken away, and re-granted until one wonders if even the grantors knew who had what. The Clan Iain paid little attention to these sheep-skins, or the feudal superiors set over them by the King and Council. Like their kinsfolk in Keppoch they continued to hold their land as best they could, usually successfully.

The lands of Glencoe had originally belonged to the Clan Cholla and passed to the Clan Dugall for a time. When that clan lost them, owing to their opposition to Bruce, the lands were given to Angus Og for services rendered, and he in turn handed them over to his son, Iain Fraoch. They appear once more in a charter given by King David II to Good John of Islay, Lord of the Isles, with many others in 1343. Later they were transferred to the families of Argyll and Stewart of Appin in turn, but whoever held them nominally of the King, the Clan Iain did not pay much attention, and frequently not much of the rental either. It is quite impossible to find if in fact they ever did pay their rents to those feudal superiors appointed by a remote foreign sovereign. Their history is a blank for hundreds of years.

Iain Fraoch was named Iain Abrachson as he had been fostered in Lochaber, and by tradition he died in Knapdale in 1358 and was buried with his father in Reilig Orain, Iona. After him there was a succession of Johns—eight of them— and it is difficult to sort them out. It was not until the end of the 15th century that we find any reference to them in the annals of Scotland. By 1500 they had lost the kindly patronage of the Lords of the Isles and an attempt was made by Argyll to oust them and the Stewarts of Appin from their lands. Decree was granted to Argyll to evict "John of the Ilis utherwyis Abroch sonne" and

Duncan Stewart from the lands of "Durroure and Glencoyne." They continued to occupy their estates, however, in defiance of this decree.

The men of Glencoe came on the scene in spectacular fashion in 1501 when they carried out a raid on Lochaweside and freed the last scion of the Isles, Donald Dubh, from his prison in the Castle of Inchconnel. This action was much admired at the time and was deservedly noted as a feat of arms worthy of the Fianna of old. They had to traverse hostile country to the heart of Argyll's domains. It was indeed a "far cry to Loch Awe," to quote the Campbell saying. But the men of Glencoe knew all the passes and paths for miles around, a knowledge acquired from their frequent marauding expeditions. This knowledge was to be very useful in later campaigns, as we shall see. On this occasion they demonstrated their loyalty to the head of their race in defiance of superiors appointed by what they regarded as an alien power.

The next time the Glencoe men are mentioned is after the middle of the 16th century. In 1563 "John Og MacAne Abrycht" was in lawful possession of his lands under Colin Campbell of Glenorchy who held them of the Crown. On the 6th May of that year a contract of protection and manrent was signed by both parties. Glenorchy undertook to defend MacIain in possession of his lands, and John Og bound himself to serve Glenorchy against all persons except the Government and Argyll. The bond was to become null and void if John Og did not at once serve against the Clan Gregor.

In 1588 a Commission of Justiciary was given by James VI to Huntly and John Grant of Freuchie and others against certain chiefs amongst whom were "John M'Ane Oig in Glencoe and Alexander M'Ane Abrycht," probably the sons of the "John Og M'Ane Abrycht" who gave the bond of manrent to Glenorchy in 1563. At this period it is clear that the Clan Iain were a menace to their neighbours, and not on this occasion only. We shall see other evidence of their predatory habits later. On the 30th June 1589 a bond of manrent was entered into by John Grant of Freuchie and Alan Cameron of Lochiel, in which the former bound himself to fortify and assist the latter against the dwellers in Glencoe. We have to remember the isolated position of the Clan Iain, far from their kinsfolk in the other branches of Clan Donald and surrounded by hostile neighbours. The nearest friends were the Macdonalds of Keppoch, far to the north beyond the high mountains of Mamore. It was fortunate for them that their narrow glen was so inaccessible.

Towards the end of the 16th century the men of Glencoe come to our notice under the most improbable of circumstances, when we find them collaborating with the Earl of Argyll. James V had enacted that a baron was responsible for the acts or misdeeds of his servants, or feudal inferiors. Argyll was accused under this act of disturbing the peace, which is a very mild way of describing what actually happened. A feud had arisen between Argyll and the Ogilvies of Glenisla away to the east. Campbell of Persie was a guest at a wedding of one of the Ogilvie family. A quarrel took place and Campbell insulted the bride and stabbed her father. Lord Ogilvie, chief of the family, drew his sword and challenged Campbell to defend himself. Campbell was quickly disarmed and driven out of the Glen in the most undignified manner. He was very fortunate not to have been hanged on the spot. Argyll swore vengeance and employed the Glencoe men to exact his retribution from the Ogilvies. In this instance the warriors of Clan Iain were only too willing to obey a superior whom they would normally have treated with disdain. They carried out the raid with their customary efficiency. They covered great distances at great speed, and the Ogilvies were taken completely by surprise. Lord Ogilvie in his appeal to the Council complained that he and his wife and children had escaped the raiders with great difficulty. He cited

Archibald, Earl of Argyll and his friends, particularly "Alan Roy M'Inoig, son to the Laird of Glencoe" (Red Alan, son of Young John) and five hundred other marauders from that country as being the prime offenders in this crime. The numbers given show that the men of Glencoe could not have been the sole offenders. The fighting strength of the Glen was normally about one hundred men, and on this occasion it is not likely that all the men turned out. They must have had some of their neighbours as allies in a raid which no doubt proved very profitable. Argyll and his accomplices were summoned to appear before the Council by the 27th October of that year (1591). They did not appear and were duly proclaimed rebels. There is no record that they ever did appear on that or any other occasion to answer for this misdemeanour, and soon afterwards they once again come before our notice.

Later in the same year the Council received serious complaints that, this time without Argyll's co-operation, they carried out a raid on the lands of Drummond of Blair. The list of offenders on this occasion included "John Og M'Ane Abrych in Glencoe, Allaster Og M'Ane Abrych his brother, and Donald Og M'Ane Abrick brother to John Og elder." These are described as living in Appin and Glencoe, lands which were regarded as under the care of John Stewart of Appin at the time. The offenders were legally his servants and tenants, and he was charged to appear before the Justice in the Tolbooth, Edinburgh, on the 7th November and to answer the charges under pain of being declared rebel. No record exists that he ever did so appear, nor do any serious consequences seem to have ensued.

Next year there was more trouble. The King and Council were told that "John MacEan Oig in Glencone," son of the aforesaid John and now Chief of the Clan, his brothers, Allaster MacEan Oig, Archibald MacEan Oig, and Alan Roy, were guilty of open aggression, murder and theft. They were summoned, but refused to find security and were duly declared rebels and outlaws. Fraser of Lovat and Mackintosh of Dunachton were appointed Commissioners to prosecute them; and yet in the same year "M'Ane Abrich of Glencone" with "MacAne of Arnamurchane" and others, were relaxed from the horn: that is, they were forgiven. The same well-worn practice prevailed: ignoring any summons to answer for their misdeeds, most criminals had only to lie low and in the course of time their crimes were forgotten by all except their victims. It was not difficult for the Glencoe men to find secluded spots in which to hide from any minions of the law approaching their Glen. They did not always escape retribution, however. One may be sure that their victims reacted vigorously on many occasions.

For some years after the raid on Blair Drummond (1591), the MacIains do not appear on record in the files of the Privy Council or elsewhere, which proves that there were periods of peace in the Glen and among the neighbours of this lively Clan. We have had to point out in other chapters that our clansmen appear on record only when in trouble, and this was abundantly true in the case of the men of Glencoe throughout their lurid history. In 1599, however, they were in trouble again.

In that year the district of Lennox in Dunbartonshire was the object of their attention. Moray and Lennox were favourite places for the western clansmen to visit to replenish their larders. This time the complainants were the Duke of Lennox on behalf of one of his tenants, and Aulay MacAulay of Ardincaple. David Craig of Drumcharrie, tenant of Lennox, lost seven good cows and a bull, valued at £140. In November of that year the men cited were "Archibald MacConeill MacIain Abrich, Ronald, Angus, Allan and John MacIain Abrich in Glencone," and they were accused of "reif, houghing of cattle, and purpose of murder." These crimes against defenceless animals just because they belonged to the victims of their raids are quite inexcusable. MacAulay escaped with his life, although the complaint seems to suggest that the MacIains only stopped short of murder because of the rapidity with which he fled to the woods. Some of his servants were taken prisoner, and the raiders retired by way of the lands of Strone and Auchingarth, the property of Lennox. There they "lifted" 32 horses and mares and 24 cows. We have no news of any reprisals following this highly successful *creach,* but in 1602 Argyll is blamed for not controlling clansmen of whom he was supposed to be the "superior" in the feudal sense, and therefore, by the act of James v, responsible for the good conduct of his "vassals." Sir George Home of Spot, Treasurer, and Thomas Hamilton of Drumcairn, King's Advocate, and Argyll became bound in the sum of 20,000 merks to observe, on his own account and that of his vassals, good rule in his domain and compensate those who had suffered by this raid. How they were able to obey this ruling does not appear on record.

In 1609 John Stewart of Acharn in Appin and one Alexander Stewart were murdered for reasons unknown. Blame was thrown upon the men of Glencoe by the widow of Acharn in 1610, and they are named in the records of the Privy Council as Angus MacIain Dubh in Dalness, Alasdair MacIain Dubh in Achtriochtan, Alan Dubh his brother, and John Og MacIain Dubh. Another accused of being implicated in the same crime was Alasdair MacIain Og, brother of the Chief, who is referred to as a "notorious thief for many years an outlaw." He had fallen into the hands of Campbell of Abermicheil, who was ordered to hand him over to James, Earl of Perth and Stewart of Strathearn, to be put on trial. In 1610 a commission was given to Hector Maclean of Duart, Colquhoun of Luss and Alan Cameron of Lochiel to apprehend the first mentioned four for trial for the murder of the two Stewarts of Appin. What happened to those four is not recorded, but the last named, being a brother of the Chief, was still in 1611 lodged in the Tolbooth awaiting trial, or under sentence. Two Macdonalds bound themselves to see that he appeared before the Lords of Council. These were Alexander Macdonald of Gargavach in Keppoch and Ronald Macdonald, his heir. We hear no more of Alasdair MacIain Og and can only assume that he suffered due punishment for his crimes.

The feud with the Stewarts of Appin, their near neighbours, continued. Seven years have elapsed since the sad story of the sins of Alasdair MacIain Og during which it seems peace reigned. In 1617, however, the men of Glencoe appear once more in the light of publicity, as usual in lawless mood. The Chief of the time is named John Abrach. In that year a Commission was issued to the Sheriffs of Edinburgh, Perth, Forfar, Aberdeen, Inverness, Argyll, Tarbert and the Steward of Strathearn by the Chancellor under the Signet to apprehend and bring to trial "John Dubh of Keills in Glencoe, John MacCondochie Mhic Gillimartyne, and John MacEane Mhic 'Illepatrick," all servants of John Abrach of Glencoe, for not answering to the charge of murdering David Bowman. We are not told who David Bowman was, or why he was murdered. The wide jurisdiction given by the Commission would suggest that this crime was of more than ordinary importance, and that the criminals, on the run from justice, might be found anywhere in the Kingdom. They do not seem to have been caught, otherwise there would surely have been some record of their trial and fate.

In the same year (1617) another Stewart was murdered by the Clan Iain. Unfortunately in all these accounts of murders we are left entirely in the dark as to why the victim met his fate. This leaves the reader to assume that the Clan were just a turbulent lot who murdered out of sheer brutality for personal gain. But there must have been a variety of motives. The Government would not allow

THE MACDONALDS (MACIAINS) OF GLENCOE

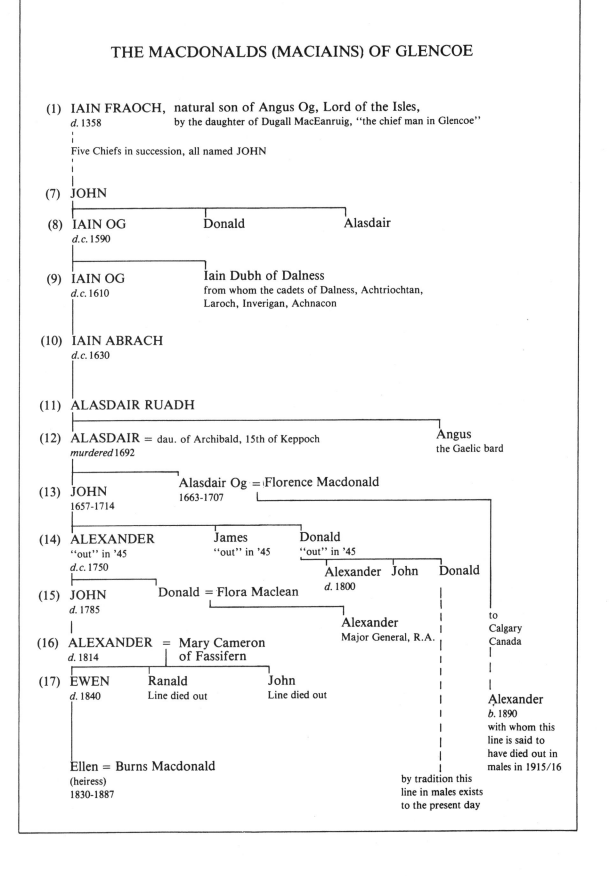

(1) IAIN FRAOCH, natural son of Angus Og, Lord of the Isles,
   *d.*1358   by the daughter of Dugall MacEanruig, "the chief man in Glencoe"

Five Chiefs in succession, all named JOHN

(7) JOHN

(8) IAIN OG   Donald   Alasdair
   *d.c.*1590

(9) IAIN OG   Iain Dubh of Dalness
   *d.c.*1610   from whom the cadets of Dalness, Achtriochtan,
                Laroch, Inverigan, Achnacon

(10) IAIN ABRACH
    *d.c.*1630

(11) ALASDAIR RUADH

(12) ALASDAIR = dau. of Archibald, 15th of Keppoch   Angus
    *murdered*1692   the Gaelic bard

Alasdair Og = Florence Macdonald
1663-1707

(13) JOHN
    1657-1714

(14) ALEXANDER   James   Donald
    "out" in '45 "out" in '45 "out" in '45
    *d.c.*1750   Alexander John Donald
                            *d.*1800

(15) JOHN   Donald = Flora Maclean
    *d.*1785
                        Alexander
                        Major General, R.A.

(16) ALEXANDER = Mary Cameron
    *d.*1814   of Fassifern

(17) EWEN   Ranald   John
    *d.*1840 Line died out Line died out

to
Calgary
Canada

Alexander
*b.*1890
with whom this
line is said to
have died out in
males in 1915/16

Ellen = Burns Macdonald
(heiress)
1830-1887

by tradition this
line in males exists
to the present day

any mitigating circumstances when a Glencoe man appeared before its justices. Usually, knowing this, the murderers took to the hills until the chase cooled off and it was safe to return.

Again, on the 15th July yet another entry appears on record. A Commission was issued to the Marquis of Huntly and the Earl of Argyll to bring to trial John Abrach the Chief and Donald Buidhe MacIain Oig mhic Iain Abraich. The last named appears in our genealogy as a younger brother of the Chief, John Abrach. These, with some others not of Clan Iain, were accused of the murder of Duncan and James Stewart. Again, there is no record of the outcome of the proceedings.

This mournful catalogue of murders laid at the door of the Clan Iain gives a very bad impression of their character, and was undoubtedly a contributory cause of the hatred shown by other clans and the Government, culminating in the massacre of 1692. One must not assume that, because the accused usually took flight and disappeared, they were therefore guilty, or that there were no extenuating circumstances. They knew very well that it would be unsafe to place themselves in the hands of a law that was heavily weighted against them. They only had to remember what happened regularly when their chiefs, and the heads of other clans too, presented themselves at Court under safe-conduct, or under invitation to attend a friendly discussion of policy. It was safer to vanish.

For seventeen years from this last recorded misdemeanour of the Clan Iain there is peace until 1634 when we find them engaged with the Gordons in a raid far from home in Buchan. The Crichtons of Frendraucht had been at feud with Huntly for a long time and were the sufferers on this occasion. The Lords of Council received complaints from the Crichtons that a number of Gordons accompanied by others, including some MacIains, had committed outrages of fire-raising and slaughter. On the 13th November a summons was issued directing the Gordons and MacIains to attend personally before the Privy Council on the 16th December to account for their actions, and further to restrain their folk. On the 13th January 1635 Alasdair MacIain Abrach, the Glencoe chief, had not appeared. He and some others were told to attend on the following Thursday. He was detained in Edinburgh and on the 5th February 1635, together with John Cameron, son of Lochiel, he was bound to remain and stay in ward in Edinburgh until further investigation was carried out by Parliament. On the 30th July he and the others concerned were committed to the Tolbooth Gaol and his privileges therein restricted until security was found for his good conduct. Once again we are left in the dark as to what transpired, for the records of the Council provide no information concerning the punishment or corrective that may have been imposed.

Like most of the other clans, the men of Glencoe threw their support behind the Royalist cause in the Civil War and played an important part in the marches, counter-marches and battles of Montrose's spectacular campaign of 1645. They acted in close concert with Donald Clanranald and his men. They provided guides for the difficult tracts of country traversed by Montrose's army, notably when they sought winter quarters in Campbell country and penetrated as far as the town of Inveraray. Angus MacAlan Dubh, a cadet of the Chief's house, was at the meeting called at Blair Atholl to decide where they should pass the winter. Angus told Montrose that if he wanted good houses, fat cattle and food of all kinds Argyll was ideal, and he could lead the army there. Like most of the Glencoe men, he knew his way around all the glens and straths from Aberdeenshire to Ardnamurchan, the breadth of Scotland, where cattle and other essential supplies could be "lifted." This decided the matter, and he skilfully guided the army through the mountain passes to Argyll territory and into the town of Inveraray itself. The course of the campaign has been related more fully in the Chapter devoted to Clanranald who took a major share in the successes of Montrose under the able leadership of their Chief and his son, Donald of Moidart.

The Clan Iain joined Montrose in November 1644 at the instigation of Alasdair MacCholla and were at the relief of the Castle of Mingary in Ardnamurchan which had been taken by Alasdair and later recaptured. Thereafter they took part in most of the activities of Montrose's army, leaving only at intervals to take home their plunder after each victory. In the march back from Inveraray to Lochaber they passed their native Glen, but kept on to take a leading part in the battle of Inverlochy. There they formed the centre of the royal army with the men of Atholl and Appin, backed by the Clanranald and Glengarry warriors, who did not remain long in the second line once battle was joined. Thus they were in the thick of that successful conflict and played their part nobly.

During the rest of the campaign they were well to the fore, led by their Chief Alasdair, son of Iain Abrach, whose son, the victim of the massacre of 1692, was now about twelve years old.

Then came the Revolution of 1688, called by some the "Glorious Revolution," but not so regarded by the clans. John Graham of Claverhouse was in London with his Regiment of Horse (The King's Own), which had been recalled with others from Scotland in the vain hope of confronting Dutch William on his advance from Torbay. Claverhouse, recently made Viscount Dundee by King James, tried to encourage that monarch to offer some resistance, but in vain. The King had lost heart. Dundee made off north with a small body of his troopers who had the confidence of their commander. Arriving in Edinburgh, he awaited the verdict of the newly-formed Convention (14th March 1689). James's letter to that body was not in the vein Dundee had hoped, and he saw that there would be no resistance in England. He could have deserted his King and changed sides to his own profit, but he chose to continue the struggle. He knew the clans were ready. He left with his small troop of horse on the 16th April and, avoiding Major-General Mackay, his old comrade in arms in the Low Countries, arrived in Inverness to find Coll of Keppoch with the Glencoe men and some Camerons in possession, levying a heavy tax on that town. Coll was in high spirits, having defeated Mackintosh at Mulroy in the previous year and subsequently harried the lands of Clan Chattan, very much to his profit. Dundee saved the town from the depredations of Coll and his men, who then went home to deliver their spoils.

While awaiting the return of the clansmen, Dundee made a lightning raid on the town of Perth, levied a monetary tax, due in his view to King James, and retired north again. Fortunately Perth had provided some replacements for his tired mounts. He made for Lochaber, where he found the clans gathering. Keppoch, Glencoe, Clanranald, Glengarry, Sleat were all there. MacIain with his two sons brought 100 tried warriors to the field. With this force of about 2500 men Dundee marched south to Blair Atholl, where the Castle was held for King James by a relative of the Earl who was away in England.

The chiefs had each received a letter from Mackay, requiring them to lay down their arms and support the new regime, and offering handsome rewards for their service. All of them replied suitably, affirming their loyalty to King James, old Alasdair MacIain of Glencoe, Glengarry and Lochiel amongst them.

From Blair the royal army marched round the back of the Hill of Lude onto the comparatively flat land which fell away to the Pass of Killiecrankie. The clans were drawn up below Urrard House on the field ever after known as *Raon*

Ruairidh in Gaelic song and story. They had the advantage of the brae. Here Dundee waited quietly while Mackay struggled through the Pass and at last drew up his line of battle. His plan was to withhold his attack until the enemy reached a position in which he could destroy them utterly and prevent their escape back through the Pass. It was late afternoon on Saturday the 17th July when Dundee attacked. On the right were the Macleans under their Chief Sir John with about 500 men. Next came young Alan with 700 Clanranald men. He was only sixteen years of age and had Donald of Benbecula as Tutor. Glengarry, commanded by the grim warrior Alasdair Dubh, numbered some 300. In the centre were Lochiel with 600 Camerons, and the Clan Iain of Glencoe under old Alasdair, a grim towering figure of a man graphically described in Latin by Dundee's standard bearer in his poem "The Graemiad." On the left wing were 500 men of Sleat with young *Dòmhnall a' Chogaidh* (Donald of the War) in command. With him as Tutor was Donald of Castleton, who had taken the Sleat men out with Montrose, and was now a grandfather. It is interesting that in this battle the Macleans were on the right, and some of Clan Donald on the left, and yet no complaint was made of the sort attributed to Clan Donald at Culloden. Nor did it seem to influence the fighting qualities of the Macdonalds on this occasion.

Dundee had trained the clansmen to hold their fire until the moment when their volleys would cause the most execution, and then go in with sword and dirk. The ground was open, giving a good field of fire to both sides. As the Highlanders attacked they had to stand a galling fire and many fell, including Sir Donald of Sleat's five cousins. The brunt of the first volley fell upon the officers, who were mostly relatives of their chiefs. Castleton's eldest son, Ranald, fell here, with James of Aird and James of Capstill.

The result was quick and decisive as far as the battle was concerned, but it was an empty victory. Dundee fell mortally wounded and died shortly after, asking how the day was going. The reply pleased him, for he is said to have murmured "It goes well for King James."

The slaughter was terrible. Mackay's men fled back through the narrow Pass and were cut down wholesale. Casualties were estimated at 2000 killed on Mackay's side. Dundee's loss was great too, about 500: and the death of Dundee meant the end of the campaign. The valorous defence of Dunkeld by the newly formed regiment of Covenanters under Colonel Cleland, turned the Highlanders back; but, worse still, it caused them to lose heart and confidence in their new general. They saw no future under Cannon and Buchan. Most of them departed home with their plunder. Few were left to suffer the final defeat at the Haughs of Cromdale in May of the next year.

Old Alasdair and his men retired by the shortest way home through Breadalbane's country, Glenlyon, over the Black Mount and across the Moor of Rannoch into their native Glen. On the way they carried out one of the most successful raids of their long and chequered career. The Campbells assessed their loss at 240 cows, 36 horses, 993 sheep, 133 goats and many household goods, even cooking pots. They estimated the value of this spoil at £7540 sterling. It must have been one of the most successful *creachs* in Highland history. But it did nothing to heal the breach between the two clans. On the contrary, it was just another though major incident in a continuing series that had for long fed the implacable hatred of the Campbells and spurred them to seek redress by whatever means that came their way.

In the eyes of the new Government of King William it was necessary to take all possible steps to quell the spirit of the Highland clans. On the 14th July of the year following Killiecrankie, MacIain was forfeited in all his lands. On the 2nd of May of that year witnesses had deponed that MacIain and Stewart of Appin had been active Jacobites. On the 11th September following, a Commission was given by the Lords of the Privy Council to the Earl of Argyll to take what force was required and proceed to their domains and thus reduce them to a state of obedience. The net was slowly being prepared in which to catch the rebellious clansmen.

The clans, however, were obdurate. Until King James gave them permission to conform to the new order, they remained ready to take up arms again. King William and the Convention in Scotland were faced with two alternatives—bribery or extirpation. The orders sent to Sir Thomas Livingstone, commander-in-chief in Scotland, were impossible to carry out. It would have taken a long time and a lot of money to destroy all the clans involved in the Killiecrankie campaign, which had already cost, on an estimate made at the time, about £150,000. The other choice was to be tried. To that end Breadalbane was entrusted with £12,000 to buy the clans off. On the 30th June 1691 he called a meeting at his Castle of Aberchallader on the Tulla Water under the Black Mount. At the outset he informed MacIain that his share of the money was already spent in compensation for the raid on Glenlyon and other lands on their passage home from Killiecrankie. The only outcome was that the chiefs promised to do nothing until October of that year. No money passed, and Breadalbane's answer to enquiries about it was unsatisfactory. Certain secret articles were entered into which showed that Breadalbane was playing a double game; but as usual he managed to come out unscathed. Sir John Dalrymple, Master of Stair, Principal Secretary of State for Scotland, accepted the blunt statement that "the money had been spent: the Highlands were quiet, and that was enough among friends." We see a lot of Stair as the story unfolds.

One other possible way of pacifying the Highlands was suggested by some, and the King himself at one stage even agreed to it. That was that the Crown should buy out the superiorities which had bedevilled the Highland clans for so long. This would not have been to the profit of such nobles as Argyll and Huntly, however, and the matter was dropped.

There remained extirpation. In August 1691 Argyll was in London in attendance on Stair. Sir Thomas Livingstone was in Scotland with 1500 horse and 5000 foot. Colonel Hill, an aged soldier who had served the Commonwealth, Charles II and James II in turn, was Governor of the fort of Inverlochy, now called Fort William. Hill had made friends of the neighbouring chiefs and was trusted by them. In August of the same year he had administered an oath of allegiance to some of them; and that was the passport given by him to Achnacon and Achtriochtan, which they had in their pockets when they were murdered.

An envoy had been sent to the Court of St Germains to secure King James's release enabling the chiefs to transfer their allegiance to the new King. That document was signed there on the 12th December 1691. The envoy, Major Menzies, sped back poste-haste, but was unable to reach Dunkeld until eleven days later. He sent an express to Livingstone with the release and begged the Privy Council to postpone operations until the chiefs had been given time to receive it, which must take some days, by which time the day of grace (31st December) would have expired. On the 5th January it was sent to the Council who decided it must be sent to "Court," by which they must have meant the King.

Meantime, as time went on and the Chiefs of Clan Cameron, Glengarry, Clanranald, Sleat, Keppoch, Appin and Glencoe failed to make their peace, Stair became more and more impatient. The King was urging him to make an end of the matter and release the regiments tied up on garrison duty in the Highlands. He hoped Breadalbane would have completed the task of winning over the chiefs before the time of mercy expired. In a letter to Breadalbane in December, Stair begs that gentleman to get on with the work, complains that the flow of money from England has stopped, and that the money already spent has done no good. To his mind the only course was to root out the whole lot even before the due date and thus dispose of the threat of further aid that might come from France or any other quarter. He thought that even if they took the oath it would be value-less, because they were only taking it at King James' behest; and if he allowed them to take such an oath, he could just as well absolve them from it on the eve of any future Rising. All this frustration served to increase Stair's hatred of the clans and he began his plans for destroying them. Sleat was far away, Clanranald safe in France, so the brunt would fall on the clans in Lochaber and the Great Glen.

As the last days of December came, all the chiefs handed in their submission except Glengarry and Glencoe. The first report sent to London included MacIain in the list. Lochiel and Appin went to Inveraray. Keppoch went to Inverness. Donald of Benbecula, tutor of Clanranald, took the oath on behalf of his ward, the young Chief in France. According to the historians of Clan Donald (*Clan Donald*, vol. 2, page 454) Alasdair Dubh of Glengarry took the oath and received pardon before the end of 1691. They do not say where he took it. Which oath did he take? The same historians say that Keppoch took the oath on the 24th of June before Breadalbane, Commissioner for the King! From these and other accounts it would seem that the oaths are mixed up in some of the records. We have seen now two oaths referred to, the first in May after Cromdale and the second in the official royal proclamation of August; but there appears to have been a third demanded by Hill in June. Perhaps this was the one taken by Keppoch on the 24th of that month? In June, Hill wrote to Melville, "Since my last the Committee of Council and the Commander in Chief thought fit to pass from their first strict order . . . [demanding surrender of arms] . . . I hope I have taken a better way and easier. I sent them a very strict oath never to take up arms against William and his Government." He goes on to say that the Camerons had come in and sworn, many Macdonalds of Brae Lochaber, the Sleat gentry (but not Sir Donald), Clanranald, and Morar. More were coming in daily. The Appin and Glencoe men desired to go to Argyll at Inveraray and he says, "I have set them a short day." Who then had come in at that time, and sworn? Surely the "middle men" or gentry of the clans, but not the chiefs.

In the event the only valid oath was that of 29th August 1691, duly pro-claimed on that day in Edinburgh. Memories of the other oaths taken by the cadets and gentry of the clans led MacIain to assume he could protect himself and his clan in the same way. And yet it is plain, from all the subsequent records, that Glengarry never did take the only valid oath by due date. The order from the King to Hill and Livingstone proves this, and at the same time gives Glen-garry the chance of taking it and ensuring his safety at a time sixteen full days after due date. In addition Hill is given full powers to compromise with Alasdair Dubh of Glengarry in any way he sees fit so long as the oath is taken in the end. The last paragraph of the same order is a very different proposition. No extension of mercy or compromise here. "*Delenda est Carthago,*" as Stair so bluntly put it, no matter what else may happen. Extirpation is the word used and the now familiar "rooting out" is as good a meaning as any, in no matter which dictionary.

In December 1691, all was quiet in Glencoe, and indeed in Lochaber after the events of the summer. Colonel Hill's offer of an oath to the clans had been taken advantage of by many of the clansmen, notably the tacksmen and cadets whose chiefs had given permission for them to make their individual peace with the Government if they so desired. Hill had been pleased with his effort and the response to the offer he had made. The tacksmen of the Glen and their dependants dwelt in fancied security, for had they not Hill's letters of indemnity in their pockets?

At Achnacon, there is a side glen running almost due south—*Gleann Leac na Muidhe* (the Glen of the Flagstones of the Churn). In this glen was a farm belonging to MacIain where he was supposed by some to have been living at this time. There are here the ruins of a fairly considerable settlement. The name of the glen indicates that it played an important part in the dairying activities of the community.

In winter the people were more concentrated than at any other time of the year. Achtriochtan, being higher up the glen than any other hamlet, was almost deserted. The tacksman himself was staying at Achnacon, leaving only a few retainers on his farm. The chief's sons were living at Carnoch; and it would seem that Alasdair and his lady had left their big house to John, their eldest son, who was in any case soon to inherit the chiefship, and who took some of the responsibility of the position off his father's shoulders. Alasdair, the younger brother, had married Elspeth Stewart of Ardsheal, and they were living not far from John. Much has been said about the fact that Glenlyon was related to young Alasdair. The relationship was in fact fairly distant. Elspeth's grandfather, Duncan Stewart of Ardsheal, had married (as her third husband) Jean Campbell, daughter of Sir Robert Campbell of Glenorchy. By her first husband, Archibald Campbell of Glenlyon, she had Robert Campbell, Captain in Argyll's Regiment, and Laird of Glenlyon. So Alasdair's wife was, one might say, Glenlyon's niece, and Alasdair, in a very distant way, Glenlyon's nephew.

The floor of the Glen, with Bidean nam Bian and Stob Coire an Lochain in the background

The two brothers, John and Alasdair, were living near to each other at Carnoch this winter. The rest of their people were in the various hamlets throughout the lower reaches of the glen between Signal Rock and the sea, the best part in which to pass the winter, low-lying and sheltered.

December drew to a close. On the 29th MacIain at last received the long awaited news from King James that he was free to take the oath and safeguard his clan from the wrath of King William. He was the last to receive Livingstone's express letter. Lochiel, Appin, Keppoch and Clanranald's Tutor had all taken the oath with little time to spare. So he set out with confidence to reach Inverlochy before the sands ran out. He had no doubt that Hill would swear him in and all would be well. He arrived at the Fort to find it crowded with troops, Hill's own regiment and some 400 men of Argyll's Regiment, the rest of which were disposed in various strategic spots. One company under Drummond, of evil memory, was at Barcaldine to overawe the Appin Stewarts. Hill received MacIain kindly as was his wont. He had a sort of private admiration for the proud old man. When MacIain asked for the oath to be administered, indicating his desire to have the distasteful formality over and done with, Hill shocked him by announcing that it was outside his power to do it, pointing out the clause in the August Proclamation that the oath was to be taken before the Sheriffs of the shires in which the applicants resided. MacIain remarked that Hill had given Achtriochtan and Achnacon his blessing and a letter to protect them. Hill could only state that that had been a previous oath of his own making, but the fact remained that now, as at this date, he must appear before the Sheriff of his shire and swear it in his presence. MacIain was dumbfounded. All his efforts had been in vain. He had waited overlong for King James's quittance; and now, at near midnight on the 29th/30th he was a good fifteen miles on the wrong side of his glen and must needs retrace his steps and get to Inveraray before midnight of the 31st, a journey of over sixty miles, impossible even in good weather.

It was not till the 5th of January that he was at last able to present himself before Campbell of Ardkinglas, the Sheriff of Argyll. On the following morning Ardkinglas gave him the oath and promised to forward it at once to the Council in Edinburgh. He kept his word; and the Chief light-heartedly set out for home, satisfied that he had now put himself and his children under the protection of the law.

The oath taken by MacIain and duly certified by the Sheriff was sent to Colin Campbell, Sheriff Clerk of Argyll, who was in Edinburgh at this time, together with a letter stating how earnest the chief had been, enclosing Hill's letter, and asking that all three be presented to the Privy Council at the earliest opportunity. He even asked Colin to report to him at once the action taken. Campbell obeyed and showed them all to the Clerks of the Council, Sir Gilbert Elliot and David Moncrieff. They were in a quandary, but, on a point of law, would have nothing to do with the matter. The Sheriff Clerk then tried a number of Privy Councillors, one of whom was Lord Stair, father of the Master. They objected, and the matter was referred to Lord Aberuchill, another Campbell. In the end it was decided to cancel the document and hand it to the Clerk of Council. It was never presented to the whole Council in session. Of course, legally they were right; but the Royal Commission, which reported later on the matter, blamed them all for not bringing all three documents before the full Council as requested by the Sheriff of Argyll.

So the oath was null and void, but MacIain back at home was ignorant of that fact. He trusted that the genial Ardkinglas would do his best for him. On his return he told his clan that all was well and they could dwell in peace, but advised his tacksmen to make sure of their safety by following his example at the first opportunity. They never did, as far as written records show, nor is it likely that they had time to do so before disaster overtook them.

A great relief settled on them all, and life resumed its normal winter routine. Meantime, all unknown to them, things were happening in London and Edinburgh which were to bring death in its most treacherous form into their beautiful valley.

By the 9th of January Stair must have heard the first report that all had submitted, for he at once wrote to Livingstone: "I could have wished the Macdonalds had not divided, and I am sorry Keppoch and Glencoe are safe." On the 11th Argyll told him he had received an express letter from Ardkinglas reporting that Glencoe had taken the oath too late, and explaining the action he had taken to forward all the documents to Edinburgh for the attention of the Council. He could not have known then that these had never been presented to the Privy Council in session; nor that they had been deleted from the records. In time he heard from his father, who knew about the transaction even if he did not take part in it, that the oath was null and void in the eyes of the negotiators in Edinburgh. On the same day as he received this news, Stair wrote to Livingstone: "Argyll tells me that Glencoe hath not taken the oath, at which I rejoice."

Between this date and the 16th there was much consultation between the King and Stair, with Breadalbane on call for advice about tactics, as his special knowledge of the terrain was of great value to those who knew little about the Glen and its surroundings. The result of their deliberations appeared on the 16th in the form of explicit orders from the King to the commander-in-chief, Livingstone, a copy of which was sent to Colonel Hill at Inverlochy.

INSTRUCTIONS FROM THE KING TO COLONEL HILL

16th Jany., 1692.

William R.

1. The copy of the paper given by Macdonald of Aughtera to you hath been shewn to us. We did formerly grant passes to Buchan and Cannon, and we do authorise and allow you to grant passes to them, and ten servants to each of them, to come freely and safely to Leith; from that to be transported to the Netherlands before the 15th March next, to go from then where they please, without any stop or trouble.

2. We doe allow you to receive the submission of Glengarry and those with him, upon their taking the oath of alledgiance and delivering up the house of Invergarry, to be safe as to their lives, but as to their estates to depend on our mercy.

3. In case ye find that the house of Invergarry cannot probably be taken in this season of the year, with the artillery and provision ye can bring there; in that case we leave it to your discretion to give Glengarry an assurance of the entire indemnity for life and fortune, upon delivery of the house and arms, and taking the oath of alledgiance. In this you are to act as you find the circumstances of the affair do require; but it were better that those who have not taken the benefit of our indemnity, in the terms within the diet prefixt by our proclamation, should be obliged to render upon mercy. The taking of the oath is indispensable, others having already taken it.

4. If McEan of Glenco and that tribe can well be separated from the rest, it will be a proper vindication of public Justice to extirpate that sect of thieves. The double of these instructions is only communicated to Sir Thomas Livingstone.

W. R.

With the copy of the King's orders to Hill, Stair included a letter similar to one sent to the commander-in-chief, but containing the following enlightening paragraph: "The Earls of Argyle and Breadalbane have promised that they [the MacIains] shall have no retreat in their bounds, the passes to Rannoch would be secured, and the hazard certified to the Laird of Weem [Menzies] to reset them; in that case Argyle's detachment with a party that may be posted in Island Stalker must cut them off." Here is abundant proof that both Argyll and Breadalbane were in the plot, and Menzies too, though the latter acted under duress, if indeed he was obliged to act at all. He was after all one of Breadalbane's protégés. It cannot be argued that the two Campbell Earls thought that this was just another of those harrying expeditions accompanied by the burning of houses and driving of cattle. It was plainly a plan for the complete cutting off of the whole clan. Escape routes far away were to be guarded—Rannoch, Glen Etive, Glen Dochart, and all the possible ways to the South which lay in the Campbell lands. Castle Stalker guarded Appin and overawed the Stewarts there. In the event we shall see how effective these dispositions were; but it seemed that nothing had been left to chance and there could be no possible escape for the unfortunate Clan Iain of Glencoe.

By the end of the month the arrangements were complete. Major Duncanson, with his second in command, Captain Drummond, had brought his company of Argyll's Regiment up to Ballachulish, thus holding the short road to Appin, close to the scene of action. The fort at Inverlochy was full of troops to the number of 800, comprising 400 from Hill's Regiment and a similar number of Argyll's. Indeed it was overcrowded, and that was the excuse given for moving a company of Argyll's to Glencoe for quartering. The passes South were held. Lt.-Colonel Hamilton, in overall command, could move unnoticed to Kinlochleven at any time, thence by the old military road over the Devil's Staircase into the headwaters of the Glen. His was the hardest task of all if he were to arrive with his troops fit for action after the gruelling climb over the Staircase in the weather prevailing. However, he had time on his side, if he cared to set out early enough, for his movements were unlikely to be perceived by any of the inhabitants of Glencoe.

There remained only one detail to attend to in order to make the whole scheme a resounding success. That essential factor was surprise. This was to be provided in the base and treacherous manner which has made the Massacre of Glencoe the most notorious crime in Scottish history, out of all proportion to the number of victims slaughtered. Many other atrocities have been committed in our nation's long history in which many times the number of men, women and children met their death; and yet these are seldom remembered, while Glencoe has never been forgotten.

On the morning of the 1st February a company of soldiers was marching along the short road from Ballachulish towards the mouth of the Glen. It was at once seen and reported to MacIain, who immediately sent word to his clansmen to hide their weapons, and called his sons to his side. After a short consultation it was decided that John and Alasdair Og should take a party of twenty men and meet the troops to find out as soon as possible their intentions. As the two young men got nearer they saw it was a company of Argyll's Regiment, a Captain, a Lieutenant and an Ensign at their head. Very soon they recognised the Captain commanding the company to be Robert Campbell of Glenlyon, uncle of Alasdair's wife. None too pleased to have a Campbell coming to their glen, they nonetheless were somewhat relieved that he was at any rate a connection by marriage, even if not a blood relation. Surely he could mean no harm.

John and Alasdair MacIain greeted Glenlyon politely and asked him his business. Glenlyon was very cordial and almost apologetic. Calling up his Lieutenant he asked him for the written orders he had received from his commander. They were billeting orders commanding the MacIains to house and feed the company, as there was no room for them in the fort of Inverlochy. An additional reason given was that they had come to collect arrears of cess and hearth money, a new tax imposed in 1690. The three officers gave their paroles of honour that they came with no hostile intentions. In spite of the obvious inconvenience of having a company of hungry soldiers to house and feed in a glen already quite densely populated, and with supplies of winter food decreasing daily, the young men told Glenlyon he was welcome and his party would have hospitality for as long as they had to stay. The demeanour of their guest was friendly and cordial; he appeared to conduct himself in all respects like a gentleman, whatever may have been going on in his mind at the time. As yet he had no certain knowledge of the part he was to be ordered to play, or that a massacre was contemplated. In all fairness one has to assume this. He was, after all, a junior officer, and the plotters had been told that what was to be done must be done secretly and suddenly. Captains and subalterns might well have been left out of the secret until the last moment when there would be little chance of their backing out. The reasons for his being sent to Glencoe were plausible enough for a simple soldier. One can hardly imagine that anyone could have lived as a guest in another's house for a fortnight with such a heavy load on his mind, and not have betrayed some of his inner thoughts.

With lighter hearts, and their fears somewhat allayed, the young men joined the company and took Glenlyon and his officers to their father who met them

Looking up Lairig Fhionnghail, with the opening of Gleann Leac na Muidhe (the escape route) on the right and Achnacon in the middle distance

with due dignity and friendship, confirming the promise of full hospitality given by his sons. The old Chief did not seem to have any hesitation in accepting the assurances of Glenlyon that the visit was an entirely friendly one, and that no harm of any kind was meant towards him or his clan. Iain Og, the eldest son, was quite happy about it all. Not so Alasdair: from the beginning he seems to have had his doubts, and it was well that he had, as things turned out. If he had been as complaisant as his father and brother there is no saying what his fate might have been.

The visitors settled down. Glenlyon and his officers chose to lodge at Inverigan, which is just about in the centre of habitation. From that point he could be in touch with his detachments scattered among the houses of the clan. Sergeant Barbour was sent to Achnacon. The Macdonalds farthest away from these concentrations were the few caretakers on the farm at Achtriochtan and the farm workers up at Gleann Muidhe on MacIain's own farm.

The soldiers—to the number of 60, according to the muster roll of October 1691, but according to other accounts 120—were distributed, three or four to a house, among the indwellers of the Glen, so that every house was under guard of its guests, who could be ready at any hour of the day or night to carry out their orders. These orders were not, of course, communicated to the troops until a few hours before the time set for action. In the meantime soldiers and clansmen lived together at close quarters under the same roof, sharing the same beds and board, like one family. The quarters must indeed have been very close, considering 60 soldiers (at the least) were living in a community of some 500 to 600 souls, already concentrated in their winter quarters.

On the 12th of February three letters were sent out:

1. COLONEL HILL TO HAMILTON

Ft. William 12 Feb. 1692

Sir, You are, with 400 men of my regt., and the 400 of my lord Argyll's Regt. under command of Major Duncanson, to march straight to Glenco and there put into due execution the orders you have received from the Commander in Chief.

Given under my hand at Fort William 12th Feb.

[*sic sub*] John Hill.

This letter is the only document incriminating Hill; and it may be said that he did not know all that the orders received from the commander-in-chief implied, as Hamilton's orders were sent to him direct from Livingstone. At this time Hamilton seems to have been at Ballachulish with Duncanson, although it is unlikely his own detachment destined to cross the Devil's Staircase was there. His letter, which follows, is headed "Ballachulish," so perhaps his troops were on the north side of the ferry, whence they would have to march round by the head of the Loch, over the Staircase and into Glencoe. No wonder they were late.

2. HAMILTON TO DUNCANSON

Ballychyllis 12 Feb. 1692

Sir, Persuant to the Commander in Chief's and my Colonel's order to me for putting into execution the King's command, you are to order your affair so as that the several posts already assigned you by you and your several detachments faln in activeness precisely at five of the clock tomorrow morning, being Saturday; at which time I will endeavour the same with those appointed from this regiment for the other places. It will be most necessary you secure those avenues on the south side, that the old fox, nor none of his cubs get away. The orders are that none be spared from seventy, of the sword, nor the Government troubled with prisoners. This all until I see you.

From your humble servant,

James Hamilton.

Please to order a guard to secure the ferry, and the boats there, and the boats must be all on this side the ferry after your men are over.

For Their Majesties' service, for Major Duncanson of the Earl of Argyll's Regiment.

From this letter it is patent that the posts assigned to the various detachments, and the part to be played by Glenylon's company, had all been thought out some days before. The instructions, too, become more explicit. All under seventy are to be killed, and the Chief must not escape.

3. DUNCANSON TO GLENLYON

12 Feby. 1692.

Sir, You are hereby ordered to fall upon the rebells the Macdonalds of Glenco and put all to the sword under seventy. You are to have special care that the old fox and his sons do not escape your hands; you are to secure all avenues, that no man escape. This you are to put in execution at five of the clock precisely, and by that time, or very shortly after it, I will strive to be at you with a stronger party. If I do not come to you at five, you are not to tarry for me, but to fall on. This is by the King's special commands, for the good and safety of the Countrey, that these miscreants be cut off root and branch. See that this be put in execution without fear or favour, or you may expect to be dealt with as one not true to King or Government, nor a man fit to carry a commission in the King's service. Expecting you will not fail in the fulfilling hereof, as you love yourself, I subscribe this at Ballychyllis, the 12 Feby. 1692.

Robert Duncanson.

This, the final written instruction, is the most virulent of all. The orders to spare none under seventy and to see that the Chief and his sons do not escape are repeated with emphasis. Then, to make sure, a threat which could hardly be more menacing, is added. It appears they were not too sure of Glenlyon.

Evening came. Glenlyon and his officers had made their usual visits during the day to take the morning draught with MacIain and his sons. They had accepted the Chief's invitation to dinner on the following night, and all seemed quite peaceful and friendly. The two young MacIains were at Inverigan spending the evening with Glenlyon playing cards. Between six and seven o'clock a runner arrived with a despatch for Glenlyon—the letter quoted above. It could be seen at once by his face that Glenlyon was taken aback by this interruption. To the anxious enquiries of the young men he replied lightly that a soldier never knew what was to happen next, but he would have to ask them to stop the game as he had work to do. He made the excuse that there was trouble in the direction of Glengarry and he had been called out in readiness to move, and John and Alasdair returned to their homes.

The hour fixed for the onslaught was five o'clock, and just before that time a servant rushed into the house and told Alasdair that soldiers were approaching with fixed bayonets. He and his wife at once fled, meeting his brother on the way. Together they collected as many of their people as they could and made for the slopes of Meall Mor. On their way they narrowly escaped running into a party of soldiers coming from the Ballachulish road, men of Duncanson's command; but they saw the soldiers before being themselves noticed, and avoided them. As they climbed along the slopes of Meall Mor they heard the fusillades at Carnoch, Inverigan and Achnacon. These same fusillades warned many of the outlying hamlets before the soldiers allotted the task of attacking them could reach the spot. It was a tactical error to use muskets, as from the time of the first shots the whole Glen was on the alert. Then, as the flames of the burning houses lit up the sky, the young men knew that their only course now was to gather as many of the survivors as possible and organise an escape.

Meantime MacIain and his wife were in bed when a knock came at the door. They replied and a servant asked who was there. A friendly voice which they recognised as Lindsay's answered that they had urgent business. The servant opened the door and Lindsay and the ensign rushed in and entered the bedroom. MacIain greeted them warmly and, calling to the servant to serve drinks to their guests, he began to dress. His back was to the visitors as he pulled on his trews. Before he could turn round and face them, they both shot him, one through the back and the other through the head. MacIain died instantly and fell by his bedside. Meantime his lady cried out and made to help her husband; but she was seized and treated in a shameful manner. Her rings were wrenched off, the assailants using their teeth to free them as they were very tightly held. Her clothes were stripped off her and she fled naked into the darkness. Somehow she managed to join a party of other fugitives, but died of her injuries the following day. The servant was murdered, and an old man of eighty who was there. Another man, Duncan Donn, who came periodically to the Glen with letters, was also shot and left for dead. The dead and dying were thrown on to the midden and left.

At Inverigan Glenlyon's men seized their host and eight men, bound them hand and foot and awaited their orders. Glenlyon gave the command and they were shot one after the other. It is here that an old story has its origin. When the nine men were seized, a woman and her baby escaped with others into the darkness. Soldiers were sent after them. After a long search one of the soldiers came up with the woman and her babe hidden under a rock. As he approached, the soldier heard the woman crooning a song he had heard his own wife singing to their child, and could not bring himself to kill the tragic pair. A dog had accompanied the woman in her flight, and the soldier killed it. Dipping his sword in its blood he returned to Glenlyon to report that the deed had been done, showing the bloody blade in proof.

At Achnacon Barbour was in charge. Eight men were sitting round the fire-side. Five o'clock seems a strange hour for such a meeting. Perhaps the general feeling of apprehension had spread. Achnacon himself sat there with Achtriochtan, the latter's brother and six more. On the stroke of five a volley of eighteen shots, fired through the windows by the sergeant and his men, laid six of them on the floor, dead or dying. Barbour came in and, seeing one of them move, asked him if he lived. Achtriochtan's brother was this man, according to the witnesses later examined at the Inquiry, and when he replied that he was sorely wounded but still alive, Barbour made as if to finish him off. Macdonald begged that he be shot, if he had to be so murdered, outside the house; and Barbour magnanimously agreed, "seeing that he had eaten his meat for so many days." The victim was dragged out and propped against the wall of the house. The morning being still dark, the firing party stood near their quarry. Suddenly, Macdonald, who was a powerful man and not so badly wounded as he had made out, leapt forward, threw his plaid over the soldier's muskets and escaped into the darkness with the shots of his would-be murderers falling harmlessly around him.

Meantime those not killed by the first volley had broken out of the back of the house and escaped.

Down at Laroch the aged Ranald of the Shield, the hero of 1645, was shot and left for dead with his son. The latter was quite dead, but old Ranald managed to crawl to the shelter of a hut nearby. There, unable to move farther on account of his wounds, he perished in the flames when the hut and other farm-buildings were set on fire. He left two grandsons, who happened to be away from home. They survived and were "out" in 1745.

Glenlyon had hardly finished his execution of the nine unfortunate bound prisoners at Inverigan when Major Duncanson, accompanied by Captain Drummond, arrived to see how things had gone. They were not at all pleased. Neither had any misgivings about their task. Drummond had already shown his hatred of MacIain at Barcaldine when he had delayed the Chief for twenty-four precious hours on his way to take the oath at Inveraray. Duncanson was now in turn to show his ruthlessness. First he upbraided Glenlyon for his inefficiency in not producing more corpses. Then he told him to get busy and find some more. At this point a young man was found still alive in the neighbourhood and dragged before the officers. Duncanson ordered Glenlyon to shoot him, and when Campbell hesitated, Duncanson himself shot the prisoner. A young boy of seven ran to Glenlyon and clasped him round the knees begging for mercy. Drummond stabbed the child through the back and he died at once. One more body for the tally.

Duncanson's troops were part of the company guarding the short road to Appin. The Major had left an officer in charge of the road block and had come on to see if his help was needed in the mopping-up operations. From the account of his meeting with Glenlyon it is plain that Campbell was tiring of the dreary business and not a little sickened by the slaughter already. The others had no such scruples, and only seemed angry that so few victims had been accounted for.

Meantime Hamilton with his company had been struggling over the Staircase. The change in the weather, unforeseen when the operation was planned, hampered him badly. This old military road leaves Kinlochleven and winds round the shoulders of hills and through streams up to a summit of 1850 feet, then for the last half mile and a half drops steeply down the "staircase" to Alltnafeadh at the headwaters of the Etive River and a mile or so from the watershed at the east end of Glencoe. The distance is in all five and a half rough miles, difficult at the best of times, but on a February morning in a blizzard, very nearly impassable. Hamilton arrived at last in the Glen before the watershed about nine o'clock and found no one there but one shepherd, an old man of eighty, one of Achtriochtan's men, whom he killed at once. The rest had fled long before and were making their way over the Lairig Eilde to Dalness. It was at this point that two officers refused to go on with the business, sickened by the murder of the octogenarian. These were Lieutenants Francis Farquhar and Gilbert Kennedy. They were immediately put under close arrest, and later sent to Glasgow. They gave evidence at the Inquiry, and it is not likely that any drastic disciplinary action was taken, in view of the popular outcry against the murders.

Finding no corpses on his way down the Glen, Hamilton was furious by the time he met the disconsolate group of officers at Inverigan, and was in no mood to listen to Glenlyon's excuses. He too poured scorn on the Captain's achievements. While they were thus arguing a soldier came up and gave them some papers he had found on two of the bodies, Achtriochtan's and another's, which proved to be the letters from Hill jealously guarded by the two unfortunates as the guarantee of their security. The letters were at once destroyed. Such evidence was best out of the way. All that remained now was to scour the ruins of the hamlets for any survivors, burn the few houses that were left and gather the stock for removal to Inverlochy. When everything possible had been done, and the corpses counted, it was found that in all 38 persons had been killed. The rest, the great majority, had vanished. The stock was collected to the number of 900 head of cattle, 200 horses, and a great number of sheep and goats, and got ready for their departure.

So ended the Massacre of Glencoe. The plan had been carried out "secretly and suddenly," but not quite entirely as conceived. Several avenues of escape had after all been left unguarded and the little clan was not annihilated. From the grandiose scheme of wiping out the Clans Cameron, Glengarry, Keppoch, Stewart, Maclean and Glencoe, the conspirators had been forced to descend to the destruction of the smallest of these, and even that had been bungled. They had incurred the ignominy, guilt and execration without achieving a fraction of their objective.

Of all the atrocities committed that morning, the murder of the Chief epitomises them all. Old MacIain, under whose orders the people of the Glen had extended hospitality to some sixty to one hundred visitors, and who himself was in the very act of ordering drinks for his guests at an unprecedented hour of the morning, was struck down by those very guests—brutally, and through the back. They did not even give him the satisfaction of one last look of scorn as he fell. This is the deed which so shocked the world at the time, and has done so ever since. And yet it was not done by the hand of his hereditary foes but by two Scots (Lowlanders it is true), not even Englishmen, under orders from their Campbell commander; and those who cause others to commit a crime have to bear the responsibility.

John MacIain, now chief of the clan, and his brother Alasdair, as we have seen, had gathered as many of the survivors as they could, after eluding Duncanson's men. As they skirted the slopes of the Meall Mor well above the floor of the Glen, they could see the fires started in the houses and hear the shots of the killers. Their shortest route from there to safety was plainly to follow the contours of the shoulder of Meall Mor into Glen Muidhe and keep going up to the head of that glen. On their way they were joined by fugitives from Inverigan and Achnacon. On the southern slopes of the hill in Gleann Muidhe they were sheltered to some extent from the north wind and snow showers, and protected from the view of the soldiers below by the dark, uncertain light of the early winter dawn.

This, the only organised party, contained some hundred and twenty souls. Men and women, young and old, children—all were represented. Young MacIain led them on, encouraging the weak and keeping them going as best he could. It was essential to be out of the Glen before day broke. A nurse carried in her arms his own son, a baby, and this child lived to become in his turn Chief of the Clan. Amongst them was a grandfather, Ewan, carrying in his arms his grandchild, Ewan Og. The mother had been killed with her husband and the old grandfather alone was left to save the baby, whose descendants live now in Canada. There were many cases such as this; and it was a sadly depleted and exhausted convoy that followed the young Chief into Appin. Some had fallen by the way, but most of them got through—the nucleus of the new Clann Iain which rose out of the ashes under the kindly care of the Appin Stewarts.

For the rest, isolated groups of two or three made their way through the other passes to Dalness, and thence, after resting, to join the main body in Appin. It is impossible to guess how many died of exposure on their way to safety. In many Macdonald families the story is still told how their ancestors were fugitives from the Massacre and fled far from their native valley, settling in distant parts of the country—Moray, Aberdeen and Perthshire—never to return. It is quite understandable that many who had seen their near relatives murdered before their eyes might never wish to see Glencoe again.

Little by little, the bolder members of the clan came back to their native valley and began to restore the houses and make ready for a full return of their families. It was not till later that official sanction was given. Meantime, not long after the disaster, Campbell of Barcaldine, as agent for Breadalbane, came to the two young MacIains and proposed that they should certify that Breadalbane had had nothing to do with the affair in any way, and in return they were offered "full restitution." How the Earl could undertake this on behalf of the Government does not appear, but it shows that one of the conspirators was feeling uneasy, although no word had yet come through that there would be any official inquiry at all.

When news of the massacre leaked out, wild rumours were current in Edinburgh first and later in London. They caused Hill no little apprehension, and in a series of letters to Lord Chancellor Tweeddale he is found explaining his own part in the proceedings and suggesting means of achieving a peaceful settlement. On 28th March he wrote: "If these poor people that remain of the Glencoe men may be accepted to mercy and pardon, taking the oath and giving security for their future peaceable living, it might be well what is done being enough for example and vindication of the public justice. I make no doubt but to keep them civil and in good order they will always, as many others do, fear such another stroak." And again: "I understand that there are some severe reflections upon the action in Glencoe, and that perhaps by many good men too. Therefore I think it my duty to give your Lordship a more particular account thereof. Glencoe came to me and I advised him to haste to the Sheriff and take the oath before the day, which he promised to do, and I would not let him stay so much as to drink but he turned about and went to Glengarry and let the time elapse, but wrote to the Sheriff three days after and what he did then was not sustained because after the day. Upon which I had several orders from the Commander in Chief and all extraordinarily strict to destroy these people and take no prisoners, and (lest I should prove remiss) another of the same orders was directed to my Lieutenant-Colonel to do the same, and after all that another order under the King's own hand to root out that sept of thieves, but by the help of a storm several of the men escaped who yet are quiet in hopes they may obtain a pardon for their lives upon giving security for their peaceable living which in my humble opinion were better than to turn them desperate and to join with other loose men and lie in every bush and glen in small parties to shoot men and rob up and down the country as they find their fittest occasions, and I doubt not but I could make them peaceable. If any censure the severity of man's justice, yet the Justice of God is to be reverenced for there was much blood on these people's hands, and either these orders must be disobeyed (that were hard pressed by authority) or else these people must have suffered what they had done."

At length the King gave in to Hill's importunity and in August sanctioned the return of the MacIains to the Glen under the protection of Hill, who was to answer for their good behaviour. So at last the little Clan was back home again, trying to make some of the houses habitable and gather enough food for the oncoming winter. Many friends helped them in this task: Keppoch, Lochiel and the Stewarts of Appin. Food came from a distance too. One notable case is on record. Far out in the Western ocean the laird of Heiskir, an island some miles to the west of North Uist, Alasdair Bàn Mac Iain 'Ic Uisdein (to give him his Gaelic patronymic), loaded his birlinn with meal and sailed through the dangerous seas of the Minch and up Loch Linnhe to the shores of Loch Leven at the mouth of Glencoe, where his grateful kinsfolk unloaded the welcome cargo. It is not to be supposed that he was the only member of Clan Donald to do such an act of kindness, but he must have been the most distant in time and space. Alexander of Heiskir was a cadet of the House of Sleat, one of the Clann Domhnaili Hearaich; so the ancestor common to himself and MacIain of Glencoe lived away back in 1300. Such ties, considered very distant in these days, were held very strongly among the Gaels, whose sense of kinship and genealogy has always been highly developed. Heiskir, and indeed the whole of Clan Donald, regarded themselves as near cousins of the unfortunate Clann Iain.

The winter passed quietly, and not much is on record to show how things went in Glencoe but the clan survived somehow. In October Hill had tried to have them placed under the "protection" of Argyll, as he deemed it necessary "they should be under some person of power and honesty to the Government." A sad and ironic turn of Fate that they should have to rely on the biggest Campbell of all for "protection"! Stewart of Appin, under whom they had been at one time, was not much better off. Argyll protected him too.

At last, in March of 1693 the Scots Parliament met after a recess of two and a half years. The Duke of Hamilton was Lord High Commissioner, and Stair and Johnstone Joint Secretaries. Stair was in Flanders with the King, so Johnstone acted at home. In a session of two months little mention was made of Glencoe in spite of the popular concern that was being expressed on all sides.

Public opinion and the repeated demands that an inquiry should be held became so urgent now that the King at last set up a Committee of Inquiry to look into the matter. The Duke of Hamilton was in charge, with orders to inquire into the slaughter and the manner in which it had been carried out. The Duke died on the 27th April, so he must have been a sick man at the time of his appointment. Anyway the results of this inquiry were deemed "defective." No one was satisfied with it, and it was soon forgotten. All it did was to make the guilty men begin to think, and wonder what they were to say if called on as witnesses. Livingstone wrote to Lt.-Colonel Hamilton that there was an agitation starting, and hinted that it might be as well to give it some thought. They had two full years to make up their minds how they should explain their actions because the next, and final, inquiry was not instituted until 1695. In that year the King wisely saw that something had to be done and, rather than be compelled to act under pressure, he appointed a Royal Commission with full powers to inquire into the whole business, call witnesses and report their findings to him and to Parliament. At long last there seemed to be a ray of hope. Perhaps justice was about to be done.

The Royal Commission was appointed at Kensington on the 29th April 1695, and sealed and registered in Edinburgh on the 20th May. The Marquis of Tweeddale, Lord High Chancellor, was at its head, with the Earl of Annandale and seven others under him. The composition of this body was impressive, being made up of the most important legal officers of the Government. It will be noted that the Lord Advocate was Sir James Steuart, who took the place when Sir John Lowther refused the office unless he were permitted to institute an inquiry into Glencoe. Annandale took the leading part in calling witnesses and conducting the business of the inquiry. He called as many witnesses as he could find. Hill was summoned to come himself and bring seven or eight of the officers or men who were present at the Massacre. The witnesses mentioned in the report include the two sons of MacIain; two Macdonalds (Archibald and Ranald); Ardkinglas, Sheriff of Argyll; Colin Campbell, Sheriff Clerk of Argyll; Lord Aberuchil; John Campbell, w.s.; Sir Gilbert Elliot; David Moncreiff, Clerk of the Council; James Campbell, a private soldier of Argyll's Regiment who had been in the

Glencoe detachment at the Massacre; Major John Forbes; Sir Thomas Livingstone; and Lt.-Colonel James Hamilton. All these attended except the last who thought it safer to absent himself, and sent a letter of apology to Annandale.

The Commission started work at once and carried out their duties well and expeditiously. Their appointment was dated the 20th May and they produced their findings on the 20th June. The Report is very full and covers much of the matter already narrated in this chapter, so it is only necessary here to extract the important parts, leaving the reader to consult for himself the full draft.

The headings under which they conducted their business were four: (1) the matters which preceded the Massacre; (2) the matter of fact with proofs and evidence taken, when and in what manner the slaughter was committed; (3) the warrants and directions that either really were, or were claimed to be, issued for the committing of it; (4) the Commissioners' opinion of the truth of the matter. They went carefully through all the evidence and found (1) that the obliteration of the oath taken by MacIain was wrong, as it was done without the warrant of the Council in full session; (2) that the Master of Stair did know that MacIain had taken the oath, even though it was taken after due date; (3) that nothing in King William's instructions warranted the slaughter, even the thing itself, far less the manner in which it was carried out; (4) that Stair's letters were the only warrant for the crime of "slaughter under trust." In support of the last finding, Stair's letters written afterwards were quoted. On the 5th March he wrote to Hill that he regretted that any of the Macdonalds had escaped. In April he told Hill not to worry, "when you are right, fear no one . . . but in the execution it was neither so full nor so fair as might have been." The general verdict was that it was a barbarous murder perpetrated by the "persons deponed against."

Parliament received the report on the 24th June, and voted *nem. con.* that His Majesty's instructions of the 11th and 16th January 1692 did ". . . contain a warrant for mercy to all, without exception, who should take the oath of allegiance, and come in upon mercy, though the first day of January 1692, prefixed by the proclamation of indemnity, was passed: and that therefore these instructions contained no warrant for the execution of the Glenco-men in February thereafter." It was then voted that the execution of the Glencoe-men, as represented to Parliament, was a murder. The method of prosecution of the guilty was delayed for decision till the following Monday. Stair's letters were considered and it was decided that they exceeded the King's Commission in their reference to the killing and destroying of the Glencoe-men. On the 28th, notice was taken of a pamphlet which had been circulated to all Members of Parliament entitled "Information for the Master of Stair." This paper stated that Stair had "been mightily prejudged by the Report of the Commission, which notices particular sentences or periods of certain letters, and from whence consequences were drawn which cannot follow upon a due consideration of the whole." The author was found to be Hew Dalrymple, younger brother of the Master of Stair. The paper was declared to be false and calumnious, an apology demanded, and the paper condemned to be burned.

Then they decided that Sir Thomas Livingstone had every reason to pass on the orders he had received from the King. On 8th July, Parliament resumed sitting and considered the case of Lt.-Colonel Hamilton and decided there was ground for prosecuting him. Duncanson came under the same condemnation and it was recommended that he should be called home from Flanders to be prosecuted, "as His Majesty shall think fit." They went on with the other cases and decided that Glenlyon, Drummond, Lt. Lindsay, Ensign Lundie and Sergeant Barbour should be brought home and tried for the "murder of the Glenco-men under trust." On 10th July Parliament sent their findings in the form of an Address to the King, with several of Stair's letters to Livingstone and Hill. There was some debate as to whether they should include the paragraph about Stair or not, but it was voted to include it.

It is patent, reading these two documents, the Report and the Address, that the efforts of the Scots lords and lawyers were bent on exonerating the King and casting the whole blame on Stair.

In the midst of all these reports and letters, so detailed and so full, where is one to find the truly guilty man, or men? The long list of accused persons falls into two main categories. The Government, which includes the King, his Secretary Stair, the Privy Council in Edinburgh, the Sheriff of Argyll and his Clerk; secondly, the Army, which includes all from the Commander-in-Chief, Livingstone, down to the last private soldier in Glenlyon's and Hamilton's companies. The fact is that all of these, in both categories, except for the Sheriff of Argyll and his Clerk, are guilty in varying degrees.

King William was guilty because he signed the order which led to the Massacre. It is little use saying that he did not know what he was signing, that he signed it among many other state papers and so escaped his eye, or that he trusted his Secretary to put the right kind of order in front of him. He ought to have read a document affecting the lives and fortunes of so many of his subjects, even if they were a remote tribe on the outskirts of his dominions. The double signature, above and below, has nothing to do with it, except that it prevented Stair's signature appearing on the paper, as it might have done had the King superscribed only. It has been said that this was an evil design of Stair's to avert blame from himself and throw it all on the King. Whether this is true or not matters little, as there are other documents and letters signed by Stair sufficient to condemn him. He is the one man of all the Government employees who must carry the blame for the Massacre. It was his rancour and hatred which urged on the others to carry out their treacherous work. He murdered the victims of the Massacre as surely as if he had done it with his own hands.

The Privy Council, or at least those members who received the letters and certified oath from Ardkinglas, are guilty for not deferring the execution until the King's mind was sought on the matter and he was given a chance to show mercy, even although his orders expressly excluded Glencoe. They had the original order to consult in which it was plain that William was willing to extend the date in certain cases, notably that of Glengarry. The Council in full session might well have given a very different opinion from that pronounced by the few members who dealt with the Sheriff's urgent appeal for consideration. In spite of his request to be informed of the action taken, it seems that he did not hear of the obliteration of MacIain's oath until too late to do anything. His powers were not great as Sheriff of Argyll, but judging by his behaviour towards MacIain, it is very unlikely that he would have been party to the cancellation. Ardkinglas and his Clerk must be judged clear of blame. They both did their best to help MacIain and avert the misfortunes that followed.

So much for the Government: the blame lies equally on the King and Stair, but on the members of the Privy Council, who dealt with the matter, to a much lesser degree. Although the Report throws much blame on them, in fairness one has to give them the benefit of some doubt. After all they acted strictly according to law and directions from above.

As for the Army commanders and soldiers, they were, of course, soldiers under orders from the political power, and might claim it was their duty to carry out orders given them by the Government, no matter what those orders were. Livingstone received and transmitted his orders without embellishing them. As far as he was concerned it was just another raid on hostile tribes and he left the details of its execution to his subordinates. Hill is a special case. His blame is much the same as Livingstone's—in being a link in the chain of orders which led inevitably to the Massacre.

Duncanson, Drummond and Hamilton can be taken together, as they, of all the soldiers concerned, showed extreme brutality, not minding how the killing was carried out so long as the tally of corpses was satisfactorily lengthy. They too planned in detail the "netting" of the Glen, and it was not their fault that any escaped. To the bitter end, they tried their hardest to add to the list, not sparing even little boys and very old men.

Glenlyon, Lindsay, Lundie and Barbour are the worst of all that grisly band. They were the ones who lived in the Glen for a fortnight before the attack, and so basely betrayed the trust put in them by their hosts.

Glenlyon is the name irrevocably linked with the Massacre. There are some extenuating circumstances in his case, and we must in fairness examine all these before condemning him out of hand. He was a Campbell and therefore disliked, to say the least, all Macdonalds. He had suffered from the predatory instincts of the MacIains in the raid of 1689 to such an extent that he had been obliged to take up employment in the Army, a thing he was not too keen on doing, but was forced to do in order to keep himself and his family alive. His character was complex. Even his kinsman, Breadalbane, had doubts as to his mental stability, as the letter of that gentleman to his agent, Campbell of Carwhin, shows. In January 1690 Breadalbane wrote: "Glenlyon ought to be sent to Bedlam as he, Duncan, used his great-grandfather. I wish I had chambered him some years ago." There follows an account of Glenlyon having raised a number of men in Argyll and led them plundering in Glenorchy and Strathfillan until challenged by the local lairds. Breadalbane goes on: "He is an object of compassion when I see him, but when he is out of my sight I could wish he had never been born!"

Perhaps there is ground for suspecting Glenlyon of some mental instability if Breadalbane is to be believed; and one might put in a plea of "diminished responsibility" in accordance with modern usage. But when all has been said in his defence, his guilt remains as black as ever. On this side of the balance we have the flagrant abuse of the sacred laws of hospitality as understood by the Gael; and he was a Gael and should have known better. That is the ingredient that sours the whole dismal business. "Slaughter under trust" are the words used by the Commission to describe the crime which has made the name of Glenlyon notorious ever since. To live with a family for a fortnight under the most friendly circumstances, to accept an invitation to dinner with that family, and then on the same day to order the murder of the head of that family, is surely the basest form of crime that could ever be imagined. That was bad enough; but although Glenlyon was not himself present at the murder of the old Chief and his Lady, he was as surely responsible as if his hand had held the pistol and fired it into MacIain's head—from the back. Much worse was the tying up of nine helpless prisoners and then having them shot one by one in front of his eyes, one of them being his own host of the past two weeks. This last atrocity seems to have sickened him, and he took no further active part in the killing, but that was just a little too late to avoid the stigma of slaughter under trust. His boasts in the Edinburgh taverns afterwards, *in vino,* do not seem to indicate any remorse or change of heart, whatever he may have suffered later.

Lindsay and Lundie were worse than their Captain. Their orders were to deal with MacIain—orders which they carried out in the most brutal manner; and then they seem to have gone mad, for to strip an elderly lady of all her clothes and tear off her rings, driving her out into the night, was beyond the command to kill only males between seven and seventy.

The military orders founded on the King's own commands changed as they were transmitted down the line. They became progressively more virulent: the element of treachery creeps in, and we have to lay the blame for that on Hamilton and Duncanson. They devised the surrounding of the folk of the Glen by a pincer movement—their two companies being the jaws of the pincer. It is not quite clear whose bright idea it was to have Glenlyon's company in the heart of the Glen for so long before the event to lull the Macdonalds into a sense of security. It may well have been the child of Breadalbane's fertile brain, but, if it was, he made sure that it did not come out at the inquiry.

We come now to that noble earl and his part in all this. He was in a way between the Government and the Army, belonging officially to neither, advising both with his special knowledge, and unobtrusively encouraging them in their designs. His character was so tortuous that it is impossible to prove his part in it. We do know he was in London and in close touch with Argyll and Stair during those vital days before the Massacre. The three dined together at times, and must have discussed the whole plot over and over again. The two Campbells in that party kept their names clear of official accusation, while Dalrymple did the writing, unfortunately for him. Breadalbane's character is succinctly summed up by Macaulay in his *History of England* thus: "He seems to have united two different sets of vices, the growth of two different regions and of two different stages in the progress of society. In his castle away in the hills he had learned the barbarous pride and ferocity of a Highland chief. In the Council chamber of Edinburgh he had contracted the deep taint of treachery and corruption. After the Revolution he had, like many of his fellow nobles, betrayed every part in turn, had sworn fealty to William and Mary, and had plotted against them. To trace all the turns and doublings of his course would be wearisome." As we have seen he managed to avoid any trouble for the private articles of the Achallader meeting by telling the Government he had undertaken to raise 1000 men of his clan for any future rising in favour of King James so that he might be in the chiefs' confidence and be able to betray their councils. Stair believed him, and he escaped. One who could evade that danger was well able to keep his designs and actions secret, so no one managed to bring him to book for any part in the Massacre. He is mentioned twice only in the Report—once in connection with the meeting at Achallader when the Glencoe-men witnessed that he had threatened to do MacIain injury for his attitude at that meeting, by which the whole business was wrecked. The second mention is when he approached, through the mediation of his agent Barcaldine, the two sons of MacIain, promising them restitution if they denied that he had any part in the plans for the Massacre. It is not apparent how he had the power to promise such restitution. Perhaps it was only an undertaking to use his good offices in trying to get their application considered. It did show, however, that he had something on his mind, if not on his conscience.

The name of Argyll does not appear in either the Report of the Royal Commission or in the Address to the King. His report to Stair that Glencoe had not come in to take the oath in time, and the fact that it was his regiment which took part in the Massacre are not sufficient to incriminate him. The other records mention him only in Stair's report that he and Breadalbane would secure the southern passes so that none should escape by those routes. In fact Argyll did not do his part in that manoeuvre, for some reason which it would be hard to prove now, and yet it was precisely through those passes that the majority of the fugitives did escape. On the evidence an impartial judge would have to acquit him, or at least pass a verdict of "Not proven."

The verdicts passed by the Commission are easily dealt with. The King was completely exonerated, and left to his own conscience. The Address from the Scots Parliament gave him a discharge in the most fulsome terms.

Stair was declared the author of the whole affair, and his fate was left to the King's mercy. William could scarcely deal harshly with his Secretary while at the same time going free from blame himself. So Stair resigned, or was retired, and given a Scroll of Discharge. The gift of certain rents and feus in Glenluce from the King followed his retiral in an almost indecently short time. In November 1695 he became 2nd Viscount Stair on the death of his father, and received an earldom in 1703. So he did not suffer much. The best one can say for him is that from the start he envisaged only a punitive expedition of a military nature against the offending clans, but as plans matured some others introduced the element of treachery which made it so reprehensible. Who those others were it is impossible to prove, but they must have had the necessary local knowledge to formulate a plan of encirclement whereby the MacIains could be trapped, and an intimate knowledge of the customs of the Gael which enabled troops to be sent into the glen and be hospitably received until the time came to strike. Argyll, Breadalbane and Hill all had that knowledge, but which of them used it is a matter for conjecture. It must have been one or all of them. Glenlyon was only their tool.

Livingstone was acquitted, and raised to the peerage as Viscount Teviot in 1696. In the New Year list of 1704 he was made Lieutenant-General and, when he died in 1711, was accorded a fine funeral and buried in Westminster Abbey.

Colonel Sir John Hill was acquitted unreservedly.

Hamilton was judged guilty of murder, and the King asked to prosecute. As we have seen he did not attend the inquiry, but left for Ireland whence he went to the Army in Flanders. All the others were judged guilty of "slaughter under trust," the most serious indictment of all, and it was asked that they be brought home from Flanders to stand trial. Nothing was done and they never appeared. Duncanson, who was certainly a good soldier, became a Lieutenant-Colonel and fell honourably in action, but was never brought to trial. Drummond, too, Glenlyon, Lindsay, Lundie, Barbour and the rest of the soldiers continued to serve in Flanders and were never tried. They just pursued the normal life of the soldier, gaining promotion as it came along, and no more said.

All these recommendations of the Commission and the Address to the King were made subject to the clause "as Your Majesty shall think fit." His Majesty did not think fit; and that was all about it. He could scarcely agree to act when he knew he was the fountain and origin of the whole dismal business, and yet had been acquitted with honour.

Some seem to have been granted "remission" for their deeds—Stair for one, and this came direct from the King. A remission was actually a somewhat doubtful benefit, if a writer who seems to have had legal knowledge is to be believed. In 1703 there appeared in Edinburgh a pamphlet or circular in the form of notes added to an account of how the Report of the Duke of Hamilton's Commission had been suppressed in 1693. It is stated therein:

> Some of the persons did get remission from K.W. concerning whom it is to be observed, first, that the taking of a remission is a tacit acknowledgment of the Crime, and taking upon them the guilt: Next, that any such remission is null and void, and will not defend them because it did not proceed upon letters of Slains [*i.e.* witnessing that the party wronged has received satisfaction] nor is there any Assithment [*i.e.* satisfaction] made to the nearest of

THE MEMORIAL CAIRN

kin; it being expressly by the Act 136, Par 8 Jac. the 6th, that remissions are null unless the Party be assithed. . . . It is to be observed that the Parliament having declared that the killing of the Glenco-men was a Murder under Trust, Credit, Assurance and Power of the Slayer, is Treason: so by the said act, these that had accession to, or were anyways airt and part of the Slaying of the Glenco-men are guilty of Treason.

P.S. You know that there never was any prosecution against any of those persons charged with this barbarous murder, but that on the contrary, by the advice of some who were about H.M., several of the Officers were preferr'd, and the whole matter slurr'd over: so that the crying guilt of this blood must lie upon them and not upon the Nation, since Parliament could do no more in it without occasioning greater bloodshed than they complain of. You know likewise that by the influence of the same persons this Report was suppressed in K.W.'s time, though H.M.'s honour required that it should have been published. (Scots Broadsides & Acts of Parliament. 1689-1707).

There it ends except that in certain quarters there was an outcry, especially from the Jacobites who demanded the blood of the criminals. Some very harsh things were said, and some very wild theories put forward. One pamphlet entitled *Gallienus Redivivus* sought to lay the blame on James Johnstone, joint Secretary with Stair. Johnstone was a staunch Protestant and Presbyterian, and the author of *Gallienus* did not like Presbyterians, so, as Stair was quite impartial in matters of religion, Johnstone had to be blamed without a shred of evidence. Letters of Johnstone show that he agreed with the King that action had to be taken, but was all against the manner in which it had been carried out. His letters make it clear that his chief concern was to exculpate the Government, lay the blame on the Army, and use it as a weapon to attack the Stair family. He wrote to Carstairs: "I have the Glencoe affairs in my hands with which I'll lash them into good behaviour cost what it will!" The other enemies of the Master and his father took advantage of the situation and Stair had to retire into the wilderness for a time, under advice from the King.

The verdict was brought in; but no sentences were ever passed. The Judge had other things on his mind and, with that callousness of which he was capable, William occupied himself with matters which were, to him, far more important. As a counter-irritant he backed the Darien scheme, which followed hard on the heels of the Glencoe inquiry, but later he let the whole project fall into ruins through fears of the vested interests of the English and Dutch companies. And very soon after that the Union of Parliaments became the engrossing topic in Edinburgh and London. Glencoe was forgotten by all but those immediately concerned—the Jacobites and the Highlanders. Stair died amid the negotiations of the Union in 1707, but was not forgotten. Underneath all the activity of the period—the death of William, the accession of Anne, the Union of 1707, and all the political manoeuvres connected with it—Glencoe still rankled, and the Rising of 1715 followed soon after the arrival of the "German lairdie," for whom the clans had less complimentary names. With the Massacre still fresh in their minds, and their memories of the last foreign king still green, they did not hesitate to take up arms again, in 1715 and later in 1745, the last desperate throw. The tragedy of Glencoe played no mean part in the events leading up to both Risings.

By 1715 the Clann Iain had recovered in a wonderful way, and Alasdair, grandson of the murdered Chief, the babe who had been carried to safety in his nurse's arms, was able to raise nearly 100 fighting men, and a similar number in 1745, which shows how miserably the Massacre failed of its object.

In 1745 the MacIains were able to show true greatness of spirit when the Prince's Army lay at Kirkliston prior to their occupation of Edinburgh. "The Prince, in his anxiety to save Lord Stair from molestation, proposed that the Glencoe men should be marched to a distance from his residence, lest memories of ancient wrongs might move them to deeds of vengeance. When the proposal was made to the Glencoe men, their reply was that, if they were considered so dis-honourable as to take revenge upon an innocent man, they were not fit to remain with honourable men, nor to support an honourable cause. It was only by much persuasion that they were induced to overlook what they regarded as an insult, and prevented from taking their departure" (*Clan Donald,* Vol. 2). They stayed, but demanded that they should provide a guard to see that no harm came to the Dalrymple estate, lest they be blamed for it.

The Rising of 1745 put an end to the Clan system, the people were scattered, the lands were bought by strangers, and only the memory of the brave men who inhabited the Glen long ago lingers in the hearts of many families of emigrants in all parts of the world. The traditions of the families who lived and died in the Glen are cherished by many notable men and women overseas, who return to seek their roots and to see the Glen of their origin.

Of all the many glens in Scotland, Glencoe is the best known not only because of the massacre, but for its wild and unparalleled scenic beauty. The Memorial Cairn at the mouth of the Glen commemorates the men and women who fell on that fateful night, and it is visited each year by clansmen who lay a wreath of remembrance there on the 13th of February. Nine trees have been planted at Inverigan where the nine unfortunate victims were bound and shot in the presence of Glenlyon and Duncanson.

The "Glen of Weeping" has now become a resort under the care of the National Trust, and visitors are drawn to see the grandeur of its hills and to hear the story of the tragedy of that stormy morning of 13th February 1692, remembered by Highlanders for its callous violation of the ancient laws of hospitality—"Slaughter under Trust."

17

The Macdonalds of Dunnyveg and the Glens
Clann Iain Mhoir

THIS IMPORTANT BRANCH of the Clan Donald was territorially the richest in the bounds of the Lordship, possessing lands in both Islay and Kintyre, and acquiring by inheritance extensive estates in the Glens of Antrim. The protection of such substantial possessions demanded constant care and jealous guardianship, and the history of the family is marked by struggles against a sensitive and acquisitive central government, and the envy and greed of aggressive neighbours bent on its dismemberment and eventual destruction.

The founder of the family was John Mor, second son of John, Lord of the Isles, by his marriage with the Princess Margaret of Scotland. John became tanister to his brother Donald who was installed as Lord of the Isles at Eigg in 1386. Thereafter he was known as John Mor Tanister and continued to exercise the functions of that office even after Donald had a son to succeed him in the Lordship. From his father John Mor received a grant of 120 merklands in Kintyre and 60 merklands in Islay, with the castles of Saddell, Dunaverty and Dunnyveg, the latter being the chiefly seat of the family throughout their reign. His marriage in 1399 with Margery Bisset, heiress of the Antrim Glens, brought the family a further accession of territory which greatly increased their power and prestige both within and beyond the Clan.

The Bissets were a Norman family who came over with the Conqueror in 1066 and later received lands in the north and south of Scotland. Those in the north died out. The southern branch flourished until 1242 when John and Walter Bisset were suspected of the murder of Patrick, Earl of Atholl. They were sentenced to exile and allowed to realise their assets and depart, ostensibly on Crusade. They chose, however, to emigrate to Ireland where they purchased extensive lands from Richard de Burgh, Earl of Ulster, and by 1300 they had the "seven lordships of the Glens." Margery, daughter of Sir Hugh Bisset of the Glens, was fifth in descent from John Bisset, and eventual heiress to the Bisset inheritance, with the acquisition of which John Mor and his successors were henceforth styled Lords of Dunnyveg and the Glens.

During the early years of the brothers Donald and John Mor, the relations of their family with England were most cordial. The one aim of the Island Lordship was to preserve its traditions and independence from the constant threat posed by the Scottish State, and it was clear that the best means of accomplishing this lay in aligning itself with England in the quarrels that continued to disturb the peace of the two countries. Thus in 1388 we find Donald, John and

THE ARMS OF CLANN IAIN MHOIR
(mid-16th century)

Godfrey visiting the Court of Richard II of England, and on the 14th July entering into a friendly alliance with that monarch. From time to time thereafter John Mor renewed the alliance and cultivated such a close relationship with the English monarch that on his deposition Richard is reported by tradition to have escaped from Pontefract and found asylum with Donald and John Mor in Islay.

The connection with Antrim had been important ever since Angus Og's bride, Agnes O'Cahan, brought over with her many gentlemen of that country. Not long afterwards, when Alexander, brother of Angus Og, was deposed, his family went to Antrim as galloglasses to O'Neill and founded families over there. Henceforth the communications between the Isles and Antrim were continuous and very valuable to any of the Clan Donald who got into trouble with the Kings of Scots. Time and again, the chiefs and warriors of Clan Donald, having raised the standard of rebellion, were able in defeat to find refuge in the Glens of Antrim; and there, too, they often found the recruits necessary to aid their return.

This traffic was not, however, always to the advantage of the Islesmen. In 1405, by which time Henry IV was on the throne of England and friendly towards Donald and John Mor, the Isles were troubled by the inroads of merchants from Dublin and Drogheda. An appeal to Henry to restrain his subjects was sympathetically received, and on the 16th September of that year John, Bishop of County Down, was able to negotiate a lasting peace between the merchants and the Isles.

In 1408 John Mor was again at the English Court. This was the year of the famous Gaelic charter granted by Donald, Lord of the Isles. This interesting document is witnessed by one "John Macdonald" who signs "with his hand at the pen," and has often been quoted as proving that John Mor was unlettered and uneducated. It is quite unlikely that one so widely travelled and so well able to undertake important diplomatic duties could not even sign his name. His brother Donald went to Oxford University, and it is reasonable to suppose that John also received an education that fitted him for the onerous tasks frequently assigned to him and accomplished with success.

At the battle of Harlaw John Mor ably assisted his brother who, we are told by the Sleat historian, placed him in command of "the lightest and nimblest men as reserve, either to assist the wings or main battle, as the occasion required." The result of that battle has been much argued, and has been discussed at length in an earlier part of this work. But however inconclusive the outcome, the battle wrought havoc amongst the Regent's forces, and John Mor contributed largely to the victory the Islesmen always claimed it to be. He also gave valiant support to his brother against the Regent's subsequent attempts to reduce Donald to submission. John Mor's conduct throughout would seem to discredit the story of a later quarrel between the two brothers over some lands in Argyll, as a result of which John had to flee for refuge in the Glens of Antrim. The sole authority for the story is Hugh Macdonald, the Sleat historian, whose version of the events contains such inaccuracies as to make the whole narration suspect and tends to be more confounded by the friendly relations which continued between the brothers till the end of Donald's life.

On his return from exile in 1424, James I set out at once to restore order and good government throughout the kingdom. After firmly dealing with the recalcitrant Lowland barons, he began to concert measures for curbing the power of the Lordship of the Isles, whose position of virtual independence he regarded as an affront to the royal authority. Casting about for means to accomplish his objective, he seized upon the expedient of trying to provoke a division amongst the Island vassals. Of these, John Mor was the most powerful, and to him the King sent an emissary named James Campbell with the suggestion, which he was careful not to put in writing, that John Mor should seize the possessions of his young nephew Alexander, Lord of the Isles. John refused to entertain such a proposal, whereupon the King resolved that he should pay the penalty. Campbell was instructed to arrange another meeting at Ard Dubh in Islay where, according to the Sleat historian:

> John came to the place appointed with a small retinue, but Campbell with a great train, and told of the King's intention of granting him all the lands possessed by Macdonald, conditionally he would, if he held of him (*i.e.* the King) and served him. John said he did not know wherein his nephew had wronged the King, and that his nephew was as deserving of his rights as he could be, and that he would not accept of these lands, nor serve for them, till his nephew would be set at liberty: and that his nephew himself was as nearly related to the King as he could be. Campbell, hearing the answer, said he was the King's prisoner. John made all the resistance he could, till, overpowered by numbers, he was killed. His death made a great noise through the kingdom, particularly among the faction in opposition to the King, *viz.* the Hamiltons, Douglasses, and Lindsays.

The "noise" referred to was serious, and the King was blamed for what amounted to a murder under trust. Campbell was arraigned in the Royal presence and accused of the murder of John Mor. Campbell strongly denied his guilt, asserting that he had only carried out the King's commands. The King denied this, and as Campbell could produce no written authority for his action, the unfortunate minion of the Crown had to pay with his life. In this way James hoped to excuse himself and vindicate the Royal honour.

The turmoil in the land caused by this act of bad faith on the King's part forced him to take drastic steps. In the same year (1427) he went with a large force to Inverness, determined to overawe the Highland chiefs. The royal invitation to attend his presence there was followed by the treacherous seizure of the principal chiefs. Some were executed at once. Others, including Alexander Lord of the Isles, and his mother, the rightful Countess of Ross, were confined to prison. Many of those detained in prison were released after a short period, amongst them the Lord of the Isles who was determined to avenge the indignity he had suffered. How he set about this has been told in an earlier chapter—his invasion of the Crown lands around Inverness and the burning of that town, his defeat as a result of the defection of the Camerons and Mackintoshes, and his submission and subsequent imprisonment in Tantallon Castle. Fortunately for the Clan, however, a bold and resolute warrior was now ready to step into the vacant leadership and strike a blow on behalf of his imprisoned Chief.

Donald Balloch was the elder of John Mor's two sons by Margery Bisset, the other being Ranald Ban, the founder of the cadet family of Largie. Donald was still quite young when his father's death elevated him to the Chiefship, and he impatiently awaited the opportunity to avenge that treacherous murder and restore the honour of the Clan by dealing a decisive stroke against the royal authority. In 1431 he was ready, and embarked on the victorious campaign which culminated in his resounding defeat of the royal army under Mar and Caithness at Inverlochy. Here he won his first of many laurels on the field of battle and added lustre to a name which was to command the respect of friend and foe alike for a generation to come.

As the course of the Inverlochy campaign has been dealt with in some detail in Chapter 10, it is only necessary here to be reminded that Donald escaped the

King's vengeance by retiring to his Glens of Antrim. There he was left in peace because of the ready resource of his neighbour Hugh O'Neill who, in response to a royal demand, sent to James a human head which he accepted as that of his formidable rebel subject. It is unlikely that Donald ventured across to Scotland thereafter during James's lifetime. The Lord of the Isles himself had remained a peaceful subject after his release and consequently provided no opportunities for a man of Donald's warlike qualities; and it was not till after Alexander's death in 1449 that he re-appeared on the scene to assume a prominent rôle in the military and political activities that for many years were to disturb relations between the Lord of the Isles and the Scottish State.

John, Lord of the Isles and Earl of Ross, was still a minor on his accession, and the veteran Donald naturally assumed the rôle of Tutor and guardian of his young cousin. We have seen in Chapter 11 how the young Lord, Earl of Ross, fell under the influence of the Earls of Douglas and Crawford, and joined their league against the Scottish Government. The rebellion which followed was led by Donald Balloch who seized and garrisoned the royal strongholds of Urquhart and Inverness, and then proceeded through Moray to Badenoch where the castle of Ruthven was demolished. The King was too occupied with the machinations of the Douglas party in the South to take any decisive action, and the Islesmen remained masters of the situation.

After his defeat at Arkinholme, the Earl of Douglas made his escape to Argyllshire and there met the Earl of Ross and Donald Balloch, with whom he concerted fresh measures to further his designs. The result was that Donald soon found himself at the head of a fleet of 100 galleys and a force of 5000 men for the purpose of harassing the West. Donald began his invasion at Inverkip, and from there proceeded to attack Arran, Bute and the Cumbraes, from which he carried away a large spoil. He then made for the island of Lismore whose bishop, Lauder, had been a party to the instrument of forfeiture against the Earl of Douglas. The attack on the island was accompanied by widespread depredations and slaughter, the bishop himself escaping with his life by taking refuge in the sanctuary of the church. The violence of these proceedings did nothing to advance the purpose of the expedition, however, and the rebellion crumbled when the expected support from the Douglas party failed to materialise.

No immediate action seems to have been taken by the King against either Donald Balloch or the Lord of the Isles for their rebellious conduct. The latter was soon received back into royal favour and in 1460 we find him at the siege of Roxburgh in the unaccustomed rôle of a loyal vassal fighting for his king. There are no records to indicate if Donald Balloch accompanied his Chief on this campaign, but the death of the King and the unsettled circumstances following that tragic event were sufficient to sever the tenuous ties of loyalty that bound them to the Government, and in 1461 we find the Lord of Dunnyveg playing a leading part in negotiations aimed at nothing less than the dismemberment of the Scottish State. The English Commissioners who met the Island Council at Ardtornish were empowered to treat with the King's "dearest cousin John, Earl of Ross, and his dear and faithful Donald Balloch or their ambassadors." In terms of the treaty, signed at Westminster in February 1462, the Lord of Dunnyveg was to share the northern part of the kingdom with John of the Isles, Earl of Ross, and the Earl of Douglas. The details of this daring scheme have already been fully dealt with in Chapter 11 of this book. The immediate result was an attempt to implement the treaty in the following year when the Island forces, under the nominal command of Angus Og, son of the Lord of the Isles, but actually led by the veteran Donald Balloch, seized Inverness Castle, expelled the garrison and proclaimed the Earl of Ross sovereign ruler of the

North and the Isles. The rebellion was premature, however, and it gradually fizzled out when hopes had faded of English help promised under the provisions of the Treaty of Ardtornish.

There is no record of any measures taken by the Government against Donald Balloch for his part in the rebellion. More decisive action might have followed had the more serious aspects of the Treaty come to the knowledge of the Government, but apart from futile attempts to bring the Earl of Ross before Parliament to answer for the conduct of his lieutenants, the history of the next twelve years is marked by an unwonted calm. Donald prudently retired to his Antrim estates, and soon after his arrival there he and his son John took the oath of allegiance to Edward of England in terms of the Ardtornish agreement. Most of the succeeding years were spent in the security of the Glens of Antrim, from which he made occasional visits to Scotland in his rôle as principal councillor of the Lord of the Isles and Earl of Ross. The first recorded visit was in 1467 when at Aviemore on 25th April he witnessed a charter granted by the Earl of Ross to his brother Celestine of Lochalsh. The second was in 1469 when he witnessed another charter at Aros granting lands to Hugh of Sleat. The third occasion is of particular interest because in a deed dated at Irvine on 8th October 1475 he is styled *Donaldus de Insulis de Glenys et de Dunnawak, miles.* The designation *miles* in this document has led some authorities to assume that the honour of knighthood had been conferred on Donald Balloch. This, however, is most unlikely. It was not unusual for such a designation to be added to the names of men of distinction who had never been so honoured, and it is extremely improbable that a man whose whole life had been spent in rebellious action against the government would receive such a mark of royal favour.

The indictment brought against the Earl of Ross as a result of the disclosure of the treasonable terms of the Treaty of Ardtornish also listed the offences of Donald Balloch, but he appears to have shared in the remarkable act of leniency which left the Lord of the Isles in possession of virtually all his possessions except the forfeited earldom. Shortly after that act of grace we find Donald living peacefully on his estates in Islay where he witnessed a charter by the Lord of the Isles on 20th August 1476. With his death later that year disappeared from the scene a formidable antagonist whose prowess in many a field throughout a long and active life had earned for him an honoured and lasting place in the annals of Clan Donald.

Donald Balloch was married twice. By his marriage with Joanna, daughter of Conn O'Neill, he had John, his successor. By his second marriage with Joan, daughter of O'Donnell of Tyrconnel, he had a daughter who married Thomas Bannatyne of Kames. John was of mature age at the time of his accession to the chiefship of his clan. He had been with his father at the signing of the Treaty of Ardtornish, but we hear nothing of him for some years thereafter, although he is likely to have been associated with his father in some of his activities. In 1481 he was living in Antrim and ruling his estates with the aid of a Council constituted after the pattern of the ancient Island Council. In June of that year we find Edward IV of England sending a commission of sundry prominent men to "the King's cousin, John of the Isles, Lord of the Glens, and his Council." Their deliberations led to the conclusion of an alliance which was confirmed later at Westminster.

John spent most of his time in Antrim and did not join in the rebellions of Angus Og and Alexander of Lochalsh. In 1493, however, after the fall of the Lordship, the Islay Chief had to appear before the King and make his peace. The monarch recognised this act of homage by making him a knight. That the son of Donald Balloch should be thus honoured is surprising unless it is viewed as part of the new royal policy to conciliate the island chiefs and attach them firmly to the royal person. In the following year, however, James tried to consolidate his hold on their lands by placing garrisons in the castles of Tarbert, Dunaverty and other strong points. The seizure of Dunaverty was resented most strongly by the newly made knight, Sir John of Islay. The King's visit ended at Dunaverty, and he had hardly embarked before Sir John and his son, John Cathanach, stormed the Castle, put the garrison to the sword, and hanged the Governor from the castle wall in full view of the King's ship. Such a flagrant act of defiance could not be ignored, and it was not long before father and son paid the penalty for their violent affront to the royal authority.

The King, on his return home, immediately declared Sir John traitor and summoned him for treason. John thought it best to ignore the summons, and returned to Islay. It might have been safer to have repaired to his lands in Antrim, the customary retreat for members of Clan Donald in trouble with the Government, but he chose to continue living in his manor house at Finlaggan in Islay. The extraordinary events which followed have been told in Chapter 15, but we relate them here to avoid interrupting the narrative.

Immediately after the fall of the Lordship, MacIain of Ardnamurchan had made almost servile submission to the King, in recognition of which he had already received some favours from the grateful monarch. Now he was used as a tool by the King to compass the destruction of Sir John and his associates in the storming of Dunaverty and its murderous result. By some means which have never been satisfactorily explained, MacIain was able to seize Sir John in Finlaggan and convey him with his son, John Cathanach, and at least two of their associates, to the presence of the King. Insidious and treacherous as it must have been, the stratagem employed by MacIain was successful in achieving its purpose, and the unfortunate prisoners were in due course summarily tried and executed on the Boroughmuir at Edinburgh. Although the capture of Sir John and his son took place in 1494, the date of their execution has not been authoritatively established; but most historians agree that it must have taken place soon after their apprehension, and not later than the beginning of the year 1495.

Although John Cathanach died on the same day as his father he had already taken the lead in his clan and we rate him fourth in line from John Mor, the founder of the House of Dunnyveg. He had married Cecilia Savage, whose family were prominent in the County of Coleraine, and by her he had at least two sons: Alexander, his successor, and Angus "Ileach," both of whom escaped their father's fate because by chance or design they had been absent in Antrim at the time of that tragedy. How long they remained there is not clear, but it is unlikely that they returned to their Islay estates during the lifetime of James iv. MacIain's reward for his part in the events of 1494 had whetted his appetite, and he was determined to extend his power by the utter destruction of the family. With this object he sent two of his sons at the head of a large force into the Glens of Antrim. The story of the expedition, as told by the Sleat historian, is that the invaders were met in Glenseich by a body of 140 men under Alexander and Angus, who decided to attack at once. The smith of Islay, on seeing his rightful master approaching, detached himself and some 50 men from the MacIain party and joined Alexander in the fray. The invaders were routed and MacIain's two sons killed. Alexander thereupon seized the boats and made straight for Islay where they landed and approached the Castle of Dunnyveg. When the Constable of that Castle learned that, contrary to expectation, Alexander was still very much alive, he handed the Castle over and told him that MacIain was hiding in the Island of Lochgorm. MacIain was forced to surrender on the condition that he resigned his claim to lands in Islay, and also

THE MACDONALDS OF DUNNYVEG AND THE GLENS

(Clann Iain Mhòir Ile)

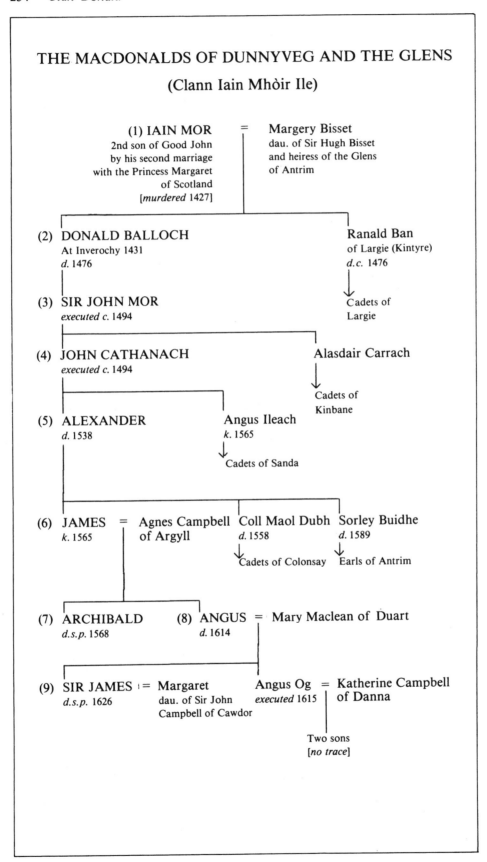

that he gave Alexander his daughter in marriage. How long Alexander remained in Islay after this romantic adventure is not certain, but we know that after the death of James IV at Flodden he was able to return and safely resume possession of his estates.

In the disturbed state of the realm after Flodden Sir Donald of Lochalsh, son of the ill-fated Sir Alexander, saw a favourable opportunity of raising the standard of rebellion in his attempt to restore the Lordship. Alexander of Islay was one of the first to support this venture in which both he and Sir Donald were inspired by the strong additional motive of avenging the deaths of their fathers at the hands of MacIain of Ardnamurchan. The final act in Sir Donald's rebellion was the invasion and laying waste of MacIain's lands, the destruction of his Castle of Mingary, and the pursuit of MacIain and his sons which ended with their deaths on the bloody field of Creag-an-Airgid. This was the only satisfactory event of the rebellion, which collapsed with the sudden death of Sir Donald in the island fort of Cairnburgh in the Treshnish Isles, west of Mull.

In spite of the prominent part he had taken in Sir Donald's rebellion, Alexander of Dunnyveg appears to have been treated with extraordinary leniency. The Islay estates, seized by James IV, were now restored with those of Kintyre, and other lands were added provided Alexander preserved good rule and gave pledges of good faith. Argyll and others of his clan, however, now began to extend their sinister designs by entering into bonds of friendship with several of the neighbouring chiefs. Amongst these was Alexander of Dunnyveg who entered into a bond of manrent with Campbell of Cawdor and for his services was to receive a five-year lease of 45 merklands in Islay, the 15 merklands of Jura and the Island of Colonsay. Although the object of such bonds of service was to provide some measure of order and security amid conditions of unsettlement, they were to be used by the House of Argyll as a means for the ruthless advancement of its own interests and the eventual assumption of the position and functions of the forfeited Lordship. Moreover, as Lieutenant of the Isles, the Earl of Argyll was able to use the influence of his office to further his designs and compel the chiefs to cultivate his favour and goodwill. It was a policy that was to lead to much disorder and bloodshed, and to inspire the eternal enmity of the vassals of the Lordship against his House.

This was the state of feeling in 1528 when the young King took the reins of government from the Regent and instituted the change of policy under which grants of land made during the Regency were all revoked. The result was consternation in the West, and the whole of Clan Donald South, with the Macleans who had also suffered from the machinations of Argyll, rose in rebellion. Roseneath on the Gareloch, the Lennox, and Craignish were laid waste, and Argyll was in such dire straits that he had to appeal for help to the Government. The Lords of Council were slow to respond and sent a very small supply of arms and no men. Apparently suspicious of Argyll's motives, they decided on 3rd August 1529 to send the herald Robert Hart to command Alexander of Dunnyveg to cease his rebellious proceedings and obey the King. This mission failed, and the Lords of Council then decided to send Argyll to force Alexander to submit. Argyll, however, was not sufficiently equipped to take immediate action, and it was not till the Spring of 1530 that a formidable expedition was prepared to reduce Alexander and other recalcitrant Western chiefs to obedience.

While these preparations were going on, the King was still hopeful of finding a peaceful settlement and offered protection to all who should come "to commune with His Majesty upon good rule in the Isles." Nine of the chiefs took advantage of this olive branch, but the Lord of Dunnyveg held aloof, suspicious of the royal policy and of the instruments chosen to enforce it.

The death of Argyll at this juncture delayed the proceedings until early in 1531. Preparations went forward with vigour, but the young Argyll was unable to bring Alexander to battle. The array of strength designed to overawe the Islesmen failed to achieve its purpose, and it was decided once again to have recourse to diplomacy.

Parliament met on the 28th April 1531 and the chiefs of Clan Donald were summoned to meet the King. They did not appear, but the summons was continued to the 26th of May, by which time negotiations between Alexander and the King had been carried on in a more friendly manner. A respite was accorded Alexander and thirty of his men to come to the royal presence. As a result, Alexander repaired to the King's Court at Stirling and received the royal pardon on the 7th June. The Council directed that, because he had obeyed the royal command, the lands he had lost under the revocation of 1528 should now be restored to Alexander on certain conditions. He was to free all prisoners taken by him in the rebellion, churchmen were to be supported in their privileges and the collection of their rents, and he was also to assist the royal chamberlains in the administration of Crown lands in Kintyre and the South Isles. At the same time, Alexander and his followers received a remission for all their crimes. As a guarantee of his future good conduct, he surrendered as hostage his young heir James, whose subsequent sojourn at Court provided him with a liberal education and exposed him to influences which were to be strongly manifested in later years.

The success of this diplomacy underlines the practical value of direct personal intercourse between the Western chiefs and their sovereign, with no self-seeking intermediary to meddle with the course of justice. We have noted this before, and we shall note it again in the course of this history. The personal intervention of the monarch seldom failed to impress the Western chiefs, if only because it represented a diminution of the power and influence of those families whose official positions were often used to advance their own private interests.

Cheated of his power as an intermediary, and resentful of the King's generous treatment of the Gaelic chiefs, Argyll at once tried to stir up trouble for Alexander by charging him with a long list of crimes allegedly committed against Clan Campbell. Although the Islay chief had already received a remission for his crimes, the Earl evidently thought that the disturbance he expected to follow this action would provide sufficient grounds for the King again to make use of his services in quelling it. His complaint being duly laid before the Council, the Islay chief was summoned to appear and answer the charges. Alexander responded at once and went to Edinburgh where he waited thirteen days to confront his accuser. Argyll failed to present himself, and Alexander finally decided to put his case in writing and submit it to the Council. This he did in a very honest statement in which he answered all the charges laid against him, pointing out that whereas he had obeyed the summons to appear, his enemy had not seen fit to confront him, and he therefore desired the Council to put his statement on record and send it to the King for his information.

This direct appeal to the sovereign had an immediate effect. It impressed the King with Alexander's desire to co-operate with the Government, and opened his eyes to the extent of Argyll's responsibility for the turbulence and disaffection amongst the Western clans in recent years. Argyll was summoned before the Council who, after a thorough examination of the facts, convicted the Earl on all counts, stripped him of all his public offices and threw him into prison. Thus was Alexander completely exonerated, Argyll's conduct of his office in the Isles utterly discredited, and the royal policy of direct personal contact with his Island subjects triumphantly vindicated.

Alexander was now in favour at Court and some of the offices taken from Argyll were given to him. For the rest of his life he kept friendly relations with the King and raised his warriors to aid him in his resistance to English aspirations in Ulster. In 1532, with a force of 7000 men of his own and allied clans in Antrim, he drove the English from that province. Letters to King Henry of England from his agent, Northumberland, in that region in 1532 express great alarm at the success of Alexander's campaign, going on to state that "The Kyng of Scottes hath plucked from the Erle of Argyle, and from his heires for ever, the rule of all the out Iles, and given the same to Mackayne [Alexander, son of John Cathanach] and his heires for ever: and also hath in like case taken from the Erle of Crafford suche lands as he had there, and given the same to the said Mackayne, the which hath ingendered a greate hatred in the said Erle's harte against the said Scottes King." Further reports in 1533 to the English King continue the tale of woe: "The Scottes also inhabit busily a great part of Ulster, which is the King's inheritance: and it is greatly to be feared onless in a short time they be driven from the same, that they bring in more numbers daily, will little by little so far encroach in acquiring and winning possessions there, with the aid of the King's disobedient Irish rebels, who do now aid them therein after such manner, that at length they will expel the King from his whole seignory there."

A letter from Archbishop Allen to the English Council shows that Alexander was hospitably received at the Court of Scotland twice within the year 1538. This is the last reference to Alexander in any records, so we must conclude that he died in that year, for in 1539 his son, James, is referred to as head of the family.

Alexander, 5th in line from Iain Mor Tanister, had by Catherine, daughter of John MacIain of Ardnamurchan: (1) Donald Mallaichte (who was physically disabled); (2) James, who succeeded; (3) Angus Uaimhreach (the Haughty); (4) Coll Maol Dubh, from whom cadets of Colonsay, Coll Ciotach and his famous son, Sir Alasdair (*fl.* 1645); (5) Sorley Buy (*Somhairle Buidhe*), founder of the line of the Earls of Antrim; (6) Alasdair Og, killed in battle in Ireland; (7) Donald Gorm, who left a son and grandson of whom little is known; (8) Brian Carrach, killed in battle in Ireland; (9) Ranald Og, of whom nothing known; (10) Meve, married to Maclean of Coll; (11) Mary, married to Hector Mor Maclean of Duart.

James, second son of Alexander, succeeded to the chiefship of a powerful clan, the most powerful of all the branches of Clan Donald, holding lands in Islay, Kintyre, and Antrim. Although he had been in Edinburgh under the King's eye since 1531, his first loyalty was to his Clan. While still in Edinburgh he had been obliged to stand surety for certain of his clansmen who had been in trouble in 1539. These were his cousins of Loup (MacAlisters) and Largie (*Clann Raghnaill Bhàin*) who had killed some MacNeills in Gigha. The MacNeills had reacted and some of James' clansmen had also been killed. This was an internal matter within the bounds of James' jurisdiction, but when the King met him next year in Kintyre, although still on friendly terms, James was obliged to surrender his brother Coll as hostage for the good behaviour of his clansmen. Coll spent three months in ward in the Castle of Edinburgh.

James v had proved himself a wise and generous monarch in his dealings with the western clans, and by his frequent visits and personal contacts had achieved more success than any of his predecessors in attaching them to the Crown. After his death, the Regent Arran tried to continue these good relations and retain the loyalty and support of the clans in the troubles that surrounded his government. The escape of Donald Dubh from Edinburgh Castle in 1543 tested the loyalty of many of the chiefs, James of Islay amongst them. He took up a neutral attitude and betrayed his secret sympathies only so far as to allow his brother Angus (the Haughty) to join Donald Dubh. Angus is in the list of the members of Council of the Isles on record on 23rd July 1545.

In April 1545, even before Donald Dubh had failed and died, Arran rewarded James of Islay generously for his neutrality, and for services rendered to the infant Queen against the old enemy, England. He was given the heritage of the lands previously held by himself and his father on lease from the Crown. Some of these were erected into the Barony of Barr in North Kintyre. Others were granted in Islay (91 merklands), in Jura (184 shilling lands), together with smaller allotments in Arran, Gigha, Colonsay and other isles.

In spite of these favours, when Donald Dubh died and the men of the Isles sought a worthy successor to carry on the campaign, James was chosen, as being the most eligible of the Island chiefs. Donald Dubh himself is said to have nominated James as his successor, as he had no legitimate issue and Donald Gormson, the next presumptive heir to the Island honours, was still a minor and thus effectively disqualified.

The Earl of Lennox was still planning the conquest of Scotland and approved of James' election as Lord of the Isles. Many of the most powerful clans of the Lordship, however, withheld their support, and James had only those of his own blood on his side. In a last desperate effort to restore the situation, James wrote to Henry of England a letter dated 24th January 1546 from Ardnamurchan. This letter, important as a record of the final appeal for aid in the story of attempts to revive the Lordship, names James as "aperand aeyr of ye Yllis," praises King Henry's support of the Earl of Lennox and promises to give him all the aid possible in the projected enterprise. He names all of his own surname, both north and south, and a few others including Clan Cameron and MacNeill of Gigha as ready to help Lennox, or any other leader nominated by Henry. He asks Henry to send an army to the Isle of Sanda to meet him there by "Sanct Patrikis day next to cowme, or yairby." The letter ends with assurances of friendship and hopes of receiving Henry's aid.

There is no record of a reply from Henry to this appeal. He either completely ignored it, or deferred consideration of it until he had dealt with more urgent matters requiring his attention. A promise of English support was vital to the success of any attempt to restore the Lordship, and when his appeal failed to bring the expected assurances James decided to abandon his claim and resume his friendly relations with the Government. This was accomplished without much difficulty as he had not indulged in open rebellion and the Regent and his Council remained unaware of his treasonable correspondence with the English King.

Relations between James and the Earl of Argyll at this time also reached a more friendly footing. Certain disputes about lands were settled by a meeting at Ardrossan with the Regent, and the new accord was cemented by the marriage of James with Lady Agnes Campbell, the Earl's sister. It was still further strengthened by a grant of the 80 merklands of Ardnamurchan, the old patrimony of the MacIains, whose fortunes were on the wane. James was required to pay only a thousand merks for these lands, a valuation scarcely high enough for such a large estate.

The Lord of Dunnyveg and the Glens, satisfied with the measures he had taken to secure his Scottish estates, now turned his attention to his lands in Antrim. With him went his brothers Angus and Coll and, probably the most famous of the family, Sorley Buy. His inheritance in the Glens, acquired through John Mor's marriage with the Bisset heiress, was shortly to be increased by the conquest of a district known as The Route. A brief description of these regions may not be out of place at this point in our history if we are to understand the events that follow.

The Glens (or Glynnis) open on the sea at irregular intervals along the east coast from Glenarm northwards to Ballycastle and lead inland to the watershed between the coast and the valley of the river Bush. Dotted along this coast are the castles of Glenarm, Red Bay, Kinbane and Dunluce, whose names appear frequently in our narrative. The obvious meaning of the Glens is clear enough, but the Irish accounts refer to the Glynnis as wooded places, which no doubt they were at that time. The account given of MacIain's efforts to harry and destroy the sons of John Cathanach and their followers in Antrim makes mention of the difficulty of finding their enemies in the thick woodlands of the Glens. They were thus an ideal place for fugitives to hide and defy pursuit.

The Route is described in the history of Antrim as the lands lying between the rivers Bush and Bann from the sea southwards to where the headwaters of the Bush join the Glens inland from Red Bay. This was the rich land of the ancient Dalriada of Ireland, and it is from the word Riada, or Reuda, that it takes its name, later to be transferred to the colony of Dalriada in Argyll which, as we know, was the beginning of the Scots kingdom of Scotland with its seat at Dunadd. The Route was the country of the O'Cahans and McQuillans. The latter were almost annihilated by the incoming Macdonnells, and the O'Cahans had been almost part of Clan Donald since the marriage of Angus Og to Agnes O'Cahan in the late 13th century.

James and his brothers had many problems to face in the disturbed conditions of Ulster. The English were pushing north to oust the Irish natives, and the intrigues of the Queen Dowager of Scotland with her native France led to the employment of French troops in that province. Angus, James' brother, brought some of these over in 1551. The Macdonnells (for that is how the Ulster Clan Donald spell their name), were suitably rewarded by the French nobles who accompanied Angus. From their lands in the Glens and the Route they invaded the district known as Clanaboy. This was O'Neill country and it lay along the coast north of the Route. It took its name (*Clan Aodh Buidhe*) from the Clan of Hugh Buidhe O'Neill. The invaders ravaged the territory and drove out their cousins, the sons of Alasdair Carrach, who had joined forces with the English. The spoil from this raid was taken for safety to the Isle of Rathlin, some four miles from the north coast of Antrim. It appears to have been a great and profitable raid, and the spoil of corn, cattle and horses that was carried away must have taken a fleet of galleys to transport to Rathlin.

The magnitude of this enterprise and the consequent anger of the O'Neills attracted the attention of the English power in Ulster. An expedition was quickly fitted out to punish the raiders and recover the spoil. The Chancellor, Sir Thomas Cusake, placed his deputy James Crofts in command of four large ships filled with troops. These approached the island and a party of four boats commanded by a certain Captain Cuffe with about 120 men led the attack. They were repulsed with great slaughter and Cuffe and two more officers were taken prisoner. James Macdonald later agreed to release his captives in exchange for his brothers Coll and Sorley who were prisoners of the English at the time. That in substance is the English account of the incident, but the disaster suffered by the enemy was of much more serious proportions if we believe the *Annals of the Four Masters* where we are told that "the Lord justice marched with a force in the beginning of harvest into Ulster, and despatched the crews of four ships

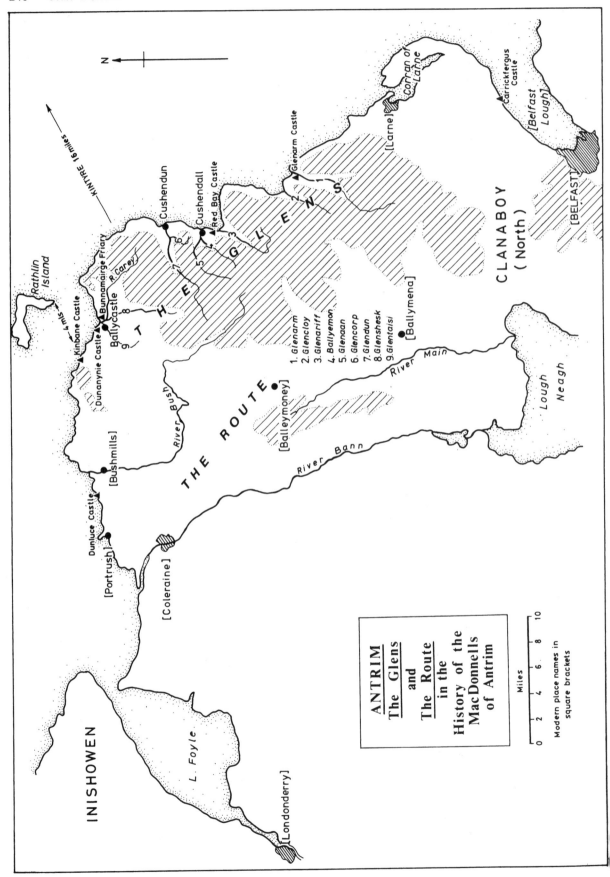

N

KINTYRE 16 miles

Rathlin Island

4 mts

Kinbane Castle

Dunanynie Castle

Bunnamairge Friary

Ballycastle

R. Carey

Cushendun

Cushendall

Red Bay Castle

Glenarm Castle

T H E   G L E N S

[Larne]

Corran of Larne

Carrickfergus Castle

[Belfast Lough]

[BELFAST]

C L A N A B O Y
(North)

1. *Glenarm*
2. *Glencloy*
3. *Glenariff*
4. *Ballyemon*
5. *Glenaan*
6. *Glencorp*
7. *Glendun*
8. *Glenshesk*
9. *Glentaisi*

[Ballymena]

River Main

Lough Neagh

T H E   R O U T E

[Ballymoney]

River Bush

[Bushmills]

[Ballymoney]

River Bann

Dunluce Castle

[Portrush]

[Coleraine]

INISHOWEN

L. Foyle

[Londonderry]

ANTRIM
The Glens
and
The Route
in the
History of the
MacDonnells
of Antrim

Miles

0   2   4   6   8   10

Modern place names in
square brackets

KINGS AND LORDS OF THE ISLES

Origins of CLAN DONALD MAIN BRANCHES

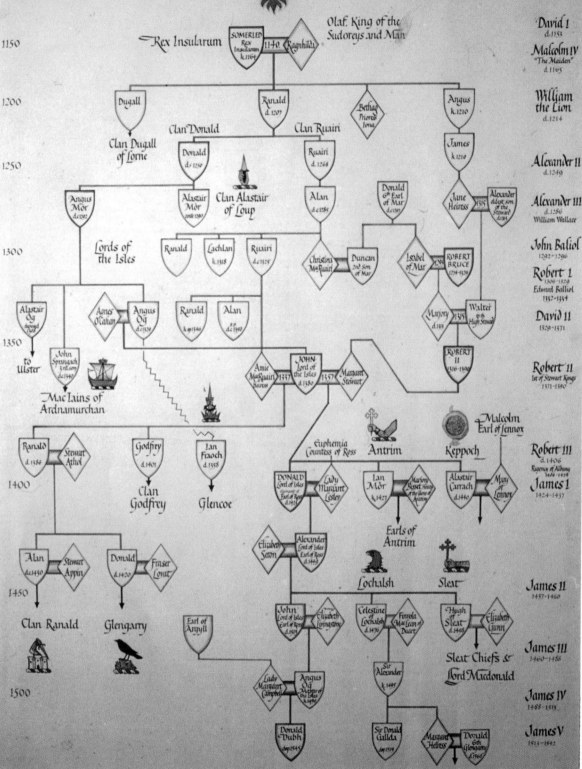

Rex Insularum — SOMERLED Rex Insularum k.1164 — 1140 — Ragnhildis

Olaf, King of the Sudoreys and Man

Dugall — Ranald d.1207 — Bethag Prioress Iona — Angus k.1210

Clan Dugall of Lorne

Clan Donald — Donald d.c.1250 — Clan Ruairi — Ruairi d.1268 — James k.1210

Angus Mór d.c.1292 — Alastair Mór unal.1299 — Clan Alastair of Loup — Alan d.c.1285 — Donald 6th Earl of Mar d.c.1301 — June Heiress — 1315 — Alexander eldest son of the Stewart d.1394

Lords of the Isles — Ranald — Lachlan k.1318 — Ruairi d.c.1325 — Christina McRuairi — Duncan 2nd son of Mar — Isabel of Mar — 1296 — ROBERT BRUCE 1274-1329

Alastair Og hanged 1308 — Aenes O'Cahan — Angus Og d.1329 — Ranald k.ap.1346 — Alan Sr. d.c.1349 — Marjory d.1315 — 1315 — Walter 6th High Steward

to Ulster — John Sprangach 3rd son d.c.1340 — MacIains of Ardnamurchan — Amie McRuairi heiress — 1337 — JOHN Lord of the Isles d.1380 — 1350 — Margaret Stewart — ROBERT II 1316-1390

Ranald d.1356 — Stewart Athol — Godfrey d.1401 — Ian Fraoch d.1358 — Euphemia Countess of Ross — Antrim — Keppoch — Malcolm Earl of Lennox

Clan Godfrey — Glencoe — DONALD Lord of Isles Consort of Earl of Ross d.1423 — Lady Margaret Leslie — Ian Mór k.1427 — Marion Bisset Heiress of the Glens of Antrim — Alastair Carrach d.1440 — Mary of Lennox

Alan d.c.1450 — Stewart Appin — Donald d.1420 — Fraser Lovat — Elizabeth Seton — Alexander Lord of Isles Earl of Ross d.1449 — Earls of Antrim

Clan Ranald — Glengarry — Earl of Argyll — Lochalsh — Sleat

John Lord of Isles Earl of Ross d.1503 — Elizabeth Livingstone — Celestine Lochalsh d.1476 — Fionola MacLain of Duart — Hugh Sleat d.1495 — Elizabeth Gunn

Sleat Chiefs & Lord Macdonald

Lady Margaret Campbell — Angus Og Master of the Isles k.1490 — Sir Alexander k.1495

Donald Dubh d.p.1545 — Sir Donald Gallda d.p.1519 — Margaret Heiress — Donald 6th Glengarry d.1560

David I d.1153

Malcolm IV "The Maiden" d.1165

William the Lion d.1214

Alexander II d.1249

Alexander III d.1286 William Wallace

John Baliol 1292-1296

Robert I 1306-1329 Edward Balliol 1332-1334

David II 1329-1371

Robert II 1st of Stewart Kings 1371-1390

Robert III d.1406 Regency of Albany 1406-1424

James I 1424-1437

James II 1437-1460

James III 1460-1488

James IV 1488-1513

James V 1513-1542

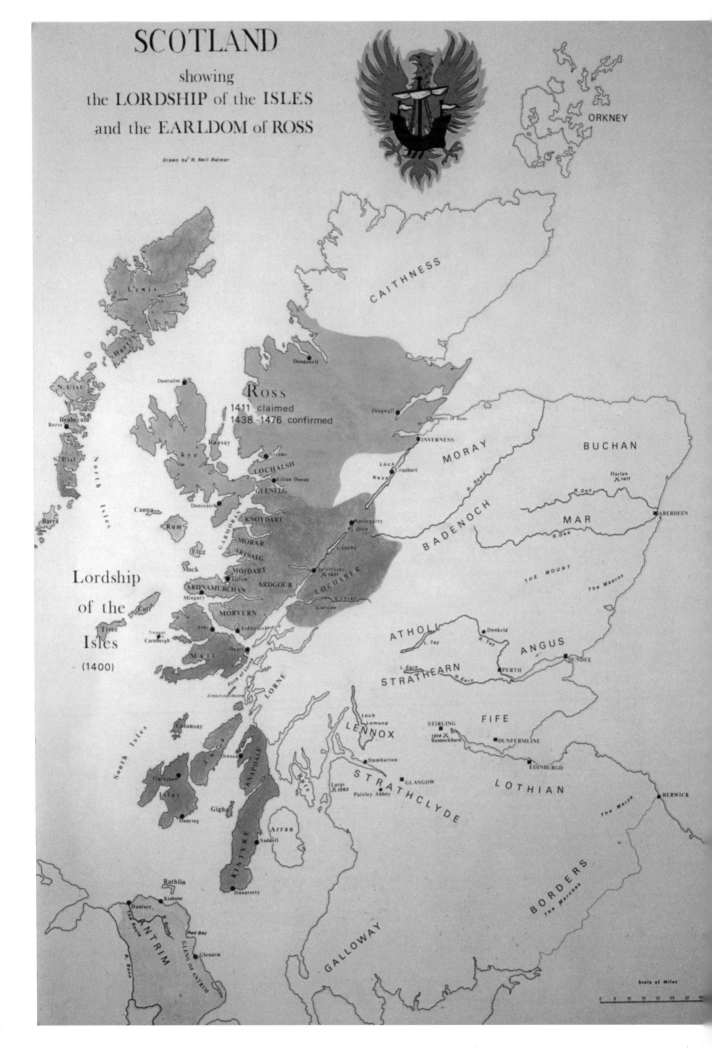

SCOTLAND

showing
the LORDSHIP of the ISLES
and the EARLDOM of ROSS

Drawn by R. Neil Balmer

ORKNEY

CAITHNESS

Dundonell

Ross
1411 claimed
1438 - 1476 confirmed

Lewis

Dingwall

Chanonry of Ross

Harris

Duntulm

N. Uist

INVERNESS

MORAY

BUCHAN

Borve

Benbecula

Raasay

Skye

Strome

LOCHALSH

Eilean Donan

Loch
Ness

Urquhart

R. Spey

Harlaw
✕ 1411

R. Don

S. Uist

Canna

Dunscaith

GLENELG

KNOYDART

Invergarry
Oloo

BADENOCH

MAR

ABERDEEN

Barra

North Isles

Rum

L. Lochy

R. Dee

MORAR

Lordship

Eigg

ARISAIG

Inverlochy
✕ 1431

LOCHABER

THE MOUNT

of the

Muck

MOIDART

The Mearns

ARDNAMURCHAN

ARDGOUR

R. Leven

Coll

Miogary

Isles

MORVERN

Glencoe

ATHOLL

ANGUS

(1400)

Tiree

Aros

Ardtornish

Dunkeld

Fraoch
Caraburgh

L. Tay

R. Tay

Mull

Duart

STRATHEARN

L. Earn

PERTH

DUNDEE

Firth of Lorne

R. Earn

Loch
Lomond

FIFE

Creach-an-Aonaich

LORNE

STIRLING

Colonsay

LENNOX

1314 ✕
Bannockburn

DUNFERMLINE

South Isles

Fladda

Jura

Scarba

ANADRALE

Dumbarton

EDINBURGH

Islay

Largs
✕ 1263

GLASGOW

LOTHIAN

Dunyveg

Gigha

Paisley Abbey

S T R A T H C L Y D E

BERWICK

Arran

Sadell

KINTYRE

The Merse

Rathlin

Kinbane

Dunaverty

BORDERS

The Marches

Dunluce

The Route

Red Bay

ANTRIM

GALLOWAY

Glenarm

R. Bann

GLENS OF ANTRIM

Scale of Miles

The Arms of

Lieutenant-General SIR JOHN MACDONALD
(Glencoe)

Quarterly; 1st, Argent, a lion rampant Gules and in a canton of the last a mural
crown Or; 2nd, Or, a dexter arm in armour couped in fess proper, the hand also
proper, holding a cross-crosslet fitched Sable; 3rd, Or, a lymphad with her oars
and sails Sable, flags flying Gules; 4th, Vert, a salmon naiant proper.   ❖
Crest, out of an Eastern Crown Or a cubit arm erect proper encircled by a laurel
wreath Vert, in the hand a dagger erect also proper, pomel and hilt Or.   ❖
Motto over the Crest NEC·TEMPORE·NEC·FATO.   ❖   ❖   ❖   ❖

The Arms of
The Right Hon. RONALD MACDONALD, MARQUESS & EARL OF ANTRIM

Quarterly, 1st, Argent a lion rampant Gules armed and holding in his dexter paw a a thistle slipped Or; 2nd, Azure a dexter hand couped at the wrist fessways Argent holding a cross-crosslet fitched paleways Gules; 3rd, Or, in the sea proper a galley with her oars disposed saltireways Sable; 4th, Parted per fess waved Argent and Vert, in the centre a salmon naiant proper. Above the Shield a Helmet answerable to his high quality over the same a Marquess Coronet with a Mantle Gules doubled Ermine and torse of his colours is set for his Crest a hand erected the fist thereof being closed proper. Supported on the dexter by a savage wreathed about the head and middle with laurel and on the sinister by a falcon proper armed, jessed and belled Or. Motto in an Escrol above all VIS · CONJUNCTA · FORTIOR . ❖   ❖

Lyon Register (Volume 1, Folio 49).

The Arms of
RANALD ALEXANDER MACDONALD OF CLANRANALD, 24th CHIEF

Quarterly, 1st, Argent, a lion rampant Gules, armed Or; 2nd, Or, a dexter hand couped in fess
holding a cross-crosslet fitchée in pale all Gules; 3rd, Or, a lymphad her oars saltireways Sable, and
in base undy Vert a salmon naiant Argent; 4th, Argent, an oak tree Vert surmounted of an
eagle displayed Or. Above the Shield is placed a chapeau Azure furred Ermine and thereon an
Helm befitting his degree with a Mantling Gules doubled Or, and on a Wreath of these Liveries
Argent and Gules is set for Crest a triple-towered castle Argent, masoned Sable and issuing from
the centre tower a dexter arm in armour embowed grasping a sword all proper, and in an Escrol
over the same this Motto MY·HOPE·IS·CONSTANT·IN·THEE. On a compartment whereon is
this word DH'AINDEÒIN·CÒ·THEIREADHE·E are placed for Supporters two bears each having
two arrows pierced through his body all proper.

Lyon Register (Volume 42, Folio 21).

The Arms of
AENEAS RANALD WESTROP M^cDONELL, Esquire
(Representer of the Family of Glengarry)

Or, an eagle displayed Gules surmounted of a lymphad Sable, her sails furled up and rigging proper, in the dexter chief point a dexter hand couped in fess of the Second and in the sinister a cross crosslet fitchée of the Third. Above the Shield is placed a Helmet befitting his degree, with a Mantling Gules doubled Argent, and on a Wreath of his Liveries is set for Crest a raven proper perching on a rock Azure, and in an Escrol over the same this Motto CRAGAN · AN · FHITHICH; on a Compartment below the Shield are placed for Supporters two bears each having an arrow pierced through his body all proper, and in an Escrol entwined with the Compartment this Motto PER · MARE · PER · TERRAS

Lyon Register (Volume 1, Folio 576).

The Arms of

Sir ALEXANDER WENTWORTH MACDONALD BOSVILLE MACDONALD, Baronet,
(Representer of the Family of Macdonald of Sleat in the Island of Skye⸺)

Quarterly, 1st, Argent, a lion rampant Gules armed and langued Azure; 2nd, Or, a hand in armour fesswise proper, holding a cross-crosslet fitchée Gules; 3rd, Argent, a lymphad sails furled and oars in action Sable, flagged Gules; 4th, Vert, a salmon naiant in fess proper. Above the Shield is placed a Helmet befitting his degree with a Mantling Gules doubled Argent, and on a Wreath of the proper liveries is set for Crest a hand in armour fesswise holding a cross-crosslet fitchée Gules, and in an Escrol over the same this Motto PER·MARE·PER·TERRAS. On a compartment under the Shield are placed for Supporters two leopards proper collared Or. ⸫ ⸪ ⸪ ⸫ ⸪ ⸫

The Arms of
ALEXANDER GODFREY MACDONALD OF MACDONALD, LORD MACDONALD

Quarterly, 1st, Argent, a lion rampant Gules, armed and langued Azure; 2nd; Or, a hand in armour
fessways holding a cross-crosslet fitchée Gules; 3rd, Or, a lymphad sails furled and oars in action Sable,
flagged Gules; 4th, Vert, a salmon naiant in fess proper, over all on an escutcheon en surtout, Or,
an eagle displayed Gules surmounted of a lymphad sails furled, oars in action Sable (as Chief of the
Name and Arms of Macdonald). Above the Shield is placed His Lordship's coronet, thereon an Helmet
befitting his degree with a Mantling Gules doubled Ermine, and on a crest coronet Or is set for Crest
a hand in armour fessways couped at the elbow proper holding a cross-crosslet fitchée Gules, and
in an Escrol over the same this Motto PER·MARE·PER·TERRAS, and on a Compartment of
rocks and heather proper issuant from the waves undy along with this Motto FRAOCH·EILEAN,
are set for Supporters two leopards proper.

Lyon Register (Volume 36, Folio 44).

to Reachrann [Rathlin] off the coast of Antrim to plunder it. James and Colla Maol Dubh, the sons of MacDonnell of Scotland, were on the island to defend the place: an engagement ensued in which the Saxons were overthrown, and not one escaped to tell the tale excepting the lieutenant who commanded them, whom the Scots kept as a prisoner until they got in his stead their own brother, namely Somhairle Buidhe MacDonnell (commonly called Sorley Boy) who had been imprisoned by the English of Dublin, a year before that time, besides another great ransom along with him."

Sorley Buy celebrated his release next year (1552) by storming the Castle of Carrickfergus on Belfast Lough and taking the Constable prisoner. James returned to Scotland where he was in high favour at Court because of his services to the Scottish interest in Ireland. During his absence his brothers Coll and Sorley Buy were engaged in a constant struggle to protect their heritage in Ulster. Faced with the hostility of both the English garrison and the native Irish they had ousted, their situation became so critical that in 1556 James was obliged to come to their support. He appointed Coll Lord of the Route and employed his considerable forces to re-establish his authority in that region. The strength of the Scottish interest in Ulster was now seen as a serious threat to English aspirations, and the newly appointed Deputy decided to take vigorous measures to drive the Scots out of the country. In 1557 he mounted a formidable expedition into Ulster. He succeeded in ravaging the Route, but was met at last by James of Islay and his brothers Coll and Sorley, at the head of a large force of their own clan and many French allies. The result was a complete victory for James and his men. Coll was confirmed in his occupation of the Route, and lived there until his death in 1558.

Coll had married a lady of the MacQuillans early in his life under romantic circumstances which are worth telling here before resuming our narrative. Coll was on his way from Scotland with his *galloglaich* (mercenaries) to the aid of the Irish chief O'Donnell against O'Neill of Tyrone. On his way he visited MacQuillan who was at war with O'Cahan, who had raided the Route in his absence. MacQuillan was living in Dunluce Castle at that time. Coll joined his force to MacQuillan's and the raid was successful: for every cow MacQuillan had lost, two were restored, and all done without the loss of a man. During the resulting festivities Coll courted MacQuillan's daughter, the fair Eveleen, whom he married later. By this lady he had two sons, Archibald, father of the famous Coll Ciotach, of whom we hear much as this story unfolds, and Ranald, of whom we hear little.

During the night, when heads were hot with wine and whisky, a quarrel arose between Coll and his host about the maintenance of Coll's mercenaries, who had been billeted on MacQuillan in accordance with the age-old custom of *bonaght,* by which mercenaries were fed and quartered, with their horses, at the expense of their employer. The feeding of so many of Coll's men no doubt imposed a great strain on MacQuillan's resources, and he planned to rid himself of the Scots by treachery. Eveleen heard of the plan and warned her betrothed in time for him to retire discreetly to Rathlin and safety.

On the death of Coll, James offered the Lordship of the Route to his brothers Alexander and Angus in turn. Both declined the offer. Sorley Buy was then given the leadership of the family fortunes in Ulster, and no-one could have excelled this stout warrior in maintaining the prestige of Macdonald of Islay in that region. He not only defended his heritage against all opposition, but in time built up the Antrim Macdonnells into one of the foremost families in that province. James continued in Ireland with his force of clansmen and French auxiliaries, and his power continued to be regarded by the English as a growing threat. By 1558 it was causing such concern that the Archbishop of Armagh urged the expulsion of all the Macdonald clan from Ulster with the aid of the native Irish.

The English Deputy's next step was doubtless designed to accomplish this end by surprising them in their Island possessions. In September of that year he attacked and harried the Isle of Rathlin, and then proceeded to Kintyre where he "burned eight miles of length and therewith James McConelles chief howse called Soudell." (In that fire many family writs and charters were lost, but were replaced by Queen Mary in the same year with the addition of some more lands, those of Kilcolmkil in Islay). Sussex also harried parts of Arran and the Cumbraes, after which adverse winds drove him back to Ireland.

Sussex now had recourse to diplomacy. He tried to inveigle James into an alliance against the native tribes, no doubt hoping that the expulsion of the Macdonalds would be all the more easily accomplished once they had helped to subjugate their Irish neighbours. He persuaded Queen Elizabeth to write to James in a conciliatory manner, expressing her satisfaction with his services to her cause. What these services may have been is not quite clear. It is true James had fought against Shane O'Neill who was Elizabeth's enemy, but not for any love of Elizabeth or her Deputy, Sussex. That had been a private feud. James refused to be drawn and both he and Sorley remained neutral during Shane's war with Sussex.

The disturbing presence of James and his clan in Ulster continued to be the subject of much concern to Elizabeth of England. In December 1561 she wrote to Mary of Scotland complaining of their conduct in what she regarded as an English province. She avers that James and Sorley were "devouring the country" and that "one James MacOnell, sometyme named Lorde of the Oute Isles" had been keeping prisoner some of her subjects taken at the Rathlin raid ten years earlier. Amongst other prisoners kept captive in James's Scottish castles were Mary, Countess of Tyrone, her son Con O'Neill, and the son of the Baron of Dungannon. Con, Earl of Tyrone, asked Elizabeth to arrange the release of these relatives of his, and this was secured in due course, no doubt in exchange for a suitable ransom.

Elizabeth's complaints served only to add to the popularity of the Dunnyveg Chief and his followers with the Scottish Crown, and the cordiality of their relations was marked by the stream of confidential communications that passed between them. More material evidence of the regard in which James was held is contained in a Letter of Tack of September 1562 in which he was granted by the Queen many more lands in Islay and Kintyre. Earlier still, in 1559, James had been granted the wardship of Mary Macleod of Dunvegan. Wardships of this kind were valuable because in many cases the heiress in ward was married off to some relative of the owner of the wardship, and they were frequently used as a means of extending the influence of powerful families like the Campbells. Mary Macleod had fallen by force or craft into the hands of Kenneth Mackenzie of Kintail, who was not willing to surrender his prize. James applied to the Court of Session, and she was delivered into the ward of the Queen with whom she remained as maid of honour from 1562 to 1565. In the end, James made over his claims to Argyll who characteristically exercised his rights in 1566 by marrying her off to his kinsman, Dugald Campbell of Auchinbreck.

Now began a feud which was to have fatal consequences for the House of Islay. It arose from a dispute with Maclean of Duart concerning the lands of the Rhinns of Islay, the western peninsula of that island. The first move was made by Maclean, and matters became so serious that the quarrel was referred to the

Privy Council. Maclean did not attend the meeting dealing with the dispute, pretending illness. James was adjudged the rightful owner of the lands, it being resolved that these were held by Maclean for personal service like those of other tenants. Later both chiefs were held prisoner in Edinburgh until they found surety for their good behaviour in a sum of £10,000. For a time peace was restored, but the hostility remained and was to become more deep-rooted with the passage of time and the lasting determination on both sides to uphold their conflicting claims.

In the meantime James was negotiating with the English Government for a satisfactory settlement of their differences in Ulster. In her anxiety to secure his assistance against their mutual enemies in that province, Elizabeth agreed to recognise James's claims in Ulster and furthermore promised to make him "Lord of all the Isles." The immediate result of these negotiations was the submission in 1564 of Shane O'Neill, one of the foremost rebels against English authority in Ireland. The way was thus cleared for Elizabeth to dispense with her agreement with James and come to an arrangement with O'Neill who, on the promise of the Earldom of Tyrone and other favourable concessions, undertook with English aid to drive all the Scots out of Ulster.

James was in Kintyre while these events were taking place, and Sorley Buy was apparently unaware of the seriousness of the threat posed by O'Neill's preparation. Shane struck before the brothers were able to join their forces, and Sorley, hard pressed and in retreat, lit beacons along the coast to warn James of his predicament. The latter immediately gathered his men and crossed the channel to the rescue, leaving his brother Alexander to follow with more reinforcements. James's castle of Red Bay was in flames when he landed at Cushendun, and Sorley was in full retreat towards Ballycastle.

The battle that followed was fought at the foot of Glentaisi on 2nd May 1565. Vainly hoping for the timely arrival of his reinforcements, James faced O'Neill's 2000 men with a force of less than half that number. The issue was not in doubt, and in the prolonged and desperate struggle that ensued some 700 of the Macdonalds, who fought "like madmen," are said to have been slain. James was critically wounded, his brother Angus was killed, and Sorley was taken prisoner with nineteen of his leading men. The battle was over when Alexander landed at Rathlin with his reinforcements, and on news of the defeat he returned to Kintyre. James was taken to Castle Corcke near Strathbane where he died of his wounds. There were well-founded rumours that he had been finished off by Shane, who turned a deaf ear to entreaties for his release not only from Argyll and others but also from the Scottish and English Courts. In a letter to the Privy Council of August 1565 Shane announced the death of this brave and remarkable Chief, whose outstanding qualities had achieved for his people a position of power and eminence unequalled in Clan Donald since the fall of the Lordship. James had raised his family's prestige to its highest level: tragically, his sons were to witness its almost total destruction.

By his marriage with Agnes, daughter of the Earl of Argyll, James had:

(1) Archibald, who succeeded and lived only a brief four years after his father;
(2) Angus, who followed Archibald in the succession;
(3) Ranald of Smerbie in Kintyre, who took a prominent part in his father's troubles with Maclean of Duart;
(4) Coll, whom we shall meet in the further history of this family;
(5) Donald Gorm of the barony of Carey in Antrim, killed in battle with the English in 1586, leaving a son, Donald Gorm Og, with whom his line died out in males;

(6) Alasdair Carrach of Glenarm, killed with his brother in the same battle of 1586, and whose line also died out;

(7) A daughter, known as *An Nighean Dubh* (the dark-haired girl), who married Hugh O'Donnell of Donegal.

In 1569, four years after James's death, his widow married Turlough Luineach O'Neill, successor to his cousin, the deceased Shane. She was known by the assumed title of "Lady Tyrone" and played a prominent part in the subsequent history of the House of Islay and the misfortunes that befell the family.

Little is known of James's successor, Archibald, whose reign was short and uneventful. During his father's life-time he had received the Barony of Barr and is described in that grant as son and heir of James. These lands were given to him, his heirs male, failing whom, to his brothers successively, or the nearest heir male of the name. The 30 merklands of Sunart were included in the grant.

Archibald tried to obtain the release of his uncle Sorley Buy, who was still a prisoner in the hands of O'Neill. In this he had the assistance of Argyll to whom he had promised to pay any expenses entailed in the process. This attempt does not seem to have succeeded in spite of Argyll's influence, although a fresh turn of events in Ireland soon secured Sorley's liberation and at the same time his captor's violent end.

Archibald died, as far as we can ascertain, in early 1569 and, having left no lawful issue, was succeeded by his younger brother Angus who in that year is on record as carrying out the functions of Chief of his Clan. His connection with the family of Argyll through his mother the Lady Agnes might well have been deemed an aid to the establishment of good relations with that powerful House. Unfortunately this was not to be the case, partly because her marriage with Turlough O'Neill had made Angus the step-son of an ambitious and turbulent neighbour in Ulster who tended to view the relationship as a useful means of exercising authority over the Islay Chief. In 1573 we find him complaining to the Council that Angus would not be "subdewit" to the Earl of Argyll, from which may be gathered that Angus was not prepared to be influenced by any matrimonial connection, however close or however deeply related to other powerful interests.

The earlier years of Angus's chiefship seem to have been peaceful, if the lack of records in the Government offices is any indication. He had fallen heir to large estates in Scotland and Ireland, and both territorially and militarily was the most powerful chief of Clan Donald. But forces were already at work which were gradually and insistently to undermine his power and lead eventually to the ruin of his House. Apart from the jealousy excited by their territorial possessions, their adherence to the old religion when the Reformation was gaining ground in the rest of the country rendered the Islay Chiefs more readily exposed to the avarice and machinations of Argyll and the King, against whose adroit diplomacy they were to prove no match. Another powerful factor in our story, already referred to, was the feud with the Macleans of Duart whose aspirations to lands traditionally belonging to the Islay Chiefs provided an ever-present source of conflict.

In the past the Macleans of Duart had become closely allied by ties of blood and marriage with the House of Islay. Hector Mor, grandfather of the present chief, had married Mary, the daughter of Alexander of Dunnyveg. Their son, Hector Og, made a politic marriage with a daughter of Argyll, by whom he had Lachlan Mor, the present Chief, and a daughter who married Angus of Dunnyveg.

Thus the two protagonists in the drama enacted between the two families were brothers-in-law, a fact which served in no way to diminish the virulence with which their claims were fought.

By his marriage with a daughter of the Earl of Glencairn, Lachlan Mor secured the support of a powerful family whose influence was to serve him well in years to come. Soon after his succession in 1578 we find him involved in hostilities with Angus of Dunnyveg. There are no records to indicate the cause or the nature of the quarrel, but we may safely conclude that it revolved around their conflicting claims to the Rhinns of Islay. We do know that their conduct attracted the attention of the Government and that both parties were obliged, under penalty of treason, to offer assurances of peaceful behaviour for a specified period.

The interval that followed was spent by Angus in extending his influence by securing bonds of friendship and service from some of his less powerful neighbours. In September 1579 he entered into a bond of manrent with James Lamont of Inveryne, and in 1580 he signed similar bonds with John Stewart, hereditary Sheriff of Bute, and with the Clan Alister Beg of Arran. In the same year he confirmed a charter by Sir Neil Mackay Vicar to Adam Mackay, likely descendants of that Brian Vicar Mackay who was the subject of Donald of Harlaw's famous Gaelic charter of 1408. Also in that year, Angus entered into an "obligation" with the Bishop of the Isles which contained the interesting stipulation that "how soon the revered father chances to comprise any lands or heritages pertaining [to] Lachlan Maclean of Duart, within the bounds of Islay [or] Kintyre . . . we shall deliver to the said reverend father thankful payment of the sums he shall comprise, and take of him just infeftment of the said lands . . . and shall fortify, maintain and defend him, his heirs and assigns in the possession of the same." By means of these bonds of service and "obligation" Angus surrounded himself with friendly neighbours and strengthened his power to contest the claims of a potential aggressor. Such precautions were rendered more necessary now that the progress of events in Ulster began to make increasing demands on his attention.

In the struggle against the English authorities in Ireland, it would appear that Sorley Buy was at this stage chiefly preoccupied with retaining undisturbed possession of the Route and was content to leave the ancient Bisset inheritance of the Glens in the effective occupation of the Islay Chief. The English Council, unaware of the tacit recognition by the two parties of this arrangement, and with the obvious intention of causing a breach between them, in 1584 confirmed a grant of the Glens to Donald Gorm, the Islay Chief's younger brother. Among the conditions were that the Castle of Olderflete was to remain in English hands, that Donald was to prevent more Scots from coming into Ulster, and was moreover to render no assistance to the Queen's enemies at home or abroad, including Sorley Buy. It was an agreement that could not long be observed in the circumstances of Irish politics of the time, and Donald enjoyed his possessions but for a brief period. In 1586, in answer to a call for aid from the hard-pressed Burkes of Mayo, Donald and his brother Alasdair Carrach entered Connaught at the head of a powerful force which included many Islesmen. They were taken by surprise at Ardnaree, and both Donald and Alasdair were killed in a disastrous defeat that put an effectual stop to Scots aspirations in Connaught.

A year earlier Angus of Dunnyveg was engaged in negotiations with the English Court with the object of establishing his title to his ancestral possessions in Antrim. These negotiations resulted in an agreement in May 1586 by which Angus was to receive the whole of the Bisset inheritance except for the Castle of

Olderflete which was to continue in English hands. The main conditions of the grant bound Angus to serve Elizabeth to the exclusion of any foreign prince, to limit the number of Scots in his service in Ireland to thirty, to provide 80 foot-soldiers for the Queen's service, and to serve against all invaders of Ireland excepting the Scots only in the event of war between the two countries. These terms are closely similar to those which bound his brother Donald Gorm, the chief difference being that Angus is not obliged to serve against Sorley Buy who was now in the process of establishing a loyal relationship with the English Court.

It is not clear how long the agreement lasted, or indeed if either party expected it to have any permanence. The English lack of confidence in the capacity or willingness of the Islay Chief to observe its terms is perhaps best illustrated by the suggestions offered to Elizabeth by some of her advisers at the time, that "the people which most annoy Ulster from Scotland are the Clan Donells, who are ever in continual wars with another sept of the people of the Isles, named MacAlanes [Macleans], and if on MacAlane Her Majesty would bestow some convenient pension, he will, I think, undertake to keep the Clan Donells continually engaged as they shall be able to send none of their people to disturb Her Majesty's subjects in Ulster." There is good reason for believing that some understanding existed between the English Court and Lachlan Mor Maclean, whose long-standing feud with the Macdonalds of Islay was viewed as a ready means of effectively restricting their activities across the Channel. Whatever the substance of that understanding or the material incentives offered, the English aim was largely achieved by the intervention of other factors which led to the revival of the feud and a more ferocious phase in the life and death struggle which not only reduced the Islay Chief's interference in Irish affairs but was to end in the downfall of his House and the loss of all its possessions.

The Castle of Dunnyveg, t
principal stronghold of the
Macdonalds of Dunnyveg
the Glens

The circumstances immediately preceding the revival of the quarrel are related in the Chapter devoted to the family of Sleat. Here it is necessary to recount only the facts. Soon after his accession to the chiefship in 1585 Donald Gorm Mor of Sleat, while on his way to visit Angus in Islay, was forced by storms to take shelter in Maclean's territory on the island of Jura. There he became the victim of the treachery of his outlawed relative, Hugh MacGilleasbuig Chleirich, who had taken refuge in a neighbouring inlet and seized the opportunity of carrying off a large number of cattle in the expectation that Donald Gorm Mor would be blamed for the outrage. In the attack that followed, many of the Sleat men were killed by the Macleans, their Chief himself escaping with his life only because he had chosen that night to sleep in his galley. Donald immediately returned to Skye, vowing vengeance against the Macleans whose action roused the bitter resentment of all branches of the Clan.

Angus of Dunnyveg's attitude at this juncture is worthy of the highest commendation for its tolerance and restraint. After visiting and commiserating with the Chief of Sleat he decided, against the urgent advice of his followers, to call on Maclean of Duart for the purpose of explaining the circumstances of the raid and persuading him to accept an amicable arrangement. Lachlan Mor of Duart was in no mood for mediation, however, and after a hospitable reception he treacherously seized Angus and all his company with the exception of his cousin Ranald who had scented the danger and made his escape. The Chief of Dunnyveg was forced under duress to surrender his rights to the Rhinns of Islay in Lachlan's favour, and to ensure the fulfilment of the agreement his brother Ranald and his young son James were held as hostages. Angus himself was released and allowed to return to Islay to complete arrangements for admitting Maclean into possession.

Such a flagrant violation of the ancient laws of hospitality must be seen as a measure of Maclean's ruthless determination to resolve the quarrel by any means that lay ready to his hand; but it would be surprising if he believed that his designs could be accomplished thus easily and without provoking reprisals of a similarly treacherous character. Shortly after these events, in July 1586, Maclean proceeded to Islay for the purpose of taking sasine of the lands and brought the young hostage James with him in his retinue as an added safeguard. Having lodged themselves in the fort of Lochgorm, they soon received a message from Angus inviting them to his residence at Mullintrae as being more suitable for their accommodation. On the most solemn assurances being offered for his safety, Lachlan eventually agreed and with a large number of his followers was received with great hospitality. After they had retired for the night their sleeping quarters were silently surrounded by several hundred of the Islay Chief's warriors. Angus went to the door of Lachlan's room and called him out on the pretext of joining him in a nightcap. Lachlan sensed his danger and was reluctant to respond, but at length yielded to Angus's insistence and appeared at the door bearing his young hostage on his shoulder. The boy, on seeing his father with drawn sword, begged him to spare Maclean's life. Lachlan was thereupon seized and placed under guard in a separate room. His followers surrendered on receiving assurances that their lives would be spared, but two held out, one of them a valued councillor of Maclean's, the other Angus Macdonald of Harris, who was the chief associate of Hugh MacGilleasbuig in the nefarious action at Jura which was the immediate cause of the renewal of this desperate feud. These two men defended their lives with great courage and were overwhelmed only when the house from which they fought had been set on fire, and they perished in the flames.

Meanwhile from Mull came a report that Angus's brother Ranald, the hostage left behind in Duart, had been executed. The author of the report is said to have been Alan Maclean, a kinsman of the Chief, who thought by this means to compass Lachlan's death and thus secure for himself the management of his estates during the young heir's minority. The reaction in Islay was immediate and devastating. Tradition has it that Angus's brother Coll, determined to exact a terrible revenge for Ranald's supposed murder, proceeded to execute two of his prisoners every day until at last only Maclean himself and John Dubh of Morvern remained. The Duart Chief would undoubtedly have shared the same fate but for an accident in which Angus broke his leg as he was on his way to witness the execution.

The violent proceedings in Islay soon came to the notice of the Government and an attempt was made to mediate in the dispute. Angus was in a strong position, holding Lachlan hostage, and he was able to impose favourable conditions in the negotiations that eventually took place. In April 1587 the Chief of Dunnyveg received a remission for his crimes and, in exchange for the release of Maclean, was given a total of eight hostages, prominent among these being Lachlan's son and heir, a son of Maclean of Ardgour, and a son of Maclean, Constable of Cairnburgh. The holding of so many hostages by one powerful chief was viewed with some apprehension by the Government, and efforts were made to have them transferred to the custody of Argyll and other Campbell men of rank. The Dunnyveg Chief, however, was not disposed under any circumstances to surrender his powerful bargaining weapon before his dispute with Maclean was satisfactorily settled.

In the month following these events Angus concluded an alliance of mutual aid against aggression with Donald Gorm of Sleat and the Chief of the Mackintoshes. With his northern borders thus secured, he felt free to attend to his affairs in Antrim where his influence had been undermined by the death of his brothers at Ardnaree and by the rising prestige of his uncle Sorley Buy. No sooner was his back turned than Maclean of Duart, regardless of the safety of the hostages still in Angus's keeping, invaded Islay and Gigha and ravaged these islands with fire and sword. According to the Maclean seanachie "all men capable of bearing arms belonging to Clan-donald of Isla" were put to death—an account no doubt exaggerated in the circumstances but nevertheless indicative of the virulence with which the enterprise was conducted.

Angus was accompanied on his return from Ireland by his mother, the Lady Tyrone, who was ambitious to heal the breach between the two families. The situation that confronted their arrival in Islay was far from favouring the pursuit of peace-making intentions, but Angus to his credit refrained from punishing his hostages and instead retaliated by attacking the Maclean lands in Mull, Tiree, Coll and Luing, exacting a terrible vengeance with the indiscriminate slaughter of man and beast.

There is no doubt that Angus's conduct at this stage was strongly influenced by the Government's evident lack of discrimination in its attitude towards the dispute. In October 1587 Maclean was given a gift under the Privy Seal of the life-rent of the lands of the Chief of Dunnyveg, these lands having been forfeited because of his refusal to surrender his hostages in accordance with the instructions issued in the previous April; and some months later more of the forfeited lands were granted to Hector Maclean, Lachlan's son and heir, who was still a hostage in Angus's keeping. Nevertheless in spite of these injustices Angus agreed to the mediation of certain powerful friends and relatives who were closely concerned with effecting a reconciliation between the two Island families. The negotiations were concluded chiefly by the Lady Tyrone, Sorley Buy and the Earl of Argyll, and resulted in an agreement under which Angus was to release his hostages in exchange for prisoners held by Maclean, chief among these being MacIain of Ardnamurchan who had been made captive some time previously in the most treacherous circumstances. The terms of the agreement were evidently observed by both sides and appear in due course to have received the sanction of the Government, because in March 1589 we find Angus and his followers being remitted for all the crimes laid to their charge in the course of the feud.

The settlement allowed Angus once again to attend to his affairs in Ireland and re-establish his waning influence in the Glens of Antrim. In this he had a common interest with the Earl of Tyrone who on this occasion invited Angus to his castle and hospitably entertained the Islay Chief and his retinue. Gifts were exchanged in token of their friendship, Tyrone giving Angus seven of his finest horses, and Angus in return presenting the Earl with Scots plaids and some "sculls," the *clogaid* or iron head-piece so highly prized by the galloglasses. The cordiality of the visit was such as to arouse the concern of the Scottish Council whose policy at this period was to cultivate a friendly relationship with England. Suspecting that they were involved in a treasonable conspiracy against the English authority in Ireland, the Scottish Council in 1590 bound Angus under severe penalties to keep the peace with Elizabeth and her subjects.

In the following year the Islay chief and Maclean of Duart were enticed to Edinburgh on pretence of discussing with the Council the ordering of affairs in their territories. By one of those acts of faithlessness which so often characterised the government's policy towards its Island subjects, the two chiefs were promptly seized and thrown into prison. Angus was not freed till the summer of 1592, and then only on stringent conditions which bound him to pay a heavy fine and provide security for the payment of Crown dues. Campbell of Cawdor undertook to become surety for the Islay Chief but, as an additional precaution, Angus was obliged to surrender his two sons James and Angus, with their kinsman Alasdair Og of Sanda, to be held hostage at the Royal Court.

Smarting with resentment over these treacherous proceedings, Angus returned to Islay with no intention of implementing the conditions of his liberation. His continued obduracy provoked the Council to further measures, threatening him with the annulment of his remission and the forfeiture of his lands; and in June 1593, having failed to respond, Angus was summoned for treason. The Islay Chief maintained his attitude of defiance, however, and a year later he was forfeited in all his estates.

It was no doubt as a result of this sentence of forfeiture that Angus's son James, who had become a Royal favourite whilst hostage at Court, was now allowed to visit Islay with a view to bringing his rebellious father to a reasonable frame of mind. James had received a knighthood and his education at Court had opened his eyes to the value of the art of diplomacy as a means of acquiring favour and territorial prestige, rather than the futile acts of rebellion which only led to an insidious erosion of the power and influence of the Island chiefs. Whatever the arguments were that he used with his father, it is clear that they were sufficiently persuasive to allow James to return to Edinburgh with proposals designed to re-establish a satisfactory relationship between the Islay Chief and the Government. In October 1596 Sir James presented to the Council a letter from his father authorising him to act on his behalf and, subject to suitable provision being made for his parents, renouncing all his lands in Sir James's favour so that the King might decide upon their ultimate fate. Sir James made submission on his own and his father's behalf, undertaking to observe the fulfilment of any conditions the King might impose. Chief of these were that (1) James was to continue hostage at Court; (2) Angus was to remove his family and immediate following from Kintyre and Gigha; (3) he was to keep good rule in Islay, Colonsay and Gigha; (4) by 25th December Angus was to present himself and his son before the King, or deliver his castle of Dunnyveg to the King's Lieutenant; after which the King was to decide on the final disposition of the lands and the conditions of their tenure.

The last of these conditions was duly fulfilled by Angus on 1st November when he gave in his submission to the King's Lieutenant at Kilkerran. Later he appeared before the King and Council in Edinburgh to hear their decision concerning his estates. The situation confronting the Council in this connection, however, was complicated by the fact that Angus was still under the sentence of forfeiture passed in 1595, and a decision was consequently postponed. Angus thus left Edinburgh with his doubts and apprehensions unresolved, and gradually fell back into his old attitude of defiance.

To add to his difficulties, the Chief of Dunnyveg's already delicate relations with the Government were to be seriously compromised by the treacherous conduct of one of his own near kinsmen. Prior to his submission to the King's Lieutenant at Kilkerran, Angus had written to his cousin James Macdonald of Dunluce, son and heir of Sorley Buy, asking him for assistance in driving the King's forces out of Kintyre. Early in 1597 James of Dunluce was invited to the Scottish Court and, in the expectation of advancing his interests at the expense of the Dunnyveg Chief, not only revealed the treasonable correspondence but put forward his own claim to the lands of Islay and Kintyre on the grounds of Angus's alleged illegitimacy. It was a blatant attempt on the part of Dunluce to establish himself in the favour of the King and benefit from the misfortunes of the head of his House; and it is gratifying to find that although he received the coveted honour of knighthood his allegations concerning Angus's illegitimacy were proved groundless, and he had to content himself with only a small portion of the lands he thought to acquire in Kintyre.

In 1598, as a result of these revelations and on account of Angus's persistent failure to fulfil the terms of the agreement of 1596, his son Sir James was once again allowed to visit him in Kintyre with a view to securing his obedience. It would appear, however, that Angus had meanwhile come to regret the renunciation of his lands in favour of his son as it became evident that the expected benefits therefrom were not to materialise. The conflict of attitudes thus created between father and son marked the beginning of a further stage in the downfall of the House of Islay. The spark was provided by a quarrel in which Sir James found his father involved with Godfrey MacAlister of Loup, who had slain his own tutor and was now at feud with Angus because he was sheltering the victim's family. In his new-found determination to reduce his father to submission and compliance with the terms of his renunciation, Sir James joined the Chief of Loup and with 300 followers surrounded Angus in his residence at Askomull. They called on Angus to surrender the tutor's family, which he very properly refused to do, and the house was thereupon attacked and set on fire, Angus and his wife barely escaping with their lives. The old chief, who was badly burned in the fire, was carried to Smerbie and there confined in irons for several months. The severity of the treatment meted out to his father by Sir James lends support to the belief that the fire at Askomull was no accident, but a deliberate act on the part of Sir James to rid the King of a troublesome subject and himself of the one obstacle that stood between him and the inheritance he already regarded as legally his.

With the assumption of his father's mantle, Sir James shed that of the courtier and with it the obligations of loyalty he had formerly sought to exact from his parent. He had found it easy to dispose of the old chief, but it was not so easy to get rid of the problems that had beset that chief throughout his reign. The violence in Kintyre attracted the attention of the Government, and preparations were made for an expedition to enforce the King's peace. As in the case of so many other similar expeditions, however, the preparations gradually petered out and it was eventually abandoned. But even while the threat of it remained, events were taking place in Islay which were to bring the age-old feud with the Macleans to its final and tragic climax.

As noted earlier, Lachlan Maclean had received in 1587 the life-rent escheat of Angus's lands in Islay. He had quite recently been granted a Crown charter which he now claimed gave him title not merely to the Rhinns but to the whole of Islay. Fuel had been added to the smouldering hatred by the incident at Askomull where Sir James's mother, who was also Maclean's sister, had been the victim of such disgraceful and unfilial treatment. On 5th August 1598 Sir Lachlan Maclean landed in Islay with a large body of men for the proclaimed purpose of taking sasine of his lands. Sir James immediately assembled his forces, determined to resist the invasion of his homeland. His training and education in Court circles disposed him towards compromise, and a meeting was arranged to take place at the head of Loch Gruinard. Here Sir James proposed that Sir Lachlan should abide by the letter of the original grant of 1587, and that in the meantime the whole dispute should be referred to the decision of the King. Sir Lachlan countered by asserting his claim to the whole island, at the same time declaring his resolve to be content with nothing less. The effect of this was to produce a complete change in Sir James's attitude, and he promptly announced his determination to agree to no decision which involved the surrender of his ancestral lands. In assuming such an uncompromising stand Sir James was no doubt influenced by the knowledge that a large proportion of Maclean's forces had been stranded on Nave Island and thus rendered inactive until relieved by the rising tide.

For Maclean it was a question of abandoning his claims or of fighting a battle which in the circumstances he was almost certain to lose. He courageously chose to fight although he was opposed by an overwhelmingly superior force strategically disposed to defend their native ground. In the words of the chronicler, Sir Lachlan "took his place in the forefront of the combat" and cut his way towards Sir James whom he was about to engage when he was shot down by one of the few gunmen taking part in the battle. The Macleans were thrown into disorder by the loss of their leader and the fierce onset of the Macdonalds, and the battle developed into a massacre. It is said that only twenty Macleans survived the conflict, leaving their Chief and 250 of his clansmen dead on the field. Sir James was wounded by an arrow, and his total casualties numbered only 30 dead and 60 wounded.

Sir Lachlan was buried at Kilchomain, six miles from the scene of the battle, in death at last undisturbed within the Rhinns which he had striven in life so long to occupy. As he lay dying he is said to have exclaimed his regret "that he had estranged Lochiel, since no other chief in the Highlands was so fitted to avenge him." The Camerons played their unexpected part, however, in the violent measures later taken to avenge his death. Tradition states that Sir Lachlan's son Hector Og, who was with the tide-bound party on Nave Island, went round enlisting the aid of the friendly clans, including the Camerons, the Macleods of Harris and MacNeils of Barra, and was soon back in Islay to exact retribution from the Macdonalds. Sir James was supported only by Maclaine of Lochbuie who had his own private feud with his kinsman of Duart. With as strong a force as he was able to muster, Sir James faced the powerful combination ranged against him, and in a bitterly fought battle at Ben Bigrie near

Dunnyveg the Macdonalds were well nigh annihilated. Sir James himself was wounded but succeeded in making his escape with a few followers to Kintyre.

No action appears to have been taken by the Government against Sir James for his part in these violent disturbances, from which it may be assumed that the Macleans were regarded as the aggressors and the death of their chief as a normal accident of war. With the end of the feud the way seemed clear for a more peaceful and permanent settlement in Islay and Kintyre, and in 1599 we find Sir James submitting some remarkably far-sighted proposals for the establishment of the royal authority within his bounds. He offered to evacuate and leave the whole of Kintyre at the King's disposal, to hand over to a royal garrison the Castle of Dunnyveg with 60 merklands for its support, and to pay £600 annually in exchange for a grant of the remaining 300 merklands in Islay. Sir James further offered to maintain his father on a yearly pension of 1000 merks in a residence appointed by the King, and as a pledge of his good faith in all these undertakings he proposed to surrender his brother as hostage and support him as long as he was held in that condition.

These proposals, which accorded well with the royal policy, were approved by the Privy Council on 6th September and authority was given for putting them into immediate effect. Sinister influences were now at work, however, and the powerful interest of Argyll and the Campbells intervened to obstruct the smooth implementation of the agreement and to thwart Sir James's efforts to secure an orderly relationship with the Government. It was about this time that Sir James married a sister of Sir John Campbell of Cawdor, and it was doubtless the latter's advice to hold out for better terms that influenced Sir James to postpone the completion of his arrangements. Cawdor's false counsel and the duplicity of Argyll, who saw his purposes better served by throwing his influence on the side of Angus and perpetuating the differences between father and son, were destined to destroy all Sir James's chances of reconciliation with the royal authority and of securing the integrity of his Islay heritage.

The first recorded act in the fresh drama that was about to surround the fortunes of the Islay family took place in 1603. On 15th August of that year the old Chief Angus entered into a bond of friendship with Campbell of Auchinbreck. Angus had been liberated from his confinement in accordance with the terms approved by the Council in 1599, but he could not easily forget the unnatural treatment he had suffered at the hands of his son. The old Chief was therefore quite ready to believe Auchinbreck when he suggested that Sir James was engaged in another plot against him. Sir James was immediately apprehended. After a spell in Angus's custody he was handed over to Campbell of Auchinbreck, who in due course surrendered him to the Earl of Argyll. When these proceedings came to the notice of the Government, Argyll was ordered to present Sir James before the Privy Council at Perth and early in 1604 he was committed to Blackness Castle. From there, after an unsuccessful attempt at escape with the aid of some of his clansmen, he was sent for greater security to Edinburgh Castle.

The preparations surrounding King James's accession to the English throne served to distract the attention of the Government from affairs in the Highlands and Isles, and as a consequence the disorders in these regions increased to a serious level. It was not till 1605, when he was firmly established in his new state, that the King felt strong enough to revive his projects for the effective settlement of the Isles. In that year Lord Scone, the King's Comptroller in Scotland, was commissioned to proceed to Kintyre and there receive the submission of the Western chiefs and their sureties for the payment of rents and other dues belonging to the Crown. Angus of Dunnyveg with many other chiefs was summoned to appear at Kilkerran and produce before the court his titles and his sureties on pain of being prosecuted with fire and sword. To lend force to the summons, a well-armed expedition was to assemble on 15th July in readiness to proceed against all those who refused to submit to the royal demands. The Castles of Dunnyveg in Islay and Duart in Mull were ordered under pain of treason to be surrendered to Robert Hepburn, Lieutenant of the King's Guard, and all boats were to be impounded to prevent the escape of the inhabitants of these islands.

Proceedings were held up by delays which were a familiar feature of such expeditions, and it was not till September that the King's Comptroller was able to hold his court in Kintyre. It was attended only by Angus and his vassals, the other Western chiefs having chosen to flout the royal summons. A complete roll was made of the Crown lands in Kintyre, and Angus paid all the arrears of rent due for his lands in both Kintyre and Islay; and as surety for his future obedience he handed over his natural son, Archibald of Gigha, who was held in custody in the Castle of Dumbarton.

In the following year the Islay chief made an earnest effort to place his relations with the Government on an orderly and amicable footing. On 8th September he submitted to the Council certain proposals in which he reiterates his former promises, engages to conduct himself as a loyal subject of His Majesty, and to continue faithfully to pay all rents due to the Crown. Furthermore, Angus bound himself to appear before the Privy Council whenever commanded to do so and in general to support the royal policy for the "reformation of the barbarity of the West and North Isles." Two days later he wrote directly to the King to ensure that he was made acquainted with these proposals. There were ample grounds for taking such a precaution. With Sir James in prison, Argyll no longer found it useful for his policies to support Angus, and his dominating influence in the Council was now employed to suppress his petition and thus more speedily accomplish his ruin. Argyll's machinations soon bore fruit. In November 1606 he concluded an agreement with the King's Comptroller under which he secured for himself the tenancy of the Crown lands of Kintyre and the island of Jura, with the right to displace their inhabitants if so desired. The agreement received the royal approval the following year, and the process was immediately started of ousting the native inhabitants and planting the regions with Campbells and their Lowland sympathisers.

On receiving news of these proceedings, Sir James made an unsuccessful attempt to escape from Edinburgh Castle, and the hostage Archibald of Gigha succeeded in escaping from Dumbarton. The whole of Clan Donald South was filled with consternation at the prospect of being dispossessed by their ancient enemies of lands they had held for hundreds of years. The old Chief was filled with resentment and, despairing of any kind of settlement with the Government, at once gathered his warriors and assembled his galleys. He was supported by his kinsman Donald Gorm of Sleat, and their combined strength frightened many of the incomers in Kintyre to flee for refuge across the Channel to Antrim. Argyll was unable to marshal sufficient forces to subdue the Islesmen, and Angus appears to have remained for the moment content with what he had so far accomplished.

Towards the end of 1607, Sir James made another attempt to regain his freedom. He had been put in irons after his earlier unsuccessful effort, but in spite of this encumbrance and with the aid of Lord Maxwell, a fellow-prisoner, whose prompting was reinforced by the consumption of a considerable quantity of wine, Sir James was persuaded that there was a good chance of success. Overpowering their keepers, they reached the Castle wall. Lord Maxwell succeeded in getting away safely, but Sir James sprained his leg in jumping and was shortly afterwards recaptured. As a direct result, instructions were immediately issued for Sir James to face trial on charges which included his recent "treasonable" breaking of ward, and the fire-raising and seizure of his father at Askomull ten years before. He was brought to trial in May 1609. While readily admitting the attempts to break ward as well as the seizure and imprisonment of his father, he strenuously denied having set fire to the house at Askomull. But the composition of the court made his conviction inevitable. He was faced by a jury of unsympathetic Lowland men of property in a court presided over by a Lord Justice commissioned by Argyll, himself the supreme criminal judge in the kingdom and an enemy dedicated to the ruin of his House. He was sentenced to be beheaded as a traitor, and this sentence would undoubtedly have been carried out forthwith had he not wisely refrained from implicating the King by producing in his defence the letter of 1598 in which the royal approval had been given of his father's detention. Whether or not he was secretly assured because of this that the ultimate sentence would not be carried out, Sir James was to spend many more years in captivity before he was able to escape and make a final and forlorn attempt to restore the fortunes of his family.

Meanwhile in Islay the royal authority as exercised through the agency of Argyll was still being set at defiance. Angus Og, the old Chief's second son, was in occupation of the Castle of Dunnyveg and refused all demands for its surrender to Argyll. In the spring of 1608 the King resolved upon another expedition to advance his projects in the Isles. A commission was granted to Lord Ochiltree as Lieutenant of the Isles and a council was appointed to advise him under the leadership of Andrew Knox, Bishop of the Isles, whose understanding of the needs and aspirations of the Islesmen made his choice as political mediator a particularly fortunate one. The expedition reached Islay in August, and Angus Og peacefully surrendered the Castle of Dunnyveg, for which he was later commended by the King who wrote: "We have remitted the rancour of our royal mind against him [Angus Og] for his treasonable keeping of the Castle of Dunnyveg, and for his disobedience to our letters, by which he was ordered to restore it to Argyll." Ochiltree placed a royal garrison in the Castle, but the fort of Lochgorm was demolished. The old Chief himself followed the King's Lieutenant to Aros in Mull where the other Western chiefs had been summoned to attend his court. On giving suitable undertakings, Angus was permitted to return home, but almost all the other chiefs were trapped whilst guests on board ship and carried off to Edinburgh and subsequent imprisonment in Dumbarton, Stirling and Blackness.

The capture of so many powerful chiefs was to afford the King a perfect opportunity for the practical realisation of his policy in the Isles. They were now compelled to listen to the royal plans for the permanent pacification of their territories, and they were set at liberty only on their promise to assist the Bishop of the Isles in carrying out the new policy and on giving substantial security for their return to Edinburgh on a date appointed. The deliberations that followed were finally to be embodied in the Statutes of Iona, which marked a significant turning-point in the turbulent history of the Highlands and Isles.

Angus of Dunnyveg was prominent among those chiefs who took part in the negotiations at Iona. The Castle of Dunnyveg was still occupied by a royal garrison in 1610, the year in which the Statutes received the royal approval. In recognition of his work, Bishop Knox was granted the King's commission as Steward of the Isles with his headquarters at Dunnyveg, of which castle he was also appointed Constable. On 10th August the Castle was formally handed over with all its stores in accordance with the royal instructions. At the same time the Bishop was given the arrears of taxes due by Angus and other tenants within his jurisdiction.

The Islay Chief was now old and tired of his hitherto constant and fruitless struggle to secure titles to his lands and preserve his heritage. The last recorded transaction in his life is to be found in a deed of 1st January 1612 by which he surrendered his patrimony in Islay to Sir John Campbell of Cawdor for the paltry sum of 6000 merks. The unhappy transaction marks the triumphant culmination of the process of insidious absorption by the Campbells of the lands of the Islay family.

The final tragedy in the story of the House of Islay was precipitated by the action of Ranald Og, a bastard son of the late Chief and, if we are to believe the chronicler, "a vagabound fellow without any residence." In the spring of 1614 Ranald Og with a few companions surprised the weakly guarded Castle of Dunnyveg and expelled the garrison. Angus Og, whose brother's continued confinement in Edinburgh left him effective leader of the clan, immediately "sent round the fiery cross, warning all those who were well affected to the King's obedience to rise and concur with him in the recovery of the House." He entrusted the siege of the Castle to Coll Ciotach, whose exploits—and those of his more distinguished son Sir Alexander, of Montrose fame—find frequent reference in this history. Ranald and his men escaped after six days, but were soon apprehended and slain, Ranald himself being taken prisoner. Angus Og occupied the Castle and made all the necessary preparations for a siege, but at the same time proclaimed his readiness to restore it to the Bishop and in fact is said to have offered it to the former garrison who, however, refused to receive it The Council suspected that the whole action was inspired by Angus Og and that Ranald's accomplices had been killed simply to cover himself. They also thought that Sir James in his prison was implicated in the design to seize the Castle, and a strict search of his papers was ordered. The result was a complete vindication of Sir James's rôle in the proceedings. His papers proved beyond a doubt that, far from encouraging Angus in his action, he had been advising him all along to surrender the Castle and conduct himself as a loyal subject of the Crown. Angus's own conduct was also placed in a favourable light by the discovery of a letter he had written to James for transmission to the Council, in which he offered to restore the Castle to the Bishop on receiving remission for any offences committed by him and his followers in the circumstances surrounding its capture.

Impressed by these revelations, the Council decided to put Angus's undertakings to the test by ordering the immediate surrender of the Castle to the Bishop, who was given a commission of fire and sword in the event of his refusal. Angus continued in possession, however, no doubt influenced by messages which, it later transpired, had been passing between him and the Earl of Argyll who, true to the predatory policy of his House, encouraged Angus in his resistance as the best means of accomplishing his family's ultimate downfall. As a result of his correspondence with Argyll, Angus became increasingly apprehensive of the Government's intentions. In these circumstances, when the Bishop arrived in Islay in September bearing a conditional pardon for Angus, but backed by a very inadequate force, Angus Og not only refused to submit but on the other hand forced the Bishop into a promise of securing for him a seven years' lease of the crown lands of Islay, possession of the Castle of Dunnyveg, as well as remission for all offences committed up to that date. The Bishop was moreover obliged to surrender his son Thomas and his nephew John Knox of Ranfurlie as sureties for the due discharge of the agreement. In reporting the failure of his mission to the Council, the Bishop provides further confirmation of the extent to which Campbell influence was responsible for the recalcitrant stance of the

Macdonalds and the measures they were taking for their defence. "They have built," he wrote, "a new fort on a loch which they have made and provisioned. Angus Og their Captain affirms in the hearing of many witnesses that he got direction from the Earl of Argyle to keep still the house and that he [the Earl] should procure him therefore the whole lands of Islay and the house of Dunavage to himself."

The Council, dissatisfied with the outcome of the Bishop's mission, were not disposed to help him out of the difficulties into which he had allowed himself to be placed. Instead the Council considered a proposal from Sir John Campbell of Cawdor in which, in return for a grant of the lands of Islay at a rental "far above any thing any responsible man of quality did ever offer for it," he undertook to accept a commission for the reduction of the island at his own expense provided he was given cannon and the services of some men expert in the "battering of housis." The proposals were viewed with the gravest concern by the Bishop for he realised how far they would strengthen the rebellious attitude of the Macdonalds and endanger the lives of the hostages at Dunnyveg. In October he voiced his feelings in a letter to the Court protesting against the proposed arrangements and expressing his conviction that no one familiar with conditions in the Isles would "think it either good or profitable to His Majesty . . . to make that name [Campbell] greater in the Isles than they are already; nor yet to root out one pestiferous clan, and plant in another little better." The situation in the South Isles, he went on to suggest, would be best resolved by the introduction of "honest men" who would be protected in their occupation by an armed force from the West of Scotland and "old soldiers out of Ireland"—in other words, a plantation similar to that which was then in progress in Ulster.

The Bishop's proposals do not appear to have attracted any direct response from the authorities, and we find him taking little part in subsequent events. When reports of the sinister plans that were afoot reached Sir James in his prison, he determined to make a last desperate effort to preserve his family inheritance. In the month of October he presented to the Privy Council a petition both submissive in tone and enlightened in its scope. He offered a rental of 8000 merks per annum for the Crown lands of Islay, in the first instance on a seven years' lease to test his obedience; but if the King preferred to retain these lands himself, he undertook to make them worth 10,000 merks a year, and to transport himself and his kinsmen to Ireland on receiving a year's rent to buy lands with in that country. He asked for forty days' freedom for the purpose of reducing the Castle of Dunnyveg, releasing the hostages, and apprehending those concerned in its seizure and retention. Finally, in the event of these offers being denied, he undertook to transport himself and his clan out of Scotland on receiving a free pardon and a royal recommendation of his services to the Estates of Holland. Amongst the sureties offered for the due performance of these undertakings it is strange to find the name of Sir John Campbell of Cawdor, from which it may be difficult to avoid the conclusion that with characteristic craft he had succeeded in deluding Sir James as to his true rôle in the events that were taking place.

No consideration appears to have been given to Sir James's offers, and the preparations for Cawdor's expedition went on apace. Towards the end of October, Cawdor was granted his commission for proceeding against Angus Og and the other rebels in Islay. Before the necessary forces were assembled, however, a fresh intrigue was set on foot which was to put the final seal on the fate of the House of Islay. The Earl of Dunfermline, Chancellor of Scotland, devised his own plan for securing the release of the hostages and, without the knowledge of the Privy Council, despatched one George Graham to Islay with instructions that were represented as having the authority of that body.

Graham succeeded in convincing Angus Og that if he surrendered the Castle and the hostages he was authorised to stop all the proceedings that were being taken against him. Having yielded up the castle and the hostages, Angus was prevailed upon to re-occupy the Castle and hold it as Constable until such time as he received instructions from the Chancellor. In the meantime he was to defend the Castle against threats from any quarter and refuse all demands for its surrender even if these came from the King's Lieutenant. It was a well-conceived plan which not only secured the safety of the hostages but at the same time enclosed Angus in a trap ingeniously designed for his destruction.

Convinced that he was acting upon the instructions of the Council, Angus refused the summons of an accredited herald to surrender the Castle and allowed the emissary to be subjected to rough treatment at the hands of Coll Ciotach. He similarly refused the summons of Sir Oliver Lambert, who reached Islay in the middle of December with the Irish section of the Lieutenant's expedition. Lambert attempted to convince Angus that Graham had no authority to negotiate, but Angus persisted in his delusion, threatening to complain to the Privy Council if Lambert attacked the Castle. Early in the following month Cawdor landed in Islay with cannon and a strong body of men, and immediately laid siege to the Castle. Shortly after the first bombardment, a parley was arranged at which Cawdor at length succeeded in bringing home to Angus the full implication of the deception carried out by Graham. Realising at last the danger of his position, Angus agreed to surrender, but on returning to the Castle and no doubt influenced by Coll Ciotach and others who suspected that no mercy would follow their submission, he withdrew his undertaking and persisted in his defiance in the vain hope of securing better terms. Cawdor continued the siege and renewed the bombardment, and on 3rd February the garrison was forced into unconditional surrender, with only Coll Ciotach and a few of his close followers successfully making their escape.

While fourteen of the rebels were immediately tried and executed by Cawdor, Angus and a number of his closest advisers were held for examination by the Privy Council on the two main counts of the original seizure of the Castle and the subsequent agreement with Graham. Among the witnesses examined on the second count was Katherine Campbell of Danna, Angus Og's wife. She declared that she was much annoyed with her father, Duncan of Danna, when he turned up at the Castle with Graham—so much so that she refused to admit them, but sent out provisions for their needs. She met her father outside the Castle later, and he told her then that although Cawdor was the King's Lieutenant, the guarantee from the Lord Chancellor borne by Graham was more valid than any warrant that Cawdor possessed. The others in the Castle believed the same to be true. When asked if any letters came during that time to her husband, she replied that one did come from Graham exhorting Angus to keep the Castle and not on any account to give it up to the Lieutenant. Katherine ably supported all her husband's three depositions, in all of which he steadfastly affirmed that he had acted in good faith on the promises of Graham, which he understood came direct from the Chancellor.

Taking all the evidence into consideration, it is obvious that Graham and the Chancellor were the prime causes of Angus Og's downfall. Graham denied he had ever made the deal with Angus, and the Chancellor denied having given any instructions other than for the release of the hostages. Any evidence that would have substantiated Angus Og's claims was quashed, and he suffered the extreme "justice" of the law on the 8th July 1615. Without doubt Angus was more sinned against than sinning.

While these tedious and devious enquiries were going on, another complication was added by the news that on the 23rd of May Sir James had at last succeeded in escaping from the strict confines of Edinburgh Castle. If Angus had any hope of proving his innocence in the recent proceedings in Islay, his chances were now rendered quite hopeless. The flight of Sir James served to convince the Council of his implication in the rebellion, and they were now resolved that both should suffer the extreme penalty for their crimes. Nor was the situation of the brothers helped by the activities of Coll Ciotach, whose piratical career subsequent to his escape from Dunnyveg had provoked the Council in April to issue a commission of fire and sword against him and his accomplices.

It was on 23rd May 1615 that Sir James, ably aided by the Chief of Keppoch, his son, and the son of the Chief of Moidart, made his escape from Edinburgh Castle, crossed the Forth by boat from Newhaven to Burntisland, and fled into the hills of Perthshire. The following day the Council sent urgent appeals to Huntly and Tullibardine offering a reward of £2000 for his apprehension, dead or alive. He and Keppoch were so closely followed that they were nearly caught near Murthlie, between Perth and Dunkeld, and had to abandon some of their baggage. At Rannoch the fugitives were met by Keppoch's clansmen who ensured his safety in the wilds of Lochaber. Passing through Moidart, Morar and Knoydart, the party arrived in Sleat. There James had a long conference with Donald Gorm Mor who, although sympathetic to his cause, was reluctant to take an active part in it. The old chief allowed some of his men to accompany him, however, and thereupon Sir James sailed to Eigg where he was joined by Coll Ciotach and his piratical crew. With the accession of some of the MacIains of Ardnamurchan Sir James now had a considerable force at his command, and the rebellion daily assumed more serious proportions. Towards the end of June he landed in Islay and without much difficulty seized the Castle of Dunnyveg, driving its defenders and the rest of Cawdor's followers out of the island. His subsequent actions were conducted in a spirit of strict moderation clearly intended to show that while he was not prepared to tolerate the presence of the Campbells in his ancestral lands he was nevertheless willing and anxious to be re-established on reasonable terms in a happy and loyal relationship with the Government. These sentiments were expressed in letters addressed to many influential nobles through the Earl of Tullibardine, and also in a petition to the Privy Council seeking their intervention on his behalf with the King, and justifying his escape on the grounds of reliable information he had received that Cawdor had secured the royal warrant for the execution of the sentence passed upon him at his trial in 1609. The letters were diverted by Tullibardine to the Council, and neither these nor Sir James's petition were ever brought before the King.

Meanwhile the Council had been initiating measures for the suppression of the insurrection. They increased the rewards for the apprehension of Sir James and his chief accomplices, and issued commissions to sundry leaders for the defence of the West against the rebel forces. Argyll was appointed Royal Lieutenant, but subsequent action was delayed because of his absence in London where he had fled to escape his creditors. The Council were at length obliged to urge the King to expedite the Earl's departure, pointing out that he and his family were largely responsible for the present disturbances as a result of their acquisition of the lands of Kintyre and Islay, and that moreover they had undertaken to preserve orderly conditions within these regions without the aid of the Government. It was not till 22nd August that Argyll at last arrived in Edinburgh and plans were finally concerted for the suppression of the rebellion and final pacification of the Isles.

In September Argyll was ready. Sir James had taken up his position at a point on the west of Kintyre near the island of Cara, where he had a force of about 1000 men supported by a small fleet. Dividing his forces, Argyll despatched one detachment by sea to attack Sir James from the west while another detachment closed the trap by a descent across country from the east. In the disorder that followed, Sir James made good his escape to Rathlin and Coll Ciotach succeeded in reaching Islay where he resumed possession of the Castle of Dunnyveg and the fort of Lochgorm. After Argyll had crossed over to Jura, Sir James returned to Islay and, collecting a force of about 500 men, prepared to make a final attempt to retrieve his fortunes. Upon this Argyll, now reinforced by some English ships of war, crossed over to Islay where he was able to land without resistance, and was joined by another strong force under Cawdor. In face of such overwhelming opposition, Sir James was forced to abandon all hope of successful resistance. He therefore sought a truce with Argyll who agreed providing the strongholds of Dunnyveg and Lochgorm were surrendered within 24 hours. This Coll Ciotach refused to do. Argyll immediately prepared his attack and Sir James, warned in time, succeeded in making his escape to Ireland followed by Keppoch and a few others desperate to save their heads. Coll surrendered his strongholds on terms which secured his own safety and that of a few of his followers but left the rest exposed to the implacable vengeance of their enemies and the summary justice of the King's Lieutenant.

Sir James eventually succeeded in reaching Spain where he was later joined by Keppoch and his son Donald Glas, for whose apprehension a reward of 5000 merks had been offered by the Council. In 1618 their exile came to be shared by their erstwhile enemy Argyll himself, whose mismanagement of affairs in his earldom and conversion to Catholicism had contributed to his fall from royal favour. It may be significant that soon afterwards Sir James and Keppoch were recalled from Spain by the King, and were granted a royal pension with remission for all their offences. Despite royal intercession, however, the Scottish Council proved reluctant to permit their return to their homelands; and although Keppoch was later allowed to live peacefully on his estates in Lochaber, Sir James never appears to have received the Council's sanction to settle in his native country. The last of his line, having no lawful issue, he died in London in 1626.

The Arms of
The Right Hon. RONALD MACDONALD, MARQUESS & EARL OF ANTRIM

Quarterly, 1st, Argent a lion rampant Gules armed and holding in his dexter paw a
a thistle slipped Or; 2nd, Azure a dexter hand couped at the wrist fessways Argent
holding a cross-crosslet fitched paleways Gules; 3rd, Or, in the sea proper a galley
with her oars disposed saltireways Sable; 4th, Parted per fess waved Argent and
Vert, in the centre a salmon naiant proper. Above the Shield a Helmet answerable
to his high quality over the same a Marquess Coronet with a Mantle Gules doubled
Ermine and torse of his colours is set for his Crest a hand erected the fist thereof
being closed proper. Supported on the dexter by a savage wreathed about the head
and middle with laurel and on the sinister by a falcon proper armed, jessed and
belled Or. Motto in an Escrol above all VIS·CONJUNCTA·FORTIOR. ⋄   ⋄

Lyon Register (Volume 1, Folio 49).

The Macdonnells of Antrim

IN THE LAST CHAPTER we recorded the fortunes of the House of Dunnyveg and the Glens from its inception about 1400 down to the last chief of the main line, Sir James, who died without issue in 1626. The only other male, his brother Angus Og, had been executed in 1615 and his two little boys with their mother, Katherine Campbell of Danna, had disappeared. Islay and Kintyre had been overrun by the Campbells, spear-headed by Sir John Campbell of Cawdor with the powerful backing of Argyll and the King. Most of the Clan Donald had to leave, some to the south-west Lowlands, others to the refuge of the family's estates in the Glens of Antrim. Two important collateral families, however, were able to keep their hold on lands in Kintyre; and we must make mention of them here before proceeding with the history of the family who eventually became the most important representers of the Clann Iain Mhòir.

LARGIE, an important estate in Kintyre, is situated along the west coast of the peninsula facing towards the Isle of Gigha. Ranald Bàn, second son of Iain Mor Tanister, received it from his cousin Alexander, Lord of the Isles, in return for the valuable support given to his more famous brother Donald Balloch in the Inverlochy campaign of 1431. Ranald's family was thereafter known as the *Clann Raghnaill Bhàin,* and they were able to maintain themselves in possession of the lands throughout all the troubles that followed in the 16th and 17th centuries. Even the clearances of 1609, which displaced the old retainers and adherents of the Clan Donald in favour of incomers from Ayrshire and Renfrewshire, left them still on their ancestral lands. Largie did not join the rebellion of Sir James, last of Islay, in 1615. Although Angus, 9th of Largie, joined in the Civil War of 1642/1646 and forfeited his lands, he was reinstated at the Restoration. His son Archibald, although quite young at the time, took part in the campaign of Viscount Dundee in 1689. He was at Killiecrankie with his uncle Donald as Tutor, who was killed early in the battle. Casualties among the officers in Dundee's army were heavy, and it is likely that young Archibald fell too because, not many days after, his brother John signed the Bond of Association at Blair. If young Archibald had been alive, he would assuredly have signed that declaration of loyalty to King James. In spite of his part in the rebellion, John was served heir to his father in 1698. The line of males continued until in 1768 John, 13th of Largie, died leaving an heiress, Elizabeth, who by her marriage in 1762 carried the name and arms of Largie to Charles Lockhart of Carnwath. Later another heiress ended the male line in the person of Mary Jane, daughter of Sir Charles Macdonald Lockhart, who married in 1837 the

Hon. Augustine Henry Moreton, second son of Thomas, 1st Earl of Ducie, who assumed the name and arms of the Macdonalds of Largie. This line exists to the present day.

SANDA is another cadet branch of the Dunnyveg line. The founder was Angus *Ileach* (of Islay), youngest son of the unfortunate John Cathanach who was executed at the end of the 15th century. At the time of this tragedy, Angus was probably already in Antrim where his brother, Alexander, joined him. When Alexander at last received his rightful inheritance as 5th of the line of Dunnyveg, he gave to Angus the lands of Sanda, Machairiach and others in Kintyre near Southend. The line continued down to the present century, but in 1960 Donald Claude Macdonald, 15th in line, died in Toronto, Canada. He matriculated arms to Sanda, but died unmarried, and the continuation of the name and arms is still in some doubt.

COLONSAY: this important family, although named "of Colonsay," was more concerned with affairs of the parent stock in Antrim, engaging in occasional sorties into Scotland on behalf of the Clan Donald in its struggle against the rising power of the Campbells in the Isles. The founder was Colla Maol Dubh (known in Irish annals as *Colla nan Capull*, as he was a notable cavalry leader of the time). He is listed in the records as fourth son of Alexander, 5th of Dunnyveg. His residence was the Castle of Kinbane, built on a white chalk cliff from which it takes its name, about 1½ miles west of Ballycastle. He took a prominent part in resisting the abortive raid on the Macdonnell lands by the English under Cusake in 1551. He died at Bunnamairge in 1558 and was buried there. He had two sons, Archibald who succeeded him, and Ranald who supported Angus of Dunnyveg in his feud with Maclean of Duart, and was the only one who escaped when Angus and his retinue were treacherously seized on their peace-making visit to Duart.

Archibald, who followed Colla Maol Dubh as head of the family, was accidentally killed in a bull-baiting incident in 1570 during his coming of age celebrations, organised in his honour by his uncle, Sorley Buy. He was succeeded by a posthumous son, the famous Colla Ciotach, whose colourful and eventful career was interwoven with the complicated struggles of the Clann Iain Mhoir against the Campbell power in Scotland and the continual pressure of the English from the Pale attempting to oust the Scots settlers as well as the native Irish from the Province of Ulster. We have had something to say about these events in the last chapter. Since 1520 the island of Colonsay had been in the possession of this branch of the Clan, and gave its name to the family. In 1558 Queen Mary of Scotland gave the Barony of Bar in Kintyre and much of the Isle of Colonsay to James, 6th of Dunnyveg, and afterwards to his heir, Archibald. The lands in Colonsay were later given to Colla Ciotach. It was there his son Alasdair was born, who was to win a knighthood and lasting fame for his service with Montrose. Their lives were spent in wars and forays during these stirring times and ended within a few weeks of each other in 1647, when old Colla was 77 years of age, and his son barely 50. It was a prolific branch of the Dunnyveg family, and many descendants of their line down to the present day are recorded.

Having dealt briefly with the notable cadets of the main family, we come now to the man who founded the fortunes of the noble family of the Earls of Antrim. This was Sorley Buy (*Somhairle Buidhe,* Somerled the golden-haired), and we shall try to tell how he came to be founder of this family and its subsequent history. *Burke's Peerage* puts his career very briefly in a paragraph, pregnant with meaning:

> Sorley Buie MacDonnell was appointed by his eldest brother Lord of the Route, Co. Antrim 1558. On his brother's death he seized the Irish estates of the family, and after conflicts with the native and English forces, he became a faithful subject of the Queen [Elizabeth], and being of Scottish birth was made a free denizen of Ireland 14th April 1573.

Seldom has the story of many lurid battles, negotiations between contending parties, and sudden violent deaths been crammed into one short paragraph. But it does epitomise the events of Sorley's active life.

This remarkable man was born in or about 1510, youngest son of Alexander, 5th of Dunnyveg. His life spanned the greater part of the 16th century, during which the troubles that followed the fall of the Lordship had widespread repercussions in Ulster. There were three factions that warred for precedence in that province: the English from the Pale seeking to expand their hold on the whole of Ireland; the native clans in Ulster—O'Neills, MacQuillans, and O'Cahans—who resented the Scots settlers of Clan Donald coming across in large numbers; and the cadets of Clann Iain Mhòir from Scotland who eventually held Antrim in a firm grip, and were for that reason unpopular with both the English and the native Irish tribes. Sorley had to steer a tortuous course among these factions in order to survive, let alone extend and consolidate his estates. And yet he was able to do just that very successfully, and leave a son who became the 1st Earl of Antrim.

Not much is known of the earlier years of Sorley's life, but he must have taken a large part in the activities of his father and brothers in the years between his birth and the first time we find him on record by name. In 1550 he was captured by the English while fighting with the Irish rebels, and after about a year spent in confinement in Dublin Castle he was liberated in exchange for an English officer. Soon after his release, under orders from his brother James, 6th of Dunnyveg, he attacked Carrickfergus. This castle appears time and again in history. It held the extreme northern frontier of the Pale, in which the English had been firmly established ever since the original invasion by Henry II in the 12th century, the frontiers being steadily extended until, in the time of Sorley, Queen Elizabeth's deputies were making strenuous efforts to drive out the natives in Antrim, and especially the Macdonnells, who were regarded as foreign intruders. Carrickfergus was therefore a very important strong-point. Sorley was highly successful, for he took the Castle and imprisoned the Constable, from whom he demanded and received a large ransom. At the same time he made his future attitude towards the English perfectly clear by firmly asserting that they had "no rygt to Yrland."

In 1555 the MacQuillans had been driven out of the Route, that fertile part of the province between the rivers Bush and Bann, and Colla Maol Dubh, Sorley's elder brother, was appointed Lord of the Route by the Chief of Dunnyveg, his brother. In 1558 Colla died and the Lordship of the Route was offered in turn to his brothers Alasdair and Angus who, however, preferred to forgo what to them seemed no sinecure, because of the constant threat from Irish tribes and English invaders. Sorley, although the youngest of the family, accepted; but very soon, in the next year, he had to defend his title against the MacQuillans, who invaded his newly acquired territories in force, and Sorley was obliged to retreat to Islay and Kintyre to recruit an army amongst his kinsfolk. This he did successfully, and in 1559 he returned to inflict a crushing defeat on the invaders at Slieve Aura, which left him undisputed master of the Route.

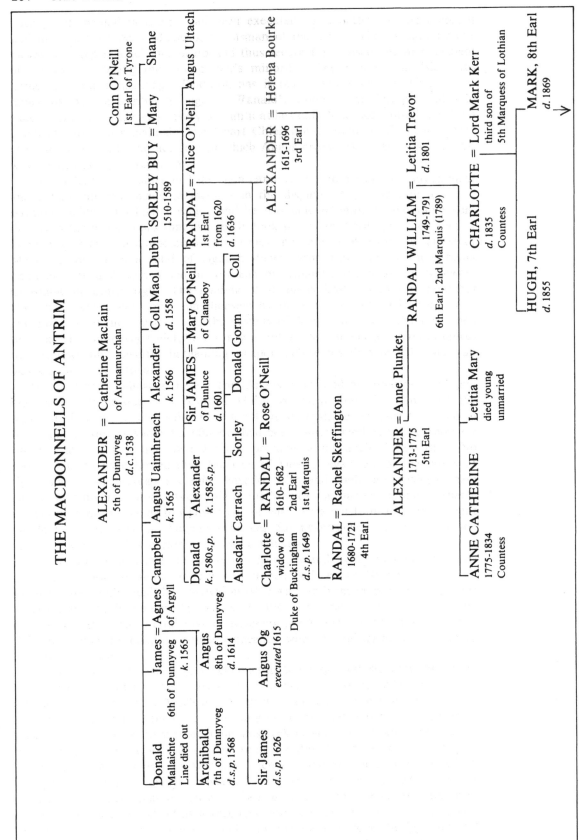

THE MACDONNELLS OF ANTRIM

During the years that followed, James of Dunnyveg and Sorley contrived to remain neutral in the disputes between the O'Neills and the Dublin government. Old Con O'Neill was received into favour by the English, and was created Earl of Tyrone with destination to his illegitimate son, Feradagh, thus ignoring his eldest legitimate son, Shane. From this time Shane became a wild and unruly character, warring with one side and the other in the struggle for power in Ulster. He first slew his half-brother, the unfortunate Feradagh, and quarrelled with his father, who shortly after died in sorrow. Shane then refused the succession to the title of Earl of Tyrone, preferring to call himself "The O'Neill," a title which implied sovereignty over the whole of Ulster. At a conference held between the English Deputy Sydney and Shane at Dundalk, neutral ground between the Pale and the Province of Ulster, Shane declared that his family had been the superiors of all the other chieftains in that Province, and that the title was his by right under the old Celtic law of Tanistry. The matter was left in abeyance until the deputy could consult the Queen. The Earl of Sussex meantime succeeded Sydney as Deputy, but stood aside while Shane laid his plans to expel the Scots settlers before tackling his more important foes, the English. The English on their side were happy to leave the extermination of James and Sorley to Shane. Thus, in spite of their desire to remain neutral, the Clan Donald of Ulster were drawn into the conflict.

Shane pursued his policy with speed and resolution. Early in April 1565, he invaded the Glens and the Route with a large force. Sorley seems to have been unprepared for such a formidable invasion, and sent over to Kintyre for help from James of Dunnyveg, who was at the time living in his Castle of Saddell in Kintyre. James quickly summoned his available forces and crossed over to Cushendun Bay where he found his castle of Red Bay in flames, with Sorley and his men hard-pressed in retreat to the north. It was the morning of 2nd May when James and Sorley drew up their united forces in preparation for what was clearly to be a decisive battle. They knew that Shane, in preparing the ground for a confrontation with his arch-enemy the English, aimed at nothing less than the total destruction of the Macdonnells in Antrim.

In the ensuing battle Sorley nearly lost all he had gained over the years of diplomacy, active rebellion, and feats of arms. Casualties among the Scots were heavy, estimated at some 600 men. James of Dunnyveg was wounded, taken prisoner and cast into a dungeon where he died later of his wounds. His death was much to be desired by both Shane and the English. Sorley himself was captured and kept in close confinement by O'Neill for two years. The disaster of the Battle of Glentaisi (or Glenshesk) marked the nadir of the fortunes of the Macdonnells in Antrim. But although many of them had been killed, they had not by any means been completely exterminated; and they remained a factor to be reckoned with, once Sorley regained his freedom.

The success went to Shane's head, and he now turned his arms against the English and their allies among the Irish. In this he was not so successful, and he was obliged to invoke the support of his erstwhile enemies. Alasdair Og was now the last of Sorley's brothers. Angus had been killed in 1565 in the war with O'Neill. James, the Chief was dead. There remained therefore only Sorley and Alasdair Og to carry the banner of Clan Donald in Ulster. Alasdair had been unable to arrive at the battle of Glentaisi in time to aid his outnumbered brothers, but he continued to prosecute the war against Shane with relentless vigour, devastating his lands in Clanaboy and carrying off large spoils.

After two years of hard fighting, Shane was reduced to such straits that he was prepared to listen to his prisoner Sorley's suggestion to open negotiations with the Macdonalds. Worsted on all sides, Shane readily agreed, and the meeting duly took place at Cushendun where he was received with traditional Highland hospitality, however great the strain his presence imposed. Towards the end of the festivities, a dispute arose over the report of a contemplated marriage between O'Neill and James of Dunnyveg's widow. O'Neill's secretary rudely protested that Shane, the hereditary Prince of Ulster, could marry whom he wished, and that the lady of his choice should consider herself highly honoured. Shane himself intervened to support his secretary with more than usual arrogance. The Macdonalds naturally resented the prospect of a marriage between Shane and the widow of their late lamented Chief, whose death in O'Neill's dungeons was being attributed at the time to causes other than his wounds. The affair developed into a violent brawl in which Shane and his retinue were cut to pieces. Shane's head was handed to the Governor of Carrickfergus, who sent it to the English Deputy in Dublin. Thus was the defeat at Glentaisi avenged, and a formidable enemy removed from the path of Clan Donald in Ulster. It accomplished little, however, towards restoring peace in that tortured province, or healing the running sore of rivalry among the three parties contending for its possession.

The violent death of his captor set Sorley free to make preparations for the speedy re-establishment of his influence in Ulster. He needed time to build up his strength and, wishing to avoid an immediate confrontation with the English power, he first attempted to negotiate a peaceful settlement by offering to acknowledge Elizabeth's suzerainty in return for her recognition of his right to the family possessions. Sorley's overtures took the English authorities by surprise, and opinions were divided as to the best course to pursue. The consequent delay was interpreted by Sorley as reluctance to consider his offer, and he resolved to strengthen his position by crossing the Channel and recruiting among his kinsmen in Kintyre. In November 1567 Sorley returned with a force of 800 men and resumed his negotiations with the English. At the same time he protected his flanks by securing the alliance of Turlough Luineach O'Neill, Shane's successor, and of Brian MacPhelim, Chief of the O'Neills of Clanaboy. Turlough had already renounced his allegiance to Elizabeth, given up his title of Earl of Tyrone, and declared himself The O'Neill, lawful Prince of Ulster.

Not content with the acquisition of these formidable allies, and dissatisfied with the progress of his negotiations with the English, Sorley decided to improve his bargaining position still further by another appeal to his kinsmen in the Isles. From this mission he returned with a mighty armament of 32 galleys and 4000 men made up largely of Donald Gorm's clansmen of Sleat and a considerable contingent of Campbells, whose accession to the cause of Clan Donald on this occasion was no doubt due to the persuasive influence of the Earl of Argyll's sister, James of Dunnyveg's widow. The appearance of this formidable combination was sufficient to drive the English from their garrisons along the Antrim coast, and Sorley quickly recovered his power and influence throughout all the territories of the Glens and the Route.

There followed a short and much-needed period of peace, during which steps were taken to strengthen the newly-formed bonds between the Macdonnells and the native Irish. The most important of these was the marriage between Turlough Luineach O'Neill and the Lady Agnes Campbell, Sorley's sister-in-law. A daughter of the 3rd Earl of Argyll, Lady Agnes was first married to James, 6th of Dunnyveg, to whom she bore six sons and at least one daughter. Her sons were Archibald, 7th Chief of Dunnyveg; Angus, 8th Chief; Ranald of Smerbie; Colla; Donald Gorm; Alasdair Carrach; and the daughter, Ineen Dubh (the black-haired girl). After her first husband died, she was usually referred to as "Lady Cantyre" in the Irish annals, and later, after her second marriage, as "Lady Tyrone." She went to and fro frequently between Antrim and Argyll, and was a powerful influence in promoting the quarrels and ambitions of her family. Her daughter, Ineen Dubh, was married at the same time to Hugh O'Donnell, another powerful chief in Ulster. Mother and daughter seemed to possess the same war-like and energetic spirit, which was to prove of inestimable value to their husbands in recruiting followers and negotiating support for their cause.

The increasing number of Scots in Ulster and their evident friendly relations with the native Irish became matters of mounting concern to the English authorities. Despite constant appeals to Elizabeth for reinforcements, they were unable to take effective measures against Sorley and the Irish rebels until 1573, when the Earl of Essex was given the task of reducing them to submission. Armed with the title of President of Ulster and his Queen's promises of more material favours to mark his success, Essex landed his forces at Carrickfergus. The local Irish tribes were subdued without difficulty after which he pushed his way into Ulster. Sorley reacted energetically, met the English at Newry in the south of the province, and routed them. Other engagements followed in which he was equally successful. Negotiations with the defeated Essex failed, as Sorley was prepared to accept nothing less than the acknowledgement of his right to both the Glens, the ancestral heritage from the Bissets, and the Route as well, which he considered his by right of conquest.

In 1575 Essex, having gathered a considerable force, marched north once again. Sorley perceived that this time the invasion was going to be much more serious, and he took the precaution of sending his women folk with their children for safety to the Isle of Rathlin.

Essex learned of this and, as his operations in the field were delayed, he sent Captain Norris with three frigates and 300 soldiers from Carrickfergus to Rathlin. There ensued one of the most tragic incidents that can be charged against English

The fortress of Carrickfergus which figured prominently in the struggle with the English power in Ulster

rule in Ireland—more disgraceful and senseless than any other in the blood-stained annals of Ulster. The small caretaker garrison of 40 men were soon forced to surrender. Norris and his soldiers were so incensed by the casualties sustained during the first attempt to reduce the fort, that no quarter was given, and about 600 men, women and children, including those consigned by Sorley to the protection of the garrison, were put to the sword. Queen Elizabeth, not fully aware of the brutal details of the operation, congratulated Essex on its military execution, asking him to "give the young gentleman Norrice the executioner of your well-devised enterprise to understand we will not be unmindful of his good services." It must be added, however, that as soon as she was advised of the magnitude of the crime committed in her name, Essex was promptly and deservedly recalled.

Sorley had been an impotent observer of the barbarous proceedings on Rathlin. He "stood on the mainland," wrote Essex in his report, "and saw the taking of the island, which made him run mad for sorrow." A few weeks later Sorley was able to exact some measure of revenge when he attacked Carrick-fergus and routed the garrison, killing about forty of the enemy and carrying off "the prey of the town." He had the additional satisfaction of killing some of "Norrey's footmen," who had taken part in the massacre at Rathlin.

Meanwhile, attempts were being made by the English authorities to divide the allegiance of Sorley's followers. They now hoped to accomplish by bribery what they were in no condition to achieve by force of arms, and the instrument they thought good for their purpose was the "Lady Tyrone," O'Neill's wife and Sorley's sister-in-law. She was known to be ambitious for her son Donald Gorm to displace Sorley in the Glens, and was prepared to engage that the property would be held by her son on whatever conditions the Queen might reasonably demand, and moreover would be defended by him against Sorley and his followers. The successful outcome of this intrigue would have deprived Sorley of the support of his kinsmen on the mainland, while it was confidently hoped that Lady Tyrone's influence with her husband would serve to disengage him from his alliance with Sorley, thus leaving the latter isolated and at the mercy of his enemies.

The progress of the negotiations was interrupted by Sorley's attack on Carrick-fergus, and in the truce that followed the English Deputy Sydney was persuaded to accept some of Sorley's proposals. He was prepared to recognise his claims to the family inheritance of the Glens, but under no circumstances could he be confirmed in the possession of the Route, which was to be restored to its original proprietors, the MacQuillans. Although Sorley insisted that the Route was his by right of conquest, he nevertheless agreed to observe the truce while the proposals were submitted to the Queen. The negotiations bore no immediate results, and the plots and intrigues continued. In 1577 O'Neill put forward a scheme for the expulsion of the Scots, with the exception of about 200 who were to be confined to the Glens, but his motives were suspect and the Lord Deputy chose to follow his own counsel in securing that desirable objective.

During the next few years the struggle continued intermittently. The English authorities were becoming increasingly alarmed by the influx of Scots to Ulster and by the continuing friendly relations between Sorley and the native Irish, including O'Neill. The latter in 1583 gave a practical demonstration of his friendship by "spoiling" the territory of the MacQuillans, who had apparently attempted to recover possession of their lands in the Route. It was also believed that O'Neill, with the aid of the Scots, was planning to invade the Pale and proclaim himself King of all Ireland, and that the King of Scots himself was actively conniving at the proceedings. The reports were no doubt greatly exaggerated, but Sir John

Perrot, the Lord Deputy, was not disposed to sit back and wait for the situation to explode. Recognising Sorley Buy as the most dangerous of all his opponents, he collected his forces and marched north unopposed as far as Dunluce, "the strongest piece of this realm," as he described it in his report. The garrison of only forty men was forced to surrender after a gallant struggle and, satisfied that he had effectively averted an imminent threat to his government, Perrot marched back through the Glens and the Route leaving widespread devastation in his wake.

Sorley had been caught napping. His movements during Perrot's operations are uncertain, but it is likely that he was on the other side of the Channel recruiting support in Islay and Kintyre. What is quite certain, however, is that Perrot had scarcely reached Dublin before Sorley was back in his territories and driving everything before him on his way to recover Dunluce. The castle fell after a sharp siege, many of the garrison were slaughtered, and Sorley marked his triumph and defiance by hanging the Governor, Peter Carey, from its walls.

Both Sorley and the English government were now forced to the conviction that a practicable arrangement concerning the destination of the disputed territories of the Glens and the Route had to be established if permanent peace was to be secured in Ulster. Mention has already been made of Lady Tyrone's intrigues on behalf of her son Donald Gorm, designed to give him possession of the family inheritance of the Glens. As a result of Perrot's invasion in 1584 an agreement was eventually reached with the Deputy whereby Donald Gorm swore allegiance to the Queen for the Bisset lands in the Glens. Donald Gorm's adherence to this arrangement, however, was more apparent than real, and he was not prepared to allow his friendly relations with Sorley to suffer as a result of it. He proved a disappointment to his English masters, who discovered he was "not so honest as was looked for," and his career as an English subject soon came to an end with an attack on one of their encampments.

A settlement was eventually reached in 1586 after Sorley offered to submit to Elizabeth on condition that his claims were recognised. In August of that year Angus of Dunnyveg was formally placed in possession of the seven baronies of the Glens, and it was agreed that Sorley was to hold these lands under Angus on such conditions as might be agreed between them. Sorley was also granted possession of the greater part of the Route on the basis of an agreed rental and other services to the English Crown. The rights of both Angus and Sorley to these territories were to be forfeited if they made any incursions upon the Queen's subjects in Ulster, or allowed the number of Scots in Ulster to exceed two hundred. There is no record of the conditions, if any, on which Angus left Sorley in possession, but he was no doubt satisfied that a peaceful solution had at last been achieved, and that he could safely relinquish his proprietary rights to one who had proved himself a worthy representative of the family and a staunch defender of its interests.

The settlement was confirmed by a visit to Dublin, when Sorley made his submission and solemnly renounced all allegiance to any foreign prince. He returned laden with gifts from the Lord Deputy and his Council, and for the rest of his days remained a loyal subject of the Queen, peacefully consolidating and restoring prosperity to the lands he had spent his life in securing against the most formidable odds. He died in 1589 at his residence of Dunanynie on Ballycastle Bay and was buried, amid the lamentations of his people, in the nearby Friary of Bunnamairge.

Sorley was married first to Catherine, daughter of Con Bacach O'Neill, 1st Earl of Tyrone, and sister of his enemy Shane. By her he had (1) Donald, who was killed about 1580, without issue; (2) Alexander, killed in a skirmish with the English in 1586, also without issue; (3) James (of Dunluce), who succeeded; (4) Randal, who succeeded James; (5) Angus, known as *Aonghas Ultach* (of Ulster), who later possessed the barony of Glenarm. By a second marriage, with a daughter of O'Hara, Sorley had another son about whom, however, little is known.

James of Dunluce, Sorley's eldest surviving son, had been made Constable of that Castle after his father's submission, and was thereafter known by that designation. Shortly after Sorley's death, the MacQuillans, who had been allotted a small part of the Route in the settlement of 1586, rose in arms against the new chief of the Macdonnells. They were, however, defeated with great loss at Ballymoney, and little more is heard of them after this time, although they continued to survive on their small estate in the Route.

While old Sorley was still alive but near his end, the defeat of the great Spanish Armada led to a romantic incident in the life of the Macdonnells of Antrim. One of the most important ships of that great fleet, the *Rata*, was commanded by Alonzo de Leyva, under whose charge were a number of high-born youths, a crew of some 800, and, according to contemporary belief, a quantity of treasure in two large chests. Having been wrecked on the coast of Donegal, Alonzo left about half his crew ashore and embarked the rest with the treasure in a galleass, the *Gerona*, with the object of seeking a friendlier refuge in Scotland. She was unable to make any headway, however, and was driven ashore into a cove still known as Port-na-Spagnis, not far from Dunluce. There she broke up and all save five on board were drowned. The story travelled far, and the Lord Deputy, Fitzwilliam, sent emissaries to recover the treasure. Not surprisingly he found none; but guns were taken to Dunluce and one "iron chest" found its way eventually to Glenarm Castle, the residence of the Earl of Antrim, where it was used to hold valuable and important documents. That there was treasure may be true, as each ship of the Armada had its own strong box containing bullion to pay for supplies, sailors' pay, and the ship's papers. But whatever may have been in the *Gerona*, little of it ever came to light. It is not likely that James of Dunluce would allow it to fall into the hands of the English, or divulge either its existence or the manner of its disposal.

From this time until 1596 we hear little of James and his Clan, from which we may assume that he dwelt in peace and security cultivating and improving his lands. The unaccustomed measure of stability he now enjoyed encouraged him to cast envious eyes on the family possessions in Kintyre. On the 26th October 1596 he wrote to King James a letter in which he referred to the services his family had given to the Kings of Scots in the past by their wars against the English in Ulster. He then went on to assert that he had a more valid claim to the lands of the Clann Iain Mhòir in Scotland than Angus of Dunnyveg, his cousin, at the same time insinuating that Angus was illegitimate. Of particular danger to Angus was the allegation the letter also contained that he had offered James substantial territorial inducements to join him in expelling the King's troops from Kintyre.

The result was an invitation to visit the Scottish Court where, early in 1597, James was received with all the marks of royal favour. But when his claim against Angus came to be examined, it was found to be quite groundless. Argyll exercised his powerful influence in favour of Angus, and the serious allegation of treasonable correspondence was found to be not proven. James had to be content with a knighthood, bestowed by a King who had come to hold him in "greit effection," and with a grant of 30 merklands in South Kintyre. Such a reward for what must be regarded as perfectly unjustifiable conduct was an ominous indication of discriminating royal favour, and of the royal policy which was destined to accomplish the eventual destruction of the House of Islay.

This visit to the King and the evidence of great cordiality on his part did not please the English power in Dublin. The governor of Carrickfergus, Sir John Chichester, accused Sir James of fortifying his castle of Dunluce with rebellious intent, and withholding rents. Sir James was defiant, and Chichester took steps to collect the arrears. His agents' methods were rough and offensive, and Sir James gathered his forces and pursued the offenders. He was met by Sir John Chichester near Carrickfergus, where the English were defeated and their commander killed. This exploit, added to his active support of the Earl of Tyrone's revolt, made Sir James most unpopular with the Dublin government, and when he died of poison in 1601, it was suspected with some reason that a secret agent of the English power had compassed the death of one of their most dedicated enemies.

Sir James married Mary, daughter of Phelim O'Neill of Clanaboy, by whom he had: (1) Alexander, known as Alasdair Carrach, but referred to frequently in the annals of the clan as Sir Alexander; (2) Sorley, who was a loyal supporter of Sir James of Dunnyveg; (3) Donald Gorm, who was engaged with the Irish Catholics in 1641; (4) Coll, whose son James was executed for his part in the Irish war of 1641.

The succession to the chiefship now became somewhat confused. The natural candidate should have been Alexander, but for some reason, either his youth or lack of other necessary qualities, he was passed over. Randal, the next brother in line to the deceased Sir James, was at the time away in Scotland, and Angus Ultach, the next brother, encouraged by his followers of Glenarm and Carey, made a move to head the Clan. Meanwhile, messengers were sent to Scotland, and Randal came back hot-foot. He was known as Randal Arranach, having been fostered with the Stewarts of Bute and Arran. During his sojourn in Scotland he had cultivated a friendly relationship with King James, who seemed to be impressed by his sincerity, his considerable diplomatic skill and other abilities which promised to make him a suitable instrument for prosecuting the royal policy in Ireland once he succeeded to the English throne. Randal's diplomatic ability was put to the test immediately on his return to Antrim where he found his brother Angus in arms and preparing to invade the territory of the Route. He opened negotiations with Angus and, aided by the good offices of an eminent Irish priest, he was able to persuade Angus to disperse his followers and recognise him as rightful head of his House.

Randal inherited his predecessor's alliance with Tyrone, and Sir Arthur Chichester, the Governor of Carrickfergus, immediately took advantage of the confusion surrounding his accession to invade and devastate the Route. It gradually became evident to Randal that Tyrone had no hope of overcoming the forces ranged against him. Moreover he clearly perceived that the whole situation in Ireland would soon be transformed with the Union of the Crowns which could take place at any time, and he had no wish to be found in a state of rebellion against a monarch whose favour he hoped to continue to merit. Towards the end of 1602, therefore, Randal broke with Tyrone and attached himself to Sir Arthur Chichester with a body of 500 foot and 40 horse. His reward was not long in coming. Recognising the value and significance of his alliance to the English cause, Sir Arthur triumphantly presented Randal before the Lord Deputy who promptly conferred upon him the honour of knighthood.

More material gains were to follow. Randal's "well-timed movements at this critical period," writes the family historian, "laid the foundation of all his subsequent honours and emoluments." Many of his expectations were to be gratified even before James had time to settle on his new throne. On 28th May 1603, only two months after the Queen's death, the King granted to Sir Randal vast estates in Antrim, confirming to him all his ancestral lands and others, "the entire region comprehending the Route and the Glynnis, and extending from Larne to Coleraine. This vast expanse comprised anciently sixteen toughs [*tuaths*] or territories, and includes the four baronies of Dunluce, Kilconway, Carey and Glenarm. The Antrim estates, as thus originally granted, contained 333,907 acres." Next year the Island of Rathlin was added.

Such generosity on the part of the King naturally excited intense jealousy in the hearts of sundry onlookers. Among them was Sir Arthur Chichester, who resented the development of what he conceived to be not only a supersession of his own authority but a final set-back to his plans for the establishment of English institutions in Ulster. Some of the native Irish tribes, and also some of Randal's kin in Islay, were not at all pleased with such an accretion of power in Sir Randal's hands. Even within his own family the threat of rebellion was posed by his nephew Alasdair Carrach's claim to be served heir to his father. His enemies spared no opportunity of misrepresenting his actions to the King. He was accused of harbouring Catholics and fostering the practices of the Roman Church, which his enemies knew could not be tolerated in the religious climate of the time. His efforts to preserve what was best in the ancient Celtic tradition were construed as opposition to the "civilising" influence of English law and customs. Sir Randal had thus a difficult course to steer amid a welter of complaints and active protests, but his refusal to be diverted from a prudent and conciliatory policy succeeded in confounding the more active of his enemies and in satisfying the more practicable claims of his own kinsmen; and he continued to retain the confidence of the King, who was not disposed to listen to the largely ill-founded grievances addressed by malcontents to his Court.

At the same time as Sir Randal was acquiring the reputation of "a promoter and patron of civility in the north of Ireland," his kinsmen in Islay were locked in the life-and-death struggles which preceded the final destruction of their House. However serious the differences between the two families might have been in the past, Sir Randal could not remain indifferent to the prospect of the Island inheritance being entirely absorbed by their ancient enemies. His friendly relations with the King could not be placed at risk by rendering active support to the embattled Dunnyveg Chief, but when Angus renounced his lands in favour of Campbell of Cawdor, Sir Randal succeeded in getting the contract cancelled by a technicality and obtained a lease of the lands in Islay for seven years in his own favour. Here as in Antrim, however, his enemies were quick to lodge complaints. Before long he was being accused of imposing excessive burdens on his tenants, and of attempting to introduce Irish 'laws and observances into the island. Sir Randal was in due course obliged to moderate his exactions and restore the ancient customs of the islanders; and the termination of the lease also marked the final severance of the Clan Donald from the ancient cradle of the race.

Despite complaints and grievances, Sir Randal maintained his good relations with the King, and marks of royal favour continued unabated. On 10th July 1614 the Castle of Dunluce, which had been excluded from the grant of 1603, was restored to Sir Randal. On 29th June 1618, he was raised to the dignity of Viscount Dunluce in the Irish peerage. This recognition of his services in "reducing to civility the barbarous people" of his domains was confirmed two years later when, on 12th December 1620, he was elevated to the still higher dignity of Earl of Antrim. These additional honours inevitably excited the envy of his opponents, and one of the immediate results was his arraignment before the Lord Deputy on a charge of harbouring Catholic priests, a heinous crime usually fraught with very serious consequences. The evidence on this occasion was indisputable, and Lord Antrim, although obliged to admit his guilt, was able to escape punishment by expressing his contrition and binding himself to refrain from such practices in the future. Another and more serious charge was the treasonable one of sheltering the sons of the late attainted Earl of Tyrone. The King, to whom he appealed for protection, rightly refused to believe that Antrim's "affection and loyalty, of which he had so many and good testimonials," would allow him to fall into such dangerous courses. Accordingly the King, aware of the animosity inspiring these efforts to discredit the Earl, saved him from the ordeal of answering the charge and instead ordered an investigation designed to root out and punish his traducers.

To add to the difficulties flowing from Lord Antrim's public involvements, a situation had been developing in his domestic affairs which was to cause considerable personal and financial embarrassment. The wardship of his son and heir, now Lord Dunluce, had been granted in infancy to the Earl of Abercorn, in whose family the King was confident he would be brought up "religiously and civilly." In course of time it was arranged that Dunluce should marry Lady Lucy Hamilton, Lord Abercorn's daughter, and the subsequent contract bound Lord Antrim in a penalty of £3000, which at that time represented a substantial sum of money. Whether the feelings of the young people concerned were taken into account is not clear, but the fact remains that Dunluce was not disposed to implement the agreement. The large penalty Antrim therefore had to pay represented a heavy burden on his estates, and delay in settlement was inevitable. In 1630 the debt was still unpaid, and the Earl had to suffer the embarrassment of a direct request from the King for a speedy settlement to allow the lady to be "speedelie provydit for and preferred to some good match."

In the same year the whole peninsula of Kintyre was exposed for sale. Three years earlier, in 1627, Antrim had attempted to purchase the lands he had formerly leased in Islay. Although the price of £5000 was agreed with Campbell of Cawdor, the negotiations were interrupted and failed to reach a settlement, no doubt due to the intervention of Argyll and his influence with the King. Now, in 1630, a final opportunity was presented for regaining a portion of the family inheritance. The barony of Kintyre, comprising the whole peninsula together with the lands in Jura, which Angus of Dunnyveg had been forced to surrender to Argyll in 1607, had been bestowed on the Earl's son James, created Viscount Kintyre in 1622. The new proprietor soon became so deeply involved in debt that he was obliged to place his estates on the market. Lord Antrim decided to place an offer on behalf of his son, Viscount Dunluce, despite a provision in the original deed of conveyance expressly prohibiting the sale of the lands to any of the Clan Donald. This legal obstacle was overcome on appeal to the King, and in January 1635 the necessary documents were subscribed, the deposit and legal fees paid, and sasine thereupon given to Archibald Stewart of Ballintoy "as attorney, and in the name and to the behoof of, Randolphe McDonnell, Viscount Dunluce."

At this stage, however, and before the formal infeftment could be accomplished, Lord Lorne, Kintyre's brother and later 8th Earl of Argyll, intervened to protest in the strongest terms against the sale. Although not disposed himself to take over the heavily burdened estates, Lord Lorne was even less inclined to suffer a member of the Clan Donald as his neighbour. With the support of leading members of his family, Lord Lorne accordingly presented a petition to the Council, pointing out the danger of restoring a branch of the Macdonalds to their old stamping-grounds. The result was a recommendation by the Council to which the King gave effect by ordering the whole proceedings to be annulled, and directing Lord Kintyre to return to the Earl of Antrim such moneys as had already been paid towards the purchase price. Thus the matter ended, and here also ended the last attempt of the Antrim family to gain a foothold in the lands of their forefathers in Scotland.

Next year (1636) on the 10th of December, Randal, 1st Earl of Antrim, died of dropsy at Dunluce and was buried in the family vault in the Abbey of Bunnamairge, which he had prepared for himself in 1621. On the eastern gable of the chapel there is a tablet bearing the inscription:

IN DEI DEI-MATRISQUE VIRGINIS HONOREM
NOBILISSIMUS ET ILLUSTRISSIMUS
RANDULPHUS M'DONNELL
COMES DE ANTRIM
HOC SACELLUM FIERI CURAVIT. ANNO DOM. 1621.

Randal, 1st Earl of Antrim, was married to Ellis (Alice), daughter of Hugh O'Neill, 3rd Earl of Tyrone, by whom he had: (1) Randal, who succeeded as 2nd Earl, and later was 1st Marquis; (2) Alexander, who succeeded his brother. There were several daughters, all of whom except one married well and left issue. The Earl also had three illegitimate sons of whom little is known except for Maurice, who was executed in 1643 for his part in the Irish rebellion of 1641.

Randal, Lord Dunluce, was 27 years old when he succeeded his father as 2nd Earl. He had been brought up by his father in the old Highland ways of training for hardship and war, and was well versed in the language, manners and traditions that were part of the accomplishments of a true Highland chief. Even his visits to the Court in London and the great houses in which he was a welcome guest did not wean him from the good old ways of those chiefs whose hardihood, strength of character and personality drew the respect and devotion of their clansmen. He was to prove a fit successor to men like his father and grandfather, Sorley Buy. It was as well he had been brought up thus, for in his time he too had to face hard times of continual change, social turbulence and political upheaval precipitated by quarrels between King and Parliament, which were to find their only solution in civil war.

After Randal had completed his schooling and travelled on the Continent, as young gentlemen did to widen their outlook, he returned to Court circles where his personal charm and manners brought him much popularity. In April 1635 he married Catherine, eldest daughter of the 6th Earl of Rutland, the lovely and wealthy widow of the 1st Duke of Buckingham, who had died by the hand of an assassin in 1628. Catherine remained a loyal and steadfast spouse throughout her relatively short life, patiently enduring the vicissitudes of fortune springing from her husband's involvement in the stirring events of the time.

The signing of the National Covenant in 1638 was the prelude to events which were to divide the country into two opposing camps. Loyalty to the King was equated with antagonism to the intolerant spirit of the Covenant, and in the inevitable conflict that followed there could be no doubt where Antrim's course lay. On 5th June 1639, while waiting hopefully at Berwick to come to terms with the Scottish army, King Charles granted a commission to the Earl of Antrim and Sir Donald Macdonald of Sleat, appointing them jointly his Lieutenants and Commissioners in the Highlands and Isles, with full powers to raise an army in the royal cause. The immediate aim was to pose a threat of insurrection which would confine the Scottish army within its own borders.

Unfortunately for Charles, this was not to happen, and after long and fruitless negotiations the army marched into England where it remained until the terms demanded for its withdrawal forced Charles to summon the Parliament which would eventually destroy him.

As an inducement to Antrim in his rôle of royal Lieutenant, the King promised to reward the successful prosecution of his mission with a grant of Kintyre. Proceeding to Ireland, he tried to raise enough forces to form a nucleus for a general rising in the Highlands, but his attempts were thwarted by the personal enmity of the Lord Lieutenant. After attending the King for a period at Oxford, he returned to Dublin in June 1640 to take his seat in the Irish House of Peers. In the following year the Irish rose in rebellion, provoked not only by an iniquitous land policy which had ruthlessly displaced native proprietors in favour of greedy English landlords, but also by the oppressive penal laws of more recent date which denied them the practice of their religion. However much his sympathies lay with the Catholics, Lord Antrim was aware of the danger of identifying the aims of the insurrection with the royal cause on account of the powerful weapon it would provide for both the Covenanting Party and the Parliament. He therefore wisely stood aloof, confining his activities to the humane tasks of preventing or alleviating the effects of excesses committed by either side. Several of his near kinsmen, however, were actively engaged in the rebellion and paid dearly in consequence. His brother Alexander and his cousin Alasdair Carrach, one-time claimant to the estates, both suffered by forfeiture, and his brother Maurice with another young cousin were executed after their capture at Carrickfergus.

Conscious of the delicacy of his position and of the natural suspicions of his enemies, Lord Antrim lived out the course of the insurrection in the shelter

Castle of Dunluce, strong-hold of the Macdonnells of Antrim

of friendly houses, frequently moving from one place of residence to another before the shifting tides of the war. It was April 1642 before he considered it wise to return to Dunluce. There he found the neighbouring town of Coleraine under close siege by Alasdair MacCholla Chiotaich (Colkitto) and his Catholic forces. The inhabitants of the town had been reduced to a state of dire privation for want of supplies, and Lord Antrim's first action was to persuade Alasdair to allow provisions into the town to relieve their distress. As a result of his intervention, 60 loads of corn and 100 head of cattle were supplied entirely at the Earl's own expense. This humane act, like many other involving substantial material sacrifices, was to receive no recognition when final scores were being settled.

The relative peace and security which the Earl hoped to secure at Dunluce were soon interrupted by the arrival of General Monro with a large force of Covenanting Scots at Carrickfergus. Monro's task was to root out the Irish Catholics and, believing that Antrim was a secret if not active sympathiser, he began operations by attacking the Earl's estates. He was no doubt prompted in taking this course by the Earl of Argyll, whose apprehensions were roused by reports of the intrigue concerning the eventual disposition of Kintyre. After reducing and setting fire to Glenarm, Monro proceeded to Dunluce and summoned the Earl to surrender. Lord Antrim, convinced that he had provided ample proof of his neutrality in the insurrection and therefore could submit in safety, made no attempt to defend the castle and yielded to Monro's demand. The result proved to be a disastrous blow to his expectations. The castle was looted of its contents and invested with a garrison of Covenanters under the command of Sir Duncan Campbell of Auchinbreck. Lord Antrim was taken to Carrickfergus where, however, the rigours of his confinement were much alleviated by the considerate treatment of his host and gaoler Lord Chichester, and by the "humanity and civility" of General Leslie and Lord Eglinton.

The Earl was soon able to escape from Carrickfergus with the aid of a retainer and, heavily disguised, he succeeded in crossing to England and joined his wife at Newcastle. From there he proceeded to York, where the Queen had arrived from Holland to concert plans in furtherance of her husband's cause. After discussion with the Queen and the Scottish nobles in attendance, it was agreed that Antrim should act on the authority of his original commission and employ every effort to cause a diversion in the Western Highlands. Early in 1643 Antrim accordingly set out to raise the necessary forces in Ireland. The capture and interrogation of one of his followers, however, betrayed his arrival, and as soon as he disembarked he was seized and taken to Carrickfergus.

After seven months in the strictest confinement, Antrim once again made his escape, this time by the help of George Gordon, an officer of the garrison who was later to marry Lady Rose, the Earl's sister. After many adventures, Lord Antrim at last succeeded in reaching the King at Oxford, in time to join with Montrose in finally securing the royal authority for a general rising in the north. Montrose was appointed "His Majesty's Lieutenant General of Scotland," and Antrim was confirmed in his original commission as Lieutenant General in the Highlands and Islands; and by an agreement dated 28th January 1644 the two engaged to act in concert for the advancement of the royal cause in Scotland.

Antrim's main task was the raising of forces in Ireland and the Isles for the invasion of Argyll's territories. The story of the brilliant campaign which now opened is described in greater detail in the next chapter: Antrim's failure to raise the promised number of troops; Alasdair MacCholla Chiotaich's landing with the Antrim contingent in Ardnamurchan, his capture of Mingary, and the destruction of his galleys by Argyll; the failure of his appeal to Macdonald of

Sleat; his fruitless recruiting march through Moray and his capture of Blair Castle in Atholl before he finally made his junction with Montrose. Alasdair was the ideal Highland warrior, brave, strong and fierce in battle: no strategist, but a formidable example of the Highland fighting chieftain capable of evoking the admiration and devotion of his followers to the terror and destruction of their enemies. Montrose was the ideal Highland general, above all capable of uniting the warring clans and suppressing their differences in the pursuit of a common purpose. The unbroken series of victories from Tippermuir to Kilsyth are spectacular examples of the results that could be achieved by an army of Highland warriors led by a man who understood their weaknesses as well as their strength, their rapid marching ability, their powers of endurance, and the terrifying effectiveness of their charge on the ground of their own choosing.

After Kilsyth, Alasdair received his knighthood at the hands of Montrose and departed to settle old scores in Argyll and Kintyre. Some 500 of the Antrim contingent remained with Montrose, to be slaughtered virtually to a man (and woman) after the defeat at Philiphaugh. Few escaped the ferocity of the victors' reprisals, which reached their foulest level at Dunaverty, where the garrison of about 400 surrendered to General Leslie and were murdered one by one at the insistence of Nevoy, the blood-thirsty and fanatical Covenanting divine. The infant Ranald of Sanda, while still a babe in arms, was brought safely away from the tragic scene by his nurse, and eventually grew up to inherit his family's estates.

In the meantime, Antrim had been elevated to the dignity of Marquis for his contribution to the campaign in Scotland and his strenuous though unsuccessful efforts to recruit additional forces for service in England. As a further mark of confidence, the King shortly afterwards sent him on a mission to the Queen at St Germains. After paying his duty to the Queen, who pressed him to renew his efforts in the King's service in Ireland, Antrim returned to Falmouth, bringing with him two Spanish frigates which Prince Charles was later to find useful in his escape to the Continent. On joining the King, he was at once sent to Scotland with the object of bringing back to the royal service the Irish troops which had been diverted to Kintyre. The Marquis continued active in the cause long after the King commanded Montrose to lay down his arms, and closely co-operated with Angus of Glengarry in his valiant efforts to marshal support for Montrose. It was only after receiving peremptory orders from the King that both Antrim and Glengarry, hard pressed by the Covenanting forces, were eventually obliged to cross over to Ireland. In May 1646 the King surrendered to the Scottish army at Newark, and in January 1647 he was sold to the English Parliament in exchange for its arrears of pay. From that moment, the Royalist cause was doomed.

Refusing to be discouraged by these events, Lord Antrim concentrated his efforts on healing the differences dividing the Irish Royalists and uniting them on the common ground of loyalty to the King. Since the differences were primarily religious in character, it was thought that the desirable unity could best be achieved by the presence of Prince Charles among them. The Irish Council accordingly invited Antrim to visit the Prince at St Germains and offer him assurances that, if he came to Ireland, both Catholics and Protestants would be united in their loyalty and support. The Prince and his advisers, however, were of the opinion that such a step would not serve the interests of the King at that juncture. In September 1648 Antrim returned to Ireland, convinced that all was lost; and with the execution of the King a few months later he ceased to take any further part in events.

The Marquis now found himself in greatly straitened circumstances. His vast estates, in common with those of other Royalists, were occupied by Cromwellian soldiers and English "adventurers," and he had been deprived of all revenue from them for years. The exigencies of his situation bore heavily upon his wife and no doubt contributed to her early death in November 1649. Antrim was reduced to despair and, wisely resolving to face the realities of the changed order, endeavoured to secure the best possible accommodation with his conquerors. In his favour in these efforts was the fact that, since his return from France, he had not participated in opposition to Cromwellian rule in Ireland. His negotiations in due course resulted in a relatively favourable settlement under which he was allowed an income of £500, later to be increased to £800, drawn from his own estates. He was also allotted certain lands beyond the Shannon in accordance with the established policy of "re-planting" the dispossessed Catholic and Royalist landowners. Antrim's brother Alexander, and their kinsman Sir James of Kilconway, were similarly treated, but it is not apparent if any of them ever took possession of these lands.

In 1653 the Marquis married Rose O'Neill, daughter of Sir Henry O'Neill of Shanes Castle, who was to outlive him by many years. Thereafter Antrim led a quiet and peaceful existence, making the best of his limited circumstances. He wisely refused to be drawn into Ormonde's ineffectual attempts to revive the Royalist cause. The relations between the two Marquises had always been notoriously bad, and Antrim's reluctance to co-operate was later to be used by Ormonde to obstruct the favourable settlement the former had every right to expect at the Restoration. When Charles returned to his throne in 1660, Antrim's enemies combined to represent to the monarch that he had betrayed his cause and thus forfeited the right to any favours he might reasonably regard as his due. Such was the strength and apparent substance of the charges levelled against the Marquis that the King refused to receive him and committed him instead to the Tower. Here he remained for several months, constantly pressing for a judicial investigation of his cause. In March 1661 he was released on his wife's petition—and on bail of the enormous sum of £20,000—to allow him to prepare his defence. He was afforded only six weeks in which to collect and present the evidence necessary to vindicate his honour, but it proved to be enough, for the Committee of the Privy Council to which it was referred by the King for examination in due course pronounced in his favour. At last the King recognised the motives of self-interest behind the slanderous charges, which were clearly designed for the most part to preserve the status quo in the dispossessed estates. He accordingly ordered Ormonde, the Lord Lieutenant of Ireland, to prepare a bill for the restoration of Antrim's possessions. The passage of the bill was delayed by the machinations of Ormonde and other enemies who placed every obstacle in its way, and it was not until the year 1665 that Antrim was at length re-instated in his inheritance.

His prolonged absence and consequent privations left Lord Antrim ill-equipped to overcome the financial difficulties that faced him on his return. He was besieged by creditors claiming large sums, most of which had been disbursed by him in the King's service during the Civil War. Lord Antrim was able to satisfy the more pressing of these claims, and did what he could to meet the remainder by making extensive improvements to his property. He was helped in his straitened circumstances by the kindly goodwill of his kinsmen in Scotland. The Chiefs of Sleat, Glengarry and Clanranald provided bonds of surety on his behalf, and the Marquis, to protect their interests, disponed in their favour the Long Liberties of Coleraine in the barony of Dunluce for the nominal rent of one grain of pepper annually.

In 1677 the Marquis matriculated the arms which are illustrated at the head of this chapter. It is noteworthy that the crest shown is "A Hand erected the fist thereof closed proper," thus departing from the traditional red hand holding a cross-crosslet fitchée, as used almost universally in arms of the chiefs and their cadets. The motto too is a new one in Macdonald arms, and even different from those used in older arms of Antrim.

Prior to his death, the Marquis made a settlement under which the estates were entailed in favour of his brother Alexander and his heirs, with remainder to Sir Donald Macdonald of Sleat, whom failing, to Donald Macdonald of Clanranald. The Marquis died without legitimate issue on 3rd February 1682 and was laid to rest in the family burial place at the Abbey of Bunnamairge.

Alexander, brother of the Marquis, succeeded to the title as 3rd Earl, the Marquisate having lapsed with the 2nd Earl as the destination was to heirs male of his body.

Alexander was born in 1615 and had thus come of age when his father, the 1st Earl, died. He spent the next three years travelling on the continent, as was the custom in noble families at that time, and on his return paid his respects to King Charles at York. Shortly afterwards, he threw in his lot with the Confederate Irish Catholic cause. He was appointed Colonel of a regiment under the militant Bishop MacMahon in 1642, and retained an active connection with the Confederacy until its surrender to Cromwell. Under the Cromwellian government, the lands settled on him by his father, which included the barony of Glenarm, were given to English "adventurers" and in return he was allotted 3500 acres in Connaught, in accordance with the policy of removing the rebellious native landowners as far as possible from the "plantations."

At the Restoration, after an interval of several years, Glenarm was restored to Alexander by Crown Charter. He served in King Charles' first Parliament as member for Wigan, and in 1685, after his accession to the Earldom, he became a member of the Privy Council in Ireland, and was appointed Lord Lieutenant of the County of Antrim by James II.

At the Revolution, he continued to support the cause of James II, and his regiment was at the Battle of Boyne where, however, his men disgraced themselves by taking to headlong flight. His lands were forfeited as a matter of course, and he was declared outlaw. Later the lands were restored to him under the Articles of Limerick. But the sentence of outlawry was still valid in England and, despite frequent petitions for its removal, remained in force until shortly before his death in May 1696.

Alexander married first the Lady Elizabeth Annesley, second daughter of Arthur, 1st Earl of Anglesey, without issue. By a second marriage, with Helena, third daughter of Sir John Bourke of Galway, he had: (1) Randal, who was born in 1680 and succeeded as 4th Earl; (2) a daughter, Mary, who married Henry Wells of Bembridge. He had also an illegitimate son, named Donald.

On the death of his father in 1696, Randal succeeded as 4th Earl of Antrim. His life was largely uneventful. When the Rising of 1715 broke out he was suspected of being sympathetic to the Jacobites and it was feared he might raise troops in their support. Complaints were lodged against him by enemies who coveted his estates, and he was for a time imprisoned in Dublin Castle. Glenarm was searched for arms and other evidence of treasonable intent, but nothing was found to substantiate the charges laid against him, and he was soon afterwards released. He died at an early age in 1721 and was buried in Dublin.

Randal, 4th Earl, married Rachel Skeffington, second daughter of the 3rd Viscount Massarene, by whom he had: (1) Alexander, who succeeded; and (2) Helena, who died unmarried in 1783.

Alexander, 5th Earl, was only eight years old when his father died; and following instructions in the will, he was put under the guardianship of the Dowager Lady Massarene and his uncle, the 3rd Viscount Massarene. This family were staunch Protestants and brought up the young Earl in that faith.

He sat in the Irish House of Lords in 1733, and was made a Privy Councillor, and Governor of County Antrim the same year. He was thus very much a Government servant, a circumstance which, coupled with his political and religious upbringing, influenced his decision to remain an inactive and neutral observer in the last great Rising of 1745.

Alexander married (1) Elizabeth Pennefather; (2) Anne Plunket of Dillons-town, C. Louth, by whom he had Randal William, who succeeded; (3) Catherine Meredyth of Newton, Meath, without issue.

Randal William, the 6th Earl, had three daughters, and no son, by his wife Letitia Trevor, whom he married in 1774. As the destination of his Earldom was to heirs male, it appeared as if the title would lapse. In 1785 he accordingly petitioned for the grant of a new patent of the Earldom in favour of heirs female, failing male issue. The petition was granted in 1785, and the Earl was re-created Earl of Antrim and Viscount Dunluce with destination to heirs male or female as prayed for in the petition.

In 1789 the Earl petitioned the King for the Marquisate, conferred upon his ancestor, the 2nd Earl, by King Charles I in 1644, to be revived in his favour. This also was granted but, as the Marquisate contained no provision for heirs female, and the Earl died in 1791 with three daughters and no son, the dignity lapsed once again, and the Earldom continued in the heirs female.

The 6th Earl died in 1791 and was buried at Bunnamairge in the family vault, leaving issue: (1) Anne Catherine, who succeeded as Countess, and by her marriage had a daughter who married the Marquis of Londonderry; (2) Letitia Mary, who died unmarried at an early age; (3) Charlotte, who succeeded her elder sister as Countess, and from whose marriage with Vice-Admiral Lord Mark Kerr in 1799 the later Earls are descended.

19

The Macdonalds of Clanranald

THIS GREAT BRANCH of the Clan Donald is descended from Ranald, son of John of Islay, Lord of the Isles, by Amie MacRuairi, heiress of Garmoran and the North Isles. Amie had three sons and a daughter, Mary, who married first Maclean of Duart, and secondly Maclean of Coll. The relative positions of the sons in her family are in some doubt. All the historians are agreed that the eldest was John, but his line ended with his only son, Angus, who died without issue. There remain Godfrey and Ranald. Although some place Ranald as second surviving son of Amie, others give second place to Godfrey. There are strong reasons, however, for assuming that Ranald was older than Godfrey. Their father during his lifetime made over by charter to Godfrey the lands of North Uist, and the Sleat historian says he held also the lands of Benbecula and Boisdale in South Uist. These were valuable lands; but the other parts of Amie's inheritance, which she brought to her husband, were vaster. While Godfrey had no written charter to his lands, Ranald had a charter from his father, confirmed by Robert II in 1373, for the districts of Moidart, Arisaig, Morar, Knoydart, Eigg Rum, Uist (presumably South Uist), as well as lands in Sunart, Ardgour, and Lochaber. From this allocation of the MacRuairi inheritance we assume that Ranald was the second surviving son, and Godfrey the youngest of all three. Again, Ranald took the lead in the installation of Donald of Harlaw at Eigg as Head of the Clan and Lordship and was apparently content to hold his estates from his half-brother, Donald, as his superior. That the men of the Isles disagreed for a time with this arrangement may have been caused by the influence of Godfrey, but we cannot be sure. The fact remains that the succession of Donald held firmly, and the men of the Isles must have agreed in the end. This is the one clear case we have on record of their will being ignored. That they finally gave Donald their full support is surely witnessed by their whole-hearted loyalty to him when he called out the warriors of the Isles to meet at Ardtornish for the Harlaw campaign in 1411. All the families of the old Lordship, those of Clan Donald and of many other independent clans within that confederacy, attended the hosting in such numbers that many had to be sent back to their homes.

Another pointer to the fact that Godfrey was younger than Ranald is that while Ranald died in 1389, three years after his father, Godfrey lived on for twelve years more, dying at Castle Tirrim in 1401. We know that Ranald was an old man even at the time of the ceremony in Eigg in 1386. On his death Godfrey was still active and able to occupy Ranald's lands to the exclusion of his nephews, Alan and Donald, who for a time do not appear in our records. The true Clan Ranald and Clan Gorrie were at variance for some time until the latter's power

The Arms of
RANALD ALEXANDER MACDONALD OF CLANRANALD,   24th CHIEF

Quarterly, 1st, Argent, a lion rampant Gules, armed Or; 2nd, Or, a dexter hand couped in fess ⁘
holding a cross-crosslet fitchée in pale all Gules; 3rd, Or, a lymphad her oars saltireways Sable, and
in base undy Vert a salmon naiant Argent; 4th, Argent, an oak tree Vert surmounted of an ⁘
eagle displayed Or. Above the Shield is placed a chapeau Azure furred Ermine and thereon an
Helm befitting his degree with a Mantling Gules doubled Or, and on a Wreath of these Liveries
Argent and Gules is set for Crest a triple-towered castle Argent, masoned Sable and issuing from ⁘
the centre tower a dexter arm in armour embowed grasping a sword all proper, and in an Escrol
over the same this Motto MY·HOPE·IS·CONSTANT·IN·THEE. On a compartment whereon is
this word DH'AINDEÒIN·CÒ·THEIREADHE·E are placed for Supporters two bears each having
two arrows pierced through his body all proper. ⁘ ⁘   ⁘ ⁘ ⁘ ⁘ ⁘   ⁘ ⁘ ⁘ ⁘

Lyon Register (Volume 42, Folio 21).

faded and Alan was able to resume his place as elder son of the founder, Ranald, and Donald founded the powerful Clan of Glengarry. The descendants of Donald have contested the claim of Clan Ranald as represented by the line of Alan, and the dispute has been carried right down to the present century. We shall have to deal with this in the chapter on The Chiefship. Meantime we take the seed of Alan as the true heads and Captains of Clanranald in their history as recorded in this chapter.

Alan was at Harlaw (1411) with two brothers: Donald who founded the Glengarry line, and another, Dugall, about whom nothing is known except that he fell in the battle. According to the Clanranald seanachie of 1819 Alan married a daughter of "John, the last Lord of Lorn," and had by her three sons: (1) Roderick, who fought at Harlaw and again at Inverlochy (1431) under the famous Donald Balloch; (2) Alan, on whom his father settled the estates of Knoydart; and (3) John, about whom we know nothing.

Alan, second son of Alan, had a family known in the Clan as *Sliochd Ailein Mhic Ailein*. The same Clanranald seanachie tells us that "this family existed for many years, but being almost always engaged in rebellion against the King of Scots, their power gradually sank, and they were at last nearly extirpated by the Clan Cameron. Alan was succeeded in his lands of Knoydart by his son, John. John was succeeded by Ranald and Ranald by Alan. This Alan was decerned to remove from the lands by decreet of the Lords of Council, 10th December 1501, in consequence of his being in non-entry. He is in the decreet designed 'Allan Ranaldson M'Eansone.' He nevertheless retained possession, but on the 12th July 1536 Cameron of Locheil obtained from the Crown a gift of non-entry duties falling due since the death of John, son of Alan, the first of Knoydart, who, it would appear, had entered with the Crown. Alan was succeeded by Angus, who together with the Clanranald, Glengarry and others, received a respite from the Crown, dated 26th August 1548, for the murder of Lord Lovat [presumably at Blàr Leine in 1544], and this respite was followed by a remission to the same persons dated 3rd March 1566. In both these deeds Angus is designed 'Angus M'Allane Vic Ranald de Knoydart.' This remission did not prevent Angus from again disturbing his neighbours, and letters of fire and sword were issued against him. The Clan Cameron and the Slioch Alasdair nan Coille at last nearly extirpated the whole race. Allan Cameron of Locheil obtained from the Crown a charter of their lands; he afterwards feued out to Donald M'Angus of Glengarry 60 pennies of them, and Glengarry obtained a charter of confirmation dated 3rd July 1613. In this way sank the Sliochd Allan Vic Allan."

From this brief account it is plain that the career of the Knoydart cadets of Clanranald was comparatively short, though turbulent and exciting like that of so many of their contemporaries. We include it here because the information we have about this family is not enough to warrant a separate chapter.

The same history states that Alan MacRanald died at his Castle of Tirrim in 1419 and was buried with his fathers in Reilig Orain in Iona. We know, however, that Alan was involved in the troubles which led to James I's judicial visit to Inverness in 1427; and that, unlike other chiefs who answered the royal summons on that occasion, he escaped serious punishment, for in the following year his name appears in the Exchequer Rolls as being owed a debt by the bailies of Inverness. The entry is valuable as evidence that Alan was alive as late as the year 1428.

Alan's son Roderick who succeeded was known as a vigorous chief who ably and loyally assisted Alexander, Lord of the Isles, in all the troubles of his time. He accompanied Alexander on the raid which ended in the sacking of Inverness in 1429 and Alexander's imprisonment in Tantallon Castle, while his mother, Countess of Ross, was held in the Abbey of Inchcolm in the Firth of Forth. He was also present with Donald Balloch at the Battle of Inverlochy where he contributed largely to the rout of the royal forces under the Earl of Mar. On many other occasions Roderick fought for the interests of the Lordship, even going as far as Ross and Sutherland on raids against the Mackenzies and the Earl of Sutherland who were at variance with the Lords of the Isles. He was not always successful in these efforts and it was with some difficulty that he managed to get his men home on one occasion in 1455, when he was defeated at Strathfleet by Robert, the brother of the Earl of Sutherland.

In spite of the loyal services rendered by Roderick to Alexander, the Island Lord's successor in 1469 granted to his brother, Hugh of Sleat, parts of the Clanranald patrimony in the Uists and Benbecula to the extent of the 30 merklands of Skirhough in South Uist, the 12 merklands of Benbecula and the 60 merklands of North Uist. No explanation is to be found for this encroachment by the Lord of the Isles on the Clanranald territories, but the legacy which Roderick was thus obliged to forgo contained the seeds of much future dissension amongst his successors.

Roderick is said to have died in 1481 and was succeeded by his eldest son, Alan. This man was not only notable, but in some opinions notorious. That he was a strong character is without doubt, and his activities were a frequent source of trouble to his neighbours. Like other members of Clan Donald, Alan resented the action of the Lord of the Isles in resigning the Earldom of Ross and actively participated in the risings that followed under Angus Og and Alexander of Lochalsh. After Angus Og's death Alan supported Lochalsh, who assumed the leadership of the Clan and set himself to recover possession of the earldom of which he might with some reason be deemed the rightful heir. In 1491 Alan joined with others sympathetic to the cause of Lochalsh, the Macdonalds of Keppoch and the Camerons, in a raid from Lochaber into Badenoch where they were joined by the Clan Chattan and Rose of Kilravock, with the object of harrying the lands of the Earl of Huntly. Thence they marched to Inverness and seized the Castle which they garrisoned. They then harried the lands of Alexander Urquhart of Cromarty and carried off a vast spoil—600 cows, 1000 sheep, and a large quantity of foodstuffs estimated at six hundred pounds in value.

Alan of Clanranald profited much from this raid, but Urquhart of Cromarty lost no time in bringing his complaint to the Lords of Council, and an act was passed the following year ordering Alan to indemnify him for his tenants' loss. Rose of Kilravock was similarly commanded to make restitution. There is no record that any such restitution was ever made by either of the parties. More appeals to the Council followed and the last time it is even mentioned is in a decree of March 1497, six years later, when Alan MacRuairi and others were ordered to relieve and keep scatheless Hugh Rose at the hands of the Laird of Cromarty, from which it would appear that Cromarty had reacted vigorously when the guilty parties refused to obey the summons of the Council.

The rebellion of Alexander of Lochalsh had the effect of bringing about the final forfeiture of the Lord of the Isles and the consequent fall of the Lordship itself. The Scottish Government was determined to make the Islanders loyal by demolishing the Celtic barrier which was supposed to stand between them and the throne. The fall of the Lordship of the Isles, however, had exactly the opposite effect. Distance from the central authority, and the still wider racial chasm that separated Celt from Saxon, rendered the attempt to bring the Highlanders into line with the rest of the Scottish population an exceedingly difficult task. The Scottish Government soon found out that it was much easier to deal with one Lord of the Isles, however rebellious, than with twenty chiefs gone rampantly wild.

In the altered circumstances, the Clan Ranald on the whole proved themselves more loyal and more willing to accept the new order of things than most of the Island vassals. On the occasion of the first visit of King James to the Highlands after the fall of the Lordship, Alan MacRuairi was amongst the few chiefs who then rendered him homage. Amid the turmoil of the time, the Chief of Clanranald kept the peace so far as his relations with the Government were concerned; but there are indications of differences with his neighbours, some of whom had recently been his brothers-in-arms. In the year 1496, the Lords of Council ordained Alan MacRuairi, Maclean of Duart, Ewen Cameron of Lochiel, Macdonald of Keppoch, and MacIain of Ardnamurchan, to find security to the extent of £500 each "yt ilk ane of yame shall be harmless and scaithless of utheris." There was, still further, a dispute between the Chief of Clanranald, John Cathanach of Dunnyveg, and MacIain of Ardnamurchan, respecting the lands of Sunart, a district the possession of which remained for many long years a source of contention between the families represented by these chiefs. The Lords of Council ordained that the rents of these lands were to remain meanwhile in the hands of the tenants, until the matter in dispute between the chiefs was finally settled by the King's advisers.

Alan MacRuairi from this time disappears almost entirely from view, and Ranald Ban, his son, assumed the chiefship, or active leadership, of the Clan. In 1498, when the King visited Kintyre and held court at Kilkerran Castle, Ranald Ban, being in high favour, waited on His Majesty. On the 3rd of August the King granted him, whom failing his brother, Alexander, a charter of 23 merklands in South Uist; and two days thereafter he granted him another charter of the 30 merklands of Skirhough, with the penny-lands of Garigriminish, in Benbecula, 21 merklands in Eigg, and 24 merklands in Arisaig, all of which were resigned in favour of Ranald by John, the son of Hugh of Sleat. The King also, on the same day, granted a charter to Angus Reochson MacRanald of the 12 merklands of Benbecula, 9 merklands in Eigg, 6 merklands in Arisaig, and the 14 merklands of Morar, all of which were resigned in his favour by John, the son of Hugh of Sleat. This Angus Reochson, who was a grandson of Ranald, the founder of the Clanranald family, seems to have been formerly in possession of Morar without any other title than what his grandfather may have granted. He was the head of a family which held Morar for several generations before the more modern family succeeded. It is to be observed that all the lands, for which the King now granted charters to Ranald Ban and Angus Reochson, formed part of the original patrimony of the Clanranald. John, the son of Hugh of Sleat, resigned these in their favour probably as an acknowledgement of their right to them, and wishing to be rid of lands of which, though he held a legal title, he never could obtain possession. Hugh Macdonald the seanachie asserts, no doubt correctly, that the lands in dispute between the families of Sleat and Clanranald were always kept possession of by the latter. Crown charters were of little value in those days, at least in the Highlands. The Chiefs of Sleat themselves held their lands without any title for a hundred years. The Charter of Confirmation to Hugh of Sleat in 1495 must be held to have been cancelled by the several subsequent charters granted to the Macleods, and others, of the same lands. But the King himself, almost immediately after his visit to Kintyre, cancelled all the charters he had granted to the Island Chiefs. His Majesty's policy was clearly to expel the vassals of the late Lord of the Isles from their possessions, bestow these on his own favourites, and thus check any claim that might be put forward by any of the Macdonald chiefs who aspired to the honours of the family of the

Isles. In the end of the year 1501, the King went through the form of summoning for illegal occupation of their lands a long array of the heads of the
Clanranald tribe, including their chief, Alan MacRuairi. No notice appears to
have been taken of the summons, and no proceedings, in consequence of their
contumacious conduct, seem to have been taken against the Islanders, the King
no doubt seeing now that less drastic measures than those he had contemplated
would be best.

Before these plans, however, were matured, whatever they may have been, the
Highlands and Islands were once more thrown into the vortex of rebellion, and
any attempt, therefore, to carry out the new policy must, meanwhile, be postponed. It appears that Ranald Ban, who had now become Chief of Clanranald, at
least *de facto,* did not join in the insurrection headed by Donald Dubh, though
it is highly probable that the other chieftains of the Clanranald were engaged in
it. The principal supporters of Donald were Lachlan Maclean of Duart, Torquil
Macleod of Lewis, and Ewen Cameron of Lochiel. But before the rebellion was
yet suppressed, Ranald Ban was one of those to whom letters were addressed by
Government soliciting their assistance in bringing the principal rebels, Maclean of
Duart and Lochiel, who had been forfeited, to justice. They were to "tak an
inbring the samyne, and herry, destroy, and byrne thar lands, and gif they
apprehend and tak and inbring any other heidsman, their complices, the takers
shall be rewarded."

As a reward for his services, Ranald Ban received a precept from the Crown,
dated 23rd August 1505, of the 20 merklands of Sleat with the "fortalice" of
Dunscaith, and the 60 merklands of North Uist, which had been resigned into the
King's hands by the late John, the son of Hugh of Sleat. The 80 merklands of
Trotternish were also let to Ranald for three years by the Commissioners of the
Crown, the Earl of Huntly becoming security for the payment of the rent, which
was to be according to the King's rental. The favours bestowed on Ranald Ban are
sufficient evidence of the high esteem in which he was held at court, but there is
nothing more certain than that he never reaped any benefit from the lands of
Sleat and Trotternish, for which he received so good a title. These remained in the
absolute possession of the Clan Uisdein, who continued bravely to hold them by
the strong hand. As further proof of the good behaviour of Ranald Ban from the
point of view of the Government, a commission, dated April 29th, 1508, is
given him with Andrew, Bishop of Caithness, and Alexander Macleod of Dunvegan, to let for five years to good and sufficient tenants the lands of Lewis and
of Vaternish, in Skye, forfeited by Torquil Macleod of Lewis. How he succeeded
in this post is not recorded, but it is difficult to believe, in view of the friendly
relationship in which he and his father stood with the Government, that their
reward for their loyalty and services was the common punishment for traitors.
Gregory alone is responsible for the statement, based on a mere conjecture, that
Alan MacRuairi was tried, convicted and executed in presence of the King at
Blair-Atholl in 1509, and that his son Ranald met with a similar fate at Perth in
1513. These conclusions are not warranted by reference to MacVurich, the
authority quoted by the learned author of the *History of the Highlands and
Islands.* MacVurich records in the *Book of Clanranald* that "Allan, after having
been before the King, and having received a settlement of his estate from King
James the Fourth, A.D. 1509, died at Blair-Athole." The same authority further
records that "Ranald Bane, son of Allan, having gone before the King to settle
finally the affairs which his father was not able to effect, died in the town of
Perth, A.D. 1514." It is quite clear that there is not in these words any foundation whatever for believing that, if these men did die, the one in Blair-Atholl and
the other in the town of Perth, it was in the violent manner alleged by Gregory.

In the long elegy on Alan and Ranald Ban by MacVurich, we should expect to find reference to events so tragic, if these chiefs had actually suffered death in the manner alleged, and there is not the faintest hint given.

But although MacVurich is generally accurate in other respects, he is seldom so in his dates. In a bond of manrent between Alexander, Earl of Huntly, and Ranald's son Dugall, dated at Inverness on the 15th day of March 1510, Ranald Ban is referred to as then dead. The last reference we can find to Ranald in the public records is in the year 1509, and he was dead in the beginning of the year 1510, on the authority of the bond referred to. In the former year King James IV granted a letter of protection to the Prioress Anne Maclean of Iona ordering all his lieges within the Isles, especially Ranald son of Alan MacRuairi, and other chiefs not to annoy the Prioress and other religious women, or exact from them anything on pretence of "sornyng or alms deeds" under the highest penalty. In the previous year letters of safe conduct had been directed "Ronaldo filio Allani Makrory" in favour of certain religious women then travelling in the Isles. The lands belonging to the Nunnery of Iona lay to a large extent within the bounds of the Chief of Clanranald. Alan MacRuairi appears in record for the last time on the 10th of December 1501 when he was summoned before the Lords of Council to answer for his continuing to hold the lands of Moidart, and others, without a title, and he appears to have been dead in 1503, in which year a letter is addressed by the Council to his son as Chief of Clanranald.

The character of Alan MacRuairi has been put in a somewhat unfavourable light by some writers of Highland history, who have not scrupled to lay almost every conceivable crime at his door. He is represented as a bold and reckless plunderer, whose whole life was consecrated to rapine, carrying his forays into every corner of the Highlands, far and near. The satire on Alan MacRuairi in the *Book of the Dean of Lismore* is a severe castigation on the redoubtable chief. The author announces the death of the "one demon of the Gael" as a tale to be well remembered, and in the fierce effusion which follows he traces the descent of Alan somewhat differently from MacVurich, the seanachie of the family:

> "First of all from Hell he came,
> The tale's an easy tale to tell."

With "many devils in his train," the "fierce ravager of Church and Cross" laid sacrilegious hands on Iona, and destroyed the priests' vestments and the holy vessels for the mass in the churches of St Mary and St Oran. The unconsecrated Vandal is further charged with burning the church of St Finnan in Glengarry, and, indeed, if there be but a grain of truth in the long catalogue of crimes of which he is accused, we should readily believe the Highlands were well rid of so great a curse. The character, however, ascribed to Alan MacRuairi by Red Finlay is very different from that given him by a contemporary bard. To MacVurich "Allan was a hero by whom the board of monks was maintained, and by whom the plain of the Fingalls was defended," a chief worthy of being lamented.

* * *

Alan MacRuairi was married first to Florence, daughter of Donald MacIain of Ardnamurchan, by whom he had four sons: (1) Ranald Ban, who succeeded; (2) Alexander, who with his son John of Moidart both succeeded later; (3) Ranald Og; and (4) Angus Reochson. By a second marriage to Isabella, daughter of Thomas, 4th Lord Lovat, he had Ranald Gallda, whose maternal connections were influential in elevating him at a later date to a brief and unpopular leadership of the Clan.

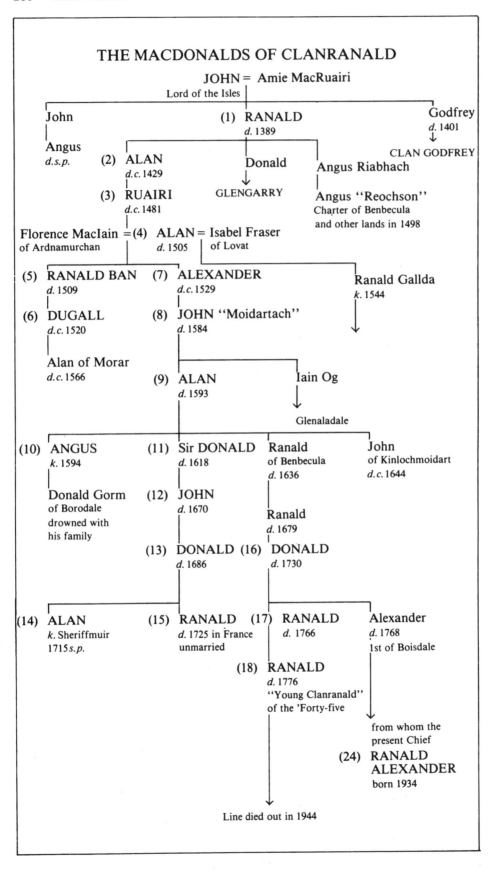

THE MACDONALDS OF CLANRANALD

JOHN = Amie MacRuairi
Lord of the Isles

John

Angus
d.s.p.

(1) RANALD
d. 1389

Godfrey
d. 1401
↓
CLAN GODFREY

(2) ALAN
d.c. 1429

Donald
↓
GLENGARRY

Angus Riabhach

Angus "Reochson"
Charter of Benbecula
and other lands in 1498

(3) RUAIRI
d.c. 1481

Florence MacIain = (4) ALAN = Isabel Fraser
of Ardnamurchan   *d.* 1505   of Lovat

Ranald Gallda
k. 1544
↓

(5) RANALD BAN
d. 1509

(7) ALEXANDER
d.c. 1529

(6) DUGALL
d.c. 1520

(8) JOHN "Moidartach"
d. 1584

Alan of Morar
d.c. 1566

(9) ALAN
d. 1593

Iain Og
↓
Glenaladale

(10) ANGUS
k. 1594

(11) Sir DONALD
d. 1618

Ranald
of Benbecula
d. 1636

John
of Kinlochmoidart
d.c. 1644

Donald Gorm
of Borodale
drowned with
his family

(12) JOHN
d. 1670

Ranald
d. 1679

(13) DONALD
d. 1686

(16) DONALD
d. 1730

(14) ALAN
k. Sheriffmuir
1715 *s.p.*

(15) RANALD
d. 1725 in France
unmarried

(17) RANALD
d. 1766

Alexander
d. 1768
1st of Boisdale

(18) RANALD
d. 1776
"Young Clanranald"
of the 'Forty-five

from whom the
present Chief

(24) RANALD
ALEXANDER
born 1934

Line died out in 1944

From the documentary evidence already cited we know that Ranald Ban had succeeded to the Chiefship in 1503 and had died by the beginning of 1510. We have seen that he kept aloof from the rebellion of Donald Dubh and in consequence enjoyed the favour of the court throughout his short reign. He was held in high esteem by his clansfolk for whom he provided the benefits of peace and protection from the turmoils that beset so many of their neighbours; and the assessment of Ranald's chiefship by the Clan historian would seem to be a fair and acceptable one when he pronounces simply that "he was good in it; for exalted was his position, and great was his sway, and good were the laws and regulations of his country during the short time he lived."

Quite a different view appears to be taken by the same historian of Dugall, Ranald's son and successor, whom he dismisses with the cryptic sentence: "Ranald left his son in the Lordship, namely Dugall, son of Ranald; but I shall leave another certain man to relate how he spent and ended his life." The references we find in the works of other seanachies are both vague and fragmentary, and at best furnish a picture of a man whose conduct rendered his chiefship extremely unpopular with the Clan. The exact reasons for his unpopularity are wrapped in obscurity, but it may be significant that one of his first acts on succeeding to the Chiefship was to enter into a bond of manrent with Alexander, Earl of Huntly. In this document, dated at Inverness on 10th March 1510, Dugall bound himself to become the Earl's man and to serve him for the rest of his life. Huntly was of all men, with the possible exception of Argyll, the most hated by the Clanranald. He had been, and was to prove over the years to come, the willing agent of the Crown in its attempt to bring the Moidart chiefs to observe the King's peace. The end of Dugall's reign was distinguished by a similar act when on 25th May 1520 he bound himself in manrent to Sir John Campbell of Cawdor, whom he promised to serve against all persons saving the King and the Earl of Huntly. The period in between was marked by serious dissensions amongst the branches of the Clan, and it is clear that the troubles were caused almost entirely by Dugall's own conduct. The situation was not improved when as a consequence the Earl of Argyll was appointed Lieutenant of the lands of Moidart, Arisaig and Morar.

All authorities seem to agree that Dugall's conduct became quite unacceptable to the Clan, and that he had eventually to be removed from the Chiefship. Moreover the whole family must have rendered themselves obnoxious, because the sons were permanently excluded from the succession. It is believed that Dugall died in 1520 or shortly thereafter, but even the manner of his death is shrouded in mystery. According to a tradition related by Fr. Charles Macdonald in his book on Moidart, Dugall was the victim of a plot by his cousins John of Moidart and his brother Alan aimed at securing the succession for their father Alexander, Dugall's uncle. To accomplish their purpose they enlisted the aid of a notorious scoundrel known as *Alan nan Corc,* who with his gang waylaid and brutally murdered Dugall as he was making his way from Arisaig to Castle Tirrim.

Even the marriage or marriages of Dugall are surrounded by a lack of documentary evidence. Father Charles, the priest of Moidart, states that he married a daughter of Cameron of Lochiel by whom he had a son, Alan, who was removed to safety after his father's death to Cameron country where he was brought up until of age. His attempts to regain his heritage failed, but he was given lands in Morar in compensation. Gregory on the other hand says that Dugall had married the daughter of Sir Alexander of Lochalsh, whose other daughter and co-heiress had married Alexander, 6th of Glengarry. Another source states that he married a daughter of Norman O'Beolan of the clerical family of Applecross. That he did marry and have legitimate issue is not questioned. Four sons survived him: (1) Alan, from whom the important family of Morar descend; (2) Lachlan; (3) Alexander; and (4) Ranald, from whom the family of Bornish descend. We have seen that the land of Morar with others were given by charter in 1498 to Angus Reochson MacRanald, having been resigned in his favour by John, son of Hugh, 1st Chief of Sleat. Alan son of Dugall succeeded to Morar in 1538 on the non-entry of the family of Angus Reochson, which had died out by then.

Alexander, 7th of Clanranald, succeeded quite legally by virtue of the charters of 1498 in favour of Ranald Ban, his heirs male with reversion to Alexander, his brother. He seems to have been a successful and popular chief within his Clan, in spite of the fact that, like his deceased nephew Dugall, he entered into a bond of manrent with Sir John Campbell of Cawdor. This bond is interesting as for the first time the "title" or name Captain of Clanranald appears in writing in the form "Alexander M'Alan, Chaptayne off the Clanranald and apyerand air of Ilanterim." There is no doubt that the name "Captain of Clanranald" is the same as "Chief of Clanranald," and has been used as such all down the years of their history to this day. "Captain" could be regarded as synonymous with the old office of "Toiseach." In olden times there could be a Toiseach as well as a chief, when a leader was required to command the clan in battle as the chief's deputy. Clanranald always made sure they had a chief of whom they approved for purposes of peace at home as well as leadership in war. We have seen this power of the clansmen at work in Dugall's time, and will see it again in the case of John of Moidart, Alexander's son and successor.

Although little is known on record or otherwise of the life of Alexander, 7th Chief, one can assume that his life was comparatively peaceful. He was thrice married and raised a large family. By a girl called Dorothy, daughter of one of the tenants of Kinlochmoidart, he had John "Moidartach" who succeeded him in the chiefship. Of his other offspring, one only need be recorded here; a daughter Catherine who married Donald Gruamach, 4th of Sleat, whose son Donald Gorm was 5th Chief of that line.

Alexander died about the year 1530. The succession now opened to whoever could claim and maintain the leadership of the Clan. The children of Dugall having been excluded for all time, the representation would naturally fall to the lot of one of Alexander's sons, failing whom their uncle, Ranald Gallda, half-brother of the deceased Alexander, was next in line. Why all the other sons of Alexander were by-passed is a mystery, and we can only assume that the strength of character and war-like qualities of John of Moidart were sufficient to overcome all obstacles. From the start he had been judged illegitimate; but even that difficulty was overcome later when he was expressly legitimated by the Privy Council and Signet on the 15th January 1531.

John of Moidart began his reign as chief in the middle of a rebellion. The prime cause of this revolt, headed by Alexander of Dunnyveg, was the Act of 1528 annulling all the charters given to the chiefs during the minority of the King. Many of the chiefs rallied to the standard, John amongst them. The rebellion petered out, however, and in May 1530 nine of the principal rebels sent in offers of submission to the King by the agency of Hector Maclean of Duart. Remission of their misdeeds was freely given on condition that they appeared in person before the King in Edinburgh before the 20th June of that year. None seemed to be willing to be first to comply, and none did, in spite of the offer of royal protection and safeguard, reinforced by an offer from Argyll of four Campbell hostages guaranteeing their safe return home. That move having failed, the

King decided to lead an expedition in person against the rebels, whereupon Alexander, realising his danger, hastened to give in his submission. His example was followed by John of Moidart and the other chiefs, and in the summer of 1531 they all received the royal pardon upon providing sureties for their future good behaviour.

For some years thereafter John of Moidart remained high in the royal favour. In 1532 he was granted a charter under the Great Seal of the 27 merklands of Moidart, the 30 merklands of Arisaig, 21 merklands in Eigg, and the 30 merklands of Skirhough in Uist. It was the first of many charters granted during this period to various members of the Clanranald family, but although the terms of some of these charters were the cause of considerable dissension within the clan, it is quite certain that John of Moidart retained the superiority over all the lands throughout his reign.

A relatively long period of peace in the Highlands was broken in 1539 when Donald Gorm of Sleat launched his attempt to restore the Lordship. Although the insurrection was short-lived and ended with Donald Gorm's tragic death at Eilean Donan, it had unfortunate results for John of Moidart and his clan. In order to prevent similar efforts in the future, the King resolved to visit the Isles and deal with the chiefs in person. The composition of the large armada which accompanied him on his progress through the Isles is dealt with in another chapter, where we have seen that John of Moidart was one of a number of western chiefs seized by the King and imprisoned in Edinburgh Castle. This enforced absence of John threw the Clanranald into some confusion. Although they regarded John as their rightful head and Captain, it was nevertheless necessary for the Clan to have an active leader. There were many claimants among the descendants of Alan MacRuairi, each one of whom might well believe he had as good a right as the man who was eventually installed in the office. This was

stle Tirrim in Moidart, the rincipal seat of Clanranald il 1715 when it was burned down and deserted

Ranald Gallda, Alan MacRuairi's son by the daughter of Thomas, 4th Lord Lovat. The latter's successor Hugh, together with the Earl of Huntly, saw in Ranald the opportunity to rid themselves once and for all of the disturbing influence of John of Moidart in their neighbourhood. The Government supported their decision, and to lend the plan a semblance of legality a charter was taken out in Ranald's name, on the 14th December 1540, of the 27 merklands of Moidart and the 24 merklands of Arisaig which had been held by the King ever since the death of Alan MacRuairi.

Backed by this parchment and the presence of Lovat and Huntly, Ranald Gallda arrived at Castle Tirrim and assumed the position of Chief. He was at once given by the King the 21 merklands of Eigg, which had been held by the Crown since the death of Dugall, 6th Chief. The clansmen were astonished by these proceedings, and not at all happy to be thus forced to accept one who was incapable of commanding their loyalty and respect. The behaviour of Ranald during his short reign as Chief was to say the least undignified, if traditional accounts of his meanness are to be believed. The real reason for his unpopularity was, of course, that he had been chosen not by the Clan, but by outsiders unfriendly to them, and was sponsored by a Government whose only aim was to disrupt their way of life and use the age-old expedient of "divide and rule." It is abundantly clear that Ranald Gallda was unable to make either his manners or his methods acceptable to the clan, and that he could never take the place of the freely chosen Chief kept prisoner in Edinburgh.

Ranald Gallda's reign was cut short by a change in Government policy following the King's death in 1542. The Regent Arran was suspicious of the aspirations of Argyll and deemed it wise to release the imprisoned chiefs whose presence in the North might act as a curb on his growing power. John of Moidart was accordingly set free and directly shaped his course for Castle Tirrim.

John was received joyfully by his Clan, and Ranald Gallda had to flee from their wrath and find refuge with his mother's fold in the East. John lost no time and began at once to gather his forces to give vent to the pent-up fury of the long months of his imprisonment.

The western clans were united under John in the expedition he now mounted against the territories of Ranald Gallda's relatives. Those who took part were the minor branches of the Clanranald: Alan of Morar, son of the murdered Dugall, Angus of Knoydart, and Alasdair of Glengarry. Ranald of Keppoch, Ewen Cameron of Lochiel, and Alasdair MacIain of Ardnamurchan joined these, the whole making a considerable army of seasoned warriors. The regions of Abertarff and Stratherrick in the Fraser country were overrun and, not content with this success, they harried Urquhart and Glenmoriston, occupying the Castle of Urquhart for a time. Bishop Lesley was of opinion that they intended occupying these lands permanently; but John was too wise a leader to imagine he could do more than carry out a successful raid on the lands which for so long had been the object of the plundering attentions of the western clans. The reaction to the raid came swiftly. Lovat and the Laird of Grant gathered their forces for a counter attack. Some writers say that this was in support of the claims of Ranald Gallda and was a serious attempt to instal him once more in Tirrim as Chief. This is unlikely, as the harrying of their lands in such a cruel manner was alone sufficient justification for their action. To make sure they had sufficient forces for their attack, they invoked the aid of the Royal Lieutenant of the North, Huntly, who needed no excuse to suppress his turbulent neighbours. Huntly raised his vassals, amongst them the Clan Chattan, and with a powerful force followed the invaders, who wisely retreated to their fastnesses in the West.

Gregory says that Huntly was able to penetrate the wilds of Moidart and instal Ranald Gallda once more in Castle Tirrim. It is difficult to believe that John, with his powerful clan and its allies, would have tamely left Huntly thus to occupy his headquarters without resistance. There is, however, no record of an engagement, and it seems certain that the punitive expedition got no farther than Inverlochy, punishing the Clan Cameron and Keppoch, and then retired. Bishop Lesley put it neatly by saying that "the Erle merching forduart with his companie maid thame [the rebels] sone to dislodge and to flie in thair awan cuntrey apoun the west seis, quhair Lawland men cuid haif no acces unto thame, and so placed the Lorde Lovat and the Laird of Grant in thair awin landis. Sua haiffing done for the moist parte that thing he come for, returnit." It is obvious, however, that Huntly did not achieve the "moiste parte" of the desired object of his expedition as the events which followed amply prove.

Huntly now retired up the Great Glen satisfied that he had done his work. On reaching Glen Spean and its junction with Glen Roy he took the road directly east on the short route via Laggan to his own country, while Lovat and the Laird of Grant made their way up the Great Glen towards their own lands in Glenmoriston and Beauly. That they risked a division of their forces at this stage suggests that they were confident that John of Moidart's clansmen had been broken and scattered. Huntly's way home was through comparatively safe country into Badenoch, but it was far otherwise with Lovat and Grant. They still had to traverse the unfriendly territory of the Glengarry Macdonalds, with a wide stretch of wild country to the north of Loch Lochy where a Highland army could march quickly and unobserved to a chosen point from which it might swoop upon the enemy below. This would give the attackers that advantage of the brae (*Cothrom a' Bhràigh*) so often sought by Highland warriors.

This is just what happened. John had followed the movements of Huntly and his allies from a safe distance ready to pounce as soon as the opportunity offered itself. When he saw Huntly break away from the main body, he swept quickly round to the north to cut off Lovat's retreat. The scene was now set for the battle, popularly known as *Blar-na-leine* (the battle of the Shirts), so called from the fact that the clansmen threw off their superfluous clothing and other encumbrances and fought in their shirts and kilts. (Other authorities state that the name should be *Blar-na-leana,* from the Gaelic word meaning a swampy meadow, a description which exactly fits the flat ground at the head of Loch Lochy where the battle was fought).

John of Moidart had with him Alasdair of Glengarry, Alan of Morar, Angus of Knoydart, Ranald of Keppoch, Ewen Cameron of Lochiel and Alasdair MacIain of Ardnamurchan. If these had called up all their followers for this expedition it would have made a very large force; but the total strength led by John of Clanranald has been estimated at about 600 men. Lovat had with him the Grants of Glenmoriston led by young Patrick Grant, and the Frasers of his own Clan, amounting according to Fraser records to about 400 men in all. The young Master of Fraser joined his father just before the battle commenced. Lovat had left him at home with strict orders to stay there, but, owing to the taunts of his stepmother who perhaps wished him dead so that her own son could succeed to the Lovat estates, he set out to join his clansmen. The young Master had just recently returned home from France, well-educated and a promising youth. Perhaps he decided he could not stay idly at home while his father and Clan were risking their lives. He accordingly left with twelve chosen men and reached the scene of the battle in time to share his father's fate.

The brave Lovat could have fled with his men eastwards although they would be passing through hostile Glengarry country. But he disdained to flee and prepared for battle, posting a detachment under one of his lieutenants called Bean Cleireach to guard his way of escape in the event of retreat.

The battle opened with the customary shower of arrows from both sides. If there were fire-arms history does not tell whether they were used in the battle. It resolved itself into the age-old slogging match of cut and thrust with the sword and axe. The battle raged all afternoon and at the end of the day the meadow was littered with the dead and dying. No quarter was asked or given. Traditional accounts tell many tales of the bravery of warriors on both sides. Ranald Gallda, although not the young man spoken of by some, fought bravely to the death. Lovat too and his son fell with over two hundred of their men. On the Clan-ranald side casualties were also very heavy, but the figure of eight survivors given in traditional accounts is obviously much exaggerated. In the year following the battle the membership of Donald Dubh's Council includes all the Clan Donald leaders with the exception of Keppoch. This is recorded in a document dated 5th August 1545 and it is also there stated that "the Captain of ClanRanald the last yeir ago in his defence slew the Lord Lowett, his son and air, his thre brother, with xiii. score of men." This account given by the victorious army is unlikely to be under-estimated. The Master of Lovat fell severely wounded and died of his wounds three days later a prisoner in the hands of Lochiel, much lamented by both sides. The bodies of Lovat, his son and that of Ranald Gallda were conveyed eventually to the Priory of Beauly where an inscription, now no longer legible, is on record in the Fraser MS which reads: *Hic jacet Hugo Dominus Fraser de Lovat, qui fortissime pugnans contra Reginalderios occubuit Julii 15 1544.*

The news of the battle caused great consternation to the Government, and especially to Huntly who must have felt he was in a measure to blame in leaving Lovat and Grant at Glen Spean, when such a bold warrior as John of Moidart was following closely on his heels. Once more he invaded and harried the lands of Keppoch and Lochiel, but failed to penetrate the Rough Bounds of Moidart beyond which the arch-enemy had retired with other leaders of Clanranald. Huntly returned to Ruthven, no doubt thinking he had accomplished his object, but his expedition was a failure and succeeded only in provoking further excesses. Keppoch, Lochiel and Glengarry retaliated at once by invading the already spoiled lands of Urquhart and Glenmoriston, from which they carried away large quantities of spoil in two successive incursions.

John of Moidart took no part in these raids. He had retired to his island dominions where he was preparing to extend his active support to Donald Dubh, who had escaped from his long confinement and was now marshalling his adherents in a second attempt to regain his inheritance. The story of this luckless enterprise has been told in another part of this work, and here it is only necessary to be reminded of the part played in the rising by Clanranald. A large proportion of the army that assembled at Knockfergus in August 1545 was led by the Chief of Clanranald and both he and his brother Ruairi, the Dean of Morvern, took leading rôles in the newly constituted Council of the Isles. Ruairi was one of the commissioners chosen by the Council to carry its proposals to the English King. He had begun his ecclesiastical career as Rector of Kilchoan in Ardnamurchan, to which were later added the parishes of Arisaig and Knoydart. He was then promoted to the Deanery of Morvern and afterwards elected to the Bishopric of the Isles in opposition to Roderick Maclean, the Regent Arran's nominee. As able with the sword as with the pen, he fought with his brother at Blar-na-leine, and then joined the seventeen chiefs who had rallied around Donald Dubh in his efforts to resurrect the ancient Lordship of the Isles and Earldom of Ross. The deliberations at Knockfergus, and the eventual resolutions reached there by the

Island Council, bear the stamp of the Dean's astuteness and learning, and his skill as a negotiator is amply manifested by the successful outcome of his mission to the English Court. Not surprisingly, Ruairi's part in these proceedings antagonised the Regent, and Roderick Maclean, brother of Duart, was preferred and appointed Bishop of the Isles. The Dean remained in Ireland after the death of Donald Dubh and lived on the bounty of his "maister" King Henry of England who, in response to an appeal addressed to him in May 1546, used his influence to restore him to his native country. He was granted a remission under the Privy Seal for a long catalogue of crimes including "treasonably passing to Ingland and Ireland, and inbringing of Inglishmen within the Ilis and uthir partis within the realm, and for burning, heirschip and destruction." Ruairi took no further part in politics and once more became a loyal subject, spending the remainder of his life quietly as Rector of Islandfinnan in his native Moidart.

After the failure of Donald Dubh's rising, and the sad death in Drogheda in Ireland of that unfortunate scion of the Isles, John and his clan returned home to Moidart. The Regent Arran had not forgotten John's long list of crimes in which he had been implicated before Donald Dubh's rebellion. This last act of treason could in no wise be ignored and he was summoned by an Act of Parliament on the 7th September 1545 to appear and answer for his crimes. He was not alone in this summons, but whoever else obeyed it is clear that John certainly did not. The summons was repeated several times and John continued his defiance. Parts of his estates had already been given by charter to others, the most recent being 30 merklands in South Uist granted to James Macdonald of Dunnyveg. None of these measures had any effect because John continued to hold his heritage by the sword.

After the departure of Donald Dubh in 1545 James of Dunnyveg, head of the Clann Iain Mhoir, was chosen to carry on the struggle to reinstate the old Lordship, but he had not the solid following of the Islesmen. The Chief of Clanranald was among the few who supported his claim. James relied on English help and when that failed it was clear his cause was lost, to the great disappointment of John of Moidart. If James had succeeded all would have been well for John in the security of the revived Lordship, but now he had still further antagonised the Regent. Other factors, however, worked in John's favour. The Regent, desirous of gaining all the backing he could find in his struggle against the aspirations of England, withdrew all the summonses against John and his fellow-rebels, and peace returned to the Isles for a space. Affairs in the Scottish kingdom once more had repercussions in the West. War was declared with England in the summer of 1547 and Regent Arran summoned all the Highland chiefs with their clans to meet at Fala Muir under the Royal Standard. Argyll and Huntly obeyed the call to arms, but few of the western clans took part, least of all the Clanranald. John had no intention of taking his men so far from home into unfriendly country to do battle against the English invaders. He knew well that, whether the battle was lost or won by Regent Arran, he would be fortunate indeed to keep his freedom. He had good cause to fear that some pretext would be found for reviving the old summons which had failed. As it happened, however, the defeat at Pinkie in September 1547 so weakened the power of the Regent that he was obliged to make his peace with the rebellious chiefs, of whom John of Moidart was the most guilty. A Special Act was passed fully pardoning John and the other leaders of his Clan for "remaining and abyding at hame fra our Soverane Ladyis oist and army, devisit and ordanit to convene upon Fala-mure . . . and for ye slaughter of ye Lord Lovet and his complices." This pardon, granted in August 1548, was to last for nineteen years, but it only meant an uneasy peace between John and the Government. For a few years he remained free from molestation by the Government and was thus able to withstand the attacks he continued to suffer at the hands of his jealous neighbours. These and other troubles in the Highlands brought the Regent to Aberdeen in the summer of 1552, where he summoned the chiefs to meet him. Many failed to respond, among them John of Moidart. Arran went on to Inverness hoping it might be a better place for the recalcitrant chiefs to attend. Memories of their treatment on a previous occasion in that town were too painful, however, and all the Island chiefs ignored the call, although some of the mainland chiefs submitted.

The Regent was now at a loss to find a way of bringing John, the arch-rebel, to heel. None of his train seemed willing to undertake an expedition into the Rough Bounds in search of the cunning John. Huntly had tried more than once and failed. There remained Argyll as the next best in line, and he was induced to undertake the thankless task. He was more confident than Huntly and promised to deliver John to the Privy Council in person. Argyll began by using the weapon of duplicity with fair promises of safe-conduct, remissions, and all the arts of diplomacy of which he was the master. None of these blandishments had any effect. John knew the Campbell methods too well, and remained defiant. Argyll had perforce to retire from the unequal contest, and the Clanranald continued to live in peace in their fastnesses, while the Government was concerned with other matters which commanded its attention.

In the autumn of 1553 there happened an incident so strange that one is at a loss to understand how it came about. One can only assume that a period of peace, undisturbed by letters of summons or force of arms, had softened the heart of the rebel chief and persuaded him of the wisdom of reaching an accommodation with the Government. On the 11th September 1553 we find John of Moidart making friends with Huntly. Our seanachies describe this unlikely event thus:

> By whatever means it may have been brought about, the spectacle of the Chief of Moidart falling on the neck of George, Earl of Huntly, at "Rovan in Badzenocht," on the 11th day of September, 1553, is both edifying and affecting. There and then, it was "appointit, concordit, and fynallie agreit betwixt ane nobill and potent Lord George, Erle of Huntlie, lord Gordon and Badzenocht, leftenent generall of the North and honorabill mene Jhone Mudyart Capitane of the Clane Ronald and his son Allan, thair Kyne, freindis, allys, and pertakkaris," to mutually forget and forgive. The Earl on his part remits and forgives the Clanranald all offences, wrongs, and disobedience in the past, "and speciall the last offence and brak maid be them, their freindis, allis, and pert takkaris, upon his gud freind, the Lord Lowett." John Moidartach, his son, and their friends, promise, on their part, to keep good rule within their bounds, and to remain true to the Earl. They further promise "faythfullie to do thar wtter deligens and laubor to cause entir and bring in the handis of the said Erll Donald Gormesson, betwixt the dait heirof and aucht days before Hallomes nixt witht all udir capitans and chieftenis within the North illis to pass to the Queen's grace, my lord guvernoris and Counsell." This, it must be admitted, is a somewhat large order. Whether or not the Chief of Moidart, now on the side of law and order, made any attempt to accomplish the herculean task of presenting before the "Queenis grace" Donald Gorme Macdonald of Sleat, and all the "udir capitans and chieftenis within the North illis," certain it is that none of them appeared either there or before "my Lord Guvenor."

This extraordinary transaction between two chiefs so diametrically opposed in aims and outlook can only be explained by assuming that John had absorbed some of the devious methods of his enemies, Argyll and Huntly. He must have known that his fair promises to bring Donald Gormson of Sleat and "all the other captains and chieftains of the North Isles" to come in and make their obeisance to the "Queenis grace" could never be kept. Huntly must have been a simple soul if he gave any credence to these promises given by one so notoriously in disgrace with the Government. It was a foregone conclusion that John could not fulfil this solemn undertaking.

In 1554 a change of Government took place which made a great difference in that body's attitude towards the recalcitrant chiefs, and especially towards John of Moidart. Any disturbances which had taken place between 1552 and this date were of a minor nature, but most of them were laid at the door of John of Moidart and his Clan. Buchanan's *History* in the following century singles out John as the arch-rebel of that time, calling him "John Muderach, Chief of the Family of the M'Reynolds, a notorious robber [who] had played many foul and monstrous pranks."

The new Regent was a very different person to her predecessor, Arran. She was a strong-minded woman who disliked any form of opposition to her plans and chose to attack rebellion at its strongest point to intimidate the others. Huntly was ordered to attack Moidart by land, and the Earl of Argyll by sea. Huntly mustered a large force of his own followers and the Clan Chattan, with some Lowland cavalry, and directed his march westwards towards the Rough Bounds of Moidart. At Abertarff at the western end of Loch Ness he halted. The Lowland cavalry had had enough of rough country already and refused to proceed any further. They had some knowledge of the sort of terrain they had still to traverse before coming to grips with the enemy. The Clan Chattan too were sullen, discontented and on the verge of mutiny, bitterly resentful of Huntly's involvement in the death of their Chief four years earlier. Huntly saw the expedition was doomed to failure even if he could have induced his troops to advance westwards.

During this time John had not been idle, and had taken up a strong defensive position at the head of Loch Moidart where the narrow pass leads over from Lochshielside. As no attack seemed to develop from that flank, he retired to his Castle Tirrim and awaited events. Argyll duly arrived with his fleet in the Loch, and finding a direct assault on that fortress impossible, contented himself with bombarding it from two angles, from under the cliffs of Dorlin and from the sea. John held out and Argyll withdrew, either because of the hopelessness of the task, or having expended all his ammunition in vain. The solid walls of the Castle defied the cannon, which in any case were not of heavy calibre.

The Queen-Regent was furious with Huntly, would listen to none of his excuses and threw him into prison. His enemies would have liked his execution, but he paid dearly for his failure. He was obliged to renounce the Earldoms of Mar and Moray recently bestowed upon him, and was exiled to France for five years. The latter part of his sentence, however, was remitted for the sum of five thousand pounds, and he was released from confinement the following year.

Mary of Lorraine was determined to reduce John to obedience and in the summer of 1555 she chose the Earl of Atholl as her instrument of justice. He duly collected a large force composed mostly of Lowlanders and arrived at Abertarff only to encounter the same disaffection amongst his troops that had foiled Huntly's expedition the previous year.

In the face of these difficulties, and believing any attempt to reduce him by force would fail, the Earl resolved to open up friendly negotiations with the rebel chief. Upon being informed of his resolution, the Queen-Regent dispatched a messenger with "cloiss writtings" to the Earl and John of Moidart, the purport of which appears to have been approval of Atholl's suggestions. The letter to John himself must have been considered by that Chief as a guarantee of Her Majesty's good faith, containing, as it no doubt did, assurances of forgiveness and protection. The Chief, agreeing to the terms offered by the Earl, and being satisfied with the assurances given, agreed to accompany Atholl, with his two sons and several of his kinsmen, to the Queen's presence at Perth. The Queen was graciously pleased to receive the Chief with great kindness and affability. But while she had him in her power she was unwilling, even at the risk of violating her pledge, to set so dangerous a rebel at liberty. The Chief accordingly, with his two sons and kinsmen, were ordered to be kept in ward, some in the town of Perth, and others in the Castle of Methven, during Her Majesty's pleasure. The conduct of the Queen in thus breaking faith with the Chief is deserving of the severest censure, as it certainly justifies the conduct of the Chief in breaking ward, as he did, as soon as the opportunity came. Besides being conduct unworthy of a Queen, it was foolish and short-sighted policy. After a short period of confinement, John of Moidart and his companions by some means effected their escape and returned home to be, if possible, greater rebels than ever. The Queen vowed the direst vengeance on the head of the rebel Chief, but the imperturbable John, who was not in the least dismayed by her threats, awaited with calmness the progress of events.

Mary appears to have taken time to mature her plans, for it was not till the following year, in the month of July, that she came north to Inverness, when she was accompanied by a formidable train of Privy Councillors. Overawed by the presence of Queen and Council, many of the rebel chiefs hastened to give in their submission, but John of Moidart, "once bitten, twice shy," sullenly stood aloof.

The Queen was greatly enraged at the continued obstinacy of John of Moidart, but she could hardly have expected the ready submission of a chief she had treated so harshly, and with whom she had so flagrantly broken her plighted faith. Force having already so often failed, it was equally vain to try diplomacy, nor did the repeated declarations of treason against him, and the confiscation of his patrimony, affect the position of the triumphant chief. So long as the Clanranald remained loyal to him, he had nothing to fear. The tide of charters which still continued to flow, and by which he was to have been overwhelmed, only intensified the loyalty of his followers. And charters were now the only weapons left to the government wherewith to punish the rebel chief. In 1558 some of his lands in South Uist were included in a charter to James Macdonald of Dunnyveg. By an agreement dated at Glasgow in July 1563, other lands in South Uist were sold by Farquhar MacAlister to James Macdonald of Dunnyveg for 1000 merks Scots. This transaction was immediately thereafter confirmed by a charter to Archibald, son and heir of James Macdonald, from Queen Mary. About the same time, the lands of Moidart, Arisaig and Eigg were granted by the Queen to Alan, the son of Ranald Gallda. In this way the lands of John of Moidart were disposed of by the Government, but no greedy robber baron of the Lowlands laying his rapacious hands on the lands of the Church held them with a firmer grip than did John of Moidart the patrimony of the Clanranald, in spite of the profusion of charters.

The upheaval caused by the Reformation struggle was not without its effect on the Highlands. As a religious movement indeed it may be said to have been almost entirely confined to the Lowlands, but the keenness of the controversy had the effect of diverting for a time the attention of those in authority from the state of the Celtic population. Very few of the chiefs affected to accept the new doctrines, and none clung more tenaciously to the old than John of Moidart and the whole body of Clanranald. From the well-known attachment of the young Queen to the old religion, it may be presumed that she was not disposed to harass unduly so strong a supporter of the old order of things as the Moidart Chief. The exact relations between him and the governing power are not now easily defined. They appear not to have been friendly on either side, though perhaps less strained than they were during the regime of the late Queen. The precept of remission in his favour in March 1566 for his not joining the royal army convened at Fala Muir in 1547, is an indication of a change of attitude on the part of the Government. This instrument of remission is evidence, besides, of the unity of the different branches of the Clanranald under their Chief, containing as it does the names of Alan of Morar, son of the deposed Chief, Angus of Knoydart, and Angus of Glengarry. The sending of "ane boy with cloiss writtingis" to John in May of the same year may certainly be construed in more ways than one. The probability is that the "boy" came on a friendly errand, and that the "cloiss writtingis" contained friendly proposals on the part of the Queen. In any case it is certain that John of Moidart continued in the same attitude of dogged resistance, and that in the following year one of the most serious questions that agitated those in authority was "be quhat meane may all Scotland be brocht to universal obedience and how may Johne Moydart and McKy be dantonit." What acts of atrocity the Chief of Moidart had recently perpetrated to have earned for him the pre-eminent distinction of being second to "all Scotland" in the measure of his disobedience, history does not record.

It is indeed most remarkable that from the death of the Queen Dowager in 1560 to the end of his life, there should be only one or two meagre notices of him in the public records. Though the peace of the Isles was seriously disturbed during that period by internal dissensions arising out of incessant feuds between neighbouring chiefs, we do not find that John of Moidart was involved in any of these. He seems to have confined his attention more to the defence of his mainland territory, and to have been busily engaged keeping at bay the Grants, the Mackenzies, and the Clan Chattan. That he was an utter terror to these clans is evident from their repeated appeals for Government help, and the many bonds of mutual defence into which they entered against the Clanranald. In a summons in name of the boy King James, dated 1st March 1567, the Clan Chattan and Clan Mackenzie are charged to assist John Grant of Freuchie against "divers wikkit personis" of the Clanranald. In a bond dated 27th July 1570, Colin Mackenzie, heir apparent of Kintail, binds himself "be the fayth and trewth" of his body to "assist, fortifie, manteine and defend" John Grant of Freuchie against the Clanranald. These and similar entries in the public records testify to the sense of insecurity which John of Moidart had inspired in the breasts of his neighbours, and the feeling of awe with which he was regarded by them.

From this year of 1570 we hear little more of John's doings until his death in 1584. Fourteen years in the life of this great chief without some account of "monstrous pranks" on his part seems very strange. We can only conclude that as old age crept on he turned his thoughts to higher things. Indeed the seanachie of the Clan records that he spent "the end of his life godly and mercifully. He erected a church at Kilmorie in Arasaig, and another at Kildonan in Eigg, and left funds to erect a chapel at Howmore in Uist, where his body was buried. . . ." Fr. Charles MacDonald in his *Moidart, or among the Clan Clanranalds,* has more to say about his interment, and it is a very different story. As Fr. Charles was priest of Moidart and steeped in the history of that region and the Clanranald, we include his version here if only for the sad commentary it provides on the respect awarded to departed greatness:

> He died at Castle Tirrim in 1584 having ruled the clan for fifty-four years. His body was conveyed to Eilean Fhionnan and buried in the church on that island. He was the last Chief of the Clanranalds buried in the same spot, most of his successors preferring Hoghmore in Uist as their final resting place. It is with regret that one has to add that the remains of this illustrious chief were in course of time disturbed and thrown out by some insignificant families who had the audacity to claim this part of the church as a proper place to intrude their own nothingness. . . . Old Moidart men aver that the Chief's skull and part of his bones were to be seen in that ghastly heap under the altar for many years until they were collected and committed once more to the earth in the little chapel used by the Kinlochmoidart family as their burial-ground. The body originally rested under one of those beautiful Iona stones with a sword carved upon it immediately in front of the altar.

The career of this Chief is outstanding in that he reigned for fifty-three years and died in his bed. That his life was turbulent and caused much disquiet to his neighbours and the Government cannot be denied. In spite of all efforts to subdue him he successfully defied a long succession of Scottish rulers and kept his lands intact by sheer strength of arms and the loyalty of his clan. He was truly a remarkable man who possessed in ample measure the outstanding qualities which entitle him to rank with the greatest of the Chiefs of Clan Donald.

John of Moidart married at least three times and had several sons. By Margaret MacIain of Ardnamurchan he had Alan, his successor. By the daughter of Alan of Knoydart he had (1) John Og, progenitor of the Glenaladale family; (2) Donald Gorm, tacksman of Griminish in 1610, whose son, Angus, was bailie of South Uist in 1619; (3) Ruairi Og, who left two sons, Donald and John. By a daughter of Neil, son of Charles (family unknown), he had (1) Ruairi Dubh; (2) Ranald, whose son, John, became Rector of Island Finnan; (3) Ian Dubh; and (4) Angus. The Clanranald History of 1819 states that John Moidart married, as his third wife, Penelope Erskine, by whom he had a daughter who married John Stewart of Appin. The date of this marriage is given as 1555.

Alan, John Og, Ruairi, Angus and Donald Gorm are all mentioned in the instrument of 1566 which remitted them and their father for their non-appearance at the hosting of Fala Muir in 1547.

Alan, son of John, now succeeded to the Chiefship in 1584. Owing to the long reign of his father, he was at this time at least fifty years of age. He had been present at the battle of Blar-na-leine in 1544, and must then have been about twenty years of age. With his father he received remission for this slaughter in 1548. From then on the history of this young chief runs parallel with his father's activities, which we have seen centred round his efforts to retain the independence of his clan in defiance of successive governments. Alan was much more involved in family differences, however, and there are certain episodes in his career which were the cause of much dissension and led to strife and bloodshed in his own time and in that of his successor.

In 1564 Farquhar, half-brother of John of Moidart, son of the late Chief Alexander by a daughter of Mackintosh, was murdered. It seems that Farquhar wished to convey the lands of South Uist to James Macdonald of Dunnyveg and the Glens for some reason unknown. This meant the loss of a considerable part of the Clanranald inheritance, the prospect of which did not by any means appeal to the family of John of Moidart. Accordingly Alan and his half-brother, Angus and Donald Gorm, killed Farquhar and put a stop to the conveyance of the lands in question. This bloody deed was regarded with complaisance by Alan's relatives judging by the fact that none objected, and in fact remission was granted to the murderers in the following year. Remissions did not usually follow so soon after such acts of blood. Perhaps the government was too occupied with the troubles crowding the last years of Mary's reign to administer the appropriate punishment in this case.

Alan's matrimonial irregularities contributed largely to the feud which arose with the Macleods of Dunvegan and was prosecuted with much bitterness throughout the latter part of the century. His first marriage was to a daughter of Alasdair Crotach, Chief of the Siol Tormoid (Macleods of Harris), widow of John Og MacDhonail Gruamach of Castle Camus. By her Alan had a son, Alan Og. Unfortunately this marriage did not last long because, while on a visit to Maclean of Duart, young Alan fell hopelessly in love with one of Maclean's seven daughters, Janet. At the first opportunity he sailed off with Janet and left his Macleod wife. This transaction is referred to without any details, by the Clanranald historian thus: "Alan had a good family, viz. Alan Og, and the daughter of Macleod of Harris was his mother: he was his first son. After her he took unto him the daughter of Maclean of Duart and had a good family by her, viz. John of Strome. He was accidentally killed by his own servant man with a stone, while they were at play shooting with a sling at Strome, Lochcarron, for it was there he was being fostered with the Laird of Strome and Glengarry."

Alan's deserted wife is said to have attracted the attentions of Ranald, Chief of the Keppoch Macdonalds. It is doubtful if a regular marriage took place as the Keppoch historians agree that Ranald's lawful wife was a daughter of Duncan Stewart of Appin, by whom he had a good family.

This desertion by Alan of the Macleod lady led to much bad blood between Clanranald and Macleod of Harris for some years to come. It was not, however, the only cause for the many feuds that existed during this period. Clanranald and the Macleods were not the only clans involved in a general state of unrest and feuding. This aspect of a general situation is clearly presented by Dr I. F. Grant in her book *The Macleods* (1959) where she says:

> The fundamental causes of the bitterest and most continuous feuds, however, were the rival claims by neighbouring chiefs for certain debatable lands, generally the most fertile in the district. Lochaber was such a battleground, but one of the most hotly contested was Trotternish.

These claims were frequently founded on charters long out of date. We have seen in earlier chapters that the granting, rescinding and re-granting of charters had been used by the King and his Council in their efforts to reduce recalcitrant chiefs when punitive expeditions had failed. It may be recalled that the forfeiture of the Lordship in 1493 was followed by a declaration by James IV that all charters given by the Lords of the Isles were null and void and new charters must be taken out. On such demands being made chiefs were naturally reluctant to surrender their titles in case they did not receive similar charters in exchange. This applied especially to chiefs in trouble with the Crown. Macleod was in dispute with Clanranald over North Uist, and with Sleat over Trotternish. Both these led to endless disputes and battles. King James VI tried to regularise matters by an act of 15th May 1598 ordaining that "all landlords, chieftains, leaders of clans, principal householders, heritors and others pretending right to any lands in the Highlands and Isles should produce their title-deeds before the Lords of

Council." Failure to obey these summons was to be punished by utter forfeiture of their lands. No doubt the wily King thought that by so doing many areas of land in the Highlands would revert to the Crown. The state of the charters granted since the fall of the Lordship was chaotic. Much of the land was held by chiefs and their tribes with no valid charter. Some chiefs, like Keppoch, regarded the grant from the now defunct Lordship as the sole valid title and disregarded subsequent charters. They still, however, kept possession of their lands.

The Bannatyne MS records three incidents in the feud between Macleod and Alan of Clanranald. In the first the crew of a Macdonald galley driven ashore during a gale in Harris were hospitably entertained until the Macleods found they were clansmen of Clanranald. By an artifice they were all killed—a sad example of the abuse of the old laws of hospitality.

In reprisal a birlinn of Macleod with thirty-six men commanded by Donald, illegitimate son of Alasdair Crotach, was seized and all starved to death.

The third instance is that of the infamous Massacre of the Cave in Eigg. A full account is given in the New Statistical Account of the Parish of the Small Isles. The story is that a Macleod galley with a crew of thirty to fifty men under command of the foster-brother of William Macleod, brother of the Chief, Alasdair Crotach, and a MacAskill was driven ashore in bad weather on the Isle of Eigg. The crew landed and asked for food for which they offered to pay. This was refused and they took some cattle which they killed and began to eat. They were then set upon and MacAskill with two other survivors were set adrift in a small boat without oars or rudder. By chance the wind carried them to Macleod country. Alasdair Crotach vowed vengeance and set sail for Eigg with six galleys. The inhabitants of that island with some from Canna and Rum made haste to hide in a large cave which had only one secret entrance. The Macleods searched the island in vain until a scout sent out to see how matters went was spotted and followed. It is said there had been a fall of snow and the scout was tracked to the cave by William Macleod, son of the Chief. A fire was lit at the mouth of the cave and all the occupants perished. Their bones were found in little heaps as if families had huddled round to perish together. Later the bones were collected and buried under a cairn (Fr. Charles MacDonald in *Moidart, or among the Clanranalds*). The date of the massacre is taken as 1577, although one account places it earlier.

About three years later the Clanranald forces invaded Skye to exact vengeance from the Macleods for their atrocious massacre in Eigg. Here again much has been written but it is enough to say that, after an alleged burning of Trumpan Church with some of the worshippers inside, the Macleods reacted strenuously. A battle ensued in which, by the waving of the famous fairy flag of the Macleods, the Macdonalds were defeated, and their bodies laid alongside a dyke which was pulled down over them to serve as their burial. This battle has been known ever since as *Blàr Milleadh Gàraidh* (Battle of the Spoiling of the Dyke) and a full account of it may be read in Nicolson's *History of Skye*.

The misfortunes Alan continued to suffer in the feud with the Macleods were not alleviated by events which took place within his own immediate family. The two eldest sons of Alan's marriage with Janet of Duart now come on the scene and, it would appear, in a very tragic manner. Alan and his wife were accustomed to spend part of the summer at a place called Keppoch in Arisaig. Here, to pass the time and practise archery, their sons used to shoot arrows at the seals which abound on that coast on the islets at the entrance to Loch na Coille. One day John and Angus, sons of Alan by Janet of Duart, with Alan Og, son of Macleod's daughter and heir apparent of his father, were engaged in this sport. Whether there was a quarrel or not is a mystery but the fact remains that Alan Og was shot with at least two arrows from the bows of his half-brothers. Historians agree it may well have been a murder inspired by Janet of Duart to remove the heir to the chiefship and thus make way for her own sons to succeed. Misfortune seems to have followed this family. John of Strome died young by accident, Alan Og was murdered as we have just seen, and John predeceased his father. Angus, who succeeded, occupied the Chiefship only for a brief period before he died, leaving a family which continued to be dogged by an unkind fate. Although Angus had five sons, none for some reason or other was able to succeed his father in the chiefship; and the eldest son with his wife and family were all drowned crossing the sea to Coll. The others seem to have left no issue.

Shortly after the murder of Alan Og steps were taken to punish the two murderers and their father who on account of their youth was regarded as responsible for their conduct. In 1588 the records of the Privy Seal read thus: "To John MacRanald, son and heir apparend to Alan McRanald of Easter Leys, his aires and assignees, ane or maa, of the gift of the escheat, etc. which pertained to Alan McIain Moidart, etc. Thro being of the said persons orderly denounced rebels, and put to the horn for the slaughter of Alan Og McAlan McIain, brother to Alexander McRanald of Keppoch and not underlying the law . . . etc. . . ." From this simplified extract it would appear that the deceased Alan Og was accepted as brother of Alexander McRanald of Keppoch. It is assumed that this Alexander was the issue of a love match between Ranald of Keppoch and the discarded Macleod wife of the Clanranald Chief. The Keppoch records make no mention of the lady. Ranald Og of Keppoch (9th Chief) married a daughter of Duncan Stewart of Appin, by whom he had his successor, Alexander (10th) known as Alasdair nan Cleas.

Alan and his son and heir, Angus, were now declared rebel and their estates forfeited and bestowed upon the family of the late Ranald Gallda who fell at Blar-na-leine. It is likely that this family still nourished hopes of gaining possession of the estates and chiefship of Clanranald.

Alan of Moidart is said to have died in 1593. By his first wife, Margaret Macleod, daughter of Alasdair Crotach of Dunvegan, he had Alan Og, who was murdered by his half-brothers. By his second wife, Janet, daughter of Maclean of Duart, he had: (1) John, who died young at Strome by accident; (2) Angus, who succeeded for one year and was killed in 1594; (3) Donald, who succeeded his brother; (4) Ranald of Benbecula; (5) John, from whom the Macdonalds of Kinlochmoidart; (6) Ruairi, of Boisdale.

The Clan Bard, MacVurich, commends Alan as a person of great piety, "a builder of churches (Eigg and Howmore), generous, open-hearted, hospitable, affable and sensible." He may, like some of his ancestors, have "spent his last years godly and mercifully."

Angus, eldest surviving son of the deceased chief, succeeded to the chiefship. His father had never taken out titles to the estates nor had he served the murdered Alan Og as his heir. In the troubles that beset the family it must have been very hard for Alan to decide which of his sons would outlive him and become heir.

Most of the information to be gathered about Angus concerns his activities in the lifetime of his father, during whose latter years he may well have acted as Captain of the Clanranald. In 1588 he was in feud with the descendants of Ranald Gallda. We find one of these, Angus MacAlan MacRanald, later receiving a remission for the slaughter of some of young Angus's retainers. In 1591 Angus signed a bond of manrent with Sir Duncan Campbell of Glenorchy "against all and sundry excepting the authority of Angus MacConill." At the same time

Campbell gave Angus a bond of protection against all persons, excepting the authority and the Earl of Argyll.

The career of Angus as chief was very short. It would seem that he survived his father by little more than a year, and the manner of his death is the subject of some doubt. MacVurich states that he "was put to death by Angus Og while he was a prisoner in Dunnyveg." Our own seanachies point out that Angus Og would hardly wish to antagonise a powerful neighbour like the Clanranald while he was at feud with the sturdy Lachlan Mor, Chief of the Macleans of Duart. There is evidence that another Angus (MacRanald), head of the Clann Domhnaill Hearaich (Cadet of the House of Sleat), had joined forces with Maclean of Duart and was burned to death in a house in Islay while a prisoner of Angus of Dunnyveg. It is likely that MacVurich confused this Angus with the Chief of Clanranald. A more plausible account of Angus's death is given by our seanachies from oral tradition thus:

> The traditions of South Uist point clearly and circumstantially to the manner in which the Chief of Clanranald appears to have met his end. The event could hardly have taken place later than 1594, and it happened in connection with the long-standing feud with the Macleods of Dunvegan which still remained unhealed. The slaughter of Macleod's kinsman, Allan Og, some half-dozen years before, would no doubt have sharply aggravated the feud and intensified Macleod's animosity to the young Chief of Clanranald. At this time Angus MacAllan, and his brother Donald Gorme, afterwards Sir Donald of Castle Tirrim, were living in South Uist, when one day word came to them through some friendly channel that the Macleods of Skye, in a fleet of six boats, with a score of men in each, numbering 120 men altogether, had landed at the *Acarsaidh fhalaich,* or hidden anchorage, on the east side of South Uist, and intended taking away with them a large spoil of cattle.

They then go on to describe in detail what happened based on strong traditions handed down in the island with place names recording certain incidents in the raid. There is little doubt that Angus met his death at the hands of the invading Macleods, and that his brother's part in the action is not above suspicion. Casualties were heavy on both sides. The Macleods got no cattle after all; and, out of the 140 men who landed in Uist, it is said that only 40 returned to Skye. These figures, as well as some of the gory details, may have been exaggerated over the years, but the fact of the death of a chief, one of their own blood, remains firmly established as having occurred not later than 1594.

The reign of Angus was so short that he is left out of the succession altogether by the Clanranald Family book of 1819, which states that he "pre-deceased his father without issue." According to some authorities Angus had no less than five sons, all of whom would seem to have died in his lifetime leaving no male heirs or in any case none who was acceptable to the clan, and he was followed in the Chiefship by his younger brother Donald.

Donald MacAlan married, after his succession to the Chiefship, Mary, daughter of Angus of Dunnyveg, and naturally backed that chief in his quarrel with Lachlan Mor of Duart. Lachlan some years previously had ravaged Clanranald lands in Eigg and Rum, ably assisted by 100 mercenaries from the Spanish ship then lying in Tobermory. These troops had been lent to Maclean in part payment for provisions supplied to the Spaniards. After assisting Maclean in harrying the small isles of Rum, Canna, Eigg and Muck, the property of Clanranald, they went to Ardnamurchan and laid siege to MacIain's castle of Mingary. Before they could reduce that fortress, they were recalled by their commander who had decided to set sail for home. Sir Lachlan sent Donald Glas, son of Maclean of Morvern, aboard to arrange the final payments due for the provisions supplied. Donald Glas was seized and held prisoner. Determined to prevent the wily Spaniard from escaping due payment of his debts, Donald somehow gained access to the ship's magazine and blew it up. The wreck is still in Tobermory Bay and still continues to be the subject of attempts that have been made ever since to locate the treasure she is said to have carried.

In revenge for these raids and spoils taken from his lands, Donald, with the aid of his father-in-law, invaded the isles of Coll, Tiree and Mull and carried off a great spoil. The feud with the Macleans was thus kept very much alive with great loss to both sides. Sir Lachlan did not react at once, but very soon an opportunity offered itself for revenge.

In the summer of 1595 Donald Gorm of Sleat and Macleod of Harris with about 500 clansmen each set sail for Ireland where they proposed to help Hugh Ruadh O'Donnell in his resistance against the inroads of Queen Elizabeth's armies in that country. Donald of Clanranald joined his forces with this armada and they went south through the Sound of Mull on their way. Sir Lachlan saw a chance to further his own interests and at the same time serve Queen Elizabeth in Ireland by preventing this large force from reaching that country. He chose his time well. The armada landed for the night on a small isolated isle. Whether this island was Calve in Tobermory Bay, or Baca, as related by the Maclean seanachie, matters little. Neither was large, and one wonders how a force of some 2000 men could have been accommodated on such a small island. The Maclean account puts the numbers at 1200 men on their side against 2500 in the invaders' contingent. A well planned night attack defeated the latter completely. The Macleans claim 350 of the invading force were killed while they themselves suffered relatively few casualties. One has to make allowance for partisanship in such accounts, but it must have been a very gallant and successful operation as our seanachies agree that Donald of Clanranald was taken prisoner with his three uncles and some of the other chiefs.

How long Donald remained prisoner in Duart Castle with Maclean is unknown, but a letter of Sir Lachlan to Queen Elizabeth in 1598 shows that Donald and Sir Lachlan had by then become reconciled. In their account of this incident the authors of *Clan Donald* are silent regarding the fate of Donald Gorm of Sleat and Macleod of Harris. But Gregory in his *History of the Western Highlands* states that Donald Gorm and Ruairi Mor Macleod reached Ireland safely with 500 men each and there joined forces with O'Donnell. Donald Gorm returned home, leaving his brother in command of the Sleat men, and Macleod remained with his men for a time; but a Privy Council order of 18th June 1595 commanded them to give no assistance to the Irish "rebels." From this it would appear that the prisoners taken by Lachlan Mor Maclean did not include the major part of the expedition, and that the Clanranald chief and his men were the main sufferers.

From a letter of Auchincross in the State Papers of the period the list of prisoners includes the three uncles of Clanranald—Donald Gorm and other two sons of John of Moidart, with the Laird of Knoydart and MacIain of Ardnamurchan.

For the next six years we hear nothing of Donald and assume he was living in peace in his Castle of Tirrim. In 1601, however, he is in alliance with Donald MacAngus of Glengarry in his long feud with Mackenzie of Kintail. Clanranald invaded and harried that district, but he does not seem to have continued in the company of Glengarry in further operations. Donald returned from Kintail through Skye to his domains in Uist. Here he found that MacNeil of Barra had been asserting his right to lands in the Boisdale district. He had some justification in this claim, as Alexander, Lord of the Isles and Earl of Ross, had in 1427 granted to MacNeil the Isle of Barra and the unciate lands of Boisdale. This charter had been confirmed by James IV at Stirling on the 12th November 1495 after the fall of the Lordship, and nothing had happened since then to affect its validity. Clanranald, however, saw it in a different light and refused to recognise claims to ownership of lands in an island which he considered part of his ancestral heritage. Donald accordingly proceeded at once to the south of the island with his forces and drove MacNeil from the island with much slaughter. From that time Boisdale remained in Clanranald hands and a notable cadet of that House followed Ruairi, brother of the Chief, in the occupation of those lands. Alexander (1678-1768), third son of Donald, 16th of Clanranald, founded this family from which the present Chief and Captain of Clanranald is descended.

Donald of Clanranald appears once more in 1605 when the "Fife Adventurers" made a second attempt to occupy the Isle of Lewis at the expense of the native Macleods. Their first attempt, encouraged by King James VI who was trying to make peace in the North Isles by planting Lowland farmers and artisans in Lewis, had failed as a result of vigorous opposition offered by the Macleods. On the second occasion, Neil Macleod of the Siol Torquil was ably assisted in his struggle by Clanranald. So successful were they that on the 16th September 1606 Mackenzie of Kintail was given a commission against Donald Clanranald and MacNeil of Barra for aiding the Siol Torquil in the person of Neil Macleod.

In his determination to impose his "civilising" influence upon the inhabitants of the Isles, the King now had recourse to proposals which were both lamentable and barbarous. These were placed before a secret Council held on the last day of April 1607 and which Huntly was called to attend. According to the minutes of this extraordinary meeting, which are preserved in an MS in the Advocates' Library, Huntly was commissioned to take possession for the King of all the North Isles with the exception of Skye and Lewis. For these he was to pay an annual due fixed by the Royal Comptroller, and was to fulfil his commission by the extirpation of the native people. Huntly undertook that he would extirpate the "barbarous people thereof" within the space of one year, and offered to pay an annual rent of 400 pounds Scots for Uist and 100 pounds for the rest of the Isles, asking only one year's respite to make the first payment. The Lords of Council agreed, drily remarking that the annual dues for the whole of the North Isles (most of which were in Clanranald country) seemed to them to be a "very mean duty"; and in seeking the approval of the King they add the comment that it would be desirable to solve the problem as soon as possible. These shameful proposals, however, came to naught. Huntly initiated certain measures in an attempt to fulfil his commission, but various disagreements arose especially in regard to the subject of rents, and the nefarious enterprise was finally abandoned in the face of opposition from powerful nobles jealous of Huntly's aggrandisement.

In the following year further measures were devised which were to have more material and lasting effects. The King's lieutenant, Lord Ochiltree, with Bishop Knox of the Isles to counsel him, held a Court at Aros in Mull at which the chiefs, amongst whom was the Captain of Clanranald, attended to hear the proposals to be made on behalf of the King. These proposals were regarded as "fair words and good promises" by Ochiltree, but the chiefs did not seem over-willing to agree. They were invited to attend a party on the royal ship to continue discussion and be entertained by the Lieutenant. All went with the exception of Angus of Dunnyveg, who had been allowed to return home, and Ruairi Macleod who suspected foul play. Once on board they were treacherously seized and made prisoner. Donald of Clanranald found himself in the royal prison of Blackness Castle where he was kept prisoner until June of 1609. Several of the captive chiefs, Donald of Clanranald amongst them, made offers of obedience to the King and Council. In his submission Donald promised to be answerable for all his lands and offered hostages for their assurance. In spite of this he was sent back to Blackness and was obliged to pay for his quarters for the remainder of his term.

* * *

We have already noted that Huntly's attempt to execute the commission granted to him in 1607 was foiled at an early stage, and that fortunately the extirpation of the "barbarous people of the Isles" was not attempted. The reasons for granting this reprieve cannot be attributed to any lofty principles on the part of the King or his Council or any change of heart in their opinion of the western clans. The scheme was abandoned on two counts only, that the sordid haggling about finances came to naught and that, in the climate of the Reformation, the Marquis of Huntly was distinctly unpopular amongst the ardent Reformers of the Protestant faith headed by the King himself. Extirpation, in the full meaning of the word, would have been impossible when applied to the island tribes headed by able chiefs like Donald Gorm, Ruairi Mor Macleod, Maclean of Duart, and the rest. A bloody civil war would have resulted with which the rebellious activities of the clans would have seemed comparatively unimportant.

Second thoughts on the King's part led to a much better way of tackling the problem. Commissioners for the Isles were appointed: Bishop Andrew Knox of the Isles, the Archbishop of Glasgow, Lord Ochiltree, and James Hay of Kingask. Of these Bishop Knox was the principal member and leader, who did all the negotiations with the chiefs which led to the Statutes of Icolmkill (Iona)—one of the most important turning points in the history of the Isles.

Knox accompanied by Angus Macdonald of Dunnyveg and Hector Maclean of Duart went to Iona in July 1609 and on the 27th of that month the articles were signed. All the chiefs present were able to sign their names. These were Angus of Dunnyveg, Hector of Duart, Donald Gorm of Sleat, Ruairi Mor Macleod, Donald of Clanranald, Lachlan of Coll, Lachlan Mackinnon of that Ilk, Hector Maclean of Lochbuy, Lachlan and Alan Maclean, brothers-german to Duart, Gilleasbuig MacQuarrie of Ulva, and Donald MacPhie of Colonsay.

The Statutes of Icolmkill of 1609 were briefly as follows:

1. Kirks, and ministers to serve them, were to be established throughout the Isles.

2. Inns for the accommodation of travellers were to be maintained: this was to ease the burden of hospitality which fell upon the chiefs and their tenants.

3. All those dwelling in the Isles were to have means of living either by their rents or by their trades. The chiefs were allowed only a certain number of retainers in their households.

4. Sorners (*i.e.* beggars and scroungers as we would call them today) were to be banned.

5. The sale of wine, except to the chiefs (who were to be rationed as to their consumption) to be banned.

6. Education to be developed. Chiefs and gentry were to send their eldest sons (or daughters) to be educated where they would learn to speak, read and write English.

7. Firearms to be banned.

8. Vagabonds, which included itinerant "bards" and beggars, to be banned.

9. The chiefs were required to keep and enforce these articles under penalties.

Later, in 1616, these articles were made considerably more stringent. Galleys and birlinns were limited. Wines and spirits (imported) were rationed to each chief's household, and later the amounts allowed to each were laid down. It is to be noted that nothing was said about whisky, which seems to have been the drink of the common people distilled on their own premises. This led naturally to an increase in the consumption of this native liquor, and caused great resentment later when excise men were sent to the Highlands to collect customs duty on its production.

The Bishop took solemn undertakings from all the chiefs present to observe these statutes.

Gregory assesses the importance of the Statutes thus: "It is a fact which may appear startling to many, but it is not less evident on that account, that the first traces of that overflowing loyalty to the House of Stewart for which the Highlanders have been so highly lauded, are to be found in that generation of their chiefs whose education was conducted on the high church and state principles of the British Solomon." He concludes that the chiefs who followed Montrose in the Civil War of 1642/1649 in the cause of Charles I were inspired by sentiments far different from those of their predecessors in previous wars and disturbances between the Crown and its rebellious subjects.

It is indeed a mystery that, after the repressive measures by parchment and armed force imposed on the clans, within so short a time they should have changed their attitude towards the Crown. Within less than forty years after the signing of the Statutes of Iona (1609) the same clans who had been obliged to conform then fought to the death from 1645 to 1745 in defence of the House of Stewart, which had for the previous 200 years tried by every means, force of arms, duplicity and legal charters, to "daunt the Isles." Perhaps the clans had always needed a head to whom to owe allegiance. In the 400 years from Somerled to Donald Dubh, that loyalty had been given willingly to the Macdonald Kings and Lords of the Isles. After the break-up of the Lordship they lacked such a head, and the Kings who preceded James VI were not very consistent in their efforts to placate the Islesmen. From the time of these Statutes Clan Donald, and the other clans who had of old been associated with them, transferred their loyalty to the Stewart family from Charles I down to Prince Charles Edward. In the end it was their undoing: the clans were broken and the clansmen scattered.

Whatever the long-term results of this statesmanlike action of the King may have been, the effect was soon felt by Donald of Clanranald. On the 15th June 1609, a month before the Statutes were ratified, Donald was set at liberty, having spent ten months in Blackness prison. Lord Ochiltree and Bishop Knox bound themselves in the sum of £5000 for his personal appearance before the King on the 2nd February 1610. In return Donald was bound under penalty to assist them in the survey they were making of the Isles, prior to the Iona meetings. Meantime Donald's son, later his successor, was to be kept strictly in the company of the Bishop as surety for his father's good behaviour. On the 7th March of the year following (1610) Donald received from the Crown a *supersedere* (release) from all his debts for a period of three years. It is likely that the King realised that the unfortunate prisoner in Blackness had not been able to administer his finances effectively, for the document notes that during his absence certain of his dependants and clansmen had incurred debts one way and another which were quite beyond Donald's power to settle, although he had done his best to do so. Relieved of this embarrassment and taking advantage of his improved relations with the Crown, Donald now set out to regularise his tenure by securing legal titles for his lands.

On the 4th of June 1610 he obtained from Donald Gorm of Sleat the 30 merklands of Skirhough, 12 merklands of Benbecula and one pennyland of Garigriminish, which had been given to Sleat in 1597 by the Crown. Then on the 24th July of the same year he obtained yet another charter registered in Edinburgh. This was a most important document from Donald's point of view. It is a long document but the gist of it is that in fulsome terms the King grants to Donald, the heirs male of his body, lawfully procreated or yet to be procreated, without division, whom failing, his heirs or assignees whatsoever, the following vast lands: 80 merklands of Moidart, 30 merklands of Arisaig, 21 merklands of Eigg, 15 merklands of Morar, 7 merklands in Arisaig, 33 merklands of Kyndies, and 6 merklands of Boisdale. Truly a generous confirmation of the lands held by John of Moidart, Donald's grandfather, in 1531. Castle Tirrim is the name given to this barony and that Castle is named his "ancestral seat."

Donald's compliance with the terms of the Statutes was already shown to have been a politic act on the part of both parties; and from this time on the Clanranald chiefs found that adherence to the King's peace was a safer mode of life than the bickering that followed the collapse of the Lordship. A symptom of this change of heart is shown by the action taken by Clanranald and Lochiel to compound their differences and make peace.

On the 28th June 1610 Donald agreed to meet Cameron of Lochiel with whom he had been at variance for some years, although the causes of the quarrel are not apparent. The two chiefs appeared before the Council, renounced all enmity, and made a peace that lasted ever after: just another proof that the King's policy of appeasement of a diplomatic kind was achieving more than many years of clumsy handling of the problem by his predecessors. Donald of Clanranald was now the friend of his monarch, and in firm occupation of his family's vast estates, even though his father and grandfather had held no feudal charter for the lands for the last eighty years.

This happy position had hardly been consolidated when Donald's peace was disturbed, this time from inside his own family. The descendants of Ranald Gallda had not forgotten the misfortunes of their grandfather. John MacAlan MacRanald, one of Ranald Gallda's grandsons, brought himself to the attention of the Council by whom he is described as a murderer, thief and unruly subject; and commissions were issued to various chiefs, but particularly Donald of Clanranald, to take up arms and apprehend him. The worthy chief now found himself in the strange position of siding with the Crown against one of his own flesh and blood even if the relationship was distant and unfriendly. The sins attributed to John MacAlan MacRanald included his banding together with his brothers to harry Donald, their Chief.

Ranald Gallda had left three illegitimate sons—John, Alan and Alexander—all of whom had managed to get a precept of legitimation on the 18th June 1555. Alan the eldest is said to have received a gift of the lands of Moidart and Arisaig, and John, the son of Alan, received the forfeited estates of Alan of Clanranald and his son Angus after the murder of Alan Og. Neither of these "gifts" took effect as the Clanranald Chief continued to hold his lands if by no other title than his own strong right hand and the support of his Clan.

Donald of Clanranald in pursuance of his commission made life difficult for Ranald Gallda's heir, who lived near Inverness where he seemed to have some holding. He complained about the treatment he had received at the hands of Donald, his Chief. What this unfriendly treatment was we do not know, but on 6th October 1612 he secured from the Sheriff Court of Inverness a decree of removal against the Clanranald Chief from the lands of Moidart and Arisaig and his Castle of Tirrim. Donald was accordingly pronounced rebel, which did not disturb him unduly for he continued to live peaceably in his domains. He still seems to have been on very good terms with the King and Council. Indeed it was about this time that he received a remission for his misdeeds in the past of fire-raising and harrying in Mull and Tiree.

During this and the following year Donald had also to contend with complications in the Isles not of his own making. Once again it came about through marital troubles in which Clanranald's own sister was involved. Ruairi MacNeil of Barra, known as the "Turbulent," had married by handfasting a daughter of Maclean of Duart by whom he had several sons. He then married in a regular fashion a sister of the Captain of Clanranald by whom another family was born. The children of the second union were feudally the legal successors to Ruairi, and differences over the question of birthright were inevitable in the circumstances. The eldest son of the first marriage was implicated in a piratical exploit involving a ship with a cargo from Bordeaux, probably in the wine trade. Clanranald captured young MacNeil and brought him to Edinburgh for trial, where he died of some cause unknown. His brothers backed by their uncle of Duart seized the eldest son by Clanranald's sister, accusing him of being implicated in the piracy, and sent him to Edinburgh. There he remained for some time; but the charge could not be substantiated, and his uncle of Clanranald was eventually successful in obtaining his release. By using his good offices and friendship with the Government he was able to secure young MacNeil's succession to his birthright, but Donald had to undertake to bring MacNeil to the Council on demand under a penalty of 10,000 merks.

It was during this period that Donald became involved once again in the misfortunes of the Macleods of Lewis, the Siol Torquil, who had received his aid some years earlier. Mackenzie of Kintail had ruined the Siol Torquil by buying out the Fife colonists and getting a commission of fire and sword against the Macleods, of whom only about thirty remained alive under siege on the rocky isle of Berisay. There they held out for three years, after which they escaped and fled to Clanranald country for safety. Kintail complained to the Privy Council, and once more Donald was in danger of being declared rebel for this act of mercy towards the unfortunate fugitives from Lewis.

In this same year (1614) the heirs of the late Ranald Gallda in the persons of John and Elizabeth, children of Angus, grandson of Ranald Gallda, renewed the attack on Donald Clanranald but had not advanced very far with their proceedings before they both died. Thus he was relieved at last from interference from that family.

During the next two years Donald was in some trouble with the authorities on account of the disorderly conduct of his clansmen. He became bound to keep order in his domain and appear in Edinburgh on the 10th of July each year to answer charges that might be brought against his clan. In obedience to this summons, Clanranald appeared with other chiefs before the Council the following year and bound himself to observe and enforce the regulations of the Statutes of Iona. He was also required to take with him certain members of his own family to answer for their good conduct. These were six: Donald Gorm MacIain, his uncle, Ruairi Dubh, his brother, Angus, son of Donald Gorm, Alasdair, son of

Iain Og, his cousin, Donald Gorm MacAngus MhicAlein, his nephew, and Ranald, son of Donald Gorm, presumably a cousin. Some of these gentlemen may have been the cause of turmoil in Clanranald country despite their chief's desire to keep out of trouble. Ranald of Benbecula and John of Kinlochmoidart are mentioned as prime offenders, and Donald had to report their doings to the Council in his attempt to maintain order amongst his clansmen. On 18th July 1615 Donald entered into a Bond of Indemnity with Donald MacAngus of Glengarry in which he undertook under heavy penalties to keep his relatives from molesting the lands of Glengarry, and at the same time pledged himself to assist Glengarry in curbing the activities of certain rebels in Knoydart.

On the 24th August 1615 he entered into a Bond of Friendship with Sir Ruairi Mor Macleod of Dunvegan, Sir Lachlan Mackinnon of Strath, and Lachlan Maclean of Coll, which would seem to mark the end of the feuds that had for long disturbed the peace of Clanranald and its neighbours.

Donald's efforts to keep his Clan out of trouble over the later years of his reign seem to have commended themselves to the King, for in the month of May 1617 he was knighted at Holyrood. He spent the last two years of his eventful life quietly at home and died in December 1618.

Donald had lived in troubled times and yet succeeded in keeping his Clan intact and in good relations with the King, which, considering the number of enterprising relatives he had round him, was no mean achievement.

By his marriage with Mary, daughter of Angus Macdonald of Dunnyveg, Donald had: (1) John, who succeeded; (2) Ranald Og, who died without issue in 1636; (3) Alexander Glas, who died without issue; (4) Donald Glas, who died without issue; (5) Marion, who married Lachlan Maclean of Torloisk, with issue.

John, 12th of Clanranald, was a minor when his father died. The date of his father's death and succession of John to the chiefship is variously recorded as 1619 and 1618. However in 1619 John, although a minor at the time, undertook all the responsibilities of an adult, and assumed the obligations left by Sir Donald. He is variously recorded as "John Moidartach," and "John M'Ranald, Captain of Clanranald," and "J. Capt. M'Ranald." He was 12th Chief of Clanranald, and we have to avoid the use of the name "John Moidartach" as several "Johns" in the Clanranald genealogy appear under that name. Owing no doubt to the prowess of the famous John Moidartach, great-grandfather of the present John, the name became popular with the succeeding chiefs.

The years that followed John's accession are full of a bewildering succession of manoeuvres in his attempts to get himself out of debt, and put his estates on a sound financial basis. Some of the measures he was obliged to resort to were the cause of considerable trouble in the early years of his chiefship.

We have seen that Sir Donald, John's father, with certain other western chiefs were obliged to appear before the Council on the 10th day of July each year to account for their doings under threat of a fine of 5000 merks. This obligation was carried on from father to son, and accordingly we find John appearing before the Council on 5th February 1619. Here Sir Ruairi Macleod sponsors him to the extent of 10,000 merks, and Donald Gorm of Sleat assists Ranald MacAlan, John's uncle, in the same way. Transactions of this sort continue to appear in Privy Council records over the next few years. In a word, John was in debt, much of which he inherited from Sir Donald, and had to find sponsors and burden his estates still further by granting superiorities to outsiders. The list of these undertakings on his part is long and complicated, and it is unnecessary to interrupt our narrative by discussing them here.

In 1627 the apparent peace that reigned in Clanranald country came to an end. Up to that time John of Moidart had been fully occupied with his financial manoeuvres. He does not seem to have had time to indulge in rebellions or excursions abroad. But now he began to involve himself in enterprises which could not fail to bring him to the notice of the Council.

We have noted in another chapter how the MacIains of Ardnamurchan, owing to the depression into which they had fallen at the hands of the Campbells, had taken up piracy as a means of restoring their fortunes. In one of these exploits John of Moidart now became involved. A ship of the Port of Leith with a valuable cargo of tea, wines and other goods was bound out of the Clyde eastwards round Cape Wrath. Near Barra Head at the south end of the Outer Isles, John's galleys caught up with her. She was boarded and her cargo plundered. It may well be that John had seen that the MacIains had been fairly successful in their nefarious industry and hoped to profit in the same manner. The spoil included 5 butts of wine, 8 casks of herring, and 300 double ells of "plaiding" worth £300. The usual "horning" followed but was relaxed shortly afterwards. The practice of putting to the horn followed by more or less immediate relaxation had become almost a matter of form. The authorities knew it would be far too expensive to pursue John into his fastness of Moidart for the sake of a few ells of "plaiding," and the matter was dropped. How the unfortunate ship-owner and underwriters of the cargo were ever compensated history does not reveal.

In 1629 the salmon fishings of Seal in the lands of the MacIains in Ardnamurchan and Sunart were invaded and exploited by the minions of Sir Donald Campbell. The MacIains regarded this as stealing and twice they attacked with the help of some of Clanranald's men and drove the invaders off. John was summoned before the Privy Council by Archibald Campbell, Lord of Lorn, to answer for the disorderly conduct of his clansmen. The matter was settled amicably and, it would appear, in John's favour.

For seven years John and his clan dwelt in peace, by which we mean they did not bring themselves to the notice of the Council as a result of any serious breaches of the King's peace. In 1636, however, the Captain of Clanranald and his men are involved in a very disreputable incident. *Susannah,* an English barque bound from St Mailles in France for Limerick, fell in with bad weather, was dismasted and blown off course northwards. Her signals were observed by the islanders of Barra and it was arranged that, for a payment of a butt of sack and a barrel of raisins, she should be towed into harbour. On reaching the shore they were met by John of Moidart at the head of 300 of his men who promptly emptied the hold of the vessel of all its contents. A young man of the ship's company was forced by John to act as agent and to sign a bill of sale for the cargo in exchange for a sum of money which was promised but never paid. The ship worth £150 was valued by her captors at £8 and that is all the owner got for both his ship and cargo. The incident throws a very lurid light on the character of John and his relatives, whose conduct on this occasion was both reprehensible and inexcusable. Horning followed as a matter of course and the usual relaxation shortly after.

Eight years of silence and presumably peace follow until in 1644 John once more comes to our notice. He does not seem to have repented of his wayward conduct in the meantime, although the church had a good pastor in South Uist. The good man's work does not seem to have borne fruit in the case of his chief parishioner, John of Moidart. Indeed the pastor, Mr Martin Macpherson, was the sufferer in the sad case we have to narrate here.

It may be that one of the sermons of the cleric had been directed against wrongdoers of the pattern of the Clanranald clansmen in general, and the Chief in particular. We shall never know; but there must have been some reason other than mere greed that inspired John to despoil the churchman. Suddenly one morning a party of John's men descended upon the pastor's land and removed all his stock—80 cattle, 88 sheep and lambs, 13 horses, utensils, corn, etc. Every thing was taken, and the minister had to retire to the shelter of Macleod of Dunvegan. It was not till 1667 that he received some small compensation after numerous petitions had been submitted to the Courts and to Parliament. That compensation was made out of some vacant stipends in Skye and John of Moidart never made any redress in spite of the decrees obtained against him, nor does he appear to have been put to the horn for his misdeeds on this occasion.

While all these domestic and local incidents were taking place, affairs in the Kingdom were undergoing rapid change. The Civil War had started in England and was soon to disturb the peace of Scotland. Charles I was in trouble with his Parliament. The National Covenant had been signed on 1st March 1638 and the Solemn League and Covenant on the 2nd August 1643, which occasioned the gibe that the Scots had sold their King. On the 17th November 1641 Charles had left Scotland, after a brief visit which led to no improvement in his relations with his Scottish subjects. The Civil War began in the next year. The Highland clans tended to hold aloof from these turmoils, but their comparatively recent transfer of loyalty to the Crown remained unaffected, and they felt the King was being badly treated. It is not to be supposed, however, that their actions from this time onwards were all inspired by sheer loyalty to the King. Another potent element entered into it. Argyll, the arch-enemy of most of them, had sided with the Covenant and against the King, and this was felt to be a very good time to challenge Campbell's power. All the western clans had suffered from the machinations and depredations of the Clan Campbell headed by Argyll who now held great power in the Covenant party. He had ably combined the rôle of Highland chief with that of courtier in the Royal presence. In the first he had several thousand brave warriors at his command, while in the second rôle he was able to profit by commissions of fire and sword, hornings and parchments to the detriment of his neighbours, and to his own aggrandisement.

From September 1644 to the same month in 1645 the Royalist cause in Scotland centred round the spectacular achievements of Montrose in his whirlwind campaign as Lieutenant-General of the King. It was truly an *Annus Mirabilis*. The part taken by John of Moidart and his clan in the ensuing campaign was important, as we shall see, but at the outset another Macdonald came on the scene whose contribution to the success of that campaign was much greater. When the Earl of Antrim raised the men of his own clan and other exiled clansmen of the Islay Clan Donald he chose Alasdair MacColla (the son of Colkitto) as his Lieutenant-General under the commission given him by the King, dated 5th June 1639, in which he names the Earl of Antrim "Lieutenant of the Isles" with "Sr. Donald McDonald of Slait, kn. baronet" as his second in command. These are given full powers to pursue and prosecute his rebellious subjects. Antrim in his turn appointed Alasdair to lead the expedition with, as his second in command, an energetic young man named Magnus O'Cahan. This name is one closely linked with Clan Donald by the marriage of Angus Og, Lord of the Isles, to Agnes O'Cahan. Moreover, Alasdair's own grandmother was an O'Cahan.

Early in July 1644 the Antrim men embarked in the *Harp* and two other vessels. On the way they captured three Parliament ships, two of which provided them with plentiful supplies for their voyage. They landed in Ardnamurchan.

There were 1600 seasoned warriors, mostly Macdonnells, well used to war in the troubles that had disturbed Ulster in the days of Antrim's grandfather and before.

As soon as they landed, the Castles of Mingary and Kinlochaline were taken and garrisoned. Alasdair went north to meet Sir Donald, who had died the year before, unknown to Alasdair. Sir James his successor was not keen to embark on what seemed a very risky venture. While this meeting was taking place, Argyll arrived with his galleys and destroyed Alasdair's shipping in Loch Eishort. The Ulster men now had no means of retreat even if they had wished. All they could do was to march east and hope to raise other clans and Royalists amongst the Gordons on their way. Montrose had left Oxford in March and was on his way north, but his movements were necessarily secret until he reached friendly country north of the Forth. Alasdair managed to communicate with Montrose and a rendezvous was fixed at Blair Atholl. Alasdair arrived there first, but he had not long encamped before Montrose arrived and reassured the Atholl men whose hostility had been causing some anxiety. The Stewarts and Robertsons then came in with their support, and Montrose had now some 2700 men. Lord Elcho, in command of the Covenanting army, was at Perth with 7000 infantry and 700 horse; and at Tippermuir, west of the city, Montrose gained the first of a series of brilliant victories against a vastly superior force. The battle of Aberdeen and the sack of that city followed, the only bad blot on the arms of the Royalists in this campaign. Alasdair's men got out of hand, and it was beyond the power of Montrose to restrain them. They had been living a hard and dangerous life ever since their arrival in Scotland, and here was a chance to recoup their losses. But it was not only a crime, it was a bad mistake as it alienated many who might have been prepared willingly to join his standard.

Alasdair had gone to the west to raise the clans. The success already attained made his task easier, and he returned to meet Montrose at Blair again, this time with reinforcements which brought the Royal Army up to some 3000 men. With him came John of Moidart, accompanied by his son and a strong force of the Clan Donald, including Sleat, Keppoch and Glengarry, supported by the Macleans, the Stewarts of Appin, the Camerons, the Farquharsons—all those in fact who would wholeheartedly subscribe to the campaign it was now determined to pursue. Argyll had disbanded his forces in the expectation that little would be attempted by the Royalist army in the winter months. To the great satisfaction of the Highland army, however, Montrose now decided to make a spectacular descent through the winter passes upon the territory of Argyll.

The army was divided into three divisions. Alasdair's men were in three battalions, commanded by James Macdonnell, Ranald Og Macdonnell and young Magnus O'Cahan; the clans of the West and Isles were under the able leadership of John of Moidart; and the rest, men from Atholl, Badenoch, some Gordons from Aberdeenshire and a few Lowland levies, were under the command of Montrose himself.

Argyll and his Campbells thought themselves safe in the country round Lochawe and Knapdale. The Royalists marched west through the fastnesses of Breadalbane, laying waste the possessions of Argyll on the way and, guided by Angus MacAilein Dhuibh of Glencoe, arrived in a very short time at the gates of Inveraray. Argyll fled across Loch Fyne and sought refuge in his castle of Roseneath on the Gareloch, leaving his subjects to look after themselves. In this march no serious atrocities are recorded. Those who resisted were killed, but judging by the number of fighting men left to face Montrose at Inverlochy two months later, there cannot have been any wholesale massacre. The country was wasted in the customary manner. Here John of Moidart and his son, Donald, rendered a signal service by raiding Knapdale and bringing 1000 head of cattle to fill the larder of the lean warriors of Alasdair and the clans. The pillage continued for many weeks until in January the Royal army marched north, across Loch Etive and into Lochaber on the way to meet Seaforth, his Mackenzies and their allied clans.

Montrose halted his march at Fort Augustus. It was a delicate situation for any general. His aim had been to attack Seaforth with his 5000 raw levies, and now from Lochaber came the news that Argyll was hard on his heels with 3000 of his men eager to avenge the disgrace of the invasion of his territory. Montrose decided to turn about and seek out Argyll, and the countermarch which followed ranks as one of the great military feats in our history.

On Friday morning the 31st January 1645 the Royal army set out guided by the Keppoch bard, Iain Lom, whose hatred of Clan Campbell knew no bounds. Their route was up Glentarff, over a pass to Glenturret, over another to Glenroy, down to Glenspean, around the shoulders of the Ben Nevis massif to the hill slopes overlooking the old Castle of Inverlochy where Argyll lay encamped. It was a march of some 38 miles through mountain passes choked with snow and down glens no less inhospitable. Food was scarce. The warriors were half starved and yet were able to arrive in sight of the Campbells by dawn on the 2nd February. Such a march in two short winter days and a long winter night was a feat worthy of the Fianna of old, and by any other commander would have been deemed insurmountable.

Argyll had retired to his galley in Loch Linnhe and left the command to Campbell of Auchinbreck. He has been criticised, rather unfairly, for "deserting" his men, but he knew he was not an experienced general, much more a courtier and statesman, while Auchinbreck was a veteran of other wars and well able to command in the field. This brave soldier had been on service in Antrim but Argyll had begged the Council of the Covenant to recall him with some 500 men to reinforce the Clan Campbell during this emergency.

The ensuing battle was short and sharp, the chase long and bloody. Auchinbreck had his Campbells in the centre, with Lowland regiments lent by Baillie on the wings, totalling 3000. Montrose commanded the centre of his 1500 tired little force—Atholl, Glencoe, Appin, some Camerons, John of Moidart with the Clanranald men, Glengarry, and Ogilvie's small body of horse. On the left, O'Cahan and the Antrim men, with Ranald Og of Dunnyveg; on the right, Alasdair and the rest of the Clan Donald of Ulster.

Montrose's flanks soon destroyed the Lowland regiments who had not yet experienced a Highland charge. Few survived to experience it again. Auchinbreck and his clansmen were on their own, outflanked and almost surrounded. They fought bravely but finally broke and fled. Auchinbreck fell with forty gentry of his clan. As far as can be estimated from various accounts of the battle, casualties were 800 on the Covenant side and only eight of Montrose's men. Iain Lom had something to sing about when it was all over, and this he did in his immortal celebration of the battle.

The victory at Inverlochy had its effect. The Royal army marched past Inverness into Moray and at Elgin Seaforth came in and joined Montrose, who sent him home to hold the North for the King. Grants and Gordons joined in greater numbers than before. Many of the Highlanders, however, collected their loot and went home to dispose of it. This was the normal course of events after a victory. It was always the great problem of any general at the head of Highland troops, and it applied even in the case of Montrose who understood both their weakness and their strength, and was above all capable of inspiring their loyalty and making the most effective use of their fighting qualities.

The recruits he found in Moray to some extent replaced that loss and he also obtained a troop of Gordon horse which was a very welcome addition. He was now able to carry out some quite bewildering marches and counter-marches through Angus, taking and sacking Dundee, and accomplishing a masterly retreat to the North before the Covenanting forces under Baillie pressing hard behind him. General Hurry had built up his forces by raising the Covenanters of Moray, and the Mackenzies of Seaforth who had changed sides again. He retreated in the direction of Inverness, and Montrose followed in the belief he was retiring to that town. But Hurry had secured additional reinforcements and turned to resume the offensive. Montrose chose his positions well at Auldearn, and on a wet dark night with dawn breaking the armies confronted each other. Marshy ground lay between and the horse were at a disadvantage. Alasdair charged impetuously as was his wont, eventually to be his undoing at his last battle. Montrose sent him relief, and after the Gordons had broken Hurry's right, Alasdair recovered and attacked with fury. Montrose followed with his foot, charging the main body in characteristic Highland fashion, and the battle became a complete rout. The Covenant side lost 2000 men and all their baggage, and Hurry escaped with his remnants to join forces with Baillie.

The victory, thus won against odds, was encouraging, but Baillie was between Montrose and the Lowlands where, if the Royalist cause was to prosper, the rest of the war should be waged. A victory there would secure the adherence of Royalist sympathisers and an overall victory might be achieved. Baillie had received reinforcements of Whigs from the South-West, but as a result of Auldearn the two opposing sides were more or less equally matched. They met at Alford where Montrose gained one of his most stubbornly contested victories, and in the subsequent pursuit virtually annihilated the Covenanting foot.

The credit for the success at Alford lies mainly with the Gordons whose popular leader, Lord Gordon, was slain in the battle, to the great grief of the whole army. Alasdair and the clans had as usual gone home to deposit their gains, but the chiefs had not remained idle for they now returned at the head of strong contingents of their clansmen which provided Montrose with the largest army he had as yet commanded. He now for the first time resolved to carry his campaign to the Lowlands and by a series of skilful movements at length succeeded in reaching Kilsyth. During the march south the rearguard was covered by Donald of Moidart, for John seems to have handed over the command to his son, who nobly discharged his duties. Twice he turned and put the advance-guard of the Covenant to flight. Baillie's army was drawn up near Kilsyth. Owing to bad advice from the Committee of Estates which accompanied his army, Baillie began a flanking movement which was seen by the clans, who lay in a valley below a ridge. Alasdair launched the clans to the attack, led by Donald of Moidart with his own and the Maclean regiments. It was a charge uphill, without the "advantage of the brae" so much favoured by a Highland army. In spite of this, Donald and the Macleans shattered the centre of Baillie's struggling infantry. The Gordons charged on the left up the valley and smote the head of Baillie's column, and within a short time the rout commenced. The Covenant lost about 4000 foot and horse, while Montrose had only a few hundred men killed. The leaders of the defeated army fled as far as they could from the fatal field. Argyll took horse to Queensferry, thence by boat to Berwick, the third flight of his by sea in this short campaign.

Montrose went on to Glasgow, which he treated generously. He allowed no looting, and some of those who disobeyed his orders were hanged. On the 4th September he withdrew his army to Bothwell. There followed his march through the Borders to the fatal disaster at Philiphaugh on the 13th.

Alasdair and the clans had meantime withdrawn to their own country laden with their spoil. On his way he harried the Campbell country, but was driven down through Kintyre, and thence to Ireland, leaving a garrison in Dunaverty at the extreme tip of that peninsula. He had hoped to return with more men from Antrim, but he became embroiled in the wars in Ireland and was eventually taken prisoner and slain.

John of Moidart and his son Donald retired in peace to their Rough Bounds. John stayed at home. At the invitation of Antrim, Donald took 300 of his clan to Ireland and, with the Glengarry men under their young chief, Angus Og, took part in the seizure of Belfast, Knockfergus, Coleraine and Derry. They were eventually defeated and taken prisoner in Queen's County, but in due course were set free and returned to their own country.

John of Moidart survived to witness the return of King Charles II in 1660. He died in 1670 in Eriskay and was buried at Howmore in Uist with his famous grandfather, the first John Moidartach. He had married Marion, daughter of Sir Ruairi Mor Macleod of Dunvegan by whom he had one son, Donald, and three daughters, one of whom, Anne, married Ranald, 2nd of Benbecula, whose son, Donald, succeeded to the chiefship of Clanranald in 1715 on the early death of the popular young Chief, Alan.

Donald, who succeeded as Captain of Clanranald, led most of his active life during his father's time as we have seen. He served Montrose well, being at times the provider of food for the troops by his skill in cattle-raiding. He fought well in attack and rearguard actions. His character is summed up by the family bard as "a harmless, bashful, affable, unpresuming man in the presence of friends; but powerful and undaunted before his enemies."

We have already recorded that Donald, at the invitation of the Earl of Antrim, went to Ireland with 300 men. The Clanranald history of 1819 is more explicit. Donald went through the Sound of Mull from his Castle of Tirrim in Loch Moidart to Colonsay, and thence to the Sound of Islay where he met a large ship laden with barley belonging to the Estates of Scotland. This he captured, and steered his course to Ireland where he landed safely. He marched first to Acha, thence to the county of Cavan, and latterly quartered his men at Kilkenny. Here a Council sat, which gave him orders to place himself under the command of General Preston. His own men with those of the Earl of Antrim, commanded by Alexander, the Earl's son, formed one regiment above 1500 strong: and of this body Donald was appointed lieutenant-colonel, and Largie's son first captain. Donald was active throughout the campaign of 1648. He was present at the taking of Belfast, Knockfergus, Coleraine and Londonderry, and continued with the King's Army till its defeat in Queen's County where he and Glengarry (Angus, later Lord MacDonell & Aros) were taken prisoners and taken to Kilkenny. They remained there until they were released by the intercession of the Earl of Antrim's lady.

He returned to visit the scenes of his Irish campaign late in 1676 and was given the freedom of the town of Londonderry. His burgess ticket bears the arms of the town and names him as "Donaldus McDonald Dux de Clanranald miles." Thereafter he dwelt in peace on his estates till his death in Canna in 1686 in his sixtieth year and was buried with his fathers in Howmore in South Uist.

Donald married first Janet, daughter of Sir Donald Gorm Og of Sleat, in 1655. She must have been the youngest of Sir Donald's four daughters who all married well into chiefly families. Her sister Margaret had married Angus of Glengarry, Donald Clanranald's companion in arms during the events we have just recorded. There is no record of any issue by this marriage: in fact the Clan-ranald history of 1819 does not mention her at all.

Donald married secondly Marion, daughter of John Macleod of Dunvegan, widow of Norman, son of Norman Macleod of Bernera. By this lady Donald had a family: (1) John "Moidartach," who died unmarried at the age of 21; (2) Alan, who succeeeded his father; (3) Ranald, who had a tack of Boisdale, and succeeded his brother; (4) Marion, who married Alan Macdonald of Morar with issue; (5) Janet, who married Donald of Benbecula with issue; (6) Mary, married in 1703 to Captain Alan Maclean with issue.

Alan, 14th Chief, succeeded his father at the early age of thirteen. He had a short but eventful life, was much loved by his clan and greatly respected by others. During his minority he was brought up by his cousin Donald, 3rd of Benbecula, as Tutor. Everything was done to educate him and instruct him in his duties as Chief. Educated at Inverness and under private tutors, he became an accomplished young man. At the age of sixteen he began his active life as Chief, taking his clan out to join Viscount Dundee.

The Killiecrankie campaign has been more fully dealt with in another chapter. It is enough to say here that young Alan was out with 500 of his Clan, but on the failure of the cause, he had to flee to France with his brother, Ranald, and find asylum at the Court of St Germains. He was thus unable to take advantage of the protection offered to those who submitted and took the oath of allegiance demanded by William before 1st January 1692. Donald of Benbecula, with the majority of the chiefs, took the oath and was thus able to preserve his own and Alan's estates from forfeiture.

While in France Alan met and married Penelope Mackenzie, daughter of Colonel Mackenzie, Governor of Tangier under King Charles II. This lady was both beautiful and accomplished. It was a love match of the most romantic kind. At this time Alan was serving in the French Army under the Duke of Berwick, and it was after peace was restored he found that his Tutor, Donald of Benbecula, had through the kind offices of the Earl of Argyll and Viscount Tarbat been able to keep his estates free from forfeiture. On the 21st July 1696 Mackenzie of Cromartie became surety for his good behaviour, and thereupon Alan returned home to resume his duties as Chief.

In 1704 Alan made up the title to his estates. In 1700 he had already given his brother, Ranald, wadset of the lands of Dalilea and others. The House of Ormiclete was improved and here with the fair Penelope he lived in peace and prosperity for all too short a time. For nine happy years the mansion of Ormiclete became the resort of many visitors to enjoy the hospitality and culture of Alan and his gifted wife. It was a happy time in the best traditions of the House of Clanranald which has always been the repository of all that is best of the ancient culture of the Gael—bardic poetry, music and "seanachas," maintaining and transmitting the historical lore of the ancient Kingdom and Lordship of the Isles. Alan was still at heart a Jacobite, and when the Hanoverian succession rekindled the old flame, he was one of the first to declare for the old House of Stewart.

After the raising of the Royal Standard on the Braes of Mar on the 6th September 1715, Alan and his clan were given an important assignment to go west into Argyll to keep as many as possible of the Campbells and their adherents out of the Rising. On the 17th September, he was at Inverlochy and was joined there by some of the Camerons and Macleans. By the 6th October he was in Strathfillan in Breadalbane country with 700 of his own men now reinforced by the Glencoe men, Stewarts of Appin, Glengarry, Sir John

Maclean, MacGregors, and some MacDougalls of Lorne. With a force now about 2400 strong he marched to Inveraray, arriving there on the 19th October. Negotiations with Sir Duncan Campbell and Sir James Campbell of Auchinbreck were unsuccessful and, after harrying Argyll's lands, Alan brought his men back to Strathfillan. The time thus gained kept a considerable force of Campbells from joining Argyll's army before the battle.

The Jacobite forces under Mar gathered at Perth where they were joined by Sir Donald of Sleat with 500 men, the Seaforths, the Chisholms and others, raising the total strength of the army to about 5000 men. On 13th November the two opposing forces met at Sheriffmuir, a spur of the Ochil Hills. The strange battle that followed has been written about so often that it is not necessary to recount it here in detail. The Clanranald men fought with their usual bravery and dash, headed by their young Chief. Alan fell early in the attack, and his men were so dismayed that they checked for an instant and halted, whereupon the impetuous Chief of Glengarry, Alasdair Dubh, shouted "Tomorrow for mourning, today for revenge!" This spurred Alan's men to further effort and the left wing of Argyll's army which faced Clan Donald was broken and put to precipitate flight. Argyll's right stood more firmly and repulsed the left wing of Mar's army for a time. In the resulting confusion each side believed the victory to be theirs, but concern for their left wings prevented them from exploiting their advantage to the full and both armies withdrew, leaving the issue for the time undecided. Mar, always a vacillating and undependable character, little trusted from the start by the chiefs, retired to Perth where his continued inaction provoked the deepest indignation and dissatisfaction amongst the clansmen.

A month later on the 16th December 1715 the long-hoped for King landed in Peterhead. James VIII, to give him his Jacobite title, was never a commanding or inspiring figure. He had suffered badly from sea-sickness during the voyage, and had a severe cold in the head for most of his brief stay in his Kingdom. He moved south via Glamis in Strathmore to Perth and met the men who had fought at Sheriffmuir. None of them was impressed by his appearance or behaviour. Any one less like a romantic and gay Prince could hardly be imagined. All enthusiasm faded, and the Highlanders began to make for their homes. This time they had little profit to take with them. For them it was a disappointing incident, as indeed it was for most of the supporters of the exiled prince, who embarked on a small French vessel, with Mar and a few others, from the Port of Montrose on the 4th February 1716 and returned to France.

For Clanranald, Alan and his men, the Rising was a disaster. Alan was buried at Innerpeffray, the burial place of the Earls of Perth. By a strange coincidence, his home at Ormiclete, where he and his beloved wife had spent so few years of peace and happiness, was burned down by accident. This strange tragedy took place about the very time Alan was meeting his death, and, still more strangely, the old Castle Tirrim too was burned shortly after Alan had departed to the war. Tradition in Moidart states that the castle was burned by order of the Chief himself, who had a presentiment that he would never return, and did not wish the enemy to find shelter in his ancestral home. Moreover, Fr. Charles Macdonald in his book *Moidart, or among the Clanranalds* states that in his own time the great-grandson of the man who fired the castle at the command of his chief was still alive at a great age and remembered the story quite clearly.

Unfortunately, Alan and his wife left no heir to the estates. So in 1716 Ranald, brother of Alan, who had accompanied him throughout the war, succeeded to the chiefship. That he assumed the leadership at once is clear from a letter he wrote to Cluny MacPherson in February 1716, but with others involved in the Rising he had to flee to the Court of St Germains which was the refuge for so many Jacobites after the collapse of their hopes.

Ranald, 15th Chief, spent all his life in exile in France. In the meantime Mackenzie of Delvin, one of the Clerks of the Court of Session, had been active on his behalf and on that of Alan's widow in an attempt to save the estates for the family. The rather complicated manoeuvres in law to achieve this object are described as follows by our seanachies (*Clan Donald,* Vol. 2, page 345):

> Mackenzie having bought the debts on the estate, obtained a decree and charter of adjudication against the estates and in his own favour. The Barony of Castletirrim [which strange to say was in South Uist] was on 9th November 1723 exposed for sale by the Trustees of Forfeited Estates, and Mr Mackenzie, in whose hands funds had been deposited for the purpose, and who was the highest bidder, purchased the lands of the Barony for £1594 17s 7d. On the 24th August 1724 a Disposition in favour of Mr Mackenzie was granted by the Commissioners, which was followed by a Charter of Resignation under the Great Seal in his favour, dated 29th November, 1725. Infeftment followed by an instrument of Sasine, dated 19th October, 1726. It was to be held in fee blench for payment of 1d. Scots yearly, if asked. The rest of the Clanranald estates were practically all held of the Duke of Argyll, who on 9th August 1719 did, as superior, obtain a decree against the Commissioners of Forfeited Estates, finding him to have a right to the property and rents of these lands in consequence of the attainder of Ranald Macdonald. On the 12th June 1727 a Charter of adjudication of all the lands other than those of the Barony of Castletirrim was granted by John Duke of Argyll in favour of Mr Mackenzie, dated 28th September, and 7th, 13th, 18th, 19th days of October 1727 (ClanRanald Charter Chest). In this way all the Clanranald estates were vested in Mr Mackenzie of Delvin; but, just as the way was paved for conveying them to the exiled chief and application for his pardon was to be made, news came of his death at St Germains, and with him the direct line of the first John Moidartach's descendants became extinct.

Ranald had never married. He died in 1725 although the date and even the year seems to be in some doubt. Communication with the exiles in St Germains must have been somewhat haphazard. The negotiations summarised above went ahead in the capable hands of Mackenzie of Delvin during the chiefship of Donald of Benbecula, 16th Chief of Clanranald.

As the representation of the Clanranald Chiefs now devolves upon the Benbecula collateral family, it would be proper at this stage to trace its origin. It proved to be also the root of several cadet families: Belfinlay, Rammerscales, Gerifliuch, Milton, and Dalilea in which we find such famous names as Flora of Milton, and Alasdair MacMhaighstir Alasdair, the bard of 1745 fame.

The founder of this important family was Ranald, fourth son of Alan, 9th Chief. It is unfortunate that we cannot attribute any great honour to this gentleman. He seems to have been a very restless man of irregular habits, mainly in his marital and extra-marital adventures. Two murders are laid at his door too, if one is to believe the "Criminal Letters" of 5th October 1633. Our seanachies in *Clan Donald* credit him with five "marriages," the *Clanranald History* of 1819 with only two, the Criminal Letters referred to above mention four, Alexander Mackenzie in his history of the Clan Donald lists two; while MacVurich confirms the five "marriages" recorded in *Clan Donald,* Vol. 3. Sifting the evidence of all these it would appear that the first two marriages took place in Ireland during Ranald's younger days, and may not have been any more than hand-fast unions, or pre-marital adventures. The first of these two "wives" was Mary, daughter of

Ranald of Smerbie (in Antrim), son of James of Dunnyveg and the Glens. By her he had Angus Mor, progenitor of the MacDonnells of Ballypatrick in the Barony of Carey in Antrim. The second was Fionnsgoth Burke of the Burkes of Connaught by whom he had three sons, Alexander, Roderick and Farquhar. This union is not mentioned by any but our own seanachies, and we are at a loss to find the source of their information. The third marriage is that with Margaret Macleod, daughter of Norman Macleod of Harris, who was the widow of Norman Og Macleod of Lewis. This lady is not mentioned by the *Clanranald History* at all, and is said to have died without issue by the two other sources. Of the only two firm marriages contracted by the polygamous Ranald, the first seems to have been with Mary, sister of Sir Donald Gorm Og of Sleat, 1st Baronet. She is said to have had a son, Donald Gorm; but three of the sources say she died without issue, having been raped by Sir Lachlan Mackinnon of Strathswordale, for which act he was attainted on 13th December 1622. The second marriage, with Margaret, daughter of Angus of Dunnyveg, is recorded as the last of three illegal unions in the Criminal Letters. By this lady Ranald had seven sons and a daughter, and these seem to have been recognised by the Clan as his lawful family from whom sprang the cadets named above.

On the 28th April 1625, John of Moidart gave his uncle Ranald and his lineal heirs of his wife, Margaret, daughter of Angus of Dunnyveg, a grant of the 13 penny lands of Borg, one penny lands of Griminish, four penny lands of Ballyna-callich, four penny lands of Belfinlay, five penny lands of Balnamanach, the 20 penny lands of Uachdar, all in Benbecula. To these were added the three penny lands of Machrimeanach in South Uist, and the ten shilling lands of Ardnish, Locheilt and Essan, all in Arisaig. These were a very large patrimony, but as Benbecula was under the superiority of the Barons of Sleat, the tenure was somewhat uncertain. Therefore, in addition to the above, his nephew granted him the whole seven penny lands of Bornish Iochdarach, the 7½ penny lands of Bornish Uachdarach, the five penny lands of Kildonan (presumably in Eigg), 10 penny lands of Garvaltos, the ten penny lands of Frobost, and the 6½ penny lands of Kilpheadar in Uist. The principal seat in this vast and somewhat dispersed estate was held to be at Ardnish in Arisaig; but actually Ranald lived in and was known by the name Benbecula. He was now a man of considerable substance, and one of the most important cadets of Clanranald.

On the 20th August 1627, in order to consolidate his hold on Benbecula, he entered into a bond with Sir Donald of Sleat, acknowledging his superiority. On the 4th March 1633 Colin, Earl of Seaforth, who had obtained the superiority of the lands of Ardnish, Locheilt and Essan in Arisaig, gave Ranald a Charter of Ratification for these lands.

Ranald continued to be turbulent and rebellious, causing concern even to his Chief, Sir Donald, who had to report him to the Privy Council. In 1618 he received a remission for the murder of one named Alasdair Roy MacDonald Roy Mhic Innes (Angus). In 1630 Ranald, on account of his irregular marital adventures, was in debt to the Church of Rome, and no doubt in order to earn some remission now came out in support of one of its persecuted members. It seems that a Catholic priest had been celebrating masses in South Uist and was apprehended by the Bishop of the Isles, for what was an illegal practice, to be taken before the Privy Council. After leaving Uist, the party was overtaken by some of Ranald's men and the priest set free. The Bishop complained to the Council, but little could be done about it in those distant isles, and the matter was dropped. Ranald died in 1636, and was succeeded in his lands by his son, Ranald of Borve, the eldest son of the fifth marriage, which was the only legal one of all five. This second Ranald proved to be a much more respectable and amenable man than his father. He took infeftment of his father's lands, and died in or about 1679.

Ranald Og married first Marion, daughter of MacNeil of Barra by whom he had Donald, his successor to Benbecula, who in 1725 became 16th Chief of Clanranald. He married secondly Anna Macdonald, daughter of John, 12th Chief, by whom he had (1) James of Belfinlay; (2) Donald Og, who died without issue; (3) Ranald; (4) Alexander of Gerifliuch, who married Margaret, daughter of Somerled Macdonald of Torlum with issue; and (5) a daughter Marion.

Donald, 3rd of Benbecula, and 16th of Clanranald fought at Killiecrankie, as we have seen, with his young Chief Alan Og for whom he acted as Tutor. He signed, with the other chiefs, the answer sent to Mackay on the 17th August 1689, and again the Bond of Association at Blair Atholl on the 24th of the same month, binding himself to bring 200 men to the King's service. Like the rest of his family he was a staunch Catholic. He profited by the legal negotiations carried through by Mackenzie of Delvin, at the instigation of Penelope, Alan Og's widow. These were successfully completed in 1726, the process being the more easily carried out because he was not personally embroiled in the Rising of 1715. The Clan Donald was greatly indebted to Mackenzie of Delvin for his timely aid during a difficult period in the life of the Clan. He acted also at this time on behalf of the friends of Sir Donald of Sleat, who was also in trouble for his involvement in the Rising of 1715.

Few years were left to Donald after his succession. Most of his life had been spent as Tutor to the young Chief, and to his brother who succeeded. He had reached a ripe old age when he died in 1730, and was buried at Nunton in Benbecula.

Donald was twice married. By his first wife Janet, daughter of Donald, 13th

Glenfinnan, where the Royal Standard was raised on 19th August 1745

of Clanranald, he had Ranald, who succeeded. By his second wife Margaret, daughter of George Mackenzie of Kildun, third son of George, 2nd Earl of Seaforth, he had (1) James, who died unmarried in 1719; (2) Alexander of Boisdale, and (3) Anne, who married John Mackinnon of Mishnish, 2nd son of Lachlan Mackinnon of Strath in Skye.

Ranald, who succeeded his father as 17th Chief, was born in 1692. He is known as "Old Clanranald" at the time of the Rising of 1745, being by then 53 years of age, and having an enterprising son, Ranald, younger of Clanranald, who led the Clan out with the Prince.

Old Ranald was of a quiet disposition and not inclined to take part in the restless affairs of his time. He did not demur, however, when Young Ranald, who was of a different character, espoused the cause of the Prince early in the events of 1745. Alexander of Boisdale, younger brother of Old Clanranald, was of a much more forceful nature. From the first he saw that nothing but disaster could accompany the Rising in the absence of substantial aid from France, and may have influenced his brother accordingly.

The events of 1745-46 have been recorded and told so often that here we need only deal with their effect upon the fortunes of Clanranald. The Prince landed from the *La Doutelle* in Clanranald country, first in the isle of Eriskay and later on the mainland of Moidart at the head of Loch nan Uamh. At the end of the episode he was to embark from the same shore with 123 other fugitives and find safety in France. The period in between was one in which the fortunes of Clanranald were closely intertwined with those of the Prince, and the consequences were disastrous for the Clan.

Loch nan Uamh, with the cairn marking the spot where the Prince first set foot on the Scottish mainland and a year later embarked for France

During the active part of the campaign of 1745/46 the old Chief remained quietly at home, and we hear little of him until the Prince had begun his wanderings, which took him back to Clanranald country, first to the mainland of Moidart and Arisaig, thence to the Outer Isles, and back again to Moidart for his final departure. During this time the old Chief did not fail in his duty, but befriended the Prince, and helped in every way possible to aid his escape. In this he was ably assisted by his lady. The story of how this was done through the agency of Neil MacEachan and Flora of Milton is too well known to require telling here.

Young Clanranald was among the first to meet the prince at Glenfinnan with some 150 men brought in by his cadet, Alan of Morar. At Prestonpans the strength of his regiment was estimated at 250; but reinforcements later brought the numbers up to between 350 and 400. Casualties at Culloden were heavy. The regiment fought bravely on every field of action as their forefathers had done. Few if any of the Clanranald men in the outer isles had been able to join their young Chief, and the regiment was composed mainly of men from the mainland estates.

After the abortive attempt to get the Prince away from Lewis and Scalpay in Harris, he had to return to South Uist where Old Clanranald met him and asked him to stay at his residence of Nunton; but, for safety, Neil MacEachan took him to the east side of the Isle in Glen Corodale where he stayed for some time. He was forced to move from one hiding place to another in Uist until arrangements were at last made for him to be escorted by Neil and Flora across the sea to Skye where they arrived on Sunday the 29th June.

Old Ranald of Clanranald, having done all he could for the Prince in his wanderings in the Long Island, had his last communication with him on the 8th of July. He was at Scotus House with Old Scotus when word was brought that the Prince was in hiding on a little island, still called *Eilean a Phrionnsa,* about a mile from Scotus. Old Ranald told the messenger that there was no more he could do to help. On the 20th September the Prince left his kingdom with about 23 officers of his now broken army, and some 100 others, in two ships. Among the clansmen who embarked with the Prince were young Lochiel, Lochgarry, John Roy Stewart, Dr Archibald Cameron (Lochiel's brother), Bishop Hugh MacDonald, and Neil MacEachan, his loyal guide and protector in his wanderings.

In the pursuit that followed Culloden, Young Clanranald sought refuge in the wilds of Moidart, but in the end found his way to Brahan Castle, where he met and married Mary Hamilton. This seems to have been accomplished without the knowledge of the Earl of Seaforth who was on the Government side during the rising, but was away from home at the time. The couple went to Cromarty and boarded a ship bound for London under the names of Mr and Mrs Black. Thence they were able to escape to the continent. In France, with the help of Prince Charles Edward and Louis XV, he entered the army, serving under Marshal Saxe.

All this time Young Clanranald was under sentence of attainder. Owing to a mistake in the bill of attainder, in which Ranald was named Donald, eventually the Judges of the Court of Session annulled the bill and Ranald was able to return to his native land. This was probably in the year 1752. He was, however, still under some suspicion and was kept in London until April 1754. He then returned home. With the aid of his father and brother, Donald of Benbecula, he was able to live on the family estates.

The Clan, as an entity, like all the others, ceased to exist after Culloden. The loyal men were hounded across the country and transported, murdered and dispossessed of their homes. The Clearances completed the destruction of the Clan as a compact unit. This sad story is a matter of history told by so many other writers that it would be useless to attempt to cover it adequately in the scope of this book.

The Arms of
AENEAS RANALD WESTROP McDONELL, Esquire
(Representer of the Family of Glengarry)

Or, an eagle displayed Gules surmounted of a lymphad Sable, her sails furled up and rigging proper, in the dexter chief point a dexter hand couped in fess of the Second and in the sinister a cross crosslet fitchée of the Third. Above the Shield is placed a Helmet befitting his degree, with a Mantling Gules doubled Argent, and on a Wreath of his Liveries is set for Crest a raven proper perching on a rock Azure, and in an Escrol over the same this Motto CRAGAN·AN·FHITHICH; on a Compartment below the Shield are placed for Supporters two bears each having an arrow pierced through his body all proper, and in an Escrol entwined with the Compartment this Motto PER·MARE·PER·TERRAS

Lyon Register (Volume 1, Folio 57b).

20

The Macdonalds of Glengarry

THE GLEN which gave its name to this notable branch of Clan Donald is in Lochaber which was a part of the old Province of Moray, ruled by the Celtic Mormaers as far back as the time of Macbeth and before. It was a very large area bounded to the east by the larger parts of Moray and Badenoch, to the north by the Earldom of Ross, to the south by Lorne, and to the west by the Rough Bounds of Garmoran. To the north-east the frontier bordering Moray was in the Great Glen at the watershed between Loch Oich and Loch Ness. This is just where the Glengarry lands start and stretch westwards to Cameron country and north to Ross. The first mention of the name as a place name is found in 1306 when Bruce gave a grant of the Glen to his nephew, Thomas Randolph, Earl of Moray.

After Bannockburn the King gave his friend, Angus of the Isles, many lands, amongst them half of Lochaber, while the other half went to Ruairi of Garmoran who held them until he was forfeited in 1325. They then went to the Lords of the Isles, who thus acquired the whole of Lochaber, and it remained in their possession until the final forfeiture in 1493. Thus the lands of Glengarry were held by the Macdonalds from the early 1300s until the middle of the 19th century, when the 16th Chief fell into debt and was forced to sell them.

How the family and Clan we know as "of Glengarry" came into occupation of those lands is a matter of some speculation, because few records exist which cast light on their history up to the fall of the Lordship. Their roots are to be found in the family of Good John of Islay and Amie MacRuairi. John made over to his eldest son Ranald many lands within the Lordship, amongst which were Garmoran, the North Isles, and a large part of Lochaber. This transfer was confirmed by Robert II in 1371.

Ranald had two sons, Alan and Donald. When he divided his vast possessions between them, he gave Garmoran and the North Isles, the old MacRuairi lands, to Alan. To Donald he gave the Stewardship of Lochaber, and it is likely that part of that territory, including Glengarry, came into Donald's legal possession later, although no record exists to prove this. MacVurich states definitely that Donald was "the second son of Ranald and that he gave him the Stewardship of Lochaber." Our seanachies agree, and trace the Chiefs of Glengarry from him. It should be mentioned, however, that the Chief of Glengarry in 1820 omits Donald from the line completely, and traces his family from Alexander, Donald's son. Another problem is presented by the appearance of one John, stated by the MS of 1450 to be an elder brother of Alexander, son of Donald, son of Ranald. This MS is regarded as very reliable by most seanachies. It states:

The children of Reginald [Ranald] were Alan and John, who was blind from his youth, and Donald and Angus Riamhach; and these are the children of Alan, *viz.* Roderic, and Huistein and John.

The children of Donald, son of Reginald, were John, whose mother was Laiglib, daughter of Cimair, and Alexander of the Woods and Angus Og, children of the daughter of Macimie [Fraser of Lovat].

MacVurich makes no mention of this John but traces the line through Alexander to Donald, son of Ranald. The Glengarry Chief of 1820 also leaves John out of the line. From the evidence available, however, we may conclude that Donald, Ranald's second son, was the founder of the Glengarry family, and that Donald's second son Alexander (*Alasdair nan Coille*) was third in line, succeeding his half-brother John who either died without issue or may have been dispossessed by Alexander. The latter died in 1460 and was succeeded by his son John, who is said to have been treacherously murdered by Lovat in 1501. John was succeeded by his son Alexander, 6th of Glengarry, and it is during his reign that the family begins to emerge from the obscurity which covers its earlier history.

It is interesting to note that in Dean Munro's *Description of the Western Isles,* written in the year 1549, no reference is made to the family of Glengarry, while the families of Sleat, Dunnyveg, Ardnamurchan, Clanranald and Keppoch are given as the five principal families of the Clan Donald at that time. It is quite evident that the family of Glengarry had not risen to the importance of the other families in the Dean's time but could be reckoned as one with the families of Moidart and Knoydart. The history of Glengarry down to the charter of 1538 is part of the history of the Clanranald. Not, indeed, until well on in the sixteenth century did the family of Glengarry act an independent part. If they ever held charters for their lands under the Lords of the Isles they are now lost. The probability is that they never held any written title for their lands prior to the grant of James v to Alexander of Glengarry in 1538. As far back as 1466, John, Earl of Ross, granted to Duncan Mackintosh, Chief of the highly favoured family of Mackintosh, the office of Bailie of his hereditary lands of Glengarry, and many others in Lochaber, including Keppoch. It is difficult to account for this favour conferred on Mackintosh by the Lord of the Isles over the heads of two cadet families of his own house; but the conferring of this important office on Mackintosh, it may be presumed, affected Macdonald of Glengarry as little as we know it did Macdonald of Keppoch, and his authority was as little regarded by the one as by the other.

Although there is no definite record of the part played by the heads of this family during the 15th century, yet it may be assumed that in the struggles of the Clan Donald, which ended in the final forfeiture in 1493, the family of Glengarry, like their kinsmen of Clanranald, played a not undistinguished part.

The fall of the Lordship of the Isles brought about many changes, both in the social and political economy of the Clan Donald families. The policy of the King was not friendly, though the great energy with which he set about restoring order among the broken clans is worthy of all praise. The first step towards receiving the allegiance of the Islanders was the insistence by the King on all the Chiefs taking out charters for their lands formerly held of the Lords of the Isles. With this purpose in view, James proceeded to the Highlands immediately after the forfeiture, and received the submission of most of the Chiefs. Among the first to submit was the Chief of Clanranald, who received two charters, dated respectively August 3rd and 5th, 1494, while at the same time Angus Reochson

MacRanald, the head of one of the branches of the Clanranald, received a charter of the lands of Benbecula and others.

Alexander of Glengarry appeared to be unwilling to accept the terms on which these Crown charters were granted, and the result was that in 1501 he was summoned for occupying the lands of Morar without a title, while Alexander, eldest son of the Earl of Huntly, had in the previous year received a grant of a portion of his lands of Glengarry. It is very evident that Alexander stood in a rebellious attitude towards the Government for many years after the fall of the Lordship of the Isles, from the fact that the lands of Glengarry are leased alternately to Huntly and Lochiel.

The attitude of the Chief of Glengarry is partly attributable to the policy of the Government. The King, no doubt with the desire to see good government established in the Highlands and Islands, committed the task of carrying out his policy to Huntly and Argyll. Having broken the power of the Island family, he delegated that power to two noblemen who were universally and deservedly detested by the clans. The one was an interloper within the Highland line; while the other, boasting of a long line of native Celtic ancestry, had risen to power on the ruins of the smaller tribes of Argyllshire, of which for centuries his family formed one. To Huntly and Argyll can be traced, without any difficulty, most of the strife which for centuries disgraced Highland history. It was surely short-sighted policy on the part of the King and his advisers to deprive of its power a family who for long years had been the kindly rulers of the Highlanders, and put it in the hands of two unscrupulous and selfish noblemen like Huntly and Argyll.

Although Alexander of Glengarry was still not on good terms with the King when Donald Dubh was released from his prison in Loch Awe by the bold men of Glencoe, he did not join that short-lived insurrection. In 1505 the unhappy Donald Dubh was handed over to the King by Maclean and confined in Edinburgh Castle, where he languished until his final effort to regain his rightful inheritance in 1543.

Meantime, when the King fell at Flodden in 1513, Sir Donald Gallda of Lochalsh thought the time ripe for another attempt to restore the Lordship. This time Glengarry joined in and headed a profitable raid on the lands of Urquhart to the east and the estates of John Grant of Freuchie, Laird of Grant. Castle Urquhart was taken and held for three years while the raiders carried off a large "creach" from the Grant lands and others. When Sir Donald Gallda died without issue in 1519, Alexander laid claim to his lands in right of his wife Margaret, sister and co-heiress of Sir Donald. To this end he made friends with the Earl of Argyll, recently appointed the King's Lieutenant of the Isles in succession to his father, who had fallen at Flodden. The lands of Morar and Lochalsh, being within the Earl's jurisdiction, were made over to Alexander of Glengarry under a bond of man-rent. The occupation of the Glengarry lands remained uncertain, however. Although crown property, they were occupied without any right or title by the "inhabitants of the Isles," in others words, by Alan MacRuairi of Garmoran, Alexander of Glengarry and others referred to in the Crown rental of 1496. In 1510 the lands and Bailiary of Glengarry had been granted to the Earl of Huntly for a period of nine years. The lease having now terminated, the chiefs of Lochiel and Glengarry made an agreement on the 21st March 1521 at Banavie, arranging how the lands should be allocated in the event of either of them obtaining possession. No immediate results followed from the agreement, but Alexander of Glengarry appears to have been more successful elsewhere. In 1524 he and Margaret, his wife, raised an action before the Lords of Council for allowing their claim to the lands of Lochalsh, and though it was not then acknowledged, they were allowed to remain in possession for the time.

Meanwhile, Alexander of Glengarry became involved in the troubles raised by Alexander of Dunnyveg, and others. In the year 1531, he was with several Macdonald chieftains, and other Islesmen, repeatedly summoned for treason; and, following the example of Alexander of Dunnyveg, he finally submitted to the King, and was pardoned for all past offences. About this time, the King granted to Ewen Cameron of Lochiel the 12 merklands of Invergarry, and others, for the yearly payment of 40 merks. Again, in 1536, the non-entry and other dues of the same lands, including the lands of Sleisgarrow in Glengarry, were granted to Donald, the son of Ewen of Lochiel. Alexander of Glengarry seems still to be in bad grace with the Government, but there is every reason to believe that he and Lochiel settled the matter of possession of the lands of Glengarry amicably, in terms of their bond of 1521.

Now had arrived the era of charters, and with it the prosperity and power of the family of Glengarry. If there was some hesitation on the part of the Chief to accept Crown charters, it was only an expression of a feeling common to all the chiefs of his time, who at length found themselves face to face with that feudal yoke from which Highlanders had striven for centuries to keep themselves free. Glengarry, after holding out longer than many of them, had at last to yield to the inevitable. On 30th March 1538 there is "ane letter maid to Alexander McAlester of Glengarry his airis and assignais of the gift of the nonentries of all and haill ye xx penny worth of land of Glengarry callit ye Slesmoyne wt ye pertinents liand in ye Lordschip of Lochabir; and of all and haill the twelf penny worth of land of ye lands of Morour with the pertinents, liand in the Lordschip of Garmoran." Alexander of Glengarry, having resigned his lands of Glengarry and Morar into the King's hands, on the 6th of March 1539, with Margaret his wife, and Angus his heir, received a Crown charter of the lands of Glengarry and Morar, half the lands of Lochalsh, Lochcarron, and Lochbroom, with the Castle of Strome.

The good relationship thus established between Alexander of Glengarry and the Government was of short duration. In the month of May of the same year the flag of revolt was raised by Donald Gorm of Sleat, who now put forward a claim to the Lordship of the Isles, and Alexander of Glengarry was among the first to join him. On the untimely death of Donald and consequent failure of the enterprise, the King hastened to the Isles to restore order amongst the clans. Realising their danger, many of the chiefs went to pay their respects to the sovereign. After cruising for some time amongst the Outer Islands, the Scottish fleet anchored in Loch-Chaluimchille, since known as Portree. Here Alexander of Glengarry and others of "MacConeyllis kin" went on board the King's ship expecting to be graciously received by the sovereign, but they found themselves prisoners instead. The King, who was delighted at this clever stroke, carried the chiefs with him to Edinburgh, where they were confined during his pleasure. John Mackenzie of Kintail was not among the chiefs taken captive by the sovereign. It was at the siege of his Castle of Eilean Donan that Donald Gorm met his death. For his services to Government, both in the Isles and elsewhere, the King bestowed on Mackenzie the lands of Laggan, Kilfinnan, and Invergarry, forfeited by Alexander of Glengarry for the part taken by him in the insurrection of Donald Gorm. From this time may be dated the bitter feud which existed between the families of Glengarry and Kintail; and now, too, we have the initiation of that policy of playing the Government game for the glorifying of the Mackenzies, pursued so persistently and successfully by the Chiefs of Kintail.

The King, satisfied that he had taught the Islesmen a salutary lesson, liberated some of the less turbulent chiefs, on their providing hostages for their future good behaviour. The rest, among whom was Alexander of Glengarry, were meanwhile kept in close confinement in Edinburgh, where they remained until shortly after the King's death in 1542, when they were set at liberty by the Regent Arran.

The angry chiefs had not long to wait before the opportunity arose for them to take their revenge for their treacherous treatment by the late King. Donald Dubh once more broke out of his prison. He was joined at once by all the loyal men of the Isles, and Glengarry was among the first to raise his clan and take a prominent part in this, the last, rising in support of the old Lordship. Glengarry was one of the seventeen chiefs who formed the Council of the Isles, and in that capacity he, with the others, signed "The Commission of the Lord of the Isles of Scotland to treat with the King of England" in 1545. It is interesting to note that he signed, with his hand at the pen, "Alexr. rannoldson of Glengarrie." This is one of the occasions when the Glengarry chiefs used that patronymic form, so often quoted by the Chief of 1820 in his wordy warfare with the Chief of Clanranald.

During this time, while the rebellion of Donald Dubh was still in progress, the quarrel between Ranald Gallda and John of Moidart came to a head. Alexander of Glengarry naturally supported John of Moidart, who was preferred by Clanranald men, and took part in the Battle of Blar-na-leine in July 1544. He followed up that victory by a raid on Urquhart and Glenmoriston in which he was accompanied by his son Angus and young Cameron of Lochiel. This was one of the most extensive and costly raids carried out on those long-suffering estates by the Western Clans. A list of the spoil, as given in D. N. Mackay's *Urquhart and Glenmoriston,* makes impressive reading. It included 1188 full grown cattle, 392 young cattle, 525 calves, 383 horses and mares, 1978 sheep, 1099 lambs, 1410 goats, 794 kids, 122 swine, 3006 bolls of oats, 1277 bolls of bear (barley), and furniture, linen and cloth valued at over £500. In addition the Laird of Grant lost 200 bolls of oats, 100 bolls of bear, 100 big cattle, 100 calves, 16 horses, 300 sheep, much furniture and household goods, 3 great boats, and other goods as well as money.

On 3rd August 1546 summonses were issued by the Government under the Royal Signet at the instance of James Grant of Freuchie and John Mor Grant of Glenmoriston against Glengarry, Angus his son, and young Cameron of Lochiel, claiming compensation for the raid. On 22nd October of the same year Freuchie and Glenmoriston were awarded damages to the amount of over £10,000 and £700 Scots respectively, which seems a very low estimate of the value of their losses. Disregarding this summons, the raiders were duly denounced at the Market Cross of Inverness, with the threat that their lands would be "apprised" by the Grants. After all had been done by law to make the offenders appear to answer for their crimes, Grant of Freuchie was given a Crown grant of all the lands owned by the Glengarry family in both Inverness and Ross, the latter being those that had come to Alexander by his marriage with the heiress of Lochalsh.

This was one of several attempts to deprive the Chief of Glengarry of his rightful inheritance over the next hundred years. All failed. In this case, as in many others, the Chiefs of Clanranald, Glengarry and Keppoch ignored parchments and summonses and eventually were given remission for their crimes. The Crown and its agents, having found it impossible to bring them personally to answer the charges, made the best of a bad job and allowed them to carry on as before. In some cases even the "criminals" were asked often to restore law and order by bringing to justice other more flagrant offenders.

In this case it is interesting to note that the Laird of Grant complained bitterly that the tenants of Glengarry, Morar, Lochalsh, Lochcarron, and Loch

Broom were exploiting the fisheries and timber stocks to the full, without paying him any rents. Letters from the Queen's Signet failed to put a stop to these practices. More letters followed requiring Glengarry to hand over the Castle of Strome to Grant within six days. All the Clanranald men were just as unwilling as Glengarry to see "foreigners" on their doorstep; and, faced with such powerful opposition, the scheme was abandoned. Alexander of Glengarry had the powerful backing of the bold John Moidartach in all these troubles, and the two together presented a formidable front which the available forces of the Crown could hardly attack with any hope of success. Clan Cameron too were frequently companions in arms with the Clan Donald men of Moidart and Glengarry on such occasions.

In 1548 Glengarry was given remission for his treasonable conduct during Donald Dubh's insurrection and also for failing to answer the Royal summons to bring his men to Fala Muir the previous year. He was also remitted for his part in the campaign of Blar-na-leine in 1544 where Lovat and his son had been killed. But it is sad to have to record that this act of forgiveness did not change his attitude towards the Government. He remained defiant. The efforts of Huntly and Argyll added to those of the Regent Arran bore no fruit, and in 1552 Arran decided that perhaps a personal visit to the Highlands in force might bring the dissidents to heel. Although some gave in their submission, Clanranald, Glengarry and Lochiel remained aloof. In 1555 the new Regent, the Dowager Queen, a much stronger character than the ineffective Arran, wrote to Rose of Kilravock deploring the outrageous behaviour of the western clans, and declaring her intention to marshal her forces for the pursuit of the evil-doers. These and similar threats, however, failed to overawe the chiefs and restore order among the Western clans.

Alexander of Glengarry died in 1560. By his wife, Margaret, heiress of Lochalsh, he had: (1) Angus, who succeeded; (2) Alan of Lundie; (3) Godfrey, who was slain by the Mackenzies at Lochcarron in 1582, leaving one son, Archibald; (4) Ranald, who fell with Godfrey; (5) Roderick, about whom nothing is known.

James Grant, 3rd of Freuchie, had died in 1553, and his son John continued to assert his claim to the Glengarry lands granted to his father by the Crown. So far from accepting this claim, any more than in the case of the old Laird of Grant, the three western clans assumed a threatening attitude, and at length Grant had to appeal to the Crown asserting that his enemies were contemplating a massive raid on the lands of Urquhart and Glenmoriston. In response to his appeal, the Council sent letters on 1st March 1567 to Lachlan Mackintosh of Dunachton and Kenneth Mackenzie of Kintail, charging them to defend the Laird of Grant against all comers, with special reference to the three clans who had caused so much trouble for so long. As far back as March 1545 the Grants, Mackintoshes, Mackenzies and other smaller clans in Ross, had formed a league against Clanranald, Glengarry and Clan Cameron, the aim being to drive Glengarry and Lochiel out of Ross-shire. This was the beginning of the long feud between the Mackenzies and Glengarry which disturbed the peace of those regions for many years to come.

Grant of Freuchie had begun to find his lands in Ross-shire an increasingly troublesome acquisition, and was now prepared to relinquish his title to these lands in the most advantageous manner possible. The Mackenzies of Kintail were rapidly increasing their power in the North at the expense of the old vassals of the Lordship, and in pursuit of their policy were employing much the same methods as the Campbells had found so profitable in the South. One of the most peaceful of these methods was to enter into matrimonial alliances with their neighbours, which led to the acquisition of lands and secured their help against their enemies. Thus Grant of Freuchie, seeing no prospect of ever obtaining peaceable possession of his lands in Ross-shire, now sought an escape from his predicament in a matrimonial alliance with his more powerful neighbour.

On the 26th July 1570 a contract of marriage was made at Elgin by which Colin Mackenzie of Kintail agreed to marry Barbara Grant, the Laird of Grant's daughter, with a dowry of 2000 merks and the half lands of Lochbroom, which had been part of the lands acquired by Glengarry by his marriage with the heiress of Lochalsh. These had been given to Grant in 1546, but never occupied or enjoyed by him. In return Mackenzie gave Freuchie a bond of man-rent undertaking to defend him against the depredations of Clanranald and Glengarry. On the 17th November 1571 at Elgin another marriage contract was entered into with Angus of Glengarry by which Donald, Angus's son, was to marry Helen, daughter of Grant, who in return was to give back to Angus the lands, including Glengarry and others, which had been acquired as compensation for the losses sustained in the great raid of 1545. Angus was to help Grant against any aggressor, saving only the King and Chief of Clanranald. At the same time the lands of Lundie were given to Alan, Angus's brother; and Angus bound himself to give Grant all necessary aid in defence of Urquhart and Glenmoriston. The result of all these negotiations was that the Laird of Grant had a powerful ally in Mackenzie of Kintail, while Angus of Glengarry regained his ancestral estates by legal charter. On July 8th 1574 King James VI granted to Angus of Glengarry a charter of the lands of Glengarry, 12 merklands of Morar, 12 merklands of Lochalsh, and 4 merklands of Lochcarron. All these had been resigned in his favour by John Grant of Freuchie in the contract of 1571.

Thus Angus succeeded in taking legal occupation of the lands he and his father had held so long in defiance of all attempts to dispossess them. Grant gained little more than a valuable alliance with Mackenzie, and a safeguard for his lands of Urquhart and Glenmoriston. Angus was now in an amicable relationship with the Crown. In 1574 he is found in Edinburgh conferring with the Lords of the Privy Council regarding the maintenance of law and order in the Highlands. At this time there had been complaints from Lowland fishermen that they had been attacked and some even murdered by Glengarry's tenants while fishing in Lochbroom, Lochcarron, and other lochs in the west of Ross. Fishing rights in coastal waters have always been a bone of contention even down to the present day, and these lochs were regarded by the local fishers as one of their main sources of livelihood. Attempts to poach on their preserves were resented bitterly, and violence and murder were resorted to at times. The King and his Privy Council too valued the fisheries highly as a great contribution to the revenue of the realm and ordained that no foreigners should be permitted to fish in those lochs "undir the pane of confiscation of their shippis and gudis and punishing of their personis at oure Soveranis will." Angus of Glengarry was given power to hold courts as and when required to deal with such offences within his "dominioun." His tenure of his new judicial office was of brief duration, however, because he died later in that same year.

Angus, 7th of Glengarry, was married three times. By his first wife, Janet, daughter of Hector Maclean of Duart, he had (1) Donald, who succeeded; (2) John who had a son, Donald Gorm. By his second wife, Margaret Macleod of Dunvegan, he had (3) Angus, and (4) a daughter, Margaret. By his third wife, a daughter of Mackenzie of Kintail, he had a daughter who married Roy Mackenzie of Gairloch.

Donald MacAngus, 8th of Glengarry, was one of the longest-lived chiefs in the Highlands. He reigned as chief for over 70 years.

The first time he appeared on record was in 1575 when he complained to the Privy Council that Lord Lovat was preventing the Glengarry men from taking their timber for sale in Inverness by boats or rafts on Loch Ness, a most convenient and cheap form of transport for them. After a short haul from their own country to the western end of that long loch, they were able to deliver their timber to market in Inverness. Donald won his case and Lovat was ordered to desist. The timber trade like the fisheries figured largely in the economy of the Highlands. Apart from petty squabbles like this Donald started his reign in peace and security.

Two years later, however, a serious threat came from an unexpected quarter. Colin, 6th Earl of Argyll, celebrated his accession to the Earldom by invading the inner isles and, after carrying away a large spoil, made preparations for invading the mainland and making Glengarry a principal point of the attack. The usual excuse was given, that he merely wished to restore law and order in that region, but the real reason was probably that Donald had provoked the Earl's resentment by opposing him in his recent activities. So formidable were the Earl's preparations that Donald was forced to appeal for protection to the Privy Council. The Council took a grave view of the situation and issued a proclamation protecting the Chief of Glengarry and his clan who, they said, were behaving peaceably like good subjects. Letters were sent to the Tutor of Lovat, Mackenzie of Kintail, Grant of Freuchie, the Chief of Mackintosh, Munro of Foulis, Ross of Balnagowan, Keppoch, and Chisholm, ordering them to "pass to assist and defend with their kin and followers Donald MacAngus and his his friends and servants." This was followed by a proclamation at the Market Cross of Inverness calling upon Maclean, Mackinnon of Strath and others not to engage in any invasion of the Glengarry lands under pain of treason. These seemed very elaborate precautions for the Council to take on behalf of a clan so often in trouble with the Council itself. It may well be that they realised the magnitude of the disturbances that would result in the Highlands if an effective stop were not immediately placed upon Argyll's nefarious schemes.

Though saved by the timely intervention of the Privy Council from an invasion by the Campbells, the Chief of Glengarry almost immediately became involved in a serious quarrel with another Clan. The relations between himself and Mackenzie of Kintail had been for some time anything but friendly, and at length their unhappy differences resulted in an open rupture between the families. The lands of Thomas Dingwall of Kildun in Lochalsh and Lochcarron, inherited by him through his mother, Janet Macdonald of Lochalsh (sister of Margaret, co-heiress of Lochalsh and wife of Alexander, 6th of Glengarry), had been acquired by purchase by the family of Kintail. But Colin Mackenzie of Kintail, who had also acquired the lands owned by Glengarry in Lochbroom, seems not to have been satisfied with this large addition to the original little territory of his family in Kintail. His great ambition appears to have been to obtain possession, by fair means or foul, of the whole of the Lochalsh family lands in Wester Ross. In any case, it is quite evident that in the quarrel with Glengarry at this time, Mackenzie was the aggressor. It suits the Mackenzie chroniclers to put a very different complexion upon it. According to them, Glengarry had behaved in a very cruel and tyrannical manner towards the native tenants of his West Coast lands, especially towards the Mathesons and the Clan Iain Uidhir, supposed to have been the original possessors of the lands of Lochalsh. The native tribes naturally sided with their near neighbours, the Mackenzies, and thus no doubt brought down upon their heads the wrath of the Chief of Glengarry. That Chief, who lived at a great distance from his West Coast property, was obliged in defence of that possession, and of such of his tenants as adhered to him, to take up his residence at Lochcarron, and place a strong garrison in the Castle of Strome. The presence of the Macdonald garrison in their midst only tended, as might have been expected, to exasperate the men of Wester Ross and provoke them to commit yet greater outrages on the adherents of Glengarry. Revolting accounts are given in the Mackenzie and other manuscripts of the reprisals on both sides, but as these are decidedly one-sided and greatly exaggerated, little reliance need be put upon them as evidence on either side. There need be no doubt, however, that the feud between the Chiefs was carried on in a savage and bloody manner, and that little quarter was given on either side. Matters at length had assumed so alarming an aspect that Glengarry was obliged to invoke the intervention of the Government.

At a meeting held at Dalkeith on 10th August 1582, Glengarry appeared personally before the Privy Council with a complaint containing very serious charges against the Mackenzies. On the last day of February of the previous year, he alleged that "great slauchters, heirschippis and skaithis" were committed upon him, his kin, friends, and servants, which he estimated at £120,000 Scots. Again, in the beginning of March, he was visited by Ruairi Mackenzie of Redcastle, brother of Kintail, and Dougal, Ruairi's brother, accompanied by two hundred persons "bodin with twa-handit swordis, bowes, darlochis, hagbuttis, pistolettis prohibite to be worne or usit, and other wappinis invasive." And finally, on 16th April, they came upon the complainer at Lochcarron, took him captive, and detained him a prisoner for forty days "in coves, craigis, woddis, and uther desert places at thair pleasour," where none of his friends had access to him. Ruairi Mackenzie and his accomplices at the same time also apprehended Ruairi, Glengarry's uncle, three of his sons, and others, his friends and servants, to the number of 33 persons. They caused the hands of these persons to be bound with their own "sarkis," cruelly slew them, and appointed that they should not be buried like Christian men, but cast forth to be eaten by dogs and swine. At the end of the complainer's captivity, he was carried to Colin Mackenzie of Kintail, and from him to Strome Castle, which the Mackenzies besieged, threatening at the same time to hang Glengarry in sight of the garrison, unless they surrendered it. The Mackenzies are still further charged with having violently taken Donald Makmorach Roy, one of Glengarry's chief kinsmen, "bait thame in his blude and be a strange exemple to satisfie their cruell and unnaturall heartis, first cut off his handis, nixt his feit, and last his heid, and having cassin the same in a peitpott, exposit and laid out his carcage to be a prey for doggis and revenus beistis." Having heard this dreadful indictment, the Privy Council passed an order charging Colin Mackenzie of Kintail, who failed to appear, to surrender the Castle of Strome to Donald of Glengarry within twenty-four hours, under pain of rebellion. Mackenzie at the same time was ordered to find sufficient caution for the safety of Donald and his friends in person and goods, and if he should fail to do so within fifteen days after being charged, he was to be denounced rebel and put to the horn.

On the 2nd day of December, David Clapen in Leith, and John Irving of Kinnock, became cautioners for Colin Mackenzie in the sum of 2000 merks, and the Chief of Kintail pledged himself to deliver the Castle of Strome to Donald of Glengarry in the event of the Council finding that he should do so. Shortly thereafter, on 15th January 1583, Kintail petitioned the Privy Council, the burden of which was a complaint against the Glengarry chief for having, as he alleged, "upon a certain sinister and malicious narration," obtained a decree charging the petitioner to deliver up the Castle of Strome. He pleaded ignorance

THE MACDONALDS OF GLENGARRY

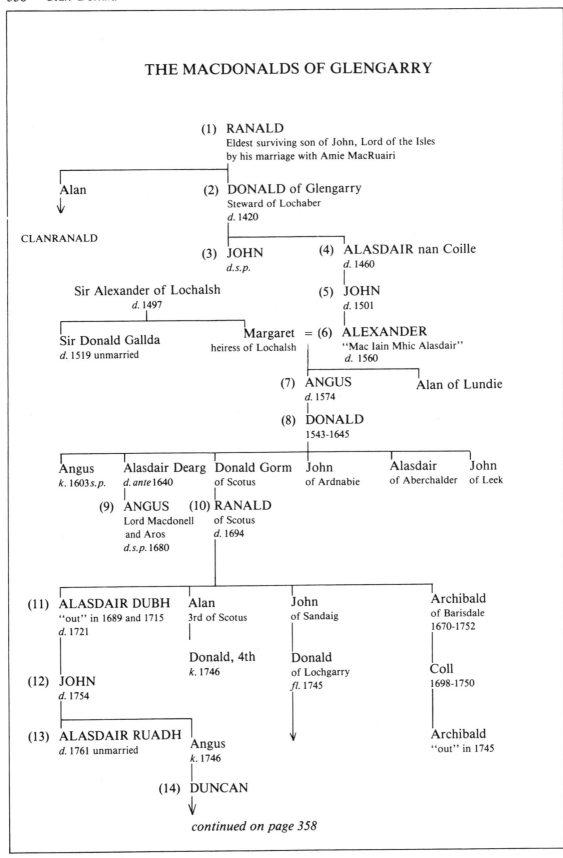

(1) RANALD
Eldest surviving son of John, Lord of the Isles
by his marriage with Amie MacRuairi

Alan

CLANRANALD

(2) DONALD of Glengarry
Steward of Lochaber
d. 1420

(3) JOHN
d.s.p.

(4) ALASDAIR nan Coille
d. 1460

(5) JOHN
d. 1501

Sir Alexander of Lochalsh
d. 1497

Sir Donald Gallda
d. 1519 unmarried

Margaret = **(6) ALEXANDER**
heiress of Lochalsh   "Mac Iain Mhic Alasdair"
d. 1560

(7) ANGUS
d. 1574

Alan of Lundie

(8) DONALD
1543-1645

Angus
k. 1603 *s.p.*

Alasdair Dearg
d. ante 1640

Donald Gorm
of Scotus

John
of Ardnabie

Alasdair
of Aberchalder

John
of Leek

(9) ANGUS
Lord Macdonell
and Aros
d.s.p. 1680

(10) RANALD
of Scotus
d. 1694

(11) ALASDAIR DUBH
"out" in 1689 and 1715
d. 1721

Alan
3rd of Scotus

John
of Sandaig

Archibald
of Barisdale
1670-1752

Donald, 4th
k. 1746

Donald
of Lochgarry
fl. 1745

Coll
1698-1750

(12) JOHN
d. 1754

(13) ALASDAIR RUADH
d. 1761 unmarried

Angus
k. 1746

Archibald
"out" in 1745

(14) DUNCAN

continued on page 358

of the charge brought against him by Glengarry, a summons having never been served upon him, either at his dwelling-house or elsewhere; and he alleged that he received the Castle of Strome by contract from Glengarry, while formerly he had been charged by the Lords of Council to deliver it to John Grant of Freuchie, as pertaining to him in heritage. He was, therefore, at a loss to know whether to give up the Castle to Glengarry or to Freuchie.

Pending further inquiry, and on the ground that he found surety, the charge against Kintail was suspended, but on condition that he should deliver the Castle to whomsoever the King might direct. By order of Council, given on 8th March 1583, the Castle of Strome, the great bone of contention, was ultimately delivered into the keeping of the Earl of Argyll.

Mackenzie's guilt is clearly proved by the fact that he made no attempt to refute the more serious charges preferred against him and his followers, his whole defence being that he held the Castle of Strome by contract from Glengarry, and the holding of the Castle of Strome was far and away the least of his offences. There is, further, the significant fact that Donald of Glengarry was confirmed by the King in all his lands in Lochalsh and Lochcarron in 1583, and by a special Retour at Inverness in 1584 he is declared heir to his grandmother in the same lands. But all doubt of the guilt of the Mackenzies is removed by the remission granted by the Privy Council in 1586 to Colin Mackenzie of Kintail, and Ruairi Mackenzie of Redcastle, for being art and part in the cruel murder of Ruairi, Glengarry's uncle, and many others, his followers, and for many other crimes.

Donald MacAngus seemed now to be again in a fair way of being independent of his opponents in the West and, to make his position all the more secure East and West, he entered in October 1585 into a bond of manrent with George, Earl of Huntly, whose bound servant he agreed to become, as his father Angus had been before him. The Chief of Glengarry, however, was destined not to possess his lands in Wester Ross in peace. He was, no doubt, largely himself to blame. The marriage contract of 1571 had not secured the end which it was hoped it would accomplish, nor had Helen Grant on probation healed the breach between the two families concerned, but, on the contrary, had widened it; and Donald found himself face to face with a wrathful father-in-law. Notwithstanding the confirmation by the King to Donald of his West Coast lands in 1583, Grant of Freuchie attempted, in 1586, to infeft Mackintosh in the same lands. But Mackintosh, exercising great discretion, made no effort to possess himself of lands which were certain to bring him more trouble than profit. During the next ten years there are no authentic references regarding the possession of these lands, nor of the relations between the Chiefs of Glengarry and Kintail, though it is evident from other sources these could not have been friendly. The only reference in the public records to Donald himself during this period is in the Acts of the Scottish Parliament for the year 1587, in which his name appears on the Roll of Landholders and Chiefs of Clans in the Highlands, appended to an Act "for the quieting and keeping in obedience of the disordurit subjectis inhabitantis of the Bordouris, Hielandis, and Ilis," commonly called from one of its principal provisions "The General Bond." In October 1592, Glengarry entered into a contract with George, Earl of Huntly, whereby he obliged himself and his friends to assist the Earl and his heirs in lawful service. The Earl, on his part, obliged himself to assist Donald of Glengarry, and to dispone to him and his heirs the davoch lands of Stramalan, Ord, and others. This bond, under ordinary circumstances, would mean very little, but in view of the recent conspiracies in which the Earl became involved, and which threatened such serious consequences, some importance must be attached to the agreement with Glengarry.

There is little reason to doubt that Huntly was the prime mover in the plot that resulted in the murder of the Earl of Murray and of John Campbell of Cawdor, and it is equally certain that with him several chiefs were deeply implicated. To fortify himself against the storm, which he knew was brewing, Huntly courted the assistance of many of the neighbouring potentates by entering into bonds of friendship with them. To the Chief of Glengarry it was a welcome opportunity to fortify himself against the Clan Mackenzie.

In the disturbed state of the country at that time it was impossible to implement the "General Bond" in full; but the King, who was always in need of funds, tried to enforce the part of it dealing with the payment of rents and taxes throughout the Isles and the West. The chiefs were reluctant to pay their dues. Accordingly, in May 1596 he called upon the defaulters to appear in person and meet him at Dumbarton. Many of them obeyed, but Donald of Glengarry held aloof and was duly proclaimed rebel and put to the horn two months later. The King saw that sterner measures were called for; and, although he himself disliked military exercises, he gave Sir William Stewart of Houston a commission to proceed north to occupy the principal fortresses in the West, with special mention of the Castle of Strome, which had been, and still was, one of the main sources of trouble between Glengarry and the Mackenzies. Another good reason was to try to keep the Clan Donald North, including Glengarry, from joining forces with Angus of Dunnyveg who was still in trouble with the King. The project was rendered unnecessary, however, by the submission of the Chief of Dunnyveg followed by that of Donald of Glengarry who appeared personally before the King in Edinburgh and bound himself and his followers to keep the peace and make due restitution for all the crimes committed by them.

In the following year, a serious attempt was made to heal the differences between Glengarry and the Laird of Grant. On 28th April 1597 they entered into a mutual bond of man-rent for defence against all except the King and the Chief of Clanranald. The old dispute about the lands of Lochcarron was also settled. Grant's rights were sustained and Glengarry agreed to pay a rent of three merks in feu for each merkland of the disputed lands. The mutual bonds of man-rent were duly confirmed, and Glengarry as a result was able to enjoy a brief period of peace undisturbed by violent disputes with his near neighbours.

But soon the old quarrel between him and Mackenzie of Kintail again broke out with, if possible, greater fury than ever, and it would appear as if Glengarry himself, or rather his son Angus, was the aggressor. At all events, in November 1601 Angus, Younger of Glengarry, accompanied by a large following of his fathers' dependents, and a "grit nowmer of brokin and disorderit Hielandmen," came down suddenly on the lands of Torridon and laid violent hands on life and property. According to the Mackenzie seanachies, the men of Glengarry committed great outrages, "cruelly slaughtered all the aged men with many of the women and children," and returned home laden with spoil. On 22nd July 1602, a complaint was made to the Privy Council at the instance of the widows of the men slain at Torridon, and their kin, against Donald of Glengarry, who is at the same time charged with accepting the fruit of the Torridon outrage "with all glaidnes of hairt." The same charges are made against Angus, his son, and a long list of Macdonalds. Neither Glengarry nor any of his followers appearing to answer to the charges preferred against them, they were all ordered to be denounced and put to the horn.

Meanwhile, Glengarry being "unexpert and unskilful in the laws of the realm, the Clan-Cheinzie intrapped and insnared him within the compass thereof," and Kintail succeeded in procuring, through the interest of the Earl of Dunfermline, a commission of fire and sword against him. Armed with this commission and accompanied by a large body of retainers, and some of the neighbouring clans, Kintail invaded Glengarry's lands of Morar, which he wasted without mercy. While the Mackenzies were thus busily engaged, the men of Glengarry in a similar manner wasted the lands of Lochalsh and Applecross.

Matters had at length taken so serious a turn from the Mackenzie point of view, that Kintail began to be apprehensive of a great rising of the Macdonalds, both North and South, to assist their kinsman of Glengarry. Mackenzie, whose sister had married Hector Maclean of Duart, naturally appealed to that chief for help; and, in hope of being able to prevent so formidable a combination of forces through Maclean's intervention, he went to see Maclean at Duart Castle. If the Mackenzie manuscript histories are to be believed, Kintail succeeded in the object of his visit to Maclean who, they assert, invaded Ardnamurchan and other Macdonald territories, and committed such outrages as to compel the interference of the Earl of Argyll. However this may be, it is certain that Glengarry received no assistance from his kinsmen in the South Isles.

Taking advantage of the absence of the Mackenzie Chief in Mull, Angus of Glengarry, at the head of a considerable body of his followers, invaded Lochcarron by sea, and went off with as much plunder as his galleys would carry. The Mackenzies, being taken unawares, were not at first able to offer any resistance, but the fiery cross was sent round, and getting into their boats they pursued Young Glengarry as far as Kylerea. At this point an engagement took place, which resulted, according to Sir Robert Gordon, in the death of Angus of Glengarry and forty of his followers, "not without slaughter of the Clan-Cheinzie likewise." The details of this and all the other engagements between Glengarry and Kintail, which are greatly exaggerated, are given with much minuteness in the Mackenzie manuscripts. There is no account given of the struggle between these families from the Macdonald point of view in any manuscript history of the clan known to us, and the Mackenzie manuscripts, which are somewhat numerous, are not to be relied upon save where they are corroborated by the public records. The final stage in this Wester Ross struggle was reached when the Mackenzies laid siege to the Castle of Strome, and compelled the Macdonald garrison to surrender. The Mackenzies afterwards caused the castle to be demolished, and its ruins now stand a picturesque object in the landscape of Lochcarron.

While these events were taking place in Wester Ross, the Government took steps to bring the protagonists to a sense of their shortcomings. On 6th August 1602, the Privy Council fined Sir Thomas Stewart of Grantully in 5000 merks, being the amount of his bond of caution for Glengarry, who had neither remained in ward himself nor conformed to his bond by entering a pledge. On 9th September, Donald of Glengarry, having lately presented a pledge for the good conduct of his men, is charged by the Privy Council with departing home, and taking his pledge with him. The Council further ordered Donald of Glengarry and Kenneth Mackenzie of Kintail, under pain of rebellion, to subscribe within three hours after being charged such forms of mutual assurance as should be presented to them, to endure till 1st May 1603. In this unequal contest between one branch of the Clan Donald and the whole Mackenzie Clan, the latter, as might be expected, prevailed and, as there was little hope of holding his lands on the Ross-shire coast in peace and safety, Glengarry at last surrendered his rights to Kintail. It is somewhat curious to find that, while he is still under the ban of the law, the King granted a commission to his "weil beloved Donald MacAngus of Glengarie to pas upoun the malefactoris and broken men of the Isles perturbaris of the quietnes thairof for thair apprehensioun." It is provided "that he be furneist with schipping at sic time as he sall have occasioun to prosequte and perseu the saidis malefactoris in sic pairtis as they hant and resort." He is further armed with full power to take any Scottish vessels that may be found in the Western Isles, and to furnish and man them for the King's service. What success attended Donald's efforts in his new and somewhat invidious position if he ever went in pursuit of the "malefactoris and broken men" of the Isles, is uncertain. That he was himself an arch-rebel is evident enough and, except on the assumption that it was deemed a wise expedient to send a thief to catch a thief, it is otherwise difficult to conceive why he should have been at such a ·time commissioned to deal with broken men. As if all his other quarrels were not enough for his energies, the Royal Commissioner, with several other Highland Chiefs, is charged to appear personally on 20th September 1603 before the Privy Council "to underly sic ordoure as sall bie prescryvit to him anent the persuit of Clangregor." But very soon thereafter he is arraigned with the Chief of this same Clan, now proscribed, and George, Marquis of Huntly, for being art and part in a great "spuilzie and slauchter" of the Clan Chattan.

The next incident in this long tale of bloody strife took place far to the East. In September 1603 Alan, 3rd in line of the Lundie cadet family, made a sudden descent upon Mackenzie lands in the Black Isle. He chose those of the minister of Killearnan, Mr John Mackenzie, who owned the neighbouring lands of Kilchrist, which gave their name to this, the notorious Raid of Kilchrist, recounted in all its gory details by many writers of Highland history. The whole district was laid waste, with much destruction of property belonging to the minister and his tenants, five of whom were killed in the course of the raid. The Chief of Kintail sent a large party to intercept the raiders, but Alan of Lundie succeeded in evading his pursuers and reached home safely, weighed down with much plunder and driving before him seventy head of cattle and nine horses.

No immediate steps were taken against Alan but many years later, in 1622, the Minister of Killearnan, who by this time had become Archdeacon of Ross, raised an action against Alan of Lundie accusing him of fire-raising and cruelly murdering Alexander, John, and Donald Mackay, Alexander Gald and another, the minister's tenants in the town and lands of Kilchrist; and further of destroying 27 dwelling houses, with barns, byres and kilns, and the theft of the cattle and horses. Alan failed to appear and was declared rebel, forfeited and put to the horn. He was saved from the ultimate consequences of his forfeiture, however, by the intervention of Sir John Grant who acquired from the Crown a gift of his lands and, on account of a debt he owed to Alan, allowed him to continue in possession. The Archdeacon then instituted proceedings against Donald of Glengarry, who might have been held responsible for the misdeeds of his relative. Donald denied all responsibility, but offered to stand trial, naming Donald Gorm of Sleat as his cautioner. Once more the worthy Archdeacon received no satisfaction, and there the matter rested.

The alleged burning of the Kirk of Kilchrist is the one circumstance that lends significance to this raid which in all other respects deserves no more notice than that accorded to many similar incidents of the time. The authors of *Clan Donald* were in their time ministers of the parishes of Killearnan and Kiltarlity, both of which are adjacent to or contain the lands of Kilchrist. As they acquired an unparallelled knowledge of the area and its local history, it is worth quoting here in full the passage in which they have demolished the myth perpetrated by so many of the earlier chroniclers of the Raid of Kilchrist:

The story of the burning of the Church of Kilchrist, with its congregation, while the piper of Allan Macdonald of Lundie marched round the building playing a piobaireachd, has, strange to say, been accepted by writers of Highland history with as much assurance as if it were based on a certified entry in the Privy Council Records. Johnson, in his account of his journey to the Western Isles, repeats the story and shifts the scene of the tragedy to Culloden. Gregory, who made the first serious attempt to clothe the legend with the halo of authenticity, quotes quite an array of authorities in support of it, one of whom would have been sufficient, and not even one of the number makes the remotest reference to the burning of the Church of Kilchrist. Others have followed the example of the author of *The History of the Western Highlands and Isles*. Many have quoted him, and no book on the Highlands is oftener quoted than that of Donald Gregory. But what are the facts? The Parish of Kilchrist had already ceased to be a separate parish, and had been joined to that of Urray in 1574, while all that remained of the church were the bare walls. Mr John Mackenzie, the principal victim of the Raid of Kilchrist, was inducted minister of Killearnan in 1602, and he had not yet been advanced to the dignity of Archdeacon of Ross, as indeed he could not be for some years to come, while the Church remained as it then was under the form of Presbyterian government. The minister of Killearnan was a son of Alexander Mackenzie of Kilchrist, whether eldest or second son matters little so far as our purpose is concerned. He certainly succeeded some member of his family as proprietor of the lands of Kilchrist, and in the process against Allan Macranald of Lundie he appears in that capacity, and not as minister of Kilchrist. He had no ecclesiastical connection whatever with that district, his sole charge then being the parish of Killearnan, where it appears he had no residence, while the duties of his cure at least on Sunday would almost if not entirely have been performed by a reader. At that time the houses of the Clergy were all situated round the cathedral in the town of Chanonry, as any one in the least degree acquainted with the ecclesiastical history of the Black Isle must know. The house occupied by the minister of Killearnan was the family residence of Kilchrist. His residence in that district is to be accounted for solely by the fact of his being the owner of the lands and not because he had any ecclesiastical jurisdiction over a parish which, with the bare walls of its church, had already been joined to the charge of another minister. Had Mr John Mackenzie been minister of Kilchrist, it would have been all the worse for him, as in that case he would have perished to a certainty in the congregational conflagration. The tradition-mongers, while they emphasise the burning of the whole congregation of men, women, and children, have forgotten to tell us by what miracle the minister escaped; but perhaps the Mackenzies of those days being probably less liturgical than their descendants later in the same century, were in the habit of meeting for public worship without a minister.

For the next five years there seems to have been peace between Glengarry and his neighbour in Kintail. In 1608 the Isles and the adjacent mainland were in turmoil. The King's Lieutenant, Lord Ochiltree, had convoked a meeting of the Islesmen at Aros where he was guilty of an act of bad faith. The chiefs were invited aboard the King's ship, the *Moon*, to a dinner following a service of prayer conducted by the Bishop of the Isles. After dinner all the chiefs present were arrested. The *Moon* weighed anchor, and sailed to Ayr, whence the chiefs were taken to Edinburgh and incarcerated in the Castles of Blackness, Dumbarton and Stirling.

The mainland chiefs, including Donald of Glengarry, were not present at the meeting at Aros and bitterly resented the treacherous conduct of the King's

Lieutenant towards their Island kinsmen. On 6th February 1609, Donald was warned by the Privy Council to give no succour to fugitives from the Isles, and was at the same time charged to aid the Council in carrying out the King's policy in the Isles. He was also warned to appear on 25th March to answer for his conduct in the interval. Failing to appear, Donald was three days later denounced rebel. To add to his troubles, while these proceedings were taking place some of Donald's men carried out a raid on the lands of Harry Stewart of Strathdee from whom they seized 28 head of cattle. Stewart complained to the Privy Council, and on 21st February 1610 the raiders were declared rebels and put to the horn. At the same time Donald was summoned to answer for his men, but failing to appear was also denounced rebel. Five years later he appealed against this judgment, declaring that he was not responsible for the raiders; and being on his good behaviour at the time, he was remitted on finding caution in the sum of 1000 merks.

On 20th December 1610 a licence was granted to Sir George Hay for 31 years to exploit the resources of the Highlands for smelting iron and manufacturing glass. The timber stocks there were valuable, as we saw earlier in this chapter. Hay was referred to the Chief of Glengarry, in whose country timber abounded, for protection during these operations which the King thought profitable "for the whole kingdom." It is refreshing to find the Glengarry men engaged in an industry other than the usual cattle-raiding. This iron-smelting enterprise seems to have lasted for many years, as in the early part of the 18th century it was still being carried on in Glengarry. We are not told how much the chief received in return for this use of his lands and the protection he gave the iron-workers; but it gave the clansmen useful employment, which must have been quite a change for many of them, not least for the measure of stability it served to introduce into their day-to-day existence.

In the same year the Chief of Glengarry had trouble with his kinsmen in Knoydart. That family was a cadet branch of the Clanranald and the last chief of the family, Ranald, 7th of the line, now raided Glengarry in a last desperate attempt to restore the family fortunes. Although there was much destruction of houses and valuable property, Donald of Glengarry for once refrained from taking the law into his own hands. Instead, he appealed for a commission of fire and sword against his kinsmen, and when the situation had become sufficiently serious the Privy Council granted such a commission to Ruairi Mackenzie of Coigeach, Macleod of Dunvegan and John Grant of Freuchie. The forces thus arrayed against him proved too much for the Knoydart chief, and Glengarry had no difficulty in occupying his lands. On 3rd July 1613 the King confirmed Donald of Glengarry in the lands of Knoydart, and they remained in the possession of the chiefs of Glengarry until the late 18th century. The Macdonalds of Knoydart henceforth ceased to have any existence as a territorial family.

Donald was by this time 67 years of age; and, his eldest son Angus having been killed by the Mackenzies in 1603, the effective leadership of the clan now devolved upon Alasdair Dearg, his second son, who is seen in this capacity in 1614 acting for his father in wadsetting the lands of Invergusaran to Alasdair Og MacIain 'ic Ailein, apparently a member of the old Knoydart family.

For the next two years all is quiet as far as our records go. But in the summer of 1615 Sir James Macdonald of Dunnyveg escaped from Edinburgh Castle and embarked on his forlorn attempt to save his patrimony. The old Chief of Glengarry took no part in Sir James's rebellion, but his son Alasdair Dearg, after having been taken captive by Sir James, eventually decided to join him but without a following. On Sir James's defeat and subsequent flight, Alasdair succeeded in evading Argyll's hot pursuit and escaping to the safety of the wilds of his own country.

Next year old Donald had more trouble, this time within his own clan. In May 1616 a raid was carried out on the Knoydart lands he had so recently acquired by a party of the Clanranald men from Moidart, led by John and Ruairi, brothers of their chief. The matter was quickly dealt with. On 18th July the chiefs of Glengarry and Clanranald met in Edinburgh and entered into a bond of friendship. In this document the injured parties are named "Alester MacEane Vc Ailein in Invergusaran, Angus MacAllan Roy in Lee, Alaster his brother in Crowlin, and Neill McRorie Vc Ean Roy in Scottos." Donald of Glengarry promised reparation, and in return the Chief of Clanranald, who here is named "Donald MacAllan Vic Ean," promised to assist his kinsman of Glengarry in "keeping his magestie's peas within all thes bounds." Donald of Clanranald furthermore undertook to help Donald of Glengarry against the rebels of Knoydart. It is interesting to note that amongst the witnesses of this document there appears the name of Archdeacon Mackenzie of Ross, the principal victim of the Raid of Kilchrist.

From this time until 1634 Glengarry was on his best behaviour and enjoyed good relations with the Government. He was frequently employed in suppressing disturbances and in curbing the lawless bands which infested the Highlands at the time. The bands of lawless "brokin lymmars" acted on their own and in many cases completely beyond the control of their chiefs, who nonetheless had to answer for their crimes. The aid of Glengarry and the Laird of Grant and other chiefs was enlisted to bring the "lymmars" to justice. On the 13th January 1635 many of the chiefs were called to meet the Council and report progress. Donald could not go on account of advanced age and ill health. His deputy, John MacRanald, presented a medical certificate signed by the Minister of Abertarff, a surgeon, and a notary testifying to the "Laird of Glengarrie his inabilitie to travel or keepe this dyet, in respect of his decrepit age, being foure score twelffe yeeres, and he is lying bedfast as the said testimonialls beiris." This is the last time Donald is heard of as responsible head of Glengarry. His grandson, Angus, son of Alasdair Dearg, who had pre-deceased old Donald, took over the active leadership of the Clan.

It was at this time that the religious and political problems besetting the kingdom began to make their impact in the Highlands where clan wars had hitherto been little influenced by either. Now the Highlands became divided on these issues. Since the Reformation the Earls of Argyll had been strong supporters of the new faith, with the notable exception of Archibald, 7th Earl who, influenced by his wife, deserted Protestantism and shared the exile of Sir James of Dunnyveg in Spain. The family of Argyll brought all their vassals to the side of the Reformers. In the North, wherever Huntly held sway, the inhabitants adhered to the old faith. In those days and for some time thereafter the chiefs set the fashion in most things, including the Church. Thus the Catholic Highlands stretched from Gordon country to the West and included Glengarry, all the Clanranald country of Moidart, Morar, Knoydart, and the outer isles.

When the Parliament in England fell out with the King the Scots Covenanters backed the Parliament. The Highlands were divided. In the far North the Covenant was successfully established. The Mackays and Sutherlands became staunch Protestants, and the Mackenzies too were gradually converted to the Covenant. The Central Highlands were for the King and the old faith, or Episcopacy. Argyll and the clans within his orbit, added to the solid Whig

INVERGARRY CASTLE

Seat of the Chiefs of Glengarry down to the 'Forty-five

South-West, made a strong Covenanting bulwark against the King and Episcopacy. The Covenanters saw little difference between Catholicism and Episcopacy and hated both.

In 1640 Argyll, acting for the Covenant, was given a commission of fire and sword to pursue "not only proven enemies to religion, but also unnatural to their country to the utter subduing and rooting them out." Glengarry was the first of the Catholic clans to suffer the attentions of the ardent Covenanting Earl who, at the head of 4000 men, laid the Glen waste from end to end. The damage done was assessed at a very high sum when compensation was later claimed. Other clans were visited by the Earl on the same occasion, executing his commission with great severity especially against those opposed to the Covenant.

Next year some of Glengarry's men apparently tried to recoup their losses. In December William Mackintosh of Torcastle and others complained to the Council that certain Glengarry men, who had previously been put to the horn, had not appeared to answer for their crimes, which included the murder of Lachlan Mackintosh and William Miller, two citizens of Inverness, as well as gathering together in arms with the intention of disturbing the peace. The complainers demanded that young Angus Glengarry, who was in town at the time, should be held in ward until satisfaction was given. He was held responsible for the sins of his clansmen, and ordered to present them before the Court. He refused to find caution for their appearance in the following June, and was thereupon imprisoned in Edinburgh Castle at his own expense. In March 1642 he petitioned the Council to be set free on condition of his finding sufficient security for presenting the offenders to justice. The Lords of the Council ruled that "the said Angus Macdonald be set at liberty because Sir John Mackenzie of Tarbett has become cautioner for him not to remove from the Burgh of Edinburgh, and to appear the first Council day in June next to satisfy the said Lords, otherwise to re-enter himself in ward in the said Castle." No more is heard of the matter; but the young Chief must have obeyed, as he was soon after at liberty again, having learned a sharp lesson in the duties and dangers of chiefship.

The Civil War between King and Parliament broke out in 1642. At first it touched the Highlands very little, but it was clear that it would soon involve the whole kingdom. As early as 1639 the King, in anticipation of trouble, had appointed Randal Macdonnell, Earl of Antrim, and Sir Donald of Sleat, as Commissioners jointly acting for the King within the whole Highlands and Isles. Now on the 28th January 1643 at Oxford, Antrim entered into an agreement with the Earl of Montrose to raise an army for the royal cause in the Isles and Ireland. Antrim's levies, commanded by Alasdair MacColla Ciotach (Young Colkitto), landed at Ardnamurchan in July 1644, and soon afterwards joined the royal standard under Montrose at Blair Atholl. The narrative of what happened during the succeeding year, aptly called the *Annus Mirabilis,* and the exploits of these two heroes, are given in full in another chapter. We tell here how the campaign affected the Chief of Glengarry and his men.

Angus did not at first join Alasdair and Montrose; but, after the initial successes, Donald Gorm, his uncle, raised the clan in Knoydart and Glengarry and joined Montrose at Blair Atholl, in time to take their part in the invasion of Argyll, the occupation of Inveraray, and the march back to Cille Chuimein (Fort Augustus). Here Montrose was joined by Angus of Glengarry with more of his clansmen, and a bond of association was drawn up which Angus signed as heir of Glengarry and was also subscribed by the heads of fifty-three families. News of Argyll's approach at the west end of the Great Glen was brought by Iain Lom, the Keppoch bard. Montrose decided to turn back and deal with

Argyll before Seaforth and he could join forces. The levies under Seaforth were not considered a serious problem. The famous forced march over impossible terrain in dead of winter, and the Battle of Inverlochy which followed, are described elsewhere in this work. Angus with his three uncles, Donald Gorm, Iain Mor and Iain Beag, were in the centre and fought with conspicuous bravery. Argyll was routed and his army virtually annihilated. Iain Lom recorded the victory in a scathing poem, in which he urges the Campbells not to forget their bonnets floating in the Lochy, and advising them to take swimming lessons before returning.

On the day of Inverlochy, Donald, the old Chief of Glengarry, died aged 102. Angus continued his active support of Montrose in the ensuing battles of the campaign. He was present at the taking of Dundee in March, and on 9th May at the great victory of Auldearn. We do not know how many Glengarry men were with Alasdair and his Antrim Macdonnells, who bore the brunt of the attack on the right wing. But they were in some force with him at Alford, where he was given command of the centre with Drummond of Balloch. The honours of that victory were due mainly to the Gordon horse on the wings, who routed the enemy leaving the foot soldiers under Angus to follow up the pursuit. The Irish contingent under O'Cahan fought with their accustomed bravery. Baillie's army was all but annihilated. Angus and his men pursued the fugitives so closely that it took relays of three horses to save Argyll from capture. Young Lord Gordon was killed in the battle and deeply mourned by his clan. He had tried to capture General Baillie in the pursuit, but was shot in the act of hauling him off his horse. His death was a serious loss to Montrose.

Alasdair, who had been recruiting in the West, now returned with 1500 men of the clans, including 500 Glengarry men. These reinforcements enabled Montrose to fulfil his aim of carrying the war to the Lowlands where he realised the issue must be decided. With an army of 4400 foot and 500 horse, the largest he had ever had, he slipped south to Kilsyth, and in one of his most spectacular battles all but annihilated the 6000 men whom Baillie brought against him. It was his last victory. The clans who fought at Kilsyth—Glengarry, Clanranald, the Macleans and others—now went home with their plunder. The newly knighted Alasdair went off with half his men to harry the Campbells in Kintyre. Only a remnant of his army was with Montrose at the disaster of Philiphaugh, which marked the end of his year of glory and destroyed the hopes of the Royalists in Scotland.

Montrose escaped to the Highlands and early in 1646 was received by Angus at his Castle of Invergarry. Spurred on by Montrose and by the devastation wrought in his absence by Argyll's Covenanters, Angus tried to raise the clans again for the Royalist cause but without success. He continued to correspond with Montrose after the Marquis was obliged by the King's command to relinquish the struggle. Towards the end of the year he succeeded in raising a regiment but, hard pressed by Leslie, the Covenanting General, he was obliged to cross over to Ireland. There Angus attached himself with his regiment to Preston's army, and was actively engaged in the campaign of 1648 until the defeat in Queen's County where he and the young Chief of Clanranald were taken prisoners. Detained at Kilkenny, they were later released at the intercession of the Countess of Antrim, and Angus was back in Glengarry by the time King Charles II landed in Scotland in June 1650.

There followed ten years of political and religious manoeuvres, the like of which have occurred but seldom in our long history. The events of the past eighteen months, and especially the execution of the King, had served to breach the alliance between the two countries and altered the alignment of sympathies in Scotland. The King's Lieutenant-General, Montrose, had fought his last campaign and paid with his life for his loyalty to the King whom his enemies were now preparing to accept as their own. With Montrose gone, the young King was entirely dependent on Argyll, and to secure the crown had to subscribe to the terms of the Covenant. Cromwell's answer was the rout of Dunbar. But the Scots refused to surrender, and Charles was crowned at Scone on New Year's Day, 1651, the crown being placed on his head by the hands of Argyll. The country now being largely controlled by Cromwell, the Royalists under Leslie and the King marched into England in the hope of gaining more support in the South. With them marched Angus of Glengarry and other Highland chiefs with their clans, to meet with utter defeat at the hands of Cromwell in his "crowning mercy" of Worcester on 3rd September 1651.

Among the few who eluded capture besides the King was Angus of Glengarry, who returned North at the head of his surviving clansmen and, continuing in arms, made determined efforts to further the Royalist cause in the Highlands where he appears to have been entrusted with the chief conduct of the King's affairs. Lilburne was appointed Commander-in-chief, Scotland, in August 1652, and the first Union of the Parliaments united Scotland and England within the Commonwealth ruled by the Protector Cromwell. Lilburne did not have many troops to enforce the new regime but, by placing garrisons in strategic places to guard the passes and prevent the rebel chiefs from joining together in numbers, he made the best use of the 12,000 infantry and 200 horse he had by the time the rebellion next broke out.

Government suspicion of Angus's conduct at this time finds expression in Lilburne's report that "Glengarry is holding meetings in the Highlands and the Isles the object unknown." Glengarry in fact started his recruiting campaign early in the year 1652. He visited his cousins of Clan Donald in the Isles and the Camerons, Macleods and Macleans. Sir James Macdonald of Sleat, Angus' brother-in-law, reported to the Governor of Inverness that "the Laird of Glengarry and some other Highlanders are drawne to an head and intend to dissquiett the peace of the country." From this it would appear that Angus had some success in gathering recruits. Lilburne became alarmed and asked Argyll to use his powerful influence to deter any who might try to join the King's party. Angus then went down into Argyll and tried to raise his friends there, even sending over to Antrim, seeking aid from his kinsfolk. The Antrim men, remembering the disastrous fate of their previous expedition into Scotland in Montrose's War, were reluctant to join another rising so far from home. Glengarry continued his efforts to raise the Royalists in arms, and now in 1652 a chance came to resume the struggle. The time seemed ripe, and in July a message was sent to Charles at St Germains asking for General Middleton to be sent to assume command.

Middleton was a trained soldier with years of active service behind him. He had fought on both sides in the Civil War. He had served with Montrose in the early days on the Covenant side. He later served on the Royalist side at Marston Moor and Worcester, had been caught and kept prisoner in the Tower of London, but managed to escape and join Charles in Paris. He was thus a good Royalist, and his experience as a soldier could be of great service. Lilburne was aware that something was afoot, warned by the suspicious behaviour of Glengarry and the arrival in Fife of a messenger from the King. About this time Charles wrote a friendly personal letter to Angus of Glengarry showing how high he stood in the King's esteem.

St Germains, August 3rd, 1652

I am promised this letter shall come safe to your handes, and therefore I am willing that you should know from myself that I am still alive, and the same man that I was when I was amongst you. I am very much troubled for what you suffer, and am usinge all the endeavours I can to free you, and before many months I hope you will see I am not idle. In the meantime, I cannot but lett you know that I am in greater straights and perplexcityes for your safetyes than you can easily apprehend; and I am thereby compelled to leave many thingis undone which would be of advantage to me and you. I could heartylie wish therefore that by your interest and negotiatione with those you have trust in, and who you know wish me well, which would be very reasonable obligatione, and would never be forgotten by me; I neede say no more to you, but that I shall be glad to receive any advice or advertisement from you that you think necessary for me, and shall alwaies remaine your very loving friend,

Charles R.

Before Middleton could arrive, the Rising began with a gathering in Lochaber, and the standard was raised at Killin on 27th July 1653. The Earl of Glencairn was appointed Commander-in-chief of the royal forces in Scotland pending the arrival of Middleton. Lord Lorne, heir of Archibald, 8th Earl of Argyll, came without his father's blessing, bringing with him some of his clan. Glengarry's meeting with Lorne was anything but friendly, and force had to be used to keep the two apart. The subsequent withdrawal of Lorne marked the beginning of the dissensions that characterised the whole campaign. At last Middleton arrived in February 1654 and, much to the annoyance of Glencairn, appointed Sir George Munro, an officer who had accompanied him from France, as his second in command. Not content with that, at a party to welcome Middleton, Munro insulted Glengarry and his men by calling them a bunch of thieves and robbers. Glengarry was furious and demanded satisfaction. A duel was with difficulty averted; but Munro then insulted Glencairn. He had been nursing a grudge against Glencairn on account of the latter's alleged ill-treatment of his brother, Munro of Foulis. In the resulting duel both Glencairn and Munro were wounded. In spite of these quarrels, Glengarry was hopeful and went to the Isles once more to raise recruits. On his return in June 1654 he wrote a letter full of hope to his King:

Most sacred Soverane,—Tho that your Majesty's forces heir upon Leutenant Generale Midlton's aryvall did not altoogether seem so strong or so numerous as possibly ether was reported or wished be our frinds, yet I dar say it wanted no indevors wee could perform, and now praised be God in som beter condition sinc, bot now since the Hollanders hes agreed with the Rebells, it is conceved if wee had the hapines off your Majesty's person to be amongst us (qhich is the humble desyr off most off your Majesty's faithfull subjects without prejudice to your Majesty's great afairs abroad) that we suld be shortly in condition to deill equaly with anie enemie in this kingdome, without qhich we shall have hard governing off our sellfs, as the Lieutenant Generall will mor punctuall inform your Majesty, to qhos relation also (feiring to be tedius) I doe referr my own chirfull indevors and concurrent with him, and my willnignes to comply with all humors for the advancing off your Majesty's servic, so that as I begunne my loyaltie so shall I end and seill it with my blood, otherwyas alive to that my greatest ambition and hapines to see your Majesty satled on your glorius and royall thron, qhich is the dayly prayers and indevors off him qho is, Sir, your Majestys most humbell, most faithfull, and most obedient servant,

—A. McDonald Glengarrie

Cathnes, Jun 5, 1654. For His Majestye the King off Great Brittane.

The Rising was conducted more or less as a guerilla war, the Royalist forces traversing the country and attacking isolated enemy units wherever they were to be found. A major confrontation was avoided until Monck brought to Scotland the reinforcements which Lilburne had been agitating for, and were only now made available as a result of the peace with Holland. Monck's forces caught Middleton at a disadvantage at Dalnaspidal near Lochgarry on 19th July. The Royalist army was in disorder, a gap of five miles separating its two divisions, and Monck was able to disperse them without difficulty. Glengarry's house was burned, and the leaders had to lay down their arms and ask for terms. Middleton escaped to France, but soon returned with fresh instructions. Angus had not been able to obtain suitable terms, and in December he is reported to be in Knoydart with "all his men at home," while Middleton is reported to be in Kintail with "not above 20 men." In the same month Angus received a letter from his King, in which he expresses due regard for his constancy in the royal cause:

> Glengarry, I have given this honest bearer in charge to say so much to you, and have written to Middleton of other particulars concerning you, which he will imparte to you, that I shall say little more myselfe then to assure you that your so constant adhearinge to Middleton in the carriage on my service when so many (from whom I expected it not) grow weary of it, and your so chearfully submitting to all these straights and distresses for my sake is very acceptable to me, and a great addicione to your former meritts. Be confident, I will not fayle of doing my parte as a good master in rewardinge so good a servant, and that when we meete, which I believe will be ere longe, you shall finde as much kindnesse as you can expect from your very affectionate frende,
>
> Charles R.

Angus still cherished hopes of keeping some forces on foot in readiness for the return of the King. In May 1655 Monck reported to Cromwell that all was quiet, "none being out but Glengarry." At last, however, he had to yield to the inevitable and come to terms with the Protector's Government. Colonel Blount received his submission at Inverness in June on terms which bound him in the sum of £2000 sterling to keep the peace and obliged him to give as sureties Sir James Macdonald of Sleat, Donald of Moidart and other prominent chieftains. Oliver Cromwell died in 1658, and on 5th October of that year his son Richard Cromwell was proclaimed Lord Protector with all due ceremony at the fort of Inverlochy in the presence of the Governor and the Sheriff. Round the dais, called at the time the "scaffold," were ranged Glengarry, Lochiel, and several of the prominent local chiefs and lairds, who were given a very "liberal colation" by the Governor, Major John Hill, whom we meet later in our history.

In November 1659 Hill was informed that the Glengarry Chief and his men were out in arms and at the old game of "herschips" and raids on peaceable folk. Hill ordered Lochiel to raise an armed body of his clansmen to deal with the offenders, and apprehend Angus if he appeared to countenance these misdeeds or protect the malefactors. Lochiel did not wish to embark on a quarrel with his erstwhile brother in arms, and took no steps to execute his commission.

With the Restoration of Charles II in 1660 the whole country looked forward to an era of political and religious freedom. For the Scots in particular it meant that they would be rid of an English army and the taxes that supported it, and once more become an independent nation with their own parliament. Those who had suffered in the Royalist cause and had been forced to make an unwilling submission under the Commonwealth might well expect now to receive the rewards of their loyal service. Foremost among these was Angus of Glengarry who expected some high honour by virtue of the fact that the exiled King had granted under his signet in his own hand several warrants creating him Earl of Ross. Instead he was raised to the peerage under the title "Lord Macdonell and Aros," with destination to heirs male of his body. He had to be content with that rather inferior title, although later in 1663 he requested that effect should be given to the earlier warrants. Furthermore he asked that the dignity of Chief of the name of "Macdonald" should be conferred upon him as representative of the ancient Lords of the Isles.

Neither of these requests was granted, for reasons which are not recorded, but it is interesting to note that an order of the Privy Council dated 18th July 1672 names Lord Macdonell "Chief of the name and Clan of Macdonald." The matter at issue affected the chief of Keppoch and eleven of his cadets and tenants who had been in trouble. Angus of Glengarry was the nearest potent chief of the Clan, and one to whom the Keppoch men looked for support, as in the case of the Keppoch murder. The difficult problem is dealt with at length in the chapter on the Chiefship, and it is necessary here only to refer to the Lord Lyon's ruling in 1947 on Glengarry's claim. In that document Lyon says

> He [Glengarry] never matriculated arms pursuant to the Statute 1672 cap. 47 [referring to Lord Macdonell and Aros' elevation to the peerage in 1661].
> Macdonell of Glengarry indeed matriculated arms 26th July 1797 (Lyon Reg. Vol. 1, p. 576); they are not the undifferenced arms of Macdonald, but there is the significant fact that the Glengarry arms are much more like the arms of the old House of Macdonald, Lord of the Isles, than those of any of the other branches.

After describing the arms, the Lyon goes on to say that the red hand and cross-crosslet appearing in chief on the arms are "an unquestionable brisur upon the undifferenced arms of Macdonald," and concludes "that the whole clan or family of Macdonald remained 'undemonstrated' by Ensigns Armorial or an ascertained representor."

It is to be noted here that the spelling of the name "Macdonell" has been used by the Glengarry clansmen ever since the original elevation to the peerage of Angus in 1661 under the name of "Lord Macdonell and Aros."

In April 1661 the act of forfeiture passed by Cromwell's Government was rescinded, and the patent of nobility granted in 1660 was confirmed. Lord Macdonell took his seat in Parliament, and immediately tried to get satisfaction from Argyll for the depredations he had suffered during the Civil War and under the Commonwealth. There is no record that he secured the satisfaction he claimed, but he was successful in having his estates more favourably assessed for purposes of tax. On his representation to Parliament that these had been over-valued, the Commissioners of the Shire of Inverness were in 1662 instructed to revert to the old rating.

On 23rd January 1663 Lord Macdonell entered into a bond of manrent and protection with Martin MacMartin of Letterfinlay on Loch Lochy side. The MacMartin estates lay along the eastern frontier of Cameron country and had suffered casualties in defending the Ford of Lochy against Mackintosh in his expeditions against Lochiel and the Keppoch Macdonalds. MacMartin was to gain considerable advantages from this bond in later years.

During the four years following his elevation to the peerage Lord Macdonell received charters under the Great Seal for all the lands he occupied, and had occupied for many years past.

In the year 1665 a serious quarrel arose between Lord Macdonell and the citizens of Inverness, who had in the past suffered much hardship at the hands of the western clans while on their "unlawful occasions." The Glengarry Chief and his men were therefore treated with some suspicion when they arrived in the town in any numbers. The story is told in full, with all the details by an "eye witness," in Alex. Mackenzie's *History of the Macdonalds.* A party of Macdonells were in the town on the 18th August 1665 on a Fair day. A quarrel arose at the Horse Market, which, starting as an argument about prices of goods on sale at the Fair, developed into a free for all, and the Glengarry men became involved. The Provost called out the Town-guard. Two men were killed and ten wounded. Glengarry demanded satisfaction in terms that could not be agreed by the Town. The matter went to the arbitration of the Privy Council, who awarded Glengarry and his men damages in the sum of £4800 Scots. Mackenzie adds to his account of this occurrence that "in 1666 the same Commissioners reported to the Town Council, that they are greatly prejudiced, hindered and crossed, by supplications and cross petitions tendered to the Privy Council, by some ill-affected and malicious neighbours, whereby they pretended and protested to be free of all personal and pecuniary fines, to be imposed upon the burgh for the unhappy tumult raised in August last with the Macdonalds: whereupon the Town Council resolved 'that the persons, protestors and complainers to the Privy Council, *viz.* John Forbes of Culloden, Duncan Forbes, his brother, William Robertson of Inshes, T. Watson, A. Forbes, A. Chisholm, and W. Cumming, being ill-affected burgesses, should not in time to come, be received as Councillors of the Burgh'."

For the last fifteen years of his life, Lord Macdonell played an active part in the affairs of the realm, as the most potent Chief of the Clan Donald on the mainland to whom the others looked for support and guidance. Once only in that time did he fail to act in the rôle of head of the "name and arms" of Macdonald, of which he constantly claimed to be the rightful representer. This was in September 1663 when the infamous double murder of the young Chief of Keppoch, Alexander, and his brother Ranald, took place at the instigation of their uncle, Alasdair Buidhe, and his son. In such a matter Lord Macdonell, as presumed head of the whole Clan, ought to have exercised his authority and taken prompt action to punish the murderers. It was left to Iain Lom, the bard of Keppoch, to enlist the aid of Sir James, 2nd Baronet of Sleat who, acting under the Royal Commission of 29th July 1665, brought the murderers to meet their fate in sudden and violent form. The act of washing the heads in *Tobair nan Ceann* prior to presenting them to Lord Macdonell was surely a rebuke underlining the failure of that Chief to do his duty.

In 1675, Glengarry turned his attention to matters outside his own clan. In the previous year the young Chief of Duart, Sir Alan Maclean, died in his 28th year, leaving one son, John, who was only four years old. The Macleans of Brolas and Torloisk were appointed Tutors to the young chief and proved to be able managers of the estates in the difficult year that followed. Archibald, 9th Earl of Argyll, who had succeeded the Marquis in 1661, claimed repayment of a large sum of money which his father had accumulated as debts incurred by the late Chief of Duart. The amount claimed came to over £27,000 sterling; but there were grave doubts as to how such vast debts had been incurred, both parties to the transactions being by then dead. In order to exact payment, other means having failed, Argyll invaded Mull with 2000 of his vassals and forced the

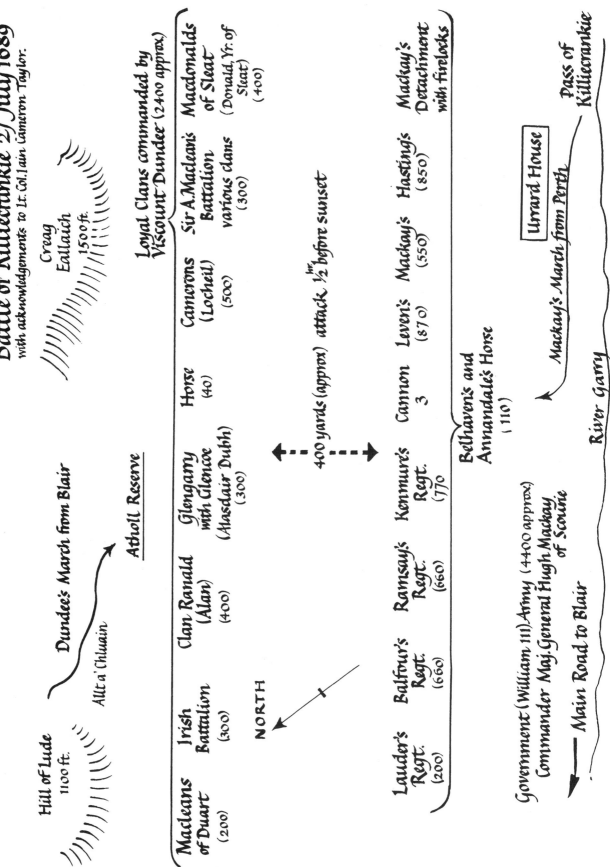

Battle of Killiecrankie 27 July 1689
with acknowledgements to Lt.Col.Iain Cameron Taylor.

Macleans to promise to pay. Next year, the Macleans having refused to pay or perhaps being unable to raise such a large sum, Argyll sent his brother Neil to invade the island and force the Macleans to submit. Violent storms destroyed the ships, and this second invasion came to nought. Here Lord Macdonell decided to intervene and took a party of his clan to reinforce the Macleans. Argyll, disappointed by this show of strength, had recourse to more peaceful means and complained to the Privy Council in Edinburgh. Although Glengarry went all the way to Edinburgh and later to London to lay the matter before the King, the dispute was eventually settled in Argyll's favour, and Maclean lost the island of Tiree to the Campbells. It is largely owing to the intervention and support of the Glengarry chief that the Macleans were not utterly ruined at this time by the vindictive and oppressive designs of Argyll.

What remained of Glengarry's life was clouded by the alarms and suspicions engendered by the disclosures in 1678 of the Titus Oates "plot," allegedly aimed at the restoration of the Papacy. As staunch adherents of the old faith, both Glengarry and Keppoch became suspect in the eyes of the Government, and in April 1679 Argyll was granted a commission to disarm and reduce them in the interests of national security. A summons to yield on pain of treason was contemptuously ignored by both chiefs, and further proceedings appear to have been suspended, the authorities no doubt being reminded of Glengarry's lifelong and undeviating devotion to the service of the Crown.

Not long afterwards, in December 1680, his eventful career came to a close. From his marriage in 1646 to Margaret, daughter of Sir Donald Gorm Og, 1st Baronet of Sleat, he had no issue and the title thus became extinct. He was succeeded by his cousin Ranald of Scotus, whose active years had been spent in Glengarry's service along with his father, Donald Gorm. Ranald was no longer a young man, and the active leadership was assumed by his son Alasdair Dubh who was to add lustre to his name and that of his Clan in the stirring events that dominated Highland history in his lifetime. Glengarry and his clansmen continued to support the House of Stewart to the tragic end, and none was more loyal to that cause than Ranald's famous son.

Eight years after Ranald's succession, that loyalty was brought to the test. The bloodless Revolution of 1688 found both sides bargaining for the support of the clans, Viscount Dundee appealing to their sense of honour and loyalty, William and his Government to their cupidity. The attempt to bribe the chiefs into attachment to the Government was destined to fail if only for the unpopularity of the Earl of Breadalbane, to whom the commission was entrusted. General Mackay, commanding the Government forces in Scotland, had equally little success in his approaches. Cameron of Lochiel deigned not to reply to his representations, while Glengarry responded in the best tradition of his House by enjoining him to emulate the action of General Monck and march south for another Restoration.

Dundee left London with a small company of his old regiment of dragoons and, snubbed in Edinburgh by the newly appointed Convention, wisely headed north where the clans awaited a leader. In him, the second Graham and worthy successor to the great Montrose, they found one whose personality and charm persuaded them to compose their differences and unite them for a common purpose. If he had lived he might have led the clans in another *Annus Mirabilis*, but it was not to be.

Dundee summoned the clans to meet in Lochaber on 18th May 1689. Alasdair of Glengarry was one of the first to arrive with some 300 of his men, bringing the total to about 2400. After a period of training in the kind of warfare he expected to wage with Mackay, Dundee made a rapid descent on Perth where he levied a toll in the name of King James, and sent a detachment to do the same in the town of Dundee. He then quickly retired to the north again. Mackay never seemed to be able to keep up with the Highland army. They were experts at forced marches across mountainous terrain. Dundee preferred to wait for a favourable opportunity to confront Mackay on ground of his own choosing. That chance came at the Pass of Killiecrankie. Mackay was marching north with over 4000 men to seize the Castle of Blair which was held for James by the Jacobites. On the 27th July Dundee had marched from Blair with no more than 2400 men and, avoiding the main road, passed round the back of the hill of Lude and drew up his line of battle on the Haugh of Urrard, facing Mackay whose men were still struggling through the narrow pass. Dundee waited until they were drawn up facing him at about 400 yards distance. His object was not to attack too early and thus allow most of them to escape back through the pass. He had the "advantage of the brae," so popular with the clansmen, and also the advantage of the setting sun which shone in the face of the opposing host. He aimed at nothing less than the annihilation of Mackay's army, although the odds against him were two to one. He knew his men were seasoned warriors, while Mackay's army, although mostly veteran troops with a sprinkling of raw levies, had yet to experience the shattering impact of a Highland charge.

At about 8 p.m. Dundee ordered the attack. The clansmen rushed forward, discharged their firearms and went in with broadsword, axe and dirk. Mackay had only time for one volley and, before his men were able to fix bayonets, a new weapon to most of them, the clans were upon them. In a few minutes the enemy broke and fled. Only the regiments under Mackay himself were able to put up a momentary resistance. Casualties were heavy on both sides. Mackay lost in killed and wounded nearly half his army, while Dundee's casualties numbered about 800, including many Highland officers killed in the forefront of the headlong onslaught.

Alasdair of Glengarry, carrying the Royal standard, and his men performed many feats of arms. Donald Gorm, his brother, killed 18 of the enemy before falling with 16 other officers of his Clan. On the left young Donald of Sleat, known later as *Dòmhnall a' Chogaidh,* lost five cousins in the first volley. Similar casualties were suffered by the other clans, but the loss of Dundee himself was the most serious of all. He fell fatally wounded early in the battle, and his death virtually ended the campaign as there was no successor capable of taking his place.

It is interesting to note that the honour of fighting on the right wing was given to Maclean of Duart and the Irish battalion. Clanranald, Glengarry, and Glencoe were in the centre, and Sleat on the extreme left. This did not in any way impair their fighting qualities, as was imputed to the Clan Donald later after Culloden, where they have often been accused of sulking for being placed on the left wing of the Prince's Army.

The advance south was stemmed at Dunkeld by the bravery of the newly formed Regiment of Foot, the Cameronians, consisting of ardent Covenanters, followers of Richard Cameron who had been martyred in 1680 at Airds Moss. Their Colonel, Cleland, fell there with many of his men, but they successfully blocked the Highlanders' march south. House to house fighting in the streets of the village was not the sort of warfare to which they were accustomed. A great many of them left for home with their booty, of which they had found an abundance in Mackay's baggage train.

The clans retired to Blair Atholl and in August entered into a Bond of Association to continue their support of King James, undertaking to meet again in September with all their available men. Glengarry was to bring to the rendezvous 200 men, Benbecula (Clanranald) and Sir Donald of Sleat a like number, and Keppoch 100.

Meantime Mackay wrote to the Chiefs advising them to lay down their arms and come to terms with the Government. Glengarry and the others signed a scornful reply in which they said: "You may know the sentiments of men of honour, we declare to all the world, we scorn your usurper, and the indemnities of his government; and to save you further trouble, we assure you that we are satisfied our King will take his own time and way to punish his rebels; although he should send us no assistance at all, we will die with our swords in our hands before we fail in our loyalty and sworn allegiance to our sovereign." One can read in the uncompromising tone of this letter the hand of Alasdair Dubh, rejecting any advances by the agents of a King whom they continued to regard as a usurper.

Cannon and Buchan, successive commanders of the remnants of the Jacobite forces, proved incapable of marshalling the support of the clans, and in July 1690 the loyalist army was disbanded. Cannon found refuge with Sir Donald of Sleat, and Buchan retired to Glengarry's residence where he continued for some time sharing that Chief's ardent hopes of another restoration. In the same month Parliament passed a decree of forfeiture against Glengarry, but Alasdair Dubh persisted in his defiance and immediately began to fortify his Castle in readiness for a siege. These warlike preparations, however, were rendered unnecessary when soon afterwards James's dispensation arrived from France releasing the Chiefs from their allegiance and permitting them to come to what terms they could with the Government.

In August 1691 the Chiefs were ordered to take the oath of allegiance to King William, the final date of registration being laid down as 1st January 1692. It seems clear that Alasdair Dubh was not yet ready to give in his submission and was causing some concern to the authorities, for on 3rd December we find Stair asking the Commander-in-chief in Scotland ". . . what force will be necessary to your garrison and the Regiment of Leven which is at Inverness, whether dragoons can subsist any time 10 or 12 miles from Invergarry, to be on hand if any occasion require, and if your being provided with a petard or some cannon may not easily be Master of Glengarry." From this it would appear that Glengarry was not expected to submit by the due date. That he had not in fact taken the oath by that date is made clear by the King's famous letter of 16th January 1692 in which it was directed that Glengarry was to be allowed, even at that late date, to take the oath and make a peaceful surrender of his Castle upon "an assurance of the entire indemnity for life and fortune." The text of the letter is given in full in the chapter on the MacIains of Glencoe, for whom paragraph 4 of the same letter prescribes an entirely different "vindication of public Justice."

Two years later, in 1694, the old Chief of Glengarry died and Alasdair Dubh assumed the official leadership which in fact he had exercised ever since his father's accession. Ranald's other sons by his wife Flora, daughter of John Macleod of Drynoch, were Angus, who succeeded to Scotus, John of Sandaig, and Archibald of Barisdale, all of whom played important parts in the later history of the clan. From Alasdair's accession until the Rising of 1715, the annals of Glengarry are uneventful, and the scanty records of the period bring to light only one matter of consequence in which he had to exert himself in the interests of his House. The Castle of Invergarry had continued to be occupied by a military garrison ever since 1692, and in 1704 Alasdair petitioned the Government claiming £150 per annum for the whole period in respect of the damage caused to house and lands and the denial to himself and his family of its amenities. He asked for the withdrawal of the troops, "all that country being still peaceable and quiet without the least apprehension of disturbance or commotion." A meeting was called to hear his cause at Fort William in the presence of Brigadier Maitland, the Governor of that fort. Glengarry was given a safe conduct to attend, but before they met, Argyll intervened with sundry claims on Glengarry's estates. The Lord Advocate, in view of this further complication, had to be asked to make up a statement to be laid before the Queen. The outcome of these negotiations is not on record, but it seems likely that Alasdair gained possession of his castle because he was once more living at Invergarry before the next Jacobite rising brought him and his men out again.

This time the foreign monarch, called by the Jacobites the "usurper," was the Hanoverian George I. He was no more popular with Glengarry and the other loyal chiefs than William had been. William at least had as his consort and partner on the throne, Mary who was the daughter of James, the exiled monarch. But George's claim was regarded by Jacobites as a very tenuous one, dating back through two female links to James VI. The Highland bards had some very uncomplimentary things to say about him, and the seeds of rebellion, always close to the surface, rapidly bore fruit.

Unfortunately the self-appointed leader who headed the Rising was the Earl of Mar, a weak and vacillating character, who had been at one time a Whig and at another a Tory, but always a self-seeker. Before George I arrived he had been Secretary of State for Scotland, and Keeper of the Signet under Queen Anne.

Before King George left the Continent, Mar had written a very fulsome letter assuring the King of his personal loyalty, pointing out his services to King William at the Revolution, and later to Queen Anne. This he followed up with a loyal address signed by many of the chiefs, amongst whom were Alasdair of Glengarry, Sleat, Keppoch, Lochiel and Maclean. This address, probably composed by Mar himself in a further attempt to demonstrate his personal loyalty and thus keep his high office in the State, was presented to the King by Mar. It was coldly received. Suspecting his loyalty, the King dismissed him from office and Mar, filled with resentment, hurriedly left for his Castle of Kildrummie, whence he sent out the invitations to the chiefs to attend the famous hunting party on the Braes of Mar. The response was massive, and after the raising of the standard in September 1715 Mar had at his command the largest force that had ever gathered in a Jacobite cause.

Glengarry played a leading part in raising the clans, as his predecessor, Angus, Lord Macdonell, had done so diligently during the Civil War and Commonwealth. This time, unfortunately, the Jacobites lacked a leader of the calibre and genius of Montrose and Dundee. If Mar had marched south the story might have been very different, but he tarried too long in Perth, and by the time the armies met at Sheriffmuir on 13th November 1715, Argyll had been allowed ample time to gather the Hanoverian forces and march north to confront Mar. They met on the northern slopes of the Ochil Hills. The ground was chosen almost by accident, but it favoured Argyll more than Mar and it suited cavalry of which the Hanoverians had a preponderance. To add to the difficulty of both sides, the flanks of both armies were almost out of sight of each other.

The Clan Donald regiments were on the right flank of Mar's army and swept irresistibly forward. Their enemies, including five squadrons of dragoons with Witham, fled from the field scarcely pausing for breath until they reached Dunblane two miles away. In the first charge young Alan of Moidart fell mortally wounded, and for a short time his clansmen faltered to be rallied at once by Alasdair Dubh's stentorian cry, "Revenge today, tomorrow for mourning!" The

Glengarry men behaved with their accustomed gallantry, inspired by Alasdair's commanding presence. Keppoch, Glencoe too, performed many feats of valour, as did the men of the Isles under young Donald and his brother.

Meantime the left of Mar's army was not faring so well. They had been thrown back by Argyll and a flanking charge by Cathcart's dragoons completed the rout. Thus on one flank Mar was victorious, while on the other Argyll was convinced he had won the day. Mar, supine as ever, did nothing to exploit the victory of his right flank, but retreated to Braco on the Allan water and bivouacked for the night.

The arrival of James himself in Scotland and entry into Perth on 6th January 1716 did nothing to rally support for his claims. His uninspiring presence served only to intensify the depression that Mar's inaction had caused amongst his supporters. The army melted away as the clans went home with their plunder, and the Rising was over when soon afterwards James left with Mar to resume his exile "over the water." Alasdair Dubh retired to his Castle where he continued to hold out until April when, realising that further resistance was futile, he surrendered to General Cadogan at Inverness and then proceeded to Edinburgh to arrange the terms of his submission. What these terms were is not recorded, but it is likely that they were more favourable than he could have hoped for because, although he was suspected of complicity in the Rising of 1719, he was able to satisfy the Government that far from having any personal involvement in that rebellion he had used his influence to dissuade his clansmen and others from taking part. Glengarry from his experience saw the weaknesses inherent in the plans for the Rising, but there is little doubt that had the outcome been other than the disaster it turned out to be, Alasdair's sword would have been once again unsheathed in the cause to which he had been so long and so firmly attached.

On the 9th of December 1716 James issued a patent of nobility, sealed with the royal seal and signed with his own hand, raising Alasdair to the peerage in the name of Lord Macdonell. It was an empty gesture, but showed the importance attached to Glengarry's part in the drama of the '15.

The remaining years of his life were uneventful. He died on 28th October 1724, universally lamented by his clan and his kinsmen in Clan Donald. "Loyal and wonderfully sagacious and long-sighted," as an impartial admirer observed, he was undoubtedly an outstanding Chief, the noble representative of a long line of bold warriors, whose loyalty to the Stewarts was steadfast through all the hardships and changing fortunes of that ill-fated House.

Alasdair was twice married. By his first wife Anne, daughter of Lord Lovat, he had a daughter Anne, who married Roderick Mackenzie, Yr. of Applecross. By his second wife Mary, daughter of Kenneth, Earl of Seaforth, he had (1) John, his successor; (2) Dr Ranald of Kylles in Loch Nevis, an "eminent physician" who was "out" in 1745; (3) Alexander; (4) William, who was killed in 1745; and (5) Isabella, who in 1713 married Roderick Chisholm of Chisholm.

Alasdair Dubh's son John, who succeeded him in the chiefship, lacked many of the heroic qualities which had distinguished his predecessors. His active life coincided with a relatively long period of peace in the Highlands and he occupied himself largely with consolidating his possessions and cultivating friendly relations with his neighbours. Thus in August 1724 he was successful in obtaining from the Duke of Argyll a charter of the lands of Knoydart to himself and his heirs male, and in 1735 he entered into a bond of friendship and association with the Grants of Glenmoriston. It does not appear that he was in favour of the Rising of 1745, in which his age if not his temperament in any case rendered him unfit to take an active part, and the distinction of leading the Clan to the Prince's standard was left to his second son Angus, in the absence of the elder son and heir Alasdair Ruadh, who was making his contribution to the cause in another sphere.

Before the landing in Moidart, Alasdair Ruadh had been chosen by the chiefs to take an address to the Prince in France, assuring him of their support provided he could bring sufficient French aid in men and money. On account of various delays, Alasdair Ruadh was unable to reach France before the Prince had sailed for Scotland. On his way back to join his clan, he was taken prisoner on the high seas when his ship was seized by two frigates of the Royal Navy. As heir to the chiefship of a notoriously Jacobite clan and a trained soldier holding a commission in the French army, he was lodged in the Tower where he remained until the Rising had been quelled. What happened to him thereafter has been the subject of considerable speculation. He appears to have been involved in Jacobite plots in London and the continent after his release in 1747, and has been credited by some writers with being a spy and double agent, but on the flimsiest evidence. What is clear is that for many years he suffered acute financial embarrassment, receiving no redress from the Prince or his father for all his sacrifices, and little aid from estates encumbered with debts and still further

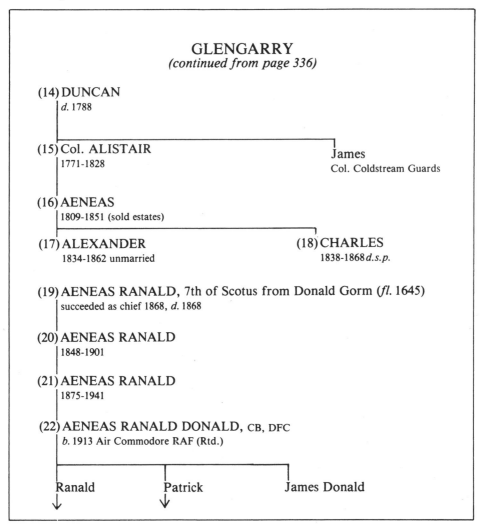

GLENGARRY
(continued from page 336)

(14) DUNCAN
d. 1788

(15) Col. ALISTAIR   James
1771-1828   Col. Coldstream Guards

(16) AENEAS
1809-1851 (sold estates)

(17) ALEXANDER   (18) CHARLES
1834-1862 unmarried   1838-1868 d.s.p.

(19) AENEAS RANALD, 7th of Scotus from Donald Gorm (fl. 1645)
succeeded as chief 1868, d. 1868

(20) AENEAS RANALD
1848-1901

(21) AENEAS RANALD
1875-1941

(22) AENEAS RANALD DONALD, CB, DFC
b. 1913 Air Commodore RAF (Rtd.)

Ranald   Patrick   James Donald

impoverished by the ravages of Cumberland's soldiery after Culloden. Succeeding to the chiefship after his father's death in 1754, he was not served heir till February 1758, and three years later, broken in health and beset by money difficulties, he died while still a comparatively young man.

As already mentioned, the old Chief of Glengarry held aloof from the Rising, but the clan was marshalled under the energetic leadership of young Angus and played a distinguished part in the whole campaign. The rout at Prestonpans was in large part due to the vehemence of their attack, and their determined rearguard action at Clifton was responsible for the repulse of Cumberland's dragoons and saving the army on its retreat to the north. The young Glengarry leader, who had meanwhile been recruiting in the Highlands, rejoined the army on the eve of the battle of Falkirk, and his strongly reinforced clansmen contributed in no small measure to the slaughter and rout that marked that victory. But for the Glengarry men the celebrations that followed were shortlived. The day after the battle Angus was accidentally shot and killed in the streets of Falkirk, and many of his clansmen who mourned his tragic loss returned to their homes.

On the eve of Culloden, old Glengarry seems at last to have thrown in his lot with the Prince and, no doubt inspired by the successes which had marked the course of the campaign, gravely compromised himself by marshalling support for the cause. In the final disastrous battle, his men were led by Donald of Lochgarry against a foe now sufficiently well instructed in the ways of meeting a Highland charge which in the past had demoralised the enemy but was now rendered ineffective by their famished and weakened condition, their want of arms and equipment, the detachment of their forces and, above all, by the wilfulness of a leader who insisted against all advice upon giving battle on ground that could hardly have been less favourable. After the battle the Prince paused at Invergarry Castle in his retreat for refuge in the West. The old Chief tried hard to come to an accommodation with the authorities, but his representations proved futile, and he and his people were subjected to the severest outrages at the hands of Cumberland's troops. He himself was taken prisoner to Edinburgh where he was confined until his release in October 1749. The remaining years of his life were spent on his estates, weighed down by debt and heavily encumbered by burdens which were passed on unredeemed at his death to his successors.

On the death without issue of Alasdair Ruadh in 1761, Duncan, the son of young Angus who had been killed at Falkirk, succeeded as 14th Chief. Duncan had a large family of whom his successor, Colonel Alistair Ranaldson MacDonell, who welcomed George IV during his Edinburgh visit in 1822, was noted as one of the most remarkable Highlanders of his day. His brother James, Colonel of the Coldstream Guards, so distinguished himself in defence of the Chateau Hougomont at Waterloo that he was acclaimed the outstanding hero of that battle. Alistair's son Aeneas succeeded as 16th Chief but found his inheritance so heavily burdened by his father's debts that he had to sell all his estates, retaining in his own possession only the Castle on the Raven Rock, the family vault at Kilfinnan and the Well of the Heads. His two sons, Alexander and Charles, having died without issue, the succession once more devolved on the Scotus family and Ranald, 7th of Scotus, became 19th Chief. Ranald's son, Aeneas Ranald Westrop MacDonell, matriculated the arms portrayed at the beginning of this Chapter. His grandson, the 22nd Chief, is Air Commodore Aeneas Ranald Donald MacDonell, C.B., D.F.C., R.A.F.(Rtd.), who has nobly upheld the martial traditions of his Clan.

Seal of Alasdair Boloyne, 8th of Keppoch
(from the Mackintosh Charter of December 1548)
S. ALEXANDRI RENALDI

21

The Macdonalds of Keppoch

THE MACDONALDS (MACDONELLS) OF KEPPOCH are also known as the Clanranald of Lochaber. Their lands lay mostly in Glen Spean and Glen Roy, a district known as Brae Lochaber. In ancient times Lochaber was a vast region bounded to the north and east by Badenoch, to the west by the Rough Bounds of Moidart and Morar, and to the south by Loch Leven and Glencoe. It first appears in historical records in 1228, when Alexander II granted the territories of Badenoch and Lochaber to Walter Comyn, whose family was eventually dispossessed by Robert Bruce in the course of his struggle for the Scottish crown. In 1309 Lochaber was granted to Angus Og of the Isles in reward for the shelter and protection he had provided for the King in his wanderings after the battle of Methven. The lands of Glen Spean and Glen Roy were later bestowed by Good John, Angus's son and successor, upon Alasdair Carrach, his youngest son by the Princess Margaret of Scotland. From that time the Keppoch Macdonalds based their claim to the lands on their undoubted right of possession, and at all times stoutly defended themselves against the encroachments of feudal superiors whose sheepskin parchments they treated with scorn.

Alasdair Carrach, progenitor of the Chiefs of Keppoch, first appears on record as Lord of Lochaber in 1394 when he entered into a contract with Thomas Dunbar, Earl of Moray, by which he was bound to protect, defend and safeguard, for the space of seven years, the possessions of the regality of Moray and all the church lands in that province, which the Earl of Moray, by a formal contract, had bound himself to protect. Alasdair promised to support the Earl against all persons for the same space of seven years, excepting the King, the Earl of Fife (afterwards the Regent Albany), and the Lord of the Isles. The Earl of Moray, in return, promised to pay the Lord of Lochaber 80 merks yearly, and to stand by him in all his affairs against all persons, excepting the King, the Earl of Fife, the Earl of Mar and Alexander Leslie, heir of the Earldom of Ross. Another clause in this contract is interesting for the picture it evokes of some of the social problems of the time. The Lord of Lochaber was also bound to prevent his own men, and "other caterans" over whom he had influence, from begging, wasting or destroying the lands of Moray, or otherwise living at the expense of the inhabitants.

For various reasons this contract was not renewed after the seven years. Chief of these was that by the death in 1394 of the Wolf of Badenoch, Earl of Ross by virtue of his marriage with Euphemia, the Countess of Ross, the succession to that rich earldom was now left wide open. Foremost among those who hoped to reap advantage from this development was Alasdair's brother Donald, Lord of the Isles, although, as a matter of policy, he decided to remain in the background and leave the initiative in Alasdair's capable hands. The lands of Moray, which the Lord of Lochaber was protecting, made a good base of operations. Alasdair launched his assault along the Great Glen from Lochaber to Inverness, taking the Castle and lands of Urquhart as a first step. How far he penetrated beyond the point is not recorded, but the march of so strong a force, now reinforced by the warriors of Isla and Kintyre under John Mor of Dunnyveg, presented such a formidable threat that Parliament at once summoned the brother for treason. Unwilling to risk the active intervention of the Government, the brothers gave in their submission. John Mor had the good fortune to receive a pardon, while Alasdair escaped with a light sentence which he served, presumably with little hardship, in the custody of his brother Donald, Lord of the Isles.

On the 20th November 1398 the Bishop of Moray lodged a complaint against "the illustrious man and potent Alexander of the Isles, Lord of Lochaber." It appears that Alasdair had given some lands and fisheries, the property of the Church, to Ranald MacAlexander (possibly a relative), John Chisholm and John White, a burgess of Inverness. The Bishop's protests, backed by threats of excommunication, proved effective, and Alasdair was obliged to withdraw and accept defeat. In 1401, however, when the seven year contract expired, he marched on Elgin, burned most of the town, and for good measure plundered the Canonry which had served as a sanctuary from ancient times. A crime of such enormity was inevitably followed by a sentence of excommunication, and Alexander, made aware of the serious consequences his action had incurred for himself and his people, hastened to make amends. Accompanied by his officers, he humbly besought and obtained absolution before the high altar of the cathedral and, as a token of earnest repentance, ordered a great torch set in gold for the church and a cross with a bell to be erected at the bounds of the sanctuary.

The next occasion on which Alasdair comes to notice is in the Harlaw campaign of 1411, when he joined his brother Donald, Lord of the Isles, with all his forces. In that momentous battle, Donald placed Alasdair and his men in the reserve commanded by John Mor of Dunnyveg, thus ensuring, according to the annalist, that the lives of all the brothers should not be hazarded at once. They all played their part, however, in securing the hard-won victory, and Alasdair continued to support Donald in his withdrawal to the West and in his subsequent quarrel with the Lord of Dunnyveg.

Many years later we find Alasdair Carrach still taking an active part in the stirring events that followed James I's return from his exile and his firm assumption of royal authority. The King's notorious visit to Inverness in 1427 resulted, as related in an earlier chapter, in the treacherous seizure of a number of chiefs, the summary execution of some and the imprisonment of others. The young Alexander, Lord of the Isles, was one of those confined to prison, albeit for a short period, and this provoked the deep resentment of all branches of Clan Donald, already inflamed by their suspicion of the King's complicity in the murder of John Mor and his execution of Alexander MacGorrie. The result was a general rising as soon as Alexander regained his freedom. The army was mustered in Lochaber, where it was joined by Alasdair and the men of Keppoch, and from there marched to Inverness, setting fire to the town and laying waste all the Crown lands in the area. With the approach of the royal army, the Islesmen retired with their spoil to Lochaber, but the desertion of the Camerons and Clan Chattan forced Alexander to sue for peace. There followed his humiliating submission to the King at Holyrood and a long period of confinement in Tantallon Castle.

Contrary to the King's expectations, Alexander's imprisonment caused a deeper rift in his relations with the clans, whose discontent and resentment now found an active response in the breast of Donald Balloch, warrior son of the murdered John Mor and cousin of the prisoner in Tantallon. In 1431 Donald raised the standard of rebellion and surprised the royal army under the Earl of Mar at Inverlochy. A large share of the victory was due to his uncle Alasdair Carrach, whose Keppoch archers poured their deadly shower of arrows upon Mar's flank and threw his army into confusion and rout. But as at Harlaw twenty years earlier, the Islesmen were unable to exploit their victory, and retribution quickly followed. Alasdair's lands in Lochaber were forfeited. They were later granted by charter to Malcolm Mackintosh, Captain of Clan Chattan, who had fought him at Inverlochy and whose desertion two years earlier had led to his nephew Alexander's defeat and subsequent imprisonment. The charter under which these lands were confirmed to Mackintosh in 1443 is remarkable for the fact that it was granted by the Lord of the Isles "for the faithful service" of one who had proved himself at once a treacherous ally and active enemy of his House. Why Mackintosh should have been thus favoured at the expense of the loyal and devoted Keppoch chief is hard to explain unless we believe that Alexander, whose release from Tantallon was followed by considerable marks of royal favour including the high office of Justiciar beyond the Forth, was obliged by the circumstances of his position to give effective confirmation of the earlier grant. Thus originated the cause of continuing conflict between Keppoch and Mackintosh, each asserting a right which no one except the other could deny— the ancient Celtic right of immemorial occupation on the one hand, and the feudal right of the written charter on the other. Almost three centuries were to pass before a settlement was finally achieved by a legal adroitness which appeared to admit the validity of the claims of each and left the honour of both untarnished.

Alasdair Carrach is assumed to have died about 1440. He was succeeded by Angus, only son of his marriage with a daughter of Malcolm, Duke of Lennox.

Angus is known in the clan as *Aonghas na Fearsaid,* so called from his place of residence at Fersit below Loch Treig. No doubt in consequence of his father's forfeiture, little or no account is to be found of Angus or his clan in the records of the time. The only mention of his name occurs in 1463, when it appears as a witness in a charter of the Earl of Ross. We know, however, that the clan supported John, Lord of the Isles, in his rebellion of 1451, and four years later joined Donald Balloch in his ravaging expedition against the Cumbraes, Bute and Arran; and it may be safely assumed that they also played their due part in the events of the year 1463, when Angus Og and Donald Balloch launched their precipitate attempt to implement the terms of the Treaty of Ardtornish.

Angus of Fersit married a daughter of MacPhee of Glenpean, by whom he had (1) Donald, who succeeded; (2) Alasdair, who became 5th Chief after the deposition of his nephew, Iain Aluinn; (3) Mariot (Margaret), who married a member of Lochiel's family.

Angus of Fersit probably died before 1478. In that year a summons was issued against John, Lord of the Isles, for providing safety and protection to Donald MacAngus, who evidently had allied himself with Angus Og in his attempt to restore the family influence in the forfeited lands of Ross. Donald remained a loyal supporter of Angus Og in his valiant struggle to retrieve the fortunes of his House. In 1483 he was present with his brother Alasdair at the battle of Lagabraad, in which Angus Og roundly defeated a strong combination of the Mackenzies and the northern clans. There is no mention of the Keppoch men in accounts of the battle of Bloody Bay, probably because that was a naval engagement fought mainly between the sea-board clans. But when the struggle, interrupted by Angus Og's tragic death, was resumed by Alexander of Lochalsh in 1491, Donald and his men joined his standard and took part in the extensive raids in Cromarty which preceded their total defeat by the Mackenzies and their allies at Park. His brother Alasdair, approaching with the rest of the clan, was unable to reach the scene in time to avert the disastrous culmination of a campaign which was to have fatal consequences for the Lordship of the Isles.

After the forfeiture of the Lordship, James IV made frequent visits to the West in pursuit of his policy of securing a stable and permanent settlement among the clans. In May 1495 he held his court at Mingary in Ardnamurchan, and Donald of Keppoch was one of the half-dozen chiefs who gave in their submission on that occasion. This was followed by an important act which made each chief answerable for the execution of summonses raised against members of his own clan. To ensure the due observance of the regulations, the Council in the following year summoned Donald and other chiefs to appear before them and bound them, "by the extension of their hands" to the Earl of Argyll as royal representative, to refrain from mutual injuries and molestation, each under a penalty of £500. Donald would seem to have established himself in the royal favour as a result of these appearances, for in the same year he was granted the crown tenancy of "Gargavach alias vocat the Inche of Lochquhabir," at an annual rental of 40 merks.

Donald's peaceful attitude, however, was of short duration. Early in 1497, William Dallas of Cantray lodged a complaint alleging violence and slaughter by the Keppoch Chief, as a result of which he had been forced to flee as far as Rathlin and later to seek the protection of MacIain of Ardnamurchan. Donald was summoned to appear before the Council and, failing to present himself, was fined in the sum of 200 merks. He remained obdurate, and was in due course forfeited in his recently acquired lands. Donald's conduct in this affair provides strong evidence of the reviving spirit of the clan and it is clearly manifested again in the events which shortly afterwards led to his death.

The manner in which Donald met his end has been made the subject of several accounts. It appears that while the men of Keppoch were engaged in a raid on the rich lands of Moray, the MacLarens of Balquhidder raided Brae Lochaber and departed with many head of cattle and other spoil. On returning from his own foray, Donald at once led his men in pursuit of the Maclarens and, having intercepted them at the head of Loch Earn, recovered his cattle after a struggle and proceeded homewards by Ben Dorain. They had not gone far when, at a place called Leachda, they were overtaken by the Stewarts of Appin, whose original design was to relieve the MacLarens of their prey, but now deemed it an easier matter to seize it from the exhausted Keppoch men. In the battle that followed, Donald of Keppoch and Dugall Stewart of Appin fought each other to the death. Tradition has embellished the story with a strange tailpiece. One of the victorious Keppoch men, known as *Domhnall Ruadh Beag* (Little Red Donald), observing the prostrate bodies of the two Chiefs, noted that Stewart was a head taller than his own chief. He promptly cut off the Appin chief's head, remarking that if Donald was at least his equal in life, he would be no less his equal in death.

Donald, 3rd Chief of Keppoch, who thus died in 1497, was married to a daughter of Cameron of Lochiel. By her he had an only son, *Iain Aluinn* (Handsome John), who now succeeded as 4th Chief.

Iain Aluinn's reign is remarkable not only for its brevity, but for the example it provides of a clan exercising its immemorial right of deposing an unpopular chief and electing another from beyond that chief's own family. The immediate cause of Iain Aluinn's deposition almost within a year of his accession sprang from his conduct in the case of Domhnall Ruadh Beag, whose equalising stroke at Leachda has just been narrated. Little Red Donald was a man of considerable prowess, and one of his more popular accomplishments was his successful preying on his neighbours of Clan Chattan. The latest of his incursions produced a strong complaint from Mackintosh, coupled with the demand that the criminal should be delivered up to justice. It appears that Iain Aluinn meekly surrendered to Mackintosh's demand, but subject to the condition that "blood should not be spilled." Mackintosh thereupon promptly fulfilled the condition and his own conception of justice by executing Donald Ruadh with a rope round his neck.

The incident clearly must have been only one of many grievances to provoke the clan's hatred of Iain Aluinn and destroy their confidence in those qualities they had a right to demand in their chiefs. Iain Aluinn was formally deposed in a solemn ceremony, and—such was the strength of feeling aroused by his conduct—his family was declared perpetually ineligible for the chiefship of Keppoch. He appears to have accepted the decision of the clan without protest, and retired peacefully to the district of Urchair where his descendants, known as *Sliochd a' Bhrathair bu Shine* (Family of the Elder Brother), flourished for many generations. A notable member of the family was his great-great-grandson Iain Lom, the Keppoch bard, who at a critical time was to vindicate the honour of the clan by wreaking a terrible vengeance upon the murderers of the Chief whose line had superseded his own.

The choice of a successor to Iain Aluinn presented not a little difficulty. Donald Ruadh Beag's branch of the clan, *Mic Ghille Mhanntaich*, asserted their influence by demanding that the vacancy should be filled by a member of their family from Barra, whence they had originally sprung. Another branch, representatives of the Clan Gorrie but long settled in Lochaber, proposed a member of the family of their founder Godfrey, Lord of Uist. The descendants of Alasdair Carrach naturally wanted the chiefship to remain in their family. The obvious candidate was Iain Aluinn's uncle Alasdair, who had already provided ample proof of his capabilities under his brother Donald's chiefship. The clan's eventual choice of Alasdair as Chief, while confirming their ancient right of election, was also in perfect accord with the old Celtic law of Tanistry under which the uncle of a rejected chief assumed command of the clan and in certain circumstances retained the office in his own family.

Unfortunately, Alasdair did not long survive his election to the chiefship. In 1498, soon after his accession, he led an incursion upon one of his neighbours and, while returning home with his booty, was ambushed and slain by a Cameron at a place thereafter known as *Carn Alasdair*, at the head of Loch Leven. Thus within the space of two years Keppoch had lost three chiefs, two of them by violent death and the other by deposition. Alasdair was known in his time as *Alasdair nan Gleann* (of the Glens), and resided generally at Torran nan Ceap, not far from Tom Beag, where his son was to build the Castle or Manor House of Keppoch.

Alasdair was married to a daughter of Donald Gallach of Sleat, who was known locally as *A' Bhaintighearna Bheag* (The Little Lady). By her he had Donald Glas, his successsor, and Ranald Og, who pre-deceased his father.

Donald Glas, 6th of Keppoch, had not long succeeded his father before he entered into a bond of mutual security with Munro of Foulis, Grant of Freuchie and others in an attempt to check the feuds and disturbances that followed the

THE MACDONALDS OF KEPPOCH

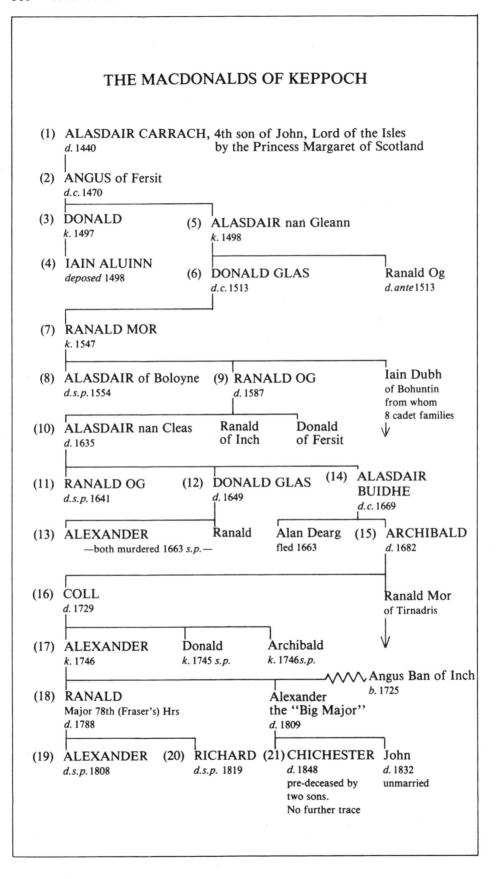

(1) ALASDAIR CARRACH, 4th son of John, Lord of the Isles
d. 1440   by the Princess Margaret of Scotland

(2) ANGUS of Fersit
d.c. 1470

(3) DONALD   (5) ALASDAIR nan Gleann
k. 1497   *k.* 1498

(4) IAIN ALUINN
deposed 1498   (6) DONALD GLAS   Ranald Og
                        d.c. 1513   *d. ante* 1513

(7) RANALD MOR
k. 1547

(8) ALASDAIR of Boloyne   (9) RANALD OG   Iain Dubh
d.s.p. 1554   *d.* 1587   of Bohuntin
                                                  from whom
                                                  8 cadet families

(10) ALASDAIR nan Cleas   Ranald   Donald
d. 1635   of Inch of Fersit

(11) RANALD OG   (12) DONALD GLAS   (14) ALASDAIR
d.s.p. 1641   *d.* 1649   BUIDHE
                                            d.c. 1669

(13) ALEXANDER   Ranald   Alan Dearg   (15) ARCHIBALD
—both murdered 1663 *s.p.*— fled 1663   *d.* 1682

(16) COLL   Ranald Mor
d. 1729   of Tirnadris

(17) ALEXANDER   Donald   Archibald
k. 1746   *k.* 1745 *s.p.*   *k.* 1746 *s.p.*

                                            Angus Ban of Inch
                                            b. 1725

(18) RANALD   Alexander
Major 78th (Fraser's) Hrs   the "Big Major"
d. 1788   *d.* 1809

(19) ALEXANDER   (20) RICHARD (21) CHICHESTER John
d.s.p. 1808   *d.s.p.* 1819   *d.* 1848   *d.* 1832
                                    pre-deceased by unmarried
                                    two sons.
                                    No further trace

rebellion of Sir Alexander of Lochalsh. At that time Munro's castle of Novar had been occupied by Sir Alexander, assisted by Donald, and the Keppoch chief was now anxious to restore friendly relations.

In 1500 Alexander, Lord Gordon, received a grant of lands in Lochaber, part of that district which had become Crown lands after the forfeiture of the Lordship. He was ordered to collect the Crown rents, by force if necessary, but it does not seem that the Chief of Keppoch paid any attention to his demands. This may account for the raid carried out in the same year by the Clan Chattan, which caused great devastation throughout the Brae. The leaders of this raid were Gillies MacPhail and Patrick MacBane, who were given a remission for their part on 9th June 1500. That remission followed so shortly after the crime gives rise to the strong suspicion that McPhail and McBane were agents acting for Lord Gordon. The punishment in this manner of a clan that had refused to pay its dues was to become an occurrence frequently resorted to by powerful superiors, with the connivance of the Crown. In the following year Donald Glas was adjudged to be in the wrong in occupying the Crown lands of Lochaber, and was accordingly ordered to remove elsewhere.

The Keppoch chief paid no heed to this attempt to oust him from his lands, but soon afterwards, when Huntly, Lovat and Munro of Foulis were given a commission to maintain the disputed lands and expel "broken men" from their bounds, Donald Glas wisely decided to submit, on which he received from Huntly a lease of the lands he then occupied. Having thus secured his tenure legally, he appears to have led a settled existence for the rest of his reign. There is no record of his participation in the stirring events of the year 1503, when Donald Dubh raised his standard of rebellion and blazed a trail of devastation through Lochaber and Badenoch. Whatever part he played must necessarily have been a minor one which did not merit the notice of a government already sufficiently taxed in its efforts to apprehend much more powerful offenders.

Donald Glas, 6th Chief, died in 1513, having married a daughter of Cameron of Lochiel, by whom he had an only son, Ranald, who succeeded.

Ranald Mor, 7th Chief, from whom the Keppoch patronymic of *Mac Mhic Raonuill* is derived, appears to have had an adventurous career. He is characterised by the bard MacFinlay in his poem "The Owl" as one who took to learning with zest, but was also a very active warrior. After John of Moidart was released from his confinement in Edinburgh and resumed his position as Chief of Clanranald, the Chief of Keppoch joined him in his subsequent campaign against the usurper Ranald Gallda and his Lovat supporters. Both he and his neighbour in Lochaber, Ewen Cameron of Lochiel, took part in the battle at Blar-na-leine in 1544 which utterly destroyed their enemies, including Ranald Gallda and both the Earl and Master of Lovat. When Huntly mounted his punitive expedition against the ringleaders, John of Moidart retreated and found refuge in the fastnesses of his Rough Bounds. Ranald Mor and Ewen Cameron of Lochiel were less fortunate. They retained their freedom for some time, but were eventually captured through the treachery of William Mackintosh, who handed them over to Huntly, the King's Lieutenant in the North. After a period of confinement in Ruthven, they were taken to Elgin and tried for complicity in the slaughter of Lovat. They were found guilty, and were beheaded in 1547, their heads being afterwards placed above the town gate.

Several of their followers were executed at the same time. These events rekindled the flame of hatred borne by the men of Keppoch against the Mackintoshes, and fuel was added by the knowledge that the slaughtered chief's wife was the sister of the man who had betrayed him. Retribution in a violent form, and uncloaked by a pretence of legality, was in due course to overtake Mackintosh when, falsely accused by a member of his own clan, he was executed in the most bizarre circumstances by Lady Huntly in the absence, though undoubtedly at the instigation, of her husband.

By his wife, Agnes Mackintosh, Ranald had two sons: Alasdair, who succeeded, and Ranald Og, who eventually succeeded his brother. A third son, Iain Dubh of Bohuntin, has been adjudged illegitimate by some, although one source names him "third lawful son of Ranald Mor," and he was accepted as such by the numerous cadet families who owe their origin to him. These are the families of Clianaig, Tulloch, Gallovie, Dalchosnie, Aberarder, Cranachan and Tullochchrom.

Alexander, 8th Chief, is known in history as Alasdair Boloyne. Shortly after his accession in 1547 he carried out a raid on Urquhart and Glenshee, from which he returned laden with booty. This appears to have been one of those raids carried out by a young chief to prove himself worthy in the eyes of his clan and capable of providing for their needs. He had been assisted by two warriors named Alasdair McGorrie and John MacInnes, both of whom figured with their chief in a respite given later under the Privy Seal, and to last for 21 years. The bewildering frequency of such respites is a sad commentary on the government's inability to impose its authority throughout the Highlands. The enforcement of its writ could be a costly exercise, and it was not often that its forces were willing to brave the lawbreakers in their remote and inaccessible territories. Thus if the threat posed by the summons failed in its purpose, the government was generally obliged to grant a remission in the fond hope that such an exercise of moderation would have a salutary influence on the subject's future conduct.

Records do not reveal how far Alasdair observed the terms of his remission, but it is evident that in the years that followed strong differences developed between him and his neighbours, the Camerons. These came to a head in 1554 when Ewen Beag of Lochiel invaded the Braes and was met by Alasdair and his men at Boloyne, behind Mulroy. During a stubborn struggle, the Camerons were put to flight after, it is said, losing their Chief in the battle. Alasdair himself was severely wounded and died later under the ministrations of a noted herbalist who was strongly suspected of poisoning the wound.

Alasdair, who died unmarried, was succeeded by his brother Ranald Og, 9th of Keppoch. Ranald appears to have been a wise chief, distinguished for his loyalty to the Crown and his desire to establish friendly relations with his neighbours. In 1563 he entered into a contract with Colin Campbell of Glenorchy for the lands of Rannoch, once part of the patrimony of the proscribed Clan Gregor. Each party bound himself to assist the other in defence of his possessions, and render mutual aid in their just quarrels. His new acquisition immediately became a source of great trouble to Ranald. The Clan Gregor were actively determined to oppose his entry into Rannoch, and the disturbances they caused reached such proportions that Keppoch and Glenorchy were given a joint commission of fire and sword against them. Their continuing hostility made the task of retaining Rannoch appear a costly and harassing burden, and eventually, after six years of turmoil, Glenorchy was persuaded to release Keppoch from his contract and resume possession of the disputed lands.

At the same time Ranald was successful in placing his relations with the Mackintoshes on a more favourable footing. He was able to accomplish this by the good offices of the Regent Moray who, on his visit to Inverness in 1569, obliged Lachlan Mackintosh to grant the Keppoch chief security of tenure in respect of the lands held of him in Lochaber, and on terms approved by the Regent. The settlement was confirmed and strengthened three years later when, on 15th June 1572, Ranald gave Mackintosh a bond of manrent and service against "all mortals" saving the King and the feudal superior. Thus the peace he sought appeared well established, and Ranald might well feel confident that the feud sparked off by his father's death was at length brought to an end.

The only other event in Ranald's life of which there is record took place in 1577. In that year the Earl of Argyll marshalled his vassals, ostensibly for suppressing disturbances in his own domains, but in fact for an invasion of the lands of Glengarry whose chief, Donald MacAngus, had provoked his resentment. Ranald was one of many chiefs summoned by the Council to oppose the Earl in defence of Glengarry, but no action became necessary as Argyll soon disbanded his forces in face of the powerful combination ranged against him.

Ranald Og died in 1587. By his marriage with a daughter of Duncan Stewart of Appin he had (1) Alexander, who succeeded; (2) Ranald of Inch; (3) Donald of Fersit; and (4) Angus, who predeceased him, about 1567.

Alexander, 10th of Keppoch, who was known as *Alasdair nan Cleas* (of the Tricks), reputedly for his sleight of hand and dexterity with cards, reigned for the long period of over forty years. For much of that time the kingdom was distracted by frequent upheavals from which it was seldom possible for the Chief of Keppoch to stand aside. Alasdair was a well-educated man of forceful character endowed with many of the qualities he needed to survive the repercussions of the plots and intrigues that followed each other in rapid succession—the deadly feud between Huntly and Moray culminating in the latter's murder in 1592, the assassination of Cawdor the same year, the Earls' Rebellion in 1594, and the constant commotion in Islay and Kintyre where his kinsmen of Clan Donald South were locked in a life-or-death struggle to retrieve the fallen fortunes of their House.

Alasdair had hardly followed his father in the chiefship when, in the quarrel between Huntly and Moray, he joined Lochiel and other Lochaber clans in supporting Huntly, while Mackintosh and Grant of Freuchie took up the cause of Moray. In 1588, Huntly, Mackintosh and Grant were given a Royal Commission to act against Keppoch and his brother Ranald with fire and sword, for raids carried out by them in the lands of Mackintosh and Grant of Freuchie in 1584. However, Huntly was not disposed to harry the lands of one of his sturdiest allies in his feud, and instead used his influence to protect the men of Keppoch against both Mackintosh and Grant.

For a time peace was restored, and in January 1589 Keppoch renewed his father's bond of manrent with Mackintosh. But, in 1592, the murder of the Earl of Moray by Huntly provoked further serious outbreaks of disorder. The supporters of the deceased Moray invaded Huntly's lands, and the Grants and Mackintosh invaded the lands of Keppoch and Lochiel. Huntly retaliated by sending Keppoch and Lochiel to harry and destroy the lands of Strathspey. From there they went to Inverness, raiding Mackintosh's lands and holding the Castle for Huntly. Owing to shortage of food, the Castle had to be given up, and Mackintosh executed Keppoch's son, Iain Dubh, and Godfrey Dubh, one of the Gorries of Brae Lochaber.

The King and his Council now intervened and gave a Commission of fire and sword to Lovat, Mackintosh and Grant against Alasdair of Keppoch and his allies, who were accused of "open oppression, murder, slaughter, sorning, theft, and other odious and capital crimes." Keppoch and Lochiel evaded the forces sent north under the Earl of Angus, and, incited by Huntly, continued their relentless devastation of the lands of Grant and Mackintosh. Such was the concern felt by neighbouring chiefs over their activities that Rose of Kilravock, whose lands lay uncomfortably close to the scene of operations, had to ask assurance from Huntly, Lochiel and Keppoch that his estates and those of his friends should not be violated during the hotilities. This undertaking was freely given on the 18th March 1593.

Next year, in the rebellion of the Catholic Earls, Keppoch and Lochiel formed part of the small army with which Huntly, Angus and Erroll opposed Argyll's vastly superior force at Glenlivet. Argyll lost the battle, but for the Earls it was an empty victory, as they had not the means to follow it up. The promised support had failed to reach them. A Spanish galleon carrying guns, ammunition and arms was driven ashore and lost in St Catherine's Dub, a rocky inlet not far from Slains Castle, the seat of the Earl of Erroll. Argyll thus became the eventual victor, and the Earls were in due course forfeited in their estates and driven into exile.

Keppoch and his friends from Lochaber now had to make their peace with Argyll, who was appointed by the King to reduce the vassals of the rebel Earls. On 3rd November 1595 Alasdair entered into a bond of service and protection with Argyll, and surrendered his son Angus as surety for his obedience. He further bound himself to go to Inveraray before Christmas 1595 under safe-conduct, provided that the Earl on his part gave Alasdair his bond of maintenance, binding him to defend him "in all kyndlie possessiounis that he may clam kyndness to." It is unlikely that either of the parties to this under-taking had the intention of adhering to its very general terms any longer than it suited his own interests. Keppoch chose to observe it for only about two years, and he resumed his old allegiance to Huntly immediately upon that nobleman's restoration to favour.

The next time we meet Alasdair of Keppoch is in 1602, when King James ordered Highland chiefs who had the "maist power" to raise men for the service in Ireland on behalf of "the Kingis majesties darrest sister, the Queen of England, having lovinglie intreated his majestie for the supply and levy of some Hielandmen, for the bettir repressing of the treasonabill rebellioun intertenit aganis hir within the cuntrey of Irland." Keppoch was told to call up 100 men, but he appears to have ignored the order. He evidently had more pressing affairs to attend to, and much closer to his own doorstep than Ireland. In April 1602 the Council had reason to complain of acts of violence and fire-raising by Keppoch in the very heart of Clan Chattan country. That they were able to penetrate so far was probably due to Mackintosh's own absence on a punitive mission against the Clan Gregor and his subsequent entanglement with the men of Atholl who had given shelter to that outlawed clan. Others besides Keppoch appear to have seized the opportunity provided by Mackintosh's absence, for Huntly and Glengarry were also cited at the same time, and denounced rebels for the same reasons.

In 1605 a serious attempt was made to secure the submission of the rebel chiefs. Lord Scone, the King's Lieutenant, summoned the chiefs of Clan Donald and others to appear before him at Kilkerran (Campbeltown) in Kintyre to exhibit titles to their lands, pay their just dues and rents, and find surety for their future behaviour. Many of the minor chiefs attended, but Alasdair nan Cleas and many others failed to appear. He had only one title, to the 40 merklands of Gargavach alone, which he held on lease from Huntly; for the other parts of the Brae of Lochaber which he occupied he had none. He remained unaffected by the threats which followed his disobedience of the royal summons, and continued relentlessly to harass his neighbours with fire and sword. The measure of his defiance during these years is evident from the list of violent crimes for which he was remitted in 1608—slaughter in Strathardle, Glenshee and Inverness, burning the house of the King's Commissary in that town, fire-raising in Atholl, and burning the house of Neil Stewart MacGilleColuim, in which one of the family died.

Two years later, in 1611, Alexander is found aiding the Government and assisting Argyll in his uprooting commission against the Clan Gregor. Some members of that proscribed clan had been given shelter by Keppoch sympathisers at Tirnadris and, upon their presence being discovered by the chief, were taken by surprise and slain. For this cruel act Alasdair was awarded the sum of £100 by a grateful Government, but his brother Ranald of Inch, who strongly disapproved of his conduct, was afterwards prosecuted by the Privy Council for not having lent his assistance in the affair. It was one of a number of incidents which caused deep antagonism between the brothers and led to a tragedy which foreshadowed the notorious Keppoch murder of half a century later. The immediate causes of both tragedies were essentially similar, involving the sensitive question of Huntly's right of Lordship. In this case Ranald of Inch had approached Huntly for a lease of the lands of Treig, which included Inverlair and Fersit. Such open recognition of Huntly's claim was taken by Alasdair as an affront to his status as head of the Clan, and he promptly went to Ranald's house, seized the document and burned it, remarking that now he had as much right to those lands as any other. Ranald is then said to have set off to see Huntly to renew the lease, but was overtaken on the way and killed by Ranald Og, the Chief's son.

We come now to a period in Alasdair's career when his resource and sagacity were taxed to the utmost. On the 23rd May 1615 Sir James of Dunnyveg escaped from his prison in Edinburgh Castle. The escape was cleverly planned by Keppoch and his son, Ranald Og, with young Clanranald as their accomplice. Successfully evading pursuit, the party crossed the Forth and, travelling by Murthlie, Methven, and the east end of Rannoch, eventually reached the safety of Lochaber. Thence they passed through the friendly territories of Clanranald and Sleat, gathering followers at various points in their progress until they finally reached Islay. Keppoch and his two sons shared in the vicissitudes of the campaign which followed and remained with Sir James until the rebellion ended with his flight to Ireland.

Meanwhile the Government had taken prompt measures for the apprehension of Sir James and those who had aided him in his escape. A reward of £5000 was offered for the recapture, dead or alive, of Sir James, and 5000 merks each for Keppoch and his son Ranald. After the rebellion collapsed and Keppoch and his two sons returned to Lochaber, a commission was given to Lord Gordon, Huntly's son, to apprehend the fugitives and bring them to justice. This presented no easy task in country like Lochaber, where the fugitives knew every place of concealment and could rely upon the loyalty and active support of their clansmen in evading their pursuers. Lord Gordon himself appears to have been half-hearted in the execution of his commission, with the result that another commission was given to him jointly with his father, the Marquis, with express instructions to speed the apprehension of the rebels; and, to assist them in their task, the Privy Council at the same time cautioned Alasdair's wife against affording any aid or comfort to her husband.

The pursuit was now pressed so closely that Keppoch decided Lochaber was no longer a safe place of refuge. With his son, Donald Glas, he succeeded in making his escape and joined Sir James of Dunnyveg in Spain. His son and heir,

Ranald, chose to remain behind in Lochaber and continued successfully to evade capture throughout his father's exile. Keppoch remained in Spain until the year 1620 when, as a result of valuable information passed by Donald Glas to King James, they were both granted permission to return. Alasdair was rewarded with a pension of 2000 merks for life and a royal remission for all his past crimes. After a period in London he was allowed to return to Scotland, but the Privy Council, who viewed with alarm the indulgence shown to the exiles, detained him in Edinburgh while a polite but urgent protest was sent to the King emphasising the danger of permitting his return to Lochaber. This protest was disregarded by the King, as were two subsequent remonstrances expressing the Council's conviction that Keppoch should not be given his freedom until adequate sureties were provided. Alasdair was forced to remain in Edinburgh for almost a year before the Council finally accepted assurances that satisfied them of his future good behaviour. In June 1622, Sir Ruairi Macleod of Dunvegan and Sir John MacDougall of Dunollie agreed to become security for Keppoch, and he was at length released from the Council's supervision and permitted to return to his home.

For the rest of his life Alasdair remained at peace with the government and with his neighbours, and the only transactions in which we find him involved are peaceful ones designed to provide security for himself and his family in their estates. In July 1628 he received from the Earl of Enzie, Huntly's son and heir, a charter granting him the lease in feu of the 4 merklands of Fersit, the 3½ merklands of Clianaig and Monassie, the 3 merklands of Breckletter, the 2 merklands of Inverlair, one merkland of Kilmonivaig, and one merkland of Loch Treig, on the east of the Water of Treig—extending in all to 15 merklands and 16 pennylands in the Barony of Lochaber. These were to be held for an annual feu-duty of 200 merks and the usual services attached to such leases. There was also a clause providing for the redemption of the lands on payment to Alasdair or his heirs of a sum of 6000 merks. Two years later, in July 1630, Alasdair assigned the lands of Fersit to his second son, Donald, and his wife, Jean Robertson, in life rent.

There is no doubt that Alasdair nan Cleas was a remarkable chief amongst the many doughty warriors of the Keppoch clan. In every branch of the Clan Donald there has been at least one chief whom we remember for outstanding character and enterprise, for valour in defending the honour of his house, and in preserving his heritage intact for his successors. Alasdair nan Cleas has an honoured place in the slender roll of such men. He reigned as chief for over forty turbulent years and died in peace. He had the benefit of a good education, made many friends from his earliest days and even seems to have inspired the affection or regard of his King, in spite of the many crimes and rebellious acts which marked his eventful life. A liberal entertainer, he successfully combined the rôles of Highland chief and friend of courtiers both north and south of the Border. The story is told that after his return from Spain he had occasion to visit an old friend, an English gentleman, whom he had known in his college days. His friend drew his attention to a valuable and handsome set of candlesticks on his table. Alasdair was suitably impressed, and agreed they were very fine, but he added that he too had a good collection of priceless articles of that kind. When his friend visited him at Keppoch later, he reminded his host of the remark he had made. Alasdair told him to wait a moment; and, as the wine circulated freely after dinner, at a signal from their master, a dozen stalwart clansmen appeared in the hall each bearing a lighted torch. "There," said Alasdair, "are my candlesticks, and no money in England or anywhere else would buy them."

Alasdair nan Cleas married Jean MacDougall of Dunollie, by whom he had:
(1) Ranald Og, who succeeded; (2) Donald Glas, who succeeded Ranald Og; (3)
Alexander, who became chief after the murder of the sons of Donald Glas;
(4) Donald Gorm of Inveroy; (5) Iain Dubh, who had been killed at Inverness in
1593; (6) Angus, from whom the cadets of Achnancoichean. Alasdair also had
five daughters, all of whom were married.

Alasdair would appear to have died in 1635, for his son Ranald Og was named
"of Keppoch" in March of the following year. Ranald spent much of his life
in the company of his father, and took his full share in the stirring events that
crowded that Chief's reign. For his part in the escape of Sir James of Dunnyveg
and in the subsequent rebellion, he was declared rebel and a reward of 5000
marks offered for his apprehension. Unlike his father and his brother Donald
Glas, Ranald chose to remain behind in Lochaber and for six years led the
precarious life of an outlaw, successfully thwarting all attempts by Mackintosh
to find him in the deep hiding-places around Loch Treig.

In 1621, after his father had returned from exile in Spain, Lord Gordon was
given a commission to find Ranald and arrest him. What followed is not
apparent, but it is probable that Ranald shared his father's remission granted
later that year, for he was able to visit London in 1622 without any hindrance.
Soon afterwards he appears in peaceful occupation of his lands and fully restored
to his former status. Huntly, remembering the support the Keppoch men had
given him in the Earls' Rebellion, no doubt employed his influence in his favour.
At the same time Ranald renewed the bond of friendship with Mackintosh. Grant
of Freuchie was not so accommodating, and the differences between them had to
be resolved by the good offices of Mackenzie of Kintail.

Ranald continued in peace from that time until, in July 1635, he was committed to the Tolbooth in Edinburgh for failing to conform to the General Band
(Bond) of 1587. He was not alone in the failure to obey that Act of Parliament,
under which all landlords and bailies of lands in the Highlands and Isles were
held responsible for the behaviour of their tenants. Neither that Act nor the
supplementary measure which followed a few years later was effective in checking
the excesses committed by "broken men" throughout the Highlands. In the end
the Privy Council realised the almost impossible task they had imposed on the
chiefs, and in March 1636, they decided to release the Keppoch Chief on
condition he found sufficient security.

Ranald's accession to the chiefship was soon to be followed by events of
much wider significance which would disturb the peace of the Highlands and
convulse the whole kingdom for many years to come. The King's attempt to
impose a new liturgy in Scotland led in 1638 to the signing of the National
Covenant and the beginning of a struggle which was eventually to destroy him.
At the head of the Covenanting Party was the Earl of Argyll, and that factor
alone was sufficient to determine the attitude of many of the Highland clans, who
had remained largely unaffected by the progress of the Reformation and tended
to align their sympathies on the side of the King. Among the first to manifest
his loyalty was Ranald Og of Keppoch, and the Earl of Argyll, quick to seize both
opportunity and advantage, obtained letters of fire and sword against him and
"other proven enemies to religion." In 1640 he invaded the Keppoch lands,
causing widespread devastation and misery, and left a garrison of 220 men behind
him to overawe the inhabitants. Such a small force, however, found it
impossible to carry out its task, and it was soon killed off or forced to flee the
vengeance of the outraged clansmen.

Ranald Og, who had married Jean, a daughter of William Mackintosh of Borlum, left no issue. There is no mention of him after the Argyll incursion against his lands, and it is assumed that he died shortly afterwards, because in October of the following year his brother Donald Glas appears as Chief. Donald Glas, as we have seen, had played a prominent part in the stirring events surrounding the fall of the House of Islay, and his loyalty to the Crown had already been confirmed by the circumstances of his recall from exile in Spain. In 1642 the differences between King and Parliament developed into open civil war. Donald joined the first attempt mounted in Scotland in the Royalist cause, the premature and abortive rising in 1644 led by the weak and vacillating Marquis of Huntly. He remained with the army until it was disbanded, but his services were soon to be claimed by a leader of a different calibre who possessed the skill and understanding to employ them to the best advantage.

James Graham, 5th Earl of Montrose, who had joined the party of the Covenant in its earlier stages, had gradually become disillusioned by the intransigence of its adherents under the leadership of Argyll. The signing of the Solemn League and Covenant, on 25th September 1643, was the culmination of a series of measures which he regarded as intolerant and oppressive, and he finally succeeded in persuading the King to accept his offer of serving the royal cause in Scotland. Leaving England with one or two companions, four horses and little baggage, he contrived to pass safely through hostile country and arrived at his kinsman's house of Tullibelton, midway between Perth and Dunkeld. Here he stayed for four days with Patrick Graham, Younger of Inchbrakie. Meantime Alasdair MacCholla Chiotaich (Young Colkitto), who had landed in the West in July, had reached Blair of Atholl with his warriors of Clan Donald of Ulster. Here he waited impatiently for the promised arrival of the King's General. The Atholl men were alarmed by the presence of the stern clansmen from Ireland, ragged and hungry after their long marches from the West, and a dangerous situation was averted only by the timely arrival of Montrose. Alasdair accepted a commission under the King's Lieutenant, and the Atholl men gathered to the Royal Standard which was raised on a knoll above the river Tilt.

It was not till after the battles of Tippermuir, Aberdeen and Fyvie that the western clans joined Alasdair during his second recruiting tour of the West. Meeting again at Blair, Clan Donald came in force, with John of Moidart, Angus of Glengarry, Donald Glas of Keppoch and MacIain of Glencoe prominent among the leaders of other loyal clans. All were united and inspired by one over-riding aim, to strike where their common enemy Argyll would suffer most; and Montrose responded with his decision to make a mid-winter descent into the very heart of Campbell territory.

Donald Glas of Keppoch and his men ably assisted John of Moidart in his forays for meat to feed the army during the invasion. Thus the problem of supplies for the winter, and shelter from the weather, was solved as promised by their guide and adviser, Angus MacAlan Dubh of Glencoe. The Keppoch men were able to take their revenge for the invasion of their lands in 1640, but although the Campbell lands were thoroughly spoiled, there is no record of unnecessary slaughter. Argyll himself had retired to Roseneath on the Gareloch, whence he addressed angry protests to the Estates in Edinburgh. In the middle of January 1645 the Royal army marched north out of Glen Shira and headed for Inverlochy and the Great Glen. News had come that Seaforth and his Mackenzies were on their way to Inverness to head Montrose off from the East and Gordon country where he could find reinforcements.

The Glencoe men and Donald's Keppoch men marched through their home lands up to Cillechuimein (now Fort Augustus) where a halt was called and, on

Iain Lom's Stone in Cille
Chaorail, ancestral burial
ground of Keppoch

the 30th January, a Bond of Union was signed by Montrose and the chiefs, Keppoch among them. Before the march was resumed, news came that Argyll had rallied his clan and was hard on their heels, panting for revenge. Montrose at once saw the danger of being caught in a trap between two powerful forces, either one of which outnumbered his own. Rightly judging the calibre of Seaforth's raw levies, he decided that the best plan was to attack and destroy the stronger jaw of the trap. He was helped to his decision by Iain Lom, the Keppoch Bard, who offered to lead the army back to Inverlochy, avoiding the Great Glen and the vigilance of Argyll's scouts.

The next phase of the campaign is one of the most interesting in an enthralling story. It was the last day of January 1645 when Iain Lom led the royal army up Glen Tarff into the hills. Climbing over the high pass into Glen Turret, they executed a spectacular flanking march through impassable terrain and winter blizzards down to Glen Roy and, skirting the foothills of Ben Nevis, arrived at dawn of 2nd February on the slopes overlooking the old Castle of Inverlochy. Argyll was taken completely by surprise and took to his galley in the Loch, leaving the command to Campbell of Auchinbreck, a tried and brave soldier. The result of the battle is well known. Once more the Keppoch men, fighting in the centre, had their revenge. The bard declined the offer of a sword from Alasdair MacCholla with the words, "If I fall in battle, who will sing your praises?" He was as good as his word. He viewed the rout from the walls of the old Castle and composed a biting and in parts scurrilous poem on the occasion, in which he incites the Campbells not to forget their bonnets floating on the river, but to get on with their swimming lessons.

The military power of Argyll was broken for the time being. In the battles of Auldearn, Alford, and Kilsyth, some of the western clans took part. Alasdair Colkitto, knighted by Montrose after Kilsyth, and no doubt believing that the Royalist cause was now well established, left to look after his own interests in Kintyre. Many of the clans went home to deliver their plunder, but 500 Ulstermen remained with Montrose to be slaughtered almost to a man after the final battle of Philiphaugh, which marked the end of the campaign and of Royalist hopes in Scotland.

While the men of Keppoch were away fighting with Montrose, the lands of Lochaber continued to suffer from the vengeful ravages of the Campbells. It was not long after their return before they retaliated. Led by Angus Og of Achnancoichean, and joined by the MacIains of Glencoe, they made a sudden descent upon the lands of Campbell of Breadalbane, seizing and driving off a large spoil of cattle. The Campbells, most of whose leading men were already assembled at Finlarig for the wedding of Breadalbane's daughter, immediately set out in pursuit and intercepted the raiders· at Stronachlachan. The fighting qualities of the Campbells had been severely impaired by the wedding festivities, and they lost heavily in the bloody struggle that followed. The survivors were driven back to Finlarig Castle, leaving many prominent Campbells dead on the field, including "32 of the laird's ablest tennentis and servands." It was also, however, a costly victory for the Macdonalds. The MacIains are said to have lost their chief, and the Keppoch men lost their leader, Angus Og, whose death was to be lamented by Iain Lom in one of his great battle poems.

The remaining years of Donald's life are a total blank and he is thought to have died about 1649. He had been married twice. By his first wife, Jean Robertson of Struan, he had no surviving male issue. His second wife was a daughter of Forrester of Kilbagie, by whom he had (1) Alexander, who succeeded as 13th Chief, and was to become the victim of the famous Keppoch Murder;

(2) Ranald, who was was murdered with his brother; (3) a daughter, who remained unmarried.

Alexander was a minor at his accession, and command of the clan was accordingly assumed by his uncle, Alasdair Buidhe. He took control at a time when Royalist fortunes had reached their lowest ebb with the execution of the King, and the Scottish estates had attempted to disavow their complicity in that tragic event by the proclamation of his son as Charles II. Alasdair espoused the royal cause with the same devotion exhibited by his predecessors and remained constant in his loyalty in face of the disastrous events of the next three years. In 1650 Montrose made his last gallant attempt to restore the Royalist fortunes, but, intercepted at Carbisdale before the clans could join his slender force, was decisively defeated, sold to his conquerors, and sent to his death in Edinburgh. Later in that same year Cromwell crossed the Tweed and scattered the Scottish army at Dunbar. The Scots proclaimed their defiance by crowning Charles at Scone on New Year's Day 1651, and then collected an army which Cromwell cunningly allowed to cross his flank to meet with disaster at Worcester. We do not know if Alasdair Buidhe accompanied the army into England, but it is not unlikely, as he was present at the coronation where he was styled "Tutor of Mcrannald" in the list of Highland chiefs. In 1652 he received from the exiled King a commission to raise troops and money for his service, no doubt in preparation for the abortive Glencairn Rising in which Alasdair fought with his allies of Lochiel and Glengarry until the dissensions of its leaders had destroyed its effectiveness. After the collapse of the Rising, it may be reasonable to assume that Alasdair, in common with other rebel chiefs, was received into the peace of the Commonwealth subject to the normal sureties, and continued in undisturbed control of his clan until the Restoration.. Shortly afterwards the young Alexander reached his majority, and there is little doubt that Alasdair Buidhe strongly resented his supersession by his nephew and actively influenced the course of the tragic events that followed.

Alexander first appears as Chief in 1661 when he was cited with others to appear before the Privy Council to find caution for themselves and their clansmen. The young Chief paid no heed to the summons, doubtless because he was already deeply involved in the quarrels sparked off by his accession. Alexander and his brother Ranald had been fostered with Sir James Macdonald of Sleat and had been sent to finish their education on the Continent. It is thus possible that Alexander returned with new ideas and an inflated conception of chiefship which were quite unacceptable to the clan. It is clear that he was unpopular from the beginning, exhibiting a degree of arrogance which the proud spirit of some of his leading clansmen found it impossible to tolerate. An early indication of his future conduct was provided by the response he made to his Tutor when Alasdair Buidhe asked him how he was to be compensated for his stewardship. The young Chief replied that the honour of having held the post should be considered sufficient reward: upon which Alasdair Buide is said to have remarked, with ominous deliberation, "If that is how it is, we shall remember you."

The immediate cause of the tragedy that followed sprang from the age-old, sensitive question of the right of lordship claimed by Huntly and passionately contested by the Keppoch chiefs. The lands of Inverlair were held by Alasdair Ruadh Macdonald, a member of Siol Dhughaill (the seed of Dugall), whose progenitor was the fifth son of Ranald, son of John of Islay by Amie MacRuairi. The family had entered Keppoch from Sunart in the previous century. It appears that Alasdair Ruadh, who had formerly held his lands from the Keppoch Chief, had taken a lease direct from Huntly during Alexander's minority. Enraged by this recognition of the hated Huntly family, the young Chief promptly fell upon the lands of Inverlair with sixty of his men, destroyed much of his property, and drove away all his cattle and horses. In January 1662 Inverlair lodged a complaint with the Privy Council, who summoned the offenders to appear before it. Keppoch's immediate answer was a counter charge, the terms of which are not on record, and in March and June 1662 he sought a suspension of the Council's proceedings against him by finding security for his appearance.

The subsequent course of events is to be gathered almost entirely from traditional accounts. Such evidence as these provide would seem to suggest that Alasdair Buidhe, the Chief's uncle, was deeply involved in the plot, if not indeed the actual instigator of it. There is no clear evidence that he was present with the murderers, although two of his sons were among those afterwards charged with the crime. In the early hours of 5th September 1663, with Inverlair and other members of his family, they broke into "the place of Keppoch, armed with swords, dirks, and other weapons" with which, according to the Privy Council Minute, they inflicted numerous ghastly wounds upon the bodies of the Chief and his young brother Ranald. Later that morning the tragic scene was visited by Iain Lom, who was to record it in mournful detail in his poem "Mort na Ceapaich," in which he lays the blame squarely on the Inverlairs. In the same poem he reminds us that the Chief and his brother had been fostered at Duntulm in the care of Sir James of Sleat: and it was fitting that, in the end, it was from that quarter that retribution came to avenge the crime.

There was no general outcry in Keppoch against the crime, a fact which may be taken as a measure of both the unpopularity of the murdered Chief and the clansmen's fear of antagonising the man who had displaced him. It is said that the criminals met at Torran nam Mionn (Hillock of the Oaths) in Glen Roy and there swore on their dirks not to divulge their parts in the plot. Iain Lom's was the only voice raised in a cry for vengeance, and it fell on deaf ears. Realising at length that justice was not to be secured in Keppoch, he determined to seek it beyond its bounds. He went first to Glengarry where the newly created Lord Macdonell and Aros was aspiring to the High Chiefship of Clan Donald and might therefore reasonably be expected to uphold the principles of law and order in all its branches. But Glengarry was clearly not disposed to embroil himself in recriminations against his close neighbour, and Iain Lom's appeal was in vain. Thence he went to Kintail, where Mackenzie also refused his aid, and eventually crossed over to Skye. There at Duntulm he addressed his appeal to Sir James of Sleat in words that spoke the poet's eloquence and erudition:

"Where do you come from?" asked Sir James.

"From Laodicea," was the reply.

"Are they hot or cold in that place?" asked Sir James.

"Abel is cold," replied the bard, "and his blood is crying in vain for vengeance: but Cain is hot and red-handed, and hundreds around are lukewarm as the black goat's milk."

The bard's eloquence prevailed, but Sir James, instead of acting on his own initiative, wisely decided to seek the authority of the government in bringing the criminals to justice. On 29th June 1665 the Privy Council granted a commission authorising Sir James to search for and apprehend the murderers, who were named as Alan Dearg and Donald of Clianaig, sons of the Tutor, Alexander Ruadh MacDugall of Inverlair and his brother, John Roy MacDugall, Donald MacColl, Dugall MacColl, Patrick Dunbar and others. Sir James selected a body of fifty men and placed them under the command of his brother Archibald, better known as *An Ciaran Mabach* and also a bard, whom he recalled from his home in North Uist to lead the avenging expedition. The party wasted no time and, guided by Iain Lom, reached Lochaber only four days after setting out from Skye. News of their approach had preceded them to Keppoch, and the criminals had gathered at Inverlair and barricaded the house in readiness for the attack. The Tutor's sons had already fled the country, Alan Dearg never to return, and his brother Donald only after a long period of exile; but seven of the murderers headed by Alasdair Ruadh put up a desperate defence and, it is said, killed many of their attackers. Only after the house was set on fire was it possible to force the besieged men out into the open, and all seven were killed as they emerged from the flames. Iain Lom cut off the heads of the seven men, reputedly with the dirk used by one of them in the murder of young Ranald, and thereupon set out with the ghastly burden to Glengarry. On his way, at a spring on Loch Oichside known to this day as *Tobair nan Ceann* (the Well of the Heads), he washed the heads one by one in a symbolic act of rebuke to the Chief who had refused to redeem the honour of the Clan. What passed between him and Lord Macdonell has not been preserved on record, but we may well believe that his macabre gift was accompanied by some well-chosen, plain-spoken words in character with the man and the occasion. The heads were afterwards sent to Edinburgh as evidence that the terms of the commission had been fulfilled, and in due course Sir James of Sleat received the Council's thanks for the "good service done to his Majesty."

Alasdair Buidhe, who had assumed the position of Chief after the murder, continued to reign without apparent opposition, and feeling secure in the knowledge that he was not officially regarded as having been involved in the plot. His remaining years were undistinguished except for one incident worthy of note in the perennial quarrel with Mackintosh. In 1667 a band of Keppoch men raided the lands of Lindsay of Edzell, the Mackintosh chief's father-in-law, and carried off a large spoil of cattle. Mackintosh retaliated by invading the Keppoch lands, recovered the cattle, and attempted to establish his hold on the lands in dispute. In this he was unsuccessful, but the quarrel was now to enter a new phase in which interested and influential observers were to make serious efforts to persuade the two clans to come to terms with each other.

Alasdair Buidhe died about 1669. He was married twice. By his first wife, a daughter of Angus Mor of Bohuntin, he had (1) Alan Dearg, who fled after the murder in 1663; (2) Archibald, who succeeded to the chiefship; (3) Alexander, who died without issue. By his second wife, whose name is not on record, he had (4) Donald Gorm of Clianaig, who also fled after the murder; and (5) Ranald na Dalaich, who died without issue.

Archibald, 15th of Keppoch, was a wise and resolute chief, possessing many qualities which made him highly popular with his clansmen. He was also an accomplished poet, and some of his works which survive are regarded as "masterpieces of wit and humour." A more serious work composed on his death-bed is to be found in the *Macdonald Collection of Gaelic Poetry*. The first reference to Archibald as Chief is in a Privy Council Order of October 1672 directing Lord Macdonell, in his presumed position of High Chief, to present Keppoch and several members of his clan before the Council for the purpose of finding caution for their tenants. The Privy Council at this period found it convenient to recognise Lord Macdonell's assumed rôle, and made frequent use of his services in their attempts to reduce the lawless activities of the clans, especially in Lochaber. His efforts were seldom successful, however, and the Council were often obliged to enlist the services of other leaders, like Sir James of Sleat, for the effective accomplishment of their purpose. His public duties tended to be sacrificed to the exigencies of his private and less lawful engagements, in pursuit of which he was sometimes prepared to accept without scruple

THE WELL OF THE HEADS

the active alliance of those whose lawlessness he was expected to suppress. For several years after 1675 Lord Macdonell had the able assistance of the Keppoch Chief in his feuds against the Campbells and in support of the Macleans in their struggle with Argyll. It was Keppoch who emerged the loser, with his lands invaded and despoiled by the Campbells, until in 1681 he was obliged to give his bond of manrent to the Campbell Earl of Breadalbane, binding himself to restrain his clansmen and others within his sphere of influence from harassing Campbell lands.

The long-lived dispute with the Mackintoshes continued under Archibald's chiefship, but a serious attempt to reconcile their differences was made when, on the suggestion of the Privy Council, a Committee of Arbitration was appointed to consider and pronounce upon the conflicting claims. It consisted of the Earls of Moray and Caithness with Sir George Munro, and their findings, which are not recorded but must have been based on purely legal grounds, do not appear to have satisfied either party and were completely disregarded by Keppoch. After a spell with the "Highland Host" sent to overawe the Covenanters in Ayrshire, Keppoch returned to face a renewal of the feud. In 1681 Mackintosh used his legal title to obtain a commission of fire and sword against Keppoch with the object of finally ejecting him from his lands, but that Chief's response was a defiant challenge to proceed if he dared, with the result that Mackintosh's commission still remained unexecuted when Archibald's son Coll inherited the problem with the chiefship in the following year.

Archibald, 15th of Keppoch, died in December 1682. By his wife Mary, daughter of MacMartin of Letterfinlay, he had (1) Coll, who succeeded; (2) Ranald Mor of Tirnadris, reputed to have married a daughter of Glengarry; (3) Alexander, who in 1718 received a tack of Gaskmore from Lachlan Mackintosh of Strone; (4) Angus Odhar, who is said to have died unmarried, but according to another account married a Fraser and lost an arm at Glenshiel; (5) Juliet, known as *Silis Nic Raghnaill,* a noted poetess, who married Gordon of Candell; (6) Catherine, who married Macpherson of Strathmashie, whose grandson was Lachlan Macpherson of Ossianic fame. Archibald had seven other daughters, all of whom were married.

Coll, 16th of Keppoch, one of the most outstanding chiefs of his time, was pursuing his studies at St Andrews when he received the summons of his clan to assume the chiefship. He was only eighteen years of age, "of low stature, but full of craft and enterprise." He was also well-educated, and these qualities he tried to put to good use soon after his accession. Early in 1683 he visited Inverness and sent messengers to Mackintosh offering to submit their differences to arbitration. Mackintosh's response to this olive branch was the immediate imprisonment of Coll in the Tolbooth without the formality of a trial. Not unnaturally, Coll was much affronted by Mackintosh's conduct and the rough reception accorded to his peaceful overtures, and he immediately in his own hand wrote a petition to the Privy Council describing the circumstances of his arrest, and begging the Council to "set him at liberty, in respect of his unwarrantable imprisonment, as said is, and that he is content to find caution to appear before the Council, at such a diet as shall be appointed upon a lawful citation to answer anything that can be laid to his charge." The petition had the desired effect, and on 1st February 1683 Coll was set free on his finding sufficient caution to appear before the Council on the 15th of March.

Mackintosh's action must be regarded as highly reprehensible in the circumstances, and it has been severely censured even by his own clan historian, who states: "Conduct such as that ascribed to Mackintosh can only be stigmatised as ungenerous and unfeeling in the extreme. To take advantage of an hereditary foe, and that foe a mere boy, on such an occasion and in such a manner, might have passed without censure a few centuries earlier, but was scarcely worth the enlightenment and politeness of a more civilised time."

The experience served to convert the peace-seeking student idealist into a hate-filled enemy more formidable than any the Mackintoshes had to face in the long history of their feud. Coll duly appeared in Edinburgh and presented his bond in accordance with the terms of his release from Inverness prison, but less than two years later both he and his cautioner were summoned to present themselves again to renew their bond. They failed to appear and a warrant was issued for their arrest. Coll had already embarked on the career which was to earn for him the significant name of "Coll of the Cows," and at the time of the summons he was occupied with the Gordons and others in harassing and despoiling the lands of Argyll. It is unlikely that the Mackintoshes escaped his attentions, nor he their retaliation, for Huntly is found complaining at this time that "all Brae Lochaber is outlawed by Mackintosh's malice." That malice was to find renewed expression when Mackintosh, in March 1688, obtained a fresh commission of fire and sword against Keppoch, this time with the active backing of the Government and the support of its regular troops. Mackintosh's preparations were carefully designed to resolve once and for all, and in his own favour, the long-standing differences between the two clans. His summons to arms went out to all branches of Clan Chattan, and the only ones who failed to answer were the Macphersons who disputed his implied assumption of the dignity of High Chief. With the regular troops under Captain Kenneth Mackenzie of Suddie bringing his total strength to about 1000 men, Mackintosh launched his invasion and took the Brae by surprise, encountering no opposition and taking up his residence in Keppoch's house, from which Coll had taken to the hills to prepare his counter-stroke.

While Mackintosh lay in fancied security at Keppoch House, already engaged in making plans for his permanent settlement, Coll was sending out the fiery cross to all the outlying glens and the bounds of his friendly neighbours. The response was encouraging, and soon he had gathered behind him sympathisers from Glengarry and Glencoe together with a body of his maternal kinsmen from the MacMartin Camerons whose chief, absent at the time in Edinburgh, was later to suffer some embarrassment for their involvement. By the 4th of August Coll was ready, having built up his strength to about 700 men and hoping to make up for his inferiority in numbers by the advantage of surprise. He advanced with his forces to Mulroy, the hill to the north-east of Glen Spean which gave its name to the battle. The Mackintoshes and their allies had set out at the same time, intending to take Keppoch by surprise, and when Coll saw what was happening he drew up his men on a ridge of the hill. They sustained the first charge without serious loss, and immediately afterwards threw themselves upon the enemy, fighting a bitter hand-to-hand conflict for almost an hour. The Clan Chattan were completely routed, leaving several of their leading men dead on the field. Mackenzie of Suddie was also killed, though accidentally and against the express wishes of Coll, who feared that casualties inflicted on the regular troops would bring the full weight of the Government's wrath down upon himself and his clan.

The Mackintosh Chief was unable on account of his age to take part in the battle, and awaited the outcome in Keppoch House where he was in due course taken prisoner. Coll treated him hospitably, and the story is told that Mackintosh proposed to settle their differences by offering him a lease of the disputed lands. Coll's response may well be imagined. He had just provided convincing and bloody proof of his ability to hold his lands against formidable odds without the aid of parchments, as his fathers had done before him. It is said that the courtesies of traditional Highland hospitality were preserved only by the timely arrival of the tardy Macphersons, to whom Coll, not caring to risk a second encounter, released his captive with all the other prisoners he had taken.

The Government bitterly resented Coll's victory over forces partly composed of its own regular troops, and immediately issued a proclamation calling upon all loyal subjects in the neighbourhood to rise and unite in a vast punitive action against the men of Keppoch. There was no response. The neighbouring clans were not disposed to help Mackintosh retrieve his lost prestige, and their sympathies lay heavily on the side of Keppoch. The Government were accordingly obliged to use regular troops, and both footsoldiers and dragoons were sent in to waste the Keppoch lands and wipe out all their inhabitants. Coll and his people evaded capture by taking to the hills and refusing to be drawn into a pitched battle. How long he could have succeeded in protecting and sustaining his people in such conditions is uncertain, but the political situation in the South saved him from the extremities a lengthy military occupation must have caused. After a month of constant pressure and pursuit, the soldiers were withdrawn to meet the threat of invasion by William of Orange, and further measures in progress against Keppoch were perforce suspended as a result of the Revolution.

Coll made good use of this fortuitous reprieve and immediately began to strengthen his position against a possible attack by Mackintosh. In February 1689 Mackintosh secured another commission of fire and sword against Keppoch, but the absence of active Government support discouraged him from risking another disastrous outcome. Shrewdly assessing the situation, Coll decided to attack. In April, with a large force of about 1000 men, he invaded the lands of his old enemy and ravaged the country as far as Inverness. From that town, which had once held him in its gaol and whose citizens had helped to swell Mackintosh's forces at Mulroy, Coll now demanded the huge indemnity of 4000 merks, threatening to burn the town if the sum were not paid promptly. For three days the citizens of Inverness were kept in suspense, and a situation fraught with possibly disastrous results was only averted by the arrival of Viscount Dundee who acted as mediator and, having negotiated a more reasonable sum of 2000 merks, gave his personal guarantee that it would be paid. Dundee's intervention thus not only relieved the citizens of Inverness, but satisfied Coll so well that he there and then agreed to join his forces.

Dundee, having failed to swing the Convention in Edinburgh in favour of King James, had fled before a charge of treason to the Highlands and was now marshalling his army in Lochaber. While he was engaged in his money-raising expeditions against Perth and the town of Dundee, Coll occupied himself in ravaging the lands of Mackintosh in Strathearn, Strathnairn and Badenoch, and burning his house of Dunachton to the ground. He also made a quick recruiting expedition to the West, with the result that when Dundee returned to Lochaber he found his army not only well supplied with provisions but greatly strengthened by contingents from Clanranald, Glengarry, Glencoe and Sleat. It was during this period that Coll is said to have earned his appellation "of the Cows," because of his deftness in tracking cattle herded out of his predatory reach, an activity in which he now had the hearty support of Young Clanranald. It was thanks to their successful enterprises that the army was so well provided for throughout its stay in Lochaber.

Before advancing to engage the enemy, Dundee decided to dispose of a possible threat to his rear. The fort of Ruthven was held by Government forces under the command of Captain Forbes, uncle of that Duncan Forbes of Culloden who was to play a distinguished rôle in events leading up to the last great Rising. Coll and his men were assigned the task of reducing the garrison. The fort was bravely defended and withstood a protracted siege in expectation of relief that never came. After its surrender, the fort was set on fire by Coll and the whole garrison taken prisoner to the camp in Lochaber.

With an army which had now grown in strength to over 2500 men, Dundee was at last ready to face Mackay, whose numerically superior forces were moving in on Blair. On the evening of 27th July 1689, he drew up his line of battle at the head of the Pass of Killiecrankie and waited for Mackay's troops to take up their positions as they emerged from the Pass. Dundee gave the order to attack as the westering sun threw its rays in the face of the enemy, and within minutes they were in confusion, running in panic before the headlong charge of the clans. Coll is said to have contributed a distinguished share to the general rout following the battle, for which he was afterwards to receive the congratulations of his exiled King. Three weeks after the battle he joined the other chiefs in the Bond of Association affirming their allegiance to King James and their resolve to continue the struggle in his cause. But the tragic death in battle of Dundee left a void in the leadership which no one was capable of replacing. The chiefs were unable to agree with either Cannon or Buchan, and the repulse at Dunkeld, followed in April by the rout at Cromdale, discouraged the clans and put an effective end to further resistance.

On his way home from Cromdale, Coll made an unsuccessful attempt to take the Castle of Rothiemurchus and then proceeded to carve a trail of devastation through the lands of Clan Chattan. So thorough was his incursion that Mackintosh complained of the extreme condition of poverty to which his people had been reduced, and in his appeal to Parliament for help assessed his losses at the astonishingly large sum of 40,000 merks.

The inevitable commission of fire and sword followed, but remained ineffective in face of the Keppoch Chiefs' defiance and the failure of Mackintosh's pleas for aid. The course of events, however, gradually forced Coll to reconsider his position. The new fort at Inverlochy placed a permanent garrison of regular troops within a short march of his lands, and even he had to recognise the impossibility of withstanding a locally based force capable of being maintained in a constant state of readiness and efficiency by an uninterrupted stream of men and munitions by sea. It was also evident that King William was now firmly seated upon the throne, and his Campbell representatives in the Highlands had the power as well as the will to destroy all those who persisted in their obduracy. Accordingly, when the Proclamation was issued in 1691 offering pardon to all who submitted before the end of the year, Coll thought it prudent to take advantage of the terms it contained. On 24th June he appeared before the Earl of Breadalbane, appointed by the King to treat with the Chiefs, and promised on his "faith and word" to submit to the Government on such favourable terms as the Earl might be able to secure for him.

It was well for Coll that he submitted when he did. He no doubt realised that his refusal to take the oath would mark him out with all his clan for total destruction in the same treacherous manner in which his kinsmen of Glencoe were later treated. After that tragedy, Coll did what he could to fix the responsibility for the massacre and courageously gave evidence against Breadalbane and Glenlyon when the extent of their implication was being investigated in Edinburgh.

Keppoch now appears to be on his best behaviour and cultivating good relations with the authorities. In 1694 he is reported to be "quyett, and in a condition to live without stealing," and Mackintosh was alone in making representations against "thatt nottorious and signall robber, murderer, and rascall." However, serious efforts were in progress to bring them together with a view to securing a stable peace. One suggestion advanced was that the Government should purchase the disputed lands and then lease them to Coll on a feu reutal. Mackintosh was reluctant to accept such an arrangement, and continued to rail against Keppoch, and against the authorities for their failure to punish him for his past misdeeds. He accused Colonel Hill, the Governor of Fort William, of aiding Coll in escaping his just dues, and petitioned the Government for a renewal of his commission of fire and sword. That such strong measures were not conceded was largely due to the influence of Colonel Hill, whose view of the utter ineffectiveness of a repressive policy was expressed in his report on the state of the Highlands in 1697, where he condemns all "discourse of a commission of fire and sword which can tend to noe advantage, but to destruction, as well as the unsettling of the countrey (now in a very peaceable condition), especially considering that (if I get orders) I can give McIntosh the possession with 12 men as well as with 1200."

A less tolerant view, however, was adopted by Brigadier Maitland, Hill's successor, who paid more heed to Mackintosh's complaints and, apparently "resolved to be very uneasy to Coll untill he gett him apprehended," was at length given the task of executing a commission of fire and sword against Keppoch. Maitland, however, appears to have taken no part in the action that followed. Mackintosh invaded the Brae with "ane considerable pairtie off good resolute men," and under cover of heavy mist managed to seize goods and cattle, left a small garrison in some hastily built wooden forts, and returned to Moy well satisfied with his work. Meantime Coll had gone to seek the aid of his kinsmen of Glengarry. He returned with a considerable force prepared to inflict another disastrous defeat upon his enemy, but the slender garrison melted away to their homes at his approach.

It became at last clear to all concerned that the differences between the two antagonists were not to be resolved by force, and Maitland with other interested parties was finally able to bring them together with a view to reaching an amicable settlement. They met at Fort William on 22nd May 1700, Mackintosh with several of his principal followers, and Coll with Sir Donald Macdonald of Sleat as his cautioner. Under the guidance of a shrewd and sagacious lawyer, an agreement was at length reached whereby Coll on the one hand was to grant Mackintosh the "three ploughs of Davoch Laggan, namely, that of Tullochrom, Aberarder and Strathchruinneachan," and Mackintosh on the other hand bound himself to give Coll a tack of the two davoch lands of Keppoch and others as possessed by his father for the space of 19 years. Coll was to pay a tack duty of 400 merks yearly for the first two years, 600 merks for the third and fourth years, and 800 merks for the fifth and subsequent years. Failure to pay the tack duty gave Mackintosh a right of access to the lands, and any molestation by Keppoch of him or his tenants was to be redeemed by his cautioner's bond of £250. Finally, Sir Donald of Sleat was further bound to secure the peaceable behaviour of Coll and his sub-tenants.

This was a remarkable document, carefully devised to make it appear that both parties preserved their ancient claims intact and were making a perfectly normal disposition of lands which were theirs by right. Thus Coll "granted" to Mackintosh the disputed lands which legally belonged to him, and Mackintosh retained his former rights by leasing them back to Coll at a reasonable rental. Implicit in the transaction was the tacit admission that Coll had the right to grant the lands which he and his forefathers had held by the sword, and

Mackintosh was perfectly satisfied with a document which witnessed the surrender of all the rights Keppoch ever claimed to possess. Thus honour was satisfied on both sides, and although some degree of friction was evident in succeeding years, the sword was henceforth forever abandoned as an instrument for enforcing rights of possession in Lochaber.

At the Hanoverian succession in 1714, Coll was one of the hundred chiefs and heads of families who signed the conventional profession of loyalty to the new regime and entrusted it to the Earl of Mar for presentation to the King. Mar was Secretary for Scotland in the previous reign, but his loyalty was suspected by the new monarch and he was soon dismissed from office. It is not clear whether Mar simply failed to present the Address of the chiefs, or the King tactlessly chose to ignore it, but the lack of royal acknowledgment had a marked effect upon the attitude of clansmen whose Jacobite spirit remained very much alive and only needed a leader to set it aflame. Unfortunately for them and the cause they served, the choice of that leadership was to fall upon the Earl of Mar, whose qualifications as an administrator in no way fitted him for an adventure which required the personality and military skill of a Dundee or Montrose to have any chance of success.

Mar, filled with resentment at his dismissal from office, left London in August 1715 with the set purpose of promoting a rising in his own country. As soon as he reached his estates on Deeside, he sent out invitations to his famous "hunting-party," and on 6th September raised the standard of King James at Braemar. Keppoch was among the first to take active military steps in favour of the cause. With the aid of Camerons and Macleans he tried to reduce Fort William, but failed in the attempt for want of heavy weapons. On raising the siege he proceeded to join Mar, by that time encamped at Auchterarder, and remained with the army for the rest of the campaign.

Meanwhile, many more clansmen had flocked to the standard at Perth, where Mar wasted valuable time waiting for promised help from France and thus allowed Argyll to build up the strength of his forces at Stirling. On 10th November Mar at last overcame his irresolution and marched out with the intention of pushing past Argyll and joining up with the Jacobite force in Lancashire. When he heard Mar had moved, Argyll at once advanced to intercept him and took up his position on Sheriffmuir at the foot of the Ochil Hills. There, on 13th November, the battle was fought in which neither side could afterwards claim the victory. The clans on Mar's right wing broke Argyll's left, which fled in confusion towards Stirling. But Mar's left wing was shattered by Argyll's right, and driven back far to the north-west. Mar had a much larger army, and with skill and determination could even then have held and thrown back Argyll who, although a much abler commander, had suffered serious losses in his outnumbered forces. Instead he retired to Perth to await the arrival in January of James, who did nothing to revive the spirits of an army discomfited by the inactivity and irresolution of its commander, and decimated by the departure for their homes of its discouraged and disillusioned Highland contingents. At the end of that month, Argyll resumed his advance with a strongly reinforced army, and Mar was relentlessly forced in retreat towards Montrose. From that port, on 3rd February 1716, he accompanied his King and several other Jacobite leaders on board a French vessel, and sailed off to France and exile.

So ended the 'Fifteen, destroyed by the inaction, vacillation and ineptitude of its leaders, leaving the clans to suffer the retribution to be exacted under the ruthless superintendence of General Cadogan. Keppoch continued in arms to the bitter end, but his men were obliged eventually to give in their submission at

Fort William. Coll himself succeeded in finding temporary refuge in South Uist, where he was joined by several other fugitives. In May 1716, in company with Ranald of Clanranald who was also sought for his part in the Rising, he escaped to France. He returned in April 1719, two months before the debâcle of Glenshiel in which, however, in common with the majority of Highland chiefs, he appears to have had no part. He no doubt considered himself fortunate in escaping the consequences suffered by many others who had played a less active rôle in the 'Fifteen, and the remaining years of his life were spent in peace, unmarked by any activities that disturbed his relations with his neighbours or brought him to the notice of the Government. The last occasion on which he appears on record is in 1722 when he received a Precept of Clare Constat from the Duke of Gordon for infefting him in the lands of Achnancoichean, Clianaig, Monessie, Brackletter, Inverlair, Kilmonivaig and Loch Treig at a yearly rental of 100 merks. He probably died in 1728 or 1729, for in the latter year his son Alexander was confirmed in the lease of Keppoch and other lands by Mackintosh.

Coll had married Barbara, daughter of Sir Donald Macdonald of Sleat, by whom he had (1) Alexander, who succeeded; (2) Donald, who was killed at Culloden; (3) Archibald, a captain in the Keppoch Regiment, who was killed at Prestonpans; (4) Margaret, who is said to have married Cameron of Erracht; (5) another daughter, who married Mackenzie of Torridon.

Alexander, 17th of Keppoch, had already, before his accession, played a distinguished part in the events of the time. In 1713 he matriculated as a student at Glasgow University, but two years later he interrupted his studies to follow the example of his father in joining the Jacobite standard. After the collapse of the rebellion he accompanied his father into exile in France, where he completed his education and served for a time in the French army, gaining valuable experience and establishing useful contacts which were to be employed to advantage at a later period. How long he remained in France is uncertain, depending as it did to some extent on his service engagement, but we know he had returned by 1722 because his name appears as witness to the Precept of Clare Constat of that year. The next twenty years of Alexander's life are a virtual blank and reflect the lull that generally existed in Jacobite activities, resulting from the people's increasing acceptance of the *status quo* and the absence of foreign entanglements that might bring the cause to life again.

There remained, however, a hard core of Jacobite sympathisers and the situation for them assumed a brighter prospect with the outbreak in 1742 of the War of the Austrian Succession. French and British involvement in the war held out the promise of French support for a Jacobite attempt, and many projects were set afoot to secure material aid from France and gain the active adherence of sympathisers at home. The prospects of French support were much improved in 1743 when Fleury's death placed the direction of French policy in the hands of Cardinal de Tencin, who possessed none of his predecessors' scruples about affording help to the Jacobites. The change of attitude was promptly noted in Scotland, and at a meeting of leading Jacobites it was resolved to take immediate steps for the restoration of the exiled King. The representatives they chose to carry their proposals to the French Court were Alexander of Keppoch and Stewart of Appin. The success of their mission was not at once apparent, but before the end of the year the long-awaited invitation to the Prince went out, and early in 1744 Charles arrived, impatient for action, at the French Court.

Preparations were immediately begun for the invasion of England. In February an expedition under Marshal Saxe set sail from Dunkirk, but was forced to turn back before a watchful British fleet to be storm-wrecked and destroyed on the coast. It was to be the last attempt by the French to lend material aid for the Stewart cause. Henceforth the Prince was on his own. After months of frustration in Paris, Charles made his momentous decision. Choosing seven men to accompany him, he embarked on the ship *La Doutelle* (*Du Teillay*) and on 16th July 1745 set sail on his desperate enterprise.

The Prince's companions, later to become celebrated in story as the "Seven Men of Moidart," were the Marquis of Tullibardine, recognised by the Jacobites as Duke of Atholl; Aeneas Macdonald, brother of Donald of Kinlochmoidart and the expedition's financier; Colonel Francis Strickland, the only Englishman in the company; and four Irishmen—the elderly Sir Thomas Sheridan, a veteran of the Boyne; Sir John Macdonald, another elderly officer who had served with the French cavalry in Spain; George Kelly, a clergyman; and William O'Sullivan, who had served in the French army and was to play a significant rôle in the campaign that was about to open. On 23rd July the party landed on the island of Eriskay in South Uist. There Charles received from Alexander Macdonald of Boisdale the discouraging news that the Chief of Sleat and Macleod of Macleod were not prepared to fulfil their earlier pledge to join him, in the absence of the expected massive support in men and arms from the Continent. Charles refused to be put out, however, and passionately believing in the efficacy of a personal appeal to the Highland clans, he set sail for the mainland and on 25th July stepped ashore at Loch nan Uamh in Moidart. There to meet him came, with some misgivings, the neighbouring chiefs and their principal men, including Young Clanranald, whose expression of loyal devotion set an example the others could not but follow.

Keppoch also had his misgivings but, like his neighbour Lochiel, he was impressed by the Prince's resolution. He immediately set about raising his clan and as a result became involved in the first action of the campaign. The stir in Keppoch alarmed the depleted garrison at Fort William, and an urgent message was sent to Fort Augustus for reinforcements. Two companies of the first Royal Scots regiment of foot were at once despatched under the command of Captain John Scott. At High Bridge, about nine miles from Fort William, they were ambushed by eleven men and a piper led by Donald Macdonald of Tirnadris, a cadet of Keppoch. The sound of the pipes mingled with powerful Highland war cries, suggesting the presence of a much larger force, threw the regular troops into confusion, and they fled in panic towards Fort Augustus. They were closely pursued by Donald, whose force was strengthened by a party of Glengarry men and the arrival of the Keppoch Chief himself with several more. They caught up with the retreating soldiers near Laggan at the head of Loch Lochy, and after an exchange of fire in which several of the enemy were wounded and a few killed, Keppoch persuaded Captain Scott to surrender. The clansmen had suffered no casualties and Keppoch, well pleased with the outcome of his first brush with the enemy, later released Captain Scott on his parole to take no further part in the campaign.

Three days after this action, the royal standard was raised at Glenfinnan. The Prince spent an anxious two hours waiting for his promised support, but his fears were relieved with the arrival together of Keppoch and Lochiel, each at the head of his men—Keppoch with 350 men, and Lochiel with 700. After the proclamation of James as King and of Charles as his Regent, they set out on 21st August marching eastwards by Kinlocheil and the Great Glen, gathering more support on the way. At Aberchalder House, at the head of Loch Oich, the Prince received intelligence that Cope was on his way to intercept him and was already in Badenoch, intending to push through the Corriearrick Pass to Fort Augustus. Charles immediately sent a detachment to secure the head of the

Pass and on the following day (27th August) crossed with the main body into Badenoch, hoping to confront the enemy and sweep him out of his southward path. But Cope had been informed at Dalwhinnie that the Highland army was already in possession of the Pass which he knew could be successfully defended against a much stronger force attacking from the south. He therefore decided to alter his line of march and take the road leading north-east from Dalwhinnie, thus leaving the way to Edinburgh open with nothing to oppose the Prince on his southward progress.

On 30th August, much against the wishes of some of the clansmen who wanted to pursue and engage Cope, Charles set out with his army for Blair, where he reviewed his troops, and on 4th September arrived at Perth, which had been occupied the day before by Lochiel and his Camerons. His triumphal entry into the city was made on the white horse taken from Captain Scott at Laggan and later presented to him by the victor in that engagement, Macdonald of Tirnadris.

The army spent a week in Perth, undergoing some much-needed training. It was also in much need of funds, and Alexander of Keppoch was assigned the task of collecting local taxes in Dundee. Accompanied by Young Clanranald, he entered the town with a force of 450 men and, having encountered no opposition, returned the next day with the city's funds and laden with a store of provisions seized from ships in the harbour.

Edinburgh was occupied by a singular piece of good fortune. Left defenceless by the retreat of Gardiner's dragoons, the Provost and magistrates of the City sent deputations to the Prince to ascertain his terms—and also to gain time, for they knew that Sir John Cope's army was already in the Forth and might rescue them from their predicament if they succeeded in protracting the negotiations. The Prince realised their intentions and decided to send Lochiel, with a detachment of Camerons and Keppoch men, to occupy the city by force if necessary. They took up their positions before the Netherbow Port, unobserved by the sentries, and as they deliberated how best to mount their assault the gate was opened to admit the coach returning with the latest deputation to the Prince. The lucky chance was immediately seized by Lochiel. He rushed in with his men and, before the night was over, had occupied without opposition all the strategic points in the city. Only the Castle remained, presenting no threat, however, to the occupying force below its guns, nor to the army encamped beyond their range in the King's Park.

Alexander of Keppoch was a member of the Council of Chiefs called by the Prince, his service in the French army being obviously regarded as a notable qualification for proffering advice on the subsequent conduct of the campaign. He fought with Clanranald and Glengarry at Prestonpans, where in the early morning of 21st September Cope's army suffered a tactical surprise leading in a few minutes to utter confusion and rout before the fierce impetuosity of an attack his troops were not trained to withstand or expect. Among the few Highland casualties was Keppoch's brother Archibald, killed in the thick of the fighting. The enemy suffered serious losses, with hundreds of men killed and most of the rest taken prisoner. The officers, deeply shamed by the defeat, were later released on parole which, however, all of them, with the honourable exception of Colonel Halkett of Lee's Regiment, were afterwards to break on the express orders of the Duke of Cumberland.

The chief significance of the battle lay in the encouragement it provided for the invasion of England, which proved to be the ruin of the whole enterprise and was launched against the better judgment of the Prince's wiser advisers. There can be little doubt that Keppoch, by virtue of his early military experience, was at one with Lord George Murray in recognising the risks attending a deep penetration to the south. Nevertheless he never faltered in his loyalty once the decision was taken, and he was one of the few who supported the Prince in his efforts to influence the Council in favour of advancing beyond Derby. In the course of the retreat, he took part in the skirmish at Clifton, which checked Cumberland's pursuit and enabled the army to continue its march in safety to Carlisle. At Falkirk he shared the right wing with the other Clan Donald regiments whose slaughter and pursuit of the fleeing dragoons caused irreparable disorder in the enemy ranks. It was in the resulting confusion of the battle that Donald of Tirnadris, Keppoch's right hand man and hero of the High Bridge skirmish, had the misfortune to be captured. Having outstripped his men in their impetuous pursuit, he strode up to a stationary body of troops he mistook for Lord Drummond's men, calling out "Why don't ye follow after the dogs and pursue them?" He was right in their midst before he realised they were part of Barrel's regiment, and he was promptly made prisoner—the only prisoner, incidentally, taken back by Hawley to Edinburgh. Another sad incident occurred the following day with the death of young Angus of Glengarry, accidentally shot in the streets of Falkirk by a Keppoch man "cleaning his piece." Although the unfortunate victim realised it was an accident and begged with his dying breath that nothing might befall the unwitting clansman, the tragedy infuriated the Glengarry men and numbers of them withdrew from the army and made for their homes as a result.

Falkirk was a resounding victory for the Prince, but such were the divisions in his command that no real advantage was taken of it. Against the advice of his most experienced officers, Charles insisted on spending two fruitless weeks continuing the siege of Stirling Castle, and it was not till the arrival of the Duke of Cumberland in Edinburgh at the end of January that he was finally persuaded to seek the safety of the Highlands and the needed reinforcements he would find there. On the 31st, as Cumberland advanced to Linlithgow, the Jacobite army moved off from Stirling, and on the following day crossed the Forth at the Fords of Frew. On the 3rd of February they were at Crieff, where a review of the army showed that desertions were fewer than had been supposed. The march was resumed in two divisions, one under Lord George Murray going by the east coast road and the other under the Prince over the mountains to the north. On 18th February the Prince reached Inverness, left defenceless by Lord Loudoun in a hurried retreat across the Kessock Ferry; and three days later the army was again united with the arrival of Lord George Murray's division, which had fought its way through blinding snowstorms on its march from Aberdeen.

To secure his western flank, the Prince despatched Keppoch and Lochiel, reinforced by Lord John Drummond's regiment and Stapleton's Irish picquets, down the Great Glen to reduce Fort Augustus and Fort William. Fort Augustus surrendered after a two-day siege, but Fort William defied all their efforts and after a month the attempt was abandoned in face of the more pressing needs of the main army. While engaged in the siege, Keppoch and Lochiel were able to visit their lands and note the ravages suffered by their people in their absence at the hands of the garrison and of the Campbells. They applied for leave to proceed against the Campbells, and this was granted by the Prince who wished to create a diversion in that area as part of a new strategy he had been contemplating; but the rapid approach of Cumberland forced him to alter his design, the permission to invade Argyll was revoked, and the two chiefs were recalled to fill the gaps in an army sadly depleted by other detachments which would fail to reach the battle in time.

Keppoch rejoined the army with 200 men on the evening of 15th April, and took part in the abortive night march intended to surprise Cumberland's sleeping encampment at Nairn. They returned worn out and hungry after that march of twenty miles, to be required almost immediately to take up their battle positions on ground that heavily favoured a well-refreshed enemy outnumbering them by several thousands. Cumberland's army of 6,400 foot and 2,400 horse was drawn up in a compact array in places six ranks deep, and with the additional advantage of heavy artillery support which was to be skilfully employed to knock the few Highland guns out of action and wreak havoc amongst the clansmen before they ever received the order to charge. The Prince's army numbered not more than 5000 men, and was drawn up in a thin oblique line that placed the Atholl and Cameron regiments on the right about 500 yards from the enemy and the Macdonalds on the left about 700 yards away. Such distances left the clans no chance of practising the kind of warfare they were used to, and Cumberland saw no reason for narrowing the gap as long as his guns were able to thin the Jacobite ranks without risk to his own men. While they impatiently awaited the order to charge, the right of the Prince's army was outflanked by four companies of the Campbell militia who broke down a dry-stane dyke and cleared a passage for themselves and the following dragoons to pour their fire upon the Atholl and Cameron regiments. It was only then that the Prince, prompted by Lochiel and Lord George Murray, at last gave the long-awaited order. It was further delayed in its transmission down the line and, such was the confusion resulting from the flanking attack and the destructive fire of the enemy artillery, it is doubtful if it ever reached some of the sections.

The Clan Chattan were the first to charge, followed by the Frasers and the Appin Stewarts, and then by the whole of the right wing. Contrary to their orders, most of them threw away their muskets and flung themselves upon the enemy with their swords and dirks, advancing in a headlong rush against the disciplined fire of line after line of seasoned troops. The Camerons and Stewarts penetrated as far as the second line before they were forced back with heavy casualties, and the whole of the right, now suffering the full weight of the Campbell flanking assault, was soon in retreat. Meantime on the left wing the Macdonalds of Glengarry and Clanranald, with Keppoch in their centre, had been suffering the enemy fire without flinching while they awaited his attack. They realised that the distance between them and Cumberland's right destroyed all possibility of success for their own characteristic method of attack, and hoped that by withholding their fire they would provoke the enemy to advance. The evidence of officers in Cumberland's army suggests that the Macdonalds made three taunting moves forward with the object of drawing their attack which, of course, did not take place because Cumberland was quite content with the results being achieved with his artillery. They continued to hesitate after the clans on their right had launched their charge, and it was at this point that Alexander of Keppoch advanced alone to face the enemy, exclaiming in frustration "*Mo Dhia, an do threig clann mo chinnidh mi?*" (My God, have the children of my clan forsaken me?). Rushing forward with pistol and drawn sword, he was almost at once hit by a musket ball which shattered his right arm. Now followed by his clansmen, he continued to advance, but was shot again in the chest, and fell never to rise again. His last words were an exhortation addressed to his kinsman Donald Roy Macdonald, who was close behind him as he fell: "God have mercy on me, Donald. Do the best for yourself, for I am gone." He was later carried by Angus Ban, his natural son, to a hut off the field in which other wounded and dying had sought refuge. But he was dead before they reached it—as it happened,

BATTLE of CULLODEN ~ 16th April 1746

(with acknowledgements to Col. Iain Cameron Taylor and the
National Trust for Scotland)

JACOBITE ARMY ~ 5000 foot (max.)

to Inverness

HORSE

mostly without horses

⊗ Prince Charles

RESERVE   others   Irish Piquets

Gordons

Atholl Cameron Appin Frazers Clan Chattan others

Clan Ranald Keppoch & Glengarry

Clan Donald

450 yds.

Walled
Enclosure
here

Argyll
Militia

Boggy
Ground.

NORTH

650 yds.

Wind from the
North East
with sleet

Hawley's Dragoons

RESERVE
Cumberland

INFANTRY LINE REGIMENTS

Bland's Cavalry

HANOVERIAN ARMY ~ 6400 foot + 2400 horse

fortunately for him because it saved him from the slow agony suffered by the other poor victims who perished in its flames on the orders of Cumberland.

The Macdonald regiments suffered heavily. Many of the officers followed Keppoch's example and charged headlong at the enemy. Young Clanranald escaped with a head wound, but among the many killed were Keppoch's own brother Donald, and old Donald of Scotus. They had reached within a few paces of the enemy when the right wing crumbled, leaving the Macdonalds without support, and the flanking movement of Kingston's Horse on their left finally forced them into retreat and a merciless pursuit along the road to Inverness. Only by the exertions of the Irish picquets of Lally's and Dillon's French regiments, who gallantly covered their retreat, were the Macdonalds saved from a much heavier toll being exacted by the bloodthirsty victors.

So ended all hope for the Stewart cause, reduced to ruin by the leadership's reckless disregard of the elemental principles of strategy and wilful refusal to accept the advice of experienced officers who knew the material with which they had to fight and the conditions in which that material might best be used. The first mistake was the decision to give battle at all in the circumstances, with much of the army dispersed on detachment, and much more engaged in a desperate search for food forced upon them by a complete and inexcusable breakdown in the commissariat. The field of Culloden itself, chosen by the Prince's sycophantic Irish advisers, was condemned by all the Prince's experienced commanders as utterly unsuitable for the type of warfare the clans were accustomed to, and was indeed of a kind calculated to give maximum assistance to the enemy. The night march to Nairn, excellently well conceived but badly executed as a result of conflicting decisions, left a still more depleted army exhausted and famished, and allowed only a few hours' rest before facing a highly disciplined, vastly superior force which had just completed an intensive course of training in how best to meet a Highland charge. The crowning mistake was in not having attacked Cumberland before he could draw up his line of battle, thus employing the clans effectively in the manner they knew best, instead of holding them frustrated and stationary to be picked off at leisure by the enemy's big guns. In the circumstances there was no way in which Culloden could have been won; and instead of ushering in a new age of Stewart rule, it was to mark the beginning of the end of Highland society, albeit perhaps to gain a more permanent existence in the minds and hearts of generations yet to come.

Alexander, 17th of Keppoch, married Jessie, daughter of Stewart of Appin, by whom he had (1) Ranald, who succeeded; (2) Alexander, known as the "Big Major"; (3) six daughters, all married, of whom Barbara is notable for her collaboration with her husband, the Rev. Patrick Macdonald of Kilmore, in the compilation of a collection of Highland music in 1784. He also had a natural son, Angus Ban of Inch, born to a Skye girl soon after his return from exile in France and, after Alexander's marriage, adopted and brought up as one of the family. Angus Ban fought at Culloden and, as we have seen, tried to save his father by carrying him off the field.

Ranald, 18th of Keppoch, was only about eleven or twelve years of age when his father was killed, and his minority was spent under the able guidance of Angus Ban. The Keppoch men were among the last to lay down their arms, and the land and its people suffered the full fury of Cumberland's troops. Many of them barely escaped with their lives from the flames of their burning houses, and all were reduced to the most pitiful level of existence by the wholesale despoliation of their livestock and property. After their eventual submission they continued to suffer the harassments of the decree of forfeiture which had been passed against the late Chief as though he were still alive. In 1748, a survey of the forfeited lands was made by David Bruce, an official from the Exchequer, but no steps appear to have been taken to enforce payment of rent by the family, although it is evident from a rent roll of 1751 that they had continued to receive the due rents of their tenants. The Commissioners on Forfeited Estates were clearly uncertain about the legal force of the decree of forfeiture as it affected Keppoch, inasmuch as all the lands were held on lease from Mackintosh and the Duke of Gordon. These lands were listed in 1751 in an affadavit made by the late Chief's widow before the Sheriff-Substitute of Inverness, and included Keppoch, Inveroybeg, Boloyne, Achaderry, Urchar and Tolly—all of which had been leased by the Mackintosh chief to Alexander of Keppoch in 1729, to be held for twelve years at an annual rental of 800 merks. The other lands possessed by Keppoch, which included Inverlair, Achnancoichean, Monessie, Clianaig, Kilmonivaig and Brackletter, were leased from the Duke of Gordon and were the subjects of the Precept of Clare Constat granted to Coll in 1722.

The situation was evenually clarified when in 1755 Mungo Campbell was commissioned to make another survey of the lands and recover unpaid rents. The young Keppoch Chief immediately appeared before the Commissioners and presented his case. In the words of the authors of *Clan Donald*, Ranald protested

> in the first place, that notwithstanding the estate which pertained to the deceased Alexander Macdonald of Keppoch, his father, had been forfeited, yet that he, as his heir male and representative, has undoubted right to the whole estates personal and real possessed by his father; that in virtue of his right and title he claimed the same before the Court of Session, where his claim was then in dependence; that he had unexceptionable evidence of the death of his father in the month of April, 1746, previous to the attainder passing into a law by which he could not have been attainted, nor his estate forfeited; and he, therefore, protested that no proceedings by Mungo Campbell by order of the Barons of Exchequer may any way hurt or prejudge his right to his father's lands or estate. Ranald further protested that notwithstanding the Barons had taken a survey and rental of the estate of Keppoch by David Bruce in 1748, and afterwards by George Douglas, Sheriff-Substitute of Inverness-shire, they never appointed a factor, and as no acts of property had been used by the barons since the attainder, but on the contrary his guardians and administrators did constantly uplift and receive the rents, profits and emoluments of these lands *bona-fide* since that period without any molestation, impediment, or opposition whatever, he therefore submitted that no process for the recovery of bygone rents is in any way competent to the Barons or their factor.

These strong, impassioned arguments were advanced in Ranald's action pending before the Court of Session, which appears in due course to have pronounced in his favour. But the effect of measures introduced after Culloden were already making their impact on the relationships between chiefs and their clansmen, and, like other chieftains who found themselves deprived of their ancient responsibilities to their people, Ranald sought an opening for his energies and inherited aptitudes further afield. In 1757 he was commissioned into the 78th (Fraser's) Highlanders raised in that year. He was wounded at the taking of Quebec in 1759, and retired on half-pay in 1763 with the rank of Captain. He devoted his period of retirement to the improvement of his lands and property, and built the present Keppoch House which, although altered and added to in later years, still retains much of the original structure.

Ranald later rejoined his regiment, and it was while serving in Jamaica that he married Sarah Cargill, by whom he had two children while serving there: (1) Alexander, who was born on 29th October 1772 and succeeded as 19th Chief; (2) Elizabeth, born 15th November 1774 and died at Keppoch in 1793. After their return home they had three more children: (3) Clementina, who was born on 8th February 1777 and remained unmarried; (4) Richard, born 26th November 1780, who succeeded his brother as 20th Chief; (5) Janet, born 26th November 1782 and married to Duncan Stewart, w.s., of Edinburgh, with issue.

Ranald was appointed Major in the newly raised 74th Highlanders in 1787, but his service with that regiment was cut short by his death the following year.

Alexander, 19th of Keppoch, was a youth of only sixteen years when his father died, and the affairs of the estate were managed during his minority by his uncle, Major Alexander MacDonell, the "Big Major." Young Alexander enlisted in the army at the age of twenty, and was wounded at the siege of Toulon in 1793. He served in the West Indies, and in 1797 was given a captaincy in the First Regiment of Foot, the Royal Scots. His regiment was with Abercromby in the Egyptian campaign of 1801, and he was again wounded in the Battle of Aboukir. In 1805 he was promoted to Major, but retired soon afterwards and went to Jamaica, where he died in 1808.

Alexander had never married, and the representation of the family accordingly devolved upon his only brother, Richard. Like his brother, father and grandfather, Richard took up a military career, enlisting as an ensign in the 92nd Gordon Highlanders in March 1808. He had a distinguished career in that regiment, serving at Walcheren (1809), in the Peninsular War, where he was wounded, and at Quatre Bras and Waterloo, where he was again slightly wounded, Most of his life was spent in service abroad, since nothing now remained of the lands his family had possessed for hundreds of years. Towards the end of his brother's chiefship, the lands had been leased to William Mackintosh, a merchant in Fort William, who held them for a brief period. Other tenants followed, among them a Macdonald of Glencoe, who died there; and the Keppoch family have been exiled from their ancestral home ever since.

Richard died of yellow fever in 1819, while serving with his regiment in Jamaica. He also had never married, and the succession fell upon his cousin Chichester, son of Alexander, the "Big Major." Of Chichester, 21st Chief, little is known beyond the meagre facts that he lived in Glasgow and Greenock, served in the Glengarry Fencibles for a short time, and died in 1848. He had two sons who went to Canada. Neither of them married, and both predeceased their father, being killed in action while serving in the army. Chichester also had a brother, John, and a sister Janet, a nun, both of whom are recorded as having died of cholera in Montreal in 1832. John, who thus predeceased Chichester by many years, does not appear to have left any issue.

In 1921 a "society of considerable importance in London" sent to Canada to trace records of the two sons of Chichester, and in the course of their researches found that no descendants of Alexander, the "Big Major," existed. Thus the modern representation of the noble family of Keppoch is to be sought among some of the collateral branches, possibly in the surviving male lines of Ranald Mor of Tirnadris There the problem must be left for the present.

The Arms of

Sir ALEXANDER WENTWORTH MACDONALD BOSVILLE MACDONALD, Baronet,
(Representer of the Family of Macdonald of Sleat in the Island of Skye—)

Quarterly, 1st, Argent, a lion rampant Gules armed and langued Azure; 2nd, Or, a
hand in armour fesswise proper, holding a cross-crosslet fitchee Gules; 3rd, Argent,
a lymphad sails furled and oars in action Sable, flagged Gules; 4th, Vert, a salmon
naiant in fess proper. Above the Shield is placed a Helmet befitting his degree with a Mantling Gules doubled Argent, and on a Wreath of the proper liveries is set for Crest a hand in
armour fesswise holding a cross-crosslet fitchee Gules, and in an Escrol over the same
this Motto PER·MARE·PER·TERRAS. On a compartment under the Shield are
placed for Supporters two leopards proper collared Or. ❖ ❖ ❖ ❖ ❖ ❖

Lyon Register (Volume 20, Folio 69).

22

The Macdonalds of Sleat

THIS IMPORTANT FAMILY, progenitors of the present Chief of Sleat and Lord Macdonald, was founded by Hugh, younger son of Alexander, Lord of the Isles, from whom they are named the *Clann Uisdein*.

Hugh first appears on record in 1460 when he, with William Macleod of Harris and "the young gentlemen of the Isles," carried out a raid on Orkney. The Orcadians apparently were warned of his approach and camped on a promontory on which he was expected to land. Hugh, however, landed on the other side of the sea-loch and the Orkney men had to change their position while Hugh put his army in order of battle. Having thus lost his advantage, the Earl of Orkney attacked with fury but was defeated with great loss and himself slain. Hugh's party carried off much booty, and on their way home stopped at Caithness where Hugh was entertained by a member of the Clan Gunn who was the Crowner of that region. Gunn's hospitality was lavish, and during the visit Hugh is said to have formed "a matrimonial alliance" with his daughter. How lawful this alliance was has been a matter of much dispute. Later writers, particularly those of other branches who wished to claim the headship of the Clan, have unhesitatingly declared the offspring of this union, Donald Gallach, to be illegitimate even by the easy-going standards of the day. The fact remains, however, that after the death of John, son of Hugh by his official wife, Fynvola MacIain of Ardnamurchan, Donald Gallach was accepted without murmur as Chief of Sleat by the men of the Clan and their neighbours; and from him the line descends to this day.

At the time of the Orkney raid Hugh had no official title to any of the lands which came eventually to the family. In fact we find that in 1463 the Earl of Ross gave a grant of the 28 merklands of Sleat to Celestine, Hugh's elder brother. These were in addition to lands in West Ross given to him the previous year, and both grants received Royal confirmation on 21st August 1464. In 1469, however, Hugh received a large grant of lands in South Uist, Benbecula and North Uist from his brother John, Earl of Ross and Lord of the Isles. These were the 30 merklands of Skirhough in South Uist, 13 merklands in Benbecula, including Griminish, the 4 merklands of Tallowmartin and 6 merklands of Oronsay, both in North Uist. At the same time he also received the 28 merklands of Sleat. All these lands were to be held of the Earl of Ross, and the terms are interesting. They were entailed on "his heirs male, lawfully or unlawfully begotten or to be begotten between him and Fynvola, daughter of Alexander Macdonald of Ardnamurchan, all of whom failing, to the heirs male of Hugh and any woman chosen by the advice of the Earl's Council or relations." The grant, which duly received the Royal confirmation, is remarkable for the terms which appear to place its ultimate destination beyond all possible dispute, thus providing Hugh's descendants with an instrument on which they were able to continue to base and maintain the validity of their succession.

Although no records exist to confirm the transaction, it must be assumed that the 28 merklands of Sleat formerly held by Celestine were resigned by him in Hugh's favour before 1469. From this time dates the occupation of the Castle of Dunscaith as the residence and stronghold of the *Clann Uisdein,* the name by which the family of Sleat has been known in the Clan, after its founder. The castle, on the west side of the Sleat peninsula, was built on what once was probably a Norse fort, and was occupied first by the MacAskills and later by the Macleods as vassals of the Lord of the Isles. The name itself is derived from the Gaelic *Dun Sgathaich,* the Castle of Sgathach, the warrior queen of early Gaelic mythology.

Hugh was now a man of substance as well as brother of Lord of the Isles, on whose Council he appears in 1474, probably taking the seat of his brother Celestine, who was by that time dead. In that capacity he was prominent in the negotiations that led to the forfeiture of the Earldom of Ross in 1476. Regarding his brother's defiance of the Royal summons as ill-conceived and futile, Hugh used his persuasion to secure his submission without unnecessary bloodshed and no doubt thus helped to reduce the severity of the measures that followed. Hugh's services on this occasion were suitably recognised by the King who, on 23rd October 1476, granted him under his Privy Seal at Edinburgh "twentie pundis worth of our landis liand in competent places in the north partis of our realme and infeft him heretably therein be charter and seasing before the feast of Whitsunday. . . ." What these lands were, or whether Hugh ever came into possession of them, it is impossible to say; but there is a persistent tradition that the early chiefs of Sleat claimed the lands of Kishorn and Lochbroom in West Ross which had been granted to Celestine in 1462, and it is possible that Hugh held these lands as reward for his services either directly from the Crown or as vassal of the Chiefs of Lochalsh. Other lands in South Uist, Arisaig and Morar also appear to have been in Hugh's superiority at this time, but no mention is made of these in the confirmation grant of 1495 although the superiority remained in the family for many years thereafter.

The lands of Trotternish in the north end of Skye, for so long in later years a subject of dispute between the Sleat chiefs and the Macleods of Dunvegan, do not seem to have constituted any part of Hugh's holdings. That they formed part of the Clan Donald possessions at this time, however, is apparent from the charter issued by Angus Og, Master of the Isles, to the monks of Iona in 1482, in which he is styled "Master of the Isles and Lord of Trotternish." Angus Og died in 1490 and the family of Sleat, after the forfeiture, claimed to be his heirs and asserted their rights to Trotternish, which they were finally able to establish and maintain against the constant efforts of their enemies to dislodge them.

In 1495, after the forfeiture of the Lordship, Hugh obtained a Crown charter confirming him in possession of all the lands granted to him in 1469. Three years later he died, leaving a securely established patrimony to a son and heir who appeared bent upon its destruction. Hugh had a large family. By his first marriage with Fynvola, daughter of Alexander MacIain of Ardnamurchan, he had John, his successor. At the time of the Orkney raid he contracted a union— the regularity of which has been questioned—with Elizabeth Gunn, daughter of the Crowner of Caithness, by whom he had Donald Gallach, so named from being fostered with his mother's family. Hugh subsequently married a daughter of Macleod of Harris, by whom he had Donald *Hearach* (of Harris), progenitor of *Clann Domhnaill Hearaich.* Hugh's other sons were illegitimate even by the lax standards of the time, and they were to cause much disunity and bloodshed in the family. These were Gilleasbuig Dubh (Black Archibald), by a daughter of Torquil Macleod of Lewis; Angus Collach, by a daughter of Maclean of Coll; and Angus Dubh, by a daughter of Maurice Vicar of South Uist.

John's reign as Chief was marked by what appeared to be a reckless determination to alienate the whole patrimony of his family. No sooner had he succeeded than he resigned to Ranald Ban of Clanranald the lands of Kendness, Griminish, the 21 merklands of Eigg and the 24 merklands of Arisaig; and more of these lands in Benbecula, Eigg and Arisaig were bestowed upon Angus Reochson, also of Clanranald, with the addition of the 12 merklands of Morar. Again, in 1505, Ranald Ban of Clanranald was given a precept from the Crown of the 60 merklands of North Uist and the 20 merklands of Sleat, with the Castle of Dunscaith, all of which had been resigned in his favour by John. The reason for John's conduct in thus dissipating the family inheritance is not easy to fathom unless we assume that, having no heirs of his body, he was resolved that the patrimony should not be enjoyed by any of his half-brothers, with whom he was never on the best of terms. Although in respect of most of the lands he surrendered his superiority was more nominal than real, and his actions may be interpreted as a practical approach to the facts and rights of actual possession, John's resignation of Sleat and North Uist is less easily understood. In the Charter of 1469 these lands had been entailed upon Hugh's heirs whatsoever, legitimate or other, and the terms of the charter were sufficiently wide to cover all possible contingencies, serving as the firm base on which the family continued to assert and maintain their rights. That charter had received the royal confirmation and, in the absence of a forfeiture, its terms rendered incompetent any individual act affecting the disposition of the inheritance.

On John's death in 1505, his half-brother Donald Gallach succeeded to what remained of the impoverished patrimony. In consequence of his brother's reckless conduct, Donald Gallach's name is not to be found in contemporary records of land tenure, and our information concerning him is derived almost entirely from traditional sources. As early as 1484 he had fought at the side of Angus Og in the battle of Bloody Bay. His next appearance is during his brief reign in which he is found occupying the Castle of Dunscaith and, in common with his brother, continuing to retain possession of their lands in Skye and Uist notwithstanding the charters granted to Clanranald. All the brothers were now to become involved in intensive broils, conspiracies and assassinations which have left a terrible stain upon the early history of Clan Uisdein.

Donald Gallach's brothers, as we have already noted, were Donald Hearach, Archibald (Gilleasbuig) Dubh and Angus Collach, all illegitimate sons of Hugh by different mothers. Archibald appears to have been discontented with the provision made for him out of the family inheritance, and the flame of discontent was fanned by his foster father, Mackinnon, who taunted him by saying that the whole of his father's estate was divided between the son of the Crowner of Caithness's daughter and the son of Macleod's daughter. The traditional historian states that from that day Archibald, whose soul was as dark as his complexion, resolved to put both Donald Gallach and Donald Hearach to death. His two half-brothers, Angus Collach and Angus Dubh, were instruments ready to his hand for carrying out the inhuman and unnatural scheme, and he promised that if they aided him he would greatly increase their patrimony. The murder of Donald Hearach was shortly thereafter accomplished in a revolting and barbarous manner, being strangled in the course of a sports feat arranged at Loch Scolpig as a cover for their wicked design.

Archibald, having carried through one part of his desperate resolve, set out from Uist for the purpose of completing it. Donald Gallach, who was then at Kishorn, was delighted to see him, and after dinner brought him out to see a galley he had on the stocks, and which he had intended to use to pay him a visit in Uist. After a careful inspection of the boat, Archibald bent down to examine the stern, and observed to his brother that there was one faulty plank at least in the galley, namely, the keel plank. Surprised that such should be the case, Donald bent down to satisfy himself as to the fault, when Archibald drew his dagger and stabbed him in the back. The blow was not immediately fatal. Donald fell, but had time to remonstrate with his brother upon the fiendish atrocity of his conduct. The latter stared for a moment at his victim, dropped his weapon, fell on his knees and, struck with remorse, poured out his lamentations, regrets, and self-reproaches, and would give the world that the deed was undone. Seeing this, the dying man begged of him to spare his son, who was a mere boy, and the murderer assured him in the most earnest manner that he would rear him with the same care as if he were his own son. Surprisingly, this promise appears to have been kept. Archibald, who though married had no family of his own, lived in the island of Oronsay in North Uist, and brought up the sons of the two murdered brothers—Donald Gruamach, the son of Donald Gallach, the heir to the chiefship and patrimony of the House of Sleat, and his cousin Ranald, the son of Donald Hearach—as if they were his own offspring. He was evidently satisfied in having the control of the Clan and the possessions of the family and, not having a son of his own, was content that in due time his nephews should enter into their kingdom.

Not long after the double tragedy, which seems to have taken place in 1506, Uist appears to have become too hot for the blood-stained Archibald, and he was forced by Ranald Ban, the Chief of Clanranald, to betake himself to the Southern Hebrides, where he joined a band of pirates, and was for about three years engaged in robbery on the high seas. Archibald eventually won the favour of the Government when, in characteristic fashion, he rounded on his partners in crime, John Mor and Alasdair Bearnach, of the Clan Alasdair of Kintyre, taking them by surprise and handing them into custody. After this he returned to his native territory, assumed the leadership of the Clan, and obtained the bailiary of Trotternish, all with the consent of the Government, who seemed to have winked at his previous enormities. He was acting in this capacity in 1510.

During the period of Archibald's piratical career, the history of Clan Uisdein in Uist is a tale of violence and lawlessness. According to the Sleat seanachie, Angus Collach, who had a hand in the murder of Donald Hearach, paid a notable visit to the Island of North Uist—a visit which proved to be his last. Angus travelled in state, taking a considerable number of followers in his train. Sunday coming round, Angus and his retinue attended divine service in the Parish Church of Saint Mary's though the sequel does not suggest the possession of profound piety. Donald Macdonald of Balranald, a gentleman of the Clan Gorraidh, was at the time from home, but his wife, a lady of the Clanranald family, was present in church. Angus Collach, meeting her after service, proposed that he and his followers should partake of the hospitality of Balranald for that night, as it was in the near vicinity of the church. This was cheerfully agreed to, but when other proposals inconsistent with the marriage vow were made by Angus, the lady of Balranald had, in the first instance, to dissemble, and afterwards contrive by stratagem to make her escape to her friends in South Uist. The result was that

60 men were sent to North Uist under Donald MacRanald, who collected a further large contingent of the Siol Ghorraidh, with whom he surprised Angus Collach at Kirkibost, killed 18 of his men, and took himself prisoner. Angus was sent to Clanranald in South Uist, where he was tied up in a sack and cast into the sea. His remains afterwards turned up on the shore at Carinish, where also they were buried. Such was the violent end of a lawless life.

Angus Dubh, another son of Hugh of Sleat, seems to have been involved in the irregularities of his brother, and was about the same time apprehended by Clanranald, and kept for a long time in close custody. One day he was let out of ward, and permitted by his guards to run on the Strand of Askernish, in South Uist, to see if he could do so as swiftly as before his incarceration. Angus, finding that his fleetness of foot was almost unimpaired, attempted to outrun his keepers, who closely pursued him, and one of them hitting him on the leg with an arrow, and the wound being considered incurable, he was put to the sword.

For the murder of Angus Collach a terrible revenge was executed by Archibald Dubh, who put to death a large number of those concerned in that miscreant's well-merited punishment. Of all the sons of Hugh of Sleat, Archibald Dubh was now the sole survivor, but each passing year brought retribution closer to the arch-villain of the triumvirate whose deeds had been the cause of so much misery and bloodshed. The story of the events that led up to his death is told with very circumstantial detail by the Sleat seanachie. According to this authority, Donald Gruamach, son of Donald Gallach, was at the time of his coming of age resident in the house of the Earl of Moray, and his uncle Archibald sent for himself and his cousin, Ranald, son of the murdered Donald Hearach, to go to see him in Uist. It was a beautiful day in summer, and Archibald and his nephews, with their gillies, were on a hunting expedition in the hills called Lea, which lie to the south of Lochmaddy. While their attendants were beating up the hill Archibald and his young kinsmen were stationed at the pass between the two Lea hills called *Bealach-a-Sgail,* waiting until the game should be driven through. Overpowered by the heat of the day, Archibald Dubh stretched himself on the heath, and fell fast asleep. This sleep was to be his last. His two nephews immediately planned his destruction, and the question was who would be the executioner. Donald Gruamach appears to have had scruples against having a hand in the deed, but on Ranald's consenting to undertake it, he is reported to have spoken these words—"*Dean, dean agus cuimhnich m'athair-sa agus t'athair fein*" (Do, do, and remember my father and your own.) The blow was struck, and this man of blood finally paid the penalty of his crimes, while tradition loves to record that on the spot where his blood flowed out neither grass nor heather ever grew—such was the detestation in which his fellow-men held the memory of Gilleasbuig Dubh.

On his uncle's death, which took place about 1518, Donald Gruamach, who was probably now of age, assumed the leadership of the Clan Uisdein as the third chief of his line. We do not find much of his history in the State Records, but it is clear that he did a great deal by his bravery and force of character to raise the status and repair the fortunes of his house. He had a difficult part to play in view of unfriendliness in high places, and no doubt the "grimness" from which he derived his name stood him in good stead in those troublous times. On 3rd July 1521, "Donald McDonald Gallych of Dunscayth" entered into a Bond of Manrent with Sir John Campbell of Cawdor "to be commyn man and servand to ane honorabyll man Sir John Campbell &c. Knycht both meself and my broder and John McKorkyll Mcloid &c. signed with my hand at the pen at Castle Meai." The following year Colin, Earl of Argyll, assigned to his brother, John Campbell

THE MACDONALDS OF SLEAT

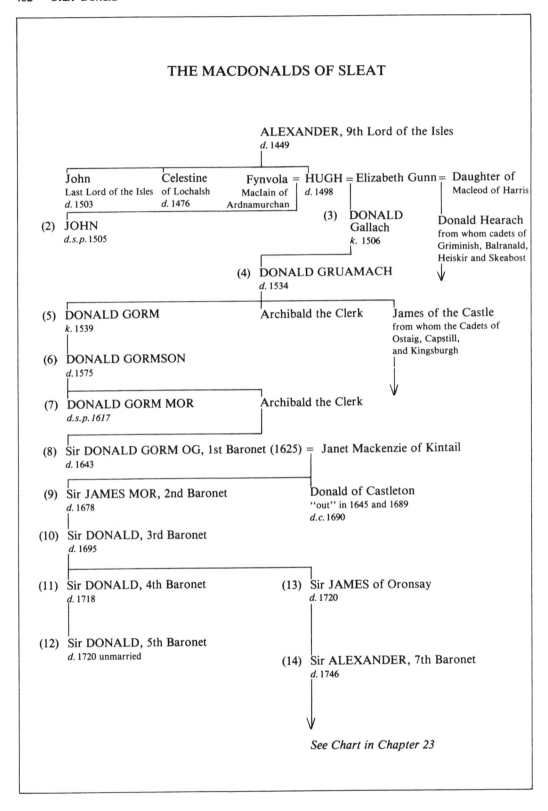

ALEXANDER, 9th Lord of the Isles
d. 1449

John — Last Lord of the Isles — *d.* 1503

Celestine — of Lochalsh — *d.* 1476

Fynvola = HUGH = Elizabeth Gunn = Daughter of
Maclain of — *d.* 1498 — Macleod of Harris
Ardnamurchan

(2) JOHN
d.s.p. 1505

(3) DONALD Gallach
k. 1506

Donald Hearach
from whom cadets of
Griminish, Balranald,
Heiskir and Skeabost

(4) DONALD GRUAMACH
d. 1534

(5) DONALD GORM
k. 1539

Archibald the Clerk

James of the Castle
from whom the Cadets of
Ostaig, Capstill,
and Kingsburgh

(6) DONALD GORMSON
d. 1575

(7) DONALD GORM MOR
d.s.p. 1617

Archibald the Clerk

(8) Sir DONALD GORM OG, 1st Baronet (1625) = Janet Mackenzie of Kintail
d. 1643

(9) Sir JAMES MOR, 2nd Baronet
d. 1678

Donald of Castleton
"out" in 1645 and 1689
d.c. 1690

(10) Sir DONALD, 3rd Baronet
d. 1695

(11) Sir DONALD, 4th Baronet
d. 1718

(13) Sir JAMES of Oronsay
d. 1720

(12) Sir DONALD, 5th Baronet
d. 1720 unmarried

(14) Sir ALEXANDER, 7th Baronet
d. 1746

See Chart in Chapter 23

of Cawdor, a Bond of Manrent which had been given to the Earl by "Donald Gromach McDonald Gallach and Alexander McAllan Mcroyrie." The assignation was signed at Inveraray, but the particular day and month are blank.

The year 1523 seems to have been a somewhat eventful one in the life of Donald Gruamach. His Bond of Manrent to Cawdor bound him to the service of that chief, and this appears to have led him into courses which do not reflect lustre on his memory. The Chief of Sleat seems to have followed Cawdor in the campaign of the Duke of Albany against England in 1523, which had a somewhat inconclusive and inglorious termination, for we find him among a number of notabilities who, along with Cawdor, received a remission for quitting the field or, as it is called in the Act of Remission, "le hame seekin" while engaged in the siege of Wark Castle. It was probably while on their way home from the borders that Sir John Campbell of Cawdor and his accomplices, among whom was the Chief of Sleat, assassinated Lachlan Cattanach of Duart, in the burgh of Edinburgh. For these and other offences Donald Gruamach received a remission in Edinburgh on 15th December 1523. In 1524 he entered into an important alliance with the Chief of Mackintosh, and in 1527 he formed a bond of a similar nature with Mackintosh, Munro of Foulis, Rose of Kilravock, the inevitable Cawdor of course heading the list. These various Bonds of Manrent and alliances in which Donald Gruamach was concerned with mainland chiefs not in his near neighbourhood, show that his support and co-operation were greatly prized, and that the Clan Uisdein, though technically "broken," were regarded as a powerful and influential community to be seriously reckoned with.

In the early years of the century, much of the disturbances afflicting Clan Uisdein and their neighbours centred on the disposition of the lands and bailiary of Trotternish. In 1498 the office of bailiary, with two unciates of the lands, was confirmed by the Crown to Alexander Macleod of Dunvegan. Only two months later, the same office with 8 merklands of the district was granted to Torquil Macleod of Lewis. The prospect of confusion and strife presented by these conflicting grants, however, was averted by the general revocation of charters which took place later in the same year. In 1505 the lands were leased for a period to Ranald Ban of Clanranald, but they appear to have come into the possession of Macleod of Dunvegan again some time before 1517, when the lease was continued until the King should reach his majority. Donald Gruamach was determined to assert and vindicate his rights to the whole district of Trotternish, and in this he was able to count on the support of his half-brother, John Macleod of Lewis, who was struggling to regain possession of his own inheritance. In 1528 their joint forces were successful in expelling Dunvegan and his vassals from the district, in return for which Donald Gruamach rendered valuable aid to the Chief of Clan Torquil in obtaining effective possession of Lewis.

Macleod of Dunvegan naturally objected to being driven out of Trotternish, and at his instance a summons was issued that same year by the Council against both the offending chiefs for his wrongful ejection. As the disturbances in the Isles continued to increase instead of diminishing, the Privy Council in 1530 ordered the tenants of the Isles, and prominent among them Donald Gruamach and Macleod of Dunvegan, to appear before the King on 24th May 1530, to consult with him for the good rule of the Isles. In the course of the same month these two chiefs and seven others of the principal island chiefs sent an offer of submission to the King, who granted them a protection against the Earl of Argyll, provided they came to Edinburgh, or wherever the King held his Court for the time, before the 30th June, and remain as long as the King required their attendance, the protection to last 20 days after their departure on their way home. In the following year both the chiefs and Ewen Mackinnon of Strathardill were frequently cited before Parliament, but failed to appear. After 1530 Donald Gruamach's career seems to have been peaceful and uneventful—at any rate we do not again find his name appearing in any of the State records of the time until his death, which appears to have taken place in 1534.

Donald Gruamach married first Catherine, daughter of Alexander Macdonald of Clanranald by whom he had Donald Gorm, who succeeded. His second marriage was with a daughter of Macleod of Lewis, by whom he had John Og, who married a daughter of Alasdair Crotach Macleod of Dunvegan without issue; Archibald the Clerk, whose two sons appear on record; and James of Castle Camus, progenitor of the *Clann Domhnaill Gruamaich*, of which the house of Kingsburgh is the most notable. There were other sons, but none appears to have been legitimate, and no record of them exists.

Donald Gorm's reign is chiefly remarkable for his attempt to restore the Lordship and the Earldom of Ross, in which he had the support of many of the Western Chiefs and particularly of the Macleods of Lewis. As already recorded in an earlier chapter, Donald Gorm began his campaign by invading and laying waste the district of Trotternish, in which the Macleods of Dunvegan had again secured a footing. He thereupon turned his attention to the mainland of Ross and laid waste the Mackenzie lands of Kinlochewe before laying siege to the Castle of Eilean Donan. The story of how Donald Gorm met his death in the course of the siege is told in the following passage from the annalist of the MacRaes, hereditary Constables of the Castle:

To return to Duncan, the son of Christopher, who was the son of Finlay, and who succeeded Malcolm MacEan Carrich, as Constable of Islandonan, . . . in John Mackenzie of Kintail's time, Donald Gorm, fifth Baron of Sleat, and thirteenth of the family, came with a strong party to the south side of Kintail, carried away a great many cattle, and killed several of the inhabitants, among whom was Sir Dugal Mackenzie, Priest of Kintail, who lived in Achyuran of Glensheal, leaving a widow, two sons and a daughter. John Du Matheson married the widow, and upon the decease of Christopher was made Constable of Islandonan. Donald Gorm, afterwards hearing that the castle was but slightly guarded, thought to have taken it by surprise. So, coming with seven or eight large boats or birlins full of men towards Islandonan, was observed by the sentinel who, suspecting their design by their number and hurry, gave the signal and cry for the country people to come and defend the castle, but, by reason of their distances, could not prevent Macdonald's landing. Only this Duncan MacGilchrist, hearing the cry and being very ready to do his master's service, in time of the greatest danger, came directly, and standing at the gate of the old tower, continued shooting his arrows at Macdonald's men, until those of the first boat of them landed, by which time he had killed and wounded severals of them. Upon his entering the tower he found none there but Matheson the Constable and the Cryer. Macdonald and his men by this time had landed and were attempting to break the castle gate, which being strongly secured by a back door of iron, and they within throwing stones upon the assailants, they were obliged to give up the attempt, and began to shoot their arrows in at the windows, by which John Du Matheson the Constable was killed; so that Duncan had now but the Cryer and one arrow to defend the fort. Macdonald having taken down the masts of some of his birlins, was looking where he might easiest make a breach and mount the wall, when Duncan took the opportunity of shooting the only arrow he had, which happened to be a barbed one, and wounding Macdonald in the master vein of the foot, he became impatient of the pain, and pulled out the arrow, not adverting it was barbed, by which means he cut the artery called in Gaelic "strurossach," and finding the blooding could not be stopped, desisted from the attack and took to their boats. Macdonald being carried to one of them by his men, few of whom escaped being killed or wounded, and before they were out of sight of the garrison he died. . . .

The short-lived rebellion thus ended tragically for the Chief of Sleat. By his marriage with Margaret, daughter of Torquil Macleod of Lewis, he had Donald Gormson, his successor, and another son, Alasdair Og, who died without issue. The new Chief was still a child on his accession and the leadership of the clan fell to his uncle, Archibald the Clerk (*Gilleasbuig Cleireach*), whose designation suggests some clerical ability but is in his case belied by the appearance of his signature "with his hand at the pen" on a list of Donald Dubh's supporters. He was, however, an able man whose shrewdness and skill were largely instrumental in preserving the freedom of his clan from the consequences of the recent rebellion. He himself moreover escaped the fate of other Western Chiefs taken captive by the King in his progress through the Isles, and in the following year succeeded in obtaining the royal pardon for the excesses committed during Donald Gruamach's campaign.

The young Chief, however, on account of his close kinship with the Lords of the Isles and the recent pretensions of his family to the forfeited honours, appears to have been regarded as a potential threat to the peace of the Isles and, if we are to believe the Sleat seanachie, efforts were made by the Privy Council to secure possession of him as hostage for the future good behaviour of the clan. He was accordingly sent in the first instance to the care of his uncle, Ruairi Macleod of Lewis, and thereafter to the English Court where his long sojourn earned for him the designation among his clansmen of Donald Gorm *Sasunnach*.

Dunscaith (*Dun Sgathaich*), fortress of the legendary Sgathach, warrior queen of the 2nd century A.D. Ancestral seat of the Sleat family from about 1469 to 1632

Meanwhile Archibald the Clerk's good relations with the Government were recognised by the grant in 1540 of a five-year lease of the whole of North Uist, excluding Church lands, and there is evidence in the Exchequer Rolls of 1542 that his annual payments were faithfully rendered. In the same year, however, the King for some obscure reason granted to Macleod of Dunvegan a charter in liferent of the lands of Trotternish. Alexander Macleod of Dunvegan had been one of the chiefs borne away by the King two years earlier, and it is difficult to understand how he had earned this mark of royal favour which was bound to lend increased bitterness to the feud between the two neighbours. Although the Macleods were unable to take infeftment and the Macdonalds continued in actual possession, the situation thus created left the feud simmering for many years to come.

The last notice we have of Archibald the Clerk is in 1545 when, as Captain of Clan Uisdein, he appears as a signatory to the "Commission from the Lord of the Isles of Scotland to treat with the King of England" issued that year from Eigg by Donald Dubh and his Island Council. Archibald probably died soon after 1545, as we find John Og acting as Tutor from that time until Donald Gormson came of age. John Og was the second son of Donald Gruamach by his second wife, a daughter of Macleod of Lewis, and he was thus a full brother of Archibald. The Sleat historian accuses John Og of murdering his brother, the Tutor, and reigning in his stead. It is more likely, however, that Archibald was now too old to carry out his duties as Captain of the Clan, and John Og was adopted as a more energetic leader capable of exercising his rôle successfully in face of threats from greedy or aggressive neighbours.

Donald Gormson probably attained his majority about the year 1553, when he is charged by Mackenzie of Kintail with taking timber from his lands. Up to this year the Highlands were in a state of constant disorder as a result of the weakness of the central government under the Regency of Arran. In 1554, however, the Queen Dowager took over the reigns of government and, determined to restore peace and order in the North, commissioned Argyll and Huntly to proceed against all those who failed to provide sureties for their good behaviour. The threat posed by these resolute measures proved effective in the case of many of the Chiefs, including Donald Gormson, who appears to have submitted and observed the peace during the remaining years of the Regency. About 1560, however, he became involved in the feud which then originated between Maclean of Duart and the Macdonalds of Dunnyveg over their conflicting claims to the Rhinns of Islay. Donald Gormson joined his kinsman of Dunnyveg in the invasion of the Maclean lands in Mull, Coll and Tiree. He appears to have suffered no serious consequences for the outrages committed against these islands, for in 1562 we find Queen Mary granting a remission to him and other ringleaders in the expedition, including his uncle James, his cousins Donald MacGilleasbuig and Angus Macdonald of Harris.

In 1565 the Earl of Argyll and the Earl of Moray were involved in the rebellion against Mary over her proposed marriage to Lord Darnley. Atholl was commissioned to proceed against the rebels, and Donald Gormson was one of those who played an active part in quelling the insurrection. About this time he seems to have adopted the new religion of the Reformation, and his later services during the Regencies of Moray and Lennox secured for him a promise that if any lands adjacent to his own were to fall into the King's hands, through forfeiture, he should be given a grant of them. This was a considerable concession, which provides ample evidence of the value placed upon Donald Gormson's services during this period by the Government.

In 1566 a strange chapter in the history of the Sleat family took place. In that year Donald Gormson put in a claim to the patrimony of the Macleods of Lewis. Ruairi Macleod of Lewis first married Janet Mackenzie of Kintail, who had a son called Torquil *Conanach* from having been fostered with his mother's people in Strath Conan. This Torquil was disinherited by Ruairi on the ground that he was not in fact his own son, and accusations of infidelity were laid against Janet, Torquil's mother. Ruairi accordingly divorced Janet and married Barbara Stewart, by whom he had another son, also named Torquil but designated *Oighre* (the heir), to distinguish him from the first Torquil. It turned out later that Ruairi had had good grounds for his suspicions, as on 22nd August 1566 a declaration was made by Sir Patrick MacMaster Martin, parson of Barvas in Lewis, before Patrick Miller, a notary public, that "Hucheon Breve of Lewis" confessed on his death-bed that he was the father of Torquil Conanach. Unfortunately in the same year Torquil Oighre, the rightful heir, was drowned crossing from Lewis to Trotternish. Donald Gormson, as nearest heir through his mother, laid claim to the succession, and did not seem at first to be opposed. Ruairi Macleod, however, was not to be cheated thus easily out of his family's rights. On the death of his second wife, he married a sister of Lachlan Maclean of Duart, by whom he had another Torquil, named Dubh, to contend in future years with Torquil Conanach for possession of the Lewis estates. Donald Gormson in consequence had to accept the situation and, thwarted in his aims in that direction, was obliged to confine his ambitions for expansion to territories nearer home.

All this time the Macleods of Dunvegan had been the legal owners, under the more recent charters, of the lands belonging by right of actual possession to the Clan Uisdein. An attempt to regularise such an anomalous state of affairs was made in 1567, when Donald Gormson entered into a contract with the Earl of Argyll for the purpose of acquiring legal titles to the estates. The terms of the contract were briefly as follows: (1) The Earl of Argyll was to get himself infefted in the lands of Trotternish, Sleat and North Uist; (2) he was for various good causes, particularly for future service, to make Donald Gormson and his heirs vassals in these lands, paying the Earl a penny more duty than he was to pay to the Crown; (3) Donald was to pay 1000 merks to the Earl as soon as he should be received as the Earl's vassal, with 500 merks additional to form part of the dowry of Mary Macleod, grand-daughter and heiress of line of Alexander Macleod, to the gift of whose ward and marriage Alexander had acquired right; (4) he was to deliver to the Earl at the same time, under penalty of all the other proceedings being declared void and null, a bond of manrent and service from himself and his successors to the Earl and his successors in the most strict form and against all and sundry, the royal authority only excepted; and upon their failure to serve the Earl with their whole force whenever they should be required, all the provisions in their favour contained in the present contract were to become null; (5) lastly, Donald was to concur with, assist, and defend Tormod Macleod, uncle of Mary, heir male of the family, when he should be required to do so by the Earl.

The contract is dated 4th March 1567, but we have no evidence that the provisions were ever implemented, though the document throws valuable light upon the favourable position occupied by the Chief of Sleat in the esteem of the powers that were. It is no less a tribute to Donald's sagacity in having brought the prestige and prosperity of his house to a level unequalled since the days of its founder. His reputation was now such that, when he joined Sorley Buy in his campaign in Ireland in 1568, he was frequently referred to as "Lord of the Oute Isles," and was by many esteemed to possess that dignity. His later years were marked by peaceful settlements which advanced the interests of his family and secured the protection of his estates. A revival of the feud with Mackenzie of Kintail in 1569 was settled before the Council at Perth to the mutual satisfaction of the two chiefs, who bound themselves to restrain their unruly vassals from molesting each other's lands. In 1572, on the strength of the promises made to him by the Regents, he received the patronage of the Bishopric of Ross and a grant of 1000 merks a year out of the Bishopric of Aberdeen. The last notice we have of this distinguished Chief is in January 1572, when he entered into an obligation with the Bishop of the Isles concerning arrears of teinds he owed to the Church in the lands of North Uist, Sleat and Trotternish. The transaction is one of the last recorded as having taken place at Dunscaith Castle, soon to be abandoned as the family stronghold in favour of Duntulm in Trotternish, no doubt in order to establish their hold more securely on that territory. Dunscaith is still, however, regarded as Lord Macdonald's "ancestral seat," as shown in the matriculation of his arms in 1947.

Donald Gormson died in 1575. By his marriage with Mary, daughter of Hector Mor Maclean of Duart, he had three sons: (1) Donald Gorm Mor, his successor; (2) Archibald, like his grand-uncle also designated "the Clerk"; and (3) Alexander, who died without issue. Donald Gorm Mor was a minor at the time of his father's death. In the year of his accession, we find James of Castle Camus and his nephews, the sons of Archibald the Clerk, acting for him in the discharge of the obligation to the Bishop of the Isles undertaken by the late Chief. The obligation to pay these dues would seem to suggest that the lands involved, although not actually confirmed to the Clann Uisdein by the Crown under charter, were nonetheless regarded as having been legally possessed by the family of Sleat.

In the division of Tutorial authority that now took place, James of Castle Camus held the bailiary of Sleat, while his nephew Donald became bailie of Trotternish. Who was responsible for North Uist does not appear. As late as 1580 the teinds due to the Bishopric of the Isles were still sadly in arrears. An Act of Council was passed raising a summons against the tutors of Donald Gorm Mor, namely Donald and Hugh, sons of Archibald the Clerk. James of Castle Camus is not mentioned in this summons, but he was in no better case than the accused, as in the following year his name appears along with Donald and Hugh when they were all declared rebels, put to the horn, and forfeited for failure to pay.

That James of Castle Camus agreed to share the Tutorial authority with his nephews, Donald and Hugh MacGilleasbuig Chleirich, was simply an acknowledgment of the power and influence that family had acquired as a result of their father's leadership of the Clan during the late Chief's minority. Hugh in particular resented the division of the Tutorship which he regarded as belonging to his family as of right, and this, together with his suspicion of his father's murder by John Og, engendered a strong feeling of bitterness which was to be the cause of much strife and discord in years to come. His brother Donald died shortly before the sentence of forfeiture passed in 1581, but Hugh was still an outlaw under that sentence when Donald Gorm Mor reached his majority in 1585. The young Chief immediately became the victim of the first of a series of acts of treachery committed against him and his house by this unscrupulous member of his family.

Donald Gorm Mor was on a voyage in his birlinn and a full complement of followers to visit Angus of Dunnyveg, when contrary winds forced him to shelter in Loch Tarbert on the west side of Jura. This loch divides the lands owned by Maclean to the north and Macdonald of Dunnyveg to the south. It so happened that the outlawed Hugh, on one of his piratical expeditions, came into the same loch at night and anchored in an adjacent bay. Donald had anchored on the Maclean side of the loch, and the wily Hugh saw his opportunity of reaping material advantage for himself at the expense of his Chief. He landed a party of his men, carried off some of Maclean's cattle and set sail before he could be caught, leaving suspicion to fall upon the Sleat Chief. The plan worked too well. Maclean's men attacked the Sleat men who, being greatly outnumbered, were defeated with great loss, Donald himself escaping with his life only because he had preferred to sleep on board his galley. It seems that Angus of Griminish, a member of the Clann Domhnaill Hearaich, was implicated in this affair with the evil Hugh. The incident led to the revival of the bitter feud between the Macleans and the Macdonalds of Dunnyveg, and was responsible for Donald Gorm becoming involved in a long quarrel marked by frequent bloody conflicts until its final resolution on the sands of Loch Gruinard in 1598.

Donald Gorm Mor returned to Skye determined to use every means in his power to exact retribution from the Macleans. That his immediate retaliatory measures were effective is evident from King James's letter of September 1585 urging Macleod of Dunvegan to assist the Macleans against the Sleat Chief. In the same year both Donald Gorm and Maclean, with Macleod of Dunvegan, were summoned to appear before the Council to consult on matters touching the "gude reull and quieting of the Ilis and Hielandis." Although the summons had little effect, it would appear that he was able to maintain good relations with the authorities, for on 20th May 1586 he entered into a bond of manrent and maintenance with the Earl of Huntly and Elgin.

The quarrel with Maclean, however, was not destined to be set at rest, and the next act in the drama was reached when Angus of Dunnyveg, after paying a visit to his kinsman in Skye, decided to play the part of mediator in the dispute. He interrupted his return voyage at Duart and, having explained to Maclean the object of his mission, was welcomed with customary hospitality. But Maclean could not forget the Rhinns of Islay, and overnight he changed from being a kindly host into a treacherous enemy. Angus and his men were cast into prison, and were later permitted to resume their voyage only on conditions which included the renunciation by Angus of his claims to the Rhinns and the surrender of hostages as surety of their fulfilment. The story of subsequent events in Islay has been told elsewhere in this work, but as a result of these proceedings the feud was later to develop into a formidable conflict involving the whole of Clan Donald and many of its minor adherents.

With the object of securing their northern frontiers, Donald Gorm and Angus of Dunnyveg now entered into an alliance with Lachlan Mackintosh of Dunachton, Captain of Clan Chattan. The pact was concluded at Inverness on 30th May 1587, and was directed mainly against Macleod of Dunvegan and Mackenzie of Kintail, whose hostility posed a dangerous threat to Donald Gorm in his forthcoming operations. Later that year the Sleat Chief launched his campaign by invading the Island of Mull. Versions of the events that followed vary from historian to historian as, in the absence of official records, these are drawn from conflicting traditional sources. The Maclean historian states that after a preliminary skirmish at a place called Sron-na-Cranalich, in which the Maclean advance guard was annihilated, Donald marched on towards the main body of the enemy. On the way Maclean of Boreray, who was a tenant of Sleat in North Uist, was seen to be downcast and of gloomy countenance. On enquiry, Boreray told Donald of a very disturbing dream in which the action was seen to take place at a pass called Leac-Li, and Donald was to be killed with great loss to his following. Donald thereupon told him to leave the company if he so desired or was contemplating any treachery. Boreray continued to follow Donald until the action took place as foretold, but changed sides during the battle, and the Sleat men were driven back to their ships with great loss. The version given by Sir Robert Gordon in his *History of Sutherland,* however, presents an entirely different picture. There he states that Macdonald "came to the very Benmore in Mull, and there killed and chased the Clan Lean at his pleasure, and so revenged himself fully of the injuries done to him and his tribe."

There followed soon afterwards another incident of which accounts are similarly unsupported by documentary evidence. We are told that as the Macdonalds were marshalling their forces on the island of Bachca, south of Kerrera, the Macleans took their superior forces by surprise and pressed home their attack with such vigour that many hundreds of the Macdonalds were killed and many more captured, including Donald Gorm Mor himself. The claim that the Macleans suffered only three casualties in this wholesale slaughter tends in itself to discredit the annalist's account of the battle, but its general inaccuracy would seem to be confirmed by the absence of any mention in the records of the period of the capture of a Chief of Donald Gorm's standing, in company with numbers of his leading clansmen.

In 1589 a settlement appears to have been reached between Donald Gorm Mor and Lachlan Maclean, although it represented but a lull in the latter's feud with the Macdonalds of Dunnyveg. In that year Donald Gorm Mor and his brothers Alexander and Archibald, James Macdonald of Castle Camus, and Hugh MacGilleasbuig Chleirich—the arch-villain of the piece, whose outrage in Jura had sparked off the feud—received a remission for all the crimes committed against the Macleans. On the strength of this remission, Donald Gorm and the two other leading participants in the late feud, Angus of Dunnyveg and Lachlan Maclean, were persuaded to go to Edinburgh for the ostensible purpose of consulting with the King and his Council on measures for securing peace and good order in the Isles. What followed was becoming a familiar feature of the treatment meted out to unwary chiefs summoned to the royal presence. All three were promptly apprehended and thrown into prison, to be released some time afterwards only on the provision of sureties and the payment of heavy fines, which the King now recognised as a useful and convenient means of replenishing his depleted treasury. Campbell of Cawdor is said to have stood surety for Donald Gorm, whose heavy fine of £4000 may be regarded as a measure of his importance in the view of the government.

Donald Gorm was again to fall into disfavour soon after these events, when Campbell of Cawdor was assassinated in 1592. Whether it was that Donald was suspected of complicity in the crime, or that the removal of his surety had encouraged him to further unlawful acts, the immediate consequence was the execution of a summons for treason against him. A sentence of forfeiture does not appear to have followed, however, and thus he was able to continue the preparations he was engaged upon with Macleod of Dunvegan for going to the aid of the Irish rebel, Hugh O'Donnell, then up in arms against Elizabeth of England. In 1594 the two Chiefs, each at the head of 500 clansmen, set out and landed on the shores of Loch Foyle, where O'Donnell came to meet them and entertained them lavishly for three days and nights. Donald Gorm on this occasion appears to have done little more than to ensure the safe junction of his forces with those of O'Donnell, and soon returned home, leaving his clansmen under the command of his brother.

By 1595 relations with the Crown seem to have improved and Donald applied to the King for a grant of the lands he was occupying at the time. In his petition he stated he would rather deal with the King direct than through an intermediary whose services might not be entirely disinterested. The proposal was favourably received, and in 1596 Donald went to Court where an agreement was reached and he was granted a charter in the same terms as that of 1469 by which Hugh, the founder, had held his lands from his brother, the Lord of the Isles. The conditions were that Donald paid 2000 merks in discharge of all feudal dues from his lands, and an annual feu-duty of £146; and Castle Camus was always to be open to the King or his officers. On 17th August of the same year Donald received a lease for five years of the Crown lands of Trotternish, of which 8 merklands were reserved to the King, who at the same time agreed that, if he did not place Lowland colonists on these lands, Donald would have first claim to them in preference to any other Highland tenant. The precept of sasine followed in December 1597. These favourable terms were completed in the year in which the King ordered all the holders of land in the Highlands and Isles to appear before the Exchequer and show their title-deeds to Crown lands, and Donald was saved from the inconvenience of exhibiting his charters on this occasion because of the recent satisfactory settlement.

In view of the security he had thus achieved for himself in his lands and the amicable relationship in which he now stood with the Crown, it is remarkable that in the following year Donald Gorm should be found offering his services to Queen Elizabeth, assuring her of the support of all the clans in fostering rebellion in Scotland, and undertaking to serve her cause against her rebellious subjects in Ireland. The document in which these offers are made is suspect not only in view of the marks of favour so recently bestowed upon Donald by the King, but also because it makes no exception in favour of his sovereign. More credibility is to be attached to his correspondence later in the year, addressed to the Lord Deputy, in which he specifically excepts King James while offering to serve Elizabeth against all and sundry. Nothing resulted from these offers, but the outlet he sought for his energies was soon to be provided by events nearer home.

Donald Gorm had married Mary Macleod, a sister of Ruairi Mor Macleod of Dunvegan. This appears to have been of the handfast type, for Donald repudiated the lady and sent her home. Tradition embellishes the incident by saying that the lady was blind of one eye, and was sent home riding a one-eyed horse, with a one-eyed gillie and a one-eyed dog. A similar story with similar unpleasant results is told about another lady in another part of the Highlands at another time. Whether true or false, however, the fact that Donald terminated the arrangement so arbitrarily stirred up the old feud.

Ruairi Mor invaded Trotternish and carried off a spoil, and Donald Gorm retaliated in like manner in the lands of Macleod in Harris. And now in these raids a notable warrior of the Sleat family emerges. This was Donald of Eriskay, grandson of James of the Castle, founder of the cadet family of Castle Camus, later known as Kingsburgh. Donald was known in the clan as *Domhnall Maclain 'Ic Sheumais*. Traditions of his exploits have been for long current in Uist and form a notable part of the history of this critical period in the life of his clan.

Following the raid by the Sleat men on Harris, the Macleods reacted with vigour and a party of some 40 men under the command of Donald Glas Macleod landed to harry the island of North Uist, which they thought an easier target than the neighbouring lands of Sleat. They made a very successful *creach* and gathered the cattle at the Temple of the Trinity in Carinish. The raiders were feasting in the outhouses of the Chapel prior to departing with their spoil, when a much smaller force of Macdonalds approached undetected. Donald of Eriskay had heard of the raid and arrived post haste in Uist, gathering as many warriors as he could on the way. His band consisted of only about 15 men, and he realised that only an adroit use of strategy would ensure his success. He accordingly divided his little force into three, sending some forward to challenge the Macleods, who thought themselves quite secure. The rest of the party he placed in two sections separated by some two hundred yards, the last being hidden behind some rising ground. The Macleods duly rushed out of the Chapel or its outbuildings, and were met by a shower of arrows expertly aimed, which cut down several of them. The first section then retreated to join their comrades in the rear. Before the Macleods came within striking distance of their foe, Donald's men met them with another shower of arrows which further cut down their number. Donald knew that his men were better bowmen and able to outdistance the Macleods with their volleys of well-directed arrows before they were able to retaliate effectively. Once more the now reduced force of the raiders was met with the combined volley of all Donald's men. The result was shattering, and a final onslaught with the sword finished the work. Donald Glas, with a few survivors, fled to the shore of Baleshare where they were overtaken and killed. During the battle Donald of Eriskay was wounded by an arrow in his thigh. Fortunately, unlike Donald Gorm at Eilean Donan, he did not snatch it out, but waited until his god-mother who was known as *Nic Coiseam,* came to his aid. Her skilful surgery removed the arrow while, to distract his attention, she and her attendant women sang a song, the words of which are still preserved in Uist.

Thanks to Nic Coiseam's skill the wound quickly healed, and not long afterwards Donald was able to set sail for Skye. His galley was half-way across the Minch when a storm blew up from the south-east and he had to run before it, ending up in the shelter of Rodel Bay, in Harris. Here Ruairi Mor was in residence. Tradition states that Ruairi, looking out of the house, remarked that even if his worst enemy were out there he would give him a night's shelter. A young MacCrimmon in Ruairi's company saw Donald approaching and ran to warn his master. As good as his word, Ruairi invited Donald and his men in for food and shelter. One can well imagine that the Macleods present were not too pleased, and when one remarked that it was three weeks to the day since the Battle of Carinish, Ruairi had difficulty in restraining his men. The time came to retire for the night and a bed was offered to Donald in the house, and a kiln nearby for his men. Donald preferred to sleep with his men, but not for long, as in the very early morning the young MacCrimmon, who was a foster-son of Donald's, woke him with the warning that mischief was afoot. We need not suspect Ruairi Mor of treachery in this case, but some of his men no doubt did not relish the idea of the victor of Carinish going free. The weather had by now moderated sufficiently for the Sleat men to embark and resume their voyage, but the flames that could be seen leaping from their recent sleeping quarters proclaimed the treachery of some Macleod whose thirst for vengeance overtook all regard for the honour of his Chief.

The feud continued to smoulder and in due course broke out with renewed violence, this time on Macleod's lands in Skye. During Ruairi Mor's absence in Argyll, the Sleat men under Donald of Eriskay invaded the Macleod lands in Bracadale and Minginish, and carried off a great spoil. The raiders gathered the cattle for the night in a corrie, known afterwards as *Coire-na-Creiche,* and in late afternoon were surprised by a large force of Macleods under the command of Alasdair Og, brother of Ruairi Mor. A desperate battle ensued. Night had fallen before the outcome was decided, and Alasdair Og with many of his men were taken prisoner. The battle of Coolin is commemorated in a pibroch, still on record, called *An Cath Gailbheach* (The Desperate Battle).

The widespread devastation caused by these recurrent outbreaks resulted in much suffering amongst the people of both clans, and the Privy Council eventually had to intervene to put an end to conditions which they described as "schamefull and barbarous slaughteris and murthouris, besydis oppin heirschipis, depradationis, and uther insolenceis." The two Chiefs were ordered to surrender themselves, Donald Gorm to Huntly and Ruairi Mor to Argyll, with whom they were bound under penalties to remain until a final settlement was reached. Angus of Dunnyveg, Maclean of Coll and other friends used their good offices to resolve the long-standing quarrel and in 1601, after meetings at Eilean Donan and Glasgow, a reconciliation was ultimately effected, with both Chiefs undertaking to preserve the peace between them and submit their differences to the arbitration of the civil authority. The case of Mary Macleod, whose repudiation by Donald Gorm had sparked off the feud, was left open with the stipulation that she was free to bring such civil action against her former husband as she might be advised to do. There is no evidence that advantage was ever taken of this apparent recognition of her rights and the injured dignity of her family.

It is not long after these events that we find the figure of Hugh MacGilleasbuig Chleirich once again casting its sinister shadow over the House of Sleat. We have already referred to the sentence of outlawry passed upon this violent character in 1581, and to his treacherous action at Jura in 1585, which led to the feud between his Chief and Lachlan Maclean of Duart. His subsequent career was marked by similar excesses and a continuing hostility towards Donald Gorm Mor and his family. In 1586 he was summoned before the Privy Council for harassing fishermen of the North Isles and adjacent mainland. In 1589 he is granted a remission for crimes committed against the Macleans. In the same year we find him as bailie of Trotternish, an office for which his lawless nature must have rendered him utterly unsuitable, and his violent conduct during his short-lived tenure made him peculiarly obnoxious to tenantry and authority alike. His dangerous character was clearly recognised by the Government when, under the terms of the settlement of 1596, Hugh MacGilleasbuig "*and none other*" was to be held hostage for the retention of Castle Camus as a royal fortress.

How long Hugh was held hostage is not apparent, if indeed he ever submitted himself to such restriction. He was certainly at large in the year 1600, for in April of that year he was summoned with others for piracy on the high seas. The "others" mentioned may well have been members of the Clan Iain of Ardnamurchan who were being harried by the Campbells and a few years later took up piracy on an extensive scale in their attempt to restore the family fortunes. It is interesting that the summons gives Hugh's abode as Waternish in Macleod country, which may be taken as a significant comment on his relations at the time with his Chief. However, when Ruairi Mor and Donald Gorm Mor made their peace in 1601, Hugh seems to have come to an understanding with his Chief and was allowed not only to live in Trotternish, but even to build himself a fine fortified house, known as *Caisteal Uisdein,* at Cuidreach on the west side of the peninsula.

As the work on his house progressed, Hugh was forming a conspiracy for the murder of Donald Gorm Mor and other leading clansmen who might stand between himself and the chiefship. The setting for his evil design was to be a feast to celebrate the completion of his new residence. Among the invitations he issued for this purpose were two which were to spell his own doom—one to William Martin, a tenant in Trotternish, whose assistance he solicited in his scheme, and the other to his Chief, containing expressions of his loyalty and affection. By some mischance the two letters were interchanged—whether by the hands of a treacherous accomplice or not, it is impossible to say—with the result that the letter intended for Martin came into the possession of Donald Gorm. Steps were immediately taken to put a final stop to the machinations of a man whose evil genius had for so long disturbed the peace and serenity of Clan Uisdein and many of its neighbours. The Chief found a ready instrument of his vengeance in that same Donald of Eriskay who on previous occasions had rendered many notable services to his House. With a strong party of men Donald of Eriskay pursued Hugh to the Sand district of North Uist and, after some difficulty, succeeded in taking him prisoner. Hugh was then carried to the Castle of Duntulm and there his long-suffering Chief consigned him to a dungeon in which, so tradition has it, he was left to die in an agony of thirst.

Apart from a visit to Ireland in 1604, and a demonstration of support in favour of the embattled Angus of Dunnyveg in 1607, Donald Gorm Mor and his clan appear to have led a relatively peaceful existence for some years. In 1608, however, the first steps were taken by the government in the initiation of certain measures which were to have a significant bearing on the future history of the Isles. The preliminary negotiations were entrusted to Lord Ochiltree, who set up his court at Aros in Mull and summoned all the principal men of the Isles to meet him there. Among those who attended were Donald Gorm Mor, Angus of Dunnyveg, Hector Maclean of Duart, Donald of Clanranald and Ruairi Mor of Dunvegan, all accompanied by leading members of their clans. Here they were asked to agree to stringent conditions which were held inseparable from the newly devised royal policy for the final settlement of the Isles. Angus of Dunnyveg, an old man harassed by enemies at his doorstep, was the only Chief who was at first prepared to subscribe to Ochiltree's proposals and was accordingly allowed

Castle Camus, on the Sound of Sleat, residence of James the Castle, son of Donald Gruamach, 4th of Sleat. Last occupied about 1650

to go home. The others were invited to attend a dinner on board Ochiltree's ship *Moon*, in which they were afterwards made captive. The only exception was Ruairi Macleod, who suspected treachery and refused to attend. The rest were borne to Ayr and sent to various prisons.

Donald Gorm was confined in Blackness Castle, but he regained his freedom soon afterwards on his undertaking to assist Bishop Knox in his survey of the Isles and providing sureties for his return to Edinburgh on an appointed day. The Bishop completed his survey in the summer of 1609, and on 23rd August the Statutes of Iona were formulated. On the following day, Donald Gorm and eight other leading Islesmen signed a bond acknowledging the royal supremacy in Church and State, and securing their loyal adherence to the provisions of the Statutes. That bond, along with the Statutes, represented a significant landmark in the history of the Isles, leading in the course of a single generation to a startling change in relations between the Crown and its Island subjects and to the growth of that strong sense of devotion to the House of Stewart first strikingly manifested in the wars of Montrose.

On the same day on which they signed the bond in Iona Donald Gorm and Ruairi Mor of Dunvegan were induced to ratify the peace they had made in 1601, and renew their assurances of friendship. Ruairi Mor, however, was an able and ambitious man and, although no longer prepared to enforce his rights by the sword, was nevertheless quick to take advantage of any legal loophole in the prosecution of his claims. In 1613 he succeeded in having himself served heir to his uncle, William Macleod of Harris, for the lands of Sleat, North Uist and Trotternish, which comprised virtually the whole patrimony of the Sleat Chiefs. On 12th June 1614 he proceeded to take sasine at Duntulm. That he was able to do so is inexplicable, because sasine is a legal formality involving the physical presence of the applicant and the actual handling of the "earth and stone" of the land in question. Although the claim was based on James v's charter of 1542 (which, however, never became operative) it is a remarkable commentary on the changed conditions now prevailing that the Chief of Sleat refrained from taking hostile action. Instead, he went to Edinburgh, and on 21st July 1614 secured a new charter for the lands of Sleat, North Uist and Skirhough, with Castle Camus and some lands in North Uist being reserved to the King. Although Trotternish is not mentioned, it appears to have remained in his possession on the terms of the lease granted in 1596.

Ruairi Macleod pressed his claims again in the following year when he sought "justice" against Donald Gorm for dispossessing him of his lands, but his petition met with no response from the Council. This was the year in which Sir James Macdonald of Dunnyveg escaped in his attempt to restore the fallen fortunes of his family. Donald Gorm refused to become personally involved, although he allowed some members of his clan to join the cause. He had, however, received Sir James in Skye, and Ruairi Mor, perceiving the advantage to be gained by implicating Donald in the rebellion, lodged a complaint against him accusing him of harbouring Coll Ciotach, one of Sir James's right-hand men and a constant thorn in the Government's side. This fresh design by Ruairi to secure the lands he coveted produced no results, although Donald Gorm, like all the other chiefs suspected of being involved in the rebellion, was summoned to Edinburgh to subscribe to more stringent conditions of tenure for his estates. The regulations imposed on the chiefs at this meeting were designed to implement and reinforce the Statutes of Iona, and in substance were as follows:

1. The chiefs were to appear annually before the Privy Council, with three of their principal cadets;

2. Each chief was to maintain only six individuals in his household, apart from his immediate family;
3. The chief's principal residence was to be specified;
4. Each chief was to be allowed only one galley;
5. All children over the age of nine were to be taught to speak, read and write in English;
6. Consumption of wine was to be restricted to four tuns per chiefly household.

Donald Gorm was not present when these regulations were signed in July 1616. On his way south he had fallen ill at the Chanonry of Ross, but on his eventual arrival in Edinburgh towards the end of August he duly subscribed to the arrangements concluded in his absence, naming Duntulm in Trotternish as his principal place of residence. We may recall that Trotternish was included in the charter granted only two years earlier to Macleod of Dunvegan, and Donald's designation of Duntulm as his principal residence is just another example of the scornful regard in which charters were held even at this late period.

Donald Gorm Mor never completely recovered from his illness, and his eventful life came to a close only a few months after his last visit to Edinburgh. He had been thrice married. His first wife was Mary Macleod, whose repudiation had been the cause of so much conflict between the two clans. His second wife was Mary, daughter of Colin Mackenzie of Kintail, and his third Marjory, a daughter of the Chief of Mackintosh. Donald Gorm Mor had no children by these marriages, and the succession devolved upon his nephew, Donald Gorm Og, the son of his brother Archibald.

The new Chief appears to have been knighted soon after his accession, for when he attended Court in the summer of 1617 he is already styled Sir Donald Gorm of Sleat. His covetous neighbour in Dunvegan had not yet relinquished his aspirations to the Sleat lands, and his restless conduct gave Sir Donald early cause to complain to the Privy Council. In April 1617 Sir Donald sought the Council's protection against Macleod's designs upon his lands in Skye and Uist. His own right to these lands he based upon the charter of 1596, no doubt on the presumption of its greater validity relative to the more recent charter secured by the late Chief as a result of Macleod's machinations in 1614. In the following year steps were taken to resolve once and for all the differences that had so long disturbed relations between the two families. On 12th March 1618 the two Chiefs resigned into the King's hands the lands of Sleat and North Uist, of which they both held charters, and Sir Donald also resigned the Clanranald lands of Skirhough and Benbecula, of which he held the superiority. A new charter was thereupon given to Sir Donald for all the lands he possessed in Skye and Uist, with the exception of Trotternish. The legal position concerning Trotternish during the preceding period is not very clear, as there is no evidence that the five-year lease granted in 1596 was renewed. It was now settled that Macleod should have possession of Trotternish until a certain sum of money was paid by Sir Donald in discharge of all his claims, after which the district was to revert to the Sleat Chief and his heirs. The disposition of the lands of Skirhough and Benbecula, however, led to a serious dispute with Clanranald in 1622, when Sir Donald was obliged to assert his rights and enforce the payment of feu-duty due to him as superior. The dispute, which involved a considerable sum of money, was eventually resolved in Sir Donald's favour by arbitration.

In 1625 Sir Donald was created a Baronet of Nova Scotia. Although others had been created before him, he was by a special clause made second in precedence to Sir Robert Gordon, the first of the order. Sir Robert's line eventually died out, with the result that the Chief of Sleat is now the premier baronet.

There is little to record in the life of Sir Donald from this time up to the eve of the Civil War. Reference has been made in earlier chapters to his appointment in 1639 as one of His Majesty's Commissioners for the Highlands and Isles, an office he shared with his kinsman, the Earl of Antrim. In his letter accompanying the commission the King promised generous rewards for his loyalty and the risks he was prepared to undertake on his behalf. He was to receive the lands of Ardnamurchan and the islands of Rum, Muck and Canna, all at the expense of Argyll and Mackinnon, whose opposition to the royal policy and championship of the Covenant had marked them out for forfeiture. Sir Donald's subsequent activities in the service of his King attracted the attention of the Scottish Parliament. In 1640 he went to England with other Scottish nobles anxious to serve their King, and although the visit was made in obedience to the royal command, he was charged to appear before Parliament to answer for various offences, including that of deserting his country. Sir Donald appears to have been successful in justifying his conduct, for he was permitted to return to his estates. The last notice we have of this Chief is in 1642 when, in accordance with the conditions imposed in 1616, he made his annual appearance before the Council in Edinburgh. He died in 1643.

Sir Donald Gorm Og, 1st Baronet of Sleat, had a large family. He married Janet, daughter of Kenneth Mackenzie, Lord of Kintail, by whom he had: (1) James, who succeeded; (2) Donald, founder of the Castleton family; (3) Archibald, known as *An Ciaran Mabach,* poet and warrior; (4) Angus of Sarthill; (5) Alexander of Paiblesgarry in North Uist; (6) Margaret, who married Angus, Lord Macdonell & Aros, Chief of Glengarry; (7) Katherine, who married Kenneth Mackenzie, 6th of Gairloch, with issue; (8) Mary, who married Sir Ewen Cameron of Lochiel, with issue; and (9) Janet, who married Donald of Clanranald in 1655.

Sir Donald Gorm is the first of the Chiefs of Sleat who gave their whole-hearted devotion to the Stewart cause and continued faithful in the service of that tragic House for the next hundred years. He was succeeded by his son, Sir James, at a time when the Civil War in England was at its height and the Marquis of Montrose had already thrown in his lot with a King from whom he vainly sought the troops to win him back his Northern Kingdom. Unlike his father, one of the King's Lieutenants of the Isles, Sir James was disposed at first to hold aloof from the struggle that was convulsing the country. When Alasdair MacColla Ciotach (Colkitto) reached him in his quest for aid and reinforcements, Sir James refused the command that was offered to him, justifying his attitude on the ground of the smallness of the Irish contingent. The opening successes of Montrose's campaign restored his confidence, however, and in a later recruiting expedition he was persuaded by Alasdair to send out about 400 of his clansmen. These troops, led by Donald Macdonald of Castleton with Alexander of Skirinish as second in command, served throughout the rest of the campaign and were among the few who rallied to Montrose after his defeat at Philiphaugh. They returned to their homes only after Montrose had received the King's explicit instructions to disband his forces and seek safety on the Continent.

Sir James now had to make his peace with the Committee of Estates. The fact that he was not personally involved in the late campaign may serve to explain the lenient terms he secured for himself and his followers. The attitude of the Committee of Estates was also no doubt influenced by the altered political alignment and their desire to secure the services of all those who had been active in the royal cause they had now themselves conditionally espoused. The outcome was an assurance by General Middleton, given on the authority of Parliament, that Sir James and his friends would be "free of all censure, pain or punishment in thair lyffes or fortunes for anie deed done by thame or anie of thame in the late rebellion." Those friends and followers who played a conspicuous part in that rebellion are listed as Donald Macdonald of Castleton, Donald Macdonald of Arnishmore, Angus Macdonald of Sarthill, Neil Maclean of Boreray, Ranald Macdonald of Barrick, Somerled MacNicol of Dreemyl, Alexander Macdonald of Skirinish and Kenneth Macqueen of Oronsay. It is interesting to note amongst these names that of Maclean of Boreray, whose father's defection at Leac-Li in 1587 was largely responsible for the overthrow of Donald Gorm Mor in that battle.

In 1648, following the secret understanding reached between the King and the Scottish Engagers, the Duke of Hamilton launched his ill-fated expedition to rescue the King from his English captors. The army was joined by large numbers of the Islesmen, including a body of Sir James's men, and they shared in the rout it suffered at Preston. With the subsequent change in political attitudes and the assumption of power by Argyll at the head of his strong pro-Covenant party, Sir James once again came under suspicion and early in 1649 was cited to find caution for his good behaviour. No doubt the citation was considered doubly necessary as a result of the King's execution and the reaction it was expected to cause throughout the country. At any rate the summons was ignored by Sir James, and he was one of the first to respond to Charles II's call for aid to oppose Cromwell's advance. He had raised his regiment by the time Charles was crowned at Scone in January 1651, and it formed part of the army which in August of the same year was utterly routed at Worcester. Only a remnant returned of those who survived the battle or escaped the transportations that followed it.

Sir James now decided to face the realities of the situation created by the King's withdrawal to the Continent and the strong but tolerant grip of Cromwell's rule in Scotland. He remained quietly at home and refused to be drawn into the plots and conspiracies of Glengarry and Glencairn and others still eager to advance the Royal cause. To many of these Sir James's conduct appeared incomprehensible, arousing their suspicion, and provoking their enmity and threats of retaliation. He was in consequence obliged to seek assurances of protection from the authorities, and these he received in due course from the Governor of Inverness in the form of a document which required all and sundry "to forbear to prejudice any of the inhabitants of the Island of North Uist belonging to Sir James Macdonald of Sleat, either by taking away of their horses, sheep, cattle or goods, or offering violence." Sir James's conduct naturally commended itself to the Government, by whom he came to be regarded as "a man of great ability and judgment"; even the Earl of Argyll expressed his estimation of him as "considerable in the Highlands and Islands." The confidence placed in him by the Government was manifested by the extensive use made of his services for securing in the Highlands the peace and stability that prevailed elsewhere in the country under Cromwell's rule. Thus in September 1653 Sir James became surety in the sum of £6000 for the appearance of Ruairi Macleod of Dunvegan before the Commander-in-chief as and when directed. At the same time he bound himself in a similar sum for the good behaviour of the Chief of Clanranald. The problem of Glengarry was a delicate and more difficult one, and it was long after the fiasco of the Glencairn rebellion before it could be said of that dedicated Royalist that he had "deported himself peacablie and quytlie and given all due obediance to his Highnesse Oliver Lord Protector." Glengarry's bond was finally secured in 1656, but such was the Government's misgivings about his future conduct that Sir James was obliged to enlist Clanranald, Morar, Benbecula and Dunvegan as additional sureties.

The favour in which Sir James stood with the Commonwealth Government afforded him a measure of security which he now used to set his affairs in order, and where possible render assistance to his less fortunate neighbours. The Clanranald had become deeply involved in debt as a result of their participation in the Civil War and other causes and Sir James, to relieve their embarrassment, took a wadset of their lands of Moidart and Arisaig for the sum of £40,000 Scots. His own lands in Skye and Uist he entailed in favour of his eldest son Donald, failing whom and the other sons and brothers of Sir James, the nearest heir male of the family. In 1657, when this deed of entail was executed, the annual value of the estates was assessed at £6050 Scots which, although much lower than at the time of his father's death, was nevertheless substantial, and was supplemented by other rents and other services paid in kind. The large population of the estates, estimated at the time at 12,000, gave him a position of considerable prominence amongst the Highland Chiefs, whose power and influence was so often measured by the strength of their following.

The restoration of Charles II in 1660 must have caused Sir James not a little anxiety in view of his conduct during the Commonwealth, but his apprehensions were to prove largely unfounded. Although a heavy fine is stated to have been imposed at the instigation of Middleton, there is no evidence of such an imposition to be found either in the proceedings of Parliament or in the records of the family. On the contrary, as early as July 1661 Sir James received from the King a Charter of Confirmation of all his lands in Skye and Uist. Four years later he was entrusted with the commission to apprehend the perpetrators of the notorious Keppoch murders—a commission which was ruthlessly executed under the direction of his brother Archibald, *An Ciaran Mabach*, and the relentless avenger Iain Lom, the Keppoch bard. For his work on this occasion Sir James received the thanks of the Privy Council, and was appointed Sheriff of the Western Isles. From this time he appears to have been regarded by the Government as the head of all Clan Donald, and as such responsible for the behaviour of all its members.

In the new capacity assigned to him, Sir James was frequently called upon to reinforce the Government's measures for the maintenance of order and stability throughout the Highlands and Isles. In 1671 he was instructed by the Council to intervene in Lochaber, at that time convulsed by a feud between the Camerons and the Macdonalds of Keppoch, and in due course restored order in that district, presenting the chief trouble-makers before the Council. Two years later he was charged to apprehend Alasdair MacIain of Glencoe, who had escaped from Argyll's custody and was accused with others of having committed murder and many outrages in the Campbell territory. In 1676 his services were again required in Lochaber in consequence of a devastating raid carried out by the Macdonalds and Camerons in a united descent upon the Campbell lands in Perthshire. Sir James does not appear to have taken the expected action on this occasion, and the reason may very well be attributed to the difficulties and harassments that were now beginning to beset him and his family at home.

Relations between Sir James and his eldest son and heir had become severely strained, and much dissension was caused by the vast debts with which the estates were burdened. The situation was so critical that it was generally feared the estates might have to be sold to satisfy the numerous creditors. The wadsetters united themselves to avert the danger, and on 1st February 1678 they signed a document in which they declared their resolve "before God Almightie with all singleness of heart and without any mentall reservation or equivocation qt. somever" to preserve the estates. The better to accomplish this, they proposed to exclude Sir James and his heir from the administration of the estates until all the debts were paid, meanwhile making each of them a suitable allowance. The wadsetters were almost all cadets of the family who had a vital interest in preserving their patrimony, and their resolute action was responsible for saving their heritage from passing into the hands of strangers.

Some time before his death Sir James matriculated his arms. These were entered in the *Register of All Arms and Bearings in Scotland* which was begun as a permanent official record in 1672. They are recorded as follows:

> First, argent, a lion rampant, gules armed or: second, azure, a hand proper holding a cross patée of Calvary, sable: third, vert, a ship ermine, her oars in saltire sable in water proper: fourth, parted per fess wavy vert and argent, a salmon naiant: crest, a hand holding a dagger proper: supporters, two leopards proper: motto, "My Hope is Constant in Thee."

The motto, replacing the traditional "Per Mare Per Terras," is always connected with the arms of Clanranald. The arms here matriculated differ in certain important respects from those later adopted by the family.

Sir James died in December 1678. He married first Margaret, only daughter of Sir John Mackenzie of Tarbat, by whom he had: (1) Donald, who succeeded; (2) Hugh of Glenmore, from whom the Glenmore and Mugstad families; (3) John of Bernisdale and Scalpay; (4) Roderick, a lawyer in Edinburgh; (5) James, of Aird in Sleat; (6) Alexander; (7) Archibald; (8) Angus; (9) Catherine, who in 1666 married Sir Norman Macleod of Bernera, with issue; (10) Florence, who married, first, Sir Norman Macleod of Dunvegan, and second, John MacNaughton of that Ilk. He married, as his second wife, in 1661, Mary, daughter of John Macleod of Dunvegan, by whom he had (11) John, of Balconie in East Ross. In addition he had one natural son, Ranald, from whom the Baleshare family descended.

Sir Donald, 3rd Baronet, succeeded his father at a difficult time. The financial state of the lands had, as we have seen, led to some friction with his father. He first comes to our notice as Chief in connection with a commission he granted to the Mackinnons of Strath to "persew, apprehend and incarcerat all thives, robberis, and sorners within the bounds of the Parish of Strath." In 1685, the abortive rebellion of the Earl of Argyll on behalf of the Duke of Monmouth's rising in England roused fears of serious trouble in the Highlands, and the services of the loyal clans were enlisted to support the newly enthroned James. Sir Donald duly raised his clan and marched to the Great Glen at Cille Chumein (later called Fort Augustus), arriving there on the 9th of June. He had not been there long before the rebellion collapsed, Argyll was taken prisoner and later executed. The Sleat men then returned home without striking a blow, and there they remained until the crisis precipitated by James's rashly bigoted policies called for another resort to arms. James's sympathisers were to be found mainly in the Highlands where the old religion still held sway and where, even amongst the Protestant clans, there was a firm belief in the hereditary monarchy as represented by the Stewarts. And, as a spur to their loyalty, there was the prospect of striking a blow at their ancient enemies the Campbells, ranged against them on the other side.

The campaign which now opened has already been recounted in an earlier chapter, and it remains for us here only to record the part played in events by the Chief of Sleat and his followers. Sir Donald was among the first to raise

Duntulm Castle, from an old
painting

Duntulm Castle as it is today.
Built on the site of an earlier
fort, it was reinforced by the
Chief of Sleat about 1630 to
secure his hold on Trotternish
against Macleod of Dunvegan.
It was vacated about 1720

his Clan and repair to Lochaber to meet King James's General, John Graham of Claverhouse, who had been made Viscount Dundee just before his departure for the North. Dundee had been in London with his troopers when William landed at Torbay, and had tried his best to induce the King to resist William's advance on London. But James had lost heart, and Dundee was forced to ride north with his faithful squadron, confront the newly appointed Convention in Edinburgh, and withdraw before their hostility to raise his standard in the Highlands. He found the clans ready to rise. The Keppoch Macdonalds were already under arms, but for quite another purpose—that of harrying the Clan Chattan and the town of Inverness. They provided the nucleus around which Dundee, like the great Montrose before him, assembled an army united in a common purpose by the loyalty his leadership inspired.

At Killiecrankie the Sleat men were on the extreme left of the army and faced that wing of Mackay's troops which alone put up any sort of a fight. They were led by young Donald, son of the Chief, and present with him was Donald of Castleton, now an old man and a grandfather, as his aide-de-camp. The losses were heavy. Mackay's troops discharged their muskets with great effect, especially on the officers at the head of their men. Before they could fix their bayonets, which at that time were screwed into the muzzle of the musket, the Highlanders were upon them, and the issue was not long in doubt. The subsequent events are a matter of history.

For the Sleat men it was a dearly bought victory, and no fewer than five of Sir Donald's principal cadets were left behind on the field. Young Donald and his men remained with the Royal army until it was obvious that Cannon and Buchan, who had taken the command, were quite incapable of holding a Highland army together. The debacle at Cromdale put an end to the rising and the clans returned home. Although the chiefs answered Mackay's peaceful overtures by declarations of unswerving allegiance to their exiled King, they remained disunited and unwilling to accept one of their own number in supreme command. The death of Dundee, whose personality and leadership alone was capable of moulding them into an effective fighting force, left them weakened by their own differences and ruined all hopes of an immediate revival of the Stewart cause.

In June 1690 a sentence of forfeiture was passed against young Donald for his active part in the rebellion. Both he and his father, however, continued staunch in their loyalty to King James, with whom they maintained a constant correspondence until the last flicker of hope had faded with the dispersal of the army and Cannon's flight to safety in the protection of Sir Donald. Although young Donald now appeared willing to come to terms, the old Chief remained obdurately impervious to the representations and entreaties of friends and intermediaries. The Government was therefore compelled to take firm measures to secure his submission, and two frigates were despatched to Skye under the command of Captains Pottinger and Douglas, with orders to reduce Sir Donald by force if other persuasion failed. The old Chief refused to be daunted, and when the frigates opened fire on his house at Armadale he rallied his men and attacked the landing party with such vigour that it was divided in two. One party fled north to the unoccupied Castle Camus, where they were later overcome and killed; the other fled south to Tormore where they were overtaken and slain at the mound of Dun Flo.

Sir Donald's success in this confrontation disposed him to discuss terms with the Government, and he sent a message to Lord Tarbat offering to submit on condition that he received a peerage and a pension, and that his son was relieved of the sentence of forfeiture. Lord Tarbat's reply, on behalf of the Government, was to point out that the new regime was now so securely established that Donald was in no position to dictate terms, and he advised him to surrender unconditionally and follow the example of other leading clansmen who had already given in their submission. In face of all such counsel and the entreaties of his friends Sir Donald appears to have remained for some time stubbornly persistent in his opposition, and although he eventually made his peace with the Government we have no record of the manner in which it was accomplished. He did not attend the meeting in June 1690 at Achallader where Breadalbane tried to bribe the chiefs into a settlement, nor is there a record of his response to a subsequent invitation from the Earl to appear before him. That invitation may have been for the purpose of reminding him of the oath of allegiance which was mandatory before the first day of January 1692. It is unlikely that Sir Donald would have submitted before he had been released from his allegiance by King James, but notwithstanding the lateness of James's authorisation it is clear that he must have been able to make arrangements that satisfied the Government in time to avert the sort of retribution that was to be visited upon his kinsmen of Glencoe.

The campaign and its aftermath had reduced Sir Donald's affairs to a serious condition, and his remaining years were spent in trying to remove some of the burdens encumbering his estates. As early as the autumn of 1692 he was granted remission of a vexatious hearth tax which had been imposed upon him, and he continued to take advantage of the good relationship he had thus early succeeded in establishing with the Government. His correspondence with Colonel Hill, the Governor of Fort William, provides further evidence of his resolution to accept the established order and pursue a peaceful mode of life. The one circumstance that clouded his last years arose from the conduct of his kinsmen of Glengarry whose tenants in Knoydart persistently harassed and molested Sir Donald's possessions in Sleat. Sir Donald was forced to complain to the Supreme Court and better relations were restored in 1694 when he was granted judgment against Alexander, Younger of Glengarry, and his offending clansmen who were bound to find sufficient caution to keep "harmless and skaithless" their neighbours across the Sound.

Sir Donald died at Armadale on 5th February 1695. He had married, on 24th July 1662, Lady Mary Douglas, second daughter of Robert, 8th Earl of Morton, by whom he had: (1) Donald, who succeeded; (2) James of Oronsay, who succeeded his brother; (3) William, from whom the family of Aird & Vallay; (4) Isabel, who married Alan Macdonald of Morar; (6) Barbara, who married Coll Macdonald of Keppoch, 16th Chief; and (7) Angus, a natural son, of whom we know nothing.

Sir Donald, 4th Baronet, succeeded to an estate burdened with debts incurred during the Killiecrankie campaign, and himself still under the cloud of forfeiture. He remained at heart a staunch supporter of the exiled House of Stewart, and perhaps to divert suspicions that he might be secretly fomenting rebellion in his territory, he lived mainly in Glasgow, "holding no correspondence with his people in the Isles," as he was afterwards to affirm in his defence. There is reason to believe, nevertheless, that he was in touch with the Jacobite cause. In 1714 he bought a small estate at Frankfield in the parish of Culross, formerly called Blair. He had not been there long when he was made prisoner by the Government on suspicion of his Jacobite leanings, although he had signed the loyal address to King George when he ascended the throne. Most of the heads of families in the Highlands had signed this document, but mainly to disarm suspicion, while in reality they still retained their loyalty to King James. This is made abundantly clear in Sir Donald's letter from Stewart of Ardsheal and Lochiel, in which they reveal the secret and united resolve of the Chiefs to restore the House of Stewart. Sir Donald's confinement was of short duration, and he was released in the autumn of 1714 through the good offices of James, 1st Duke of Montrose, who had succeeded Mar as Secretary of State.

With the accession of George I the Jacobites had good reason to believe that the tide was running in their favour. Bitter disappointment with the Union, and the recent repressive measures against those who had opposed it or were suspected of sympathy with the Stewart cause, led to a strong and mounting resentment against the Government. The first step was taken by the Earl of Mar who, frustrated in his aspirations at the Hanoverian succession, set out from London in August 1715 and a month later raised the standard of the Stewarts at Braemar. By a previously concerted arrangement, Sir Donald had proceeded to Skye to raise his clan. With a regiment of about 800 men, the largest ever put in the field by Sleat, he joined the Earl of Seaforth at Brahan and with their combined forces proceeded to disperse the hostile clans of the northern counties. Following these successes, Sir Donald marched south and joined Mar at Perth towards the end of October. Here he fell ill and had to be taken home, leaving his brothers James and William to lead the clan to battle at Sheriffmuir. On the right wing of Mar's army with the rest of Clan Donald, they acquitted themselves with honour, breaking in their charge the regular infantry who faced them and putting to rout three squadrons of cavalry. Argyll's left wing was thrown back in disorder and he was saved from utter defeat only by his flanking attack on Mar's left. The issue of the battle may have been inconclusive, but for the campaign it was decisive: Mar's ineptitude and subsequent stubborn inaction discouraged the Highland troops and they gradually melted into the hills.

The measures that followed the end of the Rising were mild compared with those that marked the final act in the drama thirty years later. The wide sympathy for the political motives of the rebellion persuaded the Government to adopt a temperate policy in the restoration of order, and an Act of Parliament was passed offering moderate terms to all those who surrendered before the last day of June, 1716. Government troops were sent to Skye and other areas where the spirit of rebellion remained alive. The Chief of Sleat, still recovering from the illness which struck him on the eve of Sheriffmuir, retired to North Uist, but on 20th April 1716 he wrote to General Cadogan, Governor of Inverlochy, informing him of his readiness to comply with the Act but regretting his inability to appear personally before him on account of his continuing illness. Sir Donald's excuse was not accepted, however, and having failed to appear by the appointed date he was duly adjudged guilty of high treason.

Forfeiture of the estates followed as a matter of course, and the Commissioner of Forfeited Estates appointed William Macleod of Hammir as factor. Macleod's administration did nothing to relieve the extreme conditions of poverty that existed at the time throughout Skye and North Uist. From one of his reports we learn that in North Uist a plague had decimated the livestock. No fewer than 745 cows, 573 horses and 820 sheep had been lost and, to add to their misfortunes, the sea was making extensive encroachments on the land, destroying habitations and endangering lives. Similar conditions prevailed in Skye where tenants in Trotternish reported the enormous loss of 485 horses, 1027 cows and 4556 sheep. The magnitude of these losses, in conjunction with the hardships suffered in consequence of the recent campaign, created a situation of extreme misery for the population and of grave concern for those responsible for their welfare.

Sir Donald, ailing and worn out by the general misfortunes, died in March 1718. By his marriage with Mary, daughter of Donald of Castleton, he had: (1) Donald, his successor and 5th Baronet; (2) Margaret, who married Captain

John Macqueen of the Royal Regiment; (3) Mary, who married John Martin of Flodigarry, with issue; (4) Isabella, who married Dr Alexander Munro, Professor of Anatomy in Edinburgh; (5) Janet, who married Norman, 22nd Chief of the Macleods of Dunvegan.

Sir Donald, 5th Baronet, did not long survive his father, whose ill-health he inherited along with forfeited estates in a critical state of impoverishment. The young Chief had been educated at the University of Glasgow, and during his short reign he employed his considerable abilities in trying to restore his estates and improving the condition of his people. Soon after his accession he petitioned the Court of Session to have his sentence of forfeiture rescinded on the ground that his father had in fact surrendered to General Cadogan even although he had failed to appear personally before him. The Court of Session gave its decision in Sir Donald's favour, but it was reversed on appeal by the Commissioners to the House of Lords. In the meantime Sir Donald had taken certain steps to relieve the condition of his tenants, and shortly before his death he was able to announce to his agent in Edinburgh that he had remitted a large proportion of the money rents of his lands in Sleat and Trotternish "because of the poverty the loss of their cattall has reduced the people to." He died before the judgment of the House of Lords was reached, but there is no doubt that, had he lived, Sir Donald would have renewed the legal struggle to restore his inheritance and continued his practical concern for the welfare of his clansmen.

Sir Donald died unmarried in the early months of 1720. He was succeeded by his uncle, Sir James Macdonald of Oronsay, 6th Baronet, who reigned but for a few short months. Sir James had fought at Killiecrankie, and with his brother William had taken over command of the Sleat contingent at Sheriffmuir where, as we have seen, they broke Argyll's left wing and put it to flight. He gave in his submission after that rebellion and remained loyal during the abortive Rising of 1719, when Seaforth and Lochiel with Spanish aid made their uncoordinated, forlorn gesture in the Stewart cause. The humiliating defeat in Glenshiel confirmed the wisdom of his decision to stand aloof from an adventure which in its execution had such little promise of success.

Sir James died in December 1720. He was twice married. By his first wife Janet, daughter of Alexander Macleod of Greshornish, he had: (1) Alexander, his successor; (2) Margaret, who married Robert Douglas of Glenbervie; (3) Isabel, who died young; (4) Janet, who married Sir Alexander Mackenzie of Coul. By his second wife Margaret, daughter of John Macdonald of Castleton, he had (5) John, whose only appearance on record is on 19th September 1723 when he is named as heir male to his father in the general provision made for the family.

Sir Alexander, 7th Baronet, was still a minor on his accession. His father had made provision for such a contingency by the appointment of tutors and curators to protect the interests of the young Chief and guide him through the troubled waters which threatened to engulf his inheritance. The principal curator was William Macdonald of Aird and Vallay, also known and recognised as the Tutor. He was a man of great courage and ability, and had fought alongside his Chief at Killiecrankie and Sheriffmuir. The others were Alexander of Gleneltin, Donald of Sarthill, and the young Chief's maternal kinsmen, Donald Macleod of Talisker and Norman Macleod of Greshornish. All these men discharged their duties with great care and good judgment, providing Alexander with a sound education, first at school in Leith and for a period of three years at the University of St Andrews, where his Highland establishment, complete with family piper and a lavish hospitality, made such a deep impression on the society in which he moved that he was given the freedom of the town in 1727.

The curators applied themselves at once to the problems surrounding the young Chief's inheritance. A petition presented to Parliament on behalf of the late Sir James's children secured the passage of an Act authorising the grant of £10,000 out of the estate of Sir Donald. Provision was made at the same time for Sir Donald's widow and children. When the estates were put up for sale by the Commissioners of Forfeited Estates, the wadsetters of the family, who were mostly cadets and included three of the curators, combined to safeguard their own interests as well as those of their Chief, and offered to become surety for the total purchase price. The transaction was entrusted to Kenneth Mackenzie, Advocate, in Edinburgh, and when the estates came up for sale in October 1723, they were purchased by him for the sum of £21,000. After disbursement of the sums awarded to the families of Sir Donald and Sir James and certain other charges, very little remained of the purchase price. In 1726, with the consent of the curators, Sir Alexander bought back the whole estate from Mackenzie, and in February of the following year he received a Crown Charter for the lands of Sleat, Trotternish and North Uist, the whole being erected into the Barony of Macdonald.

Sir Alexander came of age with the determination to improve the family inheritance. The wadsetters, who had guaranteed the purchase money for the estates, were disposed to take advantage of the relationship in which they were thus placed and tended to be dilatory in paying their dues to the Chief while making oppressive demands upon their tenants. Sir Alexander realised that in the interests of both himself and the sub-tenants, a firm stand had to be taken with the wadsetters, and he urgently applied himself to the task of redeeming his obligations to them, thereby relieving the estate of a heavy burden and the sub-tenants of a galling yoke. His policy of restoring order to his estates, however, was marred by one disreputable incident in which he was held at the time to have been deeply implicated. This was the affair of *Soitheach nan Daoine* (Vessel of the Men), which came to light in November 1739 when the magistrates of Donaghadee in Northern Ireland reported the escape of nearly 100 criminals from the ship *William,* which had been storm-driven to that port. When brought before the court they were found to include women and children, all in a sorry state of destitution. They claimed that they had been kidnapped in Skye and some of the adjacent islands, and were being shipped to slavery in the American colonies. The official inquiry which immediately followed revealed the villain of the piece to be Norman Macleod of Unish, a member of the Bernera family, who accompanied the prisoners on board. Witnesses testified that the *William* had called at several places in Skye and Harris, and that Macleod and his party had seized and forced on board many men and women, including children, who were to be sold as slaves in North America. As a result of the inquiry, the unfortunate victims were set free and most of them appear to have remained in Ireland where, it is recorded, they found employment "with the country people."

The affair seems to have been the result of excessive zeal on the part of Macleod in carrying out his remit. The estates of both Sir Alexander and Macleod of Dunvegan had for many years suffered from the depredations of thieves and beggars, and the plan was concerted of getting rid of the pests by shipping them across the Atlantic. Although the Statutes of Iona specifically allowed the execution of strong measures against beggars and sorners, it is clear that Macleod exceeded his mandate and selected his victims with little discrimination. The scandal it provoked was not lessened by the secrecy in which the affair had been conducted, and despite strenuous denials by both the Chief and his lady, it was generally believed for a long time that Sir Alexander had given open approval to the whole discreditable proceeding.

At the same time Sir Alexander was involved in another strange affair which had begun several years earlier. This was the abduction of Lady Grange, the wife of James Erskine, best known by his judicial title of Lord Grange, and younger brother of the Earl of Mar of '15 fame. Lady Grange was a daughter of Chiesly of Dalry whose violent and unstable temperament she appears to have inherited. Her conduct eventually led to a separation, but she continued to persecute her husband and finally threatened to expose him for certain treasonable practices of which she alleged she had evidence. Already suspected of Jacobite sympathies, Lord Grange was aware that any information laid against him, however groundless, was unlikely to improve his delicate relations with the Government, and might also gravely compromise certain of the Highland chieftains more actively engaged in the cause. With some of these accordingly he arranged his wife's abduction, and she was whisked away to the Island of Heiskir in North Uist, part of Sir Alexander's estate. After two years on that island, her custody was transferred to the Chief of Macleod who confined her on his island of St Kilda until proceedings for her release were instituted in 1741. That Sir Alexander was implicated in the affair is beyond doubt. Not only was his island of Heiskir used as her prison, but her custodian on that island made it plain to Lady Grange that he would not be holding her, or any other, against their will "except Sir Alexander Macdonald were in the affair." That Sir Alexander was fully aware of the situation is evident from the fact that the same custodian made frequent approaches to him concerning certain privileges desired by Lady Grange to relieve the rigours of her confinement. It is also clear, however, that he was a most reluctant participant in the affair, for during one of these approaches he is said to have expressed his regret at having been concerned in it and wished he were well out of it. There is little doubt that the involvement of Sir Alexander and other prominent men in the prolonged imprisonment of Lady Grange could only have been inspired by a genuine and over-riding concern for the protection of those supporters of the Stewart cause whose safety might well be endangered by her revelations.

Sir Alexander's reluctant and wary complicity in the affair foreshadowed the attitude he was to assume during the last great rising of the clans. His conduct in connection with that rebellion was severely criticised and condemned even by some of his own clansmen, but there are several factors which help to explain and perhaps justify the essentially realistic attitude he chose to adopt. Less than twenty years earlier his estates had been restored to him by a benevolent Government whose peaceful rule had enabled him to effect much-needed improvements on his estates and the condition of his tenantry. He was not prepared to stake his entire interests upon an adventure that was generally regarded as ill-timed and so lacking in material support as to make the possibilty of success extremely doubtful. Other chiefs were influenced by similar considerations and threw in their active lot with the Prince only after being exposed to the charm of his personality. Unlike Lochiel, Sir Alexander never had personal contact with the Prince and was thus better able to preserve the discreet, practical detachment which characterised his conduct throughout the campaign. On 23rd July 1745 the Prince landed from the *La Doutelle* on the isle of Eriskay and was received by Donald Macdonald, a cadet of Clanranald. Here he was met by Alexander of Boisdale, uncle of the young Clanranald who figured so prominently in the Rising later. The Prince asked Boisdale to go to Sir Alexander and Macleod of Macleod to solicit their help in the adventure. Boisdale, who knew the two Skye chiefs and their sympathies for the Stewart cause, knew also that, like himself, neither would be willing to risk his lands and clansfolk's welfare by supporting a cause they considered already lost for lack of support from the Continent. In spite of the Prince's entreaties, Boisdale refused to compromise himself, but agreed to convey the message to Sir Alexander and Macleod. It produced no results. A similar fate attended the efforts of young Clanranald and Alan of Kinlochmoidart who were sent on a similar mission after the Prince's Standard was raised at Glenfinnan. Sir Alexander and Macleod continued loyal to the Government, at least outwardly, but they were not prepared to take active steps in its support. When told to raise their men and report to Inverness, they replied that, thanks to the disarming act after the '15, their men were without any arms. Sir Alexander's clansmen were almost unanimously in favour of the Prince, and showed their disinclination to join any company designed to oppose him. In one of the many letters Sir Alexander wrote to the Lord President, Duncan Forbes of Culloden, he said "The men are as devoted to the young gentleman [the Prince] as their wives and daughters are!" And again Hugh of Baleshare reports to Bishop Forbes that, when Sir Alexander reviewed his clan at Portree, "the people denied rising in arms if Sir Alexander did not go and join the Prince; upon which the people all dispersed. I told Sir Alexander I was vexed at the disobedience shown by the people to their Chief. He told me to keep silence. It was all by his private orders, as it did not lay in his way to do him [the Prince] good, he had no intention to do him hurt."

On another occasion Sir Alexander met his factor, Kingsburgh, Macleod of Raasay and Captain Malcolm Macleod of Raasay at the Inn at Sconser after news had come of the victory of Prestonpans. They were suitably impressed, and Sir Alexander appeared to be in favour of raising his clan and joining the Prince. Plans were made, and they retired for the night. In the morning a messenger arrived from Forbes, the Lord President, and another from Macleod of Macleod, who was in Inverness at the time. These letters entirely changed the attitude of the Sleat Chief. The report mentions that the night before "they were a merry party," but the cold light of day and Duncan Forbes's wise counsel were sufficient to restore him to his former attitude of benevolent neutrality to the Prince's cause.

Sir Alexander's conduct throughout the period appears to have been much influenced by Duncan Forbes of Culloden, a staunch supporter of the established order, but possessing a deep understanding of the aspirations of the Highland clans and unflagging in his efforts to deflect them from a cause of which he saw the tragic, inevitable outcome. It has been said of him that his services in this respect were worth about 4000 Highland warriors to the Government. Only seven years before the Rebellion he had suggested that commissions should be granted to the Chiefs for the raising of Highland regiments, and had his advice been acted upon it is unlikely that there would have been a 'Forty-Five, and the restless energies of the clans would have been directed much earlier to the task of carving out the Empire that owed so much to their valour in later years. After Culloden, Forbes continued unremitting in his efforts to mitigate the severity of the repressive measures initiated by Cumberland, but his constant pleas for moderation went ignored by a Government bent on exacting an exemplary vengeance from a people whose very existence had come to be regarded as a perpetual threat to established order.

Sir Alexander, who provided refuge for Duncan Forbes on the eve of Culloden, was no less dedicated in his efforts to save the rebel clans from the fury of the Government, and frequently remonstrated with Cumberland for the outrages committed by his forces. His first meeting with Cumberland is noteworthy for an exchange of greetings which revealed the arrogance of the one and proud spirit of the other. "So, here comes the great rebel of the Isles! " remarked Cumberland; to which Sir Alexander boldly replied, "If, Sir, I had been a rebel, you would never have crossed the Spey." It was while on one of his missions to Cumberland that Sir Alexander died of pleurisy at Glenelg, on 23rd November 1746.

Both Sir Alexander and his wife the Lady Margaret, whose sympathies were entirely with the Jacobite cause, did all in their power to protect the Prince while he was a fugitive within their jurisdiction, and encouraged their clansmen to make possible his escape. The confidence reposed in their concern for the Prince's safety, and in the loyalty of leading members of the family, is clearly revealed in the letter in which Hugh Macdonald of Baleshare, a cadet of Sleat, described to Bishop Forbes the direction he had given to the Prince's companions on the eve of their departure from the Long Island to Skye:

> My advice was this: that as he [the Prince] lay in view of the chanell, if the chanell was clear of ships he should go of the afternoon to give him a long night, to keep close by the land of Skye, that he might have the opportunity of running ashor in case of wors, and desired him he should go to Kulin Hills in Skye, where he could get to the Laird of M'Kinnon, who would see him safely landed on the mainland . . . but advised him if he should not get to M'Kinnon, that he should without loss of time go into Sir James McDonald's country of Slet and apply to Donald M'Donald of Kingsborrow, to Archibald of Tarsquiveg and Rory M'Donald of Camiscross, all cadets of Sir James M'Donald's family. Any of the above I am confident would see him safe to the mainland.

Hugh's confidence was amply justified by the conduct of his kinsmen in Skye when Flora Macdonald and Neil MacEachan brought the Prince safely to their shore. Lady Margaret lent her active support to the measures taken to ensure the safe passage of the Prince to the mainland, providing him with financial assistance and other supplies for his material needs; and after his escape to France, she was unfailing in her efforts on behalf of those arrested for their part in his flight. There is little doubt that her influence with such men as Duncan Forbes of Culloden was responsible to some extent for the relatively lenient punishments visited upon those most nearly concerned with the Prince in his wanderings.

Lady Margaret was Sir Alexander's second wife. On 5th April 1733 he had married Anne, daughter of David Erskine of Dun, one of the Senators of the College of Justice, and widow of James, Lord Ogilvie. By her he had a son Donald, who died young. Lady Anne did not long survive the birth of her son, and on 24th April 1739 Sir Alexander married Lady Margaret Montgomery, daughter of Alexander, 9th Earl of Eglinton, by his third wife, Susanna Kennedy, daughter of Sir Archibald Kennedy of Culzean. There were three sons of the marriage: (1) James, who succeeded; (2) Alexander, who succeeded James; and (3) Archibald, who became Lord Chief Baron of the Exchequer, of whom the family of East Sheen.

Sir Alexander died long before the full consequences of the failure of the rebellion began to make themselves felt. Although his common sense had told him that the attempt was futile and would bring disaster to all, he could not have foreseen the complete break-down of the clan system that inexorably followed. The abolition of heritable jurisdictions deprived the chiefs of their ancient authority, and the emotional bond that of old existed between chief and clansman was gradually displaced by the purely commercial relationship of landlord and tenant.

The Arms of
ALEXANDER GODFREY MACDONALD OF MACDONALD, LORD MACDONALD

Quarterly, 1st, Argent a lion rampant Gules, armed and langued Azure; 2nd; Or, a hand in armour
fessways holding a cross-crosslet fitchée Gules; 3rd, Or, a lymphad sails furled and oars in action Sable,
flagged Gules; 4th, Vert, a salmon naiant in fess proper, over all on an escutcheon en surtout, Or,
an eagle displayed Gules surmounted of a lymphad sails furled, oars in action Sable (as Chief of the
Name and Arms of Macdonald). Above the shield is placed His Lordship's coronet, thereon an Helmet
befitting his degree with a Mantling Gules doubled Ermine, and on a crest coronet Or is set for Crest
a hand in armour fessways couped at the elbow proper holding a cross-crosslet fitchée Gules, and
in an Escrol over the same this Motto PER·MARE·PER·TERRAS, and on a Compartment of
rocks and heather proper issuant from the waves undy along with this Motto FRAOCH·EILEAN,
are set for Supporters two leopards proper.

Lyon Register (Volume 36, Folio 44).

23

The Chiefship

THE CHIEFSHIP of a Highland clan is a Celtic, not a feudal dignity, and from the beginning has been based on the laws and customs of the community which formed the Clan. The land belonged originally to the clan, and the advance of feudalism never deprived them of their interest in the soil nor of their right to choose their own chief. Although the chief in course of time came to hold by feudal right, his superiority over the clan lands was derived from his position as head of the clan, and not from any authority conferred upon him by his feudal tenure. No chief could be accepted as head without the tacit consent of the clan, and although the succession normally followed the feudal principle of primogeniture there were many occasions when the clan asserted their ancient rights under the old Celtic law of Tanistry and used their collective will to elect the leader of their choice or depose one who had forfeited their confidence.

It is important to distinguish between a Chief and a Chieftain. A Chief is the head of the whole Name: a Chieftain is the head of an established branch: but in view of the importance and special history of Clan Donald, whose younger sons of the Lord of the Isles were of equal status with the other great chiefs of clans who adhered to and ably supported the Lordship, the major branch chieftains came to be ranked as chiefs, while the Lord of the Isles was from 1386 regarded as the High Chief of the whole Name.

After the death of Donald Dubh, last of the main line, in 1545, his nearest heir male was Donald Gormson of Sleat, whose line claimed the rightful succession to both the Lordship of the Isles and the High Chiefship of Clan Donald.

Meanwhile the Crown had already annexed the Lordship and invested the title, Lord of the Isles, in the eldest son of the Monarch. The policy for the next 100 years was to divide and rule, and not to recognise any High Chief of Clan Donald until 1689, when the Crown duly recognised Donald Gorm's successor as "Laird of Macdonald," *i.e.* Chief of the whole Name, and his lands as the "Barony of Macdonald."

During the 350 years of the Lordship Macdonald ruled, father to son, by primogeniture, with only two interruptions. These were (*a*) when Alexander (Alasdair Og) was displaced in favour of his younger brother Angus Og, in 1308, and (*b*) when Donald of Harlaw received the sceptre from his elder half-brother Ranald, in 1386. Both Angus Og and Donald were confirmed by the consent of the Clan and the other vassals of the Isles. In the second case some of the men of the Isles had doubts, but in time all came to the conclusion that it was a wise choice, as is evidenced by the massive response to Donald's summons of his forces to Ardtornish for the Harlaw campaign.

The probable reasons for Ranald's surrender of his rights to his brother have been more fully discussed in an earlier chapter. Moreover, as far back as 1371 Good John had made provision for Ranald when he gave him a charter, confirmed by the King in the following year, of all the lands acquired by his marriage with Amie MacRuairi, Ranald's mother. These lands were to be held from the Lord of the Isles as his superior, which suggests that the transaction was a political act designed to exclude Ranald from the succession and divert it to the issue of Good John's marriage with the Princess Margaret, the King's daughter.

Donald of Harlaw's proclamation as "Macdonald and Donald of Isla," and his subsequent acceptance as such by the men of the Isles, confirmed him in the position of patriarchal head of the Clan. His successors in the office were accepted without question by all branches of Clan Donald down to 1493, when the feudal honour was forfeited. But even after that event, the clan continued to recognise Donald Dubh, the surviving representative of the family, as "Macdonald" and Chief of the Name as well as Lord of the Isles, and during his long imprisonment no fewer than three risings were attempted in his favour. These were led by Alexander of Lochalsh, Donald Gallda and Donald Gormson, and they were all aimed at the restoration of the Lordship which they regarded as the inseparable right of the Chief of Clan Donald. In the two risings led by Donald Dubh himself, he was accepted as undoubted Chief of Clan Donald and received the enthusiastic support of his clansmen and other vassals of the Lordship in his attempt to recover his lost inheritance.

With the death of Donald Dubh in 1545, the direct line of the family of the Isles came to an end, and the inheritance of the Chiefship became a subject of some importance and, in later years, of considerable controversy. In discussing the problem, it must be borne in mind that "descent descends," and one goes no farther back in the family tree of the deceased than is necessary to find an heir. In this case we need only go back to the family of Alexander, 9th Lord of the Isles and Earl of Ross who died in 1449. Alexander had three sons: John, last Lord, Celestine of Lochalsh, and Hugh of Sleat. The male line of Celestine died out in the person of Donald Gallda in 1519. Neither Donald nor his two brothers had legitimate issue in males, but Sir Alexander, son of Celestine, left two daughters, one of whom, Margaret, married Alexander of Glengarry. This marriage provided the Glengarry family with one of the grounds on which they were to base their subsequent claims.

Both Celestine and Hugh were the offspring of "handfast" marriages which, although not recognised by feudal law, were regarded as valid for purposes of succession by the canon law of the Church as well as by Celtic law. It is significant that in charters of the time neither is referred to as *bastardus* or *carnalis*. In the charter of confirmation granted to Hugh by James IV, he is referred to simply as "brother of John, Lord of the Isles," and there is no evidence to suggest that the customary charter of legitimation was required to be executed in his case before receiving feudal investiture.

Thus, without having to go any farther back amongst the collateral families of the Isles, Hugh of Sleat would appear to be the true representative of the main line, and it is in that line we follow the succession.

Donald Gormson of Sleat was still a minor when Donald Dubh died, and the question then arose as to who should take up the torch and carry on the struggle as High Chief of the Clan. The men of the Isles had to find a man of stature, near in blood to the main line. Their choice fell upon James of Dunnyveg, Chief of the Clann Iain Mhoir. Rumour had it that he had been nominated as a worthy successor to the Lordship by none other than Donald Dubh himself, but of that we have no proof. The nomination of James was not unanimous, but John of Moidart, Chief of Clanranald, was foremost in supporting him. James accepted the offer and sent letters to the Privy Council of Ireland and the English King announcing his election to the dignity. Henry VIII, whose support was essential to the plan, did not reply. The Islesmen were divided in their support and James thought it wiser to give up the attempt and return to his allegiance to James V, at whose Court he was well known ever since he had lived there as a hostage after his father had submitted to the King in 1531.

Thus the representation of the high chiefship, and any claim to reinstate the Lordship, remained with the Chiefs of Sleat and continued thus unchallenged until the Restoration of Charles II to the throne in 1660. Even before the King returned Angus, Chief of Glengarry, had been in constant correspondence with Charles making extravagant claims not only to the Chiefship of Clan Donald, but even to the Earldom of Ross. Neither of these was allowed, and Glengarry had to be content with a peerage naming him Lord Macdonell and Aros with destination to heirs male of his body.

Earlier, in 1598, the Sleat family in the person of Donald Gorm Mor had kept their claim alive. In that year Donald wrote to the Court of Queen Elizabeth styling himself "Lord of the Illis of Scotland and Chieff of the haill Clan Donald Irischemen quhairsoeuir." In the same letter he stated that the Captain of Clanranald, Glengarry, Keppoch, MacIain of Ardnamurchan and Macdonald of Dunnyveg "are sworn to follow, serve and obey him with all their forces."

When Angus of Glengarry, Lord Macdonell, put forward his claim to be recognised as Chief of the Name, Sir James, 2nd Baronet of Sleat, produced a document referred to by Hugh, the Sleat historian, who wrote about this time, as "a paper signed by all the principal men of the name wherein they acknowledge the head of the family as chief." This document, which was later registered in the Books of the Council and Session, read as follows:

> Be it kend till all men That we undersubscribers do testify and acknowledge that Sir James Macdonald of Sleat is chief of the whole Name and Family of the Macdonalds in Scotland and that we all are descended of the said Family whereof Sir James Macdonald is now undoubtedly Chief and lineally descended of the Earl of Ross which we testify by this declaration subscribed with our hands
>
> > D. Macdonald of Moydort
> > A. Macdonald of Ardnamurchin
> > G. McAlester of Loup
> > Angus McDonald of Leargue
> > Alexander Macdonald of Glencoe
> > John Donaldson Esquire.

The names of the signatories place the date of this interesting document some time between 1670 and 1678, the year of Sir James's death. They are to be identified as:

Donald, Captain of Clanranald, who reigned 1670 to 1686;
Alexander MacIain of Ardnamurchan, alive at this time;
Godfrey MacAlister of Loup, *c.* 1630 to 1698;
Alexander MacIain of Glencoe, *c.* 1640 to 1692;
Angus Macdonald of Largie, died *c.* 1680.

Following on the above document Sir James's son, Sir Donald, was officially appointed a Commissioner of Supply in 1689 as "Laird of Macdonald," his lands being described as the "Barony of Macdonald," and he was officially named by

THE MACDONALDS OF SLEAT

(continued from chart in preceding chapter)

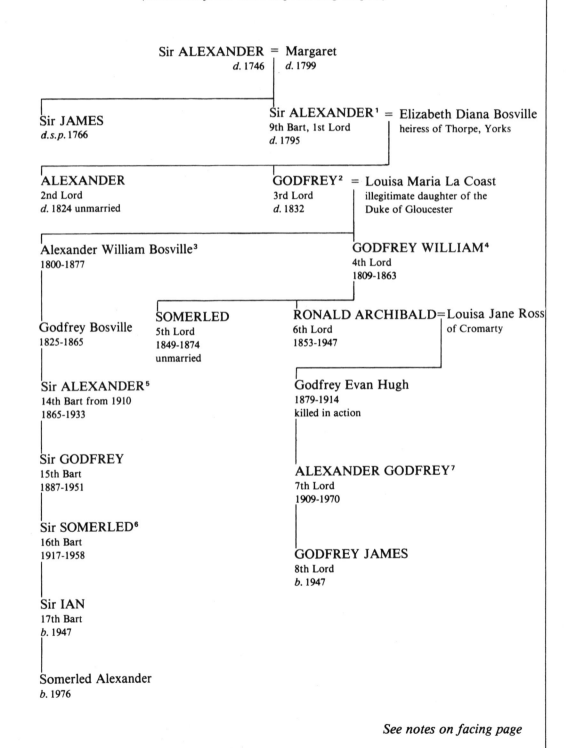

Sir ALEXANDER = Margaret
d. 1746   *d.* 1799

Sir JAMES
d.s.p. 1766

Sir ALEXANDER[1] = Elizabeth Diana Bosville
9th Bart, 1st Lord   heiress of Thorpe, Yorks
d. 1795

ALEXANDER
2nd Lord
d. 1824 unmarried

GODFREY[2] = Louisa Maria La Coast
3rd Lord   illegitimate daughter of the
d. 1832   Duke of Gloucester

Alexander William Bosville[3]
1800-1877

GODFREY WILLIAM[4]
4th Lord
1809-1863

Godfrey Bosville
1825-1865

SOMERLED
5th Lord
1849-1874
unmarried

RONALD ARCHIBALD = Louisa Jane Ross
6th Lord   of Cromarty
1853-1947

Sir ALEXANDER[5]
14th Bart from 1910
1865-1933

Godfrey Evan Hugh
1879-1914
killed in action

Sir GODFREY
15th Bart
1887-1951

ALEXANDER GODFREY[7]
7th Lord
1909-1970

Sir SOMERLED[6]
16th Bart
1917-1958

GODFREY JAMES
8th Lord
b. 1947

Sir IAN
17th Bart
b. 1947

Somerled Alexander
b. 1976

See notes on facing page

the Crown as "Sir Donald Macdonald of that Ilk," the designation only accorded to the Chief of a whole Name.

It was the custom in similar cases to make official Crown recognition absolutely clear by changing the name of the Chief's lands to that of his surname. It is clear that the Crown made very careful enquiries before acting in this case.

A similar declaration was later signed by Coll Macdonald of Keppoch in favour of Sir Donald of Sleat, Sir James's successor, and was likewise registered in the Books of Council and Session in 1726. Thus all the branches of Clan Donald, with the sole exception of Glengarry, had affirmed their acknowledgment of the Chief of Sleat as High Chief of the whole Name of Macdonald.

Next year in 1727 a Crown charter erected the Sleat estates into the lands and Barony of Macdonald. Since then, therefore, the Clan Donald have borne the usual chiefly surname of Macdonald of Macdonald. The contemporary standard 18th century work on Scottish chiefs and lairds, *The Baronage of Scotland* by Sir Robert Douglas (1694-1770), gives Sir James and Sir Donald and their successors up to Sir Alexander (afterwards created Lord Macdonald in 1776) each successively as "Macdonald of Macdonald": the entry itself being under MACDONALD OF MACDONALD.

The omission of Glengarry may be explained by the fact that the head of the family at the time was Lord Macdonell and Aros who, as related in a previous chapter, presumed upon his peerage and favour at Court to pretend to the Chiefship of the whole clan. Ever since the marriage of Alexander, 6th Chief, to the heiress of Lochalsh early in the previous century, the family of Glengarry had claimed the hegemony of Clan Donald. Celestine of Lochalsh, second son

Notes on the Chart

1. The first Lord Macdonald married the heiress of the rich Bosville estates in Yorkshire and took the name "Bosville-Macdonald."

2. Godfrey Bosville-Macdonald, 3rd Lord, eloped and lived with Louisa as man and wife in 1799. Their son Alexander William, born a year later, was adjudged illegitimate. In 1803 they married in church and thus their son Godfrey, born in 1809, succeeded to the peerage as 4th Lord Macdonald.

3. Alexander William, by Royal licence of date 26/12/1832, assumed the name "Bosville" and took the estates.

4. By private Act of Parliament of 23/7/1847 the names "Bosville" and "Macdonald" were separated—"Bosville" to the elder line and "Macdonald" to Lord Macdonald.

5. In 1910 Alexander, grandson of Alexander William Bosville (1800-1877), applied to the Court of Session and established the legitimacy of his grandfather according to Scots law. He thus became Sir Alexander Bosville-Macdonald and took the arms of Sleat, quartered with those of Bosville, and was recognised as 14th Baronet of Sleat. He added "of the Isles" to his name.

6. Sir Somerled, 16th Baronet, gave up the "of the Isles."

7. In 1947 the Lord Lyon accorded arms to Alexander, 7th Lord, as "chief of the Name and Arms of Macdonald," head of the Clan Donald.

of Alexander, Lord of the Isles, was undoubtedly the senior cadet of the Isles, but when his line failed in males with the death of Donald Gallda in 1519, and the lands went to Glengarry, it did not follow that the Chiefship of Lochalsh would descend through a female: quite the reverse, as Celtic chiefship by the law of succession and tanistry could not be transmitted through a female.

From the time of the foregoing documents down to the present day, the Chiefs of Clanranald and Glengarry agreed on two points in putting forward their claims to the Chiefship: the illegitimacy of Hugh of Sleat, and of his son Donald Gallach, and that descent from Ranald, son of Good John of the Isles, was the true line in which to seek the Chief of the name.

We have dealt with the first in the earlier part of this chapter; and, in regard to the second, it need only be pointed out that for 160 years (1386 to 1545) the line of Donald of Harlaw, descending through his son Alexander, to John, the last Lord, followed by Angus, Master of the Isles and Donald Dubh, in all five chiefs, had been accepted by the whole Clan as heads of the family and name of Macdonald, Lord of the Isles.

One thing the two chiefs of Clanranald and Glengarry could not agree upon was which of the two was the true representer of Ranald, son of Amie. This led to much wordy warfare in 1822, when the clans and all things Highland became interesting and popular, thanks to the efforts of Sir Walter Scott and the visit of George IV to Edinburgh. Chiefships became of supreme importance together with the history, genealogy, and music, and tartans of the Gael. This process was greatly accelerated by Queen Victoria and the Royal family who followed her. The Chiefships of the three main branches, Sleat, Clanranald and Glengarry, each in his own right, were accepted by their clans and the Court of Lord Lyon King of Arms, representing the Monarch, in 1822. These were:

Armadale Castle, the residence of Lord Macdonald, built by Alexander, 2nd Lord, in the early 19th century

Alexander, 2nd Lord Macdonald;

Ranald George MacDonald, Captain of Clanranald; and

Colonel Alasdair Ranaldson MacDonell of Glengarry.

Lord Macdonald stood aloof. The other two were very vocal in their claims. These hinged mainly on the question of their descent from Ranald, son of Good John by Amie MacRuairi. Both assumed that whoever could prove himself the true representer of Ranald was *ipso facto* chief of the whole Name of Macdonald. The question that had to be dealt with was which of the two could prove himself to descend directly in an unbroken line from Ranald, founder of the Clan Ranald. Glengarry declared the line of Ranald George of Clanranald to be illegitimate, quoting especially the accepted bastardy of John Moidartach, but ignoring the fact that at Blar Leine (1544) Ranald Gallda, rightful chief by primogeniture, had been killed in the battle and his family excluded. The Clan Ranald had accepted John of Moidart joyfully, and acknowledged him as their chief during the rest of his long life. Moreover John of Moidart had been granted a decree of legitimation by the Privy Council and Signet on the 15th January 1531.

Matters stood thus, with no definite verdict being arrived at, for the next 88 years. Each maintained his right to the High Chiefship of the Clan, without making any official petition to the Court of Lord Lyon King of Arms. In 1910, however, Alexander Bosville-Macdonald decided to establish the legitimacy of his line, which since his grandfather's time had been regarded as illegitimate. On the 4th June 1910, he was granted a decree of legitimacy by Lord Lyon, Sir James Balfour Paul, in the Court of Session, and assumed the Baronetcy of 14th July 1625. He thus became "Sir Alexander Wentworth Macdonald-Bosville Bt. of Thorpe," and on the 28th June 1910 he obtained a matriculation of arms in which he quartered the Sleat and Bosville arms as "14th Baronet of Sleat and Representative of the House of Macdonald of Sleat."

From this time Sir Alexander assumed the name "of the Isles" and it was used by his family down to the time of his grandson, Sir Somerled, 16th Baronet. The 6th Lord Macdonald was in hospital, and was unable to do anything to contest the assumption of the name "of the Isles," which implied Chiefship of the name. In fact Sir Alexander had established the legitimacy of his grandfather according to Scots law; but the Barony of "Slate in the County of Antrim" given to Sir Alexander 9th Baronet in 1776 came under English and Irish law, and by both those laws Sir Alexander's line was still illegitimate, and the Barony remained in Lord Macdonald's family. Thus the family of Sleat was in 1910 split in two: Lord Macdonald and Sir Alexander of Thorpe, Chief of Sleat.

The High Chiefship was still therefore in doubt, until on the 20th January 1947 Alexander Godfrey Macdonald, 7th Lord Macdonald, presented a petition to Lord Lyon to accord him a matriculation as "Chief of the Name and Arms of Macdonald." This was accorded him by Lyon on the 1st May 1947 in the following terms:

We CERTIFY AND MAKE KNOWN that the Ensigns Armorial appertaining and belonging unto the said Right Honourable ALEXANDER GODFREY MACDONALD OF MACDONALD, LORD MACDONALD, Baron of Barony of Macdonald in the Isle of Skye, Representative of the Family of Macdonald of Macdonald, Chief of the Name and Arms of Macdonald, are matriculated conform to these Presents Our Letters Patent, and are thus blasoned, *videlicet:* — quarterly, 1st, *Argent, a lion rampant Gules, armed and langued Azure*; 2nd, *Or, a hand in armour fessways holding a cross-crosslet fitchée Gules*; 3rd, *Or, a lymphad sails furled and oars in action Sable, flagged Gules*; 4th, *Vert, a salmon naiant in fess proper*; over all, on an inescutcheon *en surtout, Or, an eagle displayed Gules, surmounted of a lymphad, sails furled, oars in action Sable,* (as Chief of the Name and Arms of Macdonald); above the shield is placed his Lordship's coronet, thereon an Helmet befitting his degree with a Mantling Gules doubled Ermine, and on a crest-coronet Or is set for Crest *a hand in armour fessways couped at the elbow proper, holding a cross-crosslet fitchée Gules,* and in an Escroll over the same this Motto PER MARE PER TERRAS, and on a Compartment of rocks and heather proper issuant from waves undy along with this Motto FRAOCH EILEAN are set for Supporters *two leopards proper;* for his Lordship's badge an eagle displayed Gules, armed and beaked Sable, having a Chapeau Gules furred Ermine (for which his Lordship and his successors, Lords Macdonald, may at their pleasure substitute their peerage coronet) holding in its talons an escutcheon Or charged with an eagle displayed Gules surmounted of a lymphad sails furled and oars in action Sable, which is depicted in the first compartment, with the crest in the second compartment and a sprig of heather in the third compartment of a standard five yards in length, with his Lordship's arms in the hoist, of these Liveries, Or and Gules, and upon two transverse bands Sable this Slughorn FRAOCH EILEAN in letters also Or; by demonstration of which Ensigns Armorial he and his successors therein are to be Accounted, Taken and Received as Chief of the Name and Arms of Macdonald, Representative of the noble and princely family of Macdonald, and, in the sense and words of Sir George Mackenzie of Rosehaugh, His Majesty's Advocate, "Head of the Clan" Macdonald, amongst all Nobles and in All places of Honour, IN TESTIMONY WHEREOF We have Subscribed these Presents, and the Seal of Our Office is affixed hereto at Edinburgh this first day of May in the Eleventh Year of the Reign of Our Sovereign Lord George the Sixth, by the Grace of God, of Great Britain, Ireland and the British Dominions beyond the Seas, King, Defender of the Faith, Emperor of India, etc., and in the Year of Our Lord One Thousand Nine Hundred and Forty-Seven.

(sgd.) THOMAS INNES OF LEARNEY,
Lyon.

After his succession in 1951 Sir Somerled, the 16th Baronet, renounced the style "of the Isles," took the surname of Macdonald of Sleat as Chief of Sleat and publicly acknowledged Lord Macdonald as High Chief of Clan Donald.

Now the only absolute property as such that still nowadays must belong to the Chief of the whole Name, and can belong to nobody else is the undifferenced coat-of-arms of the Name. A Lyon Court decision is the acid test.

24

The Church

IN VIEW OF the close attachment of the Clan Cholla, and later Clan Donald, to the Church from the earliest times, it may be useful to see how the Church, Celtic and later Roman, started its influence in the regions where Clan Donald ruled.

The first Christian martyr in Britain is held to be Alban, a Roman soldier, probably of Brito-Roman origin. He served for seven years in the Roman Army, and like many another of his comrades had adopted Christianity as his faith, forsaking the Roman gods. He suffered martyrdom under the persecutions of the Emperor Valerian in about 250 A.D. At that time the rival faiths of Christianity and Mithraism were replacing the old pantheism of Greece and Rome. Christianity prevailed, and many Romans and Brito-Romans were Christians long before the legions left Britain in 410 A.D.

In Alba (Scotland) the first missionary to establish a church and monastery as a mother-church was a Pict, Ninian. His father was already a Christian, and regarded as a prince amongst the Britons of Strathclyde, the region in the south-west of Alba occupied by a tribe called by Ptolemy the Novantiae. Ninian at an early age adopted the faith of his family and travelled to Rome to study, returning by way of Tours in Gaul, where he received the blessing of the famous St Martin. Ninian left the old saint, who lent him some lay-brothers skilled in masonry and carpentry from his establishment, with a view to building a church in the land of his birth. His church was built in 397 on the Isle of Whithorn in Galloway, and from it his disciples went forth to preach the gospel in the lands of the Picts, northwards and eastwards. Ninian died in 432 A.D., the same year in which Patrick began his work in Ireland. In the forty-five years of its missionary effort much was accomplished by his church of *Candida Casa*—the "White House." Churches founded by him, or dedicated to his memory by his disciples, were established in large numbers on the eastward or Pictish side of the country as far north as Shetland, where the relics recently found on St Ninian's Isle attest the loving care bestowed on their churches. A later map showing Christian foundations in existence before Columba set foot in Iona shows the same trend, but by then they had multiplied exceedingly and a few are found in the West and the Isles. It is notable that during the period of the evangelisation of Alba by these holy men only one case of martyrdom seems to have been recorded, and that came long after St Ninian's time. St Donnan was murdered in Eigg in 617, but, it would appear, more on account of political jealousy than animosity to the new religion. When Donnan and his band of disciples made Eigg their last monastic site, a pagan amazon on the mainland was furious at the intrusion on her domains and employed a band of pirates, no doubt Vikings, to land and

IONA AS IT IS TODAY

kill them all. So tradition has it, and St Donnan became one of the few, if not the only, martyr who suffered for his faith in Alba.

The Norse overlords of the Sudereys and Man during their 350 years of occupation of the Isles were at first pagans, and behaved as such. We have seen that Iona was sacked at least twice during that period. In the late 11th century, however, Olaf, who followed Harald Haardrada as King of Norway, introduced Christianity into Scandinavia. His subjects became, at least nominally, Christians. It is doubtful if his turbulent subjects in the Isles and Dublin ever heard of this innovation until much later; still less were they imbued with the spirit of Christ for some considerable time after. In Orkney the gospel had more success, and in 1137 the magnificent cathedral of St Magnus was founded by Rognvald, nephew of Magnus, in memory of his sainted uncle.

The Celtic Church, founded by Patrick in Ireland, was the mother church of the Dalriadans and Clann Cholla from the fifth century onwards until suppressed and lost in the 12th century. Although Ninian and Patrick had visited Rome and received their training there, they had hardly returned to their countries and begun their missionary work before Rome itself came under the fierce attacks of the barbarians. The Empire broke up. The legions left Britain, and the Celtic Church was left to its own devices. There, on the outer confines of the old Empire and beyond its boundaries, the Church founded by these two great men continued to flourish. It was essentially tribal in operation and monastic in its organisation. Its doctrines were evangelical. Preaching and teaching the undiluted Gospel to the indigenous peoples was the aim of the missionaries of their Church. Cut off from the Holy See of Rome for some 150 years by the incursions of the barbarians on the continent, they preserved the faith unaffected by influences from abroad. During this interval, certain changes had taken place in the Roman Church. One of these was the method of calculating the date of Easter, and another was the form of tonsure laid down for the priests and monks. These seem to us today rather trivial matters, scarcely important enough to cause a division amongst Christians; but in 664 at the Synod of Whitby they were made the occasion for the schism between the Roman and Celtic orders. A foreshadowing of this event may be found in Skene's transcription of the manner in which the Columban mission to Gaul in 590 was received by the Church of Rome:

In the year 590 the ecclesiastical world in Gaul, in which the Franks and Burgundians were already settled, was startled by the sudden arrival of a small band of missionaries on her shores. They were thirteen in number—a leader and twelve followers. Their outward appearance was strange and striking. They were clothed in a garment of coarse texture made of wool of the natural colour of the material under which was a white tunic. They were tonsured, but in a different manner from the Gaulish ecclesiastics. Their heads were shaved in front from ear to ear, the anterior half of the head being made bare, while the hair flowed down naturally from the back of the head. They each had a pilgrim's staff, a leathern water-bottle, a wallet and a case containing some relics.

Their leader (Columbanus) was a man of commanding presence and powerful eloquence. Some learned the language of the country. The rest employed an interpreter when they preached before the laity. To ecclesiastics they spoke in the common language of the Latin Church. From the kings Columbanus soon obtained permission to settle in their territories and erect monasteries, and two monastic establishments soon arose in the recesses of the Vosges mountains at Luzeuil and Fontaines.

The position which Columbanus took up was substantially this: Your jurisdiction as Bishop of Rome does not extend beyond the limits of the Roman Empire. I am a missionary from a church of God among the barbarians; and, though temporarily within the limits of your territorial jurisdiction and bound to regard you with respect and deference, I claim the right to follow the customs of my own church handed down to us by our fathers.

The Celtic "bishops" were not dignitaries of the kind we understand by that word in later ecclesiastic history and in the Church today. They were really no more and no less than parish priests with the care of their own tribal area and independent of any interference from outside. In fact they were evangelists in the true sense of the word, owing allegiance only to their Lord and Master, Jesus Christ, whose gospel they preached and taught in its simplest form. Such a loosely knit community could not long resist the advance of the highly organised Roman Church, and its influence gradually decayed until it was entirely absorbed and supplanted by the Latin form.

Before the Gaelic Kings of the Isles transferred their allegiance to the Roman order, an attempt appears to have been made by Somerled to keep the Iona community within the orbit of the Celtic Church. In 1164, the year of his death, we find the following significant passage recorded in the *Annals of Ulster*:

> Select members of the Community of Ia [Iona], namely the arch-priest, Augustine and the lector [that is Dubsidhe] and the Eremite, Mac Gilla-duib and the Head of the Celi-De, namely Mac Forcellaigh and select members of the Community of Ia besides, came on behalf of the Colum-cille, namely, Flaithbertach Ua Brolchain's acceptance of the abbacy of Ia, by advice of Somharlidh and of the Men of Airthir-Gaedhel and of Innsi-Gall; but the successor of Patrick and the King of Ireland, that is, Ua Lochlainn and the nobles of Cenel-Eogain prevented him.

This attempt to revive the Celtic establishment in Iona failed, as it did elsewhere, in face of the aggressive and more comprehensive system of the Latin Church. From about the beginning of the reign of Reginald, son of Somerled, the Kingdom of the Isles was committed to the Church of Rome, and there were no more ardent supporters of that Church than the Clan Donald, whose benefactions were frequent and generous. The lands of the Clan Donald from Somerled downwards lay within the three dioceses of The Isles, Lismore, and Ross. The ecclesiastic history of the first, like its secular counterpart, is full of stirring episodes, having been the scene not only of St Columba's mission but also of the devastating incursions of the Viking raiders. The Diocese of the Isles was the last to attain full cathedral status, which took place in 1506. But its history as an area presided over by the Iona Community goes back much farther. During the 8th and 9th centuries the influence of Iona over the churches of mainland Alba declined, partly due to the incursions of the Norse and the removal of the relics to safer places in Ireland and eastern Alba. Many of the devoted band of priests and monks, who served their Master in that isle, suffered martyrdom at the hands of the sea-pirates, and the last great raid in 986 left the monastery in a ruined state until 1074. In that year it was restored and endowed by Margaret, wife of Malcolm Canmore. Although attempts were made later, when conditions were safer, to restore Iona to its former glory, it never recovered from the effects of the ravages to which it had been exposed. Kenneth MacAlpin in the 9th century built Dunkeld as the mother church of the

Columbans, and for a long time afterwards Iona drew its support largely from the Irish monasteries and had hardly any connection with other establishments in Scotland.

The oldest religious foundation founded and endowed by the Family of Somerled is that of Saddell in Kintyre. It seems well established that Somerled himself had laid the foundations of this Abbey, and was buried there, although Hugh of Sleat states that after his death at Renfrew in 1164, King Malcolm sent the remains to Iona for burial at his own expense. This seems hardly likely, and traditions within the Clan agree that the great Chief of the Isles was buried in Saddell Abbey.

There cannot have been much of what was later such a noble building in existence at the time of the burial of Somerled. It took some time to complete, and we may assume that Reginald continued with the good work and Donald after him, until at last it was finished about 1257. The Abbey stands in Glen Saddell, approached from the sea through an avenue of old stately trees. It was cruciform in plan and orientated to the cardinal points of the compass. *Allt nam Manaich* (the Stream of the Monks) runs down the little glen and there is a well with a cross carved on its front nearby. The ruins of the chancel, restored to make a War Memorial (1914-18), contain the carved stones of warriors, said to be those of Somerled and his son, Reginald, clad in the old Celtic manner with conical helmet, habergeon and long sword. There is also a very old cross shaft. Not much can be seen now of the walls and windows of the main structure. The following description of the Abbey and its condition at the end of last century is given by our seanachies of *Clan Donald*:

> The Church of Saddell was cruciform in structure, with the orientation and pointed arches characteristic of Gothic buildings. The Monastery lies in an exact position towards the four cardinal points. Its dimensions were at one time imposing, though little now survives beyond a mass of featureless confusion. Part of the gable of the transept and the aperture for a window alone survive; but vandalism here, as elsewhere, has done its unhallowed work, and the finished stonework of the window has almost all been removed. The minster was 136 feet long from east to west, by 24 feet broad, while the transepts from north to south measured 78 feet by 24. The conventual buildings were on the south; the dormitory was 58 feet long and there are traces of the study room. Within the arched recess in the south wall of the choir, Somerled's tomb is pointed out. The sculpture represents him as wearing a high pointed head-piece, a tippet of mail hanging over the neck and shoulders, and the body clad down to the knees with a skirt or jupon scored with lines to represent the folds. The right hand is raised up to the shoulder, while the left clasps a two-handed sword. The inscription has been worn away by the elements and has for ages been undecipherable.

Reginald installed monks of the Cistercian Order called White or Gray Friars to distinguish them from the Black Friars of the Benedictines. He endowed them with the lands of Glen Saddell, the 12 merklands of Baltebean (both in Kintyre) and the 20 merklands of Cesken in Arran. In 1257 one, Thomas, was Abbot of Saddell, notable for his piety and learning. He placed the monastery under the protection of King Haakon in 1263, which was confirmed in writing, as stated in the annals of Haakon's expedition to Largs. Friar Simon, Haakon's chaplain, died in the isle of Gigha during that expedition and was conveyed to Saddell for burial, but whether in the Abbey itself or in the *quod sacra* chapel, part of the Abbey's domains of Killean near Tayinloan, is a matter for conjecture. That Killean (Church of St John) was a cell of Saddell is certain, as before the year 1251 Ruairi, son of Reginald, gave the Abbey some five-penny lands for the service of the Church of St John. In the north transept of the old Killean Church there is an effigy of an abbot in full habit, which may be the tomb of either Abbot Thomas or Friar Simon. The last recorded burial here of a member of Clan Donald is that of Angus, Chief of Clann Iain Mhoir and father to the last chief of that race, Sir James (d. 1626). Angus is said to have died in Rothesay in October 1614, and to have been conveyed to Saddell for burial.

The most important church within the old Kingdom of the Isles was undoubtedly the Abbey Church of Iona, headquarters of the Columban Community. Queen Margaret, as we have seen, revived its establishment in 1074 but by the end of Somerled's reign it had again fallen into ruin and decay Somerled's son, Reginald, took up the torch of Christianity and resolved to restore the waste places of Iona and other foundations to their former glory. He is described by MacVurich as "the most distinguished of the Galls, that is the Norwegians, and of the Gaels for prosperity, sway of generosity, and feats of arms." That historian goes on to say that "three monasteries were formed by him: a monastery of black monks in I, or Iona, in honour of God and Saint Columchille; a monastery of black nuns in the same place; and a monastery of gray friars at Sagadul, or Sadelle." A column on the south-east under the tower of St Mary's (the name of the Iona Abbey) has the inscription *Donaldus O'Brolchan fecit hoc opus*. Here we see the well-known name of O'Brolchan, members of whose family were prominent as bishops and abbots in the Isles and Ireland. This Donaldus was Prior of Derry in Ireland and a relative of Flaherty O'Brolchan, Bishop and Abbot of Derry. Although there is no direct evidence. to that effect, it is very probable that he was Prior at the time when these buildings were erected. As he died in 1203, Donaldus was contemporary with Reginald, and the restoration must have been completed by that date. That is verified by the deed of confirmation of the Benedictine Monastery in the Vatican, carrying the date 9th December 1203. The monastery founded by Reginald for Benedictine Nuns at the same time had Beatrice, sister of Reginald, as its first Prioress. The ruins of the Nunnery are still to be seen in Iona, and have been made into a beautiful flower-garden by loving hands in memory of Beatrice, whose monumental slab is still there, bearing the inscription *Behag Nyn Shorle Ilvrid Prioressa* (Beatrice daughter of Somerled Gillebride Prioress).

The same lady is credited with the building of Trinity Chapel at Carinish in North Uist, the ruins of which still stand. Hugh of Sleat, however, ascribes the foundation to another lady of later fame, Amie MacRuairi, wife of Good John of Isla, noted for her piety and good works. The Chapel of the Trinity appears to have been the work of more than one generation, and Amie may well have restored and endowed it, although the original foundation could have been the work of the pious Bethag. In fact there are traces of work preceding the days of Somerled in the form of a beehive type of cell so closely associated with early Celtic missionaries. Yet another lady, Christina MacRuairi, aunt of Amie, gave a grant of the chapel and lands of Carinish to the Monastery of Inchaffray, so that it must have been in existence before Amie did her work of piety in embellishing it. The probability is, therefore, that the Temple or Chapel of Carinish was founded by Beatrice on the site of an ancient Culdee (Columban) temple, and endowed and repaired by the two ladies of Somerled's House in successive generations. The word "temple" is used here to describe an oratory of the early Celtic missionaries built in stone, as distinct from the older and less durable shrines built of mud and wattle or wicker.

The connection of the Lords of the Isles with the Abbey of Paisley, which is quite beyond the bounds of their domains, was maintained from the death of

Somerled to the downfall of the House of Islay, a period of over three hundred years. The cause of this connection, which was marked by frequent and lavish endowments, is thought to have originated from the tragic death of Somerled at the hands of one of his followers, and the desire of his successors to secure and maintain the good offices of the Church for his departed soul. Towards the end of his reign, Somerled's son Reginald became a monk of Paisley and granted the monastery "eight cows and two pennies for one year, and one penny in perpetuity from every house on his territory from which smoke issued, and his peace and protection wherever the monks should go, enjoining on his dependants and heirs in no way to injure them, and swearing by St Columba to inflict on the former the punishment of death and that the latter should have his malediction if they disobeyed his injunction." His wife, Fonia, who was also a sister of the convent, granted to the monks the tithe of all her goods, whether in her own possession or sent for sale by land or sea.

The Kildalton Cross in Islay, dating from about 800 A.D.

After the year 1210 Donald, son of Reginald, also joined the brotherhood of Paisley and his wife became a sister of the convent. He confirmed his father's grants both of the eight cows and the smoke tax for the salvation of himself and his wife.

Before 1295 Angus Mor, son of Donald, gave donations to the same institution as a friend and brother of the order. The grant of eight cows was commuted to half a merk in silver for each of the houses from which smoke issued, and in addition half a merk from his own mansion with his promise of peace and friendship. He added the rights of fishing in any of the waters of his domain. Further "for the salvation of his Lord and King Alexander II and his son Alexander III and for his own and his heirs'," he donated "to God and St James and Mirinus of the Monastery of Paisley and the monks there serving God and to serve God for ever," the Church of St Ciaran in his lands of Kintyre, with all its pertinents. This was confirmed by his son, Alexander. No more gifts are on record until the time of John, last Earl of Ross, who on 21st May 1455 gave to the Abbey and Convent of Paisley, "for the honour and glory of God, and of the Virgin Mary and St Mirinus, and of all the Saints, the rectories of the churches of St Kerran, Colmonell in Kintyre and Knapdale in the diocese of Argyle, given by his predecessors to them for their and his salvation." Thus we see that from the beginning to the end of the dynasty of the Isles, three of the Lords of the Isles in succession, Reginald, Donald and Angus Mor, followed at the end by John, the last Lord, left their temporal power and devoted their last days "bringing forth fruits mete for repentance" in the peaceful haven of monastic life.

The generosity of these endowments to the Abbey of Paisley was matched by the patronage extended by successive Island Lords to the churches within their own domains. Foremost among their benefactors was "Good" John of Islay, who acquired his appellation from the extent of his devotion to the interests of the Church. The Wars of Independence and the widespread unsettlement of the times had allowed the churches to fall into a state of some decay, and Good John's father, Angus Og, had played such an active rôle in the momentous events that he had little opportunity to attend to the Church's material welfare. He left to John, however, a rich and powerful inheritance from which, under the inspiration of his equally devoted wife Amie, he made the generous provisions which gained him the respect and acclaim of the churchmen of the Isles.

Finlaggan, the site of the Lord's manorial residence on the loch of that name in Islay, was one of the first establishments to receive John's attention. During the restless times of his father and grandfather, the chapel had fallen into decay. It was now re-roofed and restored with all the necessary furnishings for the service of God, and provision made for the maintenance of the monks and priests. Similar work was done for other chapels—one on the Isle of Eorsag and another on Isle Suibhne in Loch Swein. Saddell and Iona too profited by the generosity of John and Amie.

The Priory of Oronsay on the tidal isle of that name south of Colonsay is the largest of the benefactions of Good John to the Church. All traces of previous foundations, if indeed there were any, had disappeared. St Columba and his disciple Oran are said to have settled there before going on to Iona but, if so, they would have built temporary structures, such as we have described already, of mud and wattle. It may be that John founded his Priory on one of those sites. Tradition says that it was built as a cell of the Church of Kiloran in Colonsay, which was served by Augustinian canons from the Abbey of Holyrood. While some doubt surrounds the origin of this church, there is none as regards the Priory of Oronsay. MacVurich states that John, Lord of the Isles, erected the monastery of the Holy Cross long before his death, which places its foundation about the middle of the 14th century. The name of the Isle and the Priory would seem to be derived from the name of the Saint, but there are many Oronsays in the western isles. One authority quotes no fewer than twenty-two. An alternative derivation given by Professor Watson in his *Place Names* suggests the Norse words "orfisir-ey," meaning a tidal island, a description which fits all the "Orasays" or "Oronsays," and is supported by Dr Frank Knight in his book on the early Christianising of Scotland, where he quotes three authorities for this interpretation.

The naturalist Thomas Pennant visited Oronsay during his tour of Scotland about 1770, and has left us a description of the ruins as he found them. He accepts the view that the Priory was founded by the Lord of the Isles who

fixed here a priory of Canons Regular of Augustine, dependent on the abby of Holyrood, in Edinburgh. The church is fifty-nine feet by eighteen, and contains the tombs of the ancient islanders, two of warriors recumbent, seven feet long; a flattery perhaps of the sculptor, to give future ages exalted notions of their prowess. Besides these, are scattered over the floor lesser figures of heroes, priests and females; the last seemingly of some order; and near them is a figure cut in stone, of full size, apparently an abbess.

In a side chapel, beneath an arch, lies an abbot, of the name of Macdufie, with two of his fingers elated, in the attitude of benediction: in the same place is a stone enriched with foliage, a stag surrounded with dogs, and a ship with full sail: round is inscribed *Hic jacet Murchardus Macdufie de Collonsa, An. Do. 1539, mense mart. ora me ille. Ammen.* This Murchardus is said to have been a great oppressor, and that he was executed by order of the Lord of the Isles, for his tyranny. Near his tomb is a long pole, placed there in memory of the ensign-staff of the family, which had been preserved miraculously for two hundred years: on it (report says) depended the fate of the Macdufian race, and probably the original perished with this Murchardus.

e Monastery in Oronsay, as
ppeared to an 18th-century
artist

Adjoining to the church is the cloister: a square of forty-one feet; one of the sides of the inner wall is ruined: on two of the others are seven low arches, one seven feet high, including the columns, which are nothing more than two thin stones, three feet high, with a flat stone on the top of each, serving as a plinth; and on them two other thin stones, meeting at top, and forming an acute angle, by way of arch: on the fore-side are five small round arches; these surround a court of twenty-eight feet eight inches: the whole of the cloister part had been once covered. This form is peculiar (in our part of Europe) to this place. . . . Several other buildings join this, all in a ruinous state; but a most elegant cross is yet standing, twelve feet high, one foot seven broad, five inches thick.

We are indebted to Pennant for taking such careful and detailed measurements, and also for supplying some excellent wood-cuts of a view of the cloisters, details of the cross he refers to and a general view of the Priory. Although some of his sketches are a little fanciful, for example that of Staffa, we may confidently accept the accuracy of essential detail he has provided of the building, its effigies, and of the cross which still remains.

We have already referred to the Temple of Carinish and the tradition that it was founded by Beatrice, daughter of Somerled, although another tradition ascribes its foundation to Amie, the wife of Good John. Whatever the truth of its origin, it is a well-established fact that Amie restored and enlarged the chapel. Although not extensive in area, the height of the walls indicates that it was once an imposing building with some surrounding appurtenances. The Chapel of the Trinity was recognised as a sanctuary in the sense that those who had violated the law, if they reached its wall, could claim immunity so long as they were in its shelter. In Gaelic a sanctuary is called *A' Chomhraich,* a name that we find in other parts of Scotland—*A' Chomhraich* is the name of Applecross on the west of Ross, and Comrie in Perthshire is a similar derivation. During the ebb-tide, North Uist is accessible from the south by crossing the stream left by the tide. This stream is called *Sruthan na Comraich,* the Streamlet of the Sanctuary.

Amie also built the Church of Columba in Benbecula and a little oratory on the Isle of Grimsay. Her husband, the Good John, set aside eight merklands in North Uist and two farms in Benbecula for the Church in that district. She may have done much more than is recorded in our annals, but enough has been told to certify the reputation of this lady as a "devout and virtuous woman."

Succeeding Lords of the Isles followed in the tradition of their ancestors. Donald of Harlaw was, according to MacVurich, "an entertainer of clerics and priests and monks; gave lands to the monastery of Iona, and every immunity which the monastery of Iona had from his ancestors before him." He made a covering of gold and silver for the relic of the hand of Columba. He also presented vessels of gold and silver to the monastery of Icolmkill. Like some of his ancestors he retired from the world before his death and joined the brotherhood of the order in that monastery.

Godfrey, son of Good John by Amie MacRuairi, became Lord of Uist and, at his castle of Eilean Tioram on the 1st July 1389, confirmed the grant given by his grand-aunt Christina, daughter of Alan MacRuairi, of the Church of the Holy Trinity in Uist and the whole land of Carinish, with the fourpenny lands between Kirkibost and Kennerach, to the Monastery and Convent of John the Evangelist at Inchaffray.

Ranald, eldest son of Amie, received a good heritage by charter from his father. This he used to good effect, earning for himself a reputation as a "man of augmenting churches and monasteries. . . . He bestowed an unciate of land in

Uist on the monastery of Iona forever in honour of God and of Columba." On a farm in Benbecula there used to be ruins of a nunnery, which gave it the name of Nunton by which it is now known. Its stones were used when Clanranald erected his mansion to replace the House of Ormiclet, which had been burned down by accident on the night Alan Og, the Chief, fell at Sheriffmuir. Other ruins of a church are to be found on an islet in a loch at Balivanich (*Baile a' Mhanaich* or "Monk's Residence").

The old parish of Howmore (Skirhough in old records) is now part of the parish of South Uist, and there may still be seen the ruins of the Chapels of St

A "most elegant cross" in Oronsay, as seen by Pennant in the 18th century

Mary and St Columba, near to the present Church, where some of the Clan-ranald chiefs are buried. These are very old, and probably date back to the MacRuairis or the very early days of the Clanranald chiefs.

The Lords of the Isles, when they became Earls of Ross, pursued the same policy towards the Church in their mainland possessions. On 4th September 1437 we find the following grant to the Prior and Friars of Inverness:

> To all the faithful to whose knowledge the present letters shall come, Alexander de Ile, Earl of Ross and Lord of the Isles; Greeting eternal in the Lord; Know that we for the salvation of our soul and for the salvation of the souls of our fathers, ancestors, and successors have given, granted, and by this present writ confirmed to the religious men, the prior and friars of the Dominican Preachers of Inverness, twenty shillings of annual rent, of the usual money of the Kingdom of Scotland, to be paid annually at two terms of the year, *viz.*, of Pentecost and St Martins, by equal portions of our land and ferry of Easter Kessock, with the pertinents in pure and perpetual charity as freely as any annual rent is given and granted to any other religious men in the Kingdom of Scotland. In testimony of which matter we have caused our seal to be appended at Inverness, the 4th day of the month of September, in the year of the Lord 1437. These, with many others, being witnesses, *viz.*, Torquil McLoyde, Lord of Leyvhous [Lewis], George Munro of Foulis, Alexander McCullach, and Lord Blanc.

By the Roll of Rents, Feus and Maills it appears that as late as the present century, the above annual of twenty shillings was still payable by the Estate of Redcastle for the lands of Kessock, having been transferred at the Reformation to the Burgh of Inverness, and forming part of its revenues. There is also a grant by the same Earl of Ross, not apparently to the Church, but personally to the parish clergyman of Kiltearn, made 23rd March 1439:

> Be it maid kend till all men be thir present letters US Alexander the Earl of Ross and Justiciar to our Soverane Lord the King fra the north part of the water of Forth till haf giffyn to Walter of Urchard our cousin parson of Kilteyrn all the right of the lands of Finlay and Rosan within the burgh of Cromathy and his ousgang of Newaty notagane standand that the foresaid Walter is sister dochter wes ayr to the foresaid lands We gif that as of free gift to the said Walter as throw vertue of our office and throw power at 'langs til our lege lord the King, the fee as giffyn throw our gift, the Frank tenement remanand with the foresaid Walter quhilke be parte of the same at lyes upon the foresaid land as the Indenter party proports maid tharupon. And we the forsaid Alexander Earl of Ross warrands to the said Walter his ayrs and his assigneys the foresaid lands and at no man be so hardly to make grife molestation to the said Walter in the said lands onder the panes of lywis lands and guds at they may tyne agains the King and us giffyn onder our greit seil at Balkny the xxiii day of March the zeir of our Lord moiiivxxxix.

Before 1475 John, the last Lord of the Isles, and his son Angus Og, gave to the Abbey of Saddell the lands of Knockantebeg and the twelve unciates of land called Kellipull. In the year before his forfeiture, John is found exercising his rights as patron of the Church of Kilberry in Knapdale. Loss of records makes it impossible to provide a complete account of the benefactions bestowed by the Lords of the Isles upon the churches in their domains, but the examples we have given may serve to indicate the scope of their generosity and concern. However turbulent they may have been politically, their humility and dedication in spiritual matters are confirmed beyond all doubt by the munificence of their contributions to the service of the Church.

One other foundation that should be mentioned is the Church of St Columcille in Morvern, standing in the neighbourhood of the Castle of Ardtornish, an ancient seat of the Lords of the Isles and the scene of the negotiations for the notorious treaty of that name. The fragments of the Church and the tall Celtic cross that remain suggest the splendour of the original structure. It served as a Deanery, and it possesses one additional interest for its association with John of Moidart's brother Ruairi, the Dean of Morvern, who was one of the Commissioners selected by Donald Dubh's Island Council in 1545 to carry its proposals to the English Court.

The close connection between the Lords of the Isles and the Church suggests the probability that they took due advantage of the services it provided in the field of education and learning. Although literacy was not regarded as particularly important in an age when the sword was esteemed much mightier than the pen, we know that Donald of Harlaw was educated at Oxford, and his signature on the Gaelic charter of 1408 testifies to his ability at least in the art of writing. His successors may not have had the advantage of a University education, but there is reason to believe that ample use was made of the facilities available in religious establishments. Mention has already been made of the Lector, one of the dignitaries sent by Somerled to O'Brolchan in 1164. He was the man of learning in the establishment of the Church, and his functions were primarily educative, teaching the arts of reading, writing and other disciplines not only to those intended for the service of the Church, but also to members of chiefly families who were often sent to acquire the elements of knowledge considered necessary to their station. The latter were frequently given the appellation *Cleireach* (Clerk), of which several examples have been noted in the course of this history.

Throughout the period of the Lordship, Gaelic and its literature continued to be nurtured by the Church, and in Ireland literary schools arose which were often attended by family bards and chroniclers like the MacVurichs to supplement their accomplishments in their art. The end of the Lordship marked the beginning of a distinct decline in educational services throughout the Island territories. No longer were the close links with the Irish establishments maintained, but the advance of the Reformation with its disastrous effects upon the monasteries proved a serious though temporary check to educational progress; and for the best part of a century it was submerged in the feuds and struggles which followed the dissolution of that bond of social order and security in the West represented by the old Lordship.

Bibliography

Adam, Frank. *Clan Septs and Regiments of the Scottish Highlands.* Edinburgh, 1970.

Anderson, A. O. *Scottish Annals from English Chroniclers.* London, 1908.

Anderson, A. O. *and* M. O. (Eds.). *Adamnan's Life of Columba.* London and Edinburgh, 1961.

Anon. *Historical Account of the Clan Ranald.* Edinburgh, 1819.

Barbour, John. *The Bruce.* 1907.

Blaikie, W. B. (ed.). *Origins of the 'Forty-five.* Edinburgh, 1916.

Brown, P. Hume. *History of Scotland.* Cambridge, 1900.

Buchan, John. *The Massacre of Glencoe.* London, 1933.
                Montrose. London and Edinburgh, 1928.

Burton, J. Hill. *The History of Scotland.* Edinburgh, 1873.

Cameron, Alexander. *Reliquiae Celticae.* Inverness, 1882.

Cassilis, Earl of. *The Rulers of Strathspey.* Inverness, 1911.

Chambers, R. *History of the Rebellion of 1745.* Edinburgh, 1929.

Connellan, Owen (trans.). *Annals of Ireland by the Four Masters.* Dublin, 1846.

Dalrymple, Sir David. *Annals of Scotland.* London, 1776.

Daviot, Gordon. *Claverhouse.* London, 1937.

Donaldson, Gordon. *Scottish Historical Documents.* Edinburgh, 1970.

Forbes, Robert (ed. Henry Paton). *The Lyon in Mourning.* Edinburgh, 1895-6.

Grant, I. F. *Highland Folk Ways.* London, 1961.
          The Lordship of the Isles. Edinburgh, 1935.
          The Macleods. London.
          Social and Economic Development of Scotland before 1603. Edinburgh, 1930.

Gregory, Donald. *History of the Western Highlands and Isles of Scotland.* London, 1881.
          Collectanea de Rebus Albanicis. Edinburgh, 1847.

Hill, George. *The Macdonnells of Antrim.* Belfast, 1873.

Innes of Learney, Sir Thomas. *Scots Heraldry.* Edinburgh, 1934.

Jackson, Kenneth H. *The Gododdin: The Oldest Scottish Poem.* Edinburgh, 1969.

Johnstone, Chevalier de. *A Memoir of the 'Forty-five.* London, 1958.

Kermack, W. R. *The Scottish Highlands.* Edinburgh, 1967.

Knight, Frank. *Archaeological Light on Early Christianizing of Scotland.* London, 1933.

Laing, Henry. *Ancient Scottish Seals.* Edinburgh, 1850.

MacArthy, B. (ed. and trans.). *The Annals of Ulster.* H.M.S.O., 1887-95.

Macdonald, A. *and* A. *The Clan Donald.* Inverness, 1896-1904.

Macdonald, A. R. *The Truth about Flora Macdonald.* Inverness, 1938.

Macdonald, Charles. *Moidart, or Among the Clanranalds.* 1889.

Macdonald, Colin M. *The History of Argyll.* Glasgow.

Macdonald, D. J. *Slaughter under Trust.* London, 1965.

Macdonald, Hugh. History of the Macdonalds. *Highland Papers,* vol. I. Edinburgh, 1914.

Macdonald, K. N. *Macdonald Bards.* Edinburgh, 1900.

MacDonald, Norman H. *The Clan Ranald of Lochaber.* Privately published.

Macdonald, W. R. *Scottish Armorial Seals.* Edinburgh, 1904.

Macfarlane's *Genealogical Collections.* Edinburgh, 1900.

Mackay, William. *Urquhart and Glenmoriston.* Inverness, 1914.

Mackechnie, John (ed.). *The Dewar Manuscripts,* vol. I. Glasgow, 1963.

Mackenzie, Alexander. *History of the Macdonalds and the Lords of the Isles.* Inverness, 1881.

Mackenzie, A. M. *Orain Iain Luim.* Edinburgh, 1964.

Mackenzie, W. C. *The Highlands and Isles of Scotland.* Edinburgh, 1937.

Mackintosh, Charles F. *Antiquarian Notes.* Inverness, 1897.
          Further Antiquarian Notes. Stirling, 1913.

Mackintosh, Mrs Mackintosh of. *The History of the Clan Mackintosh and the Clan Chattan.* Edinburgh, 1948.

Macleod, Canon R. *The Book of Dunvegan.* 3rd Spalding Club, 1938.

Macphail, J. R. N. (ed.). *Highland Papers,* vols. I-IV. Edinburgh, 1914-34.

Martin Martin. *Description of the Western Isles* [1695]. Stirling, 1934.

Mitchell, Dugald. *History of the Highlands and Gaelic Scotland.* Paisley, 1900.

Mitchison, Rosalind. *A History of Scotland.* London, 1970.

Moncreiffe of That Ilk, Sir Iain. *The Highland Clans.* London, 1967.

Munro, R. W. (ed.). *Monro's Western Isles of Scotland and the Genealogies of the Clans* [1549]. Edinburgh, 1961.

Nicolson, Alexander. *History of Skye.* Glasgow, 1930.

Pennant, Thomas. *A Tour in Scotland and Voyage to the Hebrides,* Chester, 1774.

Porcelli, The Baron. *The White Cockade.* London, 1949.

Prebble, John. *The Massacre of Glencoe.* London, 1966.
          The Lion in the North. London, 1971.

Seanachie, A [1833]. *The Clan Maclean.* London and Edinburgh, 1838.

Skene, W. *The Highlands of Scotland.* Stirling, 1902.
          Celtic Scotland: A History of Ancient Alba. Edinburgh, 1886.

Skinner, Wm. Cumming. *Candida Casa: The Apostolic Centre of Scotland.* Dundee, 1931.

Stewart of Ardvorlich, John. *The Camerons.* Clan Cameron Association, 1974.

Watson, W. J. *The History of Celtic Place Names in Scotland.* Edinburgh, 1926.
          Bardachd Gaidhlig. Inverness, 1918.
          Macdonald Bardic Poetry. In *Clan Donald Magazine* Nos. 5 and 6.

Willcock, John. *A Scots Earl: Archibald 9th Earl of Argyll.* Edinburgh, 1907.

Wyntoun, Andrew of (ed. David Laing). *The Orygynale Cronykil of Scotland.* Edinburgh, 1872.

PRIMARY SOURCES of study and reference are to be found in the public records of Scotland and Ireland—the Acts of the Parliaments of Scotland, Calendar of Irish State Papers, Exchequer Rolls of Scotland, Records of the Rolls of Ireland, Register of the Great Seal, Register of the Privy Council, Register of the Privy Seal, Rotuli Scotiae—and in original documents preserved in family charter chests.

Select Index